Kabbalah and Ecology

Kabbalah and Ecology is a groundbreaking book that resets the conversation about ecology and the Abrahamic traditions. David Mevorach Seidenberg challenges the anthropocentric reading of the Torah, showing that a radically different orientation to the more-than-human world of Nature is not only possible, but that such an orientation also leads to a more accurate interpretation of scripture, rabbinic texts, Maimonides, and Kabbalah. Deeply grounded in traditional texts and fluent with the physical sciences, this book proposes not only a new understanding of God's image but also a new direction for restoring religion to its senses and to a more alive relationship with the more-than-human, both with Nature and with divinity.

David Mevorach Seidenberg received his doctoral degree from the Jewish Theological Seminary for his work on ecology and Kabbalah and was ordained by both the Jewish Theological Seminary and Rabbi Zalman Schachter-Shalomi. He also studied physics and mathematics at Dartmouth College, educational philosophy at Harvard University, and social ecology at the Institute for Social Ecology. He teaches Jewish thought in Europe, Israel, and throughout North America, in communities and universities and through his organization, neohasid.org, focusing on ecology and spirituality, Talmud, Maimonides, Kabbalah, and Hasidic thought; on embodied Torah, dance, and *nigunim* (Hasidic song); and on ecological and environmental ethics. In addition to scholarly articles, he was a contributing editor of the *Encyclopedia of Religion and Nature*, and his writing has been featured in *The Jewish Daily Forward, Huffington Post, The Times of Israel*, and the *Los Angeles Jewish Journal*.

"David Seidenberg's book is a tour-de-force that moves the dialog of Judaism and ecology forward in remarkably fruitful ways. This book takes a tremendous step toward reconfiguring religion, showing how we can transform some of the foundational premises of Western civilization by drawing on deeply earth-centered traditions. It is a must read for everyone interested in the impact of the Bible on the world, and for everyone studying the growth of ecotheology. *Kabbalah and Ecology* will be a seminal work for years to come."
                    Mary Evelyn Tucker, co-director, Forum on Religion and
                                                        Ecology, Yale University

"This is one of the boldest, most imaginative, and theologically significant works on Jewish Thought to appear in recent memory. With lucid expositions and meticulous scholarship, Seidenberg invites his readers to reconsider the ways we think about God, humans, animals, and the cosmos as a whole. His elegant and vibrant writing makes a persuasive case for a reverent embrace of all creation as the divine image and encourages us to ennoble our ethical postures and religious lives."
                    Nehemia Polen, Professor of Jewish Thought, Hebrew College

"A careful but exhilarating examination of ways our traditions have imagined – and might again re-imagine – our fraught relationship with the more-than-human world. Stunning in its depth!"
          Bill McKibben, founder, 350.org, author, *The Comforting Whirlwind:
                                                   God, Job, and the Scale of Creation*

"Seidenberg's *Kabbalah and Ecology* is one of the most, if not the most, original and important contributions to the growing discourse around religion and the environment of the last decade. Jewish mysticism is a woefully ignored mine of rich sources and insights for those wishing to ground their environmentalism in a spiritual base with deep roots and fertile branches. Too many works in this field are by people who are not experts, or not knowledgeable in all relevant fields. Seidenberg brings to the work truly impressive transdisciplinary learning and experience. The book deftly spans the divide between scholarship in Jewish and mystical studies and contemporary social-environmental thought and analysis. There is much here for everyone – both scholar and activist, professional and layperson, and I daresay – Jew and non-Jew. One of Seidenberg's many strengths displayed in this book is not only making accessible otherwise obscure or esoteric source material, but doing so in such a way that it virtually jumps off the page with relevance."
          Dr. Jeremy Benstein, co-founder and deputy director, The Heschel Center for
               Sustainability (Israel), author, *The Way Into Judaism and the Environment*

"What a rare find – a work that integrates theology, science, and activism in organic and well-researched ways that make sense and can impact the future. Seidenberg presents texts and ideas that many modern Jews and Christians have not encountered, and offers a fresh new look at Jewish views of humanity's role in the cosmos. Through ideas that range from Maimonides' theory of the universe as a single organism to Jewish mystical writings in which the human shares the divine image with the cosmos, Seidenberg convincingly proves to the reader that Judaism can and does support a belief system that does not elevate humans above all other species. For Jews and others who want to be part of a human world that acknowledges its interdependence with all other species, this is a crucial and irreplaceable book."

Rabbi Jill Hammer, co-founder, The Kohenet Institute, author, *The Jewish Book of Days: A Companion for All Seasons*

"People have had an intuitive knowledge that the Kabbalah and the reality map of our life on the planet are congruous to each other. It took David Seidenberg to bring this intuition into a full and rich intellectual conceptualization. This book is an important contribution that harmonizes ecology with divinity."

Rabbi Zalman Schachter-Shalomi, founder of the Jewish Renewal movement

"This rich and well-researched book into the ancient theme of the image of God is a blessing for humans and the more-than-human alike, for it restores the intrinsic dignity and sacredness of all beings. Thus it moves us beyond anthropocentrism and our narcissism as a species to our true place, not above but alongside other creatures that also reveal the God-face, in all its grandeur and diversity. While all creatures currently tremble under the ongoing diminishment of the planet, this book liberates humanity from its self-absorption and sets it free to face nakedly our responsibility to change our ways of living on Earth, so that Earth and all earth creatures may thrive anew."

Rev. Matthew Fox, author, *Original Blessing, Coming of the Cosmic Christ, Meister Eckhart: A Mystic Warrior for Our Times*

"*Kabbalah and Ecology* is a tour-de-force – serious thoughtful theology, generous and respectful to the wide range of sources and thinkers cited, developing a remarkable direction for theology. This book is stunning and will greatly enrich the conversation."

Rabbi Irving (Yitz) Greenberg, founder, CLAL National Jewish Center for Learning and Leadership, author, *The Jewish Way: Living the Holidays*

"An ecological sense of the interbreathing of all life is at the heart of both ancient Biblical thought and practice and the most advanced science of today. Rabbi Seidenberg has with impeccable scholarship unearthed how ecological ways of thinking underlie the Bible and have also permeated Kabbalah. Since Kabbalah for the last thousand years has been at or very close to the heart of Jewish thought, his work is extraordinarily important to our understanding of Judaism. His findings can help empower action to heal the web of life that has been so deeply wounded by human behavior."

Rabbi Arthur Waskow, director, The Shalom Center, author, *Tales of Tikkun, Godwrestling*

"*Kabbalah and Ecology* is an extremely detailed, careful, and well thought out attempt to fashion a Jewish theology adequate to the environmental crisis. It advances the discussion, offers important insights, and makes a real contribution to the work of helping us change our ways. At times there are instances of lovely and even poetic theological insight. This is essential reading."

Roger S. Gottlieb, Professor of Philosophy, Worcester Polytechnic Institute, author, *Engaging Voices: Tales of Morality and Meaning in an Age of Global Warming* and *Spirituality: What It Is and Why It Matters*

"Rabbi Seidenberg constructs an ecotheology from Talmud and Kabbalah wherein each species partakes in the image of God, and the awe of beholding a natural marvel is transferred onto every person. It invites us to join a conversation about humans and animals that has been going on for over a thousand years, yet, I suspect, is unknown to most conservation biologists or environmentalists."
Scott Gilbert, Professor of Biology, Swarthmore College, author,
Ecological Developmental Biology

"Most contemporary religious environmentalists have gone beyond, given up on, or at least radically reread Jewish and Christian texts that suggest a strong anthropocentrism. In this significant new work of constructive theology, Rabbi Dr. David Mevorach Seidenberg takes a different tack, arguing that we have long misunderstood these texts. What is unique about *Kabbalah and Ecology*, however, is that Seidenberg does so not with mere assertion but with scholarly rigor, delving deeply into Biblical, rabbinic, Midrashic, philosophical, Kabbalistic, Hasidic, and contemporary texts. Seidenberg provides a serious theological backbone for Jewish environmental ethics – as well as one of the most systematic contemporary Jewish theologies of any type. The more serious the scholarly or theological reader, the more powerful Seidenberg's challenge will be."
Dr. Jay Michaelson, founder, *Zeek*, contributing editor, *The Forward*, author,
Everything is God: The Radical Path of Nondual Judaism

Jacket and internal illustration: "Reflections of a Breath of Air" © Nikki Green 2015, www.nikkigreen.com.au

Kabbalah and Ecology

God's Image in the More-Than-Human World

DAVID MEVORACH SEIDENBERG

CAMBRIDGE
UNIVERSITY PRESS

32 Avenue of the Americas, New York NY 10013-2473, USA

Cambridge University Press is part of the University of Cambridge.

It furthers the University's mission by disseminating knowledge in the pursuit of education, learning and research at the highest international levels of excellence.

www.cambridge.org
Information on this title: www.cambridge.org/9781107441446

© David Mevorach Seidenberg 2015

This publication is in copyright. Subject to statutory exception and to the provisions of relevant collective licensing agreements, no reproduction of any part may take place without the written permission of Cambridge University Press.

First published 2015
First paperback edition 2016

A catalogue record for this publication is available from the British Library

Library of Congress Cataloguing in Publication data
Seidenberg, David Mevorach.
Kabbalah and ecology : God's image in the more-than-human world / David Mevorach Seidenberg.
  pages cm
ISBN 978-1-107-08133-8 (hardback)
1. Image of God. 2. God (Judaism) 3. Human ecology – Religious aspects – Judaism.
4. Bible. Old Testament – Criticism, interpretation, etc. 5. Rabbinical literature – History and criticism. 6. Cabala. I. Title.
BM610.S385   2015
296.3 – dc23   2014038241

ISBN 978-1-107-08133-8 Hardback
ISBN 978-1-107-44144-6 Paperback

Cambridge University Press has no responsibility for the persistence or accuracy of URLs for external or third-party internet websites referred to in this publication, and does not guarantee that any content on such websites is, or will remain, accurate or appropriate.

Sooner or later, technological civilization must accept the invitation of gravity and settle back into the land, its political and economic structures diversifying into the contours and rhythms of a more-than-human earth.

David Abram, *The Spell of the Sensuous*

These are the spheres in which the world of relation is built. The first: life with nature, where the relation sticks to the threshold of language. The second, life with people, where it enters language. The third: life with spiritual beings, where it lacks but creates language. In every sphere, in every relational act, through everything that becomes present to us, we gaze toward the train of the eternal You; in each we perceive a breath of it; in every You we address the eternal You, in every sphere according to its manner... But when the perfect encounter is to occur, the gates are unified into one gate of actual life, and you no longer know through which one you have entered.

Martin Buber, *I and Thou*

R' Amorai said: *Gan Eden*, where is it? He said to them: In the earth.

Sefer Bahir

For Chanina, and for Reb Zalman, z"l

Contents

Acknowledgments		*page* xi
Notes on translation, transliteration, and bibliography		xv
Overview of Kabbalah and Ecology		xvii
	Introduction: Jewish ecological thought and the challenge for scriptural theology	1

PART I MIDRASH

1. *Tselem Elohim* (God's Image) in Midrash and commentary, part 1: the angels and the heavens, the chain of Being, intellect, and speech   43
2. *Tselem Elohim* in Midrash and commentary, part 2: the body, gender, dominion, and ethics   76
3. *Tselem*, dignity, and the "infinite value" of the other   110
4. The soul and the others: humans, animals, and other subjectivities   129
5. Ethics and the others: moral fellowship with animals and beyond animals   143

    Intermediate conclusions: from Midrash to Kabbalah   169

PART II KABBALAH

    Floating Letters by Nikki Green   173

6. *Tselem Elohim* in Kabbalah, part 1: the Sefirot, the soul and body, the hypostases, and the heavens   175
7. *Tselem Elohim* in Kabbalah, part 2: the more-than-human world – holism and unifications, trees, birds, animals, and colors   208

8	Of rocks, names, and codes: the letters of Creation	233
9	*Adam Qadmon*: the universe as God's image	241
10	Gaia, *Adam Qadmon*, and Maimonides	266
11	*Qomah*: the stature of all beings	281
	Intermediate conclusions: from Kabbalah to ecotheology	312

PART III ECOTHEOLOGY

12	*Nigun, shirah*, the singing of Creation, and the problem of language	317
13	Further theological reflections	332
	Conclusions: A new ethos, a new ethics	341

Excursus 1: Nefesh *and related terms*	354
Excursus 2: The prayer of P'ri `Ets Hadar	357
Appendix: The Sefirot, the Tree of Life, and a brief history of Kabbalah	360
Bibliography of primary Jewish sources	365
Abbreviated titles	370
General index	371
Index of scriptural verses	388
Index of rabbinic sources	392

Acknowledgments

This book is especially indebted to Seth Brody, a Kabbalah scholar only a few years my elder, who shared with me a hometown, a childhood synagogue, a love for spiritual endeavor, and a passion for ecology. His very straightforward understanding of Kabbalah as a search for cosmic blessing and as an expression of human responsibility for Creation is what encouraged me to go beyond an academic vision of what Kabbalah means and to find a deep well in this field of scholarship. I imagine that large parts of this work are what he might have written had he lived to teach his Torah. I pray that he may be honored by it.

A handful of teachers have touched my life and supported my learning in key moments: Michael Paley, a Hillel rabbi who loved physics as much as Torah; Ron Kiener, who wryly taught me the rudiments of Kabbalah in the last year of Gershom Scholem's life; Shaul Magid, who bought for me my first books of Kabbalah when we were both studying at Yeshivat Hamivtar in Jerusalem; Murray Bookchin, whose work on the connections between human oppression and ecological degradation established a foundation for my own thought; Elliot Wolfson, who first exposed me to *Sefer Bahir*; Bill Lebeau, who supported me through tumultuous times at the Jewish Theological Seminary (JTS); Irene Diamond, whose understanding of ecofeminism incited some of my own breakthroughs; and Arthur Waskow, whose teachings on Torah and nuclear war in the early 1980s inspired me in 1982 to explore the Jewish response to hunger and the system of Sabbatical and Jubilee years, which began my awakening to what *Chazal* (the sages) taught about the Earth. Jacques Derrida, with whom I studied in the summer of 1986, also had a large influence on my later thinking about rabbinic texts. More concretely, Shlomo Gruber, the wizened old *buchmacher* who *schlepped* his store from Borough Park to JTS, pressed upon me several volumes that turned out to be central to my thesis. I also would like to recall two precious mentors from my year as a congregational rabbi in British Columbia, Enrica Glickman and Julian Silverman, who passed away while I was writing the dissertation this book is based on. Serendipitously, just before Tu Bishvat 2014, I stumbled upon the works of an ancestor of my great-grandmother from Aleppo, the sixteenth-century rabbi Sh'muel ben Avraham Laniado, who was, I learned, a student of Yosef Karo. Plugging into a hitherto unknown Kabbalistic lineage just as I was finishing this book felt both profound and reassuring. Most importantly, standing at the very beginning of my personal journey is my great-grandfather, Benyamin Mevorach, who came to the United States from Jerusalem Palestine in 1910 with his drum; who integrated music, joy, and kindness into his practice of Judaism and life; and who showed me the magic and theurgy of ritual. His example continually invigorates my spiritual search for holiness and community.

Since 2000, I have had the opportunity to share material that became part of this book in teaching settings around North America, as well as in Israel and Europe. I want to especially thank the Teva Learning Center (now the Teva Learning Alliance) for providing many of those opportunities, along with all my colleagues in the Jewish environmental movement who have encouraged and supported my work. Beyond the Jewish world, my relationship with Sungleska Oyate in Washington State, a Lakota-based community founded by Buck Ghosthorse, has been transformative. It also brought me together this summer with Matthew Fox. My friend and fellow Breslover-in-spirit Julian Ungar also deserves special recognition for being my first "lay reader", and I am still moved when I think about the amazing *hashgachah* that brought us side-by-side in a makeshift hostel in Uman on Rosh Hashanah 2003. I want above all to express my deepest appreciation for my "fellow fellow", Benjamin Baader, now of Winnipeg, whose support and encouragement have been constant, and whose wisdom grows ever deeper. I also want to thank my brother Steven for his constant contact during the dissertation phase and his willingness to be a resource in all matters philosophical. And I am grateful to Riqi Kosovske, who shares with me the raising of our son and who has been an ally and supporter, sharing the vision of this work through many chapters of our lives.

I would also like to thank the many people who helped in some way with the preparation of this book: David Arfa, Ben Baader, Evan Eisenberg, Gretchen Laise, Hayyim Rothman, Cara Michelle Silverberg, Nili Simhai, and especially Menachem Kallus and Jonathan Schorsch for reviewing parts of the manuscript, Emily Branton for proofreading the transliterations, Itsik Pariente for help with grammar questions, and Michael Bernstein, Lauren Deutsch, Irina Feygina, David Kaufman, Riqi Kosovske, Clementine Lazar, Larry Moss, Nili Simhai, and Alon Weinberg for helping me to review the proofs, with the obvious proviso that I am responsible for errors. Thanks also to Lewis Bateman, Shaun Vigil, Dave Morris, Tim West, Anamika Singh, and others connected to Cambridge who helped bring this book to light. Lastly, I want to thank Nikki Green (www.nikkigreen.com.au) for permission to use her exquisite artwork.

Many things have happened since the time this book was born as a dissertation in 2002. The outlines of global warming and its consequences have begun

Acknowledgments

to clearly emerge, while at the same time the movement in the United States to deny what is happening has grown stronger and stronger, especially among Orthodox Jews and Evangelical Christians. I hope that this book, rooted in the most traditional of perspectives, can be used as a resource by people within those communities to help bring their communities to the side of honoring the Creation and the Creator, not just in word but in deed.

On a personal level, in 2003 I received *s'mikhah* from R' Zalman Schachter-Shalomi. (My first ordination, from JTS, came in 1994.) Reb Zalman, as he was known, inspired many people of many generations to pray, feel, and work on behalf of the Earth, and he called on his students to bring the Jewish paradigm into alignment with his vision of ecumenism and responsibility for Gaia. Reb Zalman took a strong interest in the progress of this book, and he passed away just as it was coming to press. Of course, of all the things that have happened, nothing has been more important to me than the birth of my boy Chanina in 2004. Imagining the world of his future is what pushes me to carry on when I am feeling the least hopeful. Finally, greatest thanks are due my parents Richard and Ronnie for their financial and emotional support, which enabled me to work on this book full-time in 2002 and 2013–14. In the time between the dissertation and the book, my father passed away. It is sorrowful to not be able to share the completion of this book with him.

The seeds of this work were planted when I started keeping Shabbat at Dartmouth College in 1981. My visceral experience of an Earth-centered Judaism from that time remains the unshakeable foundation for this book, and for my Jewish practice. My experiences led me to apply for a Mellon Grant in 1982 to study the Sabbatical and Jubilee years – this began my lifelong research on Judaism and ecology. The broadest outline of this book was limned in a curriculum I wrote for the Coalition on the Environment and Jewish Life in 1996; I realized its deeper significance only later, while leading a series of "Nature and Torah" walks in Central Park for Manhattan's Congregation Ansche Chesed. I did much of the textual research as a Finkelstein fellow at the University of Judaism, fall 1997 to fall 1998. The first statement of my thesis was delivered in a lecture sponsored by the Center for the Study of Religion and Society at the University of Victoria in British Columbia in 1999, while the dissertation this book is based on was completed for JTS in 2002 in Seattle.

A large focus of this work is to highlight and call into question some of the modernist assumptions that scholars and theologians make when they read rabbinic literature and Jewish thought, and to offer alternatives to these assumptions that might bring us closer to the first meaning of these texts. I likewise expect others to offer challenges and refinements to the assumptions I make.

This book is intended to address academic, theological, and spiritual interests, which means that many elements that would be unnecessary to explain in an academic context are explained here and, conversely, many elements that would be taken for granted in a spiritual context need to be justified here. I have taken care to distinguish the homiletical and the theological from the historical and critical aspects of the discussion. I encourage each reader to use the cross-references provided to find the threads that fit her or his inclinations.

I pray this book, coming out soon after the beginning of the first Sabbatical year ever to be widely noted and observed in the diaspora, will be a meaningful step toward renewal in our relationship with the Earth and with Spirit. Most importantly, and above any intra-human concerns, I pray that we may see a flowering of relationship, a flowing of knowledge, to and from the real fields and forests, from the manifold creatures and beings, that encompass our human world and that make up the reality of Being we so often ignore. May this also be a flowering of truest praise for the One whose infinite and infinitely diverse image is held within every being.

27th of Iyyar, *Yom Hakeshet* (Rainbow Day), 5774

Notes on translation, transliteration, and bibliography

Because of the attention given to terminology in this work, most passages are translated according to the principles of concordant ("literal") translation. They are non-idiomatic and are intended, as far as possible, to reflect ambiguities in the Hebrew and to represent midrashic and philological connections between words. Important terms or words that are etymologically connected in Hebrew are sometimes given in transliteration in order to show their connection. Where the Hebrew is difficult to translate, I often include transliteration as well, and in some cases, alternative translations. Many passages translated concordantly here can be found in idiomatic translation elsewhere.

Please note that the British convention that puts punctuation inside quotation marks only if it is part of the quote ("logical punctuation") is followed.

Consonants: The system of transliteration used in this work is somewhat scientific but is meant to be readable and typeable, so it is not completely reversible to Hebrew. The common conventions of "*q*" for *Quf* ק and "*k*" for *Kaf* כ, "*kh*" for *Khaf* כ and "*ch*" for *Chet* are used. *Tsadi* צ is represented by "*ts*" rather than "*tz*". The diacritical mark (`) is used for `*Ayin* ע. *Tet* ט, *Samekh* ס, and *Vet* ב are underlined to distinguish them from *Tav* ת, *Sin* שׂ, and *Vav* ו in transliterated text; they are not underlined in book titles or names. (Consonants with *dagesh* are also not doubled.) The letter *Alef* א is represented by a single quotation mark ('): for example, *ha'el* (God). This mark is left off of words beginning with *Alef*, since it may be assumed. Aramaic words ending in *Alef* (indicating the definite article) are also transliterated without (') at the end: e.g., *d'yoqna* (image) rather than *d'yoqna'*.

Other diacritics may also be left out of names, and conventional transliterations may be used. For example: Ezra instead of `Ezra, Yehoshua instead of Y'hoshu`a (Joshua), Yitshak instead of Yits'chaq (Isaac).

Vowels: The vowel *tseirey* (a long "a" sound) is transliterated "*ei*"; where it is followed by a *Yud*, the combination is transliterated "*ey*". *Tseirey* may be

xv

transliterated "*e*" in closed syllables, especially those ending a word, e.g., *hineh* (here), and in places where "*ei*" would lead to difficult-to-read spellings. The combination *patach* or *qamats* plus Yud (a long "i" sound) is transliterated "*ay*" in the middle of a word and "*ai*" at the end of a word. Similarly, *chirik* (a long "e" sound) is transliterated "*i*", even when combined with Yud at the end of a word. For *sh'va*, only *sh'va na`* (the pronounced *sh'va*, which makes a short "i" sound) is indicated by a single quote ('). The single quote mark is also used to separate consonant or vowel combinations likely to be elided and mispronounced by an English reader: e.g., *tsomei'ach* (growing thing) or *par'tsuf* (face). It may help the reader unfamiliar with Hebrew to know that in transliteration, *sh'va na`* always appears between two consonants, while *Alef* never does.

The mark for abbreviations used in Hebrew texts is also represented by ('): for example, R' for *Rabi* or Rabbi. The mark for acronyms and numbers is represented by the similar looking ("), appearing before the last letter as it does in Hebrew: e.g., *B"N*; commonly used acronyms that have a conventional pronunciation, such as Rashi and *Chazal*, are given without this mark. Some words and names that have well-known transliterations or English renderings are spelled conventionally, such as *Rabbah* in *Midrash Rabbah*, aggadah and *aggadot*, gematria, Moshe, Sukkah, and Gemara. Words commonly used in English, like midrash and mitsvah, are not italicized; however, when given a plural Hebrew ending, they are italicized: *midrashim*, *mitsvot*.

A few other conventions have been adopted to help the reader. For translated passages, material in square brackets should be read as part of the quote, while supplemental or alternative material is placed in parentheses: for example, "were it not said (told) to them, they would [still] be beloved". When transliterated Hebrew appears alongside translation, if the English or the Hebrew is a phrase of two or more words, a space is left between the slash and that phrase: for example, "very good / *tov m'od*". When scripture is quoted, its citation appears in square brackets. When it is referred to without being quoted, its citation appears in parentheses. Also, in any rabbinic text where scripture is quoted and then followed immediately by its interpretation, the two are connected by an em dash: for example, "'in our image as our likeness'—not man without woman and not woman without man, and not both of them without Shekhinah", or "'In beginning /*B'Rei'ShiT*' [Gn 1:1]—look at the letters and see: Desiring Song / *ShiR Ta'eV*.

Page numbers preceded by "p." or "pp." always refer to pages within *Kabbalah and Ecology*. In cases where a full citation is given for passages in journal articles or book chapters, the page range is separated from the specific pages cited by a semi-colon: for example, "*Science* 252 (2004): 378–81; 380".

There are three indexes provided, along with a diagram of the Sefirot (in the Appendix). Note that the general index can also serve as a rudimentary glossary. Lastly, both the full bibliography for this book and a discussion of its methodology are published online at: www.kabbalahandecology.com.

Overview of *Kabbalah and Ecology*

This book examines precedents in Jewish thought for going beyond the strictly anthropocentric interpretation of the cosmos that characterizes Judaism and the Abrahamic traditions. The fulcrum for this examination is the idea of God's image, or *tselem*, and the ways it has been stretched in both Midrash and Kabbalah to include more than human beings. At the book's core is a transvaluation of the human–Nature relationship, indicated by a relatively new term for Nature: the "more-than-human world" (see Introduction, n.4).

One central focus is to establish a theology grounded entirely in traditional texts that envisions Creation and all creatures as participating in the divine image. Throughout, I examine precedents from Midrash, Kabbalah, and *Chasidut* (Hasidism) that differ from modernist or humanist anthropocentrism and that point toward alternative anthropologies or ways of understanding humanity. While in each case I am interested in the historical meaning of the texts, and there are many insights that I hope will make a meaningful contribution to the history of Jewish thought, the overarching purpose is to enable Jewish theology to sustain a more biocentric reading of Torah and the Jewish tradition.

The Introduction discusses the challenges that arise from ecology, beginning with general reflections on the ecological crisis and its impact on religious thought and on specific challenges faced by the Abrahamic traditions. A survey of previous work in Judaism and ecology can be found here, along with discussion about the contribution and method of this book. Broad questions are explored under the headings of "diversity", "non-human subjecthood", and "evolution". In the last section, on evolution, anthropocentrism is critiqued directly from a Maimonidean perspective. Evolution, which contradicts human exceptionalism, is discussed in light of the thought of both Maimonides and Abraham Isaac Kook. The Introduction concludes with what I call a "theological map", that is, a homiletical statement of the thesis developed herein, based on *Mishnah Avot* 3:14, which is this: When we affirm and extend the idea of God's image to other creatures, we more fully embody the image of God. This may be deemed our theological niche.

Part I of the book, on Midrash, outlines classical rabbinic anthropology and ideas about the image of God (*tselem Elohim*), the soul, and the human place in the world. This provides a basis for comparison with the texts of Kabbalah. Here it is demonstrated that the standard interpretation of *tselem* given by modern thinkers – that only human beings are in God's image – is not the best reading of rabbinic texts.

In Chapters 1 and 2, midrashic interpretations of *tselem* are organized according to whether they focus on intellectual, physical, behavioral, or ethical qualities as the essence of the divine image. *B'rei'shit* (*Genesis*) *Rabbah* is the central midrashic text analyzed, while other texts are looked at in comparison to it. A central idea in early midrash is that only half of Creation, the `elyonim*, higher or upper creatures, is in God's image, while the *tachtonim* or lower creatures are not. This metaphysical division is queried in all subsequent chapters.

Throughout these chapters, I explore the ramifications and evolution of various midrashic motifs in both medieval and modern thought. Maimonides, who adopts some remarkably eco-centric theological positions, is a frequent reference point. Here and in Chapter 4, the growing influence of anti-corporealist theology in Judaism – that is, the belief that the body is in opposition to Spirit[1] – is also traced from early midrash to later midrash to Jewish philosophy.

In Chapter 3, I tease apart the value complex that unites within the human being the ideas of *tselem*, soul, and infinite value. This value complex characterizes most modern Jewish thought. I use the term "modernist-humanist" to refer to this value complex in the rest of the book. Midrashic texts thought to be the source of these ideas are carefully analyzed to show that they do not ground human value in God's image, but in the value of Creation.

Four points are drawn from these three chapters:

1. *Tselem* according to the rabbis is not limited to human beings but includes the angels and the heavens.
2. Soul, *nefesh* or *n'shamah*, is not equated with *tselem* in early midrash.
3. The modern idea that human life has "infinite value" has no clear representation in rabbinic thought.
4. The rabbis do not connect the idea of God's image with imitating God until after the close of the Amoraic period (around the eighth century).

Focusing on these points clears space for alternative readings of the tradition. Modernist-humanist theology is not "disproven" by this. In fact, a central element in the modernist (and medieval) understanding of *tselem*, the idea

---

[1] "Anti-corporealism" can also refer to a different belief, that God has no physical body or form.

Overview xix

that God's image is realized through imitating God, is also central to any ecotheological interpretation. Rather, the modernist-humanist interpretation is shown to be a hermeneutical choice.

Chapter 4 deals with the evolution of the rabbinic understanding of soul, including the impact of Hellenism on Jewish thought and the conception that animals have souls.

Chapter 5 discusses the ethical norms applied to animals in Torah and rabbinic literature, the fact that the rabbis believed animals have moral standing and the potential to be moral actors, and how the rabbis understood stewardship and dominion. The rabbinic view of animals elucidates how the rabbis viewed the non-human other in general, including mountains, stones, and rivers, and most especially land, and how they extended a kind of moral standing to such entities.

This chapter is followed by a brief summary of the Intermediate Conclusions arrived at in Part I, as well as reflections on the idea of biophilia.

Part II, on Kabbalah, begins with a survey of ideas about *tselem* in Kabbalistic texts. Chapter 6 focuses on interpretations that extend midrashic ideas, while Chapter 7 discusses ideas that differ from the Midrash. The most important points in these chapters are:

1. In Kabbalah, *tselem* has a physical meaning that includes sexuality and the structure of our bodies and that simultaneously reflects the divine realms of the Sefirot.
2. Kabbalah sees many non-human creatures or dimensions of the earthly or lower realm as being in the divine image.

That sexuality in Kabbalah is part of *tselem* is well known but especially important, because sexuality and reproduction were defined in many classical midrashic texts as qualities we share with the lower creatures that are not *b'tselem*, not "in the image".

The second point is based on a hermeneutic essential to Kabbalah: the system of the Sefirot (attributes or vessels of God) and the name YHVH, writ upon the human body and soul, are identified as what constitutes God's image. Under the veil of esotericism, Kabbalistic texts use the same terminology to identify this divine imprint in various non-human creatures and more-than-human dimensions. Generally, elements of the *tachtonim* treated this way represent either the unification of the heavens and the earth (trees, birds), the whole of Creation, some spectrum that stands for the totality of world or cosmos (all colors, all animals), or all of the above (the *mishkan*, the rainbow).

Chapter 8 discusses the connection between *chiyut* or lifeforce and divinity in the thought of Shneur Zalman of Liady and Yaakov Lainer and whether a general theory about the extension of *tselem* to all the *tachtonim* can be grounded in these concepts.

Chapter 9 looks at how Kabbalah conceives the universe in its totality. In particular, the terminology "*Adam Qadmon*" describes the cosmos, including the Sefirotic worlds, as divinity. Some Kabbalists, especially Yosef Ashkenazi, drew the conclusion that if Adam is in God's image and the universe in the form of *Adam Qadmon* is in the human image, then Creation is *b'tselem*.

The second part of Chapter 9 discusses Shneur Zalman's description in *Igeret Haqodesh* 20 of the earthly realm as part of the living body of *Adam Qadmon*. Using the rubric of *Or Chozer*, returning or reflected light, Shneur Zalman of Liady specifically valorizes the Earth, which uniquely manifests the originary love present at the beginning of Creation.

Chapter 10 examines parallels between Maimonidean thought and *Adam Qadmon*, both of which attribute tremendous value and personhood to the whole of Creation, and between both of these and Gaia theory, which posits that the Earth is best understood as a living, whole organism.

Chapter 11 identifies several synonyms for *tselem* that evolved in Kabbalah. One in particular, *qomah*, can be traced from early Jewish texts of midrash, mysticism, and liturgy, through Kabbalistic and Hasidic thought. For Yishayah Horowitz, *qomah* came to mean **tselem in potentia**. The Ba`al Shem Tov and his disciples finally applied *qomah sh'leymah* to the idea that human intervention can reveal the divine image in other beings.

This chapter is followed by a second Intermediate Conclusions section that reviews some of the conjunctions between Kabbalah and ecotheology.

Part III looks more specifically at ecotheology. Chapter 12 focuses on language, a chief element of *tselem* according to early midrash, in the form of prayer, song, and naming. While it does discuss midrashic themes and texts, unlike other chapters it relies on modern thinkers, in particular Martin Buber and Nachman of Breslov, to elaborate the idea that all Creation has language.

Chapter 13 looks at how ideas discussed in earlier chapters line up with popular expositions of Jewish ecotheology found in the writings of Arthur Green and Arthur Waskow, and with "secular" ecotheologies. I also provide two other "theological maps" for extending *tselem* to the more-than-human world; these are analogous to the one discussed in the Introduction, but are earth-centered rather than human-centered. This chapter may be read as a second introduction to the book.

The Conclusion explores the use of historical-critical methods in constructive theology, the limitations of stewardship, and some of the halakhic and ethical implications of expanding God's image to the more-than-human. Finally, it asks: What does the theological process have to do with ecological reparation, with *tiqun* (*tikkun*), and with redemption? How do we turn theology into a living practice?

Methods for Jewish Constructive Theology, published separately online at www.kabbalahandecology.com, situates this book in the continuum of theological discourse, Jewish Studies scholarship, and literary theory. *Methods* responds to the questions that *Wissenschaft des Judentums*[2] scholars may have about combining critical analysis of texts with constructive theology.

[2] "The Scientific Study of Judaism" – the "positive-historical" school of criticism that began in the nineteenth century.

Introduction

Jewish ecological thought and the challenge for scriptural theology

> One planet, one experiment.
>
> E. O. Wilson

We live in a wondrous place, this Earth, filled with beauty and surprise. A world where the merest sparkle on the surface of the water can suggest in its variation the infinitude of the universe, the *"ru'ach Elohim m'rachefet"* – the spirit of God hovering, fluttering on the face of the waters; a world where all our senses can be filled and overflow; a world in which we share so much with even the wildest and least known creatures. As human beings we have the potential to be enchanted by all those creatures, to act in love and in faith toward them, and toward the greater mystery and unity that is all Being and that transcends all Being. As human beings, we have the potential to feel compassion for all people and all creatures we meet, and yet we have such passions and dispassions as to make us forget compassion.

Compassion does arise, naturally and spontaneously, from the moment we encounter an Other. Moral reflection can extend the reach of that compassion, even beyond the neighbor, and beyond the span of a single lifetime. But our moral vision is too easily limited to what we can imagine in our mind's eye. Religion at its best serves to magnify the power of compassion and moral vision beyond the naked eye and the "naked mind", to extend it over hundreds or thousands of years. Religion can teach us how to act to preserve life far beyond the horizon of what any of us can calculate or plan for. Religion, ritual, faith, tradition, all of them exist as guides, not just for one lifetime or for one generation, but for the proverbial seven generations, that is, for as long as any civilization will last, potentially for tens of thousands of years.

This truth is embedded in the Torah's plea to each person she addresses: "Choose life, so that you and your seed will live!" [Dt 30:19] If this is the anthropological, psychological, and metaphysical truth of religion – one of the purposes of religion, as I believe – then aside from a handful of indigenous traditions that are threatened with extinction, religion is failing. One could say that religion has already failed.

Yet we have not entirely lost our compass. Even as religion is struggling to catch up with its purpose, science can help us reclaim the inner truth of that purpose. The first way this happens is that we are becoming ever more awake to the profound miracles and intricate processes that constitute what we call life. Science has been developing the capacity to recognize, model, and study the extraordinary complexity, diversity, munificence, and wondrousness of living creatures and systems, in ways that were unimagined (to all but mystics) as recently as a few decades ago.[3] New insights into the deep nature and structure of life, at the microscopic, macroscopic, and astronomical levels, are enabling us to perceive and receive the more-than-human world we call Nature on its own terms, beyond human projections and human needs.[4] It takes only a slight shift into the language of the sacred to recognize that this knowledge practically commands us to stand in awe of Creation.[5]

Of course, science also brings us technology, and it is our technology that is bringing us to what may be the brink of a collapse. And yet, even as science teaches us how to leverage our power to move mountains, and to destroy them, science also enables us to study how human action impacts the world, and to understand how systems as enormous as the climate of the entire planet can change.[6] That is another way that science can help us recover the purpose of religion: it is enabling us to see and measure how the fabric of life can be torn apart by human profligacy and greed.[7]

---

[3] This is a consequence of many factors, including development of new technologies, especially in computing and the study of genetics, and application of the mathematics of complexity and chaos.

[4] David Abram coined the phrase "more-than-human world" in *The Spell of the Sensuous* (New York: Vintage Books, 1996) to replace the term "Nature". Abram's terminology uproots the culture/Nature dichotomy – "more-than-human" includes the human – conceptualizing the environment that surrounds us as inclusive of humanity. It not only embraces a world that is both immanent and intimately related to us, but also acknowledges that this world transcends our needs, purposes, and knowledge. See pp.34 (esp. n.102), 54, 207, and n.19 on the concept of "more-than-human". I capitalize "Nature" (except when the term is within quotes) whenever it refers to the whole natural world.

[5] Throughout, I capitalize "Creation" to refer to the universe, while "creation" refers to God's process of creating. Some quoted passages have been altered to reflect this usage.

[6] How can it be that the science of climate change incites such consternation in some fundamentalist believers of the Bible when the Torah is so insistent that climate change, and climate disaster, are the consequence for a society living out of balance, the consequence of a society that does not respect "God's preference" (to borrow the term used by Liberation theologians) for the poor and for the land? The rationalist tendency to redline those parts of the Torah that describe climate disaster as a divine consequence of sin is also problematic – for example, after much debate, the final version of the Reform movement's newest prayerbook, *Mishkan Tefila: A Reform Siddur* (New York: CCAR, 2007) once again omitted the second paragraph of the Sh'ma` prayer, Dt 11:13–21, (discussed n.412).

[7] The way science can gift us with wonder, foreboding, and tragedy was neatly exemplified over a three-day period in March 2014. On the 16th, an extraordinary announcement came that

Introduction

From the Gulf oil catastrophe of 2010 to melting glaciers, to extreme weather events like 2013's Hurricane Sandy,[8] to poisoned and depleted aquifers, to acidification of the oceans (which are more acidic than they have been in 300 *million* years[9]), the human impact is planetary in scale.[10] So too is it pervasive at the cellular level, where disruptions of fertility and growth due to petrochemicals, ozone depletion, carcinogens, and mutagens have the potential to affect any birth any place on Earth.[11] And on the level that we register most easily with our senses, the human scale of animals and plants, of valleys and rivers, species in every nation and ecosystem are imminently endangered. One does not need complex computer models to know that we are degrading Earth's carrying capacity.[12] Even without global climate change, simply by taking more and more land and habitat out of natural ecosystems and putting it into our service, we are disfiguring the face of our planet. It is at best a kind of gallows

---

scientists had detected the polarization of "gravitational waves" in the cosmic microwave background – evidence for cosmic inflation close to the beginning of time. (Whether these results will hold up is uncertain.) On the 17th, a team announced that even the most northern ice sheet in Greenland was rapidly deteriorating due to climate change (Shfaqat A. Khan et al., "Sustained Mass Loss of the Northeast Green- land Ice Sheet Triggered by Regional Warming", *Nature: Climate Change* 4 [2014]: 292–9, doi:10.1038/nclimate2161). The next day, a study of the genetic diversity of the last moas in New Zealand confirmed that 600 years ago, humans were the cause of their extinction (Morten Erik Allentoft et al., "Extinct New Zealand Megafauna Were Not in Decline before Human Colonization", *Proceedings of the National Academy of Science* 111:13 [2014]: 4922–7).

[8] One cannot know that a particular storm is "caused" by climate change, but the probability that climate change played a factor in it can be estimated. More broadly, one cannot determine what the weather would have been in the absence of climate change, because the weather itself is the change, and cause and effect are indistinguishable. This quality, related to nonlinearity, is reflected in the mathematics of chaos, which is one tool science uses to model weather.

[9] The acidity of the oceans, driven by the concentration of CO_2 in the atmosphere, is also estimated to be increasing even more quickly than at the time of the mass extinction at the end of the Permian period. See Bärbel Hönisch et al., "The Geological Record of Ocean Acidification", *Science* 335:6072 (Mar. 2, 2012): 1058–63.

[10] Not to mention the Great Pacific Garbage Patch – and the astonishing choice we have made to base our way of life on things that are intended be used once and thrown away, and to manufacture those things out of material that will last for thousands of years.

[11] "Earth" is capitalized when I am specifically referring to the whole planet as such. Otherwise, "earth" is used, including in cases where the meaning is "the entire earthly realm", and in translations. See n.61.

[12] If we take a moment to think outside our anthropocentric frame, which equates carrying capacity with "maximum number of human beings that the planet can sustain", the simple fact that so many species are at risk tells us that the Earth's capacity to nourish Life is being diminished. Calculating a numerical upper limit on Earth's "carrying capacity" is in any case naïve, because in a world that nurtures abundance, diversity, and symbiosis, the maximum sustainable human population will increase – life augments the conditions for more life. But with the resilience of Earth's systems decreasing while (and because) the human population is increasing, the limits to growth could come crashing down upon us precipitously. It may not be possible for us to know the point at which catastrophic change will occur until we have already passed it. See Marten Scheffer et al., "Catastrophic Shifts in Ecosystems", *Nature* 413 (Oct. 11, 2001): 591–6.

humor that even as so many wondrous creatures are becoming endangered or extinct, corporations are creating and patenting new sub-species.

Many scientists estimate the current rate of extinction to be precedented only by the five mass extinctions in Earth's history.[13] Add in climate disruption, and we may witness the loss, over the next 100 years, of well more than half the species that have existed on Earth for the past 20 to 55 million years.[14] And so, during the next century, we will witness the irrevocable consequences of the past century and a half of technological development. E. O. Wilson writes, "[I]f enough species are extinguished, will the ecosystems collapse, and will the extinction of most other species follow soon afterward? The only answer one can give is: possibly. By the time we find out, however, it might be too late. One planet, one experiment."[15]

Within the most industrialized societies, environmental movements have responded by calling for a transformation of culture and technology. In the less developed nations, environmentalists have called for resistance to Western technologies and to the Western path of development. In many places, the Transition Town movement, started in England and inspired by the principles of permaculture, seeks to create alternative systems of living that are resilient and sustainable. But our ability to care about what is happening arises not just from science and politics, but also from love, which, along with awe, is one of the roots of religion. And religion in turn is one of the strongest vessels for husbanding love toward social transformation.

The transformation we need to carry out will affect every aspect of human culture.[16] It has already had a profound impact on religious thought, leading to the re-evaluation of older theologies and the creation of "ecotheologies". Often

---

[13] Many consider our epoch to be the sixth mass extinction. See Elizabeth Kolbert, *The Sixth Extinction: An Unnatural History* (New York: Henry Holt, 2014) for a popular exposition of the science behind this conclusion. If this is so, the beginning of this mass extinction event dates to well before industrialization. There have already been widespread losses, for example, of all the megafauna (including elephants, saber-toothed cats, giant beavers, etc.) in the Americas and in Europe, the many species of giant bird in New Zealand (see n.7), and many of the marsupials of Australia. These losses occurred tens of thousands of years ago – even before the spread of agriculture. It is perhaps vital to notice that many of the indigenous cultures that grew in the ecological shadow of these catastrophes are profoundly sensitive to living in harmony with the Earth and the land. On this pattern applied to Hebrew thought, see p.8. This phenomenon may bear witness to the capacity of human culture to undergo exactly the kind of profound change we need today.

[14] M. C. Cadotte, B. J. Cardinale, and T. H. Oakley, "Evolutionary History Predicts the Ecological Impacts of Species Extinction", *Proceedings of the National Academy of Science*, 105 (2008): 17012–17. Paleontologists identify 55 million years ago as the time when mammals and birds began to radiate into all the species we see. Other branches of the Tree of Life are quite a bit older.

[15] *The Diversity of Life* (New York: W. W. Norton, 1992), 182.

[16] This is true not just because we must "retool" our society to become sustainable; it is also rightly argued that the roots of environmental ruin are in the bedrock of Western culture. See esp. Murray Bookchin, *The Ecology of Freedom: The Emergence and Dissolution of Hierarchy*

this creativity gets channeled toward the utilitarian purpose of making theology "relevant" to contemporary political and spiritual concerns. It is religion catching up to the present. What is at stake is far greater than that, however. Unless we can find a balance with the more-than-human world that can sustain the lives of the multitude of species, we will be awakening to a present that has no future.[17] The work of theology therefore must be directed toward the future.

It is the coming generations who will bear witness to the answer to Wilson's question. We who can only anticipate the answer are left with two fundamental questions: How can we begin turning the course of human civilization toward sustainability? And, can we begin to create the spiritual resources necessary for those generations to come who will face the problems we are creating – resources that will help them keep intact their humanity and sympathy, for all people and all life, and ultimately to thrive?

I have chosen as the focus of this book the fundament of Biblically based theology that is often the greatest source of disconnection from the natural world: the image of God. Modern and traditional theology have interpreted God's image as something that not only elevates us above Creation, but also separates and isolates us from the rest of Creation. Can we revalue the divine image, and envision Creation and all creatures as participating in this image?[18] This question is connected to many other ecological issues – animal rights, intrinsic value, stewardship, biodiversity, etc. – all of which have political implications.

But the challenge to culture and religion goes far beyond any of the explicitly political issues and ecological dangers mentioned so far. This challenge is also an opportunity to become closer, as it were, to God, to Creation, and to ourselves.

There is another reason why the question of God's image ought to be foremost in our minds. The meaning of "human", as sign, being, and species, has

---

(Oakland CA: AK Press, 2005) and "Death of a Small Planet", *The Progressive* (Aug. 1989): 19–23.

[17] While humanity might decimate the planet's biosphere, life will continue in other forms and will eventually thrive again, as it has done after every mass extinction event. We are neither able to destroy nor to "save" the Earth. However, Stephen Jay Gould ("The Golden Rule: A Proper Scale for Our Environmental Crisis", in *Eight Little Piggies* [New York: W. W. Norton, 1993], ch.2) talks about a "golden rule", a time-scale that relates to our lifespan as a species. We are only some 200,000 years into our lifespan, and yet we are facing (and causing) the end of the conditions on Earth that favor us to be here. But, as the Midrash teaches, God made and destroyed worlds before this one (n.779).

[18] The concept of "participating in God's image" is broader than the idea of "being in God's image". The term "participate" allows room for different kinds of relationship to *tselem*; different orders of Being such as rocks or animals may participate in God's image in different ways (see p.59ff.). I am drawing especially on Yosef Ashkenazi for this concept (see p.254; see also Aquinas, nn.54, 84). "Orders of Being" is a secular terminology corresponding to "orders of Creation / s̲idrey v̲'rei'shit", which is one comprehensive way of talking about Nature within rabbinic tradition (see n.936). (On space before or after a forward slash, see Notes on Transliteration.)

already been transformed by the ecological and physical sciences. The concepts of ecosystem and biodiversity, as well as ecophilosophy's critique of the cultural idea of wilderness and of Nature in general,[19] compel us to recognize that there is a more intimate relationship between culture and multifarious Nature than the Western intellectual tradition has assumed. The development of ideas of non-human agency and the recognition of emotion and of forms of language in non-human animals have led many scientists to reject Cartesian notions of the animal. Moral philosophy has begun to encompass an ecological ethos in which non-human lives and communities can be seen as ends-in-themselves. Evolutionary and genetic sciences have given us greater and greater comprehension of the relations between all life forms, while complexity and chaos theory have given us tools to quantify and affirm intuitions about the aesthetic unity of life and the more-than-mechanical coherence of the physical world.[20] The idea that humanity stands apart from Nature, and that the more-than-human world exists to serve our needs in whatever we desire, is as untenable as it is demeaning to "what the Creator has wrought".

In every dimension, we need to overcome the disconnect between our real relation to and dependence on this physical living world, and our tendency to value only those needs and ends that are strictly human. Ecological insights have altered the way we think about everything from economics to salvation. Even if there were no ecological crisis, we would still need to ask anew, in the face of deeper knowledge of who and what we are: What is God's relation to the cosmos? How does Creation, if indeed it be created, teach us about the nature of the Creator? What responsibility for the well-being of other species comes with the ever-expanding knowledge of our connection to them? As our understanding of humanity evolves, so must our theology.

---

[19] Ecophilosophers mostly reject the romantic idea of wilderness as a place empty of human presence or impact. See Max Oelschlager, *The Idea of Wilderness: From Prehistory to the Age of Ecology* (New Haven CT: Yale University Press, 1993) and Peter Van Wyck, *Primitives in the Wilderness: Deep Ecology and the Missing Human Subject* (Albany NY: SUNY Press, 1997). Culture, society, and Nature are always in dialogue, and there is no place on Earth empty of human traces. The fact that scientists detect levels of human-generated pollution in the most remote icefields and oceans underscores the reality that no phenomenon is completely isolated. Even biomes at the bottom of the ocean can be impacted by humanity, not just because of deep-sea drilling, but even because as the ocean warms, there is less mixing of layers, which means less oxygen is available.

The idea that Nature and culture are separable is difficult to defend. But much of the ecophilosophy on this question critiques the dualism between culture and Nature from a cultural-linguistic perspective; that is, "Nature" as a concept is never more than a cultural construct. The deeper (and, I would say, spiritual) implications of overcoming this dualism are explored by authors who focus on the living continuity of mind, body, and earth, such as Abram in *The Spell of the Sensuous* (the source of the term "more-than-human world"). See n.102.

[20] Scientific information related to these themes can be found in sources on the Web, so specific citations are only occasionally given, mostly where the information is new, not easily accessed, available only from a few sources, or disputed.

Jewish ecological thought

This work of evolving new ways of thinking about God, human, and cosmos is what we call constructive or creative theology. It differs from what is sometimes labeled theology in academia in that it is ultimately not about what Jewish theologians said in the past, but rather about what Jewish tradition can and should speak to the future. This may sound inimical to a clear-eyed appraisal of the history of Jewish thought. What I hope will become clear in the course of this work, however, is that all these new perspectives and questions not only push us to evolve theology, but also illuminate for us, in critical ways, the meaning of ancient texts and ideas, and the history of those texts and ideas.

JEWISH ECOLOGICAL THOUGHT

In the past thirty years of Jewish environmentalism, great leaps have been made in Jewish thought, awareness, and practice. One purpose of *Kabbalah and Ecology* is to push that work forward in a significant way. The central question of this book is: "Can we, on the basis of traditional Jewish sources, say that creatures other than human beings are in God's image?"[21] Asking this question lets us break down the wall that separates our humanity from our connection to other species, to life in general, and to the Earth itself. An ancillary question to consider is: Can we expand the meaning of God's image in a way that has integrity with the past, with tradition, and with the deepest insights of religion before modernity?

I want to acknowledge several authors who have already taken important steps toward an ecological vision of Judaism. In particular, Arthur Green, Eilon Schwartz, and Arthur Waskow have each extended Jewish ecology in new directions.[22] Arthur Waskow's work probably reached the widest audience up

---

[21] There are several significant figures for Jewish ecology whose theology will not be dealt with herein because their work does not address this central question – in particular, Bachya ibn Paquda (eleventh century, Spain) and Abraham Joshua Heschel (1907–92, Poland, United States), both of whom show extraordinary sensitivity to the natural world. On Bachya, see n.60. On Heschel, see p.96 herein, and Mike Comins, *A Wild Faith: Jewish Ways Into Wilderness, Wilderness Ways Into Judaism* (Woodstock VT: Jewish Lights, 2007), ch.4, 20–25. There are also areas of Jewish thought valuable for ecotheology that do not bear on this question, such as non-Hasidic *Musar* (ethical) literature, which is a rich resource for thinking about how to develop appreciation of and transcend consumerist attitudes toward Nature.

[22] On the contributions of all three, see Hava Tirosh-Samuelson, "Judaism", in *The Oxford Handbook of Religion and Ecology*, ed. Roger S. Gottlieb (New York: Oxford University Press, 2006), 52–3. Others whose work has significantly advanced the field include Everett Gendler and Hans Jonas. On Gendler, see Eilon Schwartz, "Judaism and Nature: Theological and Moral Issues" in *Torah of the Earth*, 2 vols., ed. Arthur Waskow (Woodstock VT: Jewish Lights, 2000), vol.2, 159–73; 163 (see n.25 for other editions of this article). On Jonas, see Lawrence Troster, "Caretaker or Citizen: Hans Jonas, Aldo Leopold, and the Development of Jewish Environmental Ethics" in *The Legacy of Hans Jonas: Judaism and the Phenomenon of Life*, eds. Hava Tirosh-Samuelson and Christian Wiese (Leiden: Brill, 2008), 373–96, as well as Tirosh-Samuelson, "Judaism", 55–6.

until the millenium,[23] though Arthur Green may have outpaced him since the publication of *Seek My Face, Speak My Name*.[24] I will return to their work in Chapter 13. Eilon Schwartz, in his article "Judaism and Nature: Theological and Moral Issues to Consider While Renegotiating a Jewish Relationship to the Natural World", questions the validity of the rigid boundary between Judaism and "paganism".[25] Evan Eisenberg's book *The Ecology of Eden* also broke new ground.[26] One of its central ideas, that the Biblical tradition may have emerged from the response of pre-Biblical Hebrews to the ecological collapse of Mesopotamian civilization, has become an important element in Waskow's teaching and in my own.[27] On a broader cultural level, the project to create a gender-liberating Judaism in the United States dating from the 1970s raised the issue of embodiment, which is an essential ingredient of a more eco-centric Judaism.[28]

---

[23] Besides *Seasons of Our Joy* (Boston MA: Beacon Press, 1982), his early and influential work on the Jewish holidays and cycles of Nature, Waskow's publications include two edited collections: *Torah of the Earth* and (with Ari Elon and Naomi Hyman), *Trees, Earth, and Torah* (Philadelphia: JPS, 1999). On Waskow, see n.58, pp.238, 240, 332ff.

[24] *Seek My Face* (New York: Jason Aronson, 1994); "A Kabbalah for the Environmental Age", *Tikkun* 14:5 (1999): 33–40; *Ehyeh: A Kabbalah for Tomorrow* (Woodstock VT: Jewish Lights, 2002), esp. 106–19; and *Radical Judaism: Rethinking God and Tradition* (New Haven CT, 2010). Green's work is discussed on pp.231, 238, 333–4.

[25] First published in *Judaism* 44:4 (1985): 437–47, "Judaism and Nature" was reprinted in both Waskow, *Torah of the Earth*, vol.2 (see n.22) and *Judaism and Environmental Ethics*, ed. Martin Yaffe (Lanham MD: Lexington Books, 2001), 297–308 (hereafter cited as "Yaffe"). All subsequent page references to "Judaism and Nature" refer to *Torah of the Earth*.

The nexus between Judaism and "paganism" deserves a book-length treatment. Further discussion is found at nn.34, 52, 403, and pp.9 (esp. n.29), 23, 122–3, 232, 272, and in *Methods*. Schwartz's work parallels a class I have taught since 1993 on what I sometimes call, tongue-in-cheek, "pagan monotheism". Jill Hammer's more recent article, "An Altar of Earth: Reflections on Jews, Goddesses and the Zohar" (*Zeek* [July 2004], www.zeek.net/spirit_0407.shtml [Mar. 2012]), touches on the same theme. Howard Eilberg-Schwartz's *The Savage in Judaism: An Anthropology of Israelite Religion and Ancient Judaism* (Bloomington: Indiana University Press, 1990) opened up space for this kind of discussion.

[26] (New York: Knopf, 1998). Eisenberg's brilliant work has not had the impact on Jewish Studies or ecotheology that it deserves. A briefer statement of Eisenberg's thesis, "The Mountain and the Tower: Wilderness and City in the Symbols of Babylon and Israel", can be found in Waskow, *Torah of the Earth*, vol.1, 18–54.

[27] See nn.13, 551. J. Richard Middleton also reads the Bible as a critique of Mesopotamian culture in *The Liberating Image: The Imago Dei in Genesis 1* (Grand Rapids MI: Brazos Press, 2005), 195–234, esp. 204–12.

[28] See Judith Plaskow, *Standing Again at Sinai* (New York: HarperCollins, 1991), 153–4. Some of the most important work in this area has been in Biblical studies. See esp. Tikva Frymer-Kensky's work *In the Wake of the Goddesses: Women, Culture and the Biblical Transformation of Pagan Myth* (New York: Fawcett Books, 1993). Jewish feminism has however largely focused on an anthropocentric egalitarian approach (cf. *Standing Again*, 231, where Plaskow's brief mention of environmental issues is the exception that proves the rule). Nevertheless, the need to account for the sensual, embodied dimensions of Jewish ritual leads to work that supports ecological reconstruction. See *Bridges*, ed. Clare Kinberg, esp. 5:2 (Fall 1995) and the article I

While some authors like Eilon Schwartz have started unearthing (or "re-earthing") a Judaism freed of the prejudices of the nineteenth century, the outdated dichotomies of that time continue to be repeated by others, particularly those who see themselves strictly as academics. Even one of the best scholars on the subject, Hava Tirosh-Samuelson, writes that, "From a Jewish perspective, 'biocentrism' is just another form of paganism that must result in idolatrous worship of nature."[29] Now, biocentrism simply means the belief that all living things have some intrinsic moral standing; there is hardly an idea that could be more compatible with ancient Jewish tradition.[30] In fact, the "Jewish perspective" that Tirosh-Samuelson refers to is not a traditional perspective at all. It is rooted in the *Haskalah* and *Wissenschaft* movements, which recast Judaism in terms of an imagined opposition between rationality and history on the one hand, and myth and Nature on the other.[31] But, as Ismar Schorsch wrote, "The celebration of 'historical monotheism' is a legacy of nineteenth century Christian-Jewish polemics, a fierce attempt by [modern] Jewish thinkers to

co-authored with Irene Diamond, "Sensuous Minds and the Possibility of a Jewish Ecofeminist Practice" in *Ethics and the Environment* 4:2 (2000): 185–95 (repr. in Roger Gottlieb, ed., *This Sacred Earth: Religion, Nature, Environment*, 2nd edn. [New York: Routledge], 391–400 and in Waskow, *Torah of the Earth*, vol.2, 245–60). Frymer-Kensky's work also has deeply ecofeminist underpinnings, as can be seen in her article "Ecology in a Biblical Perspective" in Waskow, *Torah of the Earth*, vol.1, 55–69, which does for ecology and the Bible what *In the Wake of the Goddesses* does for feminism: show that the Biblical transformation of earlier myths was broadly speaking a move toward liberation and respect, rather than a move toward oppression. See also Jeanne Kay, "Concepts of Nature in the Hebrew Bible", *Environmental Ethics* 10:4 (1988): 309–27; repr. in Yaffe, 86–104.

[29] "Nature in the Sources of Judaism", *Daedalus* (Fall 2001): 99–124; 116. Tirosh-Samuelson's example is all the more important because she provides in this same article one of the finest summaries of the subject that has been written. Tirosh-Samuelson prefaces these words with:

[I]f Jews wish to ground their approach to ecology in Jewish sources, they must come to terms with the fact that certain assumptions... conflict with Jewish tradition. For example, a Jewish environmental philosophy and ethics cannot be based on a simplistic version of pantheism that acknowledges only the world and nothing beyond the world.

Up to this point, what she says is accurate. But when Tirosh-Samuelson polemicizes against "paganism", she incorrectly interprets aspects of ecology and of Jewish tradition. For example, in comments on Nazism, paganism, and Nature (in "Judaism", in *The Oxford Handbook*, 54), she writes, "nature is also violent, competitive, ruthless... Nature does not care about the sick... Nature does not establish moral values that can create a just society." Here Tirosh-Samuelson is working from an outmoded view of both evolutionary theory (see n.75 and p.29) and moral theory (n.67). The polemic against paganism, endemic to modern Jewish thought, can lead to extreme positions, as in Manfred Gerstenfeld's "Neo-Paganism in the Public Square and Its Relevance to Judaism" (*Jerusalem Letter/Viewpoints* 392 [1998], at www.jcpa.org/jpsr/gersten-s99.htm [Oct. 2012], see esp. beginning of the section "Nature's Image").

[30] Some people draw a distinction between biocentrism, which may emphasize the moral value of individual lives, and ecocentrism, which places moral value on living systems; others use "biocentrism" to indicate both. For our purposes here, the latter usage is intended. On animal rights, see Chapter 5.

[31] For further discussion, see pp.23–4, n.81, and *Methods*.

distance Judaism from the world of paganism."³² Tirosh-Samuelson's labeling of biocentrism as "idolatrous worship" has its roots in these polemics.

The Jewish environmental movement began among quirky outsiders searching for resonance with their ideas in the mainstream community.³³ The movement has rarely questioned the dichotomy between history and Nature, which plays such a major role in the modern self-understanding of Judaism, or the dichotomy between Judaism and paganism,³⁴ though neither dichotomy is historically accurate. While Jewish environmentalism has moved far beyond the first stage of collecting what I sometimes call "pretty sayings about trees",³⁵

---

³² Schorsch adds, "But the disclaimer has its downside by casting Judaism into an adversarial relationship with the natural world." ("Tending to Our Cosmic Oasis", *The Melton Journal* 24 [Spring 1991]: 3, available at www.neohasid.org/pdf/Schorsch_OurCosmicOasis.pdf [Sep. 4, 2014].) For further discussion, see n.72 and *Methods*. In Chapter 3, I analyze an example of this depiction of Judaism. See n.363.

³³ The 1982 Jewish Environmental Conference organized by David Ehrenfeld at Rutgers University, which I attended as the youngest participant, may be seen as one of the starting points of Jewish environmentalism as a movement. The first draft of *Kabbalah and Ecology* was finished almost exactly 30 years after that conference. On this history, see Seidenberg, "Jewish Environmentalism in North America" in *The Encyclopedia of Religion and Nature* (hereafter *ERN*), eds. Bron Taylor et al. (New York: Thoemmes Continuum, 2005), 909–13, rev. www.neohasid.org/ecohasid/jewish_enviro_history/ (Mar. 2011). The earliest groups that formed were largely supplanted or absorbed by Shomrei Adamah (founded 1988), which was itself supplanted by the Coalition on the Environment and Jewish Life (COEJL, founded 1993).

³⁴ Among notable exceptions are Jill Hammer and Taya Shere's organization The Kohenet Institute, founded in 2007; Hammer's work very much parallels my own. "Paganism" is an ill-defined term that has no reality or relationship to the lifeworld of the ancient Hebrews. According to one definition of "pagan" by a scholar of the ancient world, it simply meant "'people of the place,' town or country who preserved their local customs" in the face of Christianity (Pierre Chuvin, *A Chronicle of the Last Pagans* [Cambridge MA: Harvard University Press, 1990], 9). If we are going to apply "pagan" anachronistically, it certainly includes ancient Judaism. Long-held local customs are in fact almost always related to local ecosystems. On this point, see Seidenberg, "Kashroots: An Eco-History of the Kosher Laws", www.jcarrot.org/kashroots-an-eco-history-of-the-kosher-laws (Nov. 2008); rev. www.neohasid.org/torah/kashroots (Sep. 2009), §§2, 4–6. I discuss there the rules that determine a kosher land animal: cloven hooves mean an animal can graze on rocky land unsuited for farming; chewing cud means it can thrive eating food that is not edible to people and that grows without cultivation. These rules are precisely tuned to the agriculture of hilly Canaan. Cf. Aloys Hfttermann, *The Ecological Message of the Torah: Knowledge, Concepts and Laws which Made Survival in a land of Milk and Honey Possible* (Gainesville FL: University Press of Florida, 1999), 72. Hfttermann describes ancient Hebrew society as "the first society which ever lived on this globe to establish a sustained yield form of agriculture" (201).

One curious aspect of ancient Hebrew culture is that even though it is so clearly indigenous and attuned to the land where it evolved, it insists on describing itself as not indigenous – Abraham came from Mesopotamia, the tribes invaded from Egypt, and just as "you were strangers in Egypt", so "you are strangers and sojourners" [Lv 25:23] even in the land of Israel. This subject merits in-depth treatment.

³⁵ See Lawrence Troster, "From Apologetics to New Spirituality: Trends in Jewish Environmental Theology" (www.greenwisdomrabbi.com/from-apologetics-to-new-spirituality-trends-in-jewish-environmental-theology/ [Oct 2014]). The first stage may be thought of as a kind of

Jewish ecological thought

many mainstream Jewish organizations that care about environmentalism remain uncomfortable with any challenge to these dichotomies. On the one hand, environmentalism is primarily seen as a tool for drawing stray Jews back into the fold, for strengthening "Jewish continuity".[36] On the other hand, there is so much proto-ecological material within the tradition, from the obvious topic of *bal tashchit* (not wasting or destroying) to the rhythms of the Jewish calendar,[37] Tu Bish'vat,[38] and the revolutionary ideas of *Sh'mitah* and *Yovel*, the sabbatical and Jubilee years,[39] that Jewish environmental educators have plenty to teach without stepping outside the normative framework.[40]

The newer generation of Jewish environmental organizations, including especially the farming and food movement, has nevertheless become adept at integrating alternative spiritualities and perspectives into its work.[41] The Teva Learning Center, founded in 1994 to offer outdoor education experiences to Jewish day schools, was the flagship of this movement, which now embraces numerous organizations and activities.[42] Within the Jewish Renewal

---

resource extraction. See Bradley Shavit Artson's trenchant critique of this stage ("[t]he pillaged loot gathers dust in the storehouse of ecology") in "Our Covenant with Stones: A Jewish Ecology of the Earth", *Conservative Judaism* 44:1 (Fall 1991): 14–24; 14–15.

[36] Though such considerations have their place, taking continuity to be the primary goal overlooks two essential things: first, the Jewish people, according to its own story, survives for a reason greater than self-perpetuation; and second, there is no Jewish continuity without continuity of humanity, ecosystem, and planet.

[37] On the calendar, see esp. Waskow, *Seasons*, and Jill Hammer's *The Jewish Book of Days* (Philadelphia: JPS, 2006).

[38] Copious resources for Tu Bish'vat can be found on my website, neohasid.org, and on jewcology.com, among many other sites.

[39] *Sh'mitah* and Jubilee, along with Shabbat, are fundamentally Earth-centered and are essential elements of any Jewish theology of Nature. A crucial development was the burgeoning focus on the *Sh'mitah* or Sabbatical year, in advance of the *Sh'mitah* in 2014–15. See n.47.

[40] For a good survey of all this material, see Jeremy Benstein, *The Way Into Judaism and the Environment* (Woodstock VT: Jewish Lights, 2006).

[41] Within the Jewish enviro/farming movement (especially among the younger people) it is almost taken for granted that Judaism is fundamentally Earth-centered, and many would affirm that more than humanity is in God's image – cf. the lyrics of Shir Yaakov Feinstein-Feit and Eden "Ephryme" Pearlstein's rap "To Zion": "We need a breakthrough, poetry for president / Every person has their own potential that they represent / Peace is possible but only if we first believe / Everything created is *b'tselem Elohim*!" (Darshan, 2011, www.darshan.bandcamp.com/track/to-zion [Jan. 2012]).

[42] Now called the Teva Learning Alliance, Teva was founded at Camp Isabella Freedman (now Isabella Freedman Retreat Center). The Adamah Farming Fellowship was also founded there, in 2003. In the past few years, Jewish environmental consciousness has poured itself into the farming movement, sparked by Adamah, and the food movement, focalized by Hazon (founded 2000). Other efforts include Wilderness Torah (founded 2007) and Eden Village Camp (opened in 2010). Most importantly for the advance of Jewish ecological thought, Kayam Farm at Pearlstone (founded 2006) has organized an annual conference on Jewish agricultural law. In 2013, Hazon, already the largest Jewish environmental organization in North America, merged with Isabella Freedman. Along with the proliferation of farming programs in the United States and Canada, and a network of Jewish-community-based CSA's

movement, there has also been an openness to real theological transformation,[43] while in Israel, a spiritually based environmentalism has been taking root.[44] In essence, the theology I am advocating in this book has already come into being as a way of practicing and feeling about Judaism within this network of organizations, especially among the younger generations (many of whom are now in their thirties). Bringing this approach fully into the way we understand and *think* about Judaism, and more importantly into the way we read the fullness of the Jewish tradition, is one of the next big steps.

How far have we already come in Jewish ecotheology? *Bal tashchit*, the prohibition against wasting, is a good litmus test. This principle, derived from the Torah's commandment against destroying fruit trees even during a wartime siege (Dt 20:19), is both far-reaching (in that the rabbis applied it to destroying anything needlessly, which they compared to committing idolatry) and extremely limited (in that the rabbis did not allow it to stand in the way of economic profit).[45] Mainstream Jewish environmentalism in the early days

---

organized by Hazon, there has also been a movement to bring *shechitah*, kosher slaughter, back to the small farm, using humanely and sustainably raised animals. Grow and Behold Foods (founded 2010) is the largest commercial purveyor of such meat. There is also wide interest in a kosher certification that would guarantee food is produced in an ethical manner. More recently, after a long hiatus COEJL spearheaded the effort to create a "Green Hevra" network in 2011. See Seidenberg, "Jewish Environmentalism" for a partial history. For a more comprehensive list of North American organizations, see www.jewcology.org/map-of-initiatives/ (Aug. 2014).

[43] R' Zalman Schachter-Shalomi's leadership, both as the founder of Jewish Renewal and as a revered wisdom teacher, has been instrumental. Decades ago, he coined the term "eco-kosher", taught about Gaia spirituality, and promulgated the idea that Judaism was in the process of a "paradigm shift" (*Paradigm Shift*, ed. Ellen Singer [Northvale NJ: Jason Aronson, 1993]). He also loved computer analogies and talked about "reformatting" the tradition (*Paradigm Shift*, ch.14), "updating the system files", and maintaining "backwards compatibility" (lectures). One could view *Kabbalah and Ecology* as a project to maintain backwards compatibility.

[44] The Heschel Center for Environmental Learning and Leadership and the Reform movement's Kibbutz Lotan, both founded in 1983, have had a long and lasting impact. The desert-commune experiment Hamakom (2000–05), and Tel Aviv's Bayit Chadash (2000–06), which can be categorized as Israeli Jewish Renewal, integrated Judaism and a somewhat new-age form of ecospirituality. The activist group Bustan L'Shalom (now "Bustan") organized the renegade building of a medical clinic in 2003 in Wadi al-Naam, an "unrecognized" Bedouin village near which a toxic waste dump was sited, utilizing the cob building expertise of Kibbutz Lotan. The village was receiving no medical (or other) services because officially it did not exist. See Seidenberg, "Human Rights and Ecology", *Tikkun* 23:4 (July/Aug. 2008): 48–52; 51–2, rev. 2010 at www.neohasid.org/pdf/Human_Rights_and_Ecology.pdf [Sep. 2011], and www.savethenegev. org. More recently, Yeshivat Simchat Shlomo hosted an "Eco-activist Beit Midrash" in 2005. This list represents only a fraction of what is going on in Israeli environmentalism as a whole, which is largely secular. The Jewish National Fund should also be included for its educational work, though it has often been seen as deleterious by Israeli environmentalists (see pp.305–6).

[45] If the value of a tree's wood is greater than the value of its fruit, it can be cut down (*Talmud Bavli* [Vilna: Wittwe & Gebrüder Romm, 1880; repr. Jerusalem: Tal-Man, 1981], hereafter TB, *Bava Qama* 91b). Maimonides codifies this law in *Mishneh Torah* (Jerusalem: Mechon-Mamre, n.d.), www.mechon-mamre.org/i/e506.htm (Feb. 2014), *Hilkhot M'lakhim* 6:12–13 (8–9); he also states that an *ilan s'raq*, non-food-bearing tree, may be cut down for any reason. On waste as idolatry, see TB *Shabbat* 67b, 105b. See Seidenberg, "Environment, Ecology, and

Jewish ecological thought

began and ended as a paean to *bal tashchit*. The spiritual importance of *bal tashchit* is not insignificant – idolatry is regarded as one of the chief sins – but the legal framework around *bal tashchit* makes it ineffective for preventing environmental abuses. Any Jewish environmental curriculum or theology that is serious will acknowledge these limitations. Eilon Schwartz's "*Bal Tashchit*: A Jewish Environmental Precept" is the finest exposition of the issue to date.[46]

Another litmus test is whether a curriculum or theology integrates the Sabbatical year /*Sh'mitah* and Jubilee/*Yovel*. Every seventh year in Biblical Israel was to be a *Sh'mitah*, a release, when the land was not actively farmed, and all debts were canceled. In the *Yovel* or fiftieth year, after seven *Sh'mitah* cycles, the land was redistributed, and any slave who chose not to be freed in his or her own seventh year of service was required to go free. This system of rest and renewal fulfilled on a grand social scale the ideal of Shabbat. (One might even say that the purpose of Shabbat is to practice for *Sh'mitah*.) *Sh'mitah*-Jubilee was directed equally toward creating a right relationship with the land and toward creating a right relationship between human beings.[47] There is no more radical teaching in the Torah.

---

the Bible" II, in *Encyclopedia of the Bible and Its Reception (EBR)* (Berlin: de Gruyter, 2014), vol.7, cols.974–81; 977.

[46] *Environmental Ethics* 18 (Winter 1997): 355–74 (repr. in *Trees, Earth, and Torah*, 83–106). See also Neal Loevinger, "Judaism, the Bible and Environmental Awareness" (York University, MA thesis, 1993), 36–7, 47–8 and Eric Katz, "Faith, God, and Nature: Judaism and Deep Ecology" in *Deep Ecology and World Religions: New Essays on Sacred Grounds*, eds. David Landis Barnhill, Roger S. Gottlieb (Albany NY: SUNY Press, 2001), 155–61, esp. 161. Much discussion of *bal tashchit* in Jewish environmentalism does not engage with the complexity of the issue, whether because it is apologetic toward Judaism or because it is limited in its understanding of ecology. See for example articles by Norman Lamm, Jonathan Helfand, and David Ehrenfeld and Philip J. Bentley, found in Waskow, *Torah of the Earth*, vol.1, 103–56 (esp. 109–15, 133–4, and 150–53), and Jeremy Cohen's "On Classical Judaism and Environmental Crisis" in Yaffe, 77–9. (Ehrenfeld and Bentley is also found in Yaffe, 125–35.) The *bal tashchit* section of Lamm's article was also printed separately in *Trees, Earth, and Torah*, 106–11. Leaving aside Lamm's theological remarks, his article works well as a summary of Jewish law. David Vogel ("How Green Is Judaism? Exploring Jewish Environmental Ethics", *Judaism* 50:1 [Winter 2001]: 66–81, www.faculty.haas.berkeley.edu/vogel/judaism.pdf [Apr. 2012]), also gives a more nuanced treatment of *bal tashchit*, though without reflecting critically on it.

[47] In this respect, *Sh'mitah* very much conforms to the ideals of social ecology (see n.51), and it is a profound mechanism for creating social justice. See Ellen Davis, *Scripture, Culture, and Agriculture: An Agrarian Reading of the Bible* (New York: Cambridge University Press, 2009), 92–4 and Eric Rosenblum, "Is Gaia Jewish? Finding a Framework for Radical Ecology in Traditional Judaism" in Yaffe, 183–205; 185–91. A society based on *Sh'mitah* would also not incidentally eschew the excesses and failures of both capitalism and communism. An important link can be made between *Sh'mitah* and permaculture, since the practice of *Sh'mitah* would lead people to plant perennial crops and fruit trees, which would still produce in the seventh year, instead of annual crops. The *Sh'mitah*-Jubilee system has been a centerpiece of my own teaching since 1993 (and I wrote a curriculum on "Jubilee as a Jewish Response to Hunger" in 1982), but it is only in the past two years that discussion of *Sh'mitah* has taken hold, thanks to the tireless efforts of Yigal Deutscher and Hazon. See www.hazon.org/shmita-project/educational-resources/resource-library/ for writings and curricula

Generally, Jewish environmental ethics is an area in which both traditional and academic scholars have been content to describe what Judaism already says.[48] But Jewish theology needs to catch up with the urgency of the times, the "`et la`asot". One purpose of theology is to ask, What *should* Judaism say? or, How should we revise what Judaism says in light of what we now know?

Other religious traditions are at various stages of developing a sustainable worldview.[49] By way of contrast, Christian scholars have been long involved in developing an ecotheology based on the history and texts of Christianity.[50] Their work has integrated insights from deep ecology, ecofeminism, social ecology, and even neopaganism,[51] as well as the field of ecopsychology.

Yet for Christians as much as for Jews, the central question of this book remains an open one: "Can we say that other creatures are in God's image?" This is, I think, not only the most momentous theological challenge we face, but also a challenge that is uniquely well suited to the kind of textual reasoning that characterizes Jewish thought. At the same time, the prejudices we have inherited from the past few centuries have practically made this question

---

from Deutscher, myself, Waskow, and others. See pp.126–7, 152, 166–7, 272, esp. n.888 In popular writing, see also Seidenberg, "Shmita: The Purpose of Sinai", *The Huffington Post* (May 2, 2013), also available at www.neohasid.org/pdf/shmittah-etzel-sinai.pdf. The first "Shmittah Summit" took place in March 2012 at Pearlstone Retreat Center. (Though there is consensus about focusing on *Sh'mitah*, there is no consensus about how to spell it!) On Shabbat, see n.369 and pp.125–6, 321–3 (esp. n.1039).

[48] See, e.g., Vogel. For a summary of normative Jewish environmental ethics, see also David Golinkin, "A Responsum Regarding the Environment and Air Pollution", *Responsa in a Moment* 3:2 (October 2008), online at www.schechter.edu/responsa.aspx?ID=37 (Nov. 2011). In contrast, Schwartz in "*Bal Tashchit*", Gendler in "A Sentient Universe" (*Ecology and the Jewish Spirit: Where Nature and the Sacred Meet*, ed. Ellen Bernstein [Woodstock VT: Jewish Lights, 1998], 58–68; hereafter "Bernstein"), and Eric Rosenblum in "Is Gaia Jewish?" go beyond what is normative, as do the first citations in n.46.

[49] The Harvard Divinity School conferences on religion and ecology have had a big impact on this process. The conference on Judaism, titled "Judaism and the Natural World", and the volume that issued from it, *Judaism and Ecology: Created World and Revealed Word*, ed. Hava Tirosh-Samuelson (Cambridge MA: Harvard University Press, 2002), suffered some limitations in comparison with the other conferences because the organizers, for fear of being seen as "too radical", asked presenters to discuss Nature, rather than ecology.

[50] See nn.82, 113, and p.274. I hope *Kabbalah and Ecology* will be a significant resource for Christian ecotheology. To this end, points of contact with Christianity are noted throughout.

[51] Deep ecology rejects human exceptionalism and speciesism (the idea that there is a hierarchy in the values of different species). Social ecology says that the oppression of human beings and the destruction of Nature are concomitant; see n.360. On deep ecology, including its relationship to and tension with social ecology and ecofeminism, see *Beneath the Surface: Critical Essays in the Philosophy of Deep Ecology*, eds. Eric Katz, Andrew Light, David Rothenberg (Cambridge MA: MIT Press, 2000). Ecofeminism spans a broad range of philosophies, from the social ecology interpretation that connects the oppression of women and the destruction of Nature, to the essentialist idea that women are closer to Nature and more able to build a society at peace with Nature. See *Reweaving the World: The Emergence of Ecofeminism*, eds. Irene Diamond and Gloria Orenstein (San Francisco CA: Sierra Club, 1990). Neopaganism most often personifies Nature or Earth as the Goddess. See Margot Adler, *Drawing Down the Moon* (New York: Penguin Books, 2006). On ecopsychology, see Andy Fisher, *Radical Ecopsychology: Psychology in the Service of Life* (Albany NY: SUNY Press, 2013).

unaskable. Instead, contemporary Jewish thought has limited itself to a particular understanding of the meaning of God's image, rooted in modernist and humanist ideologies, walled in by assumptions that stand in direct contradiction to deep ecology and most ecotheology.[52] We – Jews, Christians, and all for whom the Hebrew Bible is a touchstone – need to be able to peer beyond this wall, to pass beyond it, in order to create a sustainable world. There are no other significant obstacles to a free discussion within Judaism about what is our rightful place on the Earth as a people, as human beings, and as creatures.

FUNDAMENTAL ECOLOGICAL ISSUES IN JEWISH PERSPECTIVE

The very good Creation

There are a number of ecological issues that Judaism has a deeply grounded response to. One Biblical concept that every Bible reader and every Jewish denomination can affirm without controversy is the idea that Creation, in its totality, is inherently good. The idea is embedded in the Creation narrative: "Elohim saw all that He made, and here/behold: it is very good" [Gn 1:31]. Maimonides (1135–1204, Spain, Morocco, Egypt), arguably the most important Jewish philosopher of all time, explains in his *Guide for the Perplexed* (in Hebrew, *Moreh N'vukhim*) that the phrase "very good" intimates the intrinsic value and purpose of all of Creation, which is independent of humanity:

[A]ll the other beings too have been intended for their own sakes and not for the sake of something else... If you consider the Torah, the notion that we have in view will

---

[52] This does *not* mean that Judaism should suddenly or eventually conform to deep ecology or any particular ecotheology (the Torah is already in alignment with social ecology). Jewish culture has much both to teach and to learn from these other ways of seeing the more-than-human world. A Jewish engagement with these ideas, as with biocentrism in general, will require the kind of application of textual reasoning and fine distinctions that characterizes all Jewish ethics. As Neal Loevinger writes in "Deep Ecology and Biocentrism: (Mis)reading Genesis" in Bernstein, 32–40, "From a Jewish perspective, the biggest problem with this [biocentric] approach is that it obscures the real, everyday choices that people must make... Rather than being superfluous, the role of ethics is to make power differences explicit and to make past experience relevant to new situations." (38).

Any revision of Jewish theology in light of ecology must also grapple with the right relationship to the land of Israel, both because Israel is seen as more holy than other lands, and because it provides the paradigm of how to relate to land. See Artson, "Is There Only One Holy Land?" in Bernstein, 41–9. It is here that Loevinger's concerns become profoundly disquieting, given the sometimes atavistic attachment to the historical "promised land". But the Torah teaches that it is a privilege to live in the "holy land", not a right – a privilege that can be revoked when people abuse either the land or other human beings. It is that very fact – that everyone's tenure is tenuous – that makes Canaan/Israel a holy land. As "a land of mountains and valleys", only "by the rain of the heavens will she drink water" [Dt 11:11] – and so she will be subject to drought. "Always the eyes of YHVH your God are on her" [Dt 11:12] – that is, it is as if God is always assessing whether the people merit rain, "not like the land of Egypt, which... you gave drink with your foot (by pumping), like a garden of greens" [Dt 11:10], because it is not a place where people can control irrigation and disregard rainfall.

become manifest... For with reference to none of the things created is the statement made in any way that it exists for the sake of some other things. He only says that He brought every part of the world into existence and that it conformed to its purpose. This is the meaning of the saying: "And God saw that it [is] good." About the whole, it says: "And God saw everything that He had made, and, behold, it [is] very good."[53]

Maimonides' articulation of this idea was foundational for Jewish thought, as well as for Christian thought. Aquinas (1225–1274, Italy) was heavily dependent on Maimonides when he wrote that the highest good among created things "is the good of the order of the whole universe",

[for it is said:] "God saw all the things He had made, and they were very good," while He simply said of the individual works, that "they were good" [...] Thus, among created things, what God cares for most is the order of creation.[54]

Ovadiah Sforno (1470–1550, Italy) similarly comments: "The purpose of existence in its entirety is very good, more so than the specific purposes intended."[55] The affirmation found in Genesis 1:31 was incredibly important. Then, as now, it provided an imprimatur for a holistic and optimistic view of Creation. Now,

---

[53] *The Guide for the Perplexed*, trans. Shlomo Pines (Chicago: University of Chicago Press, 1963), 3:13, selected from 452–3; *Moreh N'vukhim*, trans. Yosef Kafich (Hebr.) (Jerusalem: Mossad Harav Kook, 1977), 300–301. Elsewhere in this passage Maimonides rejects the idea of "a final end of all species of beings" (see p.27). Cf. 3:25, 506. Though *Kabbalah and Ecology* focuses on Kabbalah, Maimonides could be seen as this book's most important protagonist. See esp. pp.20, 23, 71–2, 148, 160, 268ff. On Maimonides' limitations, see n.202 and p.62. For a summary of issues connecting Maimonides and ecotheology, see Seidenberg, "Maimonides" (*ERN*, 1026–7, online at www.neohasid.org/torah/rambam [Jan. 2014]). Note that in one place, Maimonides defines the meaning of "good" in the Creation story differently: "Whenever [the Torah] mentions a thing among those that exist, having been produced in time and subsisting in durable, perpetual, and permanent fashion, it says with respect to that thing that it was good" (2:30, 353). This, however, is really a lemma of the first principle, that "good" means having intrinsic value.
  In this work, I generally quote from Pines's edition, which is widely accepted among scholars. However, Moses Friedländer's translation (New York: Dover Books, 1980) is often worth reading for comparison, as are the Hebrew translations of both Kafich and Michael Schwartz (Tel Aviv University Press, 2002, www.press.tau.ac.il/perplexed/ [Sep. 2014]). Maimonides' *Guide* will be cited below as: *MN* [book: chapter], [page in Pines, unless otherwise specified].

[54] *Summa Contra Gentiles*, trans. Vernon Bourke, 3:64, paras.9–10, www.dhspriory.org/thomas/ContraGentiles3a.htm (Nov 2014), cf. 3:70, para.4. See William French, "Catholicism and the Common Good of the Biosphere", in *An Ecology of the Spirit: Religious Reflection and Environmental Consciousness*, ed. Michael Barnes (Lanham MD: University Press of America, 1990), 192. Aquinas also wrote: "For goodness, which in God is simple and uniform, in creatures is manifold and divided; and hence the whole universe together participates in the divine goodness more perfectly, and represents it better, than any single creature whatever" (*Summa Theologica*, 2nd edn., trans. Fathers of the English Dominican Province [1920] pt.1, q.47, art.1, 1:246, www.newadvent.org/summa/1047.htm [Sep. 2008]; in French, "Catholicism", 193; see also pt.1, q.15, art.2, 1:87).

[55] *ad* Gn 1:31 in *Miqra'ot G'dolot*. Throughout this work, Sforno, Rashi, ibn Ezra, and Ramban, are quoted from *Miqra'ot G'dolot* (repr., New York: Shulzinger Bros, n.d.), occasionally in comparison with online editions of their commentaries at daat.co.il.

it opens the door to look at Creation in all its diversity, with new scientific tools and renewed awe, and to understand perhaps for the first time what it really means to say "behold, it is very good / *v'hineh tov m'od*" [Gn 1:31].[56]

The next three issues of biodiversity, subjecthood (or moral agency), and evolution are not native to Jewish categories of thought, but rather arise from the theological challenges presented by a study of ecology. In each area, aspects of the Western agenda of mastery over natural forces and dominance of humans over other species have been called into question. They are keys that open the door to the inquiry about extending God's image. I will outline these issues here, along with their significance in and for Jewish tradition.

Biodiversity

The term "biodiversity" was developed by E. O. Wilson[57] almost 30 years ago to point to both the diversity of individual species and the diversity of their relationships and inter-dependencies, as well as to describe one of the chief qualities of life and living systems. More recently, Wilson coined the term "biophilia" to describe both the intimate kinship most human beings feel toward the diversity of living creatures and the human drive to know and understand life in all its forms (see p.171). If Wilson is right, and our ability to recognize and celebrate biodiversity is a fundamental part of our human makeup, then it should naturally find expression in religion.

The motif of diversity is in fact emphasized in many texts of piety and philosophy from ancient times and the Middle Ages. In one early example, *Sifra* ("The Book", on Leviticus) interprets the verse "How manifold/diverse are Your works YHVH[58] / *Mah rabu ma`asekha YHVH*" [Ps 104:24] to allude to the diversity of ecotypes (using the term in a broad sense):

[56] We know enough to think about the entelechy of Creation as a whole in a way that was never before possible. Entelechy, defined by Aristotle as the form each life takes when seen as a purposeful whole, differs from *telos*. The first term seeks meaning in the "gestalt" of a thing, whereas the second finds meaning in the final state of a thing. We can talk about the entelechy of Creation as we know it without violating the premises of ecology or evolutionary science, but we cannot talk about its *telos*. (On the spacing before and after the forward slash above, see Notes on Transliteration.)

[57] See Marjorie Reaka-Kudla, Don Wilson, and Edward O. Wilson, *Biodiversity II: Understanding and Protecting Our Biological Resources* (Washington DC: Joseph Henry, 1996), 1. Wilson dates the term to the National Forum on BioDiversity Conference that took place in 1986.

[58] In the present work, the tetragrammaton, traditionally pronounced "*Adonai*" and often translated as "Lord", is left untranslated. In this quote, the printed Talmud substitutes *H'* (standing for *Hashem*, the name) for YHVH. Various substitutions for the name (including *H'* ה, *YY* ״י, *D'* ד, *HVYH* הויה, *YQV"Q* יקוק) are used in later works to avoid writing out the letters of God's name. As with *YQV"Q*, where *Quf* takes the place of *Heh*, other divine names are "de-sanctified" with *Quf*, e.g., *Eloqim* (*Elokim*) for *Elohim*, which appears in some quotes below. The breath letter, *Heh*, is "stopped up", so to speak; conversely, the breath itself is often seen as the signature of the divine. See Abram, *The Spell of the Sensuous*, 245–53. Waskow also interprets the name YHVH (YHWH) as the sound of breath, denoting God as

When R' Akiva would reach this verse he would say: ... You have creatures growing in the sea and creatures growing on the dry land. The ones in the sea, were they to come up on the dry land they would die; the ones on the dry land, were they to go down to the sea they would die. You have creatures growing in the fire/*ur*, and creatures growing in the air/*avir*. The ones in the fire, were they to extend to the air they would die, and the ones in the air, were they to extend to the fire they would die. The place of life for this one is the death of the other, and the place of death for this one is the life of the other.[59]

Diversity is seen as one of God's praises. However, here, as in many other texts, the diversity of Creation may signify little more than evidence of God's power or wisdom,[60] with the world serving a nothing more than a palimpsest whose faint tracings serve to lead us to God. One learns, as it were, only a single

---

"YyyyHhhhWwwwHhhh, the Interbreathing of all life", so that the divine breath includes the breath of all creatures. See "The Breath of Life/Prayer", www.theshalomcenter.org/node/222 and "Nishmat: The Breath of All Life", www.theshalomcenter.org/node/229 (Philadelphia: The Shalom Center, Sep. 8, 2001).

[59] *Sifra d'Vey Rav (Torat Kohanim)*, vol.1 (Jerusalem, 1959), Sh'mini 5:7, 80b || *TB Chulin* 127a. What R' Akiva had in mind when he imagined creatures that live in fire is hard to know, but there are thermophilic species that could be described this way that have only been discovered in the past 50 years, first in 1966, in Yellowstone's hot springs, then in 1977, in hydrothermal vents at the bottom of the oceans – truly describable as habitats of fire. These vents were proposed as the place where life originated in 1988. Such life would be dependent on the abundant sulfur, rather than on dissolved oxygen, which would not have been present. (Interestingly, the parallel *TB* passage describes going down to the habitat of fire from the air and coming up to the air from the fire.) Free oxygen in both atmosphere and ocean came a half billion or more years after photosynthesis, which itself did not begin until as many as a billion or more years after the advent of the first life (scientific estimates for the beginning of photosynthesis range from 3.6 to 2.8 billion years ago). See n.873 on the Gaia hypothesis. See also nn.1013, 1081 on versions of a "universe story" that incorporate this information.

[60] Bachya ibn Paquda, in his *Torat Chovot Hal'vavot (Duties of the Heart)*, ed. Moses Hyamson (Jerusalem: Feldheim, 1970), provides many instances of this. See, for example, ch.4 of *Sha`ar Hab'khinah* (vol.1). Two typical passages read:

How astonishing too is the growth of foods from seeds...Praised be the Wise and Gracious One who causes there to be such vast effects from the [most] small and weak of causes...The wise man, when he reflects on them and understands their causes, will recognize the wisdom of the Creator's plan in them. (vol.1, 170–71, translation adapted)

And it is true, YY God, that You have not created any existing creature formless/*tohu*, nor formed it for nothing. For in it is the purpose of the universe / *takhlit ha`olam*, and it also testifies to Your wisdom and discernment and demonstrates that everything which You have made is complete without flaw, and whole without extra. It is as it says: "I know that whatever God does, it will be forever; nothing can be added to it nor anything subtracted" [Ec 3:14].

(vol.2, 396–7)

Where Bachya hints that diversity has some meaning beyond praise, as when he writes, "For in [each creature] is the purpose of the universe", he does not explore this more deeply. He may have simply meant that the purpose of the universe is the provisioning of humanity, as when he describes the world as "a house built which is set up with everything necessary to it [for] humanity, like the master of a house, who makes use of everything in it" (vol.1, 75). Similarly, he writes:

lesson from the multitude of relationships that make up the world, instead of a multitude of lessons. For this reason, the commonplace appreciation of Life's diversity as a praise of the Creator can end up being theologically sterile.

From the perspective of constructive theology, we would want to find teachings that recognize diversity to be something fundamentally desired by God, something that expresses God's love and that characterizes God's "vision" of Creation, as it were. This indeed would be a fair reading of the verse "Elohim saw everything... and behold, it is very good". One teaching from *Avot d'Rabi Natan* that leads in this direction asks, "Why is the earth[61] called *teivel*?" and answers, "Because she is enriched/seasoned/relished with everything / *m'tubelet bakol*."[62] Diversity is not just a praise of God but also a praise of the Earth and one of her essences.

> When you observe the signs of wisdom in created things, you will find that, along with testifying to the divinity and unity of the Creator, they all without exception have in them ways of being useful to humanity and intending [their] improvement / *ofaney to`elet v'kavanat taqanah*.
> (vol.1, 164–7)

Because Bachya is so eloquent about the wisdom in Nature, he is used uncritically as a resource in Jewish environmental education. Only rarely is any distinction made between what might be called Nature-positive texts, which abound in medieval Jewish thought, and ecologically significant texts, which could call on us to re-evaluate the relationship between humanity and the more-than-human world.

[61] The term used, *arets*, is translated as "land" or "earth", while *adamah* is translated as "earth" or "ground". *Arets* can refer to all land in general or to a specific land, while *adamah* refers to earth as a substance, that is, soil. Here *Chazal* are speaking about *arets*. While in some cases *arets* may in fact mean the equivalent of the whole planet, as in the phrase *shamayim va'arets*, I will translate *arets* as "earth" or "land" rather than "Earth" when it appears in rabbinic or Biblical texts, in order to preserve these ambiguities. The name for the element of earth in the four elements is `afar (dirt, usually translated as "dust").

[62] *Avot d'Rabi Natan*, ed. Salomon (Solomon) Schechter (Vienna, 1887), version A, ch.37, 110, cited hereafter as ARNA (version B is cited as ARNB). *Teivel* and *m'tubelet* share the letters TBL, suggesting a folk etymology for *teivel*. The parallel text in ARNB gives a less coherent answer to the question: "Because she is enriched with words of Torah, but the land of Israel doesn't lack anything" (ch.43, 119), while a parallel in *SifreyD* (*pisqa* 37; 70, cited by Schechter *ad loc.*) reads, "Why is [the land of Israel] called *teivel*? For she is *m'tubelet bakol*. For all the lands, there is something in this one that isn't in this one, but the land of Israel doesn't lack anything." From an ecological standpoint, this *is* more true of Israel/Canaan than most lands. Israel, sitting at the meeting place of three continents, includes an extraordinary variety of habitats and species relative to its size. See Eisenberg, *The Ecology of Eden*, 76 and Davis, *Scripture*, 49–50. It is noteworthy that while the earth as a whole is highly personified in Midrash (e.g., ARNB ch.43, quoted p.272), the land of Israel generally is not.

In Jewish liturgy, *teivel* is usually understood to mean the inhabited world. According to *A Hebrew and English Lexicon of the Old Testament* (eds. Brown, Driver and Briggs [Oxford: Clarendon, 1951], cited hereafter as BDB), *teivel* is derived from *y'vul*, produce (s.v. *y'vul*, 385). The emphasis on diversity and richness in ARNA is resonant with this derivation, even though the root of *m'tubelet* may be BLL (to mix/confuse) rather than YBL (to bear). As such, *teivel* could be an equivalent to "biosphere". In any case, for the rabbis, *teivel* and *m'tubelet* are essentially related.

Rabbinic texts such as this one still represent a primitive reading of Nature, aware of the diversity of species, but not aware of the complexity of relationships between species. But they provide a starting point for ecotheology, because they focus on the world in-itself and not only in reference to God.

Maimonides is one of the earliest and most cogent thinkers to place tremendous value on what we would define as biodiversity. He explains that "the entire purpose [of creation] consists in bringing into existence the way you see it everything whose existence is possible".[63] As discussed already, this diversity is good in itself, and each unique species is also good in itself, existing not for the sake of humanity, and not even only for its own sake, but for the sake of its participation in the whole of Creation. Even the highest revelation God gave to Moshe, the revelation of "all My goodness" [Ex. 33:19], was a revelation about the diversity of Creation, namely, that Moshe would "apprehend [the] nature [of all existing things] *and the way they are mutually connected*".[64] For Maimonides, understanding the diversity of Creation meant understanding the relationships between all the creatures, which went hand in hand with understanding God.

Nachman of Breslov (or "Bratslav", great-grandson of the Ba'al Shem Tov, 1772–1810, Ukraine) says that one task of the *tsadiq*, righteous person or saint, is to understand the nature and diversity of the creatures:

[I]n every thing there is the will of *Hashem* (the Blessed Name): so it is in the whole of Creation / *k'lal hab'riyah* . . . and so in the details of Creation / *p'ratey hab'riyah*, in each and every individual thing . . . since the Blessed Name desired that this thing would be thus, with this appearance/*t'munah*, with this power, and with this nature . . . And the righteous person searches out and seeks continually . . . to attain and to know the will of God in every thing – for example, why was it God's will that the lion should have this

---

[63] MN 3:25, 504. Maimonides is explaining that no creature is frivolous (see n.87).
[64] MN 1:54, 124. See pp.71–2 for discussion of this important passage. Cf. Aquinas, who relates the diversity of the creatures to both the goodness of the whole universe (n.54) and to God's goodness:

He brought things into being in order that His goodness might be communicated to creatures, and be represented by them; and because His goodness could not be adequately represented by one creature alone, He produced many and diverse creatures, that what was wanting to one in the representation of the divine goodness might be supplied by another.

(*Summa Theologica*, pt.1, q.47, art.1, 1:246)

While Aquinas closely follows Maimonides, he adds an emphasis not present in Maimonides: the idea that each creature represents a specific element of God's goodness. Aquinas also shifts the ontological focus from the creatures back to God, and does not mention the relationships between creatures. Hence Aquinas's teaching does not lend itself as readily to an eco-centric interpretation. This may be congruent with Aquinas rejecting the high value Maimonides placed on animals' subjectivity (see *Summa Theologica*, pt.2b, q.61, art.1, esp. 10.2, 3:1460).

Where Maimonides asserts that Creation manifestly reveals God's goodness, this appears to me to run contrary to a strict understanding of apophatic theology (the principle that we can only know what God is not, not what God is), since knowledge of God's goodness is here attained directly through the knowledge of God's creatures. On this issue, see nn.202, 876.

strength and might... and the behavior [it] has, and a little mosquito [should be] the opposite... And so with details of details / *p'ratey p'ratiyot*, as in the lion, why is this limb formed thus in it... So it is with all the creatures in the world, silent/*domem* (mineral, rock), growing/*tsomei'ach* (vegetable, plant), living/moving/*chai* (animal), speaking/*m'daber* (human) – for in all of them there are a great many differences without number, between each one and its companion. And so it is with every single individual within itself..., with the plants and trees and the rest of the particulars of Creation... and all was because of the will of the Creator. And the righteous person searches continually for these wills *r'tsonot*.[65]

For Nachman, every species and being, even every limb, reveals God's will in a unique way that demands individual understanding. Furthermore, the pursuit of understanding is a trait of righteousness. This passage provides a firm foundation on which to build a theology of diversity, which is an essential element of any theology of Nature.

Subjecthood

In addition to understanding "God's will" as it is expressed in each creature, we now have the scientific capacity to talk about the will and subjecthood of each creature itself, particularly with respect to mammals and birds. The ability

---

[65] *Liqutey Moharan* 1:17 (New York: R' Eli`ezer Shlomo Breslover, 1965), 48–9; hereafter cited as *LM*. Nachman further states that these differences correspond to the differences and kinds of beauty within the Jewish people, since the world was created for the people Israel. Could this mean that for Nachman, the only diversity and beauty that has real significance is found within the particular human group of Israel, and that we can ignore the actual beauty of Creation? On the contrary, I would claim that beauty in Creation is a primary concern for Nachman, and the midrashic twists he uses to tie this to rabbinic textuality are his way of deepening and anchoring that experience (as we also see in Nachman's interpretation of his own experience of Nature, discussed pp.331–2). This pattern of interpreting textually what was a lived experience is also found in Nachman's description of the theurgy of dance. See *LM* 1:10, 1:169 and Michael Fishbane, "To Jump for Joy", *The Journal of Jewish Thought and Philosophy* 6:2 (Dec. 1977): 371–87; repr. as "The Mystery of Dance According to Rabbi Nachman of Bratslav" in *The Exegetical Imagination*, 173–87.

Nachman's praise of Nature here may seem to contradict what Shaul Magid has noted as Nachman's antipathy to the concept of Nature ("Nature, Exile, and Disability in R. Nahman of Bratslav's 'The Seven Beggars'", *Judaism and Ecology*, 333–68, esp. 336–7, 347–50, 360). However, this antipathy is simply a result of Nachman rejecting determinism and the idea of natural law, because he insisted that every detail of the natural world was miraculous. Thus, his rejection of the concept of Nature was based on his appreciation of the more-than-human world.

For further examples of texts on diversity, see quotes from Gikatilla and Yehudah Hechasid, n.934, and Shneur Zalman, n.838, as well as curricula by this author for COEJL, "Cosmology and Biodiversity: The Divine Purpose in Creating Many Species" (www.neohasid.org/pdf/Cosmology-biodiversity.pdf [Feb. 2, 2012]), and "The Story of Noah and the Flood: Midrash Texts on the Preservation of Species and Human Responsibility" (www.neohasid.org/pdf/MidrashNoah.pdf [Sep. 2011]), both written for *Operation Noah*, ed. Mark X. Jacobs (New York: COEJL, 1996).

of scientists to measure different species' sentience, emotional intelligence, and reasoning stands in direct contrast to the behaviorism of earlier decades. Much of the work in ethology and ecology calls into question widespread assumptions that limit subjectivity and all aspects of moral agency to human beings.[66] More and more, practical and tangible studies of animal behavior have taught us that human qualities like learning, language, empathy, and altruism exist on a continuum with all the animals.[67] It has also become clear that there is no hard distinction between what we call emotion and instinct.[68]

---

[66] On the continuity between human and animal cognition, see Marc Bekoff et al. (eds.), *The Cognitive Animal: Empirical and Theoretical Perspectives on Animal Cognition* (Cambridge MA: MIT Press, 2002). On the moral front, see, for example, Inbal Ben-Ami Bartal et al., "Empathy and Pro-Social Behavior in Rats", *Science* 334:6061 (Dec. 9 2011): 1427–30. Such studies make clear that human moral judgment sits at one end of a continuum that includes other social animals. See next note.

[67] See for example Donald R. Griffin, *Animal Thinking* (Cambridge MA: Harvard University Press, 1985) and *Animal Minds* (Chicago: University of Chicago Press, 2001), Marc D. Hauser, *Wild Minds: What Animals Really Think* (New York: Henry Holt & Company, 2001), or the more controversial work of Susan McCarthy and Jeffrey Moussaieff Masson, *When Elephants Weep* (New York: Delacorte, 1995). *The Cambridge Declaration on Consciousness* (www.fcmconference.org/img/CambridgeDeclarationOnConsciousness.pdf, July 7, 2012), signed at the 2012 "Consciousness in Human and Non-Human Animals" Conference, states that the presence of consciousness in other animals is "unequivocal". For a biological interpretation of how the functioning of the mind relates to physical laws and principles that is *not* reductionist, see J. A. Scott Kelso, *Dynamic Patterns: The Self Organization of Brain and Behavior* (Cambridge MA: MIT Press, 1997).

The continuity of language with other animal behaviors and its categorization as a kind of "instinctual" human behavior has been long accepted. See Steven Pinker, *The Language Instinct* (New York: HarperCollins, 1995) and Harvey B. Sarles, *Language and Human Nature: Toward a Grammar of Interaction and Discourse* (Minneapolis: University of Minnesota Press, 1985). On the debates about animal language, see C. N. Slobodchikoff, *Chasing Doctor Dolittle: Learning the Language of Animals* (New York: St. Martin's, 2012) and Stephen R. Anderson, *Doctor Dolittle's Delusion: Animals and the Uniqueness of Human Language* (New Haven CT: Yale University Press 2004). Irene Pepperberg's famous work with Alex the African Grey parrot, and similar work by other animal researchers, has also deeply impacted the way we think about animals and language. (Noam Chomsky's vast work on grammar as a "hard-wired" function of the brain is also fundamental, though for Chomsky this distinguishes human brains from the brains of other animals.) It is equally clear that a number of other species, not just chimpanzees but crows, etc., use tools (Robert W. Shumaker et al., *Animal Tool Behavior: The Use and Manufacture of Tools by Animals* [Baltimore MD: Johns Hopkins University Press, 2011]).

[68] Even from a strictly materialist perspective, lab studies that use fMRI to image activity in the parallel structures of the brains of humans and other species provide a strong basis for attributing feeling states to animals. Strict behaviorism is no longer a tenable basis for differentiating human experience from other species. On every level, presuming that animals' emotional systems are more similar to ours than dissimilar is the most parsimonious interpretation. See Mary Midgley, "Descartes' Prisoners", *New Stateman* (May 2, 1999) and *The Cambridge Declaration*, as well as Temple Grandin and Catherine Johnson, *Animals Make Us Human: Creating the Best Life for Animals* (New York: Houghton Mifflin Harcourt, 2009).

Theologically, this resonates strongly with rabbinic texts and stories, which assumed (as did the Torah) that animals have souls (see Chapter 4). It also resonates with beliefs espoused by Maimonides. In the medieval period, Maimonides wrote,

> If you are of those who know the soul and its powers... you already know that imagination exists in most living beings. As for the perfect animal, I mean the one endowed with a heart, the existence of imagination is clear. Accordingly, humanity[69] is not distinguished by having imagination[70]

In fact, there is a preponderance of pre-modern teachings in *Tanakh* (Hebrew Bible), Midrash, and (to a lesser degree) medieval thought that ascribe subjecthood and standing to the creatures. Despite this, modern Judaism has tended to label any attribution of subjectivity or moral standing to the natural world as "pagan".[71] This misconception is a direct result of the revision of Judaism according to Hegelian ideas of the evolution of Spirit. This revision posited that Judaism was about the triumph of history over Nature.[72] This extraordinary distortion of the tradition is only beginning to be overcome as people reread the teachings of *Chazal* (the early rabbinic sages[73]) and integrate realities

---

[69] The Pines translation consistently uses "man" to mean "humanity". This has been altered here and in some quotations below.

[70] MN 1:75, 209; cf. Aristotle, *On the Soul*, 433b (3:10). See also Maimonides' discussion of animals' feelings, p.148. While the question of subjecthood is not my primary focus, many texts dicussed further on address this issue, especially in Chapters 5 and 12.

[71] To give a personal rather than scholarly example, I used to invite fellow rabbinical students to participate in *kiddush l'vanah*, the ritual sanctification of the waxing moon that addresses the moon as "you" (see the liturgy at www.opensiddur.org/moon-cycle/new-moon/kiddush-levanah [July 2, 2014]). Sometimes people would refuse, calling the ritual "pagan".

[72] See pp.8ff, 68. Though this perspective is non-traditional, it has been most strongly advocated by Orthodox thinkers like Michael Wyschogrod and Irving Greenberg. See Moshe Sokol, "Ethical Implications of Jewish Conceptions of the Natural World", *Judaism and Ecology*, 261–82, esp. 262ff. and 265. Sokol, himself a modern Orthodox thinker, strongly critiques Wyschograd's perspective, emphasizing that such a worldview cannot be coherent (see n.403). See also nn.91, 363. Another factor influencing this development was that early twentieth-century Christian scholars, anxious to prove the uniqueness of Biblical Israel, interpreted Judaism as anti-pagan and anti-Nature in the face of secularist scholarship that saw the *Tanakh* as derivative of Nature-based Near East traditions. See Middleton, *Liberating Image*, 187–8, esp. n.5. In this vein, note Steven Schwarzschild's "The Unnatural Jew", a Woody Allen-esque polemic declaiming the enmity between Judaism and Nature (*Environmental Ethics* 6:4 [1984]: 347–62, anthologized in Yaffe, 267–82 and elsewhere). Schwarzschild is sometimes used as a foil in Jewish environmental education; it would be better consigned to the dustbin.

[73] *Chazal* stands for "*Chakhamim zikhronam livrakhah*", meaning "the sages, [may] their memory be for a blessing". This acronym, along with the generic phrase "the rabbis", refers to the classical period of rabbinic Judaism (through the publication of the Talmud). Other traditional acronyms used in this book include names of specific rabbis like Ramban (R' Moshe ben Nachman, a.k.a. Nachmanides) or Rashi (R' Shlomo Yits'chaqi), with the exception of Rambam or Maimonides (R' Moshe ben Maimun), who I refer to using his Latinized name.

that science and ecology explore. Becoming more aware of these realities is an important step toward restoring Judaism to its senses, literally.

Evolution

For a Judaism in touch with its roots and its senses, evolutionary science can lead to a grand synthesis of theology and science, and also, interestingly, to a synthesis of Maimonides and Kabbalah. Among scientists themselves, evolution has many different interpretations, ranging from an expansive vision of the unity of all Being and all Life, to a reductionist interpretation of life as the so-called struggle of genes to reproduce themselves.[74] Many ecologists and ecophilosophers share some version of the expansive interpretation, while the reductionist interpretation is more common among evolutionary biologists.[75] One reason that ecology is such a fruitful interlocutor with theology, and that it dovetails so well with Jewish thought, is that it includes within itself a hermenutic that unravels scientific reductionism.

---

[74] Connie Barlow's anthology *From Gaia to Selfish Genes: Selected Writings in the Life Sciences* (Cambridge MA: MIT Press, 1991) explores the range of opinions. On the "struggle" of genes, see, e.g., Richard Dawkins, *The Selfish Gene* (Oxford: Oxford University Press, 1991), 19. Dawkins is the most well-known and ideological of the reductionist camp, who are by and large Neo-Darwinians. (Neo-Darwinism is characterized by the theory that evolutionary change is mostly driven by random genetic mutation. The reductionists see natural selection as a process acting on genes, rather than on organisms, populations, or species.) For a critique of Dawkins, see Joan Roughgarden, *The Genial Gene: Deconstructing Darwinian Selfishness* (Berkeley: University of California Press, 2009), Niles Eldredge, *Why We Do it: Rethinking Sex and the Selfish Gene* (New York: W. W. Norton, 2004), and Mary Midgley's more controversial *The Solitary Self: Darwin and the Selfish Gene* (London: Acumen, 2010). See also Stephen Jay Gould, "The Evolutionary Definition of Selective Agency, Validation of the Theory of Hierarchical Selection, and Fallacy of the Selfish Gene" in *Thinking about Evolution*, ed. Rama S. Singh (Cambridge: Cambridge University Press, 2001), 208–34. Lynn Margulis (see next note) famously called Neo-Darwinism "a minor twentieth-century religious sect within the sprawling religious persuasion of Anglo-Saxon biology" (Charles Mann, "Lynn Margulis: Science's Unruly Earth Mother", *Science* 252 [2004]: 378–81; 380).

[75] A more intellectual and less polemical argument for a gene-level perspective on evolution can be found in Ernst Mayr's "Teleological and Teleonomic: A New Analysis", in *Evolution and the Diversity of Life* (Cambridge MA: Harvard University Press, 1976), 383–403. Mayr is concerned with methodology, and his argument is appropriately limited in scope.

There is still a tendency to regard reductionist interpretations as "harder" (that is, better) science. One biologist who bucked this trend was Lynn Margulis, who developed the theory of endosymbiosis (which states that mitochondria and chloroplasts in eukaryotic cells are descendants of symbiotic bacteria that took up residence inside other ancestor cells), as well as Gaia theory (n.873). She saw evolution as driven more by symbiosis than by competition, which implies that selection can happen on the level of systems of organisms, and not just species, individuals, or at the lowest level, genes. Margulis's ideas can be accessed in her popular work *Symbiotic Planet: A New Look at Evolution* (New York: Basic Books, 1998). Another biologist who takes an integrative view of evolution is James A. Shapiro; see *Evolution: A View from the 21st Century* (Upper Saddle River NJ: FT Press, 2011).

Fundamental ecological issues in Jewish perspective

The reductive approach to science is a hallmark of modernity. In ancient and medieval times, most of what we call Western civilization was grounded in two beliefs: the first, that there is a higher level of being that is more perfect and a lower that is more corrupt or corruptible; and the second, that the whole of Creation is an organic and purposeful unity. The project of modernity may be characterized as giving up belief in organic unity while holding on to the hierarchy of Being. The meaning of this hierarchy, however, changed radically, with humanity migrating from somewhere in the middle of the chain of Being to the top, either in the place of God or right beneath God, depending on one's degree of secularism (see "The Chain of Being", Chapter 1). A postmodern ecotheology, grounded in evolutionary theory, would do the opposite: affirm the organicism of the whole, even as it rejects (or mitigates) ontological hierarchy.

In general, Jewish understandings of the purpose of creation and the role of humanity can be correlated with the question of how to interpret evolution.[76] Three perspectives can be discerned: (1) Humanity is the pinnacle and *telos* of Creation (and hence of evolution). This perspective correlates with what Bryan G. Norton calls "strong anthropocentrism", which he contrasts with "weak anthropocentrism"; here I call this "anthropo-archism".[77] (2) Humanity is part of an evolving whole and humanity's purpose is to move the whole toward greater perfection. Since perfecting Creation happens through human action, this perspective may be termed weak anthropocentrism, because it accepts the idea that humanity has a unique place in Creation while giving absolute priority only to the needs of the whole.[78] This perspective fits with spiritual interpretations of evolutionary "progress" and lends itself to a deeper reflection on stewardship. (3) Creation is inherently whole or moving toward perfection, with every species (past, present, and future) being an essential part of that wholeness or movement. This position may admit a *telos* for Creation that is not connected to any overtly human purpose, and it is closest to a biocentric perspective.

---

[76] See Michael Shai Cherry, "Creation, Evolution and Jewish Thought" (Brandeis University, PhD dissertation, 2001). His examination of evolution in Kook (205–24) and other twentieth-century theologians was the first significant study of this question. For Modern Orthodox perspectives on evolution, see Natan Slifkin, *The Challenge of Creation: Judaism's Encounter with Science, Cosmology, and Evolution* (Jerusalem: Zoo Torah, 2006).

[77] *Why Preserve Natural Variety?* (Princeton NJ: Princeton University Press, 1987), 12–14. Norton's distinction is here only an approximation, since Norton is not concerned with the theological place of humanity but rather with the hierarchy of human needs over other species. For Norton, strong anthropocentrism means that humans have the right to use Nature in any way, essentially to treat the natural world as a resource, while weak anthropocentrism admits of value in the other creatures on the basis of their aesthetic and moral significance to human beings, rather than just their "demand value" or capacity to meet consumptive needs.

[78] More than this, if the human purpose is to act for the sake of the whole then the hierarchy of anthropocentrism is turned upside down. This anthropocentrism is even "weaker" than what Norton describes as weak anthropocentrism.

Anthropo-archism, the perspective that all of Creation exists only for the sake of humanity, was expounded most emphatically by Saadyah Gaon (882–942, Egypt, Baghdad), who wrote, "When we see the many created beings, we should not be perplexed/*n'vukhim* about what among them is the goal... for the goal is humanity/*ha'adam*."[79] Saadyah went further than anyone in this respect when he asserted that even the angels and heavens exist to serve humanity.[80] Anthropo-archism is strongly represented in medieval philosophy and in modern Jewish thought, especially in the Orthodox camp.[81] It is, however, not representative of rabbinic Judaism as a whole. Though an "anthropo-archic" interpretation of Creation is reflected in individual statements found in the Midrash (see Chapter 3), wherever the perspective that Creation exists to serve humanity was expressed, it was always tempered by alternative interpretations.

In both the second and third perspectives, humanity is not the *telos* of Creation. Rather, humanity serves the *telos* of Creation.[82] Humanity receives its value from its relation to the whole of Creation, rather than being the source of value.[83] In other words, even though humanity may occupy a central and

---

[79] *Hanivchar b'Emunot v'Dei`ot* (*Emunot v'Dei`ot*), trans. Yosef Kafich (Jerusalem: Makhon Sura', 1970), art.4, introduction (www.daat.ac.il/daat/mahshevt/kapah/4-2.htm [Sep. 2012]). Maimonides' *Moreh N'vukhim*, or *Guide for the Perplexed*, may be read as a direct refutation of Saadyah's proposition. (Note that the Judeo-Arabic root for "perplexed" is also the same in both texts.) See esp. MN 3:13, quoted presently and discussed in n.84. On Saadyah, see also pp.30, 93–4.

[80] Norman Lamm, "Man's Position in the Universe: A Comparative Study of the Views of Saadia Gaon and Maimonides", *The Jewish Quarterly Review*, New Series, 55:3 (Jan. 1965): 208–234; 216–9. See n.300. This position is strongly contradicted not only by Maimonides but also by the *midrashim* discussed on p.47ff.

[81] See Schwartz, "Judaism and Nature", 161ff., esp. on Aharon Lichtenstein. Schwartz also cites the secular Yehezkel Kaufmann, n.9. Generally, this camp rejects any idea of intrinsic value in other creatures, or even in Creation as a whole, as being akin to "idolatry". Not only is that patently false – recognizing intrinsic value is not an act of worship – but it entails rejecting vital aspects of the rabbinic tradition and much of the history of Biblical and Jewish thought. See pp.9ff., 23, 232, 272, as well as *Methods for Jewish Constructive Theology*, www.kabbalahandecology.com.

[82] For a Christian take on this perspective, see Andrew Linzey, *Animal Theology* (Chicago: University of Illinois Press, 1994) ch.3, esp. 56–8. The quality of serving is what constitutes God's image in his view: "The uniqueness of humanity comes in its ability to become the servant species. To exercise its full humanity as co-participants and co-workers with God in the redemption of the world" (56). He roots this idea in the "passibility" of God; that is, that God suffers not just along with every human suffering but also along with every animal capable of suffering. On this idea in Jewish tradition, see, e.g., *Mishnah Sanhedrin* 6:5 (Philip Blackman, ed., *Mishnayoth* [New York: Judaica, 1963]). There have also been attempts to incorporate this concept into Holocaust theology, e.g., Melissa Raphael's *The Female Face of God in Auschwitz: A Jewish Feminist Theology of the Holocaust* (New York: Routledge, 2003), 125.

[83] Reformulating intrinsic value in terms of a thing's relation to the whole could still imply that humans have greater value, since they can become more connected to the whole in all its dimensions. But this value would no longer be intrinsic in an ontological sense. This is analogous to the shift that occurs when the image of God – the guarantor of intrinsic value – is

exalted place in the cosmos, the ultimate determination of value and right is not human needs but cosmic needs. The second perspective, that humanity serves a greater purpose that benefits the whole of Creation, is arguably the position of the Torah and most of Kabbalah, and both perspectives are validated in the history of Jewish thought alongside the anthropo-archic interpretation. I will presently examine Maimonides as a model for the third perspective, and then Avraham Yitshak (Abraham Isaac) Kook (1865–1935, Latvia, Palestine) representing a particular reading of Kabbalah, as a model for the second.

Maimonides is the most important Jewish source for a non-teleological interpretation of Being. He carefully explores the argument for a *telos* for Creation, explaining that this concept would only be possible if there were a beginning and end to time. While admitting that such a concept is conceivable within Judaism, he rejects this possibility:

> It should not be believed that all the beings exist for the sake of the existence of man. On the contrary, all the other beings too have been intended for their own sakes and not for the sake of something else. Thus even according to our view holding that the world has been produced in time, the quest for the final end of all the species of beings collapses... In respect to every being He intended that being itself; and whenever the existence of some thing was impossible unless it was preceded by some other thing, He first brought that thing into existence.[84]

Humanity is not the final end of Creation, or of any other species.[85]

---

no longer seen as limited to human beings, even if the divine image is still present in humans in a unique way.

[84] MN 3:13, 452; see p.15–6. This chapter is an essential foundation for any Jewish ecotheology, and one of the central chapters in *The Guide*. (The significance of this chapter is also underlined by the fact that it begins by referencing the book's title: "many are perplexed... over the final end of existence" [Kafich, 298].) The other essential chapter is 1:72, where Maimonides describes the cosmos as a single living being (see p.268ff.). See Lenn Goodman's discussion of MN 3:13 in "Respect for Nature in the Jewish Tradition", *Judaism and Ecology*, 243–5; Sokol, "Ethical Implications", 267; and George Gittelman, "Maimonides and *The Guide to the Perplexed*: An Environmental Ethic for Our Time", *CCAR Journal* (Fall 2010): 42–53; 47–8, 51. Compare Maimonides with French's analysis of Aquinas: "The vastness of God's goodness cannot be participated in, nor adequately represented by, any one creature or type of creature, even humanity" ("Catholicism", 193). See nn.54, 64.

[85] Maimonides' position here contradicts his early work. In his introduction to the Mishnah, for example, he wrote, "All existences under the sphere of the moon (= *tachtonim*, "the lower ones", see p.49) exist solely for the sake of humanity" (*Mishnah 'Im Peyrush Harambam*, vol.1 [Jerusalem: Mosad Harav Kook, 1963], *Haqdamah*, 21–2). One traditional scholar, Menachem Slae, tried to harmonize this contradiction by suggesting that in *The Guide*, Maimonides was only referring to the angels and heavenly bodies (Akiva Wolff, "Bal Tashchit: The Jewish Prohibition Against Needless Destruction" [Leiden University, PhD dissertation, 2009], 56). One could easily be led to this conclusion, since Maimonides states in *The Guide* that the human being is "the most perfect thing" that can be generated from the compounding of (sublunar) matter and that "it would be true from this point of view" to say that "all sublunar beings" – but not the heavenly bodies – "exist for his sake" (MN 3:13, 449–50; also 3:12, 444). But Maimonides is also quite clear that "this point of view" is neither his nor the ultimate

Evolutionary theorists who reject the idea of "progress" in evolution (e.g., Stephen Jay Gould) would affirm Maimonides' rejection of final ends as a hermeneutic for interpreting biological phenomena. We can only guess how Maimonides would have responded to evolutionary theory. The medievals did not conceive that Life could undergo changes on the level of species. Nevertheless, Maimonides' formulation that "the quest for the final end of all the species collapses" would fit this understanding of evolution.[86]

While Maimonides rejected final ends, he also underlined the goodness of Creation as a whole, which would ally him with most ecologists. He assiduously avoided a hierarchical interpretation of the story of creation, emphasizing that the ultimate goodness is found not in any particular creature but only in the whole. Speaking against the idea that other creatures were brought into being for the pleasure of humanity, he wrote,

What led to all this was ignorance of the nature of coming-to-be and passing-away and neglect of the fundamental principle: namely, that the entire purpose [of creation] consists in bringing into existence the way you see it everything whose existence is possible[87]

perspective and that Creation has no *telos*, no final end, human or otherwise. The correct interpretation of these passages is that Maimonides changed his mind (cf. his interpretation of the phrase "*ki tov*" in Gn 1, quoted p.16). See Lamm, "Man's Position", 223–5. For a perspective in between Slae's and Lamm's or my own, see Dov Shvarts, who understands Maimonides' position in *The Guide* to be that the other creatures aspire/conspire/desire toward the creation of the human being not because they were created to serve humanity, but because they aspire to achieve the greatest perfection of form possible for gross matter (*Central Problems in Medieval Jewish Philosophy* [Leiden: Brill, 2005], ch.2, esp. 41–5).

[86] For comparison's sake, I am bracketing out the theonomic principles that stand at the head of Maimonides' thought. Cherry (65–70) does not take note of Maimonides' rejection of teleology here, which is significant for the interpretation of evolutionary theory. He also affirms the conclusion of some *Wissenschaft* scholars that Maimonides accepted the eternality of Creation but only hinted at this position esoterically (notes, 68). While the rejection of teleology could be consistent with that position, a preponderance of evidence, including material I cite throughout, would seem to militate against this conclusion. The thesis that the world is created in time is central to Maimonides' entire project and to the structure of *The Guide*. For a survey of scholarship on this issue, see Tamar Rudavsky, *Time Matters: Time, Creation, and Cosmology in Medieval Jewish Philosophy* (Albany NY: SUNY Press, 2000), 30–34. For an extended argument against the esotericists' claim, see Daniel Davies, *Method and Metaphysics in Maimonides' Guide for the Perplexed* (Oxford: Oxford University Press, 2011) ch.2 and Kenneth Seeskin, *Maimonides on the Origin of the World* (New York: Cambridge University Press, 2006).

[87] MN 3:25, 504; Kafich, 333. Maimonides illustrates this way of thinking as follows: "That anything among His actions, may He be exalted, should be frivolous is impossible...No attention should be paid to the ravings of those who deem that the ape was created in order that man should laugh at it." Maimonides did not imagine the possibility of the extinction of species, believing that divine providence watched over each species and preserved it. (*MN* 3:17). See also Natan Slifkin, "From the Eggs of Dodos to the Horns of Aurochsen: The Extinction of Species in Jewish Thought" in *Siach Sadeh* (Summer 2011): 64–82, esp. 66–7, 72–3 (www.old.lifshiz.macam.ac.il/siach/slifkin.pdf [Sep. 2013]). However, we might wonder about Maimonides' response to those who believe that the creatures of earlier eras, such as

If the purpose of creation is to bring into existence "everything whose existence is possible", then Maimonides shares remarkable parallels with both a Spinozistic conception of the world and with contemporary scientists like E. O. Wilson, who understands the trend of evolution to be increasing diversity, or Lynn Margulis, who sees the trend of evolution as one toward greater and greater levels of symbiosis.[88] For all of them, the whole is inherently good in a way that transcends the human species.

Another important interpretation of the purpose of Life, and evolution, is found in Avraham Yitshak Kook, the chief rabbi in Palestine during the Mandate period, who draws connections between science and Kabbalistic thought. Rav Kook, as he is known, writes:

> Evolution sheds light on all the ways of God. All existence evolves and ascends... Its ascent is general as it is in particulars. It ascends toward the height of the absolute good. Obviously the good and the comprehensive (whole) all go together. Existence is destined to reach a point when the whole will assimilate the good in all its constituted particulars... No particularity will remain outside, not a spark will be lost from the ensemble.[89]

Kook underlines that evolutionary progress is a matter of perfecting the whole of Creation. Evolution toward the good entails evolution of the whole, rather than the evolution of a more perfect being that stands separate from or over against the whole.

Kook adds that "[t]he doctrine of evolution... has a greater affinity with the secret teachings of the Cabbalah [sic] than all other philosophies." Kook believed that Kabbalah was the aspect of Judaism best prepared to embrace the inner mystery of evolution.[90] His use of Kabbalah to interpret the science of his time resonates with a long line of post-Renaissance, Enlightenment, and modern Jewish thinkers who grounded science and humanism in Kabbalah.[91]

---

dinosaurs or Ediacaran fauna, only came into being to serve as steps leading to the evolution of humanity, rather than as ends-in-themselves. Would he not say that they too are "raving and ignorant"?

[88] This discussion draws on Barlow, *Evolution Extended: Biological Debates on the Meaning of Life* (Cambridge MA: MIT Press, 1995); for Wilson, see 24–9. On Margulis, see n.75 herein and *Symbiotic Planet*, 100ff.

[89] *Abraham Isaac Kook*, trans. Ben Zion Bokser (New York: Paulist Press, 1978), 221, from *Orot Haqodesh*, 2 vols. (Jerusalem: Ha'agudah L'hotsa'at Sifrey Hara'ya"h Kook, 1937), vol.2, 555 (hereafter *OHQ*). Kook thought atomic science (as it was then called) revealed a similar mystery (*The Essential Writings of Abraham Isaac Kook*, trans. Ben Zion Bokser [Warwick NY: Amity Press, 1988], 166, from *OHQ* 2, 426–7).

[90] Bokser (1978), 194–5 (*OHQ* 1, 910). See also *OHQ* 2, 537, in *The Essential Kabbalah*, trans. Daniel Matt (San Francisco: HarperCollins, 1996), 31.

[91] Some examples are Immanuel Chai Ricci (1688–1743, Italy), *Mishnat Chasidim* (Lemberg [Lvov, Galicia]: M. F. Poremba, 1858); Pinchas Eliyahu Hurwitz (1765–1821, Poland), *Sefer Hab'rit Hashalem* (Jerusalem: Y'rid Has'farim, 1990); and Elijah Benamozegh (1823–1900, Italy), *Israel and Humanity* (New York: Paulist Press, 1994). A contemporary example would

Rav Kook's thought corresponds to the ideas of a different cadre of evolutionary biologists than Maimonides, namely, those who believe there is an arrow of progress that defines evolution. Within this cadre, Kook is less anthropocentric than someone like Julian Huxley, who sees sentience and power over the environment as the two "directions" of evolution, but more anthropocentric than Francisco Ayala, who reads a kind of generalized purposefulness into the trend toward complexity.[92] I suspect that even Ayala's interpretation would have been too teleological for Maimonides.

Despite their strong differences, both Maimonides and Kook may be contrasted with the majority of Jewish thinkers, including Saadyah Gaon and (less emphatically) Bachya ibn Paquda, who understand the ultimate good of Creation and its final end to be humanity.[93] The corollary of this belief is that Creation is a mere tool and resource for humanity. This approach to the more-than-human world became one of the cornerstones of what I call "modernist-humanism". While Kook absorbed and promulgated ideas associated with modernity and humanism, both Kook and Maimonides rejected a baldly utilitarian and anthropo-archic view of Creation. Fortunately for Jewish ecotheology, some of the greatest thinkers in Jewish history have given us broad shoulders to stand on.

ANTHROPOCENTRISM AS A CENTRAL QUESTION FOR POLITICS AND THEOLOGY

Ecotheology in the monotheistic traditions has revolved around several themes, which can be grouped according to whether they are primarily theological or ethical. The ethical issues raised by ecology, which are perhaps more familiar to people, include limiting the human exercise of power through exercising responsibility, morally accounting for animal suffering and animal consciousness, internalizing the fact of our dependence on Nature and on other creatures, and defining ethical norms based on these issues. In general, these are questions

---

be Daniel Matt's *God & the Big Bang: Discovering Harmony Between Science & Spirituality* (Woodstock VT: Jewish Lights, 1998).

[92] Barlow, *Evolution Extended*, 4–20 on Huxley, 20–24 on Ayala. The emphasis on complexity found in Ayala can be interpreted to favor the human brain as the ultimate expression of evolution, even while rejecting the idea that a particular species is the climax or goal of evolution. Huxley's frame of reference, on the other hand, privileges the human gestalt, rather than an aspect of human biology. A deeper comparison can be made between Kook and Henri Bergson's view of evolution and *élan vital* (see *Creative Evolution*, trans. Arthur Mitchell [New York: Henry Holt, 1911]). One reason why Kook may be less anthropocentric than Huxley is that his theocentrism affirms the inherent moral value of all Creation. See, e.g., Bokser (1978), 230 (*OHQ* 2, 537–8); Bokser (1988), 165 and 178 (*OHQ* 2, 323 and 591). Humanity for Kook is still at the center of Creation, being the one species able to lead the whole to perfection. See Bokser (1978), 231 (*OHQ* 2, 561); Bokser (1988), 174 and 175–6 (*OHQ* 2, 565–6, 586–7).

[93] Bachya was discussed in n.60 and Saadyah on p.26.

Anthropocentrism as a central question for politics and theology

about human responsibility and the right way to balance human needs and the well-being of other species.

The theological issues include anthropocentrism (along with the metaphysical hierarchy of humans over other species), the devaluing of the physical world in relation to what is deemed spiritual or what comes after death, and the meaning of God's transcendence (*qua* absence) in relation to the physical Creation. Ecotheologians readily emphasize the immanence of God, the sacredness of all life, and the ethical importance of humility as a response to these issues, often by focusing on the mystical threads of their tradition. More generally, the focus of ecotheology is on lifting up the value of Creation in relation to two traditional axes of value: God and humanity. Of course, the theological has a profound impact on the ethical, and vice versa.

As mentioned, certain assumptions fundamental to both Christian and Jewish tradition appear to run counter to the creation of a sustainable human society. These assumptions about the human relationship to God, to other creatures, and to the Earth can be characterized by three ideas: (1) human beings alone are "created in God's image", (2) this divine image is an essence or soul that elevates human value immeasurably or "infinitely" above other creatures,[94] and (3) the true home or destiny of this soul is not found on Earth. These assumptions are also congruent with Islam's understanding of humanity's place in Creation and the soul's course.[95]

These three assumptions form the bedrock of radical anthropocentrism in our culture and within the Jewish and Christian traditions generally. They may even seem like second nature to many people. Nevertheless, the latter two assumptions are easily critiqued from within the sources of the Jewish tradition. However, the idea that humans are in God's image is firmly grounded in the Torah, the foundation of all three Abrahamic religions. The trope of God's

---

[94] However, there is no contradiction between the theology being worked out in *Kabbalah and Ecology* and the idea that there is a hierarchy that differentiates human life from the lives of other animals. The purpose here is not to overturn the value of human life, but rather to reconceptualize it in relation to other important values, such as the lives of whole species and the sustaining of life in all its complexity and diversity.

[95] Islam does not emphasize the idea of God's image, perhaps because Islam's aversion to comparing God with anything physical or metaphysical is even stronger than Judaism's. However, there is a recurring motif in the Qur'an about the angels being required to worship Adam; this motif corresponds to humans being created in God's image (see n.192). The theme of God's image does appear in the *hadith*, though the traditions in question were not regarded as authentic by all commentators. See Yahya Michot, "The Image of God in Humanity from a Muslim Perspective", in *Abraham's Children: Jews, Christians and Muslims in Conversation*, eds. Norman Solomon et al. (New York: T&T Clark, 2005), 163–74. See also Alexander Altmann's discussion of al-Ghazali and Ibn al-Arabi in "The Delphic Maxim in Medieval Islam and Judaism" (*Biblical and Other Studies* [Cambridge MA: Harvard University Press, 1963], 201–6), as well as Muhammad Suheyl Umar, "Image of God: A Note on the Scriptural Anthropology" (*The Journal of Scriptural Reasoning* 4:2 [Oct. 2004] jsr.lib.virginia.edu/vol-4-no-2-october-2004-the-image-of-god/image-of-god-a-note-on-the-scriptural-anthropology/ [Dec. 2013]), esp. n.1.

image is one of the most familiar narrative elements of Genesis, perhaps as familiar as anything else in the entire Biblical tradition. The anthropo-archic interpretation of this image has been a touchstone for ethics, political and social theory, and secular and religious ideology in the medieval and modern periods. This trope has been used to justify the division between humanity and Nature and the hierarchy of human beings over other creatures on the one hand, and universal human rights on the other. It is part of what Zalman Schachter-Shalomi might call the "system files" of Western religion.[96]

Working from a traditional framework, I will explore the variety of rabbinic anthropologies, focusing on alternative interpretations of God's image. These interpretations provide a foundation for a different anthropology, and they support a wide range of intermediate positions between a strong affirmation of the hierarchy of humans over Nature on the one hand and a rejection of this hierarchy on the other.

The elevation of individual human beings in modern civilization, grounded in the theology of God's image, has vitally positive implications as well. Many modern theologians judge the belief that humanity was created in God's image to be one of the most revolutionary and libertory insights of Biblical monotheism.[97] Moreover, the belief in humanity's divine image has been credited with laying the foundation for some of the most important and positive developments within Western civilization, including the very idea of a universal humanity, along with ethics, moral philosophy, and human rights. Without delving into the historicity of this claim, the idea of God's image in the modern period has certainly served as the ground for both secular and religious conceptions of human value (e.g., "All men are created equal"). As an imperative to create a society based on human equality, universal values, and individual uniqueness, its impact is unquestionably positive.

At the same time, one could also claim that the idea of God's image in humanity creates an absolute hierarchy of humanity over other creatures. This leads directly to human domination over the rest of the natural world. One aspect of this domination is that if we understand humans to be the only creatures in God's image, then we isolate those qualities that set human beings apart, and we similarly ignore or subjugate the qualities that we hold in common with other creatures. Thus, the idea of God's image not only justifies the subjugation of other species, it also becomes an instrument for repressing those aspects of our own being that unite us with all life.[98] In many circumstances, it can also be used to justify hierarchies of gender, race, religion, and culture.

---

[96] "The Spirituality of the Future", www.theshalomcenter.org/node/1395 (Feb. 2014).
[97] Whether this claim accurately describes the uniqueness of early Biblical religion is not critical to this discussion.
[98] From a religious perspective, this alienation from ourselves also means alienation from the divine. See next section.

Anthropocentrism as a central question for politics and theology

In various cultures, and most certainly (perhaps most extremely) in the culture of Western capitalism, people see themselves as radically separate from Nature, and readily treat other creatures as instruments to serve their own ends. Lynn White, Jr. famously claimed that this perspective has its origins in Genesis, which taught that "God planned all this explicitly for man's benefit and rule: no item in the physical Creation had any purpose save to serve man's purposes."[99] It is easy enough to critique White's claim: Genesis 1 is hardly the Torah's final statement on humanity's role in Creation, and, as Jeremy Cohen carefully documents, White's reading does not represent the historical span of Christian and Jewish interpretation.[100] However, the interpretation supposed by White is certainly part of that history, and it clearly resonates with the trajectory of Western civilization. It is not easy to know whether this trajectory was guided by theology, or whether theology is a post-facto justification of technological power and economic interests.

While many contemporary ecological thinkers are quick to blame the Bible's presumed anthropocentrism for ecological sin, there are also those who argue that the roots of environmental tragedy are not found in the human-centeredness of traditional theology, but rather in the loss of centeredness in the wake of the revolution of modern, mechanistic science. Seyyed Hossein Nasr, a contemporary Muslim philosopher, writes,

> In medieval cosmology man had been placed at the center of the Universe, not as a purely terrestrial man but as "the image of God"... By removing him from the center of things, [science] did not bestow upon man the transcendent dimension of his nature; rather it affirmed the loss of the theomorphic nature... Therefore, although on the surface it belittled the position of man in the scheme of things, on a deeper level it assisted... the Promethean revolt against the voice of heaven.[101]

Nasr outlines a dialectic in the human soul between domination and diminishment. By losing our "theomorphic" nature, he says, we lose connection also to the universe. This loss goes hand-in-hand with a willingness to act without responsibility in the world. And yet that same theomorphic image is used as an imprimatur for such actions.

---

[99] "The Historical Roots of Our Ecological Crisis", *Science*, 155 (Mar. 10, 1967): 1202–7; 1205.

[100] *"Be Fertile and Increase, Fill the Earth and Master It": The Ancient and Medieval Career of a Biblical Text* (Ithaca NY: Cornell University Press, 1989). He also lays out the very different trajectory of Christian and Jewish interpretation. See also critiques of White by J. Baird Callicott, "Genesis Revisited: Murian Musings on the Lynn White, Jr. Debate" (*Environmental History Review* 14:1–2 [1990]: 65–92) and Elspeth Whitney, "Lynn White, Ecotheology and History" (*Environmental Ethics* 15 [Summer 1993]: 151–69), as well as Whitney's summary of the literature in "White, Lynn (1907–1987) – Thesis of", *ERN* 1735–6 and Timothy Weiskel's bibliography, "The Environmental Crisis and Western Civilization: The Lynn White Controversy", www.ecoethics.net/bib/1997/enca-001.htm (Feb. 19, 1997).

[101] *Man and Nature* (London: George Allen and Unwin, 1976), 68. Nasr also writes, "With the help of the new science the only role left to man was to conquer and dominate nature and to serve his needs as an animal endowed somehow with analytical reason and thought" (72).

Moral, political, and practical questions may be impelling us to revise our theological assumptions about "what is human", but these questions should not generate our answers. Theology must respond to the "need of eternity" and not just the political needs of the moment. It may seem paradoxical that it is in the phenomenological dimension – the dimension of lived experience in which we seek, in the present, a living relationship with the divine – that one finds the firmest ground in which to root such theology.

That relationship unfolds in the more-than-human world, that is, in Nature. One reason why I use the terminology "more-than-human world" is that it reminds us that the human realm is a part of Nature, rather than standing in opposition to it. It is Nature that forms and informs human nature, teaching us what it means to be embodied and to become human.[102] Every dissonance between religion and the natural world therefore prevents us from understanding ourselves. But more-than-human also includes what is of God, and a fuller understanding of God must also embrace the diversity of Creation, which is an aspect of God's infinity.

Modern Jews, however, tend to follow the lead of medieval philosophy and focus our theological imagination on God's unity. And we focus on God's image in ourselves, thereby severing humanity from the natural world, dislocating the bone from its socket. In an anthropocentric universe, divinity is quickly reduced to a narrow set of human-centered images.

This book, behind all its talk about ancient texts, proposes that we most fully experience the meaning of the divine image not by limiting it to ourselves, but by finding it within the other creatures and dimensions of this world that embraces us. That is one way we can connect to the limitless, inexhaustible diversity inhering in what we call God. In the process, we may discover that the human/more-than-human sign of "the image of God" can become the ground for an eco-centric understanding of the human role in Creation.

---

[102] David Abram explores these issues with acuity in "Merleau-Ponty and the Voice of the Earth" (*Minding Nature: Philosophers of Ecology*, ed. David Macauley [New York: Guilford, 1996], 82–101) and in *The Spell of the Sensuous*, where he writes:

> [T]he boundaries of the body are open and indeterminate; more like membranes than barriers, they define a surface of metamorphosis and exchange. The breathing, sensing body draws its sustenance and its very substance from the soils, plants, and elements that surround it; it continually contributes itself, in turn, to the air, to the composting earth, to the nourishment of insects and oak trees and squirrels, ceaselessly spreading out of itself as well as breathing the world into itself, so that it is very difficult to discern, at any moment precisely where this living body begins and ends. (46)

I explore some implications of these ideas for Jewish thought in "Sensuous Minds". See also Seidenberg, "The Human, the Tree, and the Image of God" in *Trees, Earth, and Torah*, 263–75, esp. 269–70 and 273–4, and "Confessions of a Jewish Post-Postmodernist" (in the section "Earth"), *Response* (Summer 1995); rev. 2011, www.neohasid.org/culture/confessions (Dec. 2011).

METHODOLOGY

One of the goals of this book is to use ancient and medieval texts to challenge long-held ideas (or recently held, depending on one's time-scale) about the place of humanity in Creation. It is not surprising that ecotheologians and philosophers who reject anthropocentrism might sooner reject traditional or Biblically based religion, or appeal to some "perennial philosophy" that stands outside of so-called revealed religion, than they would appeal to such ancient voices. But my default assumption is that the deepest fixing may be found within the source and substance of what seems broken, if that source is tapped at its root. Rather than rejecting contemporary cultural norms in favor of more "advanced" ones, this work will deconstruct the religious discourse that supports those norms. Since anthropocentrism is their bedrock, its transformation would also transform every dimension of the human–more-than-human relationship. Such a process could liberate the energy and spiritual power of the Biblical traditions to help create a civilization that chooses life.

Constructive theology

To get there, it is not enough to simply deconstruct anthropocentrism. This book also constructs a "theological lens", or standpoint, rooted strictly in premodern sources, that can free us to embrace ecocentrism. To do this, I use textual moments – texts that are in some cases outliers or that represent what may be a non-normative point of view – to construct an alternative picture of what is possible within Jewish thought. Most importantly, I generally do not make claims about what is "normative" in Jewish thought. I also focus primarily not on concepts but rather on more concrete units of meaning, like a Biblical phrase or rabbinic term, which can be traced diachronically and used to tie together ideologically disparate texts.[103]

I discuss scholarly precedents for these methods in *Methods for Jewish Constructive Theology* (published online at www.kabbalahandecology.com). I will give a brief overview here.

Fundamentally, constructing theology is an act of rereading. This can be done in a way that conflicts with academic analysis and ignores contrary evidence in order to make the texts and practices of a religious tradition fit one's understanding of truth. Or, one can subject oneself to stumbling on uneven ground, examining each stone and rock, whether or not it fits one's ideology, reading and interpreting both the texts that fit one's perspective and the texts that contradict it. I anticipate that some people who think of themselves as

---

[103] The implicit theory of semiotics behind this procedure is explored in *Methods*. Though I thematize texts that lead to a new understanding of God's image (see p.208), I also try to integrate those texts that fit a modernist or strongly anthropocentric interpretation of God's image.

pure scholars will believe I have taken the former path. However, even though I can only assume that I have overlooked some important texts, it has been my goal to stay faithful to the texture, topography, and "canonized dissensus"[104] of the sources examined here.

In all cases, I have taken pains to use historical and philological methods to first analyze the texts, before using the texts themselves theologically. By completing this level of analysis first, it is possible to "do" theology in a deliberate way, to not distort the texts or override their historical meaning.[105] I focus on pre-modern texts because they can be thought of as "objective", since they are not inflected by ecological concerns. (This is similar to the way *poskim*, halakhic decisors, use precedent.) Even though my ultimate goal is theological, I also use this methodology to reach insights that may be significant for Jewish intellectual history.

Those precedents that lead to an expanded interpretation of God's image can then be used, after academic analysis, to construct a lens through which to read Judaism in ecological terms, and to revalue the significance of God's image and the sacredness of human life. This book therefore aims to open up new ways of interpreting the tradition that may affect both the way we understand the past and the way we live in the present.

The following metaphor guides my own sense of purpose: Just as biodiversity is a wellspring of richness and meaning in our lives on multiple levels, so too is human diversity, the diversity of cultures, a wellspring for humanity.[106] We need to draw on the deepest sources of this spring in order to meet challenges and adapt to changes that will come upon us in this century. Though the image of God may be problematic now because of the way it buttresses anthropoarchism, it is also a vital source of meaning in our relations to others. By using the lens of God's image to comprehend the more-than-human aspects of the world, we may come to treat the world around us not as a toolbox or resource,

---

[104] Daniel Boyarin, *Carnal Israel: Reading Sex in Talmudic Culture* (Berkeley: University of California Press, 1993), 28. In more recent work, Boyarin seems to reject this idea. Regardless, here it serves a useful purpose.

[105] I have also found ideas about counter history and redemptive texts helpful in formulating how such texts can be used theologically. See Boyarin, *Carnal Israel*, 230, and see n.945. Boyarin described a methodology of reading countertexts "redemptively" to reconstruct gender in rabbinic culture. I have modified his methodology for this book (most importantly, by using it to reconstruct intellectual history rather than cultural history – see *Methods*). David Biale's description of "counter history" is well suited to describing the methodology used here:

> Counter history is a type of revisionist historiography, but where the revisionist proposes a new theory or finds new facts, the counter-historian transvalues old ones. He does not deny that his predecessors' interpretation of history is correct, as does the revisionist, but he rejects the completeness of that interpretation. (*Gershom Scholem: Kabbalah and Counter History* [Cambridge MA: Harvard University Press, 1982], 7)

[106] Zalman Schachter-Shalomi talked about different religious civilizations being like different organs of the body of humanity, each one fulfilling a vital function.

per Heschel (p.96), but rather as a realm invested with the dignity of the divine that demands our respect, awe, and love.

KABBALAH

This work draws heavily on Midrash, Maimonides, and Kabbalah. Midrash will open the door to a diversity of thinking about God's image, breaking down what may seem like a monolithic concept. Kabbalah will be the primary vessel for developing a new theological framework (with a strong assist from Maimonides). I will use Kabbalistic precedents to establish the following ideas: (1) that specific earthly non-human creatures are in God's image, (2) that the whole of Creation is the image of God, (3) that the earth itself can powerfully manifest that image, (4) that within each creature lives a potential to express God's image, and (5) that humanity can, through right intent and consciousness, help reveal that image.

These elements of Kabbalah do not exist in a vacuum, and only some Kabbalists share all of them. But there is a greater reason why Kabbalah can be used as a vessel for so many ecologically important ideas. The Kabbalistic tradition is already aligned with a holistic sense of human purpose, because from its very origins in *Sefer Bahir*, it held that the Jewish covenant and human action serve to bring blessing to all of Creation, not just to the Jewish people, and not just to humanity.[107] That this stance can easily generate an environmental ethic can be seen in Moshe Cordovero (1522–70, Palestine), who expressed this idea most eloquently:

Being involved in this wisdom, a person sustains the world and its life and its sustenance. And this is what the Rashbi (R Shimon bar Yochai) explained, and he said that "the world is blessed because of us"[108] ... for involvement with Divinity causes cleaving, and when the human cleaves to the One who flows/guides /*hamashpi`a* (God), he causes the flow [of divine energy] necessarily, and therefore by the effect of this wisdom, he causes to flow upon the world a great flow / *shefa`rav*.[109]

In another work, Cordovero states simply of the human task, "This is the principle: [a person] should make life stream forth to all / *yihyeh no<u>v</u>ei`a chayyim lakol*."[110] As Seth Brody wrote, "The Kabbalist's goal is to become a living bridge, uniting heaven and earth, so that God may become equally

---

[107] This theme first appears in *Sefer Habahir* (eleventh century or earlier), and it appears to originate with this work. See, e.g., §§22 and 119, and see n.560 in this volume. Note that here and further on, section numbers follow the Margaliot edition (Jerusalem: Mossad Harav Kook, 1994).

[108] See p.335.

[109] *Or Ne`erav* (Jerusalem: Qol Y'hudah, 1965), 32, quoting the *Zohar* 3:144b.

[110] *Tomer D'vorah* (Jerusalem: Or Yiqar, 1969) ch.3, 20. Louis Jacobs translates: "To sum up, he should cause life to flow to all" (*The Palm Tree of Deborah* [New York: Sepher Hermon, 1974], 82).

manifest above and below, for the healing and redemption of all."[111] Kabbalah thus provides a powerful framework for rooting biocentrism and ecotheology in the ancient covenant.[112]

THE PURPOSE OF THEOLOGY

This book takes seriously the Christian call for something more than a theology about Nature, the call to formulate "a theology of Nature",[113] and it carves out building blocks that may be useable for such a theology. In a subsequent work, I hope to unite these elements in a theology of Nature. However, even the best theology is an intellectual construct that can create a static worldview, that can become an obstacle to covenantal relationship, to "thou-saying", or to an encounter with the noumenal. Theology practiced well must become a method for clearing away whatever interrupts listening, feeling, and contemplation. Rav Kook captures this goal in his extraordinary style:

Contemplate the wonders of Creation, the divine dimension of their being, not as a dim configuration that is presented to you from the distance but as the reality in which you live. Know yourself and your world... [F]ind the source of your own life, and of the life beyond you, around you, the glorious splendor of the life in which you have your being. The love that is astir in you—raise it to its basic potency and its noblest beauty, extend it to all its dimensions, toward every manifestation of the soul that sustains the universe[114]

[111] "Human Hands Dwell in Heavenly Heights" in *Mystics of the Book: Themes Topics and Typologies*, ed. Robert A. Herrera (New York: Peter Lang, 1993), 153.
[112] For a summary of ecologically important themes in Kabbalah, see Seidenberg, "Kabbalah and Ecotheology", *ERN* 945–50; rev. www.neohasid.org/kabbalah/kabbalah_and_ecotheology (June 2009). My approach sidesteps Elliot R. Wolfson's critique of the contemporary use of Kabbalistic ideas about Nature in "The Mirror of Nature in Medieval Jewish Mysticism" (*Judaism and Ecology*, 305–31). Wolfson says there that Kabbalah cannot generate "a more positive view of nature" (321). However, he assumes that the only aspect of Kabbalah relevant to ecology is the idea of Nature as divine feminine. As will become obvious, other aspects of Kabbalah are far more important. For more on Wolfson, see nn.602, 624 and *Methods*. Wolfson's perspective is frequently reflected in Hava Tirosh-Samuelson's work: see "Judaism", *ERN* 932–3; "Nature in the Sources of Judaism", 113–14; "Religion, Ecology, and Gender: A Jewish Perspective", *Feminist Theology* 13 (Sep. 2005): 373–97, but also note her very different evaluation quoted on p.240.
[113] See esp. John R. Cobb, Jr., "The Role of Theology of Nature in the Church" in *Liberating Life*, eds. Charles Birch et al. (Maryknoll NY: Orbis Books, 1990) and Sallie McFague, *The Body of God: An Ecological Theology* (Minneapolis MN: Fortress, 1993), ch.3, esp. 65–6, 78–9, and 83. See also Jurgen Moltmann, *God in Creation: A New Theology of Creation and the Spirit of God* (New York: HarperCollins, 1985), George S. Hendry, *Theology of Nature* (Philadelphia: Westminster Press, 1980), and Claude Stewart, *Nature in Grace: A Study of the Theology of Nature* (Macon GA: Mercer University Press, 1983), among others. Matthew Fox's *Original Blessing* (Sante Fe NM: Bear & Company, 1983) is also rightly understood as a theology of Nature, rather than just an ecotheology.
[114] Bokser (1978), 207 (*OHQ* 1, 83).

The purpose of theology

Kook here offers a substantive religious phenomenology of Nature and its role in moral development.[115] Theological exploration – if it "extends love to all its dimensions" – can bring us to the threshold of a radically different order of religious experience.

A theological map

The theological conclusion of this book can be stated homiletically, using a teaching attributed to R' Akiva: "He would say: Beloved is humanity/*adam*, that was created 'in the image /*b'tselem*'. Extra love [in that] it was made known to [*adam*] that he was created 'in the image', for it was said [to him]: 'for in Elohim's image He made him' [Gn 9:6]."[116]

This teaching tells us something extraordinarily important: being created in the image and being taught that one is created in the image are two separate divine acts. A parallel teaching from *Avot d'Rabi Natan* strengthens this interpretation. The text reads: "If they were created [in God's image] and it were not said (told) to them, they would [still] be beloved."[117] A corollary of this is that the Torah's revelation that we are created in God's image was not a necessary outcome of being created in God's image. It is a special act of divine grace, superadded to Creation.

One can derive two interpretations from this aspect of R' Akiva's teaching, which I offer here not as *p'shat*, the literal or contextual meaning, but as midrashic-style eisegesis. The first is that other creatures could have been created in God's image without that fact being recorded for us or told to us. The second is that the capacity to know ourselves as beloved of God flows from our ability to tell the story of God's creation of humanity.

In other words, humans have language that allows us to receive, create, and pass on a tradition that teaches us that we are in God's image. Furthermore, it is an expression of God's love to reveal, to whichever creatures it can be revealed, that they are created in God's image. If this is true, then we may emulate God, as beings created in God's image, by "telling" the other creatures that they too are in God's image. This leads to the lovely and somewhat paradoxical idea that one expression of our being in God's image is that we are able to see other creatures as beings in God's image.

Whether these others are primarily other humans, other sentient beings, or other species or even ecosystems, is a crucial question to explore. Most theologians and religious ethicists understand God's image to be concretely

---

[115] See also "A Fourfold Song", Bokser (1978), 228–9 (*OHQ* 2, 458–9).
[116] *Mishnah Avot*, variously numbered 3:13, 3:14 or 3:17. In the numbering followed by Blackman, it is 3:14. The Mechon Mamre edition (Jerusalem, 2002; www.mechon-mamre.org/b/h/ho.htm), which I also consulted throughout, numbers it 3:17.
[117] Ch.44, 124. I have emended *ARNB*, leaving out the word *lo'*, "not", after *'ilu*, which otherwise makes the passage incomprehensible. Schechter *ad loc.* interprets it the same way without actually emending the text. *Lo'* is likely a result of dittography.

manifest in the ethical space between human beings. They might say that we can only know the image of God in ourselves when we understand other human beings to be created in God's image. One of the wisdoms one can learn from ecology is that this is also true in some way of the relationship between humanity and other species. In other words, we cannot know ourselves fully as human beings in God's image without seeing the image of God in the world around us. That is the fundamental message of this book.

PART I

MIDRASH

I

Tselem Elohim (God's Image) in Midrash and commentary, part 1

The angels and the heavens, the chain of Being, intellect, and speech

The idea of God's image in the rabbinic tradition is, like almost everything within Jewish tradition, marvelously complex and multivocal. In this chapter, I will outline the fundaments of rabbinic anthropology and the varied spiritual and intellectual interpretations of *tselem Elohim* or God's image found in the early Midrash. I will also touch on the hierarchical conception of Creation sometimes referred to as the "Great Chain of Being" as it is reflected in Midrash. Lastly, I will briefly explore the difficulties of relating soul to *tselem*.

In the process of surveying the major categories of interpretation here and in Chapter 2 (which deals with physical and ethical interpretations of *tselem*), I will also focus on texts and themes that show that the midrashic understanding of God's image was not limited to human beings. The purpose of these explorations is to show that the idea of the image may be extended beyond humanity, even within a traditional or fideist theological framework.

TSELEM ELOHIM IN TORAH

The passages in Torah that touch on the idea of God's image are few and can be quickly reviewed. The most important text concerns the creation of humanity in Genesis 1. (The second story of human creation in Genesis 2 notably lacks any mention of God's image.[118]) *Tselem* appears in only two other places: the summary of Adam's life, which briefly retells the first creation story of the

---

[118] Gn 2 is equally notable for deriving the name for human, *adam*, from *adamah*, earth. The work of scripture-based ecotheology, one could say, is to integrate the *adam–adamah* relation and the *adam–tselem*–God relation. See n.492 on environmental ethics derived from reading these sources (what Biblical scholars regard as "P" and "J") separately. However, because I am interested primarily in what the Jewish tradition says about *tselem*, I perforce end up reading these sources together.

1 Tselem Elohim *in Midrash and commentary, part 1*

human "in Elohim's likeness" and reports the birth of Shet (Seth) in Adam's image, and the Noach (Noah) story, where God's image is used to underpin the ethical severity of murder.[119] The verses are as follows:

And Elohim said: Let us (or: We will) make a human/humanity/*Adam* in/with our image / *b'tsalmeinu*, according to /like/ as our likeness /*kid'muteinu*. And they will dominate/ have dominion over / exercise mastery among[120] /*v'yirdu* the fish of the sea and over the bird of the skies and over every beast/*b'heimah* and over all the land, and over every crawler crawling / *haremes haromes* upon the land. And Elohim created the human in His image /*b'tsalmo*, in Elohim's image/*tselem* He created him, male and female He created them. And Elohim blessed them and Elohim said to them: Bear fruit and multiply and fill the earth/land and occupy/subdue her /*v'khiv'shuha*, and dominate /*ur'du* the fish of the sea and the bird of the skies and every animal/*chayah* that is crawling upon the land. [Gn 1:26–8]

This is the book of Adam's generations: on the day of Elohim's creating Adam, in Elohim's likeness/*bid'mut* He created him; male and female He created them, and He blessed them, and called their name Adam in the day of their being created. And Adam lived a hundred and thirty years and bore in his likeness /*bid'muto* like his image /*k'tsalmo* and called his name Shet. [Gn 5:1–3]

One who spills the blood of the human /*dam ha'adam*, through/by the human, his blood will be spilled, for in Elohim's image/*tselem* He made the human. And you, bear fruit and multiply, swarm in the earth/land and multiply in her.[121] [Gn 9:6–7]

By way of contrast, in Genesis 2, we read:

And YHVH Elohim formed the human /*ha'adam*, dirt from the earth/ground /*ha'adamah*, and He blew into his nostrils life's breath / *nishmat chayyim*, and the human became a living animal / *nefesh chayah*. [Gn 2:7][122]

There is an enormous amount of speculation and scholarship on the meaning of *tselem* in the Biblical context.[123] The two positions around which many

---

[119] Some exegetes include Ps 39:6, "*Akh b'tselem yit'haleikh ish*", based on the *Targum* (Aramaic translation) of Psalms, which renders the phrase as "in the image of YHVH does a man walk / *bid'yoqna d'YY yit'haleikh gavra*", though the plain meaning of *tselem* here is more like shadow, that is, only an image and not more. More important is Psalm 8; see p.97. One might also reference scriptures that describe visions of God in human form, though none uses the term *tselem*. The most explicit of these would be Ex 24:10–11, Ez 1:26–7, and Da 7:9–10; see also Nu 12:8. Aramaic *targumim* in this volume are quoted from *Miqra'ot G'dolot*.

[120] Davis argues that "exercise mastery among" is the best translation (*Scripture*, 54–5).

[121] I include Gn 9:7 so it can be readily seen that all three sections in which *tselem* or *d'mut* appear mention fertility or reproduction.

[122] Here and throughout, Biblical citations follow Jewish tradition. Christian tradition numbers this verse 2:8.

[123] Gunnlaugur A. Johnson's work *The Image of God: Genesis 1:26–28 in a Century of Old Testament Research* (Stockholm: Almquist & Wiksell, 1988) is an excellent survey of Christian and secular scholarship and theology. See also James Barr, "The Image of God in the Book of Genesis – A Study of Terminology", *Bulletin of the John Rylands Library* 51 (1968): 11–26, and David Clines' superb analysis in "Humanity as the Image of God" in *On the Way to*

contemporary Biblical scholars aggregate are that (1) *tselem* refers to the physical shape of the human body or (2) *tselem* refers to the power of dominion. Christian interpretation often parallels or is intertwined with Biblical scholarship.[124] In addition, there is debate within feminist Bible scholarship about whether or not "male and female" should be considered a quality of God's image that teaches us about the nature of God.[125] Since these positions are also represented in the midrashic and Kabbalistic texts, which are the primary focus of this study, I will not dwell on the argumentation of modern Biblical scholars here.[126]

TSELEM ELOHIM IN MIDRASH

My focus for the remainder of this chapter and the following one will be on how these verses interact with rabbinic anthropology as expressed in midrashic (homiletical) literature and Torah commentary, how modern and medieval interpretations evolved from earlier interpretations, and what this teaches us about the question of human nature and humanity's place in the world. The discussion will center on the earliest midrashic texts, especially *B'rei'shit (Genesis) Rabbah* (fifth century) and elements of *Avot d'Rabi Natan*,[127] along with

---

the Postmodern, vol.1 (Sheffield UK: Sheffield Academic Press, 1998), 447–97 (esp. 448–51, 466–76, 482–95). For a brief survey of major works on *imago Dei*, see Phyllis Bird, "'Male and Female He Created Them': Gen 1:27b in the Context of the Priestly Account of Creation", *Harvard Theological Review* 74 (1981): 129–60; 129, n.1. See also Tikva Frymer-Kensky's "The Image: Religious Anthropology in Judaism and Christianity" in *Christianity in Jewish Terms*, eds. Frymer-Kensky et al. (Boulder CO: Westview, 2000), 331–3. *Contra* the physical interpretation of *tselem*, see Umberto Cassuto's notes in *A Commentary on the Book of Genesis, Part One: From Adam to Noah* (Jerusalem: Magnes, 1961), 56.

[124] In addition to Johnson, Wentzel Van Huyssteen gives a wonderful account of Christian theology about *imago Dei*, up to the present and including ecological issues, in *Alone in the World?: Human Uniqueness in Science and Theology* (Grand Rapids MI: Wm. B. Eerdmans, 2006), 110–62. Van Huyssteen reviews the four types of interpretation of *tselem* – in historical order, they are: the substantive, the functional, the relational, and the existential. He focuses on the relational and existential views as most relevant to ecology. See esp. 136–48.

[125] See Bird, "'Male and Female'", Phyllis Trible's critique in *God and the Rhetoric of Sexuality* (Minneapolis MN: Fortress, 1978), and herein, pp.78–9, 82–3, esp. n.239.

[126] Notwithstanding all argumentation about the meaning of *tselem*, the fact that *tselem* remains undefined in the Torah is due neither to reticence nor to the mysterious patterns of Hebraic thought. Rather, even though *tselem* correlates with certain consequences or practices, on the *p'shat* level it literally has no substantive content, meaning that it does not delineate a set of characteristics inhering in the human individual. Instead, it signifies a quality of relationship. See nn.124, 310.

[127] There is wide debate about the composition of *Avot d'Rabi Natan* (ARN). While many elements appear to be early versions of traditions, and are treated as such here, a number of scholars view *ARN* as a relatively late work, while some regard version B as much earlier than version A. At the very least, it is widely agreed that *ARN* preserves many early and unique versions of traditions. An argument for an early date for both versions of *ARN* can be found in Judah Goldin, *The Fathers According to Rabbi Nathan* (New Haven CT: Yale University Press,

material from the Mishnah and *Midr'shey Halakhah* (early *midrashim* that often focus more on law) such as *M'khilta*, *Sifra* (also called *Torat Kohanim*), and *Sifrey* (second to fourth century).

In addition, I use later material from *Vayiqra' (Leviticus) Rabbah* (fifth or sixth century, after *B'rei'shit Rabbah*) and *Kohelet (Ecclesiastes) Rabbah* (sixth century or later), along with *Midrash Tanchuma* (eighth or ninth century) and similarly dated books, as well as later books,[128] to trace how these ideas evolved. I will also pay special attention to mystical *midrashim* such as *Midrash Otiyot d'Rabi Aqiva* (Geonic period, eighth to tenth century, possibly earlier[129]), which may represent alternative traditions, and to aggadic traditions from the two Talmuds, which, while redacted relatively later (through the seventh century), may preserve earlier versions of traditions (as early as the second or third century). Finally, I have used *Midrash Hagadol* (thirteenth century) for the purpose of showing how earlier *midrashim* were rewritten to incorporate philosophical elements.

I will use later commentaries and philosophical works to elucidate changes in the rabbinic worldview that took place during and after the Geonic period. However, because of his cultural separation from the philosophical tradition, I treat Rashi (eleventh century, France) as someone closer to the worldview of *Chazal*.

RABBINIC ANTHROPOLOGY

Early rabbinic literature on Genesis 1 and the creation of the first human includes a diversity of interpretations concerning God's image. While there is a multitude of evidence that the image of God was a foundational element in rabbinic thought, there are relatively few passages that speculate directly about what God's image means. As Emero Stiegman explained, "[M]an's

---

1955), xxi, and in Anthony Saldarini, *The Fathers According to Rabbi Nathan* (Leiden: E. J. Brill, 1975), 12–16. See also Strack and Stemberger, *Introduction to the Talmud and Midrash* (Minneapolis MN: Fortress, 1996), 226–7. On the argument for a very late composition, see Tal Ilan, *Mine and Yours and Hers: Retrieving Women's History from Rabbinic Literature* (Leiden: E. J. Brill, 1997), 79–80 and n.47.

[128] These materials include *Pirqey d'Rabi Eli`ezer*, *P'siqta d'Rav Kahana*, and *Midrash Y'lamdeynu* in the Geonic period, as well as later books collected in *Midrash Rabbah*. A relatively late date for both recensions of *Tanchuma* goes against Solomon Buber's introduction to his edition of *Midrash Tanchuma* (Vilna: Wittwe & Gebrüder Romm, 1885), but it seems to be the current consensus (see, e.g., John Townsend, trans., *Midrash Tanhuma*, vol.1 [Hoboken NJ: Ktav, 1989], xii). It also fits what I have found with respect to *imitatio Dei* (see p.107ff).

[129] These mystical *midrashim* vary widely in their proposed dates. Some are distinguished by their preservation of what appears to be a different strain of midrashic thought, which is why they are important here. Many are especially concerned with the story of creation, *ma`aseh b'rei'shit* (more correctly: *v'rei'shit*). Those discussed here are mostly found in Shlomo Aharon Wertheimer (ed.) *Batey Midrashot* (Jerusalem: K'tav Yad v'Sefer, 1989), cited hereafter as *BM*.

foundational distinction was that he was made in the Image of God... That a divine likeness was the common inheritance of mankind was universally agreed upon by the rabbis but the question of the nature of this likeness seems not to have arisen."[130] According to Yair Lorberbaum, whose work is one of the most important studies of God's image in the Jewish tradition to date, *tselem* refers to what he calls the "iconic relation" in which the human bearer of the image is an "extensa" of its divine prototype, while the divine is, by virtue of the image, present in the human being.[131] Lorberbaum's perspective has merit, but here I will approach the meaning of *tselem* inductively, without relying on any such formulation, by studying how it is used in Midrash to explain other concepts.

We will start from one of the earliest *midrashim* on the nature of the human being and the meaning of *tselem*. In *B'rei'shit Rabbah* 8:11, four angelic qualities are seen as inherent to humans: speech, understanding (i.e., intelligence, reason), sight (perhaps also meaning "foresight"), and physically upright posture.

R' Yehoshua bar Nechemyah in the name of R' Chanina bar Yitshak and the rabbis in the name of R' Lazar (Elazar), say: He created in him four creations from above /mil'ma'lah and four from below /mil'matah. From above – he stands like the ministering angels / mal'akhey hashareit, and speaks like the ministering angels, and has knowledge in him like the ministering angels, and sees like the ministering angels... From below – he eats and drinks like an animal /kab'heimah, bears fruit and multiplies, leaves piles (excretes) and dies like an animal.[132]

---

[130] "Rabbinic Anthropology" in *Austieg und Niedergang der Romischen Welt: Principat*, II vol.19.2 (Berlin: de Gruyter, 1979), 502–3.

[131] "*Tselem Elohim* in Chazal, Rambam and Ramban" (Hebrew University, PhD dissertation [Hebr.], 1997), viii; also *Tselem Elohim: Halakhah v'Aggadah* (Tel Aviv: Schocken Publishing House, 2004), 18, 91. Lorberbaum's work, the most important on these issues to date, studies the impact of *tselem Elohim* on *halakhah* (Jewish law), especially with respect to criminal punishment. An English translation of Lorberbaum's work is forthcoming from Cambridge University Press. See also Lorberbaum, "*Imago Dei* in Judaism: Early Rabbinic Literature, Philosophy, and Kabbalah: The Teaching about God, the Human Person, and the Beginning in Talmudic and Kabbalistic Judaism" in *The Concept of God, the Origin of the World, and the Image of the Human*, ed. Peter Koslowski (Dordrecht: Kluwer Academic Publishers, 2001), 57–74 and Beth Berkowitz, *Execution and Invention: Death Penalty Discourse in Early Rabbinic and Christian Cultures* (Oxford: Oxford University Press, 2006), 53–7. Lorberbaum focuses on the meaning of *tselem* within the human community, whereas I focus on connections between *tselem* and what lies beyond the human community. Because of this, the overlap between our work is relatively small. His discussion of Kabbalah and the human body (in the chapter on Ramban), as well as his brief discussion of the term `olam malei' and the midrashic texts about procreation, are the main points of contact.

[132] *Midrash B'rei'shit Rabba'*, 3 vols., eds. J. Theodor and Chanoch Albeck (Berlin: Ts'vi Hirsch Itskovski, 1912), vol.1, 8:11, 64–5; also *B'rei'shit Rabbah* in *Midrash Rabbah* (Jerusalem: Avida' Da'at Umeyda', 1994) and at daat.ac.il/daat/tanach/raba1/tohen1.htm. The order of the text here follows Theodor; the standard edition reverses the order of qualities above and below. The parallel at *B'rei'shit Rabbah* 14:3 has "understands" rather than "has knowledge"; cf. *ARNA* ch.37 and *ARNB* ch.43 (quoted pp.58–9, 89, 283). A much later text (*Sh'mot*

This midrashic passage appears in a set of interpretations of the phrase "male and female" from Genesis 1:27. The wording of the verse here is understood disjunctively, so that "male and female He created them" is homiletically connected to the four ways that humans are like the animals, that is, **not** created "in Elohim's image". The contrasting phrase (as this midrash reads the verse), "in Elohim's image He created him", is understood without being explicitly quoted. It corresponds to the four ways humans are like the angels.[133] By ascribing *tselem* to the angels rather than to God, the midrash is able to gloss over the anthropomorphic aspects of the idea that God has an image.[134]

R' Yehoshua's teaching affirms that *tselem Elohim* is not limited to human beings. Though the connection between angels and humans is not surprising, it takes us far beyond the *p'shat* or literal meaning of the Torah verse. It also takes us beyond a modernist perspective that would limit God's image exclusively to humanity and would not countenance the idea of angels. From the perspective of rhetorical criticism, one may also notice the following: since there are *only* four created qualities "from above" that angels share with the human being, this teaching invites the reader to imagine what aspects of God's image are found in the angels that were not created in the human.

B'rei'shit Rabbah also interrogates R' Yehoshua's statement that humans see like the angels: "And an animal doesn't see?! Rather, this one [sees]

[*Exodus*] *Rabbah* 30:16; hereafter *ShmR*) describes humans as created "in the *d'mut* of the ministering angels". *B'rei'shit Rabbah* is cited hereafter as *BR* [section:paragraph]; Theodor, [page]. If no Theodor page is given then the standard edition is used. This list of eight characteristics from BR 8:11 will be used to structure chapters 1 and 2.

[133] Jonathan Schorsch suggests this teaching could be read to say that the four angelic qualities are male and the four animalistic qualities are female. There is enough evidence to rule this reading out, however, including its relation to the teaching that follows and the fact that the standard edition reverses the order of qualities above and below.

[134] Isaiah Tishby writes in *The Wisdom of the Zohar* (trans. Goldstein [London: Littman Library, 1989], hereafter WZ), "We can see from a number of passages that the rabbis were worried by theological difficulties raised by... the creation of man 'in the image of God'... They tried... to remove the basic difficulty by denying the similarity of man to God, by stating, for example, that man was created in the image of the angels" (681). Max Kadushin, however, argues that the problem of anthropomorphism was foreign to the rabbis (*The Rabbinic Mind* [New York: Bloch Publishing, 1972], 273–87). He further suggests that anxiety about anthropomorphism was a mark of pagan culture (284–5)! Whether or not Kadushin's argument is correct, it seems likely that the rabbis would agree with Rosenzweig that anthropomorphic imagery is an expression of God's nearness and presence (Michael Oppenheim, *Speaking/Writing of God: Jewish Philosophical Reflections on the Life with Others* [Albany NY: SUNY Press, 1997], 36–41). In my understanding, anthropomorphism was not a philosophical problem for the rabbis; rather, the dignity of the divine is what concerned them. Whenever anthropomorphic imagery seemed to lessen this dignity, the problem was overcome through midrash and, in the *targumim*, through glosses. In the case of *BR* 8:11, shifting the focus of the divine image from God to the angels or the heavens also explains the plural form in "Let us make a human in our image" (*viz.* Targum Yonatan's translation of Gn 1:26: "And YY said to the angels that serve before Him that were created in the second day...: Let us make a human in our image").

sideways / *ele' zeh m'tsaded* (i.e., instead of straight ahead)." If "this one" refers to the animal, as most commentators contend, then the midrash's response undermines the metaphysical boundary R' Yehoshua has drawn, since there are many animals that also see "straight ahead".[135] This is one of many examples where the attempt to draw a clear line separating humans from "the other animals"[136] is contradicted or complicated by similarities that exist between species.[137]

Though my first concern here and elsewhere in this chapter is the contextual meaning of each midrash, the fuzziness of the boundary between human and animal has implications for constructive theology as well. From the perspective of both rhetorical criticism and homiletics, such textual moments create openings for a biocentric ecotheology. Moreover, certain passages in halakhic discourse show that the rabbis were aware of the complexity of these boundaries as well.[138] Just as the boundary cases in *halakhah* (Jewish law) often define the nature and essence of the law, so too can these places of fuzzy boundaries become sites for redefining how we understand God's image in Creation.

Upper and lower creations

Immediately following the teaching of R' Yehoshua in *B'rei'shit Rabbah*, there is a second, similar tradition that uses a different terminology:

R' Tifdai (or: Tifd'ai), in the name of R' Acha: The higher/upper ones / `elyonim* were created in the image/*tselem* and likeness/*d'mut*, and don't bear fruit and multiply; and the lower ones /*tachtonim* bear fruit and multiply and were not created in the image and likeness. Said the Holiness/Holy One, blessed be:[139] Here, I am creating him in the image and in the likeness from the upper ones, bearing fruit and multiplying from (like) the lower ones.[140]

---

[135] Raptors and primates, for example. See n.234. Other commentaries on "sideways", including the idea that the midrash is referring to humans who see sideways, are discussed on p.76ff.

[136] In a theological context, it may be jarring to think of humans as animals. I would simply note that Maimonides also talks about humans and "the other animals". See pp.70, 148.

[137] See next section.   [138] For example, *TB Nidah* 22b–23a, discussed p.77.

[139] This epithet for God will always be translated as "the Holy One" hereafter, to simplify quoted passages. Its earliest form is *haqodesh barukh hu*, "the Holiness, blessed be", while its later form is *haqadosh barukh hu*, or *kudsha b'rikh hu* in Aramaic, meaning "the Holy One, blessed be". The epithet that commonly follows any mention of God, "may His name be blessed", is also left off of most of the translations herein.

[140] *BR*. The element of dominion is missing here. Had dominion been included in the qualities that make humans like the upper ones, the midrash would have neatly connected all the elements according to the verses' chiastic structure: *tselem* and dominion would be on the side of the upper ones, in contrast with procreation and being male and female on the side of the lower ones. Cohen gives an apposite reading of this problem: "[A]s R. Tifdai would have it, sexuality and the divine image are the defining characteristics of the human being, and their proper expression leads directly to the exercise of dominion" (*"Be Fertile and Increase"*, 87–8). As I interpret Cohen, he understands the potential to "fill the land" with God's image through the reproduction of the human form as both the purpose of dominion and what

This teaching about the "upper" or "supernal" beings parallels but differs from the teaching of R' Yehoshua. (I will mostly use "upper" to translate `elyon` because it is less value-laden.) R' Tifdai lines up *tselem* up with the "upper ones" instead of the angels, and reproduction with the "lower ones" instead of the animals. Instead of listing varied qualities, R' Yehoshua notes only two contraries: reproducing (i.e., being male and female) and being in the image.

The most important point shared by both teachings is that they connect sexual reproduction with mortality. In R' Yehoshua's teaching, the human "multiplies" and "dies" like an animal. Similarly, the next line of R' Tifdai's teaching imagines God saying: "If I create him from the upper ones he lives and won't die; from the lower ones, he dies and won't live."[141] Reproduction and mortality go together, eternality and God's image go together.[142]

Jeremy Cohen underscores that "the anomalous, sexual, God-like human being defies the ostensive logic of this polar opposition", while Lorberbaum understands the purpose of this union of opposites to be "to multiply and increase the image of God".[143] Cohen writes:

> Within such a framework, sexual reproduction denotes not only an attribute of the lower world, but also – along with the divine image – the essence of the singular perfection that allows humans, and humans alone, to choose between life and death.

Thus far are the areas of agreement between the two teachings.

The most important difference between them, which is extremely significant for the purposes of this book, is not what R' Tifdai says about human nature, but his use of the term `elyonim`, "upper ones", to describe the creations that are in God's image. The logic of this passage would suggest that `elyonim` includes the heavenly bodies, since they do not reproduce or die (at least not according to normal human observation). Marcus Jastrow reads the passage

---

allows humanity to have dominion. Though this reading may not be the *p'shat* of R' Tifdai's statement, it is homiletically strong. On the idea that this is the *p'shat* of scripture itself, see Lawrence Troster, "Created in the Image of God: Humanity and Divinity in an Age of Environmentalism" in Yaffe, 172–82; 178.

[141] See further discussion p.136ff. (Romans 8:12–14 presents on interesting parallel to this teaching.) BR 8:11 presumes that human beings, and animals, are mortal from the beginning of their creation. Other *midrashim* understand mortality to be a consequence of the sin of eating the fruit (n.1114). Significantly, BR 19:5 assumes that the animals were also created to be immortal. None would have died if Chavah had not fed them the fruit of the tree of knowing (usu. trans. "tree of knowledge"). See also BR 20:8, where it is Adam that feeds the fruit to the animals.

[142] Contrast this with Aristotle, who associates reproduction with a sort of eternality: "The most natural act [of an animal] is the production of an animal like itself, an animal producing an animal, a plant a plant, in order that, as nature allows, **it may partake of the eternal and the divine**" (*On the Soul*, 415a2–b7, my emphasis). In *Aristotle: The Desire to Understand* (New York: Cambridge University Press, 1988), 100, Jonathan Lear comments, "[I]n the most basic functions, nutrition and reproduction, Aristotle saw a trace of the divine. Aristotle was positing, in the form of living things, a force for the preservation of form." In Aristotle, that which preserves form is called the soul. Cf. Aquinas, *Summa Contra Gentiles*, 3:21.

[143] *Tselem Elohim*, 395–6. Cf. Mopsik, quoted n.257.

Rabbinic anthropology

this way, translating `elyonim` as "celestials".[144] If so, then R' Tifdai expands what is created in God's image to include all the heavens.

Other scholars interpret R' Tifdai, in agreement with R' Yehoshua, to be talking about angels,[145] but the evidence shows that Jastrow's interpretation of `elyonim` is the best reading of this *meimra* (saying or tradition). Most importantly, this interpretation is consistent with other examples in *B'rei'shit Rabbah* in which the phrase "upper ones" explicitly includes the host of heaven. For example, in *B'rei'shit Rabbah* 12:8, firmament, sun, and moon are generations of the heavens, created "from the upper ones / *min ha`elyonim*", while vegetation, sea creatures, and land animals are generations of the earth, created "from the lower ones".[146]

In other examples, the phrase "higher/upper ones and lower ones" is used to indicate the entire physical Creation or Cosmos – an exact equivalent to the Biblical hendiadys of "heavens and earth", which together mean the whole of Creation.[147] Similarly, *Avot d'Rabi Natan* states, "The Holy One... created the whole world entirely, and He created the heavens and the earth, upper ones and lower ones."[148]

There are also passages where `elyonim` does refer exclusively to angels. However, in many of these, unlike in R' Tifdai's teaching, *tachtonim* refers **exclusively** to humans.[149] It is clear, therefore, that in these *midrashim* (1) the

---

[144] *Dictionary of the Targumim, Talmud Babli and Yerushalmi, and the Midrashic Literature* (New York: Judaica Press, 1982) s.v. *tselem*, 1284. While Jastrow translates `elyonim` here as "celestials", elsewhere he translates it "heavenly creatures, angels" (s.v. `elyon`, 1083).

[145] Cohen writes: "For R. Tifdai... the dialectic between the angelic and beastly traits of human beings boils down to that between the divine image in which God created man and woman, and their sexuality" (*"Be Fertile and Increase"*, 86–7). Gary Porton also reads both teachings as referring to angels (*Understanding Rabbinic Midrash* [Hoboken NJ: Ktav, 1985], 168–9), as does Jacob Neusner ("Genesis Rabbah as Polemic: An Introductory Account", *Hebrew Annual Review* 9 [1985] 253–65; 257). For more on Neusner and BR, see *Methods*.

[146] Quoted p.55. Cf. BR 13:10, where the land drinks water "from the upper ones, as it is said, 'from the rain of the heavens she (the land) will drink water' [Dt 11:11]" and *Vayiqra' Rabbah* 31:1 (hereafter VR), which equates the `elyonim` with the great lights (sun and moon) when it explains that "the upper ones also need charity/*ts'daqah* from each other" and from God.

[147] BR 12:12: "the Holy One created the upper ones and the lower ones in one [act of] creation"; BR 2:2: "the upper ones and the lower ones were created in one moment... the upper ones are nourished by the radiance of the Shekhinah (divine presence), and the lower ones, if they don't struggle they don't eat"; BR 9:3: "'And God saw everything that He had made'—R' Yochanan said: A king of flesh and blood who builds a palace, he looks upon the upper ones (i.e., stories) – one glance/*r'iyah*, and upon the lower ones – one (separate) glance, but the Holy One looks upon the upper ones and upon the lower ones – one glance [altogether]." (Cf. Rashi *ad* Dt 4:35); BR 8:8: "if a great person... says, 'Why do I need to take permission from one lesser than me?'... they say to him: Learn from your Creator, for He created upper ones and lower ones, and when He came to create the human, He ruled with the ministering angels." In 8:8, the angels are explicitly distinct from the upper ones. Note also BR 38:6.

[148] ARNA ch.31, 91.

[149] In BR 78:3, the angel that Jacob wrestles represents the `elyonim`, while the *tachtonim* are the men of Esav's guard. Similarly, in VR 24:8, "the upper ones make crowns of three *q'dushot*

terminology carries a different (though derivative) meaning and (2) just as the use of "lower ones" to refer only to humans does not mean there are no other "lower" creatures, so the use of "upper ones" for angels does not mean there are no other "upper" creatures.

For these reasons, it is fair to assume that the `*elyonim* in 8:11 include the physical heavenly bodies. It is also not essential to know what R' Tifdai "originally" meant. My claim is that the redactor of *B'rei'shit Rabbah* understood R' Tifdai to mean that the physical heavens are in God's image, and juxtaposed R' Tifdai with R' Yehoshua in order to define a *machloqet* (debate) between the two, with R' Tifdai including the heavenly bodies, and R' Yehoshua excluding them. Thus, the terminology *l'ma`lah* refers to the angels only, while the terminology `*elyonim* refers to or includes the heavens.[150] Since we cannot know for certain whether this difference is integral to these traditions, or only created by how the redactor has juxtaposed them, what one can solidly claim is that, at least for one school of *Chazal*, the heavenly bodies, along with the angels, were understood to be created in God's image.

There was already Biblical precedent for regarding the heavenly bodies as having the same status as angels.[151] Other midrashic texts also draw a relationship between the heavenly lights and the likeness of God in the first human.[152]

---

for the Holy One", while *tachtonim* (in this case, the people Israel) only recite two *q'dushot*. (*Q'dushah/Kedushah* is the recitation in prayer of the doxology "Holy, holy, holy" from Is 6:3.) See also *BR* 79:8. One other example, *BR* 27:4, may refer to angels as `*elyonim* without restricting *tachtonim* to people. R' Nechemyah there interprets the phrase "God regretted/*vayinachem* that He made the human in the land" [Gn 6:6] literally as "God took comfort/*vayinachem* in having made the human as part of the earth" and not part of the heavens, for "if I had created him **above**/*mil'ma`lah*, just as he caused the lower ones to rebel, so would he have caused the **upper ones** to rebel." (Note that here *l'ma`lah* and *tachtonim* are mixed together.) It is not certain whether "upper ones" means angels or heavens in this passage, but if it means angels, "lower ones" would mean the animals, who according to some were corrupted by Adam (cf. *BR* 28:8). One also finds `*elyonim* referring strictly to angels in later works, e.g., in *PRE* ch.21, 38, where Chavah, seeing Qayin's face/*d'mut*, remarks that he is from the `*elyonim*. In context, this means from Sama'el, the archangel who, according to *PRE*, rebelled against God, rode the snake, and had sex with Chavah (see Gerald Friedlander, *Pirkê De Rabbi Eliezer* [New York: Sepher-Hermon, 1965], 151) – hence Chavah says, "I acquired a man with YHVH" [Gn 4:1].

[150] This impression is strengthened by traditions in *ARN* about the hierarchy of Creation (*ARNA* ch.37, *ARNB* ch.43) that conform to R' Yehoshua's perspective and disagree with R' Tifdai. (See pp.58–9.) The juxtaposition of R' Tifdai's opinion and R' Yehoshua's in *BR* may be similar to the way in which the Gemara initially presents a *machloqet* or disagreement between two sages. If so, we should treat *BR* 8:11 as if it were the framework for a Talmudic *sugya* whose argumentation had not yet been written down. Such an interpretation can work for a number of sections in *BR*. A thorough study of such pericopes would need to be made in order to confirm this hypothesis.

[151] For example, in Job: "Where were you in my founding the earth... when the stars of morning [were] rejoicing together, and all the children of Elohim exulted?" [38:4–7].

[152] For example, in *TB*, R' Bana'ah comes to the tomb of the patriarchs and matriarchs and hears a divine voice describing Avraham (Abraham) as "the likeness of my image/*d'mut d'yoqni*" and Adam as "my image/*d'yoqni*". He then glimpses *Adam Harishon*'s heels, saying that they

While many of these *midrashim* may be later, there is a very early midrash that supports the idea that the heavens were directly understood to be an image of God. In *Sifrey D'varim* ("The Books on *Deuteronomy*"), one finds the following exchange between Israel and Moshe:

> "And His height /*ga'avato* in constellations/*sh'chaqim*" [Dt 33:26]—All Israel gathered by Moshe. They said to him: Moshe Rabbenu, say (explain) to us what is the measure/*midah* of glory above/*l'ma`lah*. He said to them: From the lower heavens, you know what is the measure of glory above. A parable, to what does the thing compare? To one who said: I am seeking to see the glory of the king. They said to him: Go to the [king's] country and you will see him. He entered and saw a tapestry/*vilon* spread over the opening of the country and good stones (jewels) and pearls fixed in it and he could not move his eyes from it, until he fell/collapsed.[153]

Midah elsewhere in rabbinic literature is closely connected to knowing the dimensions of God's being in a theosophical sense, particularly in *Shi`ur Qomah*, while here *midah* refers to knowing God's image through the awesome beauty of the night sky and the constellations themselves.[154] A passage from the *Heykhalot* literature of early Jewish mysticism makes an even closer connection between God and the constellations: "And from [God's] form

---

"resembled sun spheres" (*Bava Bat'ra* 58a; cf. *P'siqta d'Rav Kahana*, vol. 1 [New York: Jewish Theological Seminary, 1962], 4:4, 66, and 12:1, 203; hereafter *PRK*).

[153] *Sifrey `al Sefer D'varim*, ed. Louis Finkelstein (New York: Jewish Theological Seminary, 1969), hereafter *SifreyD* (conventionally rendered *Sifre*), *pisqa* 355; 422–3. The passage concludes: "They said to him: If...you could not move your eyes from them, until you fell, were you to enter in the country, all the more so, as it is said, 'and in His height the constellations'." The standard published version of this passage suggests a greater figurative distance between God and the constellations: "From the **lower ones** you know the measure of glory of above. A parable to one that said: I am seeking to see the **face** of the king...He entered and saw a *vilon*...and he **immediately** collapsed to the earth" (*Sifrey Lid'varim*, ed. Zahava Gerlitz ([Gush Etsion: Daat, 2010], 384, daat.ac.il/daat/vl/sifri-dvarim/sifri-dvarim01.pdf). The Finkelstein version is certainly the earlier one. Cf. *Midrash T'hilim*, ed. Solomon Buber (Vilna: Wittwe & Gebrüder Romm, 1891) *ad* Ps 19:6, 165–6: the heavens are "like a king who stretched out a *vilon* over the opening of the palace. The king said: All who are wise, say what this curtain is! All who are rich, make one like it! All who are mighty, touch it!" Here, the unfathomability of the *vilon* parallels the unfathomability of the king (and of God). In the Finkelstein version, however, the *vilon* is in a sense knowable, even though it is transfixing.

I first encountered this passage in Michael Fishbane's *The Exegetical Imagination: On Jewish Thought and Theology* (Cambridge MA: Harvard University Press, 1998). Fishbane's analysis evinces some of the assumptions made in modernist scholarship. He writes: "The people surround their master and want to know the 'measure of God's glory on high.' **But Moses demurs. He then** tells them that they may infer this splendor from the lower heavens" (61, my emphasis), adding: "The central purpose of the final section...is to prevent popular knowledge of God's supernal likeness" (70). However, there is nothing "demur" in Moshe's response, and there is no suggestion in the outer story framing the parable that Moshe means to prevent the people from knowing.

[154] And what of a world where we so pollute the night sky that we cannot see the Milky Way? What then can we know of God? The *Zohar* even teaches that the very reason why human beings can speak is that we can behold the sky (see p. 319).

constellations are shimmering / *Umito'aro nitazu sh'chaqim*".[155] *To'ar*, meaning form, is used here as a synonym for *tselem*.[156] We have good reason to conclude that the `*elyonim* that are in God's image in *B'rei'shit Rabbah* 8:11 include the physical heavens.

The teachings from *B'rei'shit Rabbah* 8:11 together expand the meaning of God's image beyond the human, embracing both the angelic and the heavenly. They avoid defining God in any way, substituting the angels and/or heavens as the source of the divine image projected onto humanity. Each passage explains in its own way not just the relationship between sex/reproduction and God's image, but also the plural reference in the phrase "our image". Even on a superficial level, the meaning of *tselem* in rabbinic thought is much more diverse than a simple reading of the Torah might lead us to expect.

Though these teachings only extend *tselem* to half of Creation (and not to that half that is most important for ecology), they still move us away from the modernist and humanist interpretation that human beings alone are created in God's image. Historically, the extension of *tselem* found in Midrash provided the imprimatur for Kabbalistic theology to further extrapolate *tselem*, as will be explored in subsequent chapters.

One fundamental question that is generated both by *B'rei'shit Rabbah* 8:11 and by our contemporary crisis is: "What is a human being?" This broad question always includes within itself the ecologically pertinent questions of "What is the place of the human in the greater world?" and "What is the right relationship between the human realm and the other-than-human realms?" For the rabbis, these questions about humanity led to the conclusion that humanity was in the middle, rather than at the top, of the metaphysical hierarchy, as will be discussed in the next section. This is tremendously important for ecotheology, even though the projection of *tselem* onto the heavens otherwise has no ecological, ethical, or behavioral consequences.

From the perspective of these texts, one can see more clearly the theological import of David Abram's terminology "more-than-human world" for Nature or the natural world.[157] In rabbinic literature, human beings dwell at the horizon that divides the upper and lower realms, and humanity is what unites these realms. Abram's terminology, on the other hand, points toward the possibility of a cosmology that embraces both heavenly/divine and earthly realms – upper and lower – as one.

The chain of Being

On a superficial level, the rabbinic division between upper and lower beings would seem to conform well to the medieval idea of the "Great Chain of

---

[155] From *Heykhalot Rabbati* 24:3, transcribed in Gershom Scholem, *Jewish Gnosticism, Merkabah Mysticism, and Talmudic Tradition* (New York: Jewish Theological Seminary, 1960), 62, quoted further on p.303. Scholem notes, "The whole hymn describes the wonders of Creation stemming from God's majesty, His beauty, His stature, His crown, and His garment."
[156] See Scholem's discussion of this passage, pp.303–4.   [157] See n.4.

Being". As Jeremy Cohen wrote, "The idea that human beings straddle the colloquial fence dividing heavenly (spiritual) and earthly (material) worlds, blending characteristics of both and somehow marking the point of transition between them, enjoyed considerable popularity in ancient and medieval thought."[158] However, Cohen also notes that in the *midrashim* we have seen (as in some schools of ancient philosophy[159]), humanity occupied a middle position in the hierarchy, while in later medieval and Renaissance thought, including Jewish philosophy, humanity was more often seen as being near the pinnacle of Creation, next to God and the angels.[160]

The nature of humanity's position according to the Midrash is shown clearly in the following teaching:

All that you see, they are generations of heavens and earth, as it is said: "In beginning, Elohim created heavens and earth" [Gn 1:1]. On the second [day] He created from the upper ones / *min ha'elyonim*, as it is said: "And Elohim said: Let there be a firmament" [v.5]. On the third He created from the lower ones / *min hatachtonim*: "And Elohim said: Let the earth sprout" [v.11]. On the fourth He created from the upper ones: "Let there be lights" [v.14]. On the fifth He created from the lower ones: "Let the waters swarm" [v.20]. On the sixth He came to create Adam. He said: If I create him from the upper ones, then the upper ones will be greater than the lower ones by one creation, and there won't be peace in the world; and if I create him from the lower ones, then the lower ones will be greater than the upper ones by one creation, and there won't be peace in the world. Rather, here am I [going to] create him from the upper ones and the lower ones, for the sake of peace / *bish'vil shalom*.[161]

This midrash begins and ends with creation both above and below. Though the division between heaven and earth is breached by the creation of Adam, this breach creates balance, so that humanity's dual nature brings peace to Creation.[162] The aspects of the upper beings found in Adam do not elevate humanity above the Creation but situate it firmly within Creation.[163]

By moving between upper and lower, back and forth, the midrash emphasizes that the human role is to act as a pivot or balancing point, rather than

---

[158] *"Be Fertile and Increase"*, 85.
[159] See n.164 and discussion about the Antiochean school, p.133ff.
[160] On the shift away from a holistic view of the chain of Being in the Renaissance, see Christopher Manes, "Nature and Silence", in *Postmodern Environmental Ethics*, ed. Max Oelschlager (Albany NY: SUNY Press, 1995), 48.
[161] BR 12:8 || VR 9:9. The beginning of the parallel passage in VR emphasizes peace even more strongly. In both places, this teaching is presented as a commentary on Gn 2:7, rather than Gn 1:27.
[162] *Y'dey Moshe* (a commentary published in *Midrash Rabbah*), ad BR 12:8, even interprets R' Yehoshua's teaching in light of this midrash: "It was out of necessity that there would be for Adam four qualities/*ma'alot* like the angels and four like the *tachtonim*, so that there would not be jealousy in [Creation]." Note that *Y'dey Moshe* contrasts angels with lower ones, while BR itself either contrasts angels with animals, or contrasts 'elyonim with tachtonim.
[163] A few midrashic passages from BR, however, do fit a more anthropo-archic hierarchy. See for example BR 19:4, discussed in p.99ff.

to act as ruler.[164] In essence, seeing the human as pivot rather than pinnacle of Creation moves us away from the rigid anthropo-archism of modernist theology toward a softer anthropocentrism. This way of looking at humanity accords with ancient and medieval ideas about organicism and with many early rabbinic statements about human nature.

The motif of humanity representing balance recurs at all stages of Jewish thought, though later midrashic collections reworked this midrash so that it fit with a more dualistic metaphysical perspective. For example, a parallel to this passage from *Midrash Hagadol* ends: "On the sixth day He created the human /*ha'adam*, his body /*gufo* from the earth and his soul /*nafsho* from the heavens, in order to keep balance / *k'dey l'hakhri`a* between His creations."[165] By introducing the dualism of body and soul, *Midrash Hagadol* made the *B'rei'shit Rabbah* teaching about balancing Creation consistent with medieval philosophy. Nevertheless, despite this change, the idea persists that the human creature is in the middle of the hierarchy, balancing the whole of Creation.

In another example, from Jewish philosophy of the Renaissance period, the Maharal (Yehudah Loew of Prague, 1525–1609) uses the trope of the six days of creation to arrive at the same conclusion. He writes:

[K]now that this world that the Blessed Name created, its creation was through equilibrium/balance/*shivui*... and it shows this in that it was created in six days, for the letter *Vav* teaches about balance[166]... and you have no creation among the creatures that is more in balance than the human, and therefore the human was created on the sixth [day].[167]

---

[164] See Susan Niditch, "The Cosmic Man: Man as Mediator in Rabbinic Literature", *Journal of Jewish Studies* 34 (1983): 137–46 and Frederick McLeod, "Man as the Image of God: Its Meaning and Theological Significance in Narsai", *Theological Studies* 42 (1981): 458–68. Paulos Mar Gregorios also explores the idea of humanity as mediator or pivot of the world in *The Human Presence: Ecological Spirituality and the Age of the Spirit* (Warwick NY: Amity House, 1987); see esp. 64–5 on Gregory of Nyssa (fourth century) and 79–80 on Maximus the Confessor (seventh century), where Gregorios summarizes Lars Thunberg's *Microcosm and Mediator* (Lund: Gleerup, 1965). His brief but philosophically dense work is one of the most important texts on ecology that has come out of Orthodox Christianity. See also Irenaeus, n.436. We will see in Chapter 9 how this idea evolved into the notion of the human as the cosmic unifier.

[165] David ben Amram Adeni (thirteenth to fourteenth, Yemen), vol.1 (Jerusalem: Mossad Harav Kook, 1975), 54, ll.2–4, *ad* Gn 1:26; cf. *ad* Gn 2:7. Cf. *TanchB B'rei'shit* 15, quoted n.453. Note that *Midrash Hagadol* recasts *B'rei'shit Rabbah* using the language of *SifreyD* (see p.135), but *Midrash Hagadol*, in contrast with *Sifrey*, sees the heavens exclusively as the realm of soul, and the Earth exclusively as the realm of body.

[166] Perhaps this is because *Vav* (ו) balances upright on its end, or because *Vav* represents the center of a balance scale. More significantly, in Kabbalah *Vav* represents *Tif'eret*, the center of the Tree of Life, and the Sefirah that unifies the six Sefirot above Shekhinah/Malkhut. (See diagram, Excursus 1.) Note, however, the debate about whether Maharal alludes to Kabbalistic concepts. See Roland Goetschel, "The Maharal of Prague and Kabbalah", in *Mysticism, Magic, and Kabbalah in Ashkenazi Judaism: International Symposium Held in Frankfurt a.M. 1991*, eds. Karl Grözinger and Joseph Dan (Berlin: de Gruyter, 1995), 172–80.

[167] *Derekh Chayyim* (London: Honig and Sons, 1960), ch.2, 103.

Because the world is created through balance, the creature brought forth to complete Creation must personify balance. Humanity for the Maharal is therefore something like an embodiment of Creation.

The need of Creation as a whole to be at peace or balanced is understood in these texts as the reason why human beings are created. Homiletically, this connects with the idea that the human being is a kind of image of Creation.[168] From our perspective, it is also important that Adam is brought into being for the sake of all Creation, rather than the other way around.[169] Two midrashic images that encapsulate both elements are of *Adam Harishon* (the first human) as "the completion of the work" of creating the earth,[170] and of *Adam Harishon* as "the completion of the *challah* of the world",[171] which Jastrow translates as "the final sanctification of the world".[172] The rhetorical thrust of these passages is that humanity's unique nature does not cause us to stand apart from Creation, but rather aligns us more closely with Creation.

This is one facet of the "weak anthropocentrism" we find in rabbinic texts that runs counter to "anthropo-archism", and it leads to a very different relationship with the more-than-human world.

While these *midrashim* represent a "chain of Being" that differs from the standard medieval hierarchy, they still preserve a division between the upper and lower realms. This division seems not to be sacrosanct, however, since hierarchies of Being that interweave these realms are proposed in other texts. For example, in *Avot d'Rabi Natan* one reads:

Seven creatures [were created] this one above/*l'ma`lah* this one and this one above this one: Above all of them He created a firmament. Above the firmament He created the stars that shine forever. Above the stars He created the trees, since the trees make fruit

---

[168] See Chapter 9.
[169] Of course, some *midrashim* do describe Creation as existing for humanity's sake. For example, TB *Sanhedrin* 108a asks, Why did God destroy the animals in the flood, if it was human beings who had sinned? A teaching of R' Yehoshua ben Qorchah answers this question with a parable: A man made a wedding for his son, preparing a feast. When his son died, "he stood and destroyed his [son's] wedding canopy. He said: For nothing else did I make the canopy except for my son. Now that he has died, what [use is it] for me?... So said the Holy One: For nothing else did I create the beasts and animals except for the sake of humanity. Now that humanity is sinning, what [use are they] for me?" See also n.318.
[170] BR 12:5. The prooftext is: "I formed the earth and I created Adam upon her" (Is 45:12).
[171] BR 14:1; cf. *ShmR* 30:13; *Talmud Y'rushalmi* (Krotoszyn, Poland, 1866; repr., Jerusalem: Shilo, 1969) *Shabbat* 2:6, 5a (‖ BR 17:8). The Y'rushalmi (hereafter TY) also describes *Adam Harishon* as the *challah* and the blood of the world and its candle or lamp, correlating these with the three women's *mitsvot* enumerated in the mishnah whose neglect can cause death in childbirth: taking *challah* (see next note), sexual abstinence/*nidah* during the blood of menstruation, and Shabbat candlelighting. One could therefore interpret these *mitsvot* as either reminders of the first sin or as a means of staving off its consequences.
[172] Jastrow, s.v. *chalah*, 265. *Chalah* (*challah*) means the portion of the dough that is separated and given to the priests, but it can also mean the bread itself once it is sanctified by having this portion removed. Embedded in this image is a homily about the twofold nature of human beings, who are simultaneously united with all Creation and separated from the rest of Creation.

and the stars do not make fruit. And above the trees He created the chasing winds, since the chasing winds go to here and [then] to here, and the trees do not move from their place. Above the chasing winds He created the animal/*b'heimah*, since the animal acts (i.e., acts with will, lit. "does") and eats and drinks, and the winds do not act and do not eat. Above the animal He created Adam, since in the human there is knowledge/awareness/*dei`ah* and in the animal there is no *dei`ah*. And above the children of Adam are the ministering angels... since the ministering angels go from the end of the world and unto its [other] end and Adam is not so.[173]

Here the chain of Being ends with the familiar categorizations of humans above animals and angels above humans.[174] Though the "theographies" of *Avot d'Rabi Natan* and R' Yehoshua's *meimra* (i.e., the map each draws of the relationship between cosmos and divinity) differ, both texts use the terminology *l'ma`lah*, and neither exalts the `*elyonim*, which would include the stars and the firmament (here placed below the animals).

If the use of *l'ma`lah* does coincide with a particular school of rabbinic thought that rejected the idea that the heavens are *b'tselem*, then this *Avot d'Rabi Natan* passage, like R' Yehoshua, would be part of that school.[175] The passage does not mention *tselem*, however, and there are other details that stand in contradiction to R' Yehoshua,[176] so their relationship is uncertain at best. Also, the passage begins with the statement "Above all of them He created firmament" and then tells us what is above the firmament, suggesting that this chain of Being is more like a circle than a straight line. The passage that follows in *Avot d'Rabi Natan* similarly reflects and contradicts R' Yehoshua's teaching. It reads,

Six things were said about the children of Adam, three like an animal and three like ministering angels. Three like an animal: They eat and drink... bear fruit and multiply... and put out waste/*re`ey*... Three like ministering angels: There is understanding in them... and they walk with upright stature / *qomah z'qufah*... and they relate

---

[173] ARNA ch.37, 109.
[174] At the same time, it is closer to later medieval ideas than the previous passages, since so many things are below humanity, while only angels are above.
[175] The parallel text in *ARNB* fits R' Yehoshua's teaching even more closely, explaining that "above the children of Adam are the ministering angels... for they do not eat or drink or bear fruit and multiply; they do not sleep and they do not die" (ch.43, 120). The beginning of *ARNB* is also different in tone: "Seven things [are] one above the other... Above the earth is firmament. Above firmament are stars, in that the stars go and return/*chozrim*, and the firmament does not budge from its place. And some say that even it turns/*chozer*, like the sphere". Here the firmament is not first described, as it is in *ARNA*, as being "above all of them". Also, three of the steps in *ARNB*'s hierarchy, versus two in *ARNA*, are based on the idea that a higher level has greater locomotion than a lower one. Overall, *ARNA* seems informed by a less hierarchical model.
[176] Most importantly, eating and drinking is something that **elevates** the animals above the winds – exactly the opposite of what R' Yehoshua proposes in *B'rei'shit Rabbah*. Also, the trees stand above the stars, and the characteristic that elevates the trees above the stars – that of making fruit – is a function of reproduction – again the opposite of R' Yehoshua.

Rabbinic anthropology

things in the holy tongue... Six things were said about demons, three like the children of Adam and three like ministering angels. Three like the children of Adam: They eat and drink... bear fruit and multiply... and die... Three like ministering angels: They have wings... and know what is destined to be... and go from [one] end of the world and unto the [other] end... And some say they even change their faces to any likeness/*d'mut* that they want, and they see and are not seen.[177]

The terms "above" and "below" are missing from this text, as are any references to God's image (though the word *d'mut* appears with reference to demons!), while the level of demon has been added in between human and angel. We can presume that there is no intention of saying that demons are more in God's image than human beings. Thus, even though many details of R' Yehoshua's teaching are preserved here, the metaphysical framework behind his teaching has been erased.

This suggests that there may not have been consensus about the hierarchy of Creation among the rabbis. Several competing models could have existed, some emphasizing hierarchy and others undermining it; some holding that the heavens were closer to God's image than humans, others holding that humans were closer than the heavens.

Tracing the image

The hierarchy between upper and lower creations discussed in *B'rei'shit Rabbah* 8:11 affirms the uniqueness of humanity, stating explicitly, "the lower ones were not created in the image".[178] However, from a homiletical perspective, it is valuable to explore how we might read this hierarchy in light of the natural sciences. The contemporary recognition that the lower ones, that is, all life on the planet, participate in diverse ways in intelligence, and that the upper ones, that is, all celestial beings, are on the broadest time-scale subject to death (the sun's lifespan is in the range of ten billion years), would demand of us that we interpret the chain of Being as a continuum. In contrast, the ancients and rabbis assumed that the celestial bodies were eternal[179] – even though statements in the prophets and some *midrashim* relate the idea that the heavens will pass away.[180] There was little or no conception that new heavenly bodies could be

---

[177] ARNA ch.37, 109 ‖ *TB Chagigah* 16a, which describes angels as "flying" rather than "going".

[178] This however did not prevent the rabbis from defining ethical obligations to animals, or from attributing morality to the actions of animals. See Chapter 5, esp. p.152ff.

[179] This is why dramatic signs of transformation in the heavens, like comets and eclipses, were viewed with dread in so many cultures. It takes at least a few thousand years of human observation, along with the development of technologies for observing, before the "mortal" nature of the stars becomes clear. The fact that the rabbis understood the heavenly bodies to be created in God's image shows that they were heavily influenced by the astrological and philosophical views of their times.

[180] For example, Is 34:4, 51:6, Ps 102:26, *Targum Y'rushalmi* (also known as the fragmentary *targum*) *ad* Dt 32:1 ("the heavens and the earth do not taste death in this world, but their end is destruction in the coming world"). See also n.1030.

born.[181] For us, on the other hand, the "upper ones", that is, the sun, stars, and galaxies, have life-cycles, are born and die. Thus, the line between immortal and mortal, which for R'Tifdai divided creatures in God's image from those not in God's image, becomes quite fuzzy in light of current knowledge.

Looking at the opposite end of the rabbinic hierarchy, some of the "lower" creatures do in fact share qualities that R' Yehoshua connects with *tselem*. Especially with respect to intelligence and the rudiments of speech, modern ethology has uncovered a continuum between humans and other species that was not known to the rabbis as part of the natural world. But even within rabbinic culture, where there seems to be unanimity concerning the general question of whether animals are created in God's image, certain legendary animals are described as possessing attributes associated with *tselem* (see the section on "*Tselem*, Sexuality, Snakes, and Dolphins" in Chapter 2). Moreover, some of the interpretations of the idea that humans "see like the angels" would definitively apply to other-than-human creatures (see "*Tselem* and Vision" in Chapter 2).

In both directions, with respect to the actual mortality and "imperfection" of the *`elyonim*, as well as with respect to the intelligence, awareness, and perception of the *tachtonim*, there is a contemporary homiletical significance to these *midrashim* that goes beyond their historical meaning. The modern understanding of how the chemical elements are created further dramatizes these points. Astrophysics teaches that every atom of our bodies and of earthly matter is older in origin than the sun, that every atom heavier than beryllium was created by stellar processes, and that almost every element of our bodies was once inside a star[182] – not just our substance, but the substance of all the *tachtonim*, was a part of the *`elyonim*. Literally on the most elemental level, the division between upper and lower beings cannot be sustained.[183]

Imagining that *tselem* radiates not only to humanity but also to the stars and the angels, one is quickly led to *tselem* radiating to all the levels of Creation. Shall we reject this and say that the stuff of the heavens is not created in the image of God, as most moderns would say, or rather, that all of it, what is in

---

[181] BR 12:7 may be seen as a counterexample to this thesis.
[182] According to stellar nucleosynthesis, the "Big Bang" generated hydrogen, helium, and traces of lithium and beryllium. Beyond these, all elements up to iron were generated by nuclear interactions within stars, driven by tremendous gravitational pressure, while the majority of elements heavier than iron are derived from the force of a supernova or (as recently observed) colliding neutron stars (Joseph Stromberg, "All the Gold in the Universe Could Come from the Collisions of Neutron Stars", July 17, 2013, www.smithsonianmag.com/science-nature/215848391.html). I first studied these ideas in Benjamin Gal-Or's *Cosmology, Physics, and Philosophy* (New York: Springer Verlag, 1987); see esp. 353. Gal-Or develops an interpretation of physics he calls "Havayism", based on the name Havayah, which stands for YHVH.
[183] However, a fully emanationist model of Creation, such as Shneur Zalman's, where the substance of rocks (and ourselves) is derived from divinity and comes about "by means of numerous and powerful contractions", could readily assimilate the theory of stellar nucleosynthesis.

Intellectual and spiritual interpretations of tselem

the heavens and what is of the Earth, is somehow in the image of God? This is not a simple question. Even if we expand the concept of God's image, we would still have to ask, in what manner is all this an image of God, and with what significance? That is really the fundamental question of a Biblically-based theology of Nature.

As we have seen, the diversity of interpretations of *tselem* can be used to deconstruct the most anthropo-archic perspectives. The purpose of such deconstruction is not to erase every distinction between human and non-human animal (as if mere argument could do that), but to explore how these distinctions are conditional, so that we can build less hierarchical frameworks. For this reason, even interpretations of *tselem* that are clearly metaphysical and hierarchical can be an important basis for developing ecotheology. At various points in Jewish thought, each quality among those mentioned by R' Yehoshua – sight, posture, speech, and understanding – exists on a continuum with other animals.

To recast these ideas theologically, one could say that at each level there is a different reflection of divinity and that all of these reflections are related to each other. While at this point such a formulation is only homiletical, it grows natively from later Kabbalistic discourse, as I will show in Part II.

In the rest of this chapter and the next, I will focus on interpretations of *tselem* related to specific qualities. Broadly speaking, these interpretations can be grouped according to whether they focus on intellectual, physical, or ethical qualities. This chapter will explore interpretations of *tselem* related to the first category of intellect (including speech), while Chapter 2 will focus on physical and ethical interpretations.

While the focus in these sections will be on classical Midrash as the primary evidence of what *tselem* means to rabbinic tradition, I will also explore in some depth the ramifications of various midrashic motifs in medieval interpretation, with a particular emphasis on Maimonides. By analyzing these traditions, we gain the power to tease apart modern interpretations from the *p'shat* of classical rabbinic texts, and to establish parameters for alternative interpretations. These traditions also feed the roots of Kabbalah, which will be the focus of Part II of this book.

I. INTELLECTUAL AND SPIRITUAL INTERPRETATIONS OF TSELEM

In the Midrash, *tselem* in part signifies intellectual and spiritual awareness. *B'rei'shit Rabbah* 8:11 states that *tselem* means that a human "speaks like the ministering angels, and has knowledge in him like the ministering angels, and sees like the ministering angels". However, not only do speaking, knowing, and seeing make up a very broad spectrum of activity, but speaking and seeing are overtly physical acts. Moreover, in the Midrash all of these activities are grouped with standing, that is, with the stature of the whole body. We do not find *midrashim* that ascribe only purely intellectual or spiritual qualities (i.e., reason or "soul") to *tselem* or that apply *tselem* only to spirit but not to body. In medieval Jewish philosophy, however, it became commonplace to see God's image as reflected solely in human reason. Maimonides was the first to articulate this "anti-corporealist"[184] position (see p.67).

The shift signaled by Maimonides was also reflected in Western philosophy generally, where the understanding of reason became more and more disembodied. This trend reached its apogee in the early modern period, with Descartes' postulate *"cogito ergo sum"* and Kant's definition of the human as a "rational being", both of which define the human essence to be abstract or reflective reason.[185] Most important from the perspective of ecophilosophy is that for Kant, and for much of Western thought, having the status of a rational being was the only quality that correlated with having intrinsic value, because only a rational being can be an "end-in-itself".[186] However, ancient Greek thought did not so clearly divide reason from speech. Aristotle famously defined a human being as a *zoon logon echon*.[187] This term might be translated as "rational animal", but in context the phrase means "speaking animal" – literally, "an animal that has speech".[188]

[184] I am referring here to two interrelated positions of Maimonides: the dualism of mind and body and the belief that God has no physical body or form or description.

[185] Descartes first used the Latin phrase in *Principia Philosophiae*, pt.1, art.7, though the concept *"je pense donc je suis"* was articulated earlier in *Discours De la Méthode*, beginning pt.4. ("*Cogito Ergo Sum*", Wikipedia, en.wikipedia.org/wiki/Cogito_ergo_sum [May 2013]) Kant defined rational beings as those that could will their actions according to a categorical imperative (*Groundwork for the Metaphysic of Morals* [trans. Bennett, scribd.com/doc/147280647/Kant-Groundwork-for-the-Metaphysics-of-Morals (Dec. 2013)]).

[186] Kant did not in theory limit this status to human beings, though rationality, as he defines it, is found only in humanity. On Descartes (and Spinoza), see also n.457.

[187] "*Zoon logon echon*" was apparently Heidegger's paraphrase of Aristotle, though it is widely repeated as a quote from Aristotle himself. The closest quote in Aristotle would be *"logon de monon anthropos echei ton zoon"*, from *Politics*, 1253a, meaning, "of the animals, the human alone has speech/logos" (data.perseus.org/citations/urn:cts:greekLit:tlg0086.tlg035.perseus-grc1:1.1253a; see next note). This discussion is based in part on comments to "In Search of Zoon Logon Echon" (foureyedgremlin.blogspot.com/2010/05/in-search-of-zoon-logon-echon.html [Jan. 2012]).

[188] The *locus classicus* for this idea in Aristotle's *Politics* is connected with speech in the physical and political or practical sense, not with abstract reason. Aristotle explains:

[T]he state is a creation of nature, and . . . man is by nature a political animal . . . [T]hat man is more of a political animal than bees or any other gregarious animals is evident. Nature as we often say makes nothing in vain, and man is the only animal that has the gift of speech/*logos* . . . The power of speech is intended to set forth the expedient and inexpedient, and therefore likewise the just and unjust. (1253a ll.7–15, trans. Benjamin Jowett, *The Complete Works of Aristotle*, ed. Jonathan Barnes [Princeton NJ: Princeton University Press, 1988], 1987–8).

To be sure, one finds passages in Aristotle that define humanity in terms of reason. In the *Nicomachean Ethics*, for example, Aristotle says that perception or sentience is shared with animals, while humans uniquely have *logos*: "*leipetai de praktike tis tou logon echontos*" (1:7, 1098a, l.3; trans. W.D. Ross found at mikrosapoplous.gr/aristotle/nicom1a.htm [Sep. 2012]

Intellectual and spiritual interpretations of tselem

Corresponding to these philosophical ideas, medieval and modern Jewish theologians have tended to say that what makes humans *b'tselem* is reason. However, in ancient times, *tselem* and reason were more associated with speech, while for many theologians of the Renaissance they were more associated with free will (note that in Kant and Descartes, reason was also closely associated with free will), and in the intervening period, beginning with Maimonides, God's image was often understood to be found in purely abstract reason, dissociated from either free will or speech. It was also common in post-rabbinic thought to associate all of these qualities with the soul. The significance of each of these qualities in relation to *tselem* for Jewish thinkers was strongly linked to its significance in secular, Christian, or Muslim philosophy in the same cultural period.

Tselem as speech and understanding

In the Torah, there is no conception of intellect or imagination separate from physical speech – even reflective thought is called "speaking to one's heart". The Midrash and the *targumim*, from the earliest texts on, understand the power of language or speech to be a major part of what distinguishes humanity from other species, as we saw in *B'rei'shit Rabbah*.[189] In a similar vein, *Targum Onkelos* (attributed to Onkelos, a Roman convert to Judaism thought to have lived c.35–120) translates *"nefesh chayah"* in Genesis 2:7 as *"ru'ach m'mal'la"*, so that the verse reads, – "And He blew in his nostrils life's breath and it became in Adam the **spirit** (i.e., power) **of speaking.**"[190]

---

and in Barnes, 1735). Aristotle is analyzing the role of *logos* in attaining happiness, so in this context *logos* has the sense of practical reason – most importantly, in connection to virtue – rather than pure intellection. Also, in *De Anima*, Aristotle describes both practical and contemplative reason as uniquely human traits (III:10, 433a and III:11, 434a) and he opens the *Metaphysics* by saying it is human nature to desire knowledge, positing that human beings uniquely live by art and reasoning: *"anthropon genos chai techne chai logismois"* (980b). However, other passages in Aristotle that have been read as being about abstract rationality are clearly not describing human nature in general but only exceptional human individuals; e.g., *Ethics*, 1168b l.34–1169a l.4 and 1178a ll.2–7 (cited by Sarah Broadie in *Ethics with Aristotle* [New York: Oxford University Press, 1991], 35).

[189] This emphasis on the physical dimension of language is similar to aspects of Aristotle and dissimilar from much medieval and modern philosophy.

[190] *Targum Onkelos* changes "the *adam*" to "in Adam". Rashi (*ad loc.*) also interprets the phrase *"nefesh chayah"* to mean speech: "'And the *adam* became a *nefesh chayah*'—even a beast and a [wild] animal are called *nefesh chayah*, but this [*nefesh*] of Adam is more living than all of them, because in him was added knowing/*dei`ah* and speech/*dibur*." Sforno (*ad loc.*), perceiving weakness in this argument, gives an alternative interpretation to Rashi, connecting speech directly with *tselem*:

"And He blew in his nostrils life's breath"—a vital/animal soul / *nefesh chiyunit*, prepared to receive Elohim's image... "And the human became a *nefesh chayah*"—with all this he was only an animal/*chayah* without speaking, until he was created in image/*tselem* and likeness/*d'mut*.

The connection between speech and the divine image of humanity is emphasized in the following midrash:

> Said R' Acha: In the hour that the Holy One came to create the human, He ruled [together] with the ministering angels. He said to them: "Let us make a human [in our image]". They said to him: This one, what good is he? He said: His wisdom is greater than yours. He (God) brought before them beast and animal and bird. He said to them: This one, what is his name? and they didn't know. He made them pass before Adam. He said to him: This one, what is his name? [Adam] said: This is ox/*shor*, and this is donkey/*chamor* and this is horse/*sus* and this is camel/*gamal*. And you, [He said], what is your name? [Adam] said to him: I? It would be right/*yafeh* to be called Adam, since I was created from the ground/*adamah*. And I, [God said], what is my name? He said to him: It would be right for you to be called my Lord /*Adonai*, since you are lord/*adon* to all the creatures.[191]

This passage importantly relates the idea of naming, which is not mentioned in the Torah until the second chapter of Genesis, to the creation of Adam in God's image in the first. Here, naming – the creative dimension of human speech – places humanity above not only the animals but also the angels, who can speak but cannot name.

Naming is one of two dimensions of speech explored in *midrashim* about *Adam Harishon*, the first human. The other dimension is praise or worship. Sometimes, Adam is not the speaker but the object of worship: "Said R' Hosha`ya: In the moment that the Holy One created *Adam Harishon*, the first Human, the ministering angels erred and sought to say 'Holy/*Qadosh*' before him (to worship him)... What did the Holy One do? 'He cast upon him deep sleep' [Gn 2:21] and all knew that he was Adam."[192] Significantly,

---

While breath is the substance of speech, according to Sforno speaking remains in potentia until the implantation of the *tselem* (see also n.224).

[191] BR 17:4; also in *Midrash Tanchuma*, ed. Zundel (Jerusalem: Levine Epstein, 1968) *Chuqat* 6 and in *Midrash Tanchuma* (Buber) *Chuqat* 12 (cf. Qur'an, Sura 2:30–33). These works are cited hereafter as *Tanch* and *TanchB*, respectively. The Buber edition is also known as *Tanchuma Haqadum*. For an English translation of *Tanch*, see *Midrash Tanhuma-Yelammedenu*, trans. Samuel Berman (Hoboken NJ: Ktav, 1996), and for *TanchB*, see Townsend.

[192] BR 8:10. See Urbach, *The Sages* (Cambridge MA: Harvard University Press, 1987), 229, as well as 230, where the archangel Micha'el recognizes Adam, and 788, n.50, for parallels in apocryphal and Gnostic works. The theme that the angels wanted to worship Adam is found in several places. The trope of God diminishing Adam in order to prevent this is discussed in Chapter 9 (see p.248). On the motif of sleep, cf. *Pirqey d'Rabi Eli`ezer (Pirqey Rabi Eli`ezer*, Warsaw: Weissberg, 1874) ch.12, 21 (cited hereafter as *PRE*), which describes God setting up the human like "one of the ministering angels". There, God says that if "this one" is unique (i.e., singular) in his world and does not reproduce then the creatures will say "this one created us". Therefore, "[it is] not good, the *adam* being alone" [Gn 2:18]. Not insignificantly, the earth "heard this (that human beings would multiply) and trembled and quaked", saying, "I do not have in me the strength to feed the flocks of humanity". God promises to feed humanity at night with sleep and so share the burden with the earth. We could take this to mean that a humanity cut off from the unconscious (which includes all the ways we are connected with the more-than-human world) will destroy the earth. The outcome of this exchange between

according to *Pirqey d'Rabi Eli`ezer*, the desire to worship Adam is also shared by the animals:

> Adam looked to above and below... and he saw the creatures/*b'riyot* that the Holy One had created and he began to glorify the name of his Creator and he said, "How diverse are Your works *Hashem*" [Ps 104:24]. He stood on his feet and was described/proportioned/*m'to'ar* in the likeness of Elohim. The creatures saw him and they were afraid of him, as they thought that he created them, and all of them came to bow down to him. He said to them: "You've come to bow down to me? Come, I and you, and we will go and clothe in majesty and strength and make rule over us... the one who created us... Adam went and made Him rule over himself first and all the creatures after him and they said: "*Hashem* ruled, clothed in majesty"   [Ps 93:1].[193]

Thus the animals, like the angels, worship.[194] Instead of dividing human from animal, here speech unites them. While the speech that creates is reserved for God and the speech that names is reserved for Adam, other aspects of speech involving celebration and worship are extended to the rest of Creation, both angel and animal, higher and lower creatures (see related examples in Chapter 12, p.321ff.).

In the case of speech, as in other cases where a strong hierarchy between humanity and the other creatures is articulated, there are texts like this passage from *Pirqey d'Rabi Eli`ezer*, rhetorical "moments", in which those hierarchies

---

God and the earth is the same as what follows in *BR*: God puts Adam to sleep and creates the woman from the man. Both can be read as myths about the origin of sleep.

An interesting parallel to the theme of the angels worshipping Adam is found in the Qur'an (*Surah* 2:34, "The Cow"): "And We said to the angels, 'Bow yourselves to Adam'; so they bowed themselves, save Iblis; he refused, and waxed proud, and so he became one of the unbelievers" (trans. Arthur Arberry, *The Koran Interpreted*, vol.1 [New York: Macmillan, 1973], 33; this story is repeated six more times in the Qur'an, at 7:11, 15:29–31, 17:61, 18:50, 20:116, and 38:72–4). The midrashic story and the Qur'an are inverse images of each other: in the Qur'an, Iblis, the equivalent of Sama'el or Satan, is cast down or diminished because he will not bow to Adam; in the Midrash, Adam is cast down or diminished because the angels would have bowed down to him. It is possible that the Qur'an is dependent on early midrash for many of its details (see Abraham Isaac Katsh, *Judaism and the Koran* [New York: A. S. Barnes, 1962]). Gary Anderson, however, notes the parallels between the Qur'anic tale, the *midrashim*, and an early Christian work called *The Life of Adam and Eve*, which he thinks is a more likely source for the Qur'an. ("The Fall of Satan in the Thought of St. Ephrem and John Milton", *Hugoye: Journal of Syriac Studies* 3:1 [Jan. 2000]: paras. 1, 3, and 7, syrcom.cua.edu/Hugoye/Vol3No1/HV3N1Anderson.html [Nov. 2011]). More broadly, the Midrash seems to be wary of any transference of divine status to Adam, while the Qur'an is not. Anderson cites Altmann's suggestion that *BR* is specifically rejecting the worship of Adam by the angels found in this Christian work. Note also that the concept of divine image does **not** appear in the Qur'an explicitly (see n.95); the story in which God commands the angels to bow to Adam must be seen as its equivalent.

[193] *PRE* ch.11, 19.

[194] Though the rabbis imagine the animals initiating worship, they do not say "*Qadosh*", as the angels do in Is 6:3. The angels, already fluent in the proper prayers, need to be stopped from worshipping Adam by God, whereas when Adam stops the animals from worshipping him, he leads them in proper worship.

are deconstructed. If one chooses not to gloss over these moments, the picture of the universe found in the tradition begins to transform from one of hierarchy to one of webs or networks. A parallel transformation from hierarchical models to synergistic ones characterizes the progress of ecological science.

Before discussing the idea of disembodied intellect that was the touchstone of medieval philosophy, let us keep in mind the contrasting perspective of Elazar ben Yehudah of Worms (or Vermes; 1176–1238, Germany), who was a member of *Chasidey Ashkenaz* (the "German Pietists"). The following passage shows how concrete and physical the conception of speech could be in a mystical context separate from philosophy:

Hashem says: "Who[195] sets a mouth/*peh* for *adam*?" [Ex 4:11]—the mouth/*pi* of *Hashem* places[196] *adam*'s mouth [in him], as it is said:... "and YHVH placed a word in Bil`am's mouth" [Nu 23:5]... and it is written "I cannot go past (against) YHVH's mouth" [Nu 22:18, 24:13]. Behold, when [God] sets a word in Bil`am's mouth, he calls [it] "YHVH's mouth"... [T]he human being – all of him – resembles/*domeh* an animal; only in mouth [does a person resemble] the upper ones. And concerning this, He said: "Let us make a human in our image"—like (i.e., with) the Holy Language that is in the upper ones, and no [holy?] name can be mentioned (i.e., spoken) except by mouth.[197]

The physical mouth itself embodies God's image; besides the mouth, the rest of a person "resembles an animal". This is a far cry from the idea of *tselem* as intellect, which according to Maimonides is in God's image by virtue of its not being a corporeal organ at all.

Tselem as intellect and will: medieval Jewish thought

Intellect and will in various forms are also connected with *tselem*, as in the teaching that the human understands like the angels. However, as discussed earlier, *Chazal* did not conceive of understanding as separate from other more explicitly physical attributes. Just as the Midrash does not isolate intellect from more physical qualities, so too does Rashi in the eleventh century conjoin knowing and speaking (see n.190).

---

[195] Following Karl Grözinger (personal communication, Sep. 2013), who reads *mi* for *pi* based on ms.Munich 81, 139a.

[196] Reading *sam* (as in the verse quoted). One could read *sheim*, which would mean "the mouth of *Hashem* is the name of *adam*'s mouth".

[197] *Sodey Razaya Cheleq Bet: Sefer Hashem* (Jerusalem: Makhon Sodey Razaya, 2004), 45, quoted by Karl Grözinger in "Between Magic and Religion – Ashkenazi Hasidic Piety", in *Mysticism, Magic, and Kabbalah in Ashkenazi Judaism* (Berlin: de Gruyter, 1995), 36–7 (much thanks to Grözinger for providing the Hebrew with notations – note that my translation differs substantially). This teaching works on two levels: speech (at least prophetic speech) is a divine act, and the human mouth as the organ of speech is an image of God's mouth.

Intellectual and spiritual interpretations of tselem

Many later Jewish thinkers did, however, separate out intellect as *the* essential human quality and the source of God's image,[198] and that will be the focus of this section. Medieval texts reflect a fairly uniform understanding of this idea,[199] so I will quote just one passage from Maimonides as the example (and probable source) of this trope, from the very beginning of *The Guide*:

> The human being is made unique by a very wondrous thing that is in him, as it is not to be found in anything else that exists under the sphere of the moon, namely, intellectual apprehension... It was because of this something, I mean because of the divine intellect conjoined with man, that it is said of the latter that he is "in the image of God and in His likeness," not that God, may He be exalted, is a body and possesses shape.[200]

Maimonides emphasizes that this intellectual apprehension does not involve the body: "In the exercise of this [apprehension], no sense, no part of the body [is] used... and therefore this apprehension was likened unto the apprehension of the deity, which does not require an instrument."[201] For Maimonides, the very disembodiment of intellect is what reflects or images God.

---

[198] Philo of Alexandria (c.20 BCE–40 CE) of course articulated this idea many centuries earlier (see *On the Creation*, trans. C. G. Yonge, 23 [69], earlyjewishwritings.com/text/philo/book1.html [May 2014]), but his work had no impact on rabbinic Judaism.

[199] See Alexander Altmann, "*Homo Imago Dei* in Jewish and Christian Theology", *Journal of Religion* 48 (1968): 235–59. Altmann claims that "medieval Jewish theology... followed the Platonizing interpretation... initiated by Philo", while admitting that the medievals "substituted for [the Philonic *Logos*] Plotinus's second hypostasis, the Intellect (*nous*) or Aristotle's Active Intellect" (254). To my mind, this shift in terminology is so significant as to suggest they were not following Philo at all.

[200] MN 1:1; first line translated from Kafich, 18, balance from Pines, 23. Pines's translation begins: "Now man possesses as his proprium something in him that is very strange..." See also next note. For discussion of this passage in relation to apophatic theology, see Ehud Benor, "Meaning and Reference in Maimonides' Negative Theology", *Harvard Theological Review* 88:3 (1995): 339–60; 354–8. Benor points out the contradiction between Maimonides' general insistence on negative theology and his willingness to posit intellect as a metaphor for God in this passage. He concludes, "Maimonides did not think that we can meaningfully say only what God is not even though he did think that we can only know what God is not" (359). See also discussion of related passages in Grözinger, "Between Magic and Religion", 34–6.

[201] MN 1:1. He also states in *Mishneh Torah* (Jerusalem) *Hilkhot Y'sodey Hatorah* 4:14–15 (8) (www.mechon-mamre.org/i/1104.htm [Apr. 2012]):

> [The] soul/*nefesh* of all flesh is its form/*tsurah* that God gave to it. And the additional knowledge / *hada`at hay'teirah* found in the soul of a human being is the form of a human [who is] complete in his intellect, and concerning this form it is said in the Torah, "Let us make a human in our image as our likeness", as if to say that that there should be for him a form [capable of] knowing and grasping the intellects that have no physical body /*golem*, until he would resemble them... This [verse] is not said about the form that is recognized by the eyes... whose name is *to'ar*. And this is not the soul found in every living animal / *nefesh chayah*, through which she eats and drinks and reproduces and feels and thinks / *umargish um'harer*, except [with] the [human] intellect... And many times this form is called soul/*nefesh* and spirit/*ru'ach*. (Note that according to Maimonides, other animals feel and think.)

While the seeds for equating *tselem* with intellect are found within Midrash, Maimonides – and Jewish philosophy in general – took a radical turn away from rabbinic thought by separating *tselem* and intellect from the body.[202] This separation is one of the essential foundations for modern Jewish perspectives on the soul and the image of God in human beings. To equate this metaphysics with Judaism itself is only possible if one ignores the dissonance between medieval philosophy and classical rabbinic texts.

Contemporary Jewish culture is undergoing a transformation as people begin to pay attention to such dissonances.[203] Alon Goshen-Gottstein wrote, "The liberation of rabbinic theology from the reins of medieval theology is still underway."[204] To a large degree, that is the work of this book. However, it would be wrong to think that this resistance to medieval thought is new. While most medieval Jewish philosophers exalted the human intellect and separated it from the other qualities that the Midrash ascribed to God's image, much of Kabbalah was directed at resisting this same metaphysical hierarchy, as will be discussed in Chapter 6.[205] Furthermore, even some Jewish thinkers deeply influenced by philosophy did not accept the radical division of the intellect from the body.

For example, when Sforno interprets Genesis 1:27, he synthesizes a more classical rabbinic conception of knowledge with the medieval ideal of intellect and with his own understanding of will. Sforno emphasizes that the freedom to act is what resembles God the most in us, rather than the power of contemplation or apprehension. He writes:

"Similar to (lit. 'like') our likeness /*kid'muteinu*" in the matter of actions, since he will resemble a little bit the court above, from the perspective of acting with knowing and recognition. But their actions are without choice, and in this they do not resemble the human. And the human will resemble God, blessed be, a little bit, who acts with choice.

---

[202] See Michael Satlow, "Jewish Knowing: Monism and Its Ramifications", *Judaism* 45:4 (1996): 483–9, which deals with teaching about the Jewish tradition, where knowing is understood to come from within the body, to students immersed in Western culture, where knowing is thought of as separate from the body.

In the rest of this work, I focus on aspects of Maimonides' thought, especially his holistic view of Creation, that provide a foundation for Jewish ecotheology. Maimonides' dualism, along with his attitude toward the body, toward the sense of touch, and toward women – all connected to his elevation of the disembodied intellect – are equally incompatible with ecotheology. His attitude toward the body is moreover the foundation of the modernist Judaism I critique further on. See Seidenberg, "Maimonides" in *ERN*, 1027 (www.neohasid.org/torah/rambam/ [Jan. 2014]) and Boyarin's trenchant critique of Maimonides' attitude toward women in *Carnal Israel: Reading Sex in Talmudic Culture* (Berkeley: University of California Press, 1993), 57–60. Note, however, that Maimonides' dualism was also a rejection of Saadyah Gaon, whose interpretation of *tselem* is far more problematic (see pp.93–4).

[203] I explore these issues in "Confessions of a Jewish Post-Postmodernist".

[204] "The Body as the Image of God in Rabbinic Literature", *Harvard Theological Review* 84:2 (1994): 171–95; 171.

[205] Most especially by insisting that the body was as much in God's image as the soul.

Intellectual and spiritual interpretations of tselem

However, the choice of God always is for good and human choice is not so... and so it said, *kid'muteinu* [meaning] "similar to/approximating our likeness / *k'mo d'muteinu*", not "according to our true likeness / *kid'muteinu ha'amiti*".[206]

If our knowing makes us like the court above (angels, etc.), "in their likenesses", our freedom makes us less like them. Our freedom makes us simultaneously more like God and less like God, since God always chooses the good. Because awareness becomes evident through "action", the intellect, which may appear to operate separately from the body, must be re-embodied in order to show its relation to the divine realms.

This pattern of overlap and disjunction between humans and angels is similar to what we saw with respect to speech in the *midrashim* of the previous section. Both the power to name there and the power to choose here separate human nature from angelic nature. One might postulate that these powers are of the same essence. Here as well, the relationship between the human being, the court above, and God suggests something other than a linear hierarchy.

Though the connection between intellect and free will was made in ancient times by Philo,[207] the idea that the exercise of free will or choice is a manifestation of the image of God is not a significant theme in rabbinic literature before the sixteenth century. Sforno, who is on the cusp of the Renaissance and early modern period, is the earliest commentary on *tselem* I have seen for whom the concept of free will is central. From the Renaissance on, perhaps because of the rising emphasis on the individual, this becomes normative: the Maharal and Menasheh (Menasseh) ben Israel (1604–57, Netherlands), as well as modern commentators like Shimshon Rafael Hirsch (1808–88, Germany) and Meir Simchah Hakohen of Dvinsk (1843–1926, Latvia), all describe free will – "*hab'chirah hachofshit*" in Meir Simchah's terminology – as a main feature of *tselem*.[208]

In the preceding passages, the divine image is treated as something inherently reflected in the intellectual element within human beings. Other passages tell us that the intellect must be developed in order to show its resemblance to God, as one reads in the following example, also from Sforno's commentary:

"Walk before me /*l'fanai* and be whole/*tamim*" [Gn 17:1]. "Walk" wherever you turn "*l'fanai*" (lit. "toward my face")—as one who gazes upon Me to know My ways, according to what is possible with you, according to the idea of "I set YHVH in

---

[206] *Miqra'ot G'dolot ad* Gn 1:27. See also Sforno on speaking and God's image, n.190.
[207] In *On the Unchangeableness of God*, Philo writes that the intellect "is the only quality in us which the Father, who created us, thought deserving of freedom; and, unloosing the bonds of necessity, he let it go unrestrained, bestowing on it that [gift] most connected with himself, the power... of spontaneous will" (trans. C. D. Yonge [London: George Bell, 1890], bk.10, 352, www.earlyjewishwritings.com/text/philo/book10.html).
[208] *Meshekh Chokhmah* (Riga: Menachem Mendel Dovber, 1927), 3. Quotations from these works can be found in Martin Sicker, *Between Man and God: Issues in Judaic Thought* (Westport CT: Greenwood Press, 2001), 94–5.

front of me always" [Ps 16:8]. "And be whole"—and acquire/ take possession of the wholeness/*sh'leymut* that is possible for the human species, reason. Become wise and knowing of Me by knowing My ways, so that you become like [Me], according to what is possible for you... [A]nd this is the ultimate wholeness / *hash'leymut ha'acharon* of the human species, and the one intended by God blessed be in creation, as it says: "Let us make a human in our image as our likeness".[209]

Most importantly, Sforno underlines wholeness/*sh'leymut* as the purpose of humanity and equates this with reason.[210]

Maimonides may be the origin within Jewish theology for the idea that perfecting one's intellect allows one to come closer and closer to being formed in God's image; he is certainly its most important progenitor. According to Isadore Twersky,[211] Maimonides was the first to list imitating God as one of the commandments, stating that we should "become like /*l'hidamut* Him according to our ability".[212] Maimonides introduces the idea that this also means attaining intellectual completeness or perfection in God's image in his *Mishneh Torah*: "The additional intellect / *hada`at hay'teirah* found in the soul of a human being is the form/*tsurah* of a human complete in his intellect, and concerning this form it is said in the Torah, 'Let us make a human in our image as our likeness'".[213] The connection between imitating God and God's image is made again and again by Maimonides. He also writes about Shet (Seth):

[A]fter he had attained human perfection... it was said of him: And he begot a son in his own likeness, after his image. You know that whoever is not endowed with this form... is not a man, but an animal having the shape and configuration of man. Such a being, however, has a faculty to cause various kinds of harm and to produce evils that is not possessed by the other animals. For he applies the capacities for thought and perception... to all kinds of machinations entailing evils... and engendering all kinds of harm.[214]

---

[209] *ad* Gn 17:1. While Sforno's formulation emphasizes intellectual rather than moral development, it is structurally similar to the traditions about *imitatio Dei* explored further on. The phrase "know my ways" and Gn 17:1 are two important loci for *imitatio Dei*.

[210] The theme of wholeness underlies diverse interpretations of *tselem*. See examples from the Midrash on pp.80–81, 87–8, and from Kabbalah on pp.196, 203–4, 291.

[211] "On Law and Ethics in the Mishneh Torah: A Case Study of Hilkhot Megillah II:17", *Tradition* 24 (1989): 138–49; 142.

[212] *Sefer Hamitsvot*, trans. Yosef Kafich (Jerusalem: Mossad Harav Kook, 1957), *Mitsvot `Aseh* 8.

[213] *Hilkhot Y'sodey Hatorah* 4:14 (8) (see n.201). He also states in the *Guide*, "For the intellect that God made overflow unto man and that is the latter's ultimate perfection, was that which Adam had been provided with before he disobeyed. It was because of this that it was said of him that he was created in the image of God and His likeness" (*MN* 1:2, 24).

[214] *MN* 1:7, 33. Maimonides' interpretation explains why the Torah did not state that Adam bore Shet in his likeness at the time of Shet's birth, in Gn 3, but rather in Gn 5. See Benor's discussion about striving for moral perfection as a response to intellectual apprehension of God ("Meaning and Reference", 357–9). While this has strong ethical implications, it is quite different from the exhortations about imitating God found in Midrash. Maimonides does list moral perfection as a perfection we can attain (others being material perfection, i.e., property or wealth, and physical perfection, i.e., health and prowess – both of which he dismisses as superficial – and of course intellectual perfection) (3:54, 634–5). But the highest level of

Intellectual and spiritual interpretations of tselem

According to this passage from *Moreh N'vukhim*, practical intelligence or instrumental reason by itself is not a mark of God's image. A clever person who uses reason instrumentally for "machinations entailing evils" is a unique kind of animal, able to produce evils that cannot be produced "by the other animals", and not a human at all. Only that intelligence which develops into wisdom, through which "a person attains perfection", reflects God's image.

This is a close parallel to the interpretation of *tselem* that relates manifesting God's image to ethically imitating God.[215] In *Moreh N'vukhim*, Maimonides in fact specifies that the outcome of intellectual perfection is moral perfection:

[T]he human perfection / *sh'leymut ha'adam* in which a person can truly glory himself is [when one] reaches His apprehension, may He be exalted, according to his capacity and he knows His providence over His creations, how it [operates] in their coming into being and in their being guided/governed. And the ways of such a person, after such apprehension, will be directed continually toward lovingkindness, righteousness, and justice, to become (conduct) himself a like (aligned) with His actions / *l'hitdamut b'ma`asav* (Schwartz: "from out of becoming alike to His actions / *mitokh hidamut el ma`asav*"), may He be exalted.[216]

Though Maimonides also indicates that one can attain to moral perfection in and of itself, the nature of this perfection changes completely as one enters into apprehension of the Divine.

Even though developing the intellect "in God's image" may appear on the surface to have little to do with the physical created world, in the medieval context the development of the intellect was thought to depend on understanding and appreciating the more-than-human world in all its orders, physical and metaphysical, especially with respect to physics, astronomy, biology, and medicine. Just as Maimonides wrote that apprehending God subsumes apprehending God's "providence over His creations, in their coming into being and in their being guided", he also wrote that a person's "ultimate perfection... would consist in his knowing everything concerning all the beings that it is within the capacity of a person to know..."[217] Elsewhere Maimonides equates this kind of knowledge specifically with knowing God's goodness:

When [Moshe] asked for knowledge of the attributes... he was told: I will make all My goodness / *kol ṭuvi* pass before you [Ex 33:19]... "All My goodness" – alludes to

---

moral perfection can only be reached via apprehension of the Divine, which is predicated on intellectual perfection. See next quote.

[215] Discussed in Chapter 2, "*Tselem* and Self-Transformation: *Imitatio Dei*", p.105ff.

[216] MN 3:54, Kafich, 416. Friedländer (397) reads: "he will then be determined... to imitate the ways of God". See Menachem Kellner, *Maimonides on Human Perfection* (Atlanta GA: Scholars Press, 1990), chs.4–7. Pines translates, "The way of life of such an individual, after he has achieved this apprehension, will always have in view lovingkindness, righteousness, and judgment, through assimilation to His actions, may He be exalted" (638). This is the last sentence of *The Guide* before the coda.

[217] MN 3:27, 511. He defines this as realizing the potential of the hylic intellect, to attain what is "noble and is the only cause of permanent preservation".

the display to him of all existing things (creatures) of which it is said: "And God saw everything that He had made, and behold, it [is] very good." By their display, I mean that he will apprehend their nature and the way they are mutually connected so that he will know how He governs them in general and in detail.[218]

Maimonides' proto-ecological sensibility shines through his statement that knowledge of the creatures entails knowing "the way they are mutually connected".[219]

Maimonides explains elsewhere that concrete knowledge of the world is intimately intertwined with being able to know or infer the very existence of God:

I have already let you know that there exists nothing except God, may He be exalted, and this existent world and that there is no possible inference proving His existence, may He be exalted, except those deriving from this existent taken as a whole and from its details. Accordingly it behooves one (Kafich: "it is an absolute obligation")[220] to consider this existent as it is and to derive premises from what is perceived of its nature.[221]

For Maimonides, understanding the world, in all its complexity and unity, is the ground for understanding God; the world is more than just a kind of backdrop that inspires humans to praise God. His emphasis on knowledge of the physical world, which was part of his programmatic rejection of the Kalam,[222] became a critical contribution to the foundation of science.

---

[218] MN 1:54, 124; cf. 1:38, 87: "'And you will see My back' means you will apprehend what follows Me, has come to be like Me, and follows necessarily from My will – that is, all the things created by Me".

[219] I differ from Kafich (84, n.18), who interprets this phrase as referring only to "the connection of the world of the Intelligences to the world of the Spheres... and [their] influence on the physical world".

[220] Kafich, 125.

[221] MN 1:71, 183. In most other texts (cf. Bachya ibn Paquda, see n.60), this imperative is reduced to instilling awe for the Creator – an important part of environmental awareness, but only a first step. For Maimonides, it amounts to an entire scientific methodology; it is no exaggeration to claim that Maimonides' approach to natural philosophy became one of the foundations of scientific methodology in Western civilization. In general, there are three different approaches to science and knowing, which can be characterized as holistic, mechanistic, and atomistic. In the first category, one would place Maimonides and Leibniz, Goethe, and Einstein; in the second, Newton and the Deists; in the third (which became the accepted ideology of most of the sciences), Descartes and Bacon. On Bacon, see Carolyn Merchant, "'The Violence of Impediments': Francis Bacon and the Origins of Experimentation", *Isis* 99 (2008): 731–760 and "The Scientific Revolution and *The Death of Nature*", *Isis* 97 (2006): 513–33. On the scientific revolution in general, and especially on Newton, see Morris Berman, *The Reenchantment of the World* (Ithaca NY: Cornell University Press, 1981).

[222] The Mutakallimum (those who expounded Kalam theology) believed that each moment God created anew the "accidents" or qualities that distinguish one object or individual from another and that God could at any moment instantiate qualities that had no continuity with the previous moment. This belief undermines the assumptions that make science possible.

Intellectual and spiritual interpretations of tselem

That the intellect needs to be developed in order to reflect God's image is one of several ideas that teach that *tselem Elohim* is something that must be actualized by developing our capacities and our relationships. This entails both knowledge of God and knowledge of Creation. This hermeneutic can be applied broadly to transform the idea of God's image from something that separates us from the greater world into something that brings us closer to the more-than-human world, through our need to investigate and understand.

As already discussed, while some of the midrashic texts on *tselem* differentiate between speaking and reason or intellect, none proposes a dichotomy between the two. As one finds in Western thought more generally, earlier texts and thinkers in rabbinic Judaism associate speech and reason closely, while later thinkers begin to see reason and mind as a disembodied phenomenon, independent of physical speech. A similar pattern in the way Jewish philosophical thought comes to identify *tselem* with soul will be seen in the next section. However, in Kabbalah and its streams of influence, this trend is reversed. As I will discuss in subsequent chapters, this is one of many metaphysical premises rejected in varying degrees both by the Kabbalists and by the Hasidic rebbes after them.

Tselem and soul

The relationship between *tselem* and soul is undefined in classical Midrash. The terms *nefesh* and *n'shamah*, taken from the first chapters of Genesis, are used by the rabbis to mean "soul", and both *tselem* and *n'shamah* are interpreted as divine elements within a human being. Had the tradition intended to equate the two, one would expect to find a text that says this explicitly, especially since this would have resolved one of the major tensions between the first and second creation stories.[223] However, I have not found an early midrashic text that explicitly reads *tselem* in Genesis 1 as the equivalent of *n'shamah* or *nefesh* in Genesis 2. The Torah, as viewed through the lens of classical Midrash, was understood to describe two separate qualities, *tselem* and *n'shamah*, each of which distinguished humanity.[224]

---

[223] One hint in this direction bears inspection. The language of `elyonim` that is used to explain the meaning of *tselem* in BR is also used later in BR to interpret the phrase "*nishmat chayyim*" from Gn 2. See discussion on p.138.

[224] The Torah itself does not suggest that the *n'shamah* breathed into humanity differentiates it from the other species (cf. Gn 7:22). However, most commentaries do read this into the phrase "and He blew in his nostrils life's breath/*nishmat chayyim*". Sforno seems to disagree: "'And the human became a *nefesh chayah*' – with all this he was only an animal/*chayah* without speaking" (quoted n.190). He also pointedly states (ad Gn 1:26) that *nefesh chayah* just means another animal species: "'*Adam*'—a species from among the species of animals/*nefesh chayah* that I formed, whose name is *adam*, as it says, 'and the *adam* became a *nefesh chayah*'." Nevertheless, states Sforno, this *n'shamah* was prepared to receive Elohim's image and so become something more than animal (see n.190).

Further evidence that *tselem* and soul were seen as separate is found in the fact that early midrashic literature uniformly assumes that animals do have souls. *Chazal* believed that among the lower creatures, humans were created *b'tselem* exclusively (or almost exclusively). If they, or their redactors, believed that the image of God in a person was the soul itself, we would expect to find a corollary statement somewhere that other animals do *not* have a soul. However, no such passage exists.

What one can find, in a later-redacted teaching found in *Midrash Otiyot d'Rabi Aqiva* ("Rabbi Akiva's Midrash on Letters"), version A, is that the human soul is divine because the human is in God's image: "'A lamp of YHVH is the human soul / *nishmat adam*' [Pr 20:27]—and not the animal's soul / *nishmat b'heimah* – since she (the animal) is not created in the likeness /*bid'muto* of the Holy One, it was not said about him [*sic*]."[225] This is the only text I have found to explicitly associate the image with the soul, and it does not *equate* image with soul. Significantly, not only are we told here that animals have souls, but the passage goes on to list the many ways in which human souls and the souls of other animals are the same.

The absence of any early text equating *tselem* and *n'shamah* is striking. Any explanation is speculative, but the reason for this may be that *tselem*, prior to medieval philosophy, always included within it an element of physical form.[226] Goshen-Gottstein even claims that "the bodily meaning is the only meaning of *tselem* in rabbinic literature."[227] More accurately, *tselem* is always applied to the body, or to the whole person, rather than to the soul, which is the complement of the body.

The tension between *tselem* and *n'shamah* was picked up by Kabbalah, as will be discussed further on.[228] However, apart from Kabbalah, later Jewish thought, in both Midrash and philosophy, did equate God's image with the

---

[225] BM, vol.2, 342–95, §*Nun*, 382. Note that the pronouns should not change genders here; *n'shamah* and *b'heimah* are both feminine. If this wording does reflect the original tradition, perhaps this indicates that one pronoun referred to soul and the other to animal, which is why I read the passage as, "since the animal was not created in the likeness of the Holy One, it was not said about the animal's soul".

[226] It is also possible, though this is even more speculative, that the fact that the early Church equated the soul with the image of God negatively influenced the development of a similar idea in rabbinic literature. See Altmann, "*Homo Imago Dei*". This equation was found in the Alexandrian school, whereas the Antiochean school held positions closer to that of *Chazal*, seeing the whole person as made in God's image. See pp.133–6.

[227] "The Body", 174. On the surface, this conclusion could not contrast more strongly with Tishby, who says, "As to the idea that 'the image of God' refers to a parallel between the human body and God – the source for this is not found in aggadic literature" (*WZ* 681). However, Tishby is thinking about the way that the Kabbalah sees the image of God reflected in the physical structure and details of the body, whereas Goshen-Gottstein is focused on rabbinic teachings about the body as a whole. See p.132.

[228] p.183ff.

Intellectual and spiritual interpretations of tselem

soul, and this equation was a foundation of medieval rabbinic anthropology. For example, in *Midrash Hagadol* one reads:

"And Elohim created the human": "in his image"—this is the structure of his (Adam's) body; "in Elohim's image"—this is the soul/*n'shamah* that was put in him; for the language of "*tselem*" covers [both] the body (i.e., in the first instance, where it is not divine), and the soul/*nefesh* that is not a body.[229]

Here the *n'shamah* of Genesis 2 is equated with *tselem Elohim* in Genesis 1:27 and taken to be synonymous with *nefesh*.[230]

The development of the concept of "soul" in Midrash is explored further in Chapter 4. What I hope I have established here is simply that the idea of the soul cannot be used to interpret the early rabbinic understanding of *tselem*.

---

[229] Vol.1, 58, *ad* Gn 1:27, ll.7–9. *B'tsalmo* is taken to refer to the image of Adam, rather than the image of God. Yemen had a particularly strong relationship with Maimonides, and one could interpret *Midrash Hagadol* as a recasting of the Midrash from a Maimonidean (and dualistic) perspective. On *Midrash Hagadol*, see also p.56. Other works quoted in this volume that equate or connect *tselem* and soul include Ramban (n.299) and Sforno (n.332).

[230] The appearance of this idea in later midrash, and evidence of developmental stages leading up to it, means that this trope could be used to date various *midrashim* relative to each other.

2

Tselem Elohim in Midrash and commentary, part 2
The body, gender, dominion, and ethics

This chapter will outline physical, behavioral, ethical, and "transformational" interpretations of *tselem*. In the physical realm, themes include upright stature, gender and sexuality, and even the physiology of vision. In the behavioral realm, dominion is a paramount concern. In the ethical/transformational realm, *tselem* can be seen as the element within each person that guarantees their value as a human being – a basis for what we might call human rights; *tselem* can also act as a symbol of each person's ethical potential; that is, when a person acts ethically they bring to fulfillment the image of God in themselves.

II. PHYSICAL AND BEHAVIORAL INTERPRETATIONS OF TSELEM

While most, if not all, modern interpreters of *tselem* hear an ethical or spiritual call in the idea of God's image, not a few classical interpretations understood the idea of the image of God in humanity to be related to some physical quality. Four cases stand out: *tselem* represented in the way humans see, *tselem* as male and female, *tselem* as circumcision, and *tselem* as erect stature. Erect stature is also interpreted as a symbol of human dominion or rulership. *Tselem* as speech, discussed earlier, and *tselem* as blood, discussed under ethical interpretations of *tselem* (pp.102–3), to some degree also fit into this category, since they are essentially physical, though their primary significance is psycho-spiritual and moral.

Tselem and vision

R' Yehoshua bar Nechemyah, in *B'rei'shit Rabbah* 8:11, said that humans see "like the angels" (p.47). We might have thought this refers to foresight or vision in some intellectual or spiritual sense, but the midrash glosses this point with a wholly physical explanation: "this one [sees] sideways / *ele' zeh m'tsaded*".

Physical and behavioral interpretations of tselem 77

If "this one" refers to the animals, as most commentators contend,[231] then that would fit with *Bavli Nidah* 23a, where R' Yan'ai explains that fetuses shaped like certain animals still count as human births if "their eyes go in front of them like those of a human".[232] Indeed, the eyes of prey animals like ruminants and rodents are placed more on the sides of their heads, giving them a wider field of peripheral vision in order to detect predators.[233] Note that by this interpretation, humans would only be distinct from prey animals, not from other primates or from some predators.[234]

Grammatically, however, "*zeh*" should refer to the human.[235] Explanations based on this reading include: (1) Humans can move their eyes from side to side without turning their heads.[236] (2) Humans can turn their heads to face backwards. (3) Humans have a wider field of peripheral vision ("even though a person looks in front, he can see to the sides"). The second and third explanations are simply inaccurate. I prefer the first explanation as the *p'shat*

---

[231] See notes to l.2 in Theodor, 65. This interpretation is supported by one manuscript, which states: "this one sideward/*mats'did*, in that his eyes don't go before him" (Theodor ms.*Alef*).

[232] According to the Gemara, this includes two owl species. The significance for the Gemara is that only some miscarriages count the same as a human birth with respect to ritual impurity/*tum'ah*. Another possibility discussed is that births whose eyes (pupils) are "round/ `igul*" like a person's will incur *tum'ah*.

[233] It is perhaps significant that the midrash speaks about "*b'heimah*" – which can mean prey animals specifically (n.313). Prey animals generally have much better peripheral vision than humans, not only because of the position of their eyes, but also because the most sensitive area of their retinas, the fovea or "visual streak", is oblong, enabling them to see the whole horizon clearly.

[234] Seeing straight ahead means that there is an overlap between the visual fields of each eye, which gives an animal the ability to perceive depth. The largest degree of overlap can be found in raptors (because they hunt from the air) and primates (because they live in trees but cannot fly). In these species, the binocular field ranges from 90 to 140 degrees (for land predators, it is 75 to 110 degrees). Humans are at the extreme end of this spectrum, matched by only a few other species. (Dolphins have an equally large arc of binocular "vision", but this vision comes from sonar.)

[235] Several other differences make human vision distinct: (1) Humans have a circular area of acuity that enables us to focus on hand-oriented tasks. (2) Humans have a larger percentage of the sclera (the white of the eyes) showing than any other animal. This goes along with the ability to change focus by moving our eyes from side to side rather than turning our heads. In addition, other primates have scleras that match their skin; the white color of the human sclera enables us to signal each other with eye movements. See Hiromi Kobayashi and Shiro Kohshima, "Unique Morphology of the Human Eye and Its Adaptive Meaning: Comparative Studies on External Morphology of the Primate Eye", *Journal of Human Evolution* 40:5 (2001): 419–35. (3) Humans have a more acute sense of color than any other mammal and a much higher ratio of cones to rods. (Plenty of birds, insects, and even shrimp are more sensitive to colors, and see a wider spectrum, than any mammal.) Our color sense may be related to the need to "read" the health of diverse ecosystems that comes with being bio-generalists. Ultimately, our vision seems "destined" for things like reading, using tools, and appreciating the beauty of color. In sum, there are many ways to explain the idea that humans "see like the angels".

[236] Even most predators must turn their whole heads in order to see depth, because their eyes are less movable than ours.

(original meaning) of the text.[237] One possible way of interpreting it is that because humans can change the direction of their gaze without turning their heads, they are like the angels in Ezekiel's vision, who can change the direction they are moving in without turning.

Tselem, male and female

According to *B'rei'shit Rabbah* 8:11, the aspects of human nature that are *b'tselem* come from above, while the aspects that come from below are "male and female" and are not in the image.[238] However, one can find a strong midrashic basis for reading the clause "male and female He created them" as an elaboration of the clause, "in Elohim's image He created him". Some Biblical scholars even interpret this to be the literal meaning of the verse.[239] (It is, moreover, never the case in Biblical or rabbinic tradition that being female is described as not being in God's image.[240]) Because this interpretation of "male

---

[237] This is also the interpretation given in *Yalqut Shim`oni* (2 vols. [Jerusalem: Vegshel, n.d.], hereafter *YSh*), which explains that "an animal doesn't see except by turning its face sideways, but this one (the human) doesn't turn its face sideways" (1:14). Though *YSh*, attributed to Shimon of Frankfurt-am-Main (thirteenth century), is much later, its interpretations can be helpful, and it may preserve interesting readings of earlier manuscripts.

[238] "Rashi" (see n.514) and others (*Midrash Rabbah ad loc.*) concur with this reading.

[239] For example, Maryanne Cline Horowitz, "The Image of God in Man: Is Woman Included?", *The Harvard Theological Review* 72 (July–Oct. 1979): 175–206, or Gerhard von Rad, *Genesis* (Philadelphia: Westminster Press, 1972), 68, cited by Lorberbaum, *Tselem Elohim*, 400, n.40. Rachel Adler, in an interpretation that goes beyond gender, understands "male and female" as specifically emphasizing our sexuality:

> Sexuality, the most primary way in which humankind is at once many and one, is a metaphor for the infinitude and unity of God. Our sexuality marks us both as boundaried and boundary-transcending... Overriding the physical and emotional boundaries that keep human beings distinct from one another, it urges us to open our portals, ... to create places of co/habitation where we and the other are interlinked.

(*Engendering Judaism: An Inclusive Theology and Ethics* [Philadelphia: JPS, 1998], 118)

[240] Some feminist critics, in particular Christian feminists, have asserted that the Biblical or Hebraic tradition says exactly that. For example, editor Kari Elizabeth Borresen, in her introduction to *The Image of God: Gender Models in Judaeo-Christian Tradition* (Minneapolis MN: Fortress, 1995), 2, stated that "in early Jewish sources women are implicitly regarded as not being God-like." (Note that Borresen's work takes as its subject the "Judeo-Christian" [*sic*] tradition, but ignores rabbinic culture.) She draws this conclusion based on Anders Hultgard's "God and the Image of Woman in Early Jewish Religion" (32–47), which argues that the predominance of male animals in the sacrificial cult demonstrates the perfection of male over female in the eyes of Hebrew religion. This ignores the fact that in animal husbandry, only a few of the male animals born are needed for reproduction or as draught animals – which makes their use for sacrifices an utterly common-sense practice. (On sacrifices, see pp.144–5.) Rosemary Radford Ruether, in her concluding essay, goes even further, writing, "Hebrew thought represents the end process of [the] religious revolution against female primacy and, finally, against female presence at all in the heavens" (271). *Contra* Ruether, see Tikva Frymer-Kensky, *In the Wake of the Goddesses: Women, Culture and the Biblical Transformation of Pagan Myth* (New York, 1993; discussed n.28). (On related issues in rabbinic culture, see Daniel Boyarin, *Unheroic Conduct: The Rise of Heterosexuality and the Invention of the*

and female" serves as a homiletical support for feminist reinterpretations of scripture, it is prominent in both liberal Christian theology and Jewish feminist commentaries.[241] The midrashic connection between the image of God and androgyny is also cited by some secular feminist writers.[242]

This connection is ancient, though its fullest expression is only achieved in Kabbalah. An indicative passage can be found in *B'rei'shit Rabbah*, which responds to the tension between the first two chapters of Genesis. In Genesis 1, male and female are created at the same time, while in Genesis 2, the female is created out of the male. *B'rei'shit Rabbah* resolves this tension by asserting that the first human was created *du-par'tsufin*, with two faces or genders, one male and one female, and then divided to become a woman and a man.

Said R' Yirmiyah ben Elazar: In the hour when the Holy One created the first human, He created him [as] an androgyne/*androginos*, as it is said, "male and female He created them". Said R' Shmuel bar Nachmani: In the hour when the Holy One created the first human, He created [for] him a double-face/*di-prosopon*/ *du-par'tsufin*,[243] and sawed him and made him backs, a back here and a bac̄k [t]here, as it is said, "Back/*achor* and before/*qedem* You formed me" [Ps 139:5].[244] They objected to him: But it says, "He took one of his ribs/*ts'la`ot*..." [Gn 2:21]! He said to them: [It means] "[one] of his sides/*sit'rohi*", just as you would say, "And for the side/*tsela`* of the Tabernacle/*mishkan*" [Ex 26:20], which they translate [in Aramaic] "for the side/*seter*".[245]

Jewish Man [Berkeley: University of California Press, 1997]). Frymer-Kensky maintains that by the time the Hebrew religion evolved, female deities had already been made subservient and banished from the heavens, and that bias against women in post-Biblical Jewish culture was largely a product of Hellenistic attitudes, not of Scripture. The rabbis, on another level, taught the same thing. According to the story, when the Jewish elders were asked to translate the Torah into Greek for Ptolemy, they translated "male and female / *zachar un'qeivah* He created them" as "male with his orifices / *zachar un'quvav* He created him" (*M'khilta, Pischa* 14, 50; *BR* 8:11; *TB Megillah* 9a) – as if the first human were only male. See Judith Antonelli, *In the Image of God: A Feminist Commentary on the Torah* (Northvale NJ: Jason Aronson, 1987), 4. See also discussion of whether women are implicitly left out of God's image by circumcision, p.87ff.

[241] See, e.g., Antonelli, *In the Image*.
[242] See, e.g., June Singer, *Androgyny: The Opposites Within* (Boston MA: Sigo Press, 1989), 66–7.
[243] Variants also include "*dyu par'tsufim*", found in the standard edition, which follows ms.*Dalet* in Theodor (55). *Di-prosopon* comes directly from the Greek.
[244] Many other interpretations of Ps 139:5 are given in *BR* 8:1 and *VR* 14:1. Some read the verse temporally: "back/after/*achor*" means the human was created last, while "before" means that before punishments come to the rest of the world, they come to humans (after *TB B'rakhot* 61a); or, "after" means Adam's body was created after the rest of Creation, while "before" means *Adam Harishon*'s spirit (or the Messiah's spirit) was created at the beginning, or before the other animals (n.449). "Back and before" is also interpreted spacially – see Chapter 9 (pp.247–8.) and Porton, *Understanding*, 172–3. One more interpretation is a favorite text of Jewish environmental educators: "If a person merits they say to him, you preceded the ministering angels, and if not, they say to him, a fly preceded you" (see n.318).
[245] *BR* 8:1 ‖ *BR* 17:6, *VR* 14:1, *TB B'rakhot* 61a and `*Eruvin* 18a. *VR* reads, "a back for the male, a back for the female". *TB B'rakhot* derives this interpretation from the double *Yud* in "And He formed /*Vayyitsar*" [Gn 2:7], contrasting this interpretation with the idea that the double *Yud* stands for the *yetser to̱v* and *yetser ra`*, good and evil natures (inclinations

Though this midrash does not mention *tselem*, the androgynous character of the first human is a mark of uniqueness, contrasting with all other creatures.[246]

There are two different pictures of this "unibody" state presented here. One, the *androginos*, may be understood to mean that the human possesses a single body with two sets of genitals, while the other, *du-par'tsufin*, would mean that the human comprises two bodies, one male and one female, fused together.[247]

The *Gemara* of the *Talmud Bavli* (Babylonian Talmud) records a detailed debate between two *Amoraim* that may be correlated to the positions mentioned in this passage. Commenting on the verse "And YHVH Elohim built the *tsela`* that He took from the *adam* into a woman" [Gn 2:22], Rav and Shmuel argue about whether this means Chavah was built from a face/*par'tsuf* (a whole and equal side) of the original Adam, or from his tail/*zanav*.[248] If *androginos* means a body that was single in all respects except the genitals, then the part that God took from the first human to make a woman would be the female genitals.[249]

The Midrash also elaborates a more naturalistic view of the unification of genders, based on the Torah's explanation that a man cleaves to a woman "and they become one flesh" [Gn 2:24], as in the following passage:

"Not good[, the *adam* being alone]" [Gn 2:18]: Taught [R' Yaakov]: Anyone (man) that has no woman lives without good... R' Simon in the name of R' Yehoshua ben Levi said: Even without peace... R' Yehoshua of Sakhnin in the name of R' Levi said: Even without life... R' Chiya bar Gomdi said: He is not even a whole human / *adam shalem*, for it says: "And He blessed them and called **their** name Adam". [Gn 5:2][250]

---

or impulses). Unlike the Gemara (cf. *BR* 14:2), which refers more obliquely to the unity of genders: "'*Vayyitsar*'—two natures/forms/*y'tsirot*, a nature for Adam and a nature for Chavah". Similarly, *BR* 14:7, interpreting the statement that the human was created "dirt from the ground / *afar min ha'adamah*", explains: "'*Afar*'—male, '*adamah*'—female". For further analysis, see David Aaron, "Imagery of the Divine and the Human: On the Mythology of Genesis Rabba 8 §1", *The Journal of Jewish Thought and Philosophy* 5 (1995): 1–62.

[246] These traditions may also be conjoined with *midrashim* about *Adam Harishon* being created single. See p.114.

[247] My understanding that these are two separate positions is consistent with how I deal with terminological differences elsewhere. Boyarin, however, believes Shmuel bar Nachmani's statement is "best understood as a specification and interpretation" of Yirmiyah's (*Carnal Israel: Reading Sex in Talmudic Culture* [Berkeley: University of California Press, 1993], 43).

[248] TB *B'rakhot* 61a and `*Eruvin* 18a.

[249] Following this line of thought, it is even possible to imagine that "tail" represents the clitoris. While this interpretation may seem far-fetched, it yields a coherent reading of the aggadah. The tail would represent the elemental "animal" (as in the midrash that says Adam's tail was removed "for the sake of [his] honor/*kavod*", *BR* 14:10). Thus there may be a (not especially positive) teaching about female sexuality hidden within this idea. On *androginos* vs. *du-par'tsufin* in Kabbalah, see n.620.

[250] *BR* 17:2; Theodor, 152 || *Y'vamot* 63a; *YSh* 1:23: "is not even human". More generally, Adam is understood to include male and female, as in: "Where do we find [in scripture] that Chavah is called 'Adam'? 'Like the glory of Adam, to dwell [in the] house' [Is 44:13]." (*BR* 21:2 – "house" is understood to mean wife or woman.)

Physical and behavioral interpretations of tselem 81

We must read the preceding verse to get the full intent of Chiya bar Gomdi's teaching. To be *adam* in Genesis 5:1 means to be created in God's image. In 5:2, this *adam* is emphatically male and female together.

The emphasis up to this point is on the *sh'leymut*, or wholeness, of the couple as being in the divine image, rather than on the numerical increase of God's image through childbearing. Together, male and female constitute the image of God, independent of whether they reproduce. The ending of this passage, however, connects the image of God to reproduction: "And there are those who say he even diminishes the likeness, for it says: 'In Elohim's image He made the *adam*' [Gn 9:6]. What's written after it? 'Bear fruit and multiply'."[251]

While only male subjects are addressed by this passage, the general thrust is that any person who lives without the unity of male and female diminishes his or her own humanity and his or her capacity to reflect the divine image.[252] The following passage makes this point directly:

R' Simlai said to them: In the past Adam was created from the *adamah* and Chavah was created from the *adam*. From here and onward, "in our image as our likeness"—not man without woman and **not woman without man**, and not both of them without Shekhinah (God's presence).[253]

One may read this passage to be saying that the creation of God's likeness requires woman, man, and the Shekhinah, the indwelling or immanent aspect of God.[254] *Tselem* would then include both male and female, on the human and divine levels. Lorberbaum even contends that this tradition "makes no distinction between '[God's] image' and 'Shekhinah'; the opposite: it equates them!"[255] If so, the (divine) female would be the primary image of God.

Bi-genderedness as a kind of wholeness is taken to be an essential dimension of humanity here and in other passages. However, many teachings associating reproduction with God's image do not include this theme of wholeness. For example:

---

[251] It is possible that the ending, concerned with reproduction, is assimilated from other passages. Cf. *TB Y'vamot* 62b–63a, which includes the rest of the midrash without this ending (which appears separately a page later).

[252] How this might apply to the diversity of sexual orientations is discussed briefly further on. See n.629 on this issue in Kabbalah.

[253] *BR* 8:9 ‖ *BR* 22:2; *TY B'rakhot* 1:9; *YSh* 1:14 reads "from the beginning" rather than "in the past".

[254] However, one may also read it in line with *TB Nidah* 31a (see p.170), where a person's "father seeds the white from which [comes] bones... his mother seeds redness from which [comes] skin and flesh... and the Holy One puts in him spirit and *n'shamah*...", in which case the divine image would be derived solely from Shekhinah.

[255] *Tselem Elohim*, 393. Though the main point of the passage is to explain the plural "our image" in terms of the divine–human partnership in reproduction, this is a strong *asmakhta* (homiletical support) for my reading.

Anyone who makes void (neglects) bearing fruit and multiplying, [it is] as if he diminished the likeness. What is the reason? "For in Elohim's image He made the human" [Gn 9:6] and it's written after, "and you, bear fruit and multiply" [Gn 9:7].[256]

So we have two separate threads of interpretation, one focused on sexual or marital union, the other on reproduction.

In all three cases where *tselem* is mentioned in the Torah, procreation is also mentioned. This underlines the importance of the second thread. In fact, the theme of wholeness through union does not seem to appear in early midrash independently from the theme of reproduction. So it is unclear whether in Midrash the union of genders should be considered in itself a reflection of God's image or simply the means of creating more divine images through the mechanism of reproduction.[257]

Despite this ambiguity, there are other statements strongly linking human sexuality with divinity, even within *B'rei'shit Rabbah*, where it is taught that humans mate face-to-face because "the Shekhinah speaks with them".[258] Furthermore, for Kabbalah the unification of male and female is considered the essence of God's image (see "Male and Female", p.193ff.).

A modern use of Midrash

The connection between the androgyny of the first human and the image of God has become important in Christian, Jewish, and secular interpretations of scripture, both psychological and feminist. The idea that both male and female were present in one body, and that this bi-gendered state images God, can be used homiletically not only to transcend the binaries and hierarchies of gender, but also to introduce the idea of diversity into God's image.

In contemporary Jewish practice, the connection between androgyny and *tselem* has also become the basis for a new morning blessing in "gender-

---

[256] BR 34:14; Theodor, 326. This teaching is given in the name of R' Elazar ben Azaryah. Similar teachings are found in *Tosefta Y'vamot* 8:5 (the oldest version), TB *Y'vamot* 63b, and elsewhere (see Theodor).

[257] Reproduction of course may itself be regarded as something more than a mechanism. Mopsik, for example, interprets the Midrash to be saying,

> The fundamental role of the sexual act is not to fulfill a natural drive, or to be part of normal physical life, but to perpetuate the relationship between Creator and creation by extending the image of God through successive generations... [N]o other natural process... give[s] the Creator the chance to take part [in] his creation again. (*Sex of the Soul: The Vicissitudes of Sexual Difference in Kabbalah*, trans. Daniel Abrams [Los Angeles: Cherub Press, 2005], 61; also see 55ff.)

> Lorberbaum even more strongly emphasizes the purpose of humanity to be the multiplication of God's image (*Tselem Elohim*, 386–97). For Lorberbaum's purposes this is an important finding, while for ecotheology it is less so. While I appreciate Lorberbaum's approach, his inclusion of *Sifra Q'doshim* 4:12 under this rubric (see n.336) seems debatable.

[258] BR 20:3, discussed next section.

sensitive" prayerbooks: "Blessed be You... who made me *b'tsalmo*".[259] This blessing takes the place of two blessings related to gender in the traditional prayerbook: "Blessed be You... who did not make me a woman" (for a man) and "Blessed be You... who made me according to His will" (for a woman). The unified blessing substitutes for both, expressing a revaluing of gender.[260]

The passages cited here provide a basis for this modern interpretation of *tselem*, though one really needs to look to Kabbalah to find this idea fully spelled out. Within the Jewish Renewal movement, in fact, this blessing is interpreted as expressing the Kabbalistic idea. To the Midrash, one must add the concept that every person is on a psychospiritual level both male and female.[261]

This feminist reconstruction of the idea of God's image is an especially good model for the ecological reconstructions discussed in this work, since it is rooted solidly in older texts while addressing present and future needs. One way to frame the ecological question is to ask whether the diversity of gender that the Midrash already sees included in *tselem Elohim* can serve as a model for including an even greater diversity in *tselem Elohim* that will embrace other creatures.

Tselem, sexuality, snakes, and dolphins

The previous interpretations of gender/sexuality are premised on the idea that gender and sexuality are expressed in unique ways in the human species. In this section, I will focus on the extension of this uniqueness to specific animal species. In the discussion about animal fertility at *Bavli B'khorot* 8a, the *stam* (anonymous voice that connects material in Talmudic argumentation) proposes that species which share the same gestational period and fertile time or time of intercourse can interbreed, adding that while all other creatures have intercourse face to back, three have intercourse "face-to-face / *panim k'neged panim*, and these are: fish and human and snake / *dag v'adam v'nachash*". The Gemara asks, "How are these three different?" and answers, "When Rav Dimi came [he said]: In the West they say: [It's] because the Shekhinah speaks with them." A close parallel is found in *B'rei'shit Rabbah* 20:3, which simply

---

[259] *Siddur Sim Shalom* (ed. Harlow [New York: Rabbinical Assembly, 1985], 10), a Conservative-movement prayerbook, is one place where this blessing appears. Saying "in **His** image" of course reinscribes gender hierarchy.

[260] See Robert Gordis, "'In His Image': A New Blessing, an Old Truth", *Conservative Judaism* 40:1 (1987): 81–5. Though the blessing can be read as a reflection of the idea that the first human was *du-par'tsufim*, it can also be read as erasing gender altogether.

[261] This idea is also found in Kabbalah (e.g., TZ 56, 89b: "there is no creature that is not male and female... and when the male rules over the female, it is male, and when the female rules over the male, it is female"), though the modern interpretation tends to be more Jungian. See Seidenberg, "The Body in Kabbalah: A Study in the Process of Jewish Renewal", *New Menorah* (Summer 2003), www.theshalomcenter.org/node/127.

says, "three have intercourse face-to-face, because the Shekhinah speaks with them."

Mating face-to-face in human beings is, physiologically speaking, a consequence of our upright stature (see p.89), and standing upright is connected with *tselem*. The midrash doesn't actually explain the connection between face-to-face intercourse and speaking with the Shekhinah, but human sexual union is explicitly connected with God's image as well as with Shekhinah in *B'rei'shit Rabbah* 8:9, quoted earlier, which reads, "'In our image as our likeness'—not man without woman and not woman without man, and not both of them without Shekhinah." The Shekhinah "speaking with" humans can be understood as a more emphatic statement of the idea that reproduction in God's likeness cannot happen "without Shekhinah".

While the Gemara is only discussing animal fertility, a parallel text in *B'rei'shit Rabbah* states that the snake in Eden shared other unique attributes with Adam as well. The snake was created "ruler over beast and animal / *melekh `al hab'heimah v`al hachayah*" and "erect like Adam / *qom'miyut k'adam*" – both traits connected with *tselem*.[262] According to the Midrash, the snake sexually desired Chavah and tempted her in order to accomplish this desire; that idea is fleshed out in the image of the snake as an animal with legs and hands that stood upright and spoke.

The sexual parallel between snakes and humans is rooted in this interpretation. However, the mythical snake of Eden lost the other qualities that made it resemble Adam – specifically its legs and erect stature, its rulership, and its ability to speak – when it was cursed as punishment for inciting human beings to eat from the forbidden tree. It appears that the rabbis saw the way snakes mate as the one quality remaining that might remind us of what the snake once was.[263]

In *B'rei'shit Rabbah* 20:3, the prooftexts showing that the Shekhinah speaks with people, snakes, and fish are brought from verses about Adam and the snake in the garden, and about the fish in the book of Jonah.[264] Thus, *dag* does not mean every fish, but the species or type of "great fish" that swallowed Yonah (Jonah), that is, a whale.[265] Cetaceans, or whatever legendary creatures might have been associated with cetaceans, shared some kind of status, as it were, with humans (and snakes). Aristotle had already compared the mating of snakes, fish, and cetaceans as well, noting that they mate "belly to belly",

---

[262] 20:5. *BR* 19:1 also explains that the snake stands like a reed / `omed k'qaneh*.
[263] According to *B'khorot* 8b, snakes also have sexual intercourse ("use" each other) when the female is pregnant, "like people /k'adam*".
[264] Gn 3:14,17 and Jo 2:11. In each verse, YHVH is speaking with the animal or human, so YHVH is being equated with Shekhinah. One might wonder whether the passage only applies to these legendary animals, but the biological concerns of *BR* show that it is speaking more broadly about species.
[265] Also Rashi, *TB B'khorot* 8a, s.v. *sh'khinah imahem*.

Physical and behavioral interpretations of tselem   85

so this may have been a commonplace idea in the time of the rabbis.[266] The inclusion of the snake among creatures that mate face-to-face further reinforces the connection between God's image and these creatures.

Another passage in *Bavli B'khorot* 8a repeats this trope of a sea creature that shares some distinctive quality of sexuality with humans. The text simply reads, "The *dolfinin* bear fruit and multiply like the children of Adam. What are *dolfinin*? Said R' Yehudah: People (lit. 'children') of the sea / sea beings / *b'ney yama*." It is not certain which animals are referred to here, but the word *delfinus* or *delfus*, presumably the source for this term in the Talmud, meant dolphin in both Latin and Greek. That dolphins are like people in some important sense is reflected in their sexual or reproductive lives. Rashi's interpretation is that this means they can actually mate with humans,[267] while in Louis Ginzberg's restatement of the passage, he explains that dolphins "represent humankind in water".[268]

Biologically, a comparison between the reproduction of dolphins and humans is not far-fetched. Dolphins mate in any time or season, "face-to-face" (i.e., belly-to-belly). We might use Bruce Bagemihl's concept of "biological exuberance" for the way in which sexuality in both species serves purposes of play and intimacy rather than just reproduction (though Bagemihl argues that non-utilitarian sexual expression is part of the sexuality of most animals).[269] Dolphins also give birth to a single individual after a gestation period of eleven or twelve months, relatively comparable to human beings. Whether the connections made between the sexuality of cetaceans and humans arose from some experience with their biology, or from the image of some mythical humanoid creature, or both, in the rabbinic imagination there were living sea creatures, *tachtonim*, that were comparable to human beings.

---

[266] *The History of Animals*, 540b, ll.1–7; Barnes, vol.1, 854. See also *The Generation of Animals* I, chs.9 and 10, 718b, ll.28–36; Barnes, vol.1, 1116. On the contrast between the equality of male and female described in Aristotle's scientific works and the inequality in his political works, see Marguerite Deslauriers, "Sex and Essence in Aristotle", in *Feminist Interpretations of Aristotle*, ed. Cynthia A. Freeland (University Park PA: Penn State University Press, 1993), 158–61.

[267] Rashi's version of the text is "dolphins bear fruit and multiply *from* the children of Adam". He explains that if people have intercourse with dolphins, impregnation occurs, and that "people of the sea" means that dolphins are "half the form of a person / *tsurat adam* and half the form of a fish" (i.e., mermaids).

[268] *Legends of the Jews* (Philadelphia: JPS, 1992), 19, quoted in Loevinger, "Deep Ecology", 48. Loevinger comments, "[I]t should be fairly easy to show that dolphins have intrinsic value, and should be left alone to pursue whatever it is that makes dolphins happy. Even the writers of the midrash seem to have known that dolphins are special and unusual animals." Some contemporary researchers come to a similar conclusion. See Diana Reiss, *The Dolphin in the Mirror: Exploring Dolphin Minds and Saving Dolphin Lives* (New York: Houghton Mifflin Harcourt, 2011).

[269] *Biological Exuberance: Animal Homosexuality and Natural Diversity* (New York: St. Martin's Press, 1999). Any discussion of sexual diversity in other species must consult this remarkable book.

Returning to our first text in Chapter 1, *B'rei'shit Rabbah* 8:11 implies that sexuality in general is unrelated to God's image, while at 8:9 it affirms the presence of the Shekhinah in human sexuality. The obvious harmonization of these texts would be to assume that human sexuality is not like the sexuality of any other creature. But if snakes and whales are like humans in this respect, that cannot be correct.[270]

The Midrash already teaches that the angels, sun, and stars are connected to God's image; these *midrashim* would open the door homiletically to including "higher animals" in the list (for the rabbis, because of the influence of Genesis 2, this included the snake). Though this possibility will be fascinating for animal rights advocates, what is really significant for ecotheology is simply that these texts break down the hierarchy between upper and lower creations found elsewhere in Midrash. Such deconstructive acts on the part of the aggadah are not enough of a basis on which to establish a new theology. Nonetheless, these motifs may have provided warrant for some Kabbalists to be even more bold in extending God's image to other creatures.

Lastly, one other midrashic framework projects gender and sexuality onto the rest of Creation, specifically with respect to the waters:

In the second day [God] divided the waters... and why did the Holy One separate them? Because the upper waters are male and the lower waters are female, and when they wanted to use each other (have intercourse), this one with this, they would have sought to destroy the world.[271]

Similarly, *B'rei'shit Rabbah* describes the upper waters as male and the lower as female, saying that when the upper ask the lower to receive them, they

---

[270] Perhaps these texts disagree with the position of R' Tifdai, and all the more so with R' Yehoshua. Alternatively, R' Tifdai's statement that the lower ones were not created in the image could be meant generally, without intending to define every single species. It is common in Midrash to make general statements that sound categorical.

[271] BM, vol.1, *Seder Rabbah d'B'rei'shit* 10, 25. BR 5:4 also alludes to the desire of the waters: "the upper waters didn't separate from the lower waters except with crying" (see also YSh 2:848). Other midrashic passages have a gentler view of intercourse between upper and lower waters, as for example BR 13:13 (next note) and *ShmR* 5:9, which explains that different trees' roots reach different depths and that they are only watered equally because "the upper abyss calls to the lower and says: Rise up and I will come down, and the lower abyss says to him: Come down and I will rise up." These images are rooted in a much older mythos that sees the waters of creation as demonic forces (Jon Levenson, *Creation and the Persistence of Evil* [San Francisco: Harper and Row, 1988]). This range of attitudes toward the waters recurs in Kabbalistic texts. The Zoharic literature embellishes the myth of demonic waters in many passages. See, for example, *Zohar* 3:19a and *Zohar Chadash* 12c (ed. Margaliot [Jerusalem: Mossad Harav Kook, 1994], hereafter ZCh); WZ 539 and 582–3, respectively. *Zohar* 1:32b (WZ 581–2) harmonizes this theme with a positive image of the lower waters, identifying the demonic not with the waters' dangerous flow but rather with the north wind (i.e., G'vurah), which can freeze them and stop them from flowing.

Physical and behavioral interpretations of tselem

receive them "like [the] female...who opens for the male".[272] In Midrash, this motif is not connected in any obvious way with *tselem*, but I mention it here because Kabbalah uses exactly this trope to find the image of God at other levels of reality, building on the motif of male and female as God's image both in humanity and in the realm of the divine.[273]

Tselem as circumcision

Perhaps most astonishing of the physical interpretations of *tselem* is the idea that God's image means the absence of a foreskin: "*Adam Harishon* even came out circumcised, for it says: 'And Elohim created the *adam* in His image'."[274] If we were to take this interpretation literally, then the divine image would have no moral implications whatsoever. The midrash however also means to teach us that Adam was born circumcised as a sign of his perfection or wholeness.[275] This theme would seem to be derived from the story of Avraham's

---

[272] BR 13:13. The upper waters say "receive us /*qablunu*, you are the creation of the Holy One and we are his messengers. Immediately they receive them – that's what is written, 'the land will open' [Is 45:8], like this female who opens for the male." The waters here say the same thing as in BR 5:13 (see n.1047). Cf. *Midrash T'hilim ad* Ps 42:6, 267, where the desire of the upper male for the lower female waters brings fructification and salvation. The same passage later describes the earth rising up to meet the drops of rain. The *Zohar* draws directly on this passage: "The upper waters are male and the lower female, and the lower are sustained by the male. The lower waters call out to the upper like a female who opens up for the male and spills water, corresponding to the male water that produces seed" (1:29b, quoted in Elliot R. Wolfson, *Circle in the Square: Studies in the Use of Gender in Kabbalistic Symbolism* [Albany NY: SUNY Press, 1995], 111).

[273] This motif is also an expression of panpsychism.

[274] ARNA ch.2, 12 || YSh 1:16. The implication that God is circumcised is beyond the scope of this book. Interpreters mostly construed the passage so as to avoid that implication. For example, *Zayit Ra`anan* (*ad* YSh 1:16) glosses it: "According to its meaning, it is possible to explain that Adam was created in his [own ideal] image, for he didn't need any fixing at all." Thus he accepts that in this text, the idea of "image" is primarily physical. *Zayit Ra`anan* interprets the verse as a whole to say, "Elohim created Adam in Adam's image, in Elohim's image He created him", which explains the repetition of the word *tselem*.

[275] Other men said to be born circumcised, based on various words for completeness (*tam, tamim, shalem*) and rightness (*yashar, tov*), are: Iyov (Job), Noach, Melkhitsedek, Yaakov (Jacob), Moshe, Shmuel, and David. Shet is also born circumcised because the Torah tells us that "[Adam] gave birth in his likeness like his image /*k'tsalmo*." See parallels cited by Schechter, n.64, *ad loc*. Later examples of this theme, like *Tanch Noach* 11, understand Noach being born circumcised to be the fulfillment of a sign foretold to Adam indicating the curse of the ground was about to expire.

Seeing *b'rit milah* as a sign of perfection would seem to fit Philo's interpretation of circumcision as symbolizing or actually effecting the diminishment of sexual desire. (In the contemporary men's movement, similar interpretations are used to denounce circumcision.) However, when looked at from an anthropological perspective, circumcision actually emphasizes human and male sexuality. By permanently uncovering the corona, one gives the penis an appearance of always being erect, even when it is flaccid. (For this reason, the Greeks

circumcision: "Said the Holy One [to Avram]: Up until now you have not been whole before me, but circumcise the flesh of your foreskin 'and be whole/*tamim*' [Gn 17:1]."[276] Significantly, these passages, even while they beg the question of why circumcision is wholeness, connect *tselem* to wholeness.

If circumcision is the essence of God's image, this would imply that God's image is not inherent in every human being, and that only Avraham's male progeny are all considered to be *b'tselem*.[277] This interpretation would

---

and Romans considered a circumcised penis to be both deformed and vulgar. See Frederick Hodges, "The Ideal Prepuce in Ancient Greece and Rome: Male Genital Aesthetics and Their Relation to Lipodermos, Circumcision, Foreskin Restoration, and the Kynodesme", *The Bulletin of the History of Medicine* 75 [Fall 2001]: 375–405.) It also highlights an anatomical difference shared by human males and a few other primates, where the penis hangs separately from the body. In most other species, the penis is sheathed within the body unless aroused. (This difference may have evolved because our erect stature creates a need to communicate sexual information visually, rather than through smell.) What is certain is that circumcision does not de-emphasize embodiment, as the medieval philosophers thought. This is illustrative of a more general principle: we can best understand Torah through understanding both our bodies and our embeddedness within the more-than-human world. The difficult question is not "why circumcision?", which makes perfect sense as a compensatory ritual correlated with menarche if used to mark the entry into adolescence, as it is in Islam and in many tribal cultures. Rather, the question is, why does the Torah move circumcision from puberty to eight days after birth? Lastly, circumcision's relation to embodiment is also shown in the use of the term `orlah for both foreskin and the first three years of produce from a new fruit tree, which are proscribed to protect the tree's fertility (Lv 19:23–25). See *YSh* 1:17 and Howard Eilberg-Schwartz, "The Fruitful Cut: Circumcision and Israel's Symbolic Language of Fertility, Descent and Gender" (in *The Savage in Judaism*, 141–76) (see also n.618 on Kabbalah and circumcision).

[276] *PRE* ch.29, 50; *YSh* 1:80.

[277] Interpretations that seem to limit *tselem* to Jews are directly contradicted by Gn 9:5, where it is impossible to interpret *tselem* as applying only to Israel or only to Noach's immediate progeny. Either these *aggadot* were not meant as categorical statements about *tselem*, or Noach's (or Shet's) descendants, unlike Adam's, were all in God's image. Many later commentators take the latter approach. See, e.g., Ramban *ad* Gn 5:3. Note also discussion in *TB Sanhedrin* 59b about whether the non-Israelite descendants of Noach, Avraham, or Yitshak (Isaac) are obligated to perform circumcision.

Morton Smith discusses these issues in "On the Shape of God and the Humanity of the Gentiles" in *Religions in Antiquity* (Leiden: E. J. Brill, 1968), 315–26. Smith demolishes the claim of Jacob Jervell that the rabbis thought only Israelites were in God's image (Jacob Jervell, *Imago Dei: Gen 1,26f. im Spatjudentum, in der Gnosis, und in den paulinischen Briefen* [Gottingen: Vandenhoeck & Ruprecht, 1960], 71–121). While Smith points out many inaccuracies in Jervell's readings, and rightly concludes that in general rabbinic thought does not support Jervell's thesis, he does not adequately deal with these texts about circumcision. Smith also does not cite one other passage that could be taken to contradict his argument, from *ARNB*: "Beloved are Israel / *Chavivin Yisra'el* that they were created in the image. Were they created [in God's image] and were it not said to them, they would [still] be beloved. More love was made known to them, that they were called children to God/*Hamaqom*, for it says: 'Children are you to YHVH your God' [Dt 14:1]" (ch.44, 124). It can be argued that this passage makes no claims about the presence or absence of God's image in humanity (for example, in my reading this *meimra* hinges on the idea that if the Torah had not revealed the story of humanity's creation, Israel would have been able to deduce that they were created in God's image

contradict the normative understanding of *tselem* as a quality inherent in all human beings, and it would unravel the modern interpretation of *tselem* as a warrant for humanism and human rights, as well as the medieval interpretation of *tselem* as the human intellect. While the major voice within classical rabbinic literature affirms *tselem* as universal, these *midrashim* are a reminder that neither scripture nor rabbinic Judaism can be reduced to a single perspective.

This motif would also seem to imply that women are not in God's image.[278] However, as noted previously, where the rabbis were explicit about gender, they understood the image to equally include male and female. Moreover, the Gemara states: "a woman is like one who is circumcised / *ishah k'ma'n dim'hilah damya*".[279]

If these *midrashim* do not exclude women from the divine image, they would still seem to exclude the rest of humanity (or at least uncircumcised males). This motif of limiting *tselem* to a narrow set of people could in theory be used to undermine the hierarchy of human beings as a species over other creatures altogether. However, moving in this direction would deprive us not only of the Judaic foundation for human rights, but also of the possibility of extending *tselem* beyond human beings to the more-than-human world.

Tselem as stature

Another physical interpretation of *tselem* is that human beings are in God's image because they walk upright. This is one of the four qualities "from above" in *B'rei'shit Rabbah* 8:11 that distinguish humans ("he stands like the angels"). *Avot d'Rabi Natan* talks about walking like the angels, with "*qomah z'qufah*".[280] This fits well with anthropology's emphasis on erect posture as one of the most important markers of humanity's ancestors. Other passages indicate that erect posture is significant without specifically tying it to *tselem*. For example, the Talmud teaches that one of the qualities given to humans by God is "walking by feet / *hilukh raglayim*", that is, being bipedal.[281] The idea that the original human had gigantic (i.e., vertical) stature/*qomah* is a related motif.[282] Likewise, it is only because human beings are able to face each other with our whole bodies from head to foot that we can imagine a "double-faced" human being composed of two back-to-back bodies. Upright stature is also the physical criterion that allows human sexuality to be face-to-face and evokes the idea that "the Shekhinah speaks" with us.

---

from the passage in Deuteronomy. However, we would have benefited from knowing Smith's interpretation. Stiegman ("Rabbinic Anthropology", 503) explains this passage in light of the principle that "Israel is the norm of humanity".

[278] Other *midrashim* that talk about Chavah spoiling Adam seem to make a similar presupposition (see *BR* 14:1, quoted p.57).

[279] *TB 'Avodah Zarah* 27a. [280] *ARNA* ch.37; see p.58.

[281] *TB Nidah* 31a; see p.170. [282] See "*Adam Harishon* – the first human", p.246ff.

Not only is standing or upright stature associated with the angels, but God is also imagined to be walking. This is alluded to in the Torah in the second chapter of Genesis, which speaks of the voice or sound of YHVH Elohim "walking/*mit'haleikh* in the garden" [Gn 3:8]. This motif is elaborated upon in the more mystical *midrashim*, as for example in *Midrash Alfa-Beitot*, which explains that the first two letters of the *Alef-Bet* refer to "the Holy One who is the אב father/*av* to all, from [the world's] head to his end/*sof*, that from the beginning up until [when] the world was [still] uncreated, He was walking/going/*m'haleikh* upon the wings of the wind."[283]

A different connection is made between walking and divinity in *M'khilta d'Rabi Yishma'el* ("The Collection of Rabbi Yishmael"), which interprets the verse, "Here I am standing before you there" [Ex 17:6] in this way: "The Holy One said to [Moshe]: Every place that you find the impression of human feet / *roshem ragley adam*, there I am before you."[284] Walking upright is not just an idea or symbol of God; in itself, it becomes a carrier of divine presence.

Another meaning is found in a passage about the restoration of human glory that will take place at the time of the *Mashiach*. R' Chiya explains that people will be "with upright stature, and without fearing any creature".[285] Upright stature is thus connected to one interpretation of the dominion granted human beings (see pp.156–7). According to this interpretation, both dominion and stature were lost after Adam and Chavah ate from the tree.

Interpretations nearer to the modern era connect upright stature, or *qomah z'qufah*, not just with dominion, but with the bearing of a king among his subjects.[286] For example, Maharal states:

You will find that the human alone walks with *qomah z'qufah*, more so than all the rest of the animals... [F]or the human, since he is a king/*melekh* among the lower ones, walks upright, [in] the image/*dimyon* of the king, and the rest of the creatures walk bent over before him.[287]

Maharal also makes the astonishing claim here that "when a person is ninety [years old] he is a partial human... (because) he begins to walk hobbling, and this thing is as if he were no longer a complete human, since the superiority of the human is uprightness, and [so] he no longer has Elohim's

---

[283] *BM*, vol.2, 421.
[284] ed. Chayyim Shaul Horowitz (Jerusalem: Bamberger and Wahrmann, 1960), *Vayisa`* 6, 175 (hereafter *M'khilta*) ‖ *Tanch B'shalach* 22, cf. *Targum Yonatan, ad loc*. In context, the midrash refers to the first time God tells Moshe to bring forth water from the rock. The term *roshem* or "impression" could be taken as a synonym for *tselem* in this passage. On the connection between *RShM* and *tselem*, see p.303.
[285] *BR* 12:6.
[286] Early midrash, however, does not talk about kingship *per se*; rather, it describes humans as possessing rulership (*shilton*). This may reflect the idea that God alone can be compared to a king, or it might be rooted in an innate understanding of the human role as one of steward.
[287] *Derekh Chayyim*, ch.5, 274; cf. ch.3, 142.

Physical and behavioral interpretations of tselem

image."[288] Maharal understands upright stature in a purely symbolic manner here, without metaphysical or moral implications.[289] This does not characterize his whole anthropology,[290] but it does raise an interesting question. If we were to see *tselem* as nothing more than a symbol, this would dissolve the metaphysical hierarchy of humans over other species. Such an interpretation may appear consonant with the goals of ecotheology, but it would lead us in the opposite direction from what is intended in this work, which is not to deprive *tselem* of significance, but to allow its significance to radiate to the rest of Creation.

Tool-making

One surprising fact is that no midrashic text identifies the uniqueness of the human hand, the opposability of thumb and fingers, or the ability to make tools as one of the characteristics of God's image.[291] Perhaps the association of tools with the expulsion from the Garden of Eden and living "by the sweat of your face" [Gn 3:19] closed off that avenue of interpretation.[292]

---

[288] Ibid., ch.5, 274. The Maharal is explaining *Mishnah Avot* 5:21, which describes the stages of education and life decade by decade starting from childhood, saying, "forty is for understanding ... seventy for old age, eighty for might, ninety for hobbling/*lashu'ach*". His unique contribution is to relate this to *tselem Elohim*. Maharal's thinking parallels *Kohelet Rabbah* 1:3, which talks about the "seven worlds that a person sees": a one-year-old "appears to be a king / *domeh l'melekh*", at two and three years one is "likened to a pig", at ten one "jumps like a goat-kid", at twenty – like a horse, when "he marries a woman" – like a mule, after bearing children – like a dog. The passage ends, "When he becomes old, behold he is like a monkey." The image of a monkey implies something like "human who has less of God's image", as one finds in some Kabbalistic texts and aggadic passages like *Bava Bat'ra* 58a, which speaks of the decline in beauty of the generations after Adam.

[289] Similarly, Maharal describes the plague of boils that struck the Egyptians as one in which "their appearance and their image changed, so that they did not have *d'mut* or *tselem*" (*G'vurot Hashem* [London: n.p., 1954], 254).

[290] Most importantly, upright stature symbolizes rulership, but does not literally constitute rulership. Rather, rulership comes through actually "ruling", that is, through intellect and will. But these could not be directly represented by the body, since they were thought of as spiritual, not material, while it is the body that is *b'tselem* (*Derekh Chayyim*, 142, 243–4). Maharal also identifies another bodily quality with *tselem*: "the radiance/*ziv* of the face and its light" (143).

[291] Kabbalah and its antecedents do, however, ascribe special significance to the hand (see pp.199–200, 214), as does Bachya ibn Paquda (vol.1, 165). Several *midrashim* also emphasize that Adam was created by God in a "hands-on" manner. *ARNA* (ch.1, 8) states, "From where [do we learn] about Adam that he was created with [God's] two hands? In that it says: 'Your hands made me and You established me' [Ps 119:73]." Rashi connects this idea and *tselem* when he interprets *b'tsalmo* in Gn 1:27 to mean "with the mold made for him / *bid'fus ha'asui lo*", explaining that "everything [else] was created with speech, and [Adam] was created with hands, as it is said, 'and You laid Your palm upon me' [Ps 139:5], made with a seal/*chotam*, like a coin made by means of a stamp/*roshem*." (In contrast, according to Ps 95 everything is made with God's hands.)

[292] However, according to one midrash, agricultural tools were invented by Noach; before that people dug soil with their bare hands (*Tanch B'rei'shit* 11).

Though there is consideration in Jewish philosophy and commentary of the fact that humans live in a world of human-made things, mutually dependent on each other for the manufacture of food, clothing, and shelter, this is not usually understood to be an aspect of God's image.[293]

Maimonides does underline the connection between reason and craft when discussing the uniqueness of human social relations and interdependence, tools, and art (i.e., *techne*): "one finds in man the rational faculty in virtue of which he thinks, works, and prepares by means of various arts his food, his habitation, and his clothing".[294] However, this faculty, which includes instrumental reason, is not the same as the contemplative intellect that Maimonides describes as the divine image in humanity. Maimonides rejects instrumental reason elsewhere as being something which makes a person nothing more than a clever and harmful animal,[295] whereas in this instance he explains that the rational faculty that uses tools also "rules all the parts of the body", comparing it in that sense to the deity that rules the whole of Being. So it is unclear whether he considers tool-making and instrumental reason to be part of the divine image.[296]

---

[293] For example, Yehudah Hechasid in *Sefer Chasidim* (ed. Margaliot [Jerusalem: Mossad Harav Kook, 1992], 351, §530; hereafter, *SCh*) elaborates how each species' advantages and disadvantages are arranged so as to make all species equal (see n.934). Concerning human beings, he writes:

> And the human has good capabilities in that he dominates/*rodeh* everything, and can grab with his hand a sword and a spear and a bow and arrows and stones, and he can find food in the ground and on a tree and in bird, fish, pasture animal, wild animal, and he rides on animals and chariots (carriages) and slaughters animals to eat and takes their fur/wool for clothing and their skin for his work; and [human] disadvantages are in their [having to] labor, and by the sweat of their face they eat (after Gn 3:19), and this one kills this one, and they steal and do violence to one another, and they are terrified of sickness and death, and sad when they can't do (accomplish) their desire, for one is shamed from (before) his fellow, and they fear the Holy One and the day of judgment and *Gehinom*.

The parallel between the advantage of using hands to hold weapons and the disadvantage of being killed by each other indicates that tool-making is not seen as related to *tselem*. Surprisingly, fearing God is one of the disadvantages of *SCh*'s list but serving God is not one of the advantages.

[294] *MN* 1:72, 190–91.   [295] See p.70.

[296] In this passage, Maimonides also defines the rational faculty as the hylic intellect. Elsewhere, he describes the hylic intellect as the power of comprehension, saying that when a thing is comprehended by a person, the thing, the person, and the intellect become one (*MN* 1:68, 165). This seems much closer to an image of the divine (in fact, he uses this analogy to explain how God comprehends), but by the same token it excludes instrumental reason. Howard Kreisel discusses these distinctions in *Maimonides' Political Thought: Studies in Ethics, Law, and the Human Ideal* (Albany NY: SUNY Press, 1999), 65–7, as does Hava Tirosh-Samuelson in *Happiness in Premodern Judaism: Virtue, Knowledge, and Well-being* (Detroit: Wayne State University Press, 2003), 206–16.

One of the complexities in Maimonides' position is that he describes two divine images within the human intellect: one is the pure intellect that is in God's image, while the other is the "rational faculty", which is in the image of the spheres: "[I]t was appropriate that we

Physical and behavioral interpretations of tselem

Moshe Nachmanides or Moshe ben Nachman, known as Ramban (1194–c.1270, Spain), also mentions human activities that involve craft and tools in his explanation of what the phrase "*kivshuha*", occupy or conquer the land, means. He says that God

> gave them power and rule/*memshalah* over the land – to do according to their will with the animals and the creeping things /*sh'ratsim* and all that crawls/*zoch'ley* in the dirt, and to build and to uproot what is planted, and from her mountains to dig out brass and so forth.[297]

By this he means that people have power not only over the ground itself, but also over whatever is extracted or grows or is created from the ground (as the animals are in Genesis).[298] However, while this power is closely connected to tool-making and to dominion, Ramban does not connect dominion with God's image, though others do. Ramban even interprets "our image" as something that brings us into alliance with the earth and the *tachtonim*.[299] Moreover, he says that *k'vishah* (subduing) and *r'diyah* (dominion) are not the same.

Two earlier examples where a clear connection is made between the image of God and human tools and technology are Saadyah Gaon's commentary on *B'rei'shit* and Shabbtai Donnolo's *Sefer Chakhmoni*. After Saadyah explains that *tselem* means the human "is ruler over all", he interprets each word of the blessing of dominion to indicate another aspect of human power over the other creatures, exercised through the use of tools; God's blessing of dominion includes not only the right to take animals "with fetters, with ropes, with weapons of the hunt", but also the right to dam rivers, measure the hours,

---

> should compare the relation obtaining between God, may He be exalted, and the world to that obtaining between the acquired intellect and man; this intellect is not a faculty in the body but is truly separate from the organic body and overflows toward it. We should have compared, on the other hand, the rational faculty to the intellects of the heavens, which are in bodies" (MN 1:72, Kafich, 132, and Pines, 193). The rational faculty is only reflective of the intellect of the spheres when coupled with contemplation; otherwise, it has no relation to them at all.

[297] *ad* Gn 1:28. He also states, *ad* Gn 1:26, "the language of *r'diyah* [means] the rule of the lord over his servant".

[298] Fish and birds do not originate from the land according Gn 1:20 (and both are created from the sea according to *PRE* ch.9, 15), so Ramban derives dominion over them separately from (land) animals (*ad* Gn 1:28, on *urdu vid'gat hayam*; cf. Saadyah Gaon, n.300).

[299] Ramban explains *tselem* in the same place (*ad* Gn 1:26) as follows:

> [God] said about the human, "Let us make", as if to say... I and the earth, we will make Adam, for the earth will bring forth the body from her elements, like she did with the animals / *biv'heimah uv'chayah*, as it's written: "*Hashem Elohim* formed the human, dirt from the ground", and He would give the *ru'ach* from His exalted mouth / *pi `elyon*... and it said "in our image, as our likeness" because [the human] would resemble the two of them... and here, the human resembles the lower ones and the upper ones in form/beauty/*to'ar* and majesty... in wisdom and in knowledge and in the ability for action / *kishron hama`aseh*, and in likeness truly, for his body would be like the lower ones and his soul/*nafsho* like the upper ones.

plow the land, extract gold, eat animal flesh, and many other things.[300] Donnolo more subtly writes that human actions can in some ways resemble God's actions, both in the sense that God grants the prophets the power to perform miracles and in the sense that, just as God built and sustains the world, so too do people sustain their households, "build and found... and sow and grow and plant and do".[301]

Saadyah's perspective is also not strongly reflected in later medieval texts.[302] The theme's relative absence from other commentaries furnishes us with a powerful argument that we need not affirm the modernist idea that technological power elevates humanity above Nature in a metaphysical sense. There could be no clearer contradiction than this to Bacon's call for a science and technology that would allow "the human race to recover that right over nature which

[300] Quoted by Jeremy Cohen in *"Be Fertile and Increase"*, 184–5, and "On Classical Judaism and Environmental Crisis" in Yaffe, 76–7. (I combine these overlapping quotations here.) After Saadyah explains that *tselem* means the human "is ruler over all", he interprets each word of the blessing of dominion as indicating another aspect of human power and tool use:

The word *v'yirdu* ("they shall dominate [Cohen: rule]") includes the entire range of devices with which man rules over the animals... with fetters and bridles... with ropes... with weapons of the hunt... [and] with cages... The word *vid'gat* ("over the fish") includes the stratagems for catching fish... their consumption, the extraction of pearls... the use of... skin and bones... and He added the word *hayam* ("of the sea") to include man's subjugation of water; for he finds it within the ground and raises it out... And thus he dams rivers... and he uses it to power mills... and [it hints at] the construction of ships and boats... And His word *uv'of* ("and over the birds") corresponds to... snares... the process of taming... the preparation of them for foods... and potions. And He added *hashamayim* ("of the sky") to include the ability of man to understand the heavenly sphere and its composition... and to prepare... instruments for measuring the hours... And with the word *uvab'heimah* ("and over the cattle") He gave him authority to lead and... to make use of them all, to eat the flesh... to heal from that which is medicinal, to ride on those suited for riding like mules, and to know all their diets, that is, how to feed them. And the words *uv'khol ha'arets* ("and over the whole earth") hint at... building houses, fortresses and battlements... plowing the land... sowing diverse seeds... extracting gold, silver, iron and copper... fashioning utensils and jewels... [and] tools for agricultural work... for carpentry... for the weaving of cloth... and for writing utensils... And with the words *uv'khol haremes* ("and over all the creeping things") he gave man [understanding] to confine bees in hives to make honey for him (Hebrew added)

Cohen remarks, "in their length and elaboration of dominion Saadyah's comments are exceptional" (*"Be Fertile and Increase"*, 186). It is also exceptional and significant that Saadyah combines practical intelligence and tool-making with "the ability to understand the heavenly sphere", which in other commentators is associated with attaining knowledge of the divine.

[301] *Sefer Chakhmoni*, a commentary on *Sefer Y'tsirah*, one of the earliest mystical texts, published with *Sefer Y'tsirah* (Jerusalem, 1961), 127.

[302] Perhaps Maimonides' strong objections to this perspective moderated others from adopting it wholesale. Saadyah is, however, cited for his views on the superiority of humanity over other creatures. See, e.g., Shimon ben Tsemach Duran (1361–1444, Spain, Algeria), *Magen Avot* (Brooklyn NY: Light Publishing, 1946) *ad Mishnah Avot* 3:14, 50b. Duran also says that *tselem Elohim* means the image that is the most honored in Creation, rather than the image of the divine.

Physical and behavioral interpretations of tselem

belongs to it by divine bequest."[303] If technological power is not an essential part of dominion or of God's image, then there is no "divine right over nature" in Bacon's sense.

A connection between God's image and the use of tools can be found in more modern texts, as for example in Pinchas Eliyahu Hurwitz of Vilna's book *Sefer Hab'rit* ("The Book of the Covenant"), which appeared in 1797:

> The substance/*mahut* of "loving [one's] fellows/neighbors" is that a person should love [every member of] the whole human species, from whatever people he might be and whatever language he might be, because he is a human in His (God's) likeness and in His image like himself, and engaged in settling the world or building or plowing... or selling or whatever craftwork... for the needs of the world... and he prepares the world/*teivel* through his wisdom and perceives and researches and he fashions/*taqein* wondrous tools and works through the idea in his heart that he works on.[304]

Sefer Hab'rit connects the work people do with the completion of the world: "For by means of these things the world/`olam* stands, according to its order/fixing/perfection /*k'tiquno*, and it sustains itself in its wholeness, and all things are found 'that Elohim created to do' and that he (the person) did, and 'here, very good' are they for every human being."[305]

This text is the earliest precedent that I have found for the modern idea of *tiqun `olam* (*tikkun olam*), that is, the idea that human beings have an imperative to perfect or fix the world through tangible action in the social realm.[306] The idea of *tiqun `olam* in *Sefer Hab'rit* is essentially optimistic about both human nature and worldly human power, and it parallels how *tiqun `olam* is understood among contemporary Jews as social justice. Obviously, there are also strong contrasts between the paradigm of social justice and Pinchas Eliyahu's technological paradigm, though *Sefer Hab'rit* does link *tiqun* with love for one's fellow. Both, however, extol progress.

Pinchas Eliyahu continues in this passage to focus on the social nature of the human endeavor:

---

[303] Quoted from *Novum Organum* in Norton, *Why Preserve Natural Variety?* (Princeton NJ: Princeton University Press, 1987), 141. Of course, one cannot deny that practical intelligence and technological prowess elevate humanity in terms of power, and may even be called "Godlike", but this is the exact contrary of the aspect of mind and spirit that Maimonides equates with *tselem*. I do not mean to proscribe what *we* should believe about *tselem*, but this fact should give us pause. See further discussion, p.91ff. There is no question that Lynn White's criticism of Biblical dominion applies to Bacon's use of the trope. On Bacon, see also n.221.

[304] (Berlin, 1797; repr. Jerusalem: Y'rid Has'farim, 1990), 526. The impact of modern humanism is very clear in this work, one of the earlier attempts to integrate science with tradition (see n.91 for other examples). Zalman Schachter-Shalomi first drew my attention to this work.

[305] Ibid.

[306] By this I mean to distinguish both Hurwitz's idea of *tiqun `olam* and the modern progressive idea of *tiqun `olam* from the Lurianic understanding, in which the world shattered first by divine act and then by human sin must be repaired through mystical unifications.

For a human is not formed for the sake of himself alone; the existence of every human is for the sake of another human, like the saying of the sage: all the earth and what fills it were created for the sake of the human species, and [within] the human species itself, a person was created for the sake of his fellow/neighbor.

This text shows how classical humanism, for all its profound good, can devalue the more-than-human world in order to value other human beings.[307] All Creation, as seen here, represents resource material for human beings to use, to the extent that even the phrase "very good" from Genesis 1 is understood as referring to an expansive list of human actions, rather than to the whole of Creation.

In contrast, Abraham Joshua Heschel, on the other side of modernity from Hurwitz, decried that our power to make tools devalued the natural world:

Our age is one in which usefulness is thought to be the chief merit of nature; in which the attainment of power, the utilization of resources is taken to be the chief purpose of man in God's Creation. Man has indeed become primarily a tool-making animal, and the world is now a gigantic tool box for the satisfaction of his needs... Nature as a tool box is a world that does not point beyond itself. It is when nature is sensed as mystery and grandeur that it calls upon us to look beyond it.[308]

This change in civilization's relationship to Nature was engendered by the loss of belief in the organic unity of Creation. That loss is possibly the most significant shift from the medieval to the modern period.[309]

---

[307] While precedents for Hurwitz's interpretation can be readily found, it is not clear to me which sage articulated the exact idea Hurwitz refers to. I am inclined to view this simply as Hurwitz's refashioning of the tradition that each person should say *"bishvili nivra' ha`olam"* (p.117). Note that both Calvin (Commentary *ad* Luke 10:30 [www.ccel.org/ccel/calvin/calcom33.ii.vii.html]) and Luther (*Weimarer Ausgabe*, quoted in *An Introduction to Ecclesiology*, Veli-Mati Kärkkäinen [InterVarsity, Downers Grove IL, 2002], 46–7, esp. 21.346), also expressed the idea that a person was created for the sake of their neighbor.

[308] *God in Search of Man* (New York: Farrar, Straus & Cudahy, 1955), 34, 36. See Ellen Bernstein, "Environment, Ecology, and the Bible" III, *EBR*, vol.7, cols.981–2.

[309] See Chapter 10, p.268ff. I have not attempted to trace this shift, though doing so would be important to further understanding these issues. David Abram does an admirable job of describing its phenomenology in *Becoming Animal: An Earthly Cosmology* (New York: Random House, 2011), 154–5:

[A] conception of the cosmos as an immense interior or enclosure seems to have been common to a large majority of human cultures... There was a great intimacy to this vision of the cosmos, with its invisible but ordered spheres enveloping the earth, cradling this world in their grand embrace... We can hardly imagine the visceral disorientation and sheer vertigo precipitated by [the Copernican] shift, as first the spheres holding the planets and then the outermost sphere of fixed stars abruptly dissolved into a boundless depth. Europeans soon found themselves adrift in a limitless space, a pure *outside*.

Here Abram is working from an analogy of the universe as home rather than as body, but the shift to exteriority and away from the sense of being within – whether people see themselves as inside the home of the universe or as part of the body of the universe – is the same in either case. See also Morris Berman, *The Reenchantment of the World* (Ithaca NY: Cornell

Physical and behavioral interpretations of tselem 97

In order to respond to ecology and to develop ecotheology, we must restore organicism to our theological universe, just as new developments in science have restored an organic view of the physical universe (see Chapter 10).

Tselem as dominion and rulership

It is plausible to argue that dominion is the *p'shat*, the "original" significance, of *tselem* in Genesis 1.[310] One may certainly read Psalm 8:5–9 as a kind of interpretation of Genesis 1:26–8 in this vein:

What is a person, that You would remember him, and a child of Adam, that You would take account of him? And You would make him lacking little from *Elohim*, and glory and majesty You made crown him. You would make him rule/*tamshileihu* over the works of Your hands; all was set under his feet. Sheep-flock and oxen, all of them, and also beasts of the fields; bird of the skies and fish of the sea, what passes over the ways of the seas.

The mention of animals from the three realms mentioned in Genesis 1:28 (in reverse order), and the specificity of the name *Elohim*, bolster the argument that this Psalm is a direct commentary on those verses.

The Midrash also teaches that the animals submit to humans when humans are in God's image:

"And dominate /*ur'du* the fish of the sea"—said R' Chanina: If [a person] merited, "dominate! /*ur'du*" [the animals]; and if not, "they will be dominated /*yeiradu*" [by the animals]. Said R' Yaakov of K'far Chanan: The one that is "in our image as our likeness" – "dominate! /*ur'du*"; the one that is not in our image and in our likeness – "they will be dominated /*yeiradu*".[311]

University Press, 1981) and Carolyn Merchant, *The Death of Nature: Women, Ecology, and the Scientific Revolution* (New York: HarperCollins, 1990), chs.1, 4.

[310] See Jan J. Boersema, *The Torah and the Stoics: On Humankind and Nature* (Leiden: Brill, 2001), 61–7. According to the *p'shat* of the Torah, there also seems to be no essence or characteristic that defines *tselem*; rather, *tselem* is something that structures relationships: between people and animals in Gn 1, and among people themselves in Gn 9. As Jonathan Schofer writes, "Neither [Gn 1 nor Gn 9] specifies exactly what part of humans constitutes the divine image, but both cite the motif to uphold particular practices" ("The Image of God: A Study of an Ancient Sensibility", *The Journal of the Society for Textual Reasoning* 4:3 [May 2006], jtr.lib.virginia.edu/volume4/number3/TR04_03_r02.html). The attempt to define the content of God's image (that is, to give it a substantive interpretation – see n.126), which saturates the Christian and Jewish traditions, is important from a theological and a historical perspective, and that history is the focus of much of this book. But the way the Torah uses this term stands separate from any substantive definition. See discussion p.160.

[311] BR 8:12; Theodor, 65. The vocalization *yeiradu* follows Israel Einhorn (*Peyrush MHR"Z, ad loc.*, in *Midrash Rabbah*, 46). However, some interpreters read *yardu*, "they will go down" – taking the root as YRD rather than RDH. Incidentally, one could argue that this passage alludes to the idea of *imitatio Dei*; that is, if one **acts** with merit then one is in God's image. Jastrow in fact glosses "in our image and likeness" as "who imitates the Creator" (*s.v. tselem*, 1284) or as "the good man" (*s.v. radi, radah*, 1458). However, the *p'shat* is that a person is

According to R' Yaakov, there is an intimate connection between *tselem* and dominion: the animals submit to human beings, perhaps even are tamed by them, because of God's image. If the *tselem* within each person is located in the way others treat them, then these others include the animals as well. But this *tselem* can be lost.[312]

Whether the change in the animals' behavior is brought about through divine fiat or because the animals themselves sense the change is not clear here. However, the Gemara at *Shabbat* 151b states explicitly that "a wild animal / *chayah* does not rule over a person until he appears to [it] to be like a prey animal /*b'heimah*".[313] In other words, when the animals no longer recognize the divine image in a person, they no longer respect or submit to him.

The teaching that follows, also in R' Yaakov's name, depicts God saying, "Let the one who is our image and our likeness come and dominate what does not resemble our image as our likeness." This is a clear expression of the idea that God's image equals rulership, even subjugation. However, Julius Theodor states that this is a later addition not found in any manuscript.[314] Therefore, we can tentatively say that in early midrash, *tselem* is not *equated* with dominion. In summary, both human dominion and its relationship to *tselem Elohim* are conditional and contestable (see further discussion, p.158ff.).

If one looks at some later commentaries, however, one finds that dominion over the environment is sometimes taken to be an incontrovertible human right. Saadyah Gaon provides the most extreme example of this, suggesting that God's blessing and God's image give human beings, from the very beginning of their creation, not only dominion over the other creatures and the power to manipulate land and sea, soil, rock, and water (n.300), but also the right to eat animal flesh.[315] Even though Ramban gives a similar interpretation of dominion (p.93), he does not describe dominion as an expression of *tselem*. (Ramban also excludes eating animals – see p.141. In fact, Saadyah is the only commentator I have seen who imagines humans having the right to eat animals before the flood.)

---

by nature *b'tselem* but may lose that nature, rather than that someone must accomplish deeds or acquire virtue in order to become *b'tselem*.

[312] If this parallels R' Chanina's teaching then one loses God's image when one no longer has merit. One way to interpret the difference between the two is to say that for R' Yaakov, losing God's image must be a consequence not just of a lack of merit, but of actively committing some grave sin (cf. *BR* 22:12, quoted p.156). Jonathan Schorsch notes that, taken out of context, "the one that is not in our image" in R' Yaakov's teaching could be the animals themselves (personal communication, Mar. 2014).

[313] *Chayah* often means wild animal vs. *b'heimah*, domesticated animal, but here *chayah* means predatory animal. *B'heimah* can similarly mean prey animal.

[314] 65–6.

[315] According to Saadyah, God's intention in Gn 1:29 was that the first human beings would *temporarily* be vegetarian, until the various animal species could establish themselves. Of course, the same conditions would have prevailed after the flood, when Noach was given permission to eat animals (*"Be Fertile and Increase"*, 187).

Physical and behavioral interpretations of tselem   99

The *targumim* equate dominion with rulership, and many commentaries follow suit; I presume that Psalm 8 does as well.³¹⁶ Though *B'rei'shit Rabbah* does not explicitly define either dominion or *tselem* in terms of rulership, it connects Adam with rulership: "[I]n the hour that the Holy One created *Adam Harishon*, He made him rule over all / *hish'litu `al hakol* (i.e., over animals and over the land). The cow would listen to the plowman and the furrow would listen to the plowman".³¹⁷ Another section similarly reports (with much debate), "R' Yehudah bar Simon said: Everything that was created after its fellow rules/*shalit* over its fellow... And Adam was created after all to rule over all."³¹⁸

---

³¹⁶ On Psalm 8, see p.97. Some examples from commentaries and *targumim* in *Miqra'ot G'dolot* are: "and they will rule /*v'yishl'tun*" (*Targum Onkelos*); "they rule over all / *sholtim bakol*" (Rashi); and from commentaries on *Midrash Rabbah*: "'*ur'du*'—[this is] the language of dominion and rule / *l'shon r'diyah umemshalah*" (*Chidushey Haradal*, David Luria, 1797–1855, Lithuania); "they will rule / *yimsh'lu*" (*Matnot K'hunah*, Yissachar Berman, sixteenth century, Poland); "the human/humanity is the one who dominates and rules / *ha'adam hu harodeh v'hamoshel*" (*Yafeh To'ar*, Shmuel Yafeh, 1525–95, Turkey).

³¹⁷ BR 25:2. Note that rulership is also given as the interpretation of "fill the land and occupy/subdue her". The passage continues: "When Adam sinned when [the cow and the furrow] rebelled against him... When Noach arose, they rested /*nachu*."

³¹⁸ BR 19:4. BR is quite conflicted over R' Yehudah's premise. The anonymous voice of the midrash enumerates four examples that contradict him: (1) the firmament was created after the heavens but supports them, (2) the plants were created after the firmament but they need its waters, (3) the "lights/*m'orot*" (i.e., the sun) were created after the plants but they ripen plants' fruits (and so serve them), and (4) the birds come after the lights but do not rule them (though R' Yehudah disputes the last example, because the giant *ziz* bird covers the sun with its wings when it flies). Not only this, but the same midrash portrays the snake using R' Yehudah's argument, that what comes after rules over what comes before, in order to tempt Chavah to eat from "the tree of knowing good and bad" (the literal translation of `*ets hada`at tov v'ra*`):

> [The Creator] ate from this tree and created worlds, and He said to you both do not eat from [the tree] so that you will not create other worlds... Hurry and eat so that (lit. "until") He will not create other worlds and those [worlds] will rule over you/*bakhem*.

> Thematically related *midrashim* also do not incorporate R' Yehudah's premise. According to the *Tosefta*, Adam was created last so that "should a person/*adam* be overbearing, they say to him, the mosquito preceded you" (*Sanhedrin* 8:4 || *TB Sanhedrin* 38a). *Tosefta* gives a string of alternative explanations, one of which is that the guests were invited only after the banquet was ready (cf. *BR* 8:6). Though intensely anthropocentric, this reading does not portray Adam and Chavah as rulers. BR 8:1 and VR 14:1 integrate these perspectives, again without incorporating the idea that what comes last rules: "if a person merits they say to him, you preceded the ministering angels (BR) / all the work of creation (VR), and if not they say to him, a fly preceded you (BR), a mosquito preceded you, (this) slime worm/*shilshul* preceded you". (Theodor, 56, excludes this saying from BR as a later addition. Other *midrashim* suggest that the land began generating mosquitoes and flies and fleas only after Adam and Chavah ate from the forbidden tree [BR 5:9 and 20:8, cf. *ARNB* 42, 117], though 5:9 suggests this was a latent punishment for the land's "sin" of not bringing forth trees whose wood tasted like their fruit.)

> Though BR does not in the end endorse the idea that what comes last rules, a passage from *B'midbar* (*Numbers*) *Rabbah* (hereafter *BmR*), a twelfth-century midrash, makes this claim without any equivocation:

Medieval commentaries draw an unequivocal connection between rulership and *tselem*.[319] For example, Avraham ibn Ezra (1089–1164, Spain), quoting Saadyah Gaon, states, "the explanation of 'in our image as our likeness' [is] rulership/*memshalah*".[320] Many *m'forshim* (commentators) agree with this interpretation,[321] and Maharal went so far as to equate upright stature with being a king.[322] There are, however, medieval texts in which other animals share the quality of rulership.[323] Maimonides, moreover, explicitly rejects any connection between dominion and *tselem*, even though he pairs dominion with rulership.[324]

> "An *apiryon* (palanquin) Shlomo (Solomon) the King made for himself" [So 3:9]—this is the world... "its inside inlaid [with] love" [So 3:10]—[this means] that after all the work of creation, He created Adam and Chavah to rule over all of them / *limshol b'kulam*... and so it says, "She sent out her maidens, she would call out" [Pr 9:3]—they are "... the daughters of Jerusalem (i.e., Israel)" [So 3:10], [so] that all the creatures would fear them and be ruled by / subject to them, like it says, "there will be a terror of you and dread of you" [Gn 9:2].
>
> (*Naso'* 12:4)

Significantly, *BmR* equates rulership with the "terror and dread" of Gn 9:2 – something we do not find in *BR*. In fact, "terror and dread" are explicitly not connected with *r'diyah*, according to *BR* 34:12 (discussed p.159). (The first part of the *BmR* passage, quoted n.661, strikes a very different tone. Note that the *Tosefta Sanhedrin* 8:4 and *Bavli*, *TB Sanhedrin* 38a interpret the maidens of Pr 9:3 to be Adam and Chavah, so *BmR* is essentially equating the part of humanity that deserves to rule with Israel.) In any case, if each creation does rule over what came before and rulership is what constitutes *tselem*, this would create a homiletical connection between the other creatures and *tselem*.

[319] Christian theology came to this equation far earlier. See Frymer-Kensky, "The Image: Religious Anthropology in Judaism and Christianity", 324.
[320] *ad* Gn 1:26. On Saadyah, see n.300.
[321] Shabtai Donnolo (913–82, Italy), for example, wrote in *Sefer Chakhmoni* that the human is created in God's image so "that he would be governor and guardian and lord of all the creatures... to rule /*limshol* in the world and to reign and have dominion / *limlokh v'lirdot* over every creature in the land and the seas" (126). See n.879. Yosef Kimhi (also "Kimhi", 1105–70, Spain, France) wrote, "As for image and likeness... [i]n what does [man] resemble Him? In the image of dominion and the likeness of rulership" (*The Book of the Covenant of Joseph Kimḥi*, trans. Frank Talmage [Toronto: Pontifical Institute of Mediaeval Studies, 1972], 40).
[322] See p.90.
[323] For example, Elazar ben Yehudah of Worms writes:

> "And the image of their face: the face of a human" [Ez 1:10] – because Adam of all the *par'tsufin* rules over them all, therefore the human was [described] first... "and the face of a lion to the right" since the lion is (most) important among the creatures next to /besides Adam, for he is king among the wild animals /*chayot*... "and the face of an ox from the left"... an ox is king among domestic animals /*b'heimot*, "and the face of an eagle"... an eagle is king among the birds.
>
> (*Sefer Sodey Razaya* [Jerusalem: Makhon Sha`arey Ziv, 1985] *Ot Lamed*, 148)

Humanity may be the preeminent wordly image of ruler, but is by no means the only one.
[324] *MN* 3:13, 454, discussed p.160. Maimonides does give another interpretation of God's image that involves a radically different understanding of dominion. In *MN* 3:8 (431–2), he describes how the intellect, which is in God's likeness, must impose its dominion over the "earthy matter" that is the substance of the body. In other words, one's intellect should control one's desires.

Physical and behavioral interpretations of tselem

As we have seen, many midrashic passages consider the heavenly bodies to also be in God's image. The fact that the root *MShL*, meaning rule, is connected with the sun, moon, and stars in Genesis 1 (Gn 1:16,18), and is elsewhere associated with dominion, would homiletically support this idea. Other *midrashim* extend the idea of rulership beyond the heavens, to include all the elements of creation. For example, alongside the well-known midrashic idea that God ruled with the angels in creating the human, alternative stories elaborate that all the works or creatures ruled with God in the creation of humanity.

"Let us make a human"—with whom did He rule/*nimlokh?* R' Yehoshua in the name of R' Levi said: With the work/*m'la'khah* of the heavens and the earth ... R' Shmuel bar Nachman said: With the work/*ma`aseh* of each and every day.[325]

Rulership here is attributed to the whole Creation, including the lower ones, who are the work of the Earth. More significantly, in *Avot d'Rabi Natan*, the Earth itself (*arets*) is said to rule with God:[326]

She is called "*arets*" because she ran /*rats'tah*. A parable, to what does the thing compare? To a king that called to his retinue/*pamalya* (*familia*), and one ran and stood before him, and [so] the king **made him ruler**/*shilton*. So did the Holy One call to all that came into the world, and the *arets* ran and stood before him.[327]

Here, and many places in Midrash, the lines that demarcate upper and lower are broken down in a way that creates a homiletical bridge between God's image and the Earth.

---

[325] *BR* 8:3. An early attestation to this teaching can be found in Justin Martyr's *Dialogue with Trypho* (second century), where he adjures the Jewish Trypho to not "repeat what your teachers assert, – either that God said to Himself, 'Let Us make,' just as we, when about to do something, oftentimes say to ourselves, 'Let us make'; or that God spoke to the elements, to wit, the earth and other similar substances of which we believe man was formed..." (*The Ante-Nicene Fathers*, eds. and trans. Alexander Roberts and James Donaldson [Grand Rapids MI, 1985–1987], ch.62, www.earlychristianwritings.com/text/justinmartyr-dialogue trypho.html [June 2002]). (Justin, of course, understands the verse as God the Father speaking with the figure of Christ.) *BR* 8 continues in a different vein: R' Ami says God consulted with His heart (§3); R' Chanina, with the ministering angels (§4); R' Yehoshua of Sakhnin, with the souls of the righteous (§7). The difference between *m'la'khah* and *ma`aseh* in this passage is unclear to me, though following the methodology I have used elsewhere, the different vocabulary should correlate with some difference in the positions of R' Levi and R' Shmuel.

[326] This theme is important in later Kabbalistic traditions. See p.217.

[327] *ARNB* ch.43, 119. See p.272. The passage does not explain at what point or for what purpose God called on the elements or creatures. The subtext may be similar to that of *BR* 8:3. A parallel at *BR* 5:8 reads, "'And [God] called to the dry-place/*yabashah*, land/*arets*' [Gn 1:10]— Why did He call her name *arets*? Because she ran /*rats'tah* to do the will/*ratson* of her Possessor /*qonah*."

III. ETHICAL AND TRANSFORMATIONAL INTERPRETATIONS OF TSELEM

There are two distinct paths taken in interpreting *tselem* as an ethical idea. The first path, the one taken by classical Midrash, is that the image of God in one's fellow human being calls upon each person to act with regard for the other – anyone who harms or despises another human being desecrates the image of God in them. Thus, the image of God represents a notion similar to intrinsic value.[328] This interpretation is other-centered. The second is that the image of God represents a potential within a person that becomes fulfilled by imitating God through ethical behavior toward others – in classical terms, *imitatio Dei*. This interpretation is focused on the self and its transformation. The first sections that follow explore ideas of *tselem* that are other-centered, while the last section explores the later medieval and modern idea of *tselem* as *imitatio Dei*.

Tselem and the other

Blood and the image

The *locus classicus* of the idea that *tselem* teaches us about the intrinsic value of a human being is the verse, "One who spills the blood of the human, by the human his blood will be spilled, for in Elohim's image He made the human" [Gn 9:6]. One very clear expression of this idea can be found in *M'khilta*:

> How were the ten word-acts/*dib'rot* (commandments) given? Five on one table/tablet and five on one tablet [opposite each other]. It's written, "I am YHVH your God" [Ex 20:2] and opposite that, "You will not murder" [Ex 20:12]. The scripture is telling that anyone who spills blood, scripture lays it upon him as if he diminishes the likeness of the king ... as it is said, "One who spills the blood of a human, [his blood will be spilled]" and [then] it's written, "for in Elohim's image He made the human".[329]

According to *M'khilta*, the meaning of *tselem* is embedded within the ten commandments themselves. The significance and inviolability of human life is grounded in and flows from the image of God in each person.

If every human being has innate value, this verse leaves open the question of what happens to the value or image of God in someone who commits murder. Though the consequence of murder is clear – that the killer may be killed – it yields two possible interpretations. One is that the murder of another human is

---

[328] Note, however, that this "intrinsic" value (1) depends on relationships and (2) is not immutable.

[329] *Bachodesh* 8, 233. *M'khilta* includes a parable about a king's icons/*ikonin*, images/*ts'lamim*, and coins. The parallel at *BR* 34:14 simply says, in the name of R' Akiva, "one who spills the blood of a human, scripture lays it upon him as if he diminishes the *d'mut*", while *YSh* 1:299 draws on both. Cf. *ShmR* 30:16, where a more elaborate parable is drawn, which states, "one who kills a person/*nefesh* ... it is as if he removed the icons of the king, and he is sentenced and has no life, for the human is created in the *d'mut* of the ministering angels".

Ethical and transformational interpretations of tselem

so great a desecration that it outweighs the image of God in the one who kills;[330] the other is that the image of God in the one who kills is somehow destroyed by the commission of murder. The latter interpretation is found in some medieval commentaries to Genesis 9:5, "But your blood for your lives/*nafshoteichem* I will seek, from the hand of every animal I will seek it". While the *p'shat* of this verse seems to be that God will seek the life of an animal that takes the life of a human being, Ramban reads it to mean that God may send animals to kill anyone who has killed a human being.[331]

The significance placed upon human life implies that other animals' lives are less significant. Sforno explains Genesis 9:5,7 thus: "I (God) will seek your bloods for the sake of your souls/*nafshoteichem*,[332] which are more important to me /*etsli* than the souls of the rest of the animals [...] and the reason why the blood of a human will be sought after (requited), and not the blood of the rest of the animals, [is] 'because in Elohim's image He made [him]'." (See further discussion in Chapter 4, "Animal Souls in the Rabbinic Tradition".)

Tselem *is greater than love*

A general ethical principle is also rooted in *tselem* according to a teaching in the name of Ben Azai. Ben Azai argues that the ethical demand that flows from God's image or likeness is greater than the command to love one's fellow human being. The earliest version of Ben Azai's teaching in *Torat Kohanim* reads:

R' Akiva says: "And you will love your fellow/friend (usually trans.: 'neighbor') like yourself" [Lv 19:18]—this is a great principle in the Torah. Ben Azai says: "This is the book of Adam's generations [... in Elohim's likeness He made him]" [Gn 5:1]—this is a greater principle than this (than "love your fellow").[333]

---

[330] This interpretation appears to be the *grundnorm* for *halakhah*. Thus the rabbis explained the Torah's prohibition against letting the body of a hanged criminal remain hanging after sunset (Dt 21:23) to be a matter of respecting God's image. See Lorberbaum's analysis (*Tselem Elohim*, 278ff.).

[331] See p.156 under "Animals as Agents of Divine Punishment".

[332] I have translated *nefesh* as "soul" in Sforno, while in the Torah verse he quotes, I translate *nefesh* as "life". This reflects the evolution of the term in Jewish thought. That this is Sforno's intent is clear, for he writes here:

"[H]e was made in Elohim's image"—in the image of the separate essences / *ha`atsamim hanivdalim* that are called "*Elohim*" (!)...[for] he put power into the separate essences, or into one of them, to cause the flow of intellect/ *koach hasikhli* upon every prepared subject, which is every one of the human species / *min ha'enoshi*. And in being a human in God's image, which is his human soul / *nafsho ha'enoshit*... he is an intelligent animal / *chai maskil*.
(*ad* Gn 9:7)

[333] *Sifra Q'doshim*, 4:12, 42b. Ben Azai's declaration, "*Zeh k'lal gadol mizeh*", is interpreted in accord with most commentaries (see Theodor, 236–7, n.12). David Darshan (sixteenth century, Poland), in his commentary on the parallel passage in *TY Nedarim* (9:4, 41b), cites a manuscript that spells out this interpretation: "Said R' Akiva: They said a great principle in the Torah: 'And you will love your fellow like yourself'. And Ben Azai **added**: And it said

Torat Kohanim does not quote the end of Genesis 5:1, "in Elohim's likeness He made him". It is possible that Ben Azai is simply teaching that all humanity is obligated to each other because all are related through Adam. But *B'rei'shit Rabbah*'s version of this tradition does include the end of 5:1. The standard published version reads:

Ben Azai said: "This is the book of the generations of Adam"—this is a great principle in the Torah. R' Akiva said: "And you will love your fellow like yourself"—this is a great principle in the Torah. For you shouldn't say: Since I was despised, let my friend be despised. Said R' Tanchuma: If you did so (despise your friend), know whom you despise, [for] "in Elohim's likeness He made him".[334]

Theodor notes the many versions of this teaching where Ben Azai follows Akiva, and reconstructs the original teaching as such:

R' Akiva said: "And you will love your fellow... Ben Azai said: "This is the book of the generations of Adam"—this is a greater principle in the Torah, for you shouldn't say: Since I was despised, let my friend be despised. Said R' Tanchuma: If you did so (despise your friend), know whom you despise, [for] "in Elohim's likeness He made him".[335]

The exact intent of Ben Azai's teaching is defined in later versions and commentaries. According to one interpretation, which is less relevant to our immediate discussion, "one's fellow" only includes all Jews, whereas "Adam's generations" is greater because it includes all human beings.[336] The other important interpretation, which is relational, is that the principle of loving one's fellow like oneself depends on one's feeling of love for oneself, which is something changeable, while the principle of *tselem* roots the idea of respect and honor in the ground of divinity, which transcends one's feelings.[337]

We can also make sense of the standard version, however. There, R' Tanchuma seems to both unify the two principles and magnify Ben Azai's, explaining that one despises not only the image of God but even despises God. Homiletically, one might say that we need Akiva's and Ben Azai's principles,

---

something greater than this, and so it's written: 'in Elohim's image He made the human' [Gn 9:6]." (*Peyrush Haqatsar*, ad loc. Darshan's interpretation is given in n.337.)

[334] BR 24:7. Theodor, 237, chooses as his primary text: "'This is the book...' [is] a great principle in the Torah. R' Akiva said: 'Love...' [is] a greater principle than it."

[335] Theodor, 237. In all versions, the end of the verse used by Ben Azai is quoted.

[336] See Lorberbaum, *Tselem Elohim*, 398–9. In *Derekh Haqodesh* (Husiatyn, Ukraine: Dov'vey Sif'tey Y'sheinim, 1907), Vidal Tsarfati (d.1619, Morocco) explains Ben Azai's message to be that "all [people] are the generations of Adam, [so] also all of us are in one image, in one *chotam*, in one *tsurah*. We are also sealed/stamped with the likeness of Elohim, and we need to treat another with honor and dignity/*silsul* [due] Elohim, and not to shame our fellow" (391). Lorberbaum believes that the word "*toldot*" or generations, which Ben Azai quotes, is meant to emphasize procreation, though this interpretation feels a bit forced to me.

[337] For example, Ben Azai's teaching is explained by Darshan in this way: "It is in the hand (authority) of a person and in his domain to humble himself and to forgo/forgive his honor, but the honor of his fellow he does not have the authority to forgo" (9:4, 41b).

Ethical and transformational interpretations of tselem

the former based on love for when the feeling of love is there, and the latter based on the principle of universal humanity, when love is transient.

The interpretations I have grouped under "*Tselem* and the Other" are fundamentally relational, and even the last interpretation cited, which approaches the idea of the intrinsic worth of each individual, still does so through the notion of relationship. They differ in this regard from most modern interpretations of *tselem*, which regard the divine image as an objective property of human life that guarantees its intrinsic value. The meaning of being human in the preceding interpretations is manifested by how individuals are treated, that is, by ethical principles, rather than by some ontological essence like the "soul", whose value stands independent from the relationships and interactions between human beings. Other *midrashim* that ground the modernist interpretation of intrinsic value are examined in Chapter 3, rather than here, because, perhaps surprisingly, they are not teachings about *tselem*.

Tselem *and self-transformation*: imitatio Dei

There is one other level of ethical interpretation of *tselem* that is perhaps most important for ecotheology. According to this interpretation, we become like God and reflect God's image when we are righteous or compassionate or perform righteous and compassionate acts, thereby imitating God. Unlike ethical interpretations of *tselem* rooted in the other, here the image of God within oneself is what calls forth or embodies righteousness. The imperative to imitate God either derives from or perfects the image of God within a person. More generally, by doing good one comes closer to some ideal of virtue.[338] I call this interpretation "transformational" to distinguish it from other categories of ethical interpretation, since the image of God represents a potential that must be realized through action that corresponds to or engenders a transformation of the individual.

Most previous scholars have assumed that *imitatio Dei* and *tselem* or *imago Dei* (to use the parallel Latin terminology) are related concepts. The Midrash frequently exhorts its readers to become like God through *rachamim*, or mercy and compassion, and acts of *chesed* or lovingkindness.[339] However, as Solomon Schechter described, all of these texts fall under the rubric of *kedushah*

---

[338] An interesting twist on this is that a person embodying righteousness or compassion radiates the image of God to other people as an exemplar. This interpretation was suggested to me not by any Jewish source, but by Vladimir Lossky, an Orthodox Christian theologian, who writes, "Man created 'in the image' is the person capable of manifesting God in the extent to which his nature allows itself to be penetrated by deifying grace" (*In the Image and Likeness of God* [Crestwood NY: St. Vladimir's Seminary Press, 1974], 139).

[339] The verses that are important *loci* for *midrashim* about *imitatio Dei* are: Gn 17:1 ("Walk before me and be whole"), Lv 19:2, 20:26 ("Become holy for I am holy"), Dt 13:5 ("After YHVH your God you will walk"), Ps 25:10 ("All YHVH's paths are kindness and truth"), Mi 6:8 ("Walk humbly with your God"). The most well-known example may be the following:

(*q'dushah*) or holiness, which is connected to the people Israel rather than to humanity.³⁴⁰ Not one of them relates to or mentions *tselem*, which first and foremost applies to all humankind.³⁴¹ If we examine the evolution of *imitatio Dei*, we can trace the moment when imitating God becomes assimilated to the concept of God's image.

In an early teaching from *M'khilta*, *imitatio Dei* is derived from the Song of the Sea, specifically from the verse "[This is my God] and I will glorify Him / *V'anveyhu*" [Ex 15:2]. "Abba Shaul says: [This means] 'I will be like Him / *Edmeh lo*'—just as He is merciful and gracious, so you be merciful and gracious."³⁴² A parallel passage in the *Bavli* reads: "Abba Shaul said: '*V'anveyhu*'—become similar / *hevey domeh* to [the Holy One]. Just as He is gracious and merciful, so you be gracious and merciful."³⁴³ Even though one could connect the words *edameh* and *domeh* with *d'mut* because they share the same root, the verse Abba Shaul comments on refers strictly to Israel.³⁴⁴ It is only Israel, who is rescued from the sea, who knows God's miracles, who can say, "I will be like Him".

The parallel teaching in *Torat Kohanim* shows that this is the correct way to read Abba Shaul's statement: "'Become holy for I am holy' [Lv 19:2]—Abba Shaul says: The retinue/household/*pamalya* of the king, what is placed on them? To be imitating/*m'chaqeh* the king."³⁴⁵ Only Israel is called to be holy; only

> Why is it written: "After YHVH your God you will walk"?—And would it be possible for a human to walk after the Shekhinah, and wasn't it already said, "For YHVH your God is a consuming fire" [Dt 4:24]? Rather [it means] to walk after the Holy One's qualities/*midot*. Just as He clothes the naked ... so should you clothe the naked; just as the Holy One visits the sick ... so should you visit the sick; just as the Holy One comforts mourners, so should you comfort mourners; just as the Holy One buries the dead ... so should you bury the dead.
>
> (TB Sotah 14a)

> A parallel version of this teaching has import for mitigating climate change: "[J]ust as the Holy One from the beginning of the creation of the world was engaged in nothing but planting ... so you too at first engage in nothing but planting, as it's written: 'When you will come unto the land' [Lv 19:23]." (VR 25:3; cf. ARNB 31, 67, top, and Tanch Q'doshim 8, beginning)

---

³⁴⁰ *Some Aspects of Rabbinic Theology* (Woodstock VT: Jewish Lights, 1993), ch.13, esp. 199–207. Schechter's precision comes from his insistence on describing rabbinic thought using native rabbinic categories. Max Kadushin, whenever he discusses imitating God, follows Schechter, for similar reasons. See, e.g., *Organic Thinking: A Study in Rabbinic Thought* (New York: Bloch Publishing, 1938), 142–3.

³⁴¹ It is, however, possible to read *imitatio Dei* into BR 8:12 (see n.311) and *SifreyD*, *pisqa* 306 (n.440).

³⁴² *Shirah* 3, 127. Abba Shaul's comment explains the difficult word *v'anveyhu*, which he apparently reads as though it were "*v'ani hevey hu*", "I will be[come] Him".

³⁴³ *Shabbat* 133b.

³⁴⁴ The connection between *domeh* and *d'mut* is explicitly made in later literature (see, e.g., Maimonides, quoted p.90, and *Tiquney Zohar*, p.197). *D'mut* would be mentioned if it were intended.

³⁴⁵ *Q'doshim* 1:1, 86a. Note that the verb *m'chaqeh* is not found in *Tanakh* with this meaning; according to BDB, it is late Hebrew.

Ethical and transformational interpretations of tselem

Israel is part of the *pamalya* of the Holy One.[346] The *Torat Kohanim* passage is the oldest of this group of traditions, and we can assume it illustrates its earliest evolution. Not only is there no connection with *d'mut* here (the root *ChQH* is found instead of *DMH*), but the whole point of Abba Shaul's teaching is that the rest of humanity, which is not included in the commandment to be holy, is not called to imitate the Holy One.[347]

As we have seen, none of the earlier midrashic teachings about *tselem* invoked imitating God. In early rabbinic literature, though following, imitating, emulating, or becoming like God are mentioned frequently, they are never associated with *tselem*.[348] Micheline Chaze also reaches this conclusion: "In rabbinic texts, we do not find any explicit association at all between the image of God... and the imitation of God".[349]

The first *locus classicus* I have found that draws a connection between *imitatio Dei* and the image of God comes after the Talmudic period, in *Midrash Tanchuma*.[350] This is fittingly also the earliest text where *imitatio Dei* is applied to Adam rather than to Israel.

---

[346] The earth is also described as the *pamalya* of the king. See *ARNB* ch.43, 119 (quoted p.101 and discussed p.272), where the earth receives the distinction of rulership that according to many commentators makes humanity *b'tselem*.

[347] Visotzky (personal communication, Sep. 2002) believes a connection is made in these passages between *imago Dei* and *imitatio Dei*. On behalf of his position, one could argue that some traditions about *tselem Elohim* are applied to Israel alone (see n.277). However, the fact that no explicit connection is ever made between *imitatio Dei* and *imago Dei* in any early text, while this connection is explicitly mentioned by almost every Jewish commentator and philosopher after a certain period, strongly militates against Visotzky.

[348] Nevertheless, almost every article I have read on these subjects makes no distinction between *imago* and *imitatio Dei*, even when discussing early rabbinic texts. See David S. Shapiro's heavily reprinted article, "The Doctrine of the Image of God and *Imitatio Dei*", *Judaism* 12 (1963): 57–77, which appears in *Contemporary Jewish Ethics*, ed. Menachem Kellner (New York: Sanhedrin, 1979) and other collections, or the recent example (which relates *imitatio Dei* to stewardship) of Frymer-Kensky, "The Image", 334–6. Grözinger similarly writes:

> [T]he Talmudic sages believed that man may become the image of God *by acting morally like God*. The Midrash Tanhuma puts this in the following way: "The Holy One, blessed be He, is called 'Just' and 'True'. Therefore He has created man in His image... that man might be just and true like God himself!" (citing *B'rei'shit* 7, quoted presently, which is post-Talmudic)... For the Talmudic sages, therefore, it is primarily the ethical behaviour which enables man to become the image of God.
>
> ("Between Magic and Religion", 30–31, my parens., emphasis)

[349] *L'imitatio Dei dans le Targum et la Aggada* (Leuven Belgium: Peeters, 2005), 24, my trans. In the original, Chaze Writes:

> [D]ans le judaïsme rabbinique, les deux notions, image initiale et imitation de Dieu par l'homme, ne sont généralement pas mises en relation[...]Dans les textes rabbinique, nous n'avons trouvé nulle part l'association explicite entre l'image de Dieu... et l'imitation de Dieu; l'image de Dieu justifie cependant le respect, corollaire de celui pour Dieu, envers les autres hommes (21, n.28, and 24).

[350] On the dating of *Tanchuma*, see n.128.

"And YHVH Elohim said: Here, the human [is/was like one from us]" [Gn 3:22]— This is what scripture said: "See, this alone I found, that *Ha'elohim* made the human virtuous/straight/*yashar*" [Ec 7:29]. The Holy One, who is called righteous and virtuous / *tsadiq v'yashar*, did not create the human in His *tselem* except in order that he should be *tsadiq v'yashar* like Him.[351]

Tanchuma goes on to debate at length whether or not humans are evil by nature, with God protesting, "You make [your nature] evil!"[352] It concludes, "Even so, the Holy One made the human *yashar*. The evil impulse / *yetser hara`* stood and degraded him /*m'navlo*."[353]

This passage is the only example I have found in what is considered classical rabbinic literature where the terminology of *tselem* is explicitly related to *imitatio Dei*. The fact that *Tanchuma* but no earlier midrash reflects this connection fits with the idea being a product of the Geonic period, perhaps influenced by Judaism's interactions with ethical philosophy under Islam.[354] After *Tanchuma*, this same idea becomes normative in midrash and in the evolving body of Jewish philosophy (see p.70), with numerous midrashic texts teaching that we are *b'tselem Elohim* when we act mercifully according to the "the ways of YHVH".

[351] Tanch B'rei'shit 7 (cf. TanchB Noach 4, quoted p.149). The connection between God's image and imitating God was made centuries earlier by Christian theologians, who taught that Christ restored the image of God in humanity that was lost after the fall. It was also often grounded in the relational aspect of the Trinity. (This may explain why the idea did not penetrate rabbinic thought earlier, when so many other Christian ideas did.) There were, however, Christian authors who drew a connection between *imago* and *imitatio Dei* without reference to Christ, such as Leo the Great (c.400–461, Italy), who wrote, "[W]e shall find that man was made in God's image, to the end that he might imitate his Creator, and that our race attains its highest natural dignity, by the form of Divine goodness being reflected in us, as in a mirror" (*Sermons* 12:1 in *Nicene and Post-Nicene Fathers*, second series, vol.12, 121). (See also 2 Corinthians 3:18.) It therefore seems plausible that later midrashists arrived at this trope through Christian influence. See n.354.

[352] See Schechter, *Some Aspects*, 268–9.

[353] This statement is the *nimshal* or explanation of a *mashal*, a parable, which again discusses the image of God: There was "a king who made a gold image/*tselem* in his likeness/*d'mut*, and he erected it in the entrance of his palace. A bird dwelled on it and crapped it /*v'nivlo*." (The *Zohar* adopts this language – see n.948.) Other parables relating *tselem* to royal images or statues are discussed nn.329, 444. In "The Image of God: Notes on the Hellenization of Judaism", Morton Smith writes, "[T]he prominence given by the rabbis to the notion of man as an image of God... reflects the influence of the cult of statues of the rulers on the Hellenistic world and the Roman Empire." (*Bulletin of the John Rylands Library* 40 [1958]: 473–512; 480–81) On this motif, see Goshen-Gottstein, "The Body as the Image of God in Rabbinic Literature". Needless to say, applying the concept of the royal image to every human being was revolutionary and democratizing. Many Biblical scholars assume that this was also the intent of *tselem Elohim* in Genesis itself. See Middleton, *Liberating Image*, 206–7, and Samuel E. Loewenstamm, "*Chaviv Adam Shenivra' B'tselem*", *Tarbits* 27 (1957): 1–2.

[354] This does not mean that the concept was inherited from Islam – in fact, the idea of God's image is largely a peripheral motif in Islamic theology. However, under the relatively liberal dispensation of Islam at that time, Jewish theology may have more readily absorbed Christian influences.

Ethical and transformational interpretations of tselem

Ultimately, the diversity of interpretations of *tselem* compels us to view the significance of *tselem* as an open question. One of the most promising directions for the evolution of *tselem* is the transformational interpretation discussed in the introduction: that we may know ourselves to be in God's image when we respond to others, including not just human beings but also the world and other creatures, as though they had the sanctity of God's image. Thus the equation of *tselem* with imitating God is a foundation of both modernist and ecological ethics. Which way we turn this idea is more determined by how we need to evolve than by what is the "true" meaning of God's image.

3

Tselem, dignity, and the "infinite value" of the other

A CRITIQUE OF MODERNISM

In this chapter I will closely read *Mishnah Sanhedrin* and other midrashic texts on the worth of humanity that have become the basis for a modernist and humanist interpretation of *tselem* as intrinsic or infinite value. Because these texts are not directly related to *tselem*, they were not dealt with in Chapters 1 and 2. My purpose here is to show that *Chazal*'s teachings as found in these texts differ in important ways from the interpretation given to them by modern readers. Even when they are homiletically compatible with such modern interpretations, one finds that the significance of each individual is tied in rabbinic texts to the significance of Creation, rather than to God's image. What this means for ecotheology will be explored at the end of the chapter.

As elaborated in the previous chapter, the idea that *tselem* indicates the significance of human life is rooted strongly in Genesis 9:6, which states that one person who kills another will himself be killed, "for in Elohim's image He made the human". This is further developed through the midrashic understanding that harm done to another person desecrates God's image. However, unlike in Torah and Midrash, where *tselem* acts as an operator to illuminate the proper relationship between human individuals, in modern theology *tselem* is often taken to be an abstract expression of human value. Many theologians take this argument a step further, describing the image of God as a kind of coinage of infinite value. Irving (Yitz) Greenberg is the most important proponent of this view. He writes, "Infinite value, equality, uniqueness – these are the characteristics inherent in the very fact of being human. To know persons as

A critique of modernism

they really are, to recognize them in all their distinctiveness, is to know them as an image of God."[355]

Greenberg calls these the "three dignities", and through them he develops a Jewish foundation for human rights and other extraordinarily important ideas about inter-human ethics. Here I will focus only on Greenberg's first dignity, infinite value. Greenberg writes elsewhere, "A world in which humans are grounded in the infinite is a world in which humans have infinite value."[356] God is infinite and beyond measure; so too is the value connected to God's image, and hence the value of each and every human life.

I would characterize this way of thinking as radical theological humanism.[357] *Tselem*'s reformulation as "infinite value" is unique to modernity and can be traced to Kant and Hegel via Christian thought.[358]

---

[355] "Seeking the Religious Roots of Pluralism: In the Image of God and Covenant", *Journal of Ecumenical Studies* 34:3 (Summer 1997): 385–94; 387. Greenberg originated this interpretation of the "three dignities" implied by the image of God. Greenberg's importance as a theologian in the contemporary Jewish world, his adherence to Orthodox Judaism, and his well-articulated humanism – which in intra-human areas of concern leads him to a refined moral sensitivity – make him the most important advocate of this position. Steven Kepnes, an academic and Jewish philosopher, similarly interprets *tselem Elohim* as "the infinitely valuable spark of uniqueness within us" ("Adam/Eve: From Rabbinic to Scriptural Anthropology", *The Journal of Scriptural Reasoning* 4:2 [Oct. 2004]: jsr.lib.virginia.edu/vol-4-no-2-october-2004-the-image-of-god/adameve-from-rabbinic-to-scriptural-anthropology/ [Dec. 2013]). I will elaborate on Kepnes's position further on. Greenberg's interpretation contrasts with others that emphasize dignity but do not lead as readily to devaluing the other-than-human, such as in William Schweiker, "The Image of God in Christian Faith: Vocation, Dignity, and Redemption" in *Christianity in Jewish Terms*, eds. Tikva Frymer-Kensky et al. (Boulder CO: Westview, 2000), 347–56 and Joseph Soloveitchik, discussed p.122ff.

While infinite value is a relatively new conception, Greenberg's other dignities have ancient roots. Gregory of Nyssa is one of the earliest theologians to articulate an idea of human dignity and equality rooted in God's image; this formed the basis of his rejection of all forms of slavery. See Donald L. Ross, "Gregory of Nyssa", *Internet Encyclopedia of Philosophy* (Martin TN, 2006), www.iep.utm.edu/gregoryn (Sep. 2012).

[356] "The Third Great Cycle of Jewish History" in *Wrestling with God: Jewish Theological Responses During and After the Holocaust*, eds. Steven T. Katz et al. (Oxford: Oxford University Press), 536.

[357] On the general malaise in our relationship with Nature and the effect of humanism on our ability to listen to the more-than-human, see Christopher Manes, "Nature and Silence", in *Postmodern Environmental Ethics*, ed. Max Oelschlager (Albany NY: SUNY Press, 1995), 48.

[358] The idea of infinite value or worth was not applied to human beings earlier than the Enlightenment. "Infinite value" in earlier times was used in reference to the blood of Jesus. But understanding that this blood was shed for the sake of a human soul, one would be led easily to the idea of that the soul itself has infinite value. The earliest example I have found of this is in the sermons of George Whitfield (1714–70, England, America; www.ccel.org/ccel/whitefield/sermons.xlix.html [Oct. 2013]). In the same time period, Kant ascribed intrinsic infinite value to the will of the individual.

> [A]ctions exhibit the will that generates them as the object of an immediate respect... This esteem lets the value of such a turn of mind be recognized as dignity or intrinsic value, and

Greenberg believes that he derived this terminology from Samuel Belkin.[359]

As a theological version of humanism, this position may adopt *in extremis* the following assumptions: (1) the Biblical proposition that humans are created in the image of God means that no other aspect of Creation is in God's image; (2) since the image of God is found only in humanity, only human beings have moral standing or intrinsic value; (3) everything else can only have instrumental value – even, some would say, Creation as a whole. The over-focus on humanity, which I will refer to as modernist-humanism, can lead to a kind of moral anemia about the world around us, and to a paucity of imagination, so that the only needs we recognize are our own.[360]

---

puts it infinitely above any price; to compare it with, or weigh it against, things that have price would be to violate its holiness, as it were. (*Groundwork*, 33)

Kant is responding to an economic system that gives a price to every value. As he explains, regarding an individual's will and reason in this way violates their holiness. Hegel seems to be the first to apply the idea of infinite value to the human individual *per se*. He writes, "The individual subject is the object of divine grace; each subject, or man as man, has on his own account an infinite value", which he associates with freedom ("Hegel's Lectures on the History of Philosophy, Part Two, Philosophy of the Middle Ages", www.marxists.org/reference/archive/hegel/works/hp/hpmiddleages-introduction.htm [Aug. 2013]). Christian writers after Kant and Hegel who feature the idea of the soul's infinite value or worth prominently in their writings include Charles Finney (1792–1875, United States), Philip Schaff (1819–1893, Germany, United States), Adolf Harnack (1851–1930, Germany), and James Orr (1844–1913, Scotland). See e.g. Finney, "The Infinite Worth of the Soul" (1850, online at www.gospeltruth.net/1849-51Penny_Pulpit/501222pp_worth_of_soul.htm [Sep. 2014]). Orr in particular also equates "the infinite value of man" with the image of God (*God's Image in Man, and Its Defacement in the Light of Modern Denials* [London: Hodder and Soughton, 1905], 27, 261–2). On the influence of Kant on Christian ideas about human dignity, see Ron Highfield, "Beyond the 'Image of God' Conundrum: A Relational View of Human Dignity", *Christian Studies Journal* 24 (Jan. 2010): 21–32.

[359] Personal communication, Aug. 2013. Belkin was the second president of Yeshiva University. Belkin talks about "the sacredness of the human personality and the infinite worth of the individual" in *In His Image: The Jewish Philosophy of Man As Expressed in Rabbinic Tradition* (Westport CT: Greenwood Publishing Group, 1979), 148. Greenberg also cites lectures by Joseph Soloveitchik on the mishnah from *Sanhedrin* and dates his own use of the terminology "infinite value" to a lecture given at Wurzweiler School of Social Work in 1967. The German Protestant theologian Helmut Thielicke (1908–86) developed a concept of the "infinite worth" of the individual at nearly the same time, though there is no indication of influence in either direction. See Karen Lebacqz, "Alien Dignity: The Legacy of Helmut Thielicke for Bioethics" in *On Moral Medicine: Theological Perspectives in Medical Ethics*, eds. Stephen E. Lammers and Allen Verhey, 2nd edn. (Grand Rapids MI: Wm. B. Eerdmans, 1998), 184–92. Thielicke, however, describes this worth as coming from outside the human individual, from God; hence, he calls it "alien". His tone is very different from Greenberg's: "Even the most pitiful life still shares in the protection of this alien dignity" ("The Doctor as Judge of Who Shall Live and Who Shall Die", *Who Shall Live?* [Philadelphia: Fortress, 1970], 172). Greenberg is not wont to describe any life as "pitiful". For more on Thielicke, see p.125.

[360] There are other real-world consequences: of the very many Jewish groups working on social justice and human rights, virtually none give consideration to environmental issues, even though global warming will cause greater societal decompensation and deterioration of human

A critique of modernism

Importantly, Greenberg has been updating his theological ethics to respond to life as "a continuum". In our correspondence, he has written that his current understanding is that "all forms of life have value, dignity, uniqueness. The higher the form of life the more it has these dignities, and must be treated accordingly."[361] Here, however, I am concerned with exploring the way his published theology is used and is reflective of recent Jewish thought. Nearly all modern Jewish thinkers (including Orthodox) adopt a modernist-humanist perspective that devalues the more-than-human world, where the value of the human being is defined over against the value of all other aspects of Creation.[362] Again, in Greenberg's (published) words, "Judaism proclaimed that human beings, created in the image of God, are commanded to reshape the world, to conquer nature for the benefit of humanity."[363]

It is also true that this is not only a modern phenomenon. While my focus here will be on the modernist metaphysics of Greenberg and others, elsewhere in Jewish philosophy, most prominently with Saadyah Gaon, we also find the idea that the whole Creation only has instrumental value.[364] But in a time when our

---

rights and equality, and greater increase in poverty, than any other challenge faced by civilization. It should be obvious that a just economy can only be founded upon ecological well-being. One exception is American Jewish World Service, which emphasizes sustainability in its development work. See Seidenberg, "Human Rights". By the same token, it is critical for environmentalists to recognize that how we treat the more-than-human world is intimately bound up with how we treat each other. As Murray Bookchin, the founder of social ecology, wrote, "[t]he domination of nature by man stems from the very real domination of human by human" (*Ecology of Freedom*, 65), which implies that justice within society is a prerequisite for a just relation to the more-than-human world.

[361] Feb. 2014. Greenberg's forthcoming book on these issues is titled *The Triumph of Life*.

[362] The obvious exceptions would be Abraham Joshua Heschel, Franz Rosenzweig, Martin Buber, and Avraham Yitshak Kook. Kook's work has already been discussed (p.29–30, 38–9). See n.21 on Heschel. Rosenzweig affirmed the moral standing of the whole of Creation and also affirmed that the potential moral standing of other creatures is made real through the process of redemption (see *The Star of Redemption*, trans. William Hallo [New York: Holt, Rhinehart and Winston, 1971], Part Two, Book Three, "Redemption or The Eternal Future of the Kingdom", and the epilogue titled "Threshold" that follows). Buber, however, is probably the more significant thinker for this book's purpose (see Chapter 12).

[363] From Greenberg's discussion of Nature and Sukkot in his work *The Jewish Way: Living the Holidays* (New York: Touchstone, 1988), 105–6. According to Greenberg and many others, "a major characteristic of the Jewish religion [is] the shift from nature to history". This assumption originates in polemics – see pp.9–10, 23, esp. n.29. Greenberg remarks that the holiday of Sukkot "focuses equally on the importance of nature [as on history], as no other Jewish holiday does" and that "[t]his contradiction (!) underscores the divine genius of the Torah; it expresses the deepest values when it transforms a nature festival into a historical holiday... This represents the movement from human passivity and acceptance of nature-as-destiny to a drive for liberation." He is also aware of the questions raised by ecology. He writes, "The liturgy sings of the need for roots and the acceptance of nature's gifts. There are controls over what can be done to nature." However, like many Jewish scholars, Greenberg, in this work at least, was hampered by accepting the dichotomy between history/Judaism on one side and Nature/paganism on the other. See further discussion in *Methods*.

[364] See n.300.

WHO SUSTAINS ONE LIFE: `OLAM MALEI'

Greenberg writes that the idea that the image of God has "infinite value" is "the logical validation of the classic rabbinic statement that 'to save one life is equivalent, in scripture's eyes, to saving a whole world.'"[365] There are two early passages in rabbinic literature that articulate slightly different versions of this statement, *Mishnah Sanhedrin* 4:5 and *Avot d'Rabi Natan A* ch.31. The primary reference Greenberg gives is the mishnah: "Adam was created single/*y'chidi* to teach you that anyone who destroys/*m'abeid* one life / *nefesh achat*, the scripture lays it upon him as if he destroyed a full world / `*olam malei'*, and anyone who sustains/*m'qayem* one life, the scripture lays it upon him as if he sustained a full world."[366] The moral implications of human individuality are expressed most strongly here, in one of the earliest texts I will have occasion to cite. However, this text presents a challenge for Greenberg's interpretation of *tselem*: the value of human life in this mishnah is not established with reference to God's image, but only with reference to the value of Creation. I will return to this point further on.

In the Mishnah, the inner context of this teaching follows an exegesis of the story of Qayin and Hevel (Cain and Abel). At the same time, the outer frame describes how this teaching was used to exhort witnesses to fulfill their moral duty in the trial of a capital offense – specifically, to not give condemnatory testimony unless they were absolutely certain of it. In context, the Mishnah's interpretation of "destroying a full world" is that killing a person is like killing all of their would-be descendants.[367] While the Mishnah makes clear that the phrase "destroying one life / destroying a world" refers to the killing of Hevel and the potential execution of the accused, it is less clear what "sustaining one life" refers to.

The parallels in *Avot d'Rabi Natan* are given a completely different context that makes fuller sense of this teaching. Both versions begin with the statement, "Through ten sayings the world was created" (from *Mishnah Avot* 5:1) – underlining that the value of Creation is the main reference point for this

---

[365] Greenberg, "Seeking the Religious Roots", 386, n.3. Similarly, Kepnes, "Adam/Eve": "What does it mean to be created in the tselem Elokim [*sic*], the image of God? It means to possess the complexity, unity and the infinite value of a world." For both, infinite value is equivalent to uniqueness. See, however, the continuation of Kepnes on p.120.

[366] *Nefesh* in this context means life or person, inclusive of the body, rather than soul. The word "soul" may also be used this way in English (e.g., "twenty souls were lost").

[367] This is profoundly significant for Lorberbaum's thesis about procreation, and allows him to connect `*olam malei'* directly with *tselem* (*Tselem Elohim*, 377). However, I think the connection is only *in potentia* here, and the primary meaning is really found in *ARNA*, cited presently.

Who sustains one life: `olam malei'

tradition. *Avot d'Rabi Natan A* asks, "And then how do those who come into the world need this?"; that is, Why do people need to know that the world was created through ten sayings rather than one?[368] The answer is that it teaches the magnitude of observing the commandments or sustaining a life: "it's to teach you that anyone who does one mitsvah, or keeps one Shabbat, or sustains one life, the scripture lays it upon him as if he sustained a full world that was created through ten sayings."[369] Similarly, when one "transgresses one transgression, or profanes one Shabbat, or destroys one life", one "destroys a full world that was created through ten sayings".[370] This text teaches something very important for our purposes: there are actions like keeping of Shabbat that are not directed at saving another person that "sustain a full world". What is compared to a full world in this *girsah* (version) is not the person whose life is saved or sustained, but rather the type of act that saves or sustains life.

Avot d'Rabi Natan B is closer to the Mishnah than version A. The inner teaching from *Mishnah Sanhedrin* was a response to the textual question, Why was the human created as a single creature and only afterward divided into male and female, unlike the other animals, which were created separately as male and female from the outset? Version B derives the same question from the specific wording of the verse, "Not good, the *adam* being alone" [Gn 2:18], rather than from the general picture of Adam's creation. I read this passage as follows:

"Not good [being alone]"—and then what need is there for all who come into the world that they should come here [this way, i.e., alone]? To teach you that anyone who destroys one life, the scripture lays it upon him as if he destroyed a full world, and anyone who sustains one life, the scripture lays it upon him as if he sustained a full world.[371]

---

[368] In the Mishnah and *ARNB*, the question is, "Couldn't the world have been created with one saying? But [it was created this way] to exact punishment from the wicked who destroy the world" (i.e., to multiply their punishment by ten).

[369] *ARNA* ch.31, 90–91. The explicit mention of Shabbat alone out of all the *mitsvot* is significant, since Shabbat is the festival that celebrates Creator and Creation, and its violation happens through the assertion of human dominion over Creation. *Seder Eliyahu Rabba'* 10 similarly understands sustaining a life to mean giving charity, *ts'daqah* (*Tana' d'Vey Eliyahu* [Warsaw, 1912], 59, also quoted in Kadushin, *Organic Thinking*, 131).

[370] A related interpretation is found in *SCh* 103, §43, in a discussion about *lashon hara`* (harmful speech): "One who troubles a person, it is as if he troubled a full (complete) world (based on mishnah), for everything that is in the world is in the human (based on *ARN*)." See further discussion about microcosm and macrocosm, p.242ff. The application of the Mishnah's formula to merely "troubling" another person is characteristic of the heightened moral sensitivity or anxiety found in *SCh*.

[371] *ARNB* ch.36, 90. The bracketed words in this quote are based on the following reading of this passage:

By ten speech-acts/*ma'amarot* the world was created... [The tenth one was] "And Elohim said: Not good, the *adam* being alone". R' Yirmiyah would establish [as the tenth, instead of this verse,] "And Elohim created the great lizards". (New thought:) "Not good"—and then what need is there for all who come into the world that they should come here [alone]?", etc.

Whereas in the Mishnah, one finds a homiletical interpretation of the Torah's narrative about *Adam Harishon*, I understand the midrash here to be focusing on the reality that, like *Adam Harishon*, but unlike most other animals, human beings are usually born into the world alone, since a human pregnancy usually gestates only one baby at a time.[372] This slight change from *Mishnah Sanhedrin* would strengthen the moral intent of the *meimra*, placing it upon existential grounds.

In all three texts, the intrinsic value of the full world or Creation is the ground for the value of the human individual. These teachings, and all the other teachings in these pericopes (sections), are not about the image of God in human beings, but rather about the image of Creation in human beings.[373] The term `olam malei' was interpreted in parallel ways by Stiegman. I think Stiegman's reading comes very close to the *p'shat* of the text:

> As a human being develops, there forms within him the other creatures over which he will come to marvel. The image corroborates man's understanding of his centrality and leadership in creation; but, unlike its Hellenistic counterpart, it keeps him close to his earthly setting.[374]

This is an extraordinary reframing of what anthropocentrism might mean.

FOR MY SAKE THE WORLD WAS CREATED

The uniqueness of each human individual is also emphasized in these traditions. Again, we read in *Mishnah Sanhedrin*:

> Schechter, however, interprets it differently, attaching the quote "not good" to the previous phrase, and adding the following words in bold: "R' Yirmiyah would establish [as the tenth] 'And Elohim created the great lizards' **and he would delete** /v'gorei`a, 'Not good'. And then what need is there (etc.)" (n.1 to *ARNB*). Schechter's emendation fixes one problem but creates others. Note also that one cannot use *ARNA* to interpret *ARNB* here. The wording is different, and more importantly, *ARNB* has already answered the question "Why was the world created through ten speech-acts instead of one?" at the beginning of the pericope (n.368). It may be that the question found at the beginning of *ARNA* migrated to the end of *ARNB*, at which point a new meaning was improvised. A parallel at *BR* 17:1 includes none of these extra elements or difficulties.

[372] Indeed, some species that bear a single individual at a time, like elephants or dolphins, not to mention apes, tend to possess qualities of intelligence, self-awareness, and/or memory that we associate with humans.

[373] See Abraham Joshua Heschel's analysis in *Torah Min Hashamayim Ba'aspaklariyah shel Hadorot* (New York: Shontsin, 1962), 220–23; *Heavenly Torah: As Refracted Through the Generations*, trans. Gordon Tucker (London: Continuum, 2006), 261–4. Heschel sees our mishnah as the expression of the Ishmaelite school, in opposition to Akiva's teachings (discussed p.102): "Not all the Sages agreed with Rabbi Akiva's doctrine of the Divine Image. Many followed the immanentist approach and saw humanity as a reflection of the terrestrial realm, the microcosm balancing the macrocosm of creation" (222 [Hebr.]; 263 [Engl.]). Irrespective of the historicity of the claim that these positions were held by Akiva and Yishmael, Heschel's perception that the different sets of vocabulary reflect different ideas about the significance of human life is plausible, and congruent with what I argue elsewhere.

[374] "Rabbinic Anthropology", 502.

For my sake the world was created

Adam was created single... to tell of the greatness of the Holy One, for a human/*adam* coins so many (or: a hundred) coins with one seal/stamp/*chotam*[375] – all of them are similar, this one to that one... [T]he Holy One coins every *adam* with Adam Harishon's seal, and one is not similar to his fellow.[376] And therefore, each one must say: For my sake the world was created / *bish'vili nivra' ha`olam*.

This teaching is again not explicitly about *tselem*, though it would make sense to draw a connection between Adam's seal and God's image.[377]

What does it mean, however, to say "For my sake the world was created"? This teaching can be interpreted homiletically to be an expression of the intrinsic value and infinite worth of a single human life, as modern theologians readily do.[378] The context, however, suggests a more subtle meaning. Rather than being about the infinite *value* of a person, this teaching is about the infinite diversity of human forms.[379] Because each person is as unique as the first created human, unique in relation to the whole of Creation, each person can say the world was created for her sake. Each person in this sense is like a species unto him or herself, with as much standing as an entire species (see discussion next section).

One finds yet another understanding of these teachings in a series of statements from the *Bavli*, whose subject is not humanity in general, but rather the God-fearing individual:

Every person that has fear/awe of the heavens, his words are heard, as it is said, "The end of the word/matter/*davar*, everything is (has been) heard, fear *Ha'elohim* [and keep His commandments, for this is the whole human]" [Ec 12:13][380] etc. What is [the meaning of], "for this/*zeh* is the whole human"? R' Elazar said: The Holy One said: The whole entire world was not created except for the sake of this one / *bish'vil zeh*. R' Abba bar

---

[375] Note the use of *chotam* in a way that parallels "image". See further discussion of this term and this passage, pp.302–3.
[376] God's power is expressed through diversity. [377] Heschel, *Torah*, 263.
[378] Greenberg, "Seeking", 386 and 387 (top). See also David Novak, *Jewish Social Ethics* (New York: Oxford University Press, 1992), 145ff. In *Natural Law in Judaism* (New York: Cambridge University Press, 1998), 128, Novak writes that for Saadyah Gaon "man is the end of this purposeful, orderly creation. Saadiah well appropriated a teaching of the Mishnah: 'Everyone should say that for my sake the world was created.'" However, one cannot equate Sa'adyah's interpretation with the Mishnaic statement itself, as Novak does here. While the theme that humanity is the purpose and completion of Creation – alongside other countervailing teachings – is found in several places in Midrash (see n.169), the statement "for my sake the world was created" is not a claim about the species, but about the human individual. See Stiegman, "Rabbinic Anthropology", 500.
[379] Kepnes ("Adam/Eve") similarly explains our passage thus: "[T]he mishna [*sic*] is saying that implicit in the fact that humans are created by God is the value of human diversity. In reflecting on this point the mishna makes one of the most beautiful statements about the value of every human life in all of the Torah." (Torah here means Jewish tradition, rooted in the oral Torah.)
[380] The Gemara reads the verse as though it said, "everything is heard *from the one who* fears God".

Kahana said: This one is equal to the whole world. R' Shimon ben Azai says:... The whole entire world was not created except to join to this one / *l'tsavot l'zeh*.[381]

Here it is not the case that every human individual is worthy of saying, "the whole world was created for me", but only the one who is tempered by reverence.[382] Notably, the last tradition, from Ben Azai, is strikingly different in tone: The world was created to become connected with the righteous ones of humanity. Connection, more than hierarchy, characterizes humanity's unique place in relationship to the rest of Creation, according to this *meimra*.

PSYCHE VERSUS METAPHYSICS

Is the claim that the world was created for the sake of humanity a metaphysical or ontological claim, or a kind of psychological guidance? On the level of *p'shat*, it is always hard to ascribe a metaphysical meaning to aggadic material; this is even more true for the mishnah in question, where the setting, to exhort witnesses in a trial, is strictly homiletical. From our own homiletical perspective, a further question might be, what is the best human context for this teaching?

One characteristic Hasidic interpretation gives a strictly psychological reading that I find both inspiring and elucidating. According to Simchah Bunam, a person must have two slips of paper in his pockets, one of which reads, "For my sake the world was created", and the other, "I am dirt and ashes / *Anokhi `afar v'eifer*" [Gn 18:27].[383] The trick to knowing the truth of our own nature is knowing which slip of paper to pull out when. (It is so easy in my experience to pull out exactly the wrong slip.)

Nachman of Breslov explained *bishvili* in a different but equally humble way: "since the world was only created for my sake, I need to see and look into repairing the world / *tiqun `olam* in every moment, and to fill the lack (needs) of the world".[384] This interpretation is already implied in a well-known midrash from *Kohelet Rabbah*:

---

[381] *B'rakhot* 6b. *L'tsavot* can also mean "to attend to"; Jastrow gives both definitions (s.v. *tsavah*, 1267).

[382] Without context, one would assume *Adam Harishon* was the subject being discussed here, because the first human is indeed comparable to the whole species.

[383] Martin Buber attributes this teaching to Simchah Bunam of Przyscha (1765–1827, Poland) in *Tales of the Hasidim: Later Masters* (New York: Schocken Books, 1948), 249–50.

[384] LM 1:5, 10. Noson (Natan) Sternhartz of Nemirov (1780–1844, Ukraine), the disciple who recorded most of Nachman's teachings, also transformed those teachings into prayers. Concerning this lesson, he suggested:

> One could start by saying in the bitterness of his soul, "wasn't the world created for me?"... He may feel so far from this that it is hard for him to talk about it, but this in itself will enable him to pour out his heart like water to God when he looks at how far he is... because of his deeds. This is how he will be able to start the conversation, and go on to express all the diseases of his heart and pains of his soul.
>
> (*Liqutey T'filot* [Jerusalem: Keren Yisra'el Odesser], intro., 3–4; trans. based on www.breslov.org/bookshelf/gate/tefilo4.html [July 2011])

How far from arrogance are this sentiment and Nachman's interpretation of the mishnah!

Psyche versus metaphysics

In the time that the Holy One created the first human, He took him and brought him around all the trees of *Gan Eden* and said: See my works, how lovely and praiseworthy they are, and all I created, *for your sake I created it*. Put your mind [to this], that you don't ruin or destroy my world, for if you bring ruin, there is no one who will repair after you.[385]

The meaning of *bish͟vili* in these teachings is not that we have the right to use the world, but rather that we have responsibility for the world.

Also in *Kohelet Rabbah*, one midrash rhetorically questions the position of *Mishnah Sanhedrin*. R' Yehoshua ben Qorchah asks, "Who was created for the sake of whom / *mi niv͟ra' bish'vil mi*? Was earth/*arets* created for the sake of a (human) generation, or a generation created for the sake of the *arets*?"[386] The phrase "for my sake the world was created" is also inverted in the teaching that the human was created "from the upper and lower ones for the sake of peace / *bish'vil shalom*"—that is, "for the sake of the peace of Creation I was created" (see p.55). Embedded in the interplay between these differing views is a profound understanding of mutuality between humanity and the whole of Creation, despite the fact that the fundamental perspective remains anthropocentric.

I argued previously that the statement *bish'vili niv͟ra' ha`olam*, as it is framed in *Mishnah Sanhedrin*, may actually be comparing the uniqueness of each individual human being to the uniqueness of each species. Lenn Goodman similarly reads the whole of this mishnah:

Indeed, the argument in the human case is recognized as a special case of the argument in behalf of nature at large and the species it contains. For the Mishnah predicated the special sanctity of each human life on the likeness of each human being to a world or a natural kind... Note the order of the argument: Not, thou shalt respect and protect nature because it is the abode of human beings, but rather: thou shalt respect and protect human lives because they are, in their own way, miniature worlds and complete natural kinds.[387]

If Goodman is correct, then a good interpretation of this tradition would be: The world was created for the sake of each and every species, each one of which is unique, but the world was also created for the sake of each and every human individual, because each human individual is as unique as an entire species.[388]

The direct implication of this is that individual species are worthy of the ethical distinction of being treated as ends-in-themselves. We can derive a beautiful reading of what this might mean by adding a few words to Kepnes:

---

[385] *ad* Ec 7:13, "See the work of Elohim – who is able to fix what He (interpreted as 'he', i.e., *Adam*, in the midrash) has made crooked." See Goodman's analysis of this aggadah in "Respect for Nature in the Jewish Tradition", *Judaism and Ecology: Created World and Revealed Word*, ed. Hava Tirosh-Samuelson (Cambridge MA: Harvard University Press, 2002), 228.

[386] *ad* Ec 1:4, "A generation goes and a generation comes, and (while) the earth is standing forever." The midrash is asking, if the earth was created for humanity, shouldn't a generation last as long as the earth? The answer it gives is quoted at the end of n.782.

[387] Goodman, "Respect for Nature", 228.   [388] On this theme, see *MN* 2:40, 381–2.

The image of God, then, does not work like a mold or mirror, giving us like attributes; rather it is a kind of inverted mirror or prism which gives each of us our unique light. It is a spark of diversity which makes us uniquely us. And if we stay with the metaphor of the *tselem Elokim* [sic] as the infinitely valuable spark of uniqueness within us *and within each species*, perhaps we could gain a deeper understanding of the nature of God. God, the creator and source of difference, uniqueness, value, and oneness, must himself be the infinitely different, unique, valuable and one.[389]

I have added the words in italics, "and within each species". Doing so takes nothing away from Kepnes' vision of the power of individuality, yet it fully incorporates basic ecological ideas. Similarly for Heschel, who wrote "God means: *Togetherness of all beings in holy otherness.*"[390] When he explains these words, he appears to apply them ethically to human beings alone. Yet for us, they may be true in a way that Heschel could not anticipate. These rereadings fit in with one of the more important conclusions of this book: we must expand our definition of *tselem* if we want to "gain a deeper understanding of the nature of God." For, as Kepnes wrote, "God, the creator and source of difference, uniqueness, value, and oneness, must be the infinitely different, unique, valuable and one."

Whether or not one accepts Goodman's biocentric reading and this rereading of Kepnes and Heschel, one element remains incontrovertible: the teaching in *Mishnah Sanhedrin* grounds the value of the individual in the value of Creation.[391]

ONE PERSON EQUALS THE WHOLE CREATION

There is one more teaching in chapter 31 of *Avot d'Rabi Natan A* that relates to the notion of infinite value even more strongly than what we have already discussed. According to R' Nechemyah, "one human weighs equal to / is balanced against / *shaqul k'neged* the work of Creation".[392] While this teaching does not say that the value of each person is "infinite", it certainly assumes that each person's value, like the value of Creation, is unsurpassable. Though the term *shaqul* can be interpreted in several ways, this tradition resonates strongly with the modernist position that the human individual has "infinite value".

R' Nechemyah derives this teaching from the use of the word *toldot*, "generations", to refer to both Creation and human beings in the verses, "These are the *toldot* of the heavens and the earth" [Gn 2:4] and "This is the book of Adam's *toldot*" [Gn 5:1]. From here, one may interpret that this passage is

---

[389] Kepnes, "Adam/Eve".
[390] *Man Is Not Alone: A Philosophy of Religion* (New York: Farrar, Straus and Giroux, 1976), 109. Cf. 121: "Neither stars nor stones, neither atoms nor waves, but their belonging together... all bodies are interdependent, affect and serve one another." Heschel, like Kepnes and Greenberg, brings *Mishnah Sanhedrin* 4:5 to buttress his point. Thanks to Yariv Chen and Fred Dobbs, who pointed out these passages to me.
[391] Much of this argument is summarized in Seidenberg, "Human Rights", 48–50.
[392] *ARNA* ch.31, 91.

comparing the nature and complexity of a human being with the nature and complexity of the heavens and the Earth.[393] Though this teaching also does not mention the divine image, the end of one of the verses used as prooftexts, Genesis 5:1, does include the term *d'mut*. Just as with the concept `olam malei'`, if this passage teaches us anything about the *tselem* in humanity then it must perforce teach that the heavens and earth as a whole **are equally in God's image**.

THE MEDIEVAL REJECTION OF UNIVERSALISM

There is another obstacle in these texts to any humanistic exegesis: the standard published version of *Mishnah Sanhedrin* reads "anyone who destroys a single life *from Israel*, it is as if he destroyed a full world".[394] Either the editors of this version thought that only Jews bore *tselem Elohim* or they thought that `olam malei'` had no connection with the image of God. Either way, such a limitation of the ethical sphere to Jewish people would obviously be anathema to Greenberg (as well as to any ecotheology that would extend *tselem* and moral standing beyond humanity).

While there is midrashic evidence that some of the early rabbis limited *tselem* to Jews, this was not the normative position. Those who did limit *tselem* held that the *tselem* implanted in humanity was lost because of Adam's sin, with the exception of certain righteous individuals, until it was restored through Abraham and his seed.[395] As an aside, this dynamic illustrates how the question of *tselem* in the more-than-human world is isomorphic to the question of chosenness. Just as the Jewish people being chosen can entail the "de-selection" of every other people, so too can *tselem* readily be limited to

---

[393] This reading is borne out by one manuscript, which states, "what are generations of creation and making there, here also are generations of creation and making" (Schechter *ad loc.*; cf. *Tanch*, quoted p.245, where the *mishkan* is "*shaqul k'neged* the whole world and the formation of the human"). Note that a single human is compared to the whole creation in *ARNA*, rather than the human species. It would be logical for this principle to apply all the more to humanity as a whole. However, where we do find parallel language in *BR* (13:3 *ad* Gn 2:5), humanity is compared not to Creation, but to the rain and the land: "Three things are equal/*sh'qulin* one to the other: land, and human, and rain / *arets v'adam umatar*." The teaching that follows indicates that the rabbis here were not making a metaphysical statement, but rather describing *the human perspective*: "if there is no land there is no rain, and if there is no rain there is no land, and if there are not both of them, there is no humanity." Other phrases from *ARNA* and *Mishnah Sanhedrin* are echoed here: "[God's] full name / *sheim malei'* (YHVH Elohim) is mentioned for a full world / `olam malei'`" – meaning that from Gn 2:1 on, the creation of the world was already complete, even though plants had not yet grown and human and animals were yet to be formed. The next teaching reads, "Said R' Hosha`ya: The might of the rains / *g'vurot g'shamim* is difficult, for it weighs equal to the entire work of creation / *sh'qulah k'neged kol ma`aseh v'rei'shit*" (13:4; cf. *D'varim Rabbah* 7:7, *TB Ta`anit* 7a, "Great is the falling of rains *y'ridat g'shamim*, for it weighs/*sh'qulah* as [much as] the resurrection of the dead", and *YSh* 2:287).

[394] See Margaliot, *SCh* 103, n.7.   [395] See pp.88–9 and notes.

human beings or even Israel. Conversely, if being chosen does not imply a negation of relationship between God and "all the peoples" then, similarly, *tselem* need not sanctify humanity to the exclusion of all other species.[396]

EXISTENTIALISM AND PERSONALISM

According to Joseph Soloveitchik's existentialist interpretation of *tselem Elohim* in *The Lonely Man of Faith*, God's image represents "man's inner charismatic endowment as a creative being. Man's likeness to God expresses itself in man's striving and ability to become a creator."[397] Since this understanding of *tselem* does not directly reference the more-than-human world, it does not push us to devalue non-human creatures, even though it also does not provide a foundation for recognizing their intrinsic value. Another existentialist interpretation of *tselem*, from Gedaliah Fleer, a chief exponent of Breslover *Chasidut*, is even more ecologically significant: "Since we are created in the divine image, that is, as replicas of the emanations that are perfect and limitless, we too must *constrict* our existence", according to the principle of divine *tsimtsum* or contraction.[398] For Fleer, divine power, and the image of divinity, can be reflected in the capacity to restrain one's power and restrict one's impact.

Soloveitchik himself, however, also emphasized a relationship to Nature based on domination. According to his reading, "Adam the first" (the *Adam* of the first chapter of Genesis) teaches us that a human being must be "aggressive, bold, victory-minded" and must "harness and dominate the elemental natural forces and . . . put them at his disposal."[399] For Soloveitchik, "man acquires dignity through . . . his majestic posture *vis-à-vis* his environment." Soloveitchik's Adam the first was at least balanced by "Adam the second", the steward and servant of Genesis's second chapter and the lonely man of faith of the book's title, who "looks for the image of God . . . in every beam of light, in every bud and blossom".[400] Even Adam the first may become a steward.[401] However,

---

[396] This raises a critical question: If in the past it has been so easy to radically "diminish the image" by limiting it to Israel, is it then any more radical to "increase the image" by extending it to include the Earth? This also brings us to a point of tension concerning Kabbalah: while Kabbalah is a source for so many inferences about *tselem* in Nature, it is also the body of Jewish literature most comfortable with limiting *tselem* to Jews (see, e.g., p.228).

[397] (New York: Doubleday, 1965), 12.

[398] Perle Besserman, *A New Kabbalah for Women* (New York: Palgrave Macmillan, 2005), 137. On *tsimtsum*, see n.906, and on *tsimtsum* as an environmental value, see Eisenberg, *The Ecology of Eden*, 430, 432.

[399] *Lonely Man*, 17 and 13, also quoted in Sokol, "Ethical Implications", 274. See Sokol's discussion there.

[400] *Lonely Man*, 22. I assume that Soloveitchik is using "image" informally here to simply express connection. If he means *tselem* specifically then there is a huge depth to explore here.

[401] Soloveitchik states, "Dignity of man express[es] itself in the awareness of being responsible and of being capable of discharging his responsibility". Here he gives the example that finding the cure to a disease creates a responsibility to treat people who have it. (Cf. n.408.) If that is

Existentialism and personalism

other thinkers writing in a similar vein have readily adopted a stance of antagonism toward Nature. To give one example, Nehama Leibowitz, in her popular study series on the *parshiyot* of the Torah, quotes Julius Guttmann, who connects God's image with the existential philosophy of personalism. Guttmann writes:

> Zelem [sic] refers to the personal relationship that can only be found between "persons"... Only as long as man is a person can he preserve his relationship with God. [This means that] man is a world of his own and he is not required to merge himself in nature... Man is not subservient to the world. The forces of nature are not supernatural ones that are superior to him. But **he stands on the side of God against/*mul* nature.**[402]

Guttman reworks `olam malei' to mean that a person is "a world of his own... on the side of God against (or: opposite) nature". Thus, the hermeneutical principle that connected a human being intimately with Creation in rabbinic thought becomes a principle that uproots a person from Creation. It is, furthermore, hard to imagine from a Jewish perspective how God could be "against Nature", as the translator has inflected it, though this idea would be perfectly intelligible in the framework of Gnosticism.[403] Such "traditional" readings are quite distant from the rabbinic tradition. At the same time, they are simply alternative theologies, based on plausible homiletical readings, so they are not inherently less valid than the ecological reading explored in this work. But neither are they any more valid. More importantly, from the perspective of what we need to find *tiqun*, healing, in our relationship with God and Nature, they are part of what needs to be healed.

From a textual point of view, Guttmann's sentiments are easily refuted. From an ecological point of view, however, even more subtle existential or modernist interpretations, like the one found in *The Lonely Man of Faith*, are deeply limited. Nevertheless, Soloveitchik gives considerable standing to the more-than-human world elsewhere in his work: "Human life is evaluated as

---

> true then it must also be true that once humanity does take control of its environment, it must heal the Earth's diseases that are caused by humanity, since by doing *t'shuvah* (transforming) we would have the power to cure them.

[402] *Studies in Bereshit*, trans. Aryeh Newman (Jerusalem: World Zionist Organization, n.d.), 2–3, 6, my emphasis and parens. I have adduced the translator's version to illustrate a point. However, the term *mul*, here rendered as "against", may also be translated as "opposite", that is, facing, rather than opposing, nature.

[403] See Sokol's excellent discussion of this question, "Ethical Implications", 261–4, and see n.24. Citing Michael Wyschograd's "Judaism and the Sanctification of Nature" (*The Melton Journal* [Spring 1992]: 5–7) and Schwarzchild's "The Unnatural Jew", Sokol writes:

> [T]his putative opposition between Judaism and nature... is to my mind incoherent. How can Judaism, or any religious tradition, be in "conflict" with (Wyschograd's phrase) or in "confrontation" with (Schwarzchild) nature?... Does it make sense to say that Judaism disapproves of trees or grass, or the processes which account for their growth and decline? No more than it makes sense to say that Judaism is opposed to the Pythagorean theorem. (262)

the apex of the bio-pyramid – what was termed *tzelem* [*sic*] – and plant as its base. But the difference consists only in degree, not in kind."[404]

THE CHALLENGE OF HISTORY AND OURSELVES

Though there is some congruence between modernist ideas about the value of human life and rabbinic ideas about human uniqueness, the two ways of thinking are distinct. Though the rabbis affirmed the limited control people were able to exert over the natural world in their time and place, they did not define humanity in a way that cut people off from the rest of Nature. If the rabbis were comfortable with a more modest definition of human standing, why are modernist theologians generally insistent on a more radical one?

If we consider the modernist approach in light of the assaults on humanity that were part of the previous century – most importantly for Jewish thinkers, the Holocaust – this makes good sense. As Greenberg has noted, "the religious enterprise after this event must see itself as a desperate attempt to create, save, and heal the image of God wherever it still exists".[405] Even though *Chazal* were

---

[404] *The Emergence of Ethical Man* (Jersey City NJ: Ktav, 2005), 44–5, in a chapter titled both "Man as a Carnivorous Being" and "Man as a Part of Nature", 31–47. Not only does Soloveitchik describe the slaughter of animals as *chamas* ("misappropriation", by his definition; usu. trans. "violence"), his interpretation of *tselem* there is radically different from that in *The Lonely Man of Faith*. See David Errico-Naga, "Vegetarianism and Judaism: The Rav's Radical View", *Kol Hamevaser* 5:3 (Feb. 6, 2012): 13–14. Integrating these varied facets of Soloveitchik's thoughts would be invaluable.

[405] "Cloud of Smoke, Pillar of Fire: Judaism, Christianity and Modernity after the Holocaust" in *Auschwitz: Beginning of a New Era? Reflections on the Holocaust*, ed. Eva Fleischner (New York: Ktav, 1977), 42. He also states, "Judaism and Christianity . . . stand or fall on their fundamental claim that the human being is . . . of ultimate and absolute value". Greenberg also discusses these issues in "The Third Great Cycle of Jewish History", in *Living in the Image of God: Jewish Teachings to Perfect the World: Conversations with Rabbi Irving Greenberg*, Shalom Freedman (New York: Jason Aronson, 1998), 37, and in many other places. One would be hard pressed not to support modernist theologians like Greenberg on this point, since the corruption they are fighting against goes so very deep.

It is worth noting that Tirosh-Samuelson also regards "all late-twentieth-century Jewish ecological thinking . . . as a belated response to the catastrophe of the Holocaust, a determination of the Jewish people to renew themselves" ("Judaism", *The Oxford Handbook*, 53). My experience of the relationship between the two is quite different. One trend that emerged after the Shoah, which may have had some influence on the nascent Jewish environmental movement, is that many of the early leaders grew up with and rejected a Holocaust-focused educational curriculum that inculcated Jewish identity through fear. Instead, we embraced as the core of our Jewish identities positive Torah principles about the land. For twenty-first-century Jewish environmentalism, the Shoah has little relevance even in a back-handed way, but Zionism does, for a less than obvious reason. The back-to-the-land/farming sector of Jewish environmentalism, which has grown exponentially, has opposite valences for different people: for some it represents a complement to Zionism, and for others, an alternative. Thus, that sector is a kind of safe space within the North American Jewish community where people with very differing perspectives on Israel can work closely together.

also fighting a materialistic and (in some periods) murderous culture under Rome, there is tremendous difference between the oppression veiled under *pax Romana* and the extermination carried out by the Nazis, where killing itself was a political goal and not just a tactic.

Even without that historical background, modern theologians may feel pressure to elevate humans higher in order to protect some idea of humanity from the erosion of modern materialism (whether that be capitalist or communist), which can reduce people to consumers and objects for manipulation. As Helmut Thielicke (1908–86), a German Protestant theologian whose work paralleled Greenberg's (see n.359) stated, "Only if human life is unconditionally sacred and humanity is made the measure of all things are we protected against its being made a thing or tool and thus consigned to the scrap heap, as machines are when they wear out and are no longer of use."[406]

For the ancient rabbis, moral and ethical calculations about human life were not based on monetary or exchange value.[407] While such moral reasoning is endemic to modern American society[408] and to capitalism in general, it would make no sense in the framework of traditional *halakhah*, where exchange is overridden by Shabbat and Shabbat is overridden by *pikuach nefesh*, saving a

---

[406] *Being Human... Becoming Human* (New York: Doubleday, 1984), 9. Like Greenberg, Thielicke finds in the Holocaust a negative touchstone to anchor human value ("The Doctor as Judge", 172). In complete contrast to Greenberg, he has no trouble advocating the sterilization of certain categories of "mental defectives" (150–53) and has a much more muscular and troubling idea about how humanity should use and control Nature (152, 165).

[407] Valuations did happen for other purposes, *viz.* for determining the amount a person owed to the priests if they vowed to give to the Temple "their worth" (*Mishnah `Arakhin*) or for determining the compensation due for an injury.

[408] An example of cost–benefit thinking that struck me dumb, back when I was beginning the dissertation *Kabbalah and Ecology* is based on, came from an essay by the Institute for Policy Innovation (a group with ties to pharmaceutical companies) broadcast by National Public Radio on Mar. 21, 2001 (KUOW, 4:45 PM). The issue was supplying low-cost AIDS drugs to Africa. The essayist explained that the pharmaceutical companies face "an ethical and economic dilemma" because they need to stay profitable in order to develop drugs for the future; the situation was actually compared with the question of whether Coca-Cola should have to supply its products at lower cost. No distinction was made between supplying drugs to save lives and supplying other types of products. Of course, once one has decided what the moral imperatives are, questions of cost must be dealt with, but triage is tantamount to murder when preserving corporate profit margins is the limiting factor.

An aggadah about Alexander the Great could be applied to this ethos. Alexander, visiting the court of a foreign king, witnesses a case in which treasure has been found buried in land that one party has sold to another. When each party insists that the treasure belongs to the *other* party, the king decrees that their children should marry and thus share it. Seeing Alexander's shock at the verdict, the king asks Alexander what he would have done. Alexander says that both parties would have been killed and the treasure taken for the government. The king then asks, "Does the rain fall for you? Does the sun shine for you?" When Alexander responds yes, the king surmises that it is only for the sake of small animals that the heavens provide his land with sustenance (*BR* 33:1 ‖ *TY Bava M'tsiy`a* 2:6, 8b; *Tanch Emor* 6; and other places).

human life. In the context of modernity, however, there is a real need to place human life above any exchange value by labeling it "infinite".[409]

Finally, another reason for moderns to be more absolutist about human value is the loss of belief in the organicism of Creation that was a consequence of the Enlightenment scientific revolution. Organicism, which was part and parcel of ancient and medieval theology, anchored human standing in the standing of the natural world. Alongside being in the image of God, the highest value that could be assigned to a human being by *Chazal* was that he or she was like the natural world, like an `*olam malei'*. Once the idea of organicism was shattered, no dimension in the more-than-human world was left to shore up human standing.[410] The ancient idea of the image of God, because it resonated with the Enlightenment apotheosis of the individual, remained as the sole affirmation of human standing.

There are many positive aspects to the modernist formulation of "infinite value", especially with respect to human rights. We can see this in the work of groups like B'Tselem, whose very name is derived from this interpretation of the Torah. The value of Greenberg's formulation in such areas is immense. It is also true that in a world where people are both able and willing to balance human life against profit, there is tremendous pressure and need to argue for the absolute value of human life. But the negative aspects of doing so are also tremendous, for there can be no moral standing for other creatures or for Creation as a whole that is not trumped by the idea of "infinite value". Alternative ethical constructions based on human life trumping other *social* values and needs can better preserve life's sanctity in face of the onslaught of modernity.[411]

In the modernist-humanist framework, it is too easy to forget that the more-than-human world is an essential area of moral concern, not only from an ecological perspective but also from the Torah's perspective. That this *is* the Torah's perspective is clear. The Torah laws that safeguard the health and humanity of society as a whole deal with justice in the broadest sense, not only for the poor but also for the land. This is especially true for the laws of *Sh'miṭah*, the sabbatical year (often spelled *Shmita*), and *Yovel*, the Jubilee

---

[409] On this point, Greenberg cites the sale of a Van Gogh painting for $82,500,000 as an example of the finite value of "an image of the human" ("Seeking the Religious Roots", 386). Cf. Kant's idea of infinite value, n.358.

[410] See discussion, pp.25, 270ff.

[411] For example, the Declaration of Helsinki on the use of human subjects in medical research states, "Concern for the interests of the subject must always prevail over the interests of science and society" (I.5, 1975–1996 www.en.wikipedia.org/wiki/Declaration_of_Helsinki [Oct. 2013]). The interests and life of the individual take precedence over other *human* interests, over society and science, which might otherwise be allowed to trump them – which means that they are functionally of "infinite" or unsurpassable value in comparison with the competing cultural values. But the need of other species to survive transcends and cannot solely be defined by human interests or culture. Importantly, the Declaration of Helsinki was a response to the atrocities of Nazi medical experimentation.

The challenge of history and ourselves

year. According to the Levitical section on *Sh'mitah*, when the rights of the land conflict with the needs of people, the rights of the land take precedence (Lv 26:34,43).[412] Not only that, but wild animals have the right in the *Sh'mitah* year to forage freely on land that would normally be cultivated (Lv 25:7). The Torah is explicit that our moral frame of reference must extend beyond the human world. (The latter rule also suggests that *Sh'mitah* is a kind of return to Eden, where all the creatures shared the same food supply.[413]) Even from the perspective of human needs – most especially the need for justice – we must not put on moral blinders that prevent us from empathizing with the more-than-human creatures and ecosystems around us. Justice can never be complete without justice for the land.

This concern ought not to diminish the profound significance of Jewish teachings on human life. However one chooses to interpret the idea that a person is a full world, it clearly has normative ethical content, teaching us that each human life is profoundly significant. It may also teach us about the relative priority of an individual human life compared with individuals of other species. However, it does not teach us the "infinite" value of human life, and, most importantly for this work, it does not teach us about the meaning of *tselem*.

To return to the article I used as the starting point for this discussion, Greenberg used his interpretation of `olam malei'* and *tselem* to provide a theological basis for pluralism. His goal was to answer "doubts about the authenticity of pluralism [which] grow out of the widespread feeling that any tradition of ultimate significance should make absolute claims."[414] *Tselem* for Greenberg guarantees not just the value of each human being but also the value of each person's perspective: "Part of every truth is the fact that an image of God is speaking it; that is to say, a being of infinite value, equality, and uniqueness is speaking it."[415]

This is a powerful, beautiful idea, and Greenberg's theological support for human dignity and pluralism has been practically and spiritually important in

---

[412] See p.166ff. and Seidenberg, "Genesis, Covenant, Jubilee, Shmitah and the Land Ethic", www.jewcology.com/resource/Genesis-Covenant-Jubilee-Shmitah-and-the-Land-Ethic (neohasid.org, 2010). (Cf. *Mishnah Avot* 5:7.) This is also the perspective of the second paragraph of the *Sh'ma`* prayer: "And it will be, if listening you will listen to my commandments... that I will give the rain of your land... Watch yourselves, lest your hearts turn astray... and [YHVH] shuts the heavens and there will be no rain... and you will be lost from off the good land that YHVH is giving you" [Dt 11:13–17]. It is easy to read these words as a simple warning about how God punishes disobedience, but they are rooted in a deeper reality that revolves around the *mitsvot* of Shabbat and *Sh'mitah*. Ultimately, fundamentally, the Torah is about sustainability, as it says here: "Set these my words on your heart... in order that you may increase your days and the days of your children upon the face of the ground... like the days of the skies over the land" [Dt 11:18–21], or more generally, "Choose life, in order that you will live" [Dt 30:19].
[413] See Seidenberg, "Genesis, Covenant, Jubilee" and "Shmita: The Purpose of Sinai". On the connection between *Sh'mitah* and Eden, see also Davis, *Scripture*, 60–61.
[414] "Seeking the Religious Roots", 386.   [415] Ibid., 390.

the Orthodox community (where some sects reject the universality of humanism) and in the wider Jewish world. I would suggest, however, that there are other theological strategies for supporting pluralism which are less consequent upon devaluation of the more-than-human. For example, Walter Brueggemann, who also derives pluralism from the concept of *tselem*, draws a parallel between the multivocality of the human personality and the multivocality of the image of God in *Tanakh* (Bible). Critiquing standard interpretations of the image of God, he writes:

> Because our notion of God is characteristically one-dimensionally monotheistic, monolithic, and monarchic, i.e., reduced and domesticated, we imagine that "image of God" that is most faithful, full, and effective when we become unified personalities capable of "willing one thing," i.e., so centered that all parts of our person, all parts of our body are unified in a single identity and commitment.[416]

For Brueggemann, this way of thinking cuts us off not only from God's diversity but also from our own selves. Reconnecting with that diversity can strengthen our resistance to what he deems to be the oppression of modern society:

> Given the sense of God as an endlessly negotiated person, it is exactly the biblical text and the biblical community of faith which can bear witness to the "many selves of the self," and which can protest against the ideological closure that a technological, one-dimensional society requires of the self.[417]

While Brueggemann's theology is no less anthropocentric or modernist than the other theologies discussed in this chapter, it is far more amenable to ecotheology. Not only does the "monolithic" understanding of God cut us off from ourselves, as Bruegemann asserts, but it also cuts us off from the diversity of the more-than-human world. Conversely, connecting the diversity of God's image to the more-than-human world is a desideratum not only for ecotheology, but also for the redemption of our own humanity and psychic well-being. Brueggemann's insistence that God's image is most profoundly expressed through diversity also calls us to include in our moral purview the more-than-human world, which is the living ground of our experience of diversity.

---

[416] "'In the Image of God'...Pluralism", *Modern Theology* 11:4 (Oct. 1995): 455–69; 459.
[417] Ibid., 460.

4

The soul and the others

Humans, animals, and other subjectivities

> The human species emerged catching, dreaming, and thinking animals and cannot be fully itself without them.
>
> Paul Shepard, *The Others*

> Who knows if the spirit of the children of Adam rises upward, and if the spirit of the beast descends below, to the earth?
>
> *Ecclesiastes* 3:21

Tselem is not the only qualifier dividing human beings from the more-than-human world. The concept of the soul, so bound up with *tselem* in later Jewish thought, also defines a kind of border between kingdoms, dividing humans from all the other animals. This chapter outlines early rabbinic ideas about the human soul, the souls of animals, and their interrelations, and discusses the evolution of these ideas. Though the concepts of soul and *tselem* are distinct in early rabbinic literature, as shown previously, both concepts ground the value of the human individual in similar ways. Nevertheless, the rabbis universally understood animals to have souls as well. This is one of several motifs and ethical principles that suggest a notion of intrinsic value in non-human species.

THE SOUL, HUMAN AND ANIMAL

In both medieval and modern theology, the divine *tselem* and the human soul are elements in the Jewish (and Christian) understanding of the human makeup that correspond to the concept of intrinsic value in ethics. The evolution of the concept of the human soul in Jewish thought, explored in the first two sections of this chapter, sometimes parallels and sometimes diverges from the evolution of *tselem*.

The idea that the soul is the source of human uniqueness is often paralleled by the devaluation of other-than-human species. However, there are intermediate steps on the way to this idea that point toward alternative theologies, theologies that can nourish a deeper relationship with the more-than-human world. These dimensions will be explored in "Animal Souls in the Rabbinic Tradition", and they will inform our understanding of the ethical duties toward animals defined by the rabbis in the next chapter.

Nefesh and *n'shamah* in the Torah

In the Torah itself, there is no concept of soul distinguished from the body. Though both *n'shamah* and *nefesh* are often translated as soul, *n'shamah* means embodied breath and *nefesh* means animate self in the embodied sense, without metaphysical connotations; the contrasting term *ru'ach* means breath that is not embodied, such as spirit and wind.[418] (Note that in one case, *nefesh* may be interpreted in a less material sense as life-breath.[419]) One thing *nefesh* and *n'shamah* cannot mean is "soul" in the ancient Hellenistic sense of immortal part or personality. Another thing neither can mean is soul in opposition to physical matter or the body.

It has been taught many times by many scholars that there is no metaphysical vocabulary, as we understand it, in the Torah. This generalization overlooks many nuances, which I will discuss momentarily, but it remains a useful starting point for discussion. (Some scholars, as discussed in the next section, apply a similar perspective to the rabbis.) Urbach's statement of this principle is illustrative. He wrote,

> In the Bible a monistic view prevails. Man is not composed of two elements – body and soul, or flesh and spirit... [T]he term *nefesh* is not to be understood in the sense of psyche, anima. The whole of man is a living soul... *Nefesh*, *guf*, and *ruach* [sic] form an indivisible entity... This unity finds expression in a lack of differentiation between the word and the substance in the Hebrew tongue.[420]

Urbach's choice of terms for his example shows the strong influence of rabbinic vocabulary. *Guf*, meaning body, is strictly a post-Biblical term. As Byron Sherwin, critiquing this passage, stated, "[I]n Hebrew scriptures, no distinct term for the body exists... The word *guf* used to designate the body in post-Biblical literature only appears in Hebrew Scripture to denote a corpse... Nor does the term *nefesh* denote soul as is often thought. Rather, *nefesh* usually refers to the person..."[421] Stiegman insightfully comments on Urbach that, "[w]hat

---

[418] See Excursus 1. [419] Specifically, Genesis 35:18; see Excursus 1. [420] *The Sages*, 214–5.
[421] "The Human Body and the Image of God" in *A Traditional Quest: Essays in Honour of Louis Jacobs*, ed. Dan Cohn-Sherbok (Sheffield: JSOT Press, 1991), 77, n.1. Even with the meaning corpse, *guf* (as *gufah*) appears only in a single verse, 1Ch 12:10. *Nefesh* can also mean corpse. See Excursus 1.

The human soul in the rabbinic tradition

is indivisible is composed... Biblical man is a unity, not a monad."[422] Simply put, the word *nefesh* in Torah means body, but body as subject, not body in a materialist or reductionist sense.[423]

The idea of soul in Jewish tradition is rooted in Biblical verses that seemingly reject the division of soul and body. The fact that *nefesh chayah* is applied to the other animals in Genesis 1 and to human beings in Genesis 2 also creates a hermeneutical roadblock to the idea that soul is uniquely human. There is no way to completely separate either the soul from the body or the human soul from the other animals on the basis of scripture.[424] The radical embodiment of *nefesh* in the *Tanakh* thus serves as an anchor that prevents the development of a completely dualistic conception of soul and body.[425]

If the Torah lacks a metaphysical vocabulary, it more importantly lacks a vocabulary that distinguishes between animate and inanimate (e.g., *nefesh* can mean both living body and corpse, *basar* means flesh and meat, `*ets* means tree and wood, *qol* means voice and sound, *ru'ach* means wind and spirit).[426] As such, the Torah provides a solid, holistic foundation for understanding the human being. Thus, we can break down the division between body and soul by re-rooting words like "soul" in the soil of the indigenous culture that birthed the Torah. Doing this would reset the meaning of these "reserved terms" for Western thought, and bring us closer to the meaning and spirit of the ancient tradition.

THE HUMAN SOUL IN THE RABBINIC TRADITION

With the convergence of Hellenistic and Jewish thought in the period preceding the rabbis, the idea of a soul separate from the body gradually took

---

[422] He adds, "it is time to become more precise and to allow the question whether the case for anthropological holism in the Bible has not been overstated" ("Rabbinic Anthropology", 513).

[423] See Excursus 1.

[424] BR suggests two readings that erase the amphibolousness of *nefesh chayah*. According to the first, *nefesh chayah* in Gn 1 actually refers to *Adam Harishon*, so that neither occurrence of *nefesh chayah* refers to the other animals (BR 7:5, 8:1, see n.449). According to the second, *nefesh chayah* in Gn 2 means that God created *Adam Harishon* with a tail (like an animal/ *chayah*) and then removed it, so that both occurrences in effect refer to the other animals (BR 14:10).

[425] Thus, even in Kabbalah, which elaborates several levels of soul that differentiate human beings from other creatures, the term *nefesh* is inclusive of a level of soul found in animals.

[426] See Excursus 1. From an earlier period of scholarship, Thorlief Borman's *Hebrew Thought Compared with Greek* (Philadelphia: Westminster Press, 1960) is a worthwhile exploration of these ideas. Johannes Pedersen similarly writes: "[T]he Israelite does not distinguish between a living and a lifeless nature" (*Israel: Its Life and Culture* [London: Oxford University Press, 1926], 155) and "The Israelites do not acknowledge the distinction between the psychic and the corporeal" (479). For Pedersen, this goes far beyond the question of body and soul in the human being: "Earth and stones are alive, imbued with a soul..." Though such statements may be criticized as essentializing, they illuminate important Biblical themes. On *basar*, see p.131.

root. Both *nefesh*[427] and *n'shamah* were used for soul, sometimes interchangeably, though eventually the idea of the human soul became fixed to the term *n'shamah*.[428] Nevertheless, while the rabbis ultimately accepted the idea that the human soul was uniquely divine and in some sense immortal, they insisted that there could be no life after death without a bodily resurrection. Many readers of the tradition interpret this doctrine as a rejection of the Hellenistic notion that the soul could exist independently of the body. To give two examples, Will Herberg states, "The Hebraic (i.e., rabbinic) conception avoids alike the pitfalls of naturalism and of body-soul dualism... In the age-old vision of the resurrection, it is the whole man, not his 'soul' alone, that is revived to share in the fulfillment of human destiny."[429] Goshen-Gottstein similarly claims, "The distinction between spirit and matter is not known in rabbinic literature... [This] is reflected in rabbinic eschatology. The future life takes the form of resurrection of the dead, rather than eternal life of the soul."[430]

While these claims may be overstated, it is true that there are no radical *ontological* distinctions between spirit and matter in rabbinic texts, which seemingly reject the spirit–body or mind–body dualism endemic to Greek thought. As Lorberbaum writes, "man is not comprised of ontologically discrete and differentiated elements, such as body and soul... [S]oul [is not] an entity separate from the body but rather... the vital and animating principle of the body."[431]

The question is not one of metaphysics *per se*, but whether one identifies the self or personality primarily with the soul, or with the body and soul together.[432] Boyarin in *Carnal Israel* explains this distinction between Hellenism (as he defines it) and rabbinic culture in this way: "[F]or rabbinic Jews, the human being was defined as a body – animated, to be sure, by a soul", whereas "for Hellenistic Jews [and] Christians, the essence of the human being is a soul housed in a body," elaborating that the Platonic conception of the human being is one "for which the soul is the self, and the body only the

---

[427] *Nefesh*, however, could also mean body, as one sees in *Sefer Y'tsirah*, a mystical work that correlates letters and planets with different body parts, each of which is described as being created "in the *nefesh*" (3:5–9 and 4:5–11).

[428] While some idea of the soul appears in the earliest rabbinic texts, it did not achieve a terminologically fixed form until later midrash. This suggests that the concept was undergoing rapid and significant transformation in early rabbinic culture.

[429] *Judaism and Modern Man* (New York: Atheneum Press, 1973), 70. Similarly, Sherwin: "In rabbinic literature, body/soul dualism does not really exist" ("Human Body", 77). When the Reform movement rejected the idea of resurrection in favor of a purely spiritual afterlife, they essentially capitulated to this dualism.

[430] "The Body", 176–7. Goshen-Gottstein also claims that "nowhere is the soul regarded as divine". This accurately describes the rabbinic idea of *tselem*. However, while *tselem* always has a physical element, *n'shamah* need not.

[431] *Tselem Elohim*, vii (in English).   [432] See, e.g., VR 4:8, discussed presently.

The human soul in the rabbinic tradition

dwelling place".[433] Further on, I will show that this dividing line may correspond with the division between the Alexandrian and Antiochean schools of Hellenistic Christian thought, and that the rabbinic tradition was aligned with the latter school.

Burton Visotzky took Boyarin to task for these characterizations, claiming that Boyarin denied that the rabbis were heavily influenced by Hellenism.[434] As part of his critique, Visotzky brings several texts to show that the rabbis participated in a significant way in Hellenistic ideas, the most important of which is a homily in *Vayiqra' Rabbah*. The verse that this homily is based on is Ps 103:1, "My soul, bless YHVH", which, as understood by the rabbis, represents the Psalmist speaking to his own soul as an intimate other or "You". The *Vayiqra' Rabbah* text continues in this vein:

This soul/*nefesh* fills the body as the Holy One fills His world... Let the soul come that fills the body and praise the Holy One who fills the world. This soul bears the body and the Holy One bears the world... Let the soul that bears the body extol (etc.) The soul outlasts the body and the Holy One outlasts the world. Let the soul (etc.) This soul is unique/*y'chidah* in the body and the Holy One is unique in the world. Let the soul (etc.) This soul does not eat in the body and there is no eating before the Holy One. Let the soul (etc.) This soul sees and is not seen and the Holy One sees and is not seen. Let the soul (etc.) This soul is pure in the body and the Holy One is pure in His world. Let the soul (etc.) This soul does not sleep in the body and for the Holy One, there is no sleeping before Him. Let the soul (etc.).[435]

There is a clear acceptance of a division between soul and body here. Note, however, that the speaker exhorts the soul as if it were other, and does not identify the self with the soul. Consequently, the aggadah fits rather neatly into the anthropology described by Boyarin as rabbinic. Its purpose is to connect the soul to God, rather than to alienate the soul from the body.

Most scholars would agree that if we want to make sense of the presence of Hellenistic ideas within rabbinic teachings, we must distinguish between the rabbis' participation in Hellenism as a culture, and their rejection of a particular aspects of Hellenistic ideology. However, as far as I know, no one has differentiated between the various schools of Hellenistic thought that the rabbis might have internalized or rejected. It turns out that the division between Antiochean and Alexandrian Christian theologians concerning the image of God, a concept that for both schools was bound up with soul, corresponds

---

[433] *Carnal Israel: Reading Sex in Talmudic Culture* (Berkeley, University of California Press: 1993), 5, 31.
[434] "Intersexuality and the Reading of Talmudic Culture", *Arachne* 1:2 (1994): 238–42. Vistozky's claim seems to be incorrect, however. Even though Boyarin contrasts "rabbinic Jews" with "Hellenistic Jews", he understands both to be cultural trends mediated and shaped by Hellenism. See *Carnal Israel* (33, 45) and *Border Lines: The Partition of Judaeo-Christianity* (Philadelphia: University of Pennsylvania Press, 2011), 18–20. The second half of this article, by Gwynne Kessler, though also critical, does not make this claim.
[435] VR 4:8.

almost exactly to Boyarin's division between Hellenistic ideas the rabbis accepted and ideas they rejected. According to Frederick McLeod, "While Alexandrian and Augustinian traditions located our 'image of God' in the higher 'regions' of our rational soul, the Antiocheans looked upon this phrase as being attributable to our whole person as a unique, living composite of body and spirit".[436]

Simply put, the rabbis embraced Antiochean Hellenism and rejected Alexandrian Hellenism. The harmonious relationship between body and soul posited in the *Vayiqra' Rabbah* passage and throughout rabbinic literature definitively contradicts the Alexandrian school of Hellenistic thought, as does the fact that in cases where body, soul, and *tselem* are all mentioned, *tselem* is associated first with the body. It seems then that Alexandrian Hellenism is what people have in mind when speaking about the opposition between "Hellenism" and "rabbinism".[437]

It is not only a geographical coincidence that the more dualistic form of Hellenism espoused by the Alexandrian school resembles what we find much earlier in Philo, whereas the Antiochean school was concordant with the rabbis' ideology and cosmology. In fact, there were significant relations between the rabbinic Jewish community and the Christian community in Antioch.[438] What

---

[436] "Anne Morrow Lindbergh's *Gift From the Sea* as a Religious Myth", *An Ecology of the Spirit*, 226. See also n.164, as well as McLeod's book-length treatment of this subject, *The Image of God in the Antiochene Tradition* (Washington DC: Catholic University of America Press, 1999). The more holistic anthropology of Antioch can also be found in Irenaeus (second century, Anatolia, Gaul), whose work predates the division between Antioch and Alexandria. Irenaeus wrote:

> Now the soul and the spirit are certainly a part of man, but certainly not the man; for the perfect man consists in the commingling and the union of the soul receiving the Spirit of the Father, and the mixture of that fleshly nature *which was also moulded after the image of God*... But when the spirit here blended with the soul is united with the body, the man becomes spiritual and perfect because of the outpouring of the Spirit, and *this is he who was made in the image and likeness of God* (*Against Heresies* 5.9.1, my emphasis).

See discussion in Bernard McGinn, "Humans as *Imago Dei*: Mystical Anthropology Then and Now", in *Sources of Transformation: Revitalising Christian Spirituality*, eds. Edward Howells and Peter Tyler (New York: Continuum, 2010), 27; see also 27–8 on Maximus the Confessor.

[437] This may be because the Catholic Church and Western Christianity excluded and ultimately condemned and anathematized Antiochean theology, in the First Council of Ephesus (431 CE) and the Second Council of Constantinople (553 CE). Part of the work of Christian ecotheology is to reclaim the Antiochean heritage.

[438] See Pieter W. van der Horst, "Jews and Christians in Antioch at the End of the Fourth Century" in *Japheth in the Tents of Shem: Studies on Jewish Hellenism in Antiquity* (Leuven Belgium: Peeters, 2002), 109–18. Stories about Abba Yehudah or Abba Yudan at *TY Horayot* 3:7, 48a (other editions, 3:4) and *VR* 5:4 also indicate a strong connection between the rabbis of Palestine and the Antioch Jewish community. Perhaps most significantly, the son of rabbinic patriarch Gamliel (Gamaliel) (V or VI) and Theodore of Mopsuestia (c.350–428, Antioch, Anatolia), who was one of the earliest exponents of the Antiochean school, were both pupils of the pagan rhetorician Libanius (314–383, Antioch). On Gamliel, see van der Horst, "Jews and Christians", 116 and "The Last Jewish Patriarch(s) and Graeco-Roman Medicine" in

is significant about the rabbinic affirmation of resurrection is not the fact itself, but the way in which it is of a piece with their overall anthropology, which is congruent with Antiochean anthropology.[439]

This pattern is confirmed in what is perhaps the earliest rabbinic expression of duality between soul and body, found in *Sifrey D'varim*:

> [S]o would R' Sim'ai say: All creatures that were created from the heavens, their soul/*nafsham* and their body/*gufam* are from the heavens, and all creatures that were created from the earth, their soul and their body are from the earth, except for this human, for his soul is from the heavens and his body is from the earth.[440]

While this passage affirms that the human soul comes from the heavens and the human body from the earth, it also asserts a worldview in which souls and bodies exist at all levels – the souls of other earthly creatures come from the earth, while the bodies (and souls) of the heavens come, naturally, from the heavens. There is not one realm of soul and another of body. The passage strongly rejects Alexandrian dualism and falls neatly within the rabbinic anthropology of the human as cosmic unifier. This is the same anthropology espoused by the Antiochean school.[441]

This text represents the precision with which the rabbis employed Hellenistic tropes. Rabbinic culture embraced a moderate version of Hellenism, and emphasized the importance of embodiment within that framework,

---

Japheth, 32–6; and see Visotzky, "Midrash, Christian Exegesis, and Hellenistic Hermeneutic" in *Current Trends in the Study of Midrash*, ed. Carol Bakhos (Leiden: Brill, 2006), 111–31; 120–21. On Theodore, see next note. While here I imagine the rabbis as intentionally rejecting Alexandrian Hellenism, they may have simply absorbed the version of Hellenism that was more influential in their time and place.

[439] Both Alexandrian and Antiochean theologians accepted the idea of the bodily resurrection of the dead. But whereas for the Alexandrian school, resurrection meant the transformation of the body into something disassociated from the corruption of the material world, for Antiochean Theodore of Mopsuestia, the incorruptible body was a sign of Creation's wholeness, and included the material world:

> God made the whole of Creation one cosmic body, containing all things, visible and invisible... Although these differ among themselves, God's intent is that all things be bound into one reality. For He created the human being to be fashioned with a visible body that is related to the material Creation... and of an invisible soul that is akin to those invisible... The Lord said that He would restore us by raising us up and making us immortal, so that no one should ever fear that the common bond [uniting] Creation would ever again be changed and be dissolved (McLeod, *Theodore of Mopsuestia* [New York: Routledge, 2009], 92, commentary *ad* Romans 8:19).

[440] *Pisqa* 306; 340–41. Visotzky does not cite this text. The passage continues:

> Therefore if a person/*adam* did Torah and did the will of his Father in the heavens, behold he is like the creatures above/ *shel ma'lah*, for it is said, "I said, you are Elohim, and the sons of the highest / *uv'ney 'elyon* all of you" [Ps 82:6]. [If h]e didn't do Torah and didn't do the will of his Father in the heavens, behold he is like the creatures below/ *shel matah*, for it is said, "so like Adam you will die" [Ps 82:7].

[441] McLeod, *Theodore of Mopsuestia*, 226–7.

while strongly rejecting the extremes we find in the Alexandrian school and Philo.

It is also intriguing that those rabbinic texts that speak of a clear duality between body and soul among the early *midr'shey aggadah* are found in *Vayiqra' Rabbah*;[442] the only one found in *B'rei'shit Rabbah* has a radically different tone.[443] Moreover, statements that sound like they might be talking about the immortality of the soul in *B'rei'shit Rabbah* are consistently concerned with *tselem*.[444] For example, in a teaching already quoted, "Said the Holy One: If I create him from the upper ones [alone] he lives and won't die [in this world]; from the lower ones, he dies [in this world] and won't live [in the coming world]",[445] what gives permanence is *tselem*, rather than *n'shamah*.

Even more importantly, all the passages in *B'rei'shit Rabbah* that do speak of soul as distinct from the body still clearly show that the soul was characterized as physical and embodied.[446] For example, *B'rei'shit Rabbah* 14:9 reads,

---

[442] See esp. *VR* 4:5–8, and see 34:3 in n.444.

[443] *BR* 22:9, quoted following page. How these considerations may help with dating these texts or distinguishing between rabbinic schools of thought remains to be explored. Visotzky has done preliminary work in this direction in *Golden Bells and Pomegranates: Studies in Midrash Leviticus Rabbah* (Tübingen: Mohr Siebeck, 2003), ch.9. He suggests that *VR* "received the notion of equality of body and soul from an earlier source" but "actively undermines it by its redactive strategy" (94). Nevertheless, his picture of how these ideas developed differs from my own, and he equates soul and image, without providing a basis for this equation (e.g., 90). See next note.

[444] Contrast this with two vignettes about Hillel, one concerning *tselem* and one concerning *nefesh*, which teach a similar lesson from completely opposite vantage points (*VR* 34:3 ‖ *ARNB* 30, 66). In both stories, as Hillel takes leave of his students, they ask him, "Where are you going?" In the first story,

He said: [I am going] to do a mitsvah. They said: What is this mitsvah? He said: To wash at the bathhouse. They said: Is this a mitsvah? He said: If it's so that with the icons of kings that they erect in theaters and circuses, the one who is responsible for them washes them and scrubs them ... I who am created in the image and likeness / *b'tselem uvid'mut* ... all the more so!

Here *tselem*'s significance is purely physical, even though *tselem* is highly honored. In the second story about going to the bathhouse, Hillel says: "[I am going] to show kindness to this guest in [my] house. They said: Every day you have a guest? He said: This poor soul/*nafsha*, is he not a guest in the body? Today he is here, tomorrow he is not here." The duality between soul and body in these two stories is not found in *BR*, but it still fits with our description of rabbinic/Antiochean vs. Alexandrian metaphysics – that is, the speaker does not identify the self with the soul. Most importantly, *tselem* and soul are on opposite sides of the body–soul duality.

[445] *BR* 8:11 ‖ *BR* 14:3. See p.49 ("Upper and Lower Creations"). Cohen interprets this unit as follows: "Tifdai's second homily indicates that, unlike the angel and the beast, humans can determine their own destiny; their merits will yield for them the deserts of the upper world or those of the lower" (*"Be Fertile and Increase"*, 86).

[446] Cf. *BR* 14:10, which equates *n'shamah*, *nefesh*, and *ru'ach*. Also, in 14:9, *n'shamah* is interpreted to mean breath/*n'shimah*, and we find two opposing statements about the role of the *n'shamah* during sleep: the first, that she remains in the body to keep it from growing cold, the

The human soul in the rabbinic tradition

By five names is the soul/*nefesh* called: *nefesh, ru'ach, n'shamah, chayah* (living one), *y'chidah* (unique one). *Nefesh* – this is the blood... *Ru'ach* – for she rises and falls, [as in:] "Who knows if the *ru'ach* of human beings goes upward?" [Ec 3:21]. *N'shamah* – this is the visage/character/*ofah*[447]... *Chayah* – that all the limbs die and (i.e., unless) she lives in the body. *Y'chidah* – that all the limbs are two by two [but] she is singular in the body.[448]

These names are given as synonymous expressions for each other, without any structure defining their interrelationships, in the same way that *Avot d'Rabi Natan* explores the derivation of ten names for earth. *N'shamah*, its Biblical correlates *nefesh, ru'ach*, and *chayah* (sometimes read: *chiyah*), along with the strictly rabbinic term *y'chidah*, were mostly used without metaphysical distinctions.[449]

One explicit reference to *n'shamah* may contradict this schema. Concerning the death of Hevel, we read:

"The voice of your brother's bloods [are] screaming to me from [the surface of] the ground" [Gn 4:10]—[this means that] she (the voice of Hevel's blood) could not go up above/*l'ma`lah*, for as yet no soul/*n'shamah* had gone up to there; and below/*l'matah* she could not stand (i.e., stay or sink into the ground), for as yet no *adam* had been buried there, and [so] "his blood was cast upon the trees and the stones".[450]

The soul is somehow destined to survive the body and potentially to ascend *l'ma`lah* (though the author gives equal weight to the idea that the soul would remain *l'matah*). However, even here no metaphysical framework is developed.

---

second, that "she fills the body, and when a person sleeps, she ascends above to draw down life for the body." All these teachings emphasize the soul's embodiment. Contrast this with texts in n.449 on *ru'ach* and *nefesh*.

[447] Admiel Kosman reads this as "breath" ("Breath, Kiss, and Speech as the Source of the Animation of Life", 96–124, in *Self, Soul, and Body in Religious Experience*, eds. Albert Baumgarten et al. [Leiden: Brill, 1998], 105).

[448] BR 14:9; Theodor, 133. Despite the fact that *chayah* means wild animal elsewhere in *Tanakh*, the connection between *chayah* and *nefesh* in Gn 2:7 is so strong that it was also included as a term for soul. The midrash, however, seems to have added *y'chidah* without any textual basis. Note that the printed version reads *ofiyah* rather than *ofah*.

[449] Two teachings understand *ru'ach* to be separate from and pre-existent to the body. One equates the spirit/*rucho* of *Adam Harishon* (or the spirit of the Messiah) with the "spirit of God / *ru'ach Elohim* hovering over the face of the waters" [Gn 1:2] (BR 8:1); the other equates it with the "living soul / *nefesh chayah*" [Gn 1:24] mentioned before animals are created (BR 7:5, 8:1). Yet another passage states that God, when creating the human, shared rulership with "the souls of the righteous / *nafshoteihen shel tsadikim*" (BR 8:7). Together, these passages suggest a metaphysics in which some dimension of soul/spirit pre-exists the body, though *ru'ach* here may mean something closer to archetype.

[450] BR 22:9; cf. Jb 16:18, Ez 24:7–8. The last phrase comes from *Mishnah Sanhedrin* 4:5, where it has a different meaning. The mishnah explains why "bloods" is plural – Hevel's blood was divided upon the surfaces of the trees and stones. In BR, the phrase "cast upon trees and stones" illustrates that the voice, connected with the bloods, could neither ascend to heaven nor sink into the ground. Thus the phrase, rather than being commentary, is the subject of commentary.

Since soul was elsewhere identified with blood,[451] it is possible that voice and blood and soul are considered synonyms here, or that they are so thoroughly intertwined as to be indistinguishable.

Lastly, there is a passage found in both *B'rei'shit Rabbah* and *Vayiqra' Rabbah* that touches directly on these issues: "'And YHVH Elohim formed him dirt from the ground'—from the lower ones; 'and He blew in his nostrils life's breath / *nishmat chayyim*' [Gn 2:7]—from the upper ones."[452] This passage could be used *homiletically* to say that the *n'shamah* (*nishmat*) is the part of the human being that is formed in God's likeness, since, like *tselem*, the *nishmat chayyim* comes "from the upper ones". However, it only invokes the term *n'shamah* within quotation marks, so to speak, as part of a scriptural phrase. It does not appear here as a rabbinic category or a theological term, but rather as a handle to connect the midrash to scripture. The very fact that the passage does not define or specify its terminology enabled it to serve the differing goals of the redactors of *B'rei'shit Rabbah*, for whom the chief divine element was *tselem*, and *Vayiqra' Rabbah*, for whom that element was the soul.[453]

Though Goshen-Gottstein's claim that the rabbis do not know the soul as divine (n.430) does not fit some of the texts we have examined, it does describe *B'rei'shit Rabbah*, and the school or schools it represents. *B'rei'shit Rabbah* does not express the understanding that the soul is immortal or "divine".[454]

In contrast with Midrash, medieval thought developed a fully metaphysical conception of soul and used various terms for soul that were synonymous in Midrash to bear the weight of complex ideas about levels of the soul. The soul was generally understood in medieval philosophy in terms of Aristotle's division into three aspects: growth, movement, and logos (speech or reason).[455] Some Kabbalistic systems simply transformed the three-part model, while others elaborated a four- or five-part model, dividing rational from spiritual and so on, with the trend toward more and more elaborate rungs of soul culminating in Lurianic Kabbalah.[456] The five names given for soul in

---

[451] Not just in Torah (see Excursus 1, p.355), but also in *BR* 14:9 (previous quote).

[452] *BR* 12:8; *VR* 9:9. *Nishmat* is the construct state of the word *n'shamah*.

[453] Later *midrashim* removed this ambiguity by rewriting the midrash. For example, *TanchB B'rei'shit* 15 reads, "What did the Holy One do? He created an *adam* from below /*mil'matan* and a *n'shamah* from above /*mil'ma`lan*." Cf. *Midrash Hagadol ad* Gn 1:26, quoted p.56.

[454] Other outlying texts were mentioned in n.449.

[455] That is, the "vegetative soul", or that which nurtures simple physical growth, also called the natural soul or *nefesh tiv'i*, found in all living things; the "animal soul", or *nefesh b'hemi*, that which allows for desire, will, and locomotion; and the rational soul, *nefesh sikhli*, thought to be found only in humans.

[456] Tishby examines the use of different terms for soul in various stages of the Kabbalah (*WZ* 684–714). He focuses on the *sui generis* aspects of Kabbalah's concept of soul, and demonstrates that within Zoharic literature, several systems of thought coexisted. For example, he observes, "In *Midrash ha-Ne'elam nefesh hayyah* [sic] ... is thought of as the terrestrial, vital soul, which is derived from the earth and whose chief function is to give life and strength to the body. In the main corpus of the *Zohar*, however, *nefesh hayyah* is the holy soul, which is emanated

B'rei'shit Rabbah 14:9 became paradigmatic nomenclature for these different parts, defining the soul's structure.

Most importantly, in the anthropology of the medieval thinkers, whether philosophically or Kabbalistically oriented, the most valued level of the soul, the level that was essentially part of divinity, was identified as uniquely human (or uniquely Jewish). I have mainly bracketed out these issues, and do not intend to explore them further here, however fascinating, though they are important signposts for understanding the intellectual history of Judaism. My goal is rather to clear away old metaphysics in order to make space for new, living relationships. Acknowledging the metaphysical height that separates the human soul from other souls in these texts, we can move beyond this to talk coherently about the souls of animals, and the intrinsic value of animals, in the rabbinic tradition.

ANIMAL SOULS IN THE RABBINIC TRADITION

As mentioned, the biggest obstacle in modern theology to extending moral significance to animals is the belief that animals do not have souls. In the metaphysics of the Cartesians, this belief was broadened to the idea that animals do not have feelings and are best regarded as machines – a belief which became justification for the horrific treatment of animals in the name of research.[457] While *Chazal* did distinguish between human and animal souls, the idea that

---

from the Shekhinah, 'the upper creature' (*hayyah elyonah*)" (WZ 704). The fact that these metaphysical hierarchies were reversed within Zoharic literature itself shows how unaxiomatic ideas about the soul were. For a Lurianic description of the soul's structure see p.183ff.

[457] According to John Cottingham, this was not Descartes' position ("'A Brute to the Brutes?': Descartes' Treatment of Animals", *Philosophy* 53 [1978] 551–9). Claude Bernard (1813–78), a French physiologist, took Descartes' ideas to mean that animals could not really "feel" anything, even pain. Bernard would carry out extended vivisections – leaving animals nailed to boards and half-dissected – in a time when anesthesia had not yet been developed. Bernard wrote,

The physiologist is no man of fashion. He is a scientist, absorbed by a scientific idea which he pursues: he no longer hears the cries of animals, he no longer sees the blood that flows. He sees only his idea, and perceives only organisms concealing from him problems which he intends to discover (*An Introduction to the Study of Experimental Medicine*, trans. Henry Copley Greene [New York: Dover Publications, 1957], 103, trans. adapted).

Descartes may have also carried out vivisections. See Articles XVI and L in the first part of "The Passions of the Soul" (in *The Philosophical Works of Descartes*, vol.1, eds. Elizabeth Haldane and G. R. T. Ross [New York: Cambridge University Press, 1931], 339–40, 356). Spinoza, who is extolled by ecophilosophers for equating God with Nature, is almost as problematic as Descartes, though he does assert that animals feel:

[T]he law against killing animals is based upon an empty superstition and womanish tenderness rather than upon sound reason. The law, indeed, of seeking one's own profit teaches us to unite in friendship with men, and not with brutes, nor with things whose nature is different from human nature... I by no means deny that brutes feel, but I do deny that, on this account, it is unlawful for us to consult our own profit by using them for our own pleasure and treating

an animal has no soul is neither a rabbinic nor a Torah perspective. To the extent that one can speak of the idea of soul in Torah, animals are also in possession of a soul. Most importantly, the Torah repeatedly equates the blood of an animal with its *nefesh* (Gn 9:4, Lv 17:10–12, Dt 12:23–5). *Nefesh* in this context is usually (and equally correctly) translated as life, but in the animistic worldview of the Torah, the life (or lifeforce) *is* the soul.[458] In rabbinic literature, *Tanchuma* teaches, "It's written: 'A righteous [person] knows the soul of his animal / *nefesh b'hemto*' [Pr 12:10]. The Righteous One of the world (God) even understands the soul of His animal (that is, the animals in the ark), even when He is angry."[459] A passage in *B'rei'shit Rabbah* reads, "'[The fruit of the righteous is a tree of life] and one who acquires souls/*n'fashot* is wise' [Pr 11:30]—for he (Noach) fed and nourished [the animals] the whole twelve months in the Ark."[460] When we take care of the other animals, we are taking care of *souls*.

> them as is most convenient for us, inasmuch as they do not agree in nature with us, and their feelings are different from our emotions.
> (*Ethic*, trans. Hale White [London: Trubner & Co., 1883] IV, 37, Note 1, 209)

The idea that we are too different in nature from the other animals to befriend or be allies with them goes back to the Stoics. See Richard Sorabji, *Animal Minds and Human Morals* (Ithaca NY: Cornell University Press, 1993), ch.14. On Augustine's adoption of that position as decisive for Christianity, see 195ff. By way of contrast, Maimonides (*MN* 1:75, 209) teaches that animals have imagination and feelings exactly like us, and that this directly entails certain ethical obligations. See p.148. For further discussion of Spinoza, see K.L.F. Houle, "Spinoza and Ecology Revisited", *Environmental Ethics* 18:4 (Winter 1997): 417–31; 422ff. Susan Board, *Ecological Relations: Towards an Inclusive Politics of the Earth* (London: Routledge, 2002), 146–50; and Stephen David Ross, *The Gift of Truth: The Gathering Good* (Albany NY: SUNY Press, 1997), 101–9. Ross is quite generous to Spinoza in how he reinterprets this passage (as well as another passage about women he calls "heinous"). However, he does not discuss the following passage:

> Excepting man, we know no individual thing in Nature in whose mind we can take pleasure, nor anything which we can unite with ourselves by friendship or any kind of intercourse, and therefore regard to our own profit does not demand that we should preserve anything which exists in Nature excepting men, but teaches us to preserve it or destroy it in accordance with its varied uses, or to adapt it to our own service in any way whatever.
> (*Ethic*, IV, Appendix 26, 247)

[458] See Excursus 1 and further discussion, p.144ff. and n.471.
[459] *TanchB Noach* 10; *Tanch Noach* 7, ad Gn 8:1, "And Elohim remembered Noach and every animal and every beast with him in the ark..." The implication is that only God can truly understand the soul of an animal, which is to some degree closed off from us who are dependent on speech. *Tanch* is particularly rich in passages that assume a deeply moral relationship between other animals and humans, and between other animals and God. Scholarship examining how this reflects *Tanch*'s cultural context would be valuable.
[460] *BR* 30:6; a parallel passage in *TanchB Noach* 2, reads:

> "And one who acquires souls is wise"—this is Noach, who acquired souls, and was nourishing them and feeding them... The twelve months that Noach did in the ark, he did not taste the taste of sleep, not in the day and not in the night, for he was busy feeding the souls that were with him, so "one who acquires souls", this is Noach.

Scripture itself also questions the distinction between human and animal souls: "Who knows the *ru'ach* of the children of Adam, if she rises upward, and the *ru'ach* of the beast, if she descends below, to the earth?" [Ec 3:21]. The rhetorical thrust of Ecclesiastes' question is that human and animal souls are of the same nature and could possibly go to the same place. Obviously, the verse is consistent with the pessimistic tone of Ecclesiastes. Nevertheless, this destabilization of the division between other animals and humans recurs in various commentaries. For example, Ramban quotes Ecclesiastes when he explains why the first humans did not have permission to eat meat:

[T]his was because the ones who possess a moving soul / *ba`aley nefesh t'nu`ah* (animals) have a little of the superiority in their soul that makes them similar /*nidmu* to the ones who possess a rational soul / *ba`aley hanefesh hamaskelet* (humans), and in them there is choice/freedom/*b'chirah* concerning their good and their sustenance, and they flee from pain and death, and [so] scripture says: "Who knows (etc.)"[461]

According to Ramban's reading of the verse, humans were not permitted to eat meat because the nature of an animal's soul is too similar to the nature of a person's.

This close connection between human and animal souls is reflected even in the passage from *Midrash Otiyot d'Rabi Aqiva* quoted previously, in one of the few passages that discusses an intrinsic difference between the human soul and the animal soul:

Nun: Why is the *Nun* [in two forms], one crouched/*ravuts* (נ), and one straight and standing (ן)? Because the *n'shamah* of the creatures was created through him (through *Nun*). For each and every soul/*n'shamah* sometimes is crouching, sometimes is straight. In the time that Adam crouches, his soul crouches, and in the time that Adam straightens, his soul straightens, as it says: "A lamp of YHVH is the human soul / *nishmat adam*, searching all chambers of the womb" [Pr 20:27].[462]

This passage can be said to deconstruct the difference between the human and other animals, imagining the human soul "crouching" like a four-legged animal and standing straight like a human. This agenda is discussed explicitly in the next teaching, which begins with a question: "'A lamp of YHVH is the human soul' — and not the animal's soul / *nishmat b'heimah*. But is it not [said that] the human soul and the animal soul all go to one place?" (based on the verse from Ecclesiastes). In response, the teaching enumerates many ways in which humans and other animals are the same. Finally, after describing the way a human soul – but not an animal soul – is judged after death, it asserts that the animal soul "is not created in the *d'mut*". Nevertheless, the rhetorical flow of the passage has the effect of bracketing that conclusion, indicating that the answer was considered less than obvious.

---

[461] *ad* Gn 1:29. Ramban adds that after the flood, "the body of an animal/*chai*, which does not talk, became permitted after death, [but] not the soul itself." See n.486.

[462] BM vol.2, §*Nun*, 381–2, also discussed p.74.

These passages taken together underscore that the perspective of *Chazal*, even through most of the Geonic period, was one of weak anthropocentrism, moderated by the assumption that animals have souls. In Kabbalah, this assumption fed the idea that human souls could be reincarnated into animals.[463] Most importantly, at no point in classical Jewish thought were animals regarded as machines, as non-sentient, or as non-feeling.

---

[463] See Gershom Scholem, "Gilgul", *Encyclopedia Judaica*, 2nd edn., eds. Michael Berenbaum and Fred Skolnik (Detroit: Macmillan, 2007), 7:603 (hereafter *EJ*).

5

Ethics and the others
Moral fellowship with animals and beyond animals

> How can the blood of this one that did not sin be spilled by the hand of a sinner?
> *Sefer Chasidim*, §373

> We are human only in contact, and convivality, with what is not human.
> David Abram, *The Spell of the Sensuous*, 22

The previous chapter explored the idea that animals have souls. This chapter will explore other dimensions of the human–animal relationship in Jewish thought, and how they played out in ethical terms. Consequently, while the main purpose of this book is to consider the intrinsic value of all species and ecosystems, the issues discussed here will mainly relate to animal species and "animal rights". Because this chapter falls outside the subject of *tselem*, I will deal with some of the relevant Kabbalistic literature here, rather than revisiting these themes in Part II. The final sections will look at ways in which the ethical norms and ideals related to animals were extended to all Creation, especially in the work of kabbalist Moshe Cordovero.

THE OTHERS: ETHICS EXTENDED TO ANIMALS

Paul Shepard, in his book *The Others: How Animals Made Us Human*, writes, "[T]he human species emerged catching, dreaming, and thinking animals and cannot be fully itself without them. I return to the animals as Others in a world where otherness of all kinds is in danger, and in which otherness is essential to the discovery of the true self."[464] Shepard calls on us to understand our humanity in relationship to the other creatures.

---

[464] (Washington DC: Island Press, 1997), 4–5. David Abram's *Becoming Animal* also touches these issues on a deep level, though it is not as apropos as one might imagine from the title.

Animal ethics, animal rights, and animal sacrifice

It is very clear both in the Torah and in the halakhic application of its rules by the rabbis that the animals we use have some kind of status as ethical ends.[465] Laws about the suffering of animals, about not muzzling domestic animals to prevent them from eating when they work, about not taking the life of a mother and child together, as well as many of the laws concerning kosher slaughter, appear to have consideration for the subjectivity and intrinsic needs of the creatures we care for.[466] Wild animals had the right to enter the agricultural fields and eat during Sabbatical year (Lv 25:7). Also, when wild animals were caught and slaughtered, their blood was given a burial (Lv 17:13 – see n.476). That animals have standing is reflected at an even more fundamental level in the Torah's use of the same vocabulary for human and animal bodies. Both an animal and a human are called *nefesh* (see Excursus 1), and the substance of both is called *basar*, flesh.

Yet the Torah did permit the eating of certain animals, which meant that it needed to make some kind of distinction between human and animal bodies. Instead of doing this by denying the subjecthood and subjectivity of animals, as later Western thought did, ancient Hebrew culture used rituals to symbolically inscribe different meanings on animal and human bodies. The sacrificial system of the *qorbanot* (animal offerings) found holiness in an animal's body by dividing up the body into sanctified parts, whereas the purification system of *tum'ah* and *taharah* (cultic impurity and cultic purity) found holiness in the human body by valorizing its wholeness and reconstituting its unity through immersion in *miqveh* and related rituals.

The Temple or *beyt hamiqdash*[467] existed as the ground and center where these two symbolic systems and ritual regimes interacted.[468] Sacrifices in the

---

[465] It was a commonplace in the ancient world that animals had some kind of legal standing (Beth Berkowitz, "Animals as Legal Subjects in Roman and Rabbinic Law", Association for Jewish Studies Conference, 2011).

[466] Despite the consistency of these laws and the insistence of *Chazal* that tsa`ar ba`aley chayyim (the prohibition against causing suffering to animals) is *d'orayyta*, from the Torah (*TB Bava M'tsiy`a* 32b), many medieval authors saw their purpose as edification, without concern for the subjectivity of animals themselves (p.147ff.). Modern Jewish theologians and ethicists have oft repeated these ideas uncritically (or polemically – see nn.477–8). A more accurate picture can be found in Goodman, "Respect for Nature in the Jewish Tradition" (*Judaism and Ecology*), 245–52, and Seidenberg "Animal Rights in the Jewish Tradition", in *ERN* 64–6 and at www.academia.edu/1063285/Animal_Rights_in_the_Jewish_Tradition (Apr. 2011).

[467] Literally, "the house of the sanctuary", but the rabbis use the term in a way that suggests something more than just an enclosure for the altar.

[468] See Seidenberg, "Brit Taharah: Reconstructing the Covenantal Body of the Jew", in *Sh'ma* 25/486 Jan. 20 (1995). The secret of the red heifer ritual (Nu 19) may be hidden in the need to connect these two systems. The *parah adumah* must be wholly red/*adumah* (i.e., earth-colored) like Adam/*adamah*, and wholly burnt. Its ashes were used to restore the wholeness of the human body in the case of its most extreme breach, contact with a human corpse (*nefesh* in the Torah), in a ritual incorporating other red items – cedar wood, hyssop, and crimson. In

The others: ethics extended to animals

Temple overcame the tension between the intrinsic value of an animal's life and its use-value for us. The sacrificial process harvested, as it were, the intrinsic value of the animal for an end greater than human needs or desires, something we might term its "holiness-value".[469]

Fundamentally, this holiness-value was located in the blood of the animal, which the Torah insists again and again is the *nefesh* or life of the animal – here rightly interpreted as soul in the animistic sense.[470] Because of this sanctity, the only valid use for the blood was on the altar.[471]

Human beings were required by the Torah to allow animals to meet their intrinsic needs.[472] The use-value that animals have for human beings was also weighed against the intrinsic needs of each animal in any moral calculus undertaken by the rabbis.[473] These intrinsic needs were determined by each species' nature, as well as by a generalized rabbinic understanding that animals were sentient and could suffer, and that they had their own purposes and potential for relationship beyond their use-value to us. This is reflected in the rabbinically derived Torah prohibition against sterilizing animals, as well as in other *mitsvot*, such as the prohibition against muzzling an animal that is being used to thresh grain (Dt 25:4).

---

the red heifer ritual, the redness of blood was externalized and the body of the animal was kept whole – thereby combining elements of the *taharah* system and the *qorbanot*. Both the sacrifice of the heifer and the ritual of purification that used its ashes happened outside the Temple and the camp. These rituals thus formed the second pole of a circuit, whose opposite pole was the *mishkan* or Temple altar, where perfect whole humans offered the blood and parts of perfect animals. Cf. Lev 14, which describes the ritual for purification from *tsara`at*/leprosy, which also happened outside the camp.

[469] See Seidenberg, "Kashroots: An Eco-History of the Kosher Laws", www.jcarrot.org/kashroots-an-eco-history-of-the-kosher-laws (Nov. 2008); rev. 2009, www.neohasid.org/torah/kashroots (Sep. 2011).

[470] On these verses, see p.140. In essence, the *nefesh* was localized to the blood so that the *basar* or flesh could become permitted for eating. See Seidenberg, "Kashroots". The prohibition against eating blood is repeated without reference to *nefesh* at Lv 7:26–7, 19:26; Dt 12:16, 15:23.

[471] See esp. Lv 17:10–12. Similarly, the *cheilev* of sacrificed animals, that is, the omentum and visceral fat found on the kidneys and liver, was offered on the altar and forbidden to be eaten (Lv 7:23–7). For wild ruminants like deer, which could be eaten but not sacrificed, the Torah also required their blood be covered with earth (see n.476). The *cheilev* of a wild animal, however, could be consumed, because it did not have the sanctity of the soul.

[472] The question of whether these needs should be ascribed primarily to individual animals or to species is related to a well-known *machloqet* or debate between Maimonides and Ramban about *shiluach haqein*, the mitsvah to send the mother bird away when taking the eggs or chicks (Dt 22:6–7), and *oto v'et b'no*, the prohibition against sacrificing an animal and its parent on the same day (Lv 22:28). Maimonides declares that the reason for the mitsvah is to avoid causing suffering to individual animals (see p.148). Ramban rejects Maimonides' reasoning and expounds several other reasons, which include the Torah forbidding anything that would "uproot" (or have the appearance of uprooting) an entire species (commentary *ad* Dt 22:6; see n.477). The debate between Maimonides and Ramban parallels contemporary debates between animal rights activists and environmentalists.

[473] Seidenberg, "Animal Rights in the Jewish Tradition", 64.

Since the intrinsic needs of an animal can override its use-value to humans, these needs represent a modified notion of intrinsic value, and the obligation to respect these needs functions as the equivalent of rights. Moreover, even when the use of an animal was clearly permitted, the rabbis called into question whether this represented the ideal of righteousness. When Rebbe (R' Yehudah Hanasi) commands a calf seeking refuge from slaughter to return to its place, telling it, "Go, you were made for this [purpose]", they (i.e., the angels) say, "Since he shows no mercy let afflictions come on him", and they afflict him with sickness and pain.[474] The conflicted message of this story is that even the proper use of an animal's life could not be fully justified from the perspective of righteousness.

Suffering and tsa`ar ba`aley chayyim

The experience of animals as subjects, and their capacity to feel pain, led to the codification of laws against causing needless suffering to animals, *tsa`ar ba`aley chayyim*. Some mystical interpretations of Jewish law attribute a kind of personhood to animals in their attempts to understand the reason behind *tsa`ar ba`aley chayyim*, as in this passage from Yehudah Hechasid (1150–1217, Germany) in *Sefer Chasidim*:

[I]f [a person] causes needless pain to animals / *tsa`ar ba`aley chayyim b'chinam*... he comes to judgment for causing pain to animals... [Thus] the sages explained "in that day I will strike every horse" [Zc 12:4] [to mean that] the Holy One is destined to punish the humiliation of horses from their riders[475]

Humiliation can only be a sin against persons, so to speak, whether they be two- or four-footed. Similarly, the characteristic innocence of animals is invoked in the same work to understand the significance of the commandment to cover the blood of a slaughtered wild animal:

[W]hen a person slaughters an animal or bird, he should think in his heart, this one that did not sin was slaughtered... [H]ow then can a person who is full of sin overcome spilling blood / *sh'fikhut damim* (a term usually meaning murder of a human being) and *Gehinom* (Hell)? And he should consider how the Holy One commanded him to cover an animal's or bird's blood (Lv 17:13), lest the angel [having] authority over them should say, "How can the blood of this one that did not sin be spilled by the hand of a

---

[474] TB Bava M'tsiy`a 85a || BR 33:3. Rebbe is healed after he protects rodents living in his house, invoking the verse "and His mercies are over all His works" [Ps 145:9]. Rebbe receives from heaven what he gives to the creatures.

[475] §44, 104. See next source, as well as 425–7, §§666–70 (on §666, see n.515). SCh in these sections demonstrates a unique sensitivity toward animals. Though Haym Soloveitchik has disagreed with this characterization (lecture discussion, Association for Jewish Studies Conference, 2002), it appears to me to be incontrovertible.

sinner whose sin is like scarlet and worm", and [thus] they [become] sealed in the blood decreed for death.[476]

The limitations of *Sefer Chasidim*'s notion of the personhood of animals are also clearly demonstrated here, where the mitsvah becomes a way of tricking the animal's angel into not recognizing the sin of the human slaughterer. Nonetheless, the exhortation is not to commit subterfuge, but to respect the subjecthood of the animal even in the process of using its life for our own sustenance.

This strong sensitivity, however, was generally lost when Jewish philosophy became predominant. Many of the medieval philosophers declared that the purpose of laws commanding kindness or compassion toward non-human animals was purely instrumental, teaching us nothing about animal subjectivity. The *only* purpose of these rules, according to them, was to prevent people from becoming cruel (i.e., to each other), or even simply to command obedience. (Many medieval and modern thinkers incorrectly interpret Ramban as though he held this position.[477]) Some modern halakhists and theologians even

---

[476] §373, 273. In rabbinic parlance, this mitsvah is sometimes called *kavod ladam* or *k'vod hadam*, "respecting the blood". Cf. Rav Kook, who says that the purpose of covering the blood is to "hide your shame [about eating meat] and your moral weakness" (*Chazon Hatsim'chonut v'Hashalom*, ed. David Cohen [Jerusalem: Nezer David, 1983], 23; trans. Jonathan Rubenstein, *A Vision of Vegetarianism and Peace*, www.jewishveg.com/AVisionofVegetarianismandPeace.pdf [Sep. 2013], 15). Another interpretation is that the blood is given a kind of burial (*BR* 22:8, discussed p.154). Avraham ben Aharon Yosef Tcharek (c.1870–1940, Poland, Palestine) also wrote that since "the life/*nefesh* of all flesh is its blood with its soul" [Lv 17:14], one has to cover it "as for a person, where one needs to bury him" (*Divrey Avraham* [Jerusalem: Ha'ivri, 1927], 21a). See further sources on *q'vurah* and *kavod ladam* at "Mitsvat Kisui Hadam" (Hebr.), §8, www.malchuty.org/2009-06-16-14-01-37/821-2012-10-25-07-39-50.html (Nov. 2013). For further discussion, see pp.154, 349.

[477] See, for example, Simcha Feuerman, "What is Our Responsibility to Other Creatures? A Jewish Perspective on Animal Suffering and Conservation", www.canfeinesharim.org/what-is-our-responsibility-to-other-creatures/ (July 2013). If, for Ramban, one purpose of these laws was "that we should not become cruel", it did not exhaust their meaning, and therefore was *not* the same as the radically human-centered position described above. For example, the command to send away the mother bird if one wishes to take the chicks or eggs, called *shiluach haqein* (Dt 22:6–7), was also a prohibition of actions that could destroy a species (which Feuerman acknowledges), and it had the further mystical significance of honoring *Binah*, "the mother of the world" (commentary *ad* Dt 22:6), while *shechitah* (kosher slaughter) honored the soul of the animal (*ad* Gn 1:29, see n.486). It was because laws against animal suffering appear overtly motivated by compassion that Ramban used them to show that *all* the *mitsvot* contained mysteries beyond their obvious meanings. On the evolution of interpretations of *shiluach haqein*, see Natan Slifkin, "Shiluach haKein: The Transformation of a Mitzvah" (Jerusalem, 2010), www.zootorah.com/RationalistJudaism/ShiluachHaKein.pdf (Sep. 2013). On *shiluach haqein* embodying an ethos of sustained yield harvesting, see Aloys Hfttermann, *The Ecological Message of the Torah: Knowledge, Concepts and Laws which Made Survival in a Land of Milk and Honey Possible* (Gainesville, FL: University Press of Florida, 1999), 123–5.

now understand *tsa`ar ba`aley chayyim* in this way, resisting any ascription of moral significance to the lives of animals.[478]

If the tendency of rationalist philosophy was to negate the suffering of animals and turn the *mitsvot* about animals into mere character lessons for human beings, Maimonides, the tradition's most celebrated and significant rationalist, completely rejects this idea:

> It is forbidden to slaughter [an animal] and its young on the same day, this being a precautionary measure to avoid slaughtering the young animal in front of its mother. For in these cases animals feel very great pain, *there being no difference regarding this pain between humankind and the other animals*. For the love and the tenderness of a mother for her child is not consequent upon reason, but upon the activity of the imaginative faculty, which is found in most animals just as it is found in humankind.[479]

We will continue to see how Maimonides' philosophy avoids the most egregious aspects of medieval and modern anthropocentrism and provides a critical foundation for Jewish and monotheistic ecotheology.[480] His example proves that there is no inherent contradiction between adopting a thoroughly rationalist interpretation of Judaism and rejecting anthropocentrism.

> Incidentally, the idea that the Torah forbids actions that could destroy a species, while given a more biocentric reading by Ramban, can be interpreted anthropocentrically. Don Yitshak Abravanel (1437–1508, Portugal, Spain) wrote that "this commandment is given not for the sake of the animal world but rather so that it shall be good for humankind when Creation is perpetuated, so that one will be able to partake of it again in the future" (quoted by Eliezer Diamond in "Jewish Perspectives on Limiting Consumption", Bernstein, 80–87; 85). However, this is far from Ramban's interpretation. See, David Vogel, "How Green Is Judaism? Exploring Jewish Environmental Ethics", *Judaism* 50:1 (Winter 2001): 66–81; 67.

[478] See, for example, J. David Bleich, "Vegetarianism and Judaism", *Tradition* 23:1 (Summer 1987): 86–9; 84. Bleich's tendentiousness can readily be seen if one compares his presentation of Rav Kook with David (Dovid) Sears's in *The Vision of Eden: Animal Welfare and Vegetarianism in Jewish Law and Mysticism* (Jerusalem: Orot, 2003). See also Seidenberg, "Animal Rights in the Jewish Tradition", 65–6.

[479] *MN* 3:48, 599, my emphasis. See discussion in "Maimonides", *ERN* 1027. Maimonides conjoins this mitsvah, called *oto v'et b'no*, with *shiluach haqein*: "If...the mother is let go and escapes...she will not be pained by seeing that the young are taken...In most cases this will lead to people leaving everything alone" (600). Imagine the shock he would feel were he to see Jews so eager to do the mitsvah of *shiluach haqein* that they were taking away eggs from nesting birds without any intention of using them, as occurs in the Haredi community. This custom emerged in part because of a Zoharic teaching (see *TZ* 23a) that *shiluach haqein* is *intended* to arouse suffering in the mother bird, so as to arouse God's compassion (Slifkin, "Shiluach haKein", 17–18, 26ff.). This example is a stark reminder that Kabbalah can be at odds with ecology.

[480] See related passages herein, on pp.15–16, 23ff., 27ff., 160, 268ff. What led Maimonides to this unique valuing of other animals alongside humans? His metaphysics was certainly anthropocentric. One might speculate that his radically theocentric view compressed the difference between humanity and non-human species, yet most other theocentric thinkers were anthropoarchic (see Sokol, "Ethical Implications", 271–5). Rather, his attitude may flow from his "cosmocentrism" (see p.270).

The others: ethics extended to animals

Stewardship and mercy as *imitatio Dei*

Though one can outline moral models that transcend anthropocentrism (as we will see further on), stewardship is a more normative framework for Jewish ethics toward animals. According to the classical model of stewardship, a steward administers a fiefdom for the benefit of a lord. Applying this to environmental ethics, humans steward Creation not for the good of future generations (which still implies human ownership even if that ownership is deferred), but rather for the sake of God, who is the focus of both human `avodah and Nature's unfolding.

Our caretaking toward the other animals was understood by the rabbis to be related to God's caretaking and to God's image. *Tanchuma* asks: "Why is Noach called righteous? Because he fed the creatures of the Holy One, and **became like his Creator** / *na`aseh k'bor'o*. Thus it says: 'For the Lord is righteous, loving righteous deeds' [Ps 11:7]."[481] For us, as for God, righteousness is related to taking care of other creatures.

God's mercy is often typified in Midrash by the verse "and His compassion/mercies /*rachamav* are over all His creatures" [Ps 145:9].[482] This same verse delineates how human beings should act toward other living creatures.[483] Later texts also understand God's mercy through the lens of God's relationship to the creatures. A sixteenth-century example can be found in Cordovero's *Tomer D'vorah*:

[A person's] mercies should be distributed to all the creatures, not despising them and not destroying them, for so is the highest (divine) wisdom distributed to all the creatures, silent and growing and moving and speaking (mineral, animal, vegetable, human).[484]

Cordovero here cites the story about Rebbe, already mentioned. According to Cordovero, being merciful implies that we have an obligation of spiritual stewardship, such that how we use other creatures must bring benefit to their souls. Only then is it "permitted to uproot the growing thing and to kill the animal, the debt [being outweighed] by the merit".

While the model of stewardship in Jewish tradition is still anthropocentric, it assumes that animals have spiritual needs, that there is an inherent value in our relationships with other creatures, and that these relationships can positively actualize the meaning of God's image. It also limits human power: we administer Creation on God's behalf, properly taking only to fulfill what God needs from us, and caring for the other creatures as God would care for them.

---

[481] *TanchB Noach* 4. The standard edition of *Tanch* leaves out "*v'na`aseh k'bor'o*" (*Noach* 5). Note that *Tanch* is the earliest text where an explicit connection is made between *imitatio Dei* and God's image. See pp.107–8.
[482] e.g., *Tanch Noach* 6.   [483] e.g., *BR* 33:3, *TB Bava M'tsiy`a* 85a (n.474), and *Zohar* in n.497.
[484] Ch.3, 20, quoted at greater length pp.163–5, 186. On the anthropology underlying Cordovero's ethics, see pp.189–90, 252.

As such, true stewardship is an important step toward connecting with the more-than-human world.

Beyond stewardship

From the perspective of environmental ethics, stewardship, though important, is a limited basis for changing the way we live. Stewardship still assumes a hierarchy that *separates* humans from the natural world, and the human self-image as caretaker over other species can encourage arrogance rather than mutuality. It is inherently prone in its secularized version to cast humans in the role of the powerful, wise masters of the earth, whose needs are still the measure of all things.[485]

Commentaries on Noach reflect this dynamic when they explain that because the animals came under Noach's care, they became like his possessions, and he could now kill and eat them. Ramban for examnple says Noach was granted permission to eat the animals because "their existence was because of him".[486] Thus, after Noach and his family emerge from the ark, Noach's role changes, from caretaker and steward to master, and the animals' new relationship to humankind becomes one of "terror and dread" rather than dominion.[487] The meaning of this change is explored further on p.158ff.[488]

One midrash in *B'rei'shit Rabbah* directly criticizes stewardship. The passage in question concerns the dove Noach sent out from the ark to see if dry land had yet appeared, who brought back an olive leaf (Gn 8:8–11). In the midst of a debate about whether the olive leaf came from Israel or from the Garden of Eden, R' Abahu asks: If the dove had come from Eden, why did she return to Noach with an olive leaf, which is bitter, instead of "something

---

[485] See Eisenberg's critique in *The Ecology of Eden*, 285–88.

[486] *ad* Gn 1:29: "Because Noach rescued [the animals] to keep the species in existence, [God] gave them (the people) permission to slaughter and to eat, because their (the animals') existence was because of him /ba`avuro." However, Ramban adds:

> [W]ith all this, [God] did not give permission for the soul/*nefesh* (i.e., the blood) and forbade [any] part [taken] from a living-animal / *eiver min hachai*... and this is the reason for *shechitah* and what [it means] that *"tsa`ar ba`aley chayyim* is from the Torah" (*TB Bava M'tsiy`a* 32b) and this is [the reason for] our blessing... "who commanded us concerning *shechitah*".

A possible consequence of stewardship, in this view, can be a kind of moral insensitivity. But Ramban suggests that we are protected from that outcome by the laws prohibiting blood and *eiver min hachai*.

[487] "Bear fruit and multiply and fill the land, and a terror of you and dread of you will be over all" [Gn 9:1–2].

[488] There is moreover an understanding in the current-day Jewish community that permission to eat meat was granted Noach as a concession to human violence. The sources for this view are explored in Sears, *The Vision of Eden*, 155ff. See also Richard Schwartz, *Judaism and Vegetarianism* (New York: Lantern Books, 2001), 1–15. Rav Kook is the most important proponent of this interpretation – see *Chazon Hatsim'chonut v'Hashalom*, 9, 13; *A Vision of Vegetarianism and Peace*, 2–3, 6; also excerpted in Sears, 338–40.

The others: ethics extended to animals

special, cinnamon or balsam"? The answer, he says, is that the dove was hinting to Noach, "better is bitterness from [*Gan 'Eden*] and not sweetness from beneath your hand."[489]

This midrash decries the loss of wildness that comes when humans are caretakers of other creatures – even when we are merciful caretakers. Both humanity and the creatures themselves suffer this loss. Shepard also reflects on a similar dynamic: "The idea of 'mercy' toward animals, with its detached overriding of nonhuman life and its assumptions about 'lower' and 'higher' life forms, seems to me... dangerous and anemic."[490]

One Torah-based model of our relationship to the creatures and the land that goes beyond stewardship is described in J. Baird Callicott's "Genesis and John Muir".[491] Callicott suggests that an entirely different Biblical anthropology emerges if we just look at the passages identified with the so-called "J" or Yahwist source (primarily, for this purpose, the second and third chapters of Genesis). These passages develop what Callicott calls a "citizenship model", in which humanity is created to live in close communion with the other creatures.[492] The separation of humanity from the other creatures, represented in Genesis 1 by God's image, is according to Callicott only found in the "P" or Priestly source. In "J", not only is the idea of God's image absent, but those characteristics that separate humanity from the other creatures, emblemized by knowledge of good and evil (which is not given by God), and by the need to work the soil that comes with expulsion from the garden (which is a

---

[489] *BR* 33:6; Theodor, 311, discussed further p.345. In *TB Sanhedrin* 108b, the dove speaks to God directly, rather than to Noach: "Said the dove before the Holy One: Master of the world, may my food be bitter like olive and given over in (by) Your hand, and may it not be sweet like honey and given over by a hand of flesh and blood".

[490] *The Others*, 5. Shepard contrasts the idea of merciful stewardship, which is dominant in our culture, with the idea found in other cultures that animals are the interlocutors of humanity, in which he finds "[a] humility to which I am attracted – not civilized 'kindness' but rather curiosity, receptive courtesy, gratitude, and respect for the power of animals." From a religious perspective, mercy and humility should go hand-in-hand. But that is Shepard's point: an ethical model based on human intervention and moral superiority is flawed and will too readily be distorted toward the kind of "anemic mercy" that "overrides nonhuman life".

[491] In Callicott, *Beyond the Land Ethic: More Essays in Environmental Philosophy* (Albany NY: SUNY Press, 1999), 187–220. See also Callicott, *Earth's Insights: A Survey of Ecological Ethics from the Mediterranean Basin to the Australian Outback* (Berkeley: University of California Press, 1997), 14–21.

[492] Alongside the citizenship model, Callicott identifies the stewardship model, which has become normative in Christian and Jewish ecological thought, and which comes from reading "J" and "P" together, and the despotic model, which Callicott derives from just reading the first chapter of Genesis and related "P" texts. Neither extreme is representative of traditional Jewish thought, which reads the Torah as one whole. (Note, however, that Callicott's models do correspond to Soloveitchik's Adam I and Adam II.) See also Theodore Hiebert's important work, *The Yahwist's Landscape: Nature and Religion in Early Israel* (New York: Oxford University Press, 1996), 149ff. ("Creation as Redemption: The Human as a Citizen of the Earth"), esp. his discussion of Callicott and "J" and "P", 155–162.

kind of dominion), are not seen as a positive expression of humanity's divine status. Rather, they are the result of the deterioration in humanity's relationship with the divine.

Callicott's citizenship model closely parallels Aldo Leopold's "land ethic". Though I deeply appreciate Callicott's perspective, I believe that a true citizenship model can also be derived from the whole Torah – including not just "J" but also the verses about God's image. The Torah's rich and still futuristic land ethic, embodied in the laws of *Sh'mitah* and *Yovel* – also designated by Biblical scholars as part of "P" – fulfills in spirit and praxis Aldo Leopold's vision of a world where the righteousness of an action is determined by whether it "preserve[s] the integrity, stability, and beauty of the biotic community".[493]

Animals as teachers, exemplars, and moral agents

Even though, as good stewards, we may learn *about* the creatures in order to better manage them, the Midrash also suggest that we must learn *from* them. The dove, venturing from the ark, returned as Noach's teacher, rather than Noach's charge. (The midrash, however, does not tell us that Noach understood the dove's message!) Other *midrashim* explicitly see animals as teachers. For example, one midrash asks, exactly how did Adam and Chavah learn how to bury the dead?

> Adam and his partner *l`ozro* came and cried [over Hevel (Abel)], and they did not know what to do... One raven whose companion died said: I will teach Adam this is what to do. He set down his friend and dug in the earth before their eyes and buried him. Adam said: Like the raven, this is what we will do.[494]

The raven accomplishes two *mitsvot*, burying the dead and comforting Adam and Chavah in their mourning, both of which also fall under the rubric of imitating God. Homiletically, this suggests that the ways in which we imitate God's kindness can make us similar to the other creatures, rather than different from them.

A Talmudic passage similarly explains that even without the Torah, we could learn ethical commandments by observing different species of animals.[495] The

---

[493] "The Land Ethic", *A Sand County Almanac* [New York: Ballantine Books, 1986], 239. See discussion p.167, and n.1039.

[494] PRE ch.21, 38–9. In the parallel passage from *Tanch B'rei'shit* 10, God sends two *tahor* (cult-pure) birds to Qayin. One kills the other and then buries him "with his hand *lb'yado*". Here the moral agency of the creatures is significantly reduced. Both of these *midrashim* may derive from the Qur'an, *Surah* 5:31. In BR 22:8, it is the birds and the pure (kosher) animals that bury Hevel.

[495] TB `Eruvin 100b: "Were the Torah not given, we would learn modesty from the cat, and [not] stealing from the ant, and [prohibitions concerning] sexual contact from the dove, manners/ *derekh erets* from the rooster".

The others: ethics extended to animals

thread that unites these *midrashim* is that the animals come to us as moral exemplars; they are not mere vassals or objects to be taken care of. Other *aggadot* treat animals as subjects with moral agency. The *Bavli* tells a story about R' Pinchas ben Yair's donkey, who refuses to eat untithed grain (*tevel*), to illustrate the saying, "The Holy One does not even allow a righteous person's animal to sin, so much more so the *tsadiq* himself." When the grain finally gets tithed, she eats. R' Pinchas declares, "This poor [animal] is going to do the will of her Possessor (God), and you feed her *t'veilim*?!"[496] We are dealing not just with a sinless donkey, but one who is a pious *chasidah*![497]

Here we can ask: Is this merely a fabulistic way of talking about other species? We could ask the same question of the story in the book of Numbers about Bil`am's ass, who is given the power of speech in order to say *what she was already thinking and feeling*. These stories about Bil`am and R' Pinchas illustrate one difference between the righteous and the wicked: the righteous give voice to and are aware of the intentions of their animals. While they may seem more fable than theology, they are rooted in a way of understanding the world.

Other ideas about animal agency arise from this perspective. For example, in a passage that comments on the phrase "Elohim remembered Noach and every animal" [Gn 8:1], all creatures are imagined as receiving the divine capacity to be merciful:

R' Yehoshu [of Sakh'nin] in R' Levi's name said: "*H'* is good to all", and He gives from His mercies for the creatures / `*al hab'riyot* (or: to the creatures /*liv'riyot*) (Theodor: so that they will be merciful with each other).[498]

---

[496] TB *Chulin* 7a–b ‖ TY *Dema'i* 1:3, 4a; cf. BR 60:8, ARNA ch.8, 38. In *Dema'i*, R' Pinchas's students ask, "Did we not learn, Rabbi, that the one who takes grain for an animal is free from [the obligation of] tithing?" He answers, "What [else] can we do for this poor thing, since she is strict with herself!" In another story from this same sugya of *Chulin*, R' Pinchas contests with a morally determined river (n.1048).

[497] Pinchas's donkey continued to attract attention in Kabbalah. The *Zohar* turns her into a superhero who destroys robbers, and who leads R' Pinchas to R' Shim`on Bar Yochai when Pinchas does not know the way (3:200b–202b). This section also includes other motifs of a sentient natural world. Birds come to shelter R' Shim`on. When they tire themselves taking turns shading the *chevraya*, R' Pinchas sends them away, saying, "It was enough of a burden for those birds before, and we do not want to be a burden for animals, because it's written: 'and His mercies are over all of His works' [Ps 145:9]." As the birds leave, trees spread their branches over each sage's head, and a spring spontaneously wells up. So the story of R' Pinchas's donkey attracts several other stories that depict a morally significant *and conscious* world that revels in the blessing of the righteous.

[498] BR 33:3; Theodor, 304. Theodor reads the statement that follows in the name of R' Abba as an elaboration of R' Yehoshua. In the context of Noach, Yehoshua points to the relationships between the animals. However, the story that illustrates R' Abba's teaching strictly concerns human beings, while two other stories in this chapter concern human mercy *toward* animals. While "*b'riyot*" or creatures can mean humanity, there are many cases where it is ambiguous, as here, where modern readers might assume it refers only to humanity, or where it definitively means all creatures (see *PRE* ch.11, quoted p.65).

According to R' Yehoshua of Sakh'nin (as interpreted by Theodor and "Rashi" – see n.514), the most profound expression of God's mercy or compassion is that God gives the creatures the capacity to show compassion to each other.[499]

The rabbis also extend moral agency to animals by depicting them receiving reward for their good deeds. This is how *Tanchuma* explains why the animals in the ark merit being saved: "'And Elohim remembered Noach and every animal' [Gn 8:1]—If [God] remembered Noach, why also animal and beast? May the name of the Holy One be blessed, who never deprives any creature/*b'riyah* of its reward. [If] even a mouse has preserved its family (i.e., species), and did not mix with another species, it is worthy to get a reward."[500] According to *Tanchuma*, the animals on the ark merited to be saved because they had properly performed the mitsvah of procreation.[501] They were not simply saved for Noach's sake, as one might conclude based on a superficial reading of Genesis.

Similarly, according to *B'rei'shit Rabbah* 22:8, because the birds and wild animals buried Hevel after Qayin killed him, they received the reward of having their blood buried when they are slaughtered.[502] Other *midrashim* focus on the righteous behavior of the dogs of Egypt, who were silent when the children of Israel left. Because of this, their descendants (i.e., all dogs) have the right to eat any meat that is not kosher, as it says, "to the dog you will cast it" [Ex 22:30].[503]

---

[499] This perspective is compatible with the recent research in ethology. See Introduction, p.21ff.
[500] *TanchB Noach* 11, referring to the midrash that the animals were destroyed in the flood because, along with the humans, they were having sexual intercourse between species (cf. *BR* 28:8, *TB Sanhedrin* 108a). Cf. the contrasting midrash cited in n.1027.
[501] In addition to *TanchB Noach* 11, see also *Noach* 18, which describes the animals that merited entering the ark as *tsadiqim*, and *Tanch Noach* 11, which describes them as *k'sheirim*, "kosher", i.e., upright in the moral sense, because they had not engaged in sexual relations with other species. *TanchB* also teaches that the animals "did not conjoin for being fruitful and multiplying" while in the ark, for "so did the Holy One command them" (*Noach* 17).
[502] According to Yaakov Chayyim Sofer (1870–1939, Iraq, Palestine), *Kaf Hachayyim* (Jerusalem: Moshe Sofer, 1965), this was *"midah k'neged midah"* – the mitsvah to bury a wild animal's blood (*kavod ladam*) is a direct reward for their burying Hevel (*Yoreh Dei`ah*, vol.2, 58). For more on *kavod ladam*, see pp.144–6 and nn.476. On the meaning of *kavod ladam* for our time, see p.349, esp. n.1116.
[503] *M'khilta* reads:

"To the dog you will throw it / *lakelev tishl'khun oto*" [Ex 22:30]—to teach you that the dog is more honored than the servant…to teach you that the Holy One does not cancel/wrest/*m'qapei'ach* the reward of any creature, as it is said: "and against all the children of Israel a dog will not sharpen/*yecherats* its tongue" [Ex 11:7]. Said the Holy One: Give him his reward.   (*Kaspa* 20, 321)

Similarly, *ShmR* 31:9:

Said the Holy One: You are indebted/obligated/*chayavim* to the dogs, for in the hour that I killed the firstborn of Egypt…the Egyptians were sitting all night and burying their dead, and

The others: ethics extended to animals

These examples suggest a hierarchy of moral agency. The animals are rewarded as representatives of species; Noach is saved because of his individual righteousness; his family is saved largely because of their relationship to him. We have in this schema three tiers: individual, familial or clan-based, and species-based. There are also three tiers of mitsvah. The mitsvah or righteousness a mouse performs by reproducing is a reflection of its species-nature. The mitsvah of caring for the animals performed by Noach and his family is appropriate to human beings and represents a greater level of freedom. *Tanchuma* describes this as the capacity to "become like one's Creator". Finally, and more subtly, the midrashist's ability to find moral agency in a mouse is an expression of the human capacity for empathy and personification, and the human drive to find moral meaning. Homiletically, one could say that this is what it means to see things from God's perspective or to become like God, or, more broadly, to embody God's image.

As the preceding sections should make clear, even though the Jewish tradition generally espouses a hierarchy that sets humans above any other animal, this hierarchy is not one in which humans have infinite intrinsic value and animals have only use-value. Rather, animals also have moral or intrinsic value, or, as I have defined it, intrinsic needs that have moral value.

Animals as agents of divine punishment

Beyond this, various authorities also thought humans could become prey to animals, with God's approval. This perspective is represented in interpretations of Genesis 9:5, "But your blood for your lives I will seek, from/by the hand of every animal / *miyad kol chayah* I will seek it, and from/by the hand of the human". According to Rashi (*ad loc.*), the reason the verse states, "I will

> the dogs barked at them, and at Israel they didn't bark...therefore..."to the dog you will throw it".
>
> *YSh* 1:187 incorporates both passages, adding to them a vignette often appended to the last section of *Pereq Shirah*. According to this story, R' Yisha`yah (or Osha`yah) fasted eighty-five fasts to receive an answer to the question, Why do dogs merit to sing a song of praise to God? The angel who answers him cites Ex 11:17, saying that dogs even merited that their excrement be used to tan parchment for *t'filin*, *mezuzot* and Torah scrolls. And then the angel admonishes the rabbi: "Turn yourself back (away from) what you asked and don't continue in this matter, as it's written: 'Who watches/*shomer* his mouth and his tongue, keeps/*shomer* his soul from trouble' [Pr 21:23]." Essentially, the angel tells Yisha`yah to behave at least as well as the dogs in Egypt. See also *TB Shabbat* 155b, which derives dogs' rights from Pr 29:7. For a modern reading of the *M'khilta* passage, see Emmanuel Levinas, "The Name of a Dog, or Natural Rights" in *Difficult Freedom: Essays on Judaism* (Baltimore MD: Johns Hopkins University Press, 1990), 150–53. Levinas reflects on a dog who made his home for a short time in the Nazi labor camp where Levinas was interned, and who joyfully greeted the inmates when they returned from forced labor. See also John Llewelyn's analysis of animal rights in light of this essay, "Am I Obsessed by Bobby? (Humanism of the Other Animal)" in *Re-Reading Levinas* (Bloomington: Indiana University Press, 1991), 234–46.

seek your blood from... every animal", is that God is *warning the animals* that they may no longer kill people as prey. This was necessary because God had declared the people of the flood generation to be *hefqer*, open targets to be preyed upon. Some commentators also read the phrase *miyad kol chayah* in an opposite manner, to mean that post-flood, God will send animals to kill a person who has murdered.⁵⁰⁴ Ramban, for example, writes, "It is possible that the reason for the phrase 'from every animal' is that vengeance against the one who spills blood will be from the hand of every animal... and it is saying, 'I will avenge him by the hand of /*b'yad* (by means of) every animal, for I will send against the murderer all the wild animals, and I will also send against him the human.'"⁵⁰⁵

Ramban's reading contrasts with Sforno, who strongly underlines the hierarchy between humankind and all the animals. Sforno writes, "If he (the victim) merits, 'by the hand of every animal I will seek [to rescue] him, and by the human hand'... If he does not merit this... and he is killed... I will seek the life of the one who was killed from the hand of his brother who killed him... but *not* by the hand of the animal."⁵⁰⁶

The idea that animals may take vengeance for murder is not only expressed here. In *B'rei'shit Rabbah*, Qayin is beset by the animals after he murders Hevel: "R' Yitshak (Isaac) said: Beast and wild animal and bird gathered in to take retribution for Hevel's blood."⁵⁰⁷ Rashi relates this teaching to Qayin's statement that "anyone finding me will kill me" [Gn 4:14]. According to Rashi, Qayin pleads, "Until now I would instill fear /*pichad'ti* over all the wild animals/*chayot*... and now because of this sin the animals won't fear me, and they will kill me immediately/*miyad*". In response, God "'made a sign/*ot* for Qayin' [Gn 4:15]—He made fear of him return over all".⁵⁰⁸

---

⁵⁰⁴ This perspective is also reflected in halakhic midrash, which states: "'from every animal'—even without warning/*hat'ra'ah*" (*TB Sanhedrin* 57b; *YSh* 1:61). *Hat'ra'ah* refers to the stricture in Jewish law that a person can only receive the death penalty if that person was warned before committing the crime that its punishment was death. The import of the *Bavli* is that even without warning, death could be meted out by a court in Noach's time. The *Bavli* derives this from the idea that God may send animals, who kill without warning, to mete out punishment. (*BR* 34:14 instead derives this point from the words, "by a human his blood will be spilled" [Gn 9:6]. The *Bavli* instead uses this phrase to prove a different halakhic point, that capital punishment could be meted out with only one witness in Noach's time, rather than the two required in a Jewish court.)

⁵⁰⁵ *ad* Gn 9:6. Ramban *ad* Gn 9:5 discusses the more straightforward explanation that God will seek death of any animal who kills a human. However, he rejects that explanation, because an animal does not have the awareness needed to be able to receive punishment or reward.

⁵⁰⁶ *ad* Gn 9:5–6. According to Sforno, animals may be enlisted to kill an assailant in order to rescue a potential victim, but not in order to punish a murderer. See also p.103.

⁵⁰⁷ *BR* 22:12.

⁵⁰⁸ *ad* Gn 4:15, *s.v.* "YHVH made for Qayin a sign". One interpretation of Rashi's comment is that Qayin lost God's image when he killed his brother. The sign, substituting for the image, prevents him from being killed by the animals, but does not restore his dominion over them. Rashi further explains: "[T]here weren't any humans/children of *Adam* left, only his mother

The others: ethics extended to animals

Lastly, the Torah itself outlines that God will bring animals to prey upon the people as a chastisement: "I will send out against you the animal of the field / *chayat hasadeh* and she will make you childless and cut off your animals and diminish you" [Lv 26:22].[509] In this context, the animals, who should have been allowed to share the Sabbatical year produce from the land alongside the people, instead take the people themselves as their due.

Civilization, according to some anthropologists, is founded on an order in which humans can take from Nature and predate upon other animals, but are not to be taken as prey by other humans or animals. These passages show that such an order was seen as normal by commentators, but not as necessary. In other words, under certain circumstances, the lives of the animals may take precedence over a human life. Importantly, according to some of these interpretations, animals participate in the moral order in a direct and sentient way, responding to signs and fulfilling commands. More generally, animals have a role to play in the moral order, whether as subjects sensing the loss of God's image, or as tools executing God's judgment.

Midrashim discussed in the previous three sections reflect a worldview in which animals can, within the limits of their own nature, be moral actors. This is in some sense the converse of the approach of sociobiology and evolutionary biology, where every behavior is understood as a computation to maximize genetic survival. In the simple will to survive, the Midrash recognizes the qualities of mercy and mitsvah. Though humans may have a unique and profound perspective on mercy, it is not humans alone that can show mercy, nor is it humans alone that may execute judgment or justice. Both capacities can emerge out of instinctual behavior and out of the interplay of species that shapes the actions of each creature.[510] Human beings, we might say, are uniquely able to bring this reality into consciousness, both through our actions and through understanding the relationships between other creatures.

---

and father, and from them he would not be afraid." (The locution "they will kill me *miyad*" can be read as an allusion to Gn 9:5, "from the hand/*miyad* of every animal".)

[509] This is the third of six curses for not observing the Sabbatical year, which describe the unraveling of the relationship between the people and the land, marked by who eats what or whom. See Davis, *Scripture*, 99–100. The thread of this progression is woven in and out with other threads, but here is what it looks like when we pull it out: (1) "you will sow your seed for emptiness, for your enemies will eat it" [v.16]; (2) "you will completely use your strength for emptiness, and your land will not give her produce and the tree of the land will not give his fruit" [v.20]; (3) as quoted above, the wild animals will eat you; (4) "you will be gathered (i.e., like a harvest) into your cities... and I will break the staff of bread against you... you will eat, and you will not be satisfied" [v.26]; (5) "you will eat the flesh of your sons and your daughters' flesh you will eat" [v.29]; (6) "you will be lost in the nations and the land of your enemies will eat you" [v.38]. Because the Jewish people was in exile for so long, the last curse does not sound like the worst one; because we love our children, it is the fifth that sounds the worst. But symbolically, if the land eats us, this represents the final step: a complete reversal of the right relationship between people and land.

[510] See nn.66–8 on cognitive ethology and related research.

Dominion

Any discussion of animal ethics must come to some understanding of dominion. Dominion is equally important to understanding *tselem*, since according to Midrash it is the presence of *tselem* that sustains human dominion over the animals.[511] Returning to the creation story, what does "Let them have dominion" or "They will dominate" mean? What was its content?

As many commentaries understood it, the first humans were only allowed to eat plants and fruit.[512] The Talmud in *Sanhedrin* therefore interprets dominion to mean the right to use animals for work.[513] However, if one takes Genesis 2 to be filling in details about Genesis 1 (as was normative), it would seem that humans had no need to work the land with implements or draught animals until after they were expelled from *Gan Eden*. So dominating the animals could not have meant using them, at least not *ab initio*.

"Rashi" on *B'rei'shit Rabbah*[514] instead describes Adam's relationship with the animals this way: "Adam would call them and they would come, for they were in his *r'shut*/domain."[515] According to this, dominion or *r'diyah* means the power to name, "he would call them", and to tame, "and they would come". This also means the animals related to humans without fear,[516] and had both the capacity to respond to language and the desire to respond.

---

[511] See pp.97–8. See Cohen, "Be Fertile and Increase", esp. 68–76 and 81.

[512] See, e.g., *TB Sanhedrin* 59b. In the Jewish environmental world, some read this as proof that the ideal human state is to be vegetarian. Contrast this perspective with Saadyah Gaon, discussed n.315. (Note, however, that Hevel's sacrifice of animals in Gn 4:4 is pleasing to God, and that according to *TB `Avodah Zarah* 8a, Adam offered up a bull when he and Chavah saw the sun rise the first time. So the killing of an animal must have been understood as permitted.)

[513] *TB Sanhedrin* 59b. The Gemara then comes up with fabulistic examples of how fish and birds and "the creeping/crawling animal / *chayah haromeset*" can be used for work. The example given of a "crawling animal" that can work is the *nachash*, the snake or serpent, before it was cursed. Of course, in Eden, the snake was not yet crawling.

[514] Though this commentary is published in the name of Rashi, Yonah Frankel (*Midrash v'Aggadah*, vol.3 [Tel Aviv: Open University, 1996], 904) says it was written by an Italian author from the same period.

[515] ad BR 34:12 (discussed further on). *R'shut* is a rabbinic term, but it is related to *net/reshet* in the *Tanakh*, which derives from YRSh, meaning to take possession or inherit (*BDB s.v.* YRSh). *SCh* (§666, 425) similarly states that Noach and his sons had no dominion over the animals, and in fact posits that the permission to eat animals precludes dominion and vice versa.

[516] This does not explain why *BR* says terror and dread **returned**, meaning they were present before the flood. The actual Rashi's Torah commentary can be used to explain this. Rashi says that the animals feared Qayin before he murdered Hevel, and that fear "returned" only when Qayin was given a sign by God (see p.156). This implies that if there was no fear between humans and animals in the garden, there was fear after Adam and Chavah were expelled. This motif dovetails with the aggadah that Nimrod became a great hunter because he possessed the cloak of skin God had given to Adam, and that Nimrod would wear it in the field and "all the animals and birds in the world would come and gather around him" (*BR* 63:13). The understanding of this aggadah is that after the flood, terror was placed upon the animals, so that the only circumstance in which they would come toward humans was when they were

The others: ethics extended to animals

This is very nearly the opposite of the "terror and dread" that according to Torah characterized the animals' response to human beings after the flood. When Noach and all the other creatures leave the ark, God says, "Bear fruit and multiply and fill the land, and terror of you and dread of you will be over all" [Gn 9:1–2]. Far from being a restatement of dominion, the power of dominion in Genesis 1 is replaced by "terror and dread", while the power of conquest/*kibush* over the land is simply absent.[517] *B'rei'shit Rabbah* explains that a shift had taken place: "Terror and dread returned [after they left the ark], but dominion/*r'diyah* did not return."[518]

What does it mean to say that *r'diyah* did not return? First, if indeed dominion exists only when the *tselem* of God is present, as taught elsewhere (see p.97), then this would imply that the image of God had left humanity.[519] Second, "terror and dread", qualities one might have thought were descriptive of human dominion, are not what constitute dominion at all.[520] If so, we see here the trope that to become less like God means to lose one's connection and mutuality with other creatures. This midrash (and perhaps the Torah itself) had in mind two different models of power, one defined as rule or dominion and characterized by mutuality, the other characterized by fear (i.e., just rule vs. tyranny). However, a medieval restatement of the idea of dominion in the *Zohar* (or *Sefer Hazohar*, "The Book of Radiance") – the most canonical, literary, and encompassing work of Kabbalah – does equate the elements of *tselem* and dominion with terror and dread:

When the Holy One created the world, He made all the creatures of the world, each and every one in its image... and after He created the human/ *bar nash* in the high/upper image / *d'yoqna ila'a*, and made him rule over all the others through this image; for all the time a human remains/stands in the world, all these creatures of the world

---

deceived – specifically, when they were lulled by a reminder of the Edenic relationship that once existed between them and human beings.

[517] Even the power of reproduction is somehow altered. At the end of this charge to Noach and his children, God says, "And you, bear fruit and multiply, **swarm**/*shirtsu* in the land and multiply in her" [Gn 9:7]. This sounds like an increase in the power of reproduction, and it may be read as a way to ameliorate humanity's destruction by the flood. However, it may also indicate that the humans have become more like the sea and land creatures that swarm in Genesis 1, and less like God. In fact, the same word, used to describe the population increase of the Israelites in Egypt ("*vayishr'tsu*", Ex 1:7), is interpreted this way by Sforno ("they inclined to the ways of swarming things/*sh'ratsim*"), and Azaryah Figo (1579–1647, Italy), in *Binah La`itim*, wrote, "they were as swarming beast and as the lowest of animals, whose whole purpose is to satisfy their passions" (quoted in Roni Weinstein, *Juvenile Sexuality, Kabbalah, and Catholic Reformation in Italy* [Leiden, Netherlands: E. J. Brill, 2009], 119).

[518] BR 34:12.

[519] According to this passage, *r'diyah* did return in the time of Shlomo (Solomon). Shlomo's dominion is represented in Midrash by Shlomo controlling demons, or by understanding the speech of the animals. On the latter, see p.325.

[520] According to some modern interpreters of the Bible, "terror and dread" define exactly what dominion means according to the "P" source (e.g., Callicott, discussed pp.151–2).

raise/*zaq'fin* [their] head and gaze on the person's high image, so that they will be in fear and trembling before him, as it says: "terror of you and dread of you will be over every animal" [Gn 9:2]—these words are when they look and see in him that image and the soul in him. Said R' Elazar: ... [W]hen a person does not follow the ways of the Torah, that holy image goes away from him, and then the beasts of the wilderness and the birds of the skies are able to rule over him.[521]

The equation of human rulership or dominion that came before the flood with the animals' "terror and dread" *after* the flood is not something we see in early midrash.[522]

Maimonides dealt with these complications in a radically different manner, by divorcing dominion from *tselem*. He explained that dominion is neither a commandment nor an imperative, but merely a description of human nature:

Similarly [to the heavenly bodies, which give light and rule over time by their nature], it says of man, And have dominion over the fish of the sea, and so on, which dictum does not mean that humanity was created for the sake of this, but merely gives information about man's nature with which He, may He be exalted, has stamped him.[523]

As a part of human nature, the capacity for dominion represents a potential that is not yet actualized at the beginning of the story. Maimonides' comparison also reminds us that rulership is not unique to humanity, but is also associated with the heavenly bodies. He further states that dominion should benefit the ruled, just as the rule of the stars benefits the creatures, rather than the other way around. Finally, Maimonides believed that it was both a moral and intellectual imperative to make oneself in God's image. Therefore, his assertion that the verses about dominion are merely descriptive and not imperative indicates that in his opinion, dominion over Creation is unrelated to God's image.

Intrinsic value

One cannot account for the complexity of rabbinic ideas about animals, unless one goes beyond the idea that only humans have intrinsic or essential value. Emero Stiegman's characterization of the rabbinic worldview is helpful in this regard. He writes:

---

[521] *Zohar* 1:191a; WZ 785-7 and in Scholem, *On the Mystical Shape of the Godhead*, trans. Joachim Neugroschel (New York: Schocken Books, 1991), 269 (hereafter *OMG*). Cf. *Ra`ya Mehemna* 3:123b, quoted p.228. The *Zohar*, promulgated near the end of the thirteenth century, is believed by scholars to have been written by Moshe de León (c.1250-1305), possibly with his fellow Kabbalists. The edition of the *Zohar* consulted throughout is *Sefer Hazohar*, 3 vols., ed. Reuven Margaliot (Jerusalem: Mossad Harav Kook, 1984). Electronic editions of Zoharic literature found on hebrew.grimoar.cz were also consulted.

[522] For a later midrash (maybe only a century or so before the *Zohar*) where this equation appears, see end of n.318.

[523] *MN* 3:13, 454. See also *MN* 1:7, discussed pp.70-71.

[M]an is not considered the measure of all things. Nature is not measured against him in metaphysical categories... Things were not forced to coalesce; each was seen, not "objectively", but... in its specific, separate relationship to its Maker... [S]uch a view... compels an acceptance of creatures, not according to their supposed nature, but according to their concrete relationships, to God not least. Man also, then, is not seen as an essence, but as related.[524]

If Stiegman's characterization is correct, then there may be no idea of intrinsic value at all in rabbinic thought, but rather an idea of relational value, such that even God's image in humanity represents not essence but significance, expressed in terms of a symbolic and moral relationship to the divine (see n.310). Since other creatures also stand in relation to God and to each other, they too share in this value.[525] The reason why individual humans must be treated as ends-in-themselves is not because humanity has intrinsic value over against all other species. Rather, a person's value comes from the potential significance of their *relationships* with other humans, with other creatures, and with God. Stiegman speculates that "[p]erhaps this explains why the rabbis could affirm man's centrality in creation and his dominion without reducing the world to a mere complex of useful functions."[526]

I discussed earlier the idea that Noach's stewardship of the animals resulted in a hierarchy in which human need was the measure of all things. It is possible instead to see in Noach's actions a fulfillment of the intrinsic needs felt by both human beings and other animals. The relationships Noach and his family have with the animals on the ark reflect a natural human impulse to care for other creatures and to relate to them as moral subjects. This impulse is a part of human nature, which we can identify with biophilia (*per* Wilson).[527] Acting on it fulfills an intrinsic human need that can only be attained when other species are treated as ends rather than as means. We can achieve this when we recognize some aspect of intrinsic value in them.

This perspective is consonant with rabbinic ethics in general, since the rabbis see ethical behavior as part of the natural order. That is already indicated by the fact that in rabbinic parlance, normal ethical behavior is called *derekh erets*, "the way of the earth".[528] Human behavior is part of the more-than-human world and exists within a continuum of animal behavior.[529] Homiletically speaking, seeing the image of love or caring in the actions of non-human creatures may also entail seeing the image of God in them.

[524] "Rabbinic Anthropology", 500.
[525] Aquinas's distinction may be helpful here. He says that God loves rational creatures with "the love of friendship" but loves all creatures with "the love of desire" (*Summa Theologica*, pt.2a, q.20, art.2, ro.3, 1:115).
[526] "Rabbinic Anthropology". [527] See p.340ff.
[528] On *derekh erets*, see Kadushin, *Organic Thinking*, 117–67. According to *Chazal*, "Ethics/ the way of the land comes before Torah / *Derekh erets qadmah laTorah*" (VR 9:3 and other places).
[529] See nn.66–8.

THE OTHER OTHERS: INCLUDING THE REST OF CREATION

Beyond animals – do all beings have moral standing?

Thus far I have focused on the subjectivity and moral standing of animals, and the Midrash would support that focus. Sentience and the capacity to suffer provide a normative basis for animal rights and for the attribution of ethical standing. But the conception of the Torah is far broader than that. For example, a kind of subjectivity is ascribed to the trees when, in teaching the laws of warfare, the Torah prohibits cutting down fruit trees, saying, "Is the tree of the field a person, to come before you in the siege?" [Dt 20:19]. Midrash picks up on this, stating for example that when a fruit tree is cut down, its cry goes "from one end of the world and unto its other end".[530]

Rabbinic literature abounds in stories rooted in an animistic or mythical understanding of reality such as this.[531] In the Torah, the rock at Qadesh-Barne'a is treated as a subject with a kind of personhood, for Moshe is told to speak to it in order to bring forth water (Nu 20:7–11). The later midrash reflects the animistic (or panpsychic) dimension of this story. According to *Midrash Hagadol*, the rock begins to bleed when Moshe strikes it the first time instead of speaking to it. God asks, "For what reason are you bringing forth blood?" and the rock answers, "Because Moshe hit me."[532] In *Yalqut Shim'oni*, we are taught that this rock was the same one that Moshe struck earlier in the Israelites' desert odyssey; since the rock had "grown up", it could now take instruction like a learned student, instead of being struck like a young schoolchild.[533] Arguments about appropriate pedagogy notwithstanding, these *midrashim* evince a vibrant sense of aliveness in the more-than-human world that transcends sentience.[534]

I discussed earlier (p.103ff.) how Ben Azai and R' Tanchuma used God's image to affirm that one must not despise (*m'vazeh* מבזה) one's fellow. This

---

[530] PRE ch.34, 68. Goodman cites *Yalqut Reuveni* to Genesis, "Respect for Nature", 254. In *SifreyD*, R' Yishmael even applies this stricture to fruit: "the mercy/pity/*chas* of the Place /*Hamaqom* (God) is on the fruit of the tree... just as the verse cautions you concerning the tree that makes fruits, all the more so the fruits themselves" (*pisqa* 203; 239).

[531] Michael D. Swartz, in "Bubbling Blood and Rolling Bones" (in *Antike Mythen: Medien, Transformationen und Konstruktionen*, eds. Ueli Dill and Christine Walde [Berlin: de Gruyter, 2009], 440–45), explores this dimension in rabbinic thought.

[532] vol.4, 362–3, ad Nu 20:11 ‖ *Midrash T'hilim*, 344, ad Ps 78:20. Even the *p'shat* of the story (the simple contextual meaning) seems to espouse the idea that everything in the world can be spoken to and treated as sentient. Moshe's sin is his failure to demonstrate this reality to the people.

[533] YSh 1:764. While most of YSh is based on earlier texts, Hyman, *M'qorot Yalqut Shim'oni* (Jerusalem: Mossad Harav Kook, 1974), 524, does not recognize an earlier source for this passage.

[534] Whether or not this was more than a matter of poetry and play in Midrash, it became a lived understanding in Kabbalah.

The other others: including the rest of creation

interpretation gives great symbolic value to the image of God in human beings, but it does not eliminate an obligation to treat other creatures with honor. Parallel traditions explicitly extend the moral realm beyond humanity. We read in *Mishnah Avot*, again in the name of Ben Azai: "Don't be despising/scornful / *Al t'hi baz* בז to any person/*adam*, and don't be rejecting / *v'al t'hi maflig* to any thing/*davar*, for you don't have a person who does not have his hour, and you don't have a thing that does not have its place."[535] The moral directive concerning human beings, "Don't despise anyone", is here paralleled by a directive to not reject any "thing". In context, "thing" would include animals, plants, rocks, possibly even human artifacts.

Similarly, from the commandment to not make steps going up to the altar, the midrash learns that one should show respect even to the rocks of the sanctuary. One version of this idea, which again uses the root *BZH* (in the term *bizayon* מיון), reads:

> "Do not go up steps to my altar [and expose your nakedness]" [Ex 20:22]—if this is true with stones, that do not have in them awareness/*da`at*, neither for bad nor for good, that the Holy One said: Do not act with them in a despising manner / *minhag bizayon*, then it is a rule [that even more so applies to] your fellow, who is in the likeness/*d'mut* of the One who spoke and the world was, that you should not act with him in a despising manner.[536]

The need to show respect even to something that has no awareness only strengthens the directive not to despise humans. The idea of God's image is used here to include beings that are not in God's image within the universe of moral responsibility.

All of these texts apply the priniciple "Do not do to others what is hateful to you" more broadly than is understood in any normative anthropocentric ethic. They provide a model for how moral categories may be extended beyond the realm of sentient creatures. From the perspective of constructive theology, Ben Azai's dictum in *Avot* that every thing has its place could be reframed as "Everything has its ecological niche; everything serves the needs of its own ecosystem."[537]

Looking ahead to the ways these ideas are formulated in Kabbalah, one finds that the same ideas and vocabulary are beautifully interwoven in Cordovero's *Tomer D'vorah*. Cordovero builds his ethics upon this principle of not despising, using the same terminology that referred to honoring humans to exhort his reader to honor every single creature:

---

[535] 4:3.   [536] *M'khilta Bachodesh* 11, 245.
[537] Ben Azai's distinction between the "hour/*sha`ah*", when each person may shine (so to speak), and the "place/*maqom*", where every thing may shine, begs for interpretation. It could be said that a person's truest hour unfolds in historical time when that person's unique qualities come to bear, whereas the significance of each thing is found in relation to its rightful place, that is, its home or *oikos* (from which we derive "ecology" and "economy").

[It is good medicine for a person] to honor the creatures/*nivra'im* entirely/all of them, since he recognizes in them the exalted quality of the Creator / *ma`alat haborei'* who "formed the human with wisdom"[538] and so [it is with] all creatures – the wisdom of the One who forms /*hayotser* is in them, and he [can] see himself that they are so very very honored, for the One who forms [them] cares for all... And it is even evil in the eyes of the Holy One if they despise any creature/*b'riyah* of His creatures, and this is [why] it says: "How manifold/diverse are Your works / *Mah rabu* רבו *ma`asekha*" [Ps 104:24] – ...*rabu* [like] the language of "*rav* רב *beyto* / important in the house [of the king]" [Es 1:8] – very important... and it is worthy for a person to understand through them wisdom, and not despising/*bizayon* [...] Moreover, [a person's] mercies/compassion need to be distributed to all the creatures, not despising them and not destroying them, for so is the upper/highest wisdom distributed to all the creatures, silent and growing and moving and speaking.[539]

Here again the instruction to not despise is given the broadest application possible. Cordovero evinces great passion when he brings this principle to bear on practical issues. He continues:

[Therefore a person should] not uproot a growing thing except for need, nor kill any animal / *ba`al chayyim* except for need. And he should choose a good death / *mitah yafah* for them, with a carefully examined knife, to show mercy however is possible. This is the principle: compassion/*chemlah* [should be] over all existences, to not hurt them... unless [it is] to raise them from level to level / high to higher, from growing to living, from living to speaking, for then it is permitted to uproot the growing thing and to kill the animal, the debt [being outweighed] by the merit.[540]

Differing from normative *halakhah*, Jewish ethics or law, Cordovero understands necessity not in terms of human need, but rather in terms of the need of each living thing to fulfill its divine purpose. *Tsorekh gavoha*, the need of the divine realms, is a common consideration in Kabbalah, but it is also not the primary consideration given here. Rather, the elevation of each creature serves the need of each creature itself.

To focus again on the question of animals, the expression Cordovero uses for proper slaughter, "*mitah yafah*", is especially poignant and significant. It derives from a rabbinic dictum that one must choose a good or easy death for a

---

[538] Quoting the morning blessing for the body and its functions.
[539] End of chs.2 and 3 19, 20; *Palm Tree* of Deborah, 78, 83ff. Cf. *Tomer D'vorah*, 16; *Palm Tree of Deborah*, 71.
[540] Isaac of Syria (also called Isaac of Nineveh, an Orthodox Church Father, d. c.700) explored similar themes (though in a descriptive rather than proscriptive fashion) when he wrote,

> What is a charitable heart? It is a heart burning with charity for the whole of Creation, for humans, for the birds, for the beasts, for the demons – for all creatures. He who has such a heart cannot see or call to mind a creature without his eyes becoming filled with tears by reason of the immense compassion that seizes his heart, a heart that is softened and can no longer bear to see or learn from others of any suffering, even the smallest pain, being inflicted upon a creature (discourse 81, quoted by Vladimir Lossky in *The Mystical Theology of the Eastern Church* [Crestwood NY: SVS Press, 1976], 111).

The other others: including the rest of creation

person who is going to be executed by the court. In the *Tosefta* and the Talmud, this principle is derived directly from the commandment, "Love your fellow like yourself / *V'ahavta l'rei`ekha kamokha*" [Lv 19:18].⁵⁴¹ By appropriating this terminology, Cordovero concretely extended the commandment to love one's neighbor to all animals, specifically with respect to slaughter. While Cordovero does not directly cite Leviticus, Yishayah (Isaiah) Horowitz (1562–1630, Prague, Palestine, also known as the Shlah) does. Specifically, in his work *Sh'ney Luchot Hab'rit* ("The Two Tables of the Covenant"), he quotes the Talmud's formulation, "'And you will love your fellow like yourself'—choose a good death for him", and comments, "this means *shechitah* (slaughter) without a mistake/*p'gimah*."⁵⁴²

For Cordovero, other creatures, plant or animal, are ends-in-themselves. In Part II, we will see how this sensitivity was closely tied to the idea that other creatures participate in the divine image. Here I want to highlight that for Cordovero, any use of plant or animal must in a spiritual sense benefit the plant or animal that is being used. While Cordovero articulated this principle more strongly than other Kabbalists, his work remains the foundation for all subsequent Kabbalistic ethics. Applied halakhically, this framework would revolutionize the laws of *bal tashchit*, refocusing those laws on spiritual aid rather than material profit.

Lenn Goodman provides a rational framework for extending moral standing to non-sentient creatures that may be helpful here. He ascribes what he calls "virtual subjecthood" to other creatures, which he distinguishes from the "personhood" ascribed to human beings.⁵⁴³ He reads the Torah's injunction against cutting down fruit trees in this light:

The trees are assigned interests, and their interests are made vivid, rhetorically, by pleading the trees' defenselessness: they cannot withdraw into the city... They are innocent, and it follows that they should be spared. The trees have interests, and because they have interests, they have deserts⁵⁴⁴

Goodman describes these as "phased deserts", as opposed to "absolute deserts like the right of the accused to a trial". This is a helpful framework for understanding how one may assign moral standing to other creatures, without necessarily equating human lives with the individual lives of other species. Importantly, the standing of other creatures is sufficient to command us.

---

⁵⁴¹ Tosefta *Sanhedrin* 9:3; TB *Sanhedrin* 45a, 52b, *Pesachim* 75a, *K'tubot* 37b.
⁵⁴² *Sh'ney Luchot Hab'rit*, 4 bks. in 2 vols. (Jerusalem: Book Export Enterprises, n.d.), vol. 2:3, *Torah Shebikhtav, Parshat R'eh*, 82b (hereafter *ShLH*). Horowitz connects this with the principle that human beings can reincarnate as animals. Shlah is an acronym taken from the title of this work.
⁵⁴³ "Respect for Nature", 230ff., 253, 257. For Goodman, virtual subjecthood, associated with obligations of consideration and protection, is related to Spinoza's *conatus*, the "project" of being of a thing. On personhood, see 234.
⁵⁴⁴ Ibid., 254.

However, most formulations of Jewish ethics focus on interactions between people. In fact, Jewish thought came to divide the *mitsvot* into two categories: "between human and God / *beyn adam lamaqom*", and "between human and his/her fellow [human] / *beyn adam l'chaveiro*". But we have seen that the ethical world of the rabbis and the Kabbalists was much larger. We have the opportunity to expand these categories, both to come to a truer reading of tradition and to root ecotheology in Judaism.[545] When we talk about the inter-subjective or relational *mitsvot* – literally "between a human and his friend" – we could begin to include in this the fellowship we have with other animals and all life. That would require us to transition from a stewardship model to a model that embraces other creatures as subjects. Likewise, the terminology for *mitsvot* between humanity and God – literally "between a human and the Place" – suggests an expansive framework that would include the land. In fact, for the Torah, our relationship to the land is the primary medium through which we enact our relationship to God.[546] In any case, however we do it, we must add to the two traditional categories of *mitsvot* two more kinds of *mitsvot*: those between people and other creatures, and those between people and the land.

The land as subject

Our framework thus far does not account for the Torah's own preference for the land over humanity. The Torah portrays the land as a subject, with interests, rewards, and rights that take priority over our needs.[547] Especially in the laws of the Jubilee and *Sh'mitah* years (Lv 25) – and in the consequences that are supposed to befall the people if they do not observe these laws (Lv 26) – it is clear that God is ready to take the side of the land of Israel against the Jewish people.[548] Humanity as a social order, as a species, and all the more so as a collection of individuals, has no moral standing when its interests conflict with the intrinsic interests of the land, who will "enjoy her Sabbaths" [Lv 26:34,43] – even if that means the people are exiled or wiped out.[549]

---

[545] See Jeremy Benstein, "'One Walking and Studying...': Nature vs. Torah" in Yaffe, 222.
[546] Traditionally, *Sh'mitah* and *Yovel* would be included under this same rubric, since their observance was seen as a way of showing one's trust in God. Benstein suggests both categories be put under a new rubric: *"beyn adam l'olamo"* – "between human and his/her world".
[547] Goodman briefly discusses the virtual subjecthood of the land ("Respect for Nature", 257). I do not here deal with other halakhic dimensions of land stewardship that may have more to do with taking care of people, and which would also be important in a fully developed theology of Nature, such as *migrash*, the command to leave enough undeveloped arable land around every city free for farming (Lv 25:34; *TB Sotah* 27b).
[548] See n.509. It is incorrect to view this as a consequence of not observing the *mitsvot* in general.
[549] See sec. "Jubilee and Land Rights" in Seidenberg, "Human Rights", as well as Seidenberg, "Genesis, Covenant, Jubilee, Shmitah and the Land Ethic", www.jewcology.com/resource/Genesis-Covenant-Jubilee-Shmitah-and-the-Land-Ethic (neohasid.org, 2010). From the divine perspective, the human social order has value or validity only when justice encompasses

The other others: including the rest of creation

This is the land ethic of the Torah, which is congruent with the more radical statements of deep ecology (in which the needs of the ecosystem come *before* human needs), and with the idea of a land ethic articulated first by Aldo Leopold in 1949. Leopold's most important argument, *vis-à-vis* the moral value of human society, is that human beings as a species are citizens of the land and not rulers over it – in other words, from the perspective of a land-centered ethic, we are on a par with other species.[550] The Torah's ethic is also a natural outgrowth of the connection between Adam and *adamah* in Genesis 2, and a corollary of the idea that God put the human in the garden of Eden "to serve her /*l`ovdah*", a phrase that uses the same idiom otherwise reserved for serving God.[551] In all these tropes, the highest ethical priority is given to the land or, in modern terms, to the ecosystem, while all the creatures – even human beings – find their place and ethical status in the greater context of the land.[552]

In this light, the Midrash's personification of the land or the earth (e.g., earth is called "*arets*" "because she ran/*rats'tah* to do [God's] will/*ratson*"[553]) is more than poetic. And the Midrash's derivation for the divine epithet Place/*maqom*

---

the land as both a moral subject and a covenantal partner. What has intrinsic value is not humanity but justice, which is humanity's potential. On *Sh'mitah* and eco-justice, see also Rosemary Radford Ruether, *Gaia & God: An Ecofeminist Theology of Earth Healing* (New York: HarperCollins, 1992), 211–13.

[550] "The Land Ethic", in *A Sand County Almanac*, 237–61, online at www.neohasid.org/stoptheflood/the_land_ethic (Mar. 2007). Be cautioned, however, that Leopold makes great errors in reading the Bible here and elsewhere – presumably he was relying on secondary interpretations. He wrote, for example, "Conservation is getting nowhere because it is incompatible with our Abrahamic concept of land" (*A Sand County Almanac*, xviii). See Yaffe, intro., 2–6, as well as my notes to *The Land Ethic* on neohasid.org.

Other aspects of the Biblical tradition resonate with a deep ecology perspective as well. On wisdom literature, for example, see Eric Katz, who focuses on Job in "Faith, God, and Nature: Judaism and Deep Ecology", 153–4, 164–6, and Katharine J. Dell, "The Significance of the Wisdom Tradition in the Ecological Debate", in *Ecological Hermeneutics: Biblical, Historical and Theological Perspectives*, eds. Cherryl Hunt et al. (London: Continuum, 2010) 56–69; on Proverbs, see Davis, *Scripture*, 139–54; on the prophets, see, among many others, Davis, *Scripture*, 14, 120–38, 155–78. The Midrash also posits the primacy of the land in many passages (see p.271ff.).

[551] As in "*ul`ovdo b'khol l'vav'chem*" in the second paragraph of the *Sh'ma`*, "and you will serve [YHVH your God] with your whole heart" [Dt 11:13]. *L`ovdah* is often translated "to work her", that is, to use the way one uses a draught animal – but no one would ever translate the phrase *l`ovdo* to mean "you will work YHVH". In fact, some *midrashim* also understand *l`ovdah* to mean spiritual service (e.g., PRE ch.12, 21, which sidesteps the incongruity, in the eyes of the author, of `*avodah* or service being directed toward the garden by taking the object of service to be Torah). Discussion of these issues must be grounded in the meaning of agriculture to the ancient Hebrews (Davis, *Scripture*, 56–9). Ploughing and sowing were seen as ways of serving the land; agriculture was meant to be a sacrament. Agriculture that destroyed the earth, like Mesopotamia's, was seen as violating not only the land but also the purpose of humanity. See Eisenberg, *The Ecology of Eden*, 70, 75, 80–90.

[552] See Davis, *Scripture*, 82–3, 91–4; see also Paul Thompson, *The Spirit of the Soil: Agriculture and Environmental Ethics* (New York: Routledge, 1995).

[553] BR 5:8. See pp.101 and 272ff.

is even more significant: "[God is called] *Hamaqom*, because God is the place of the world."[554] The relationship of God to the world is the relationship of place to what is situated in a place – so that God is context, totality, but also so that the ecosystem, the land, functions as an image or symbol of God.

We have seen that the moral universe includes the more-than-human world. Adding to this the rights of the land would challenge us to develop an ethics that goes far beyond the limited reality of anthropocentrism. I will return to this challenge in the Conclusions chapter.

---

[554] BR 68:9; also *Tanch Ki Tisa'* 27. This terminology lends itself to a panentheistic interpretation, as one finds in Chayyim of Volozhin (1749–1821, Belarus region), *Nefesh Hachayyim* (Wickliffe OH: A. D. Goldberg, 1997), who explains *maqom* this way:

> Just as they said that the soul fills the body, so does the Holy One fill the world... and there is no limb/*eiver* empty of Him (the author uses the formula of *Tiquney Zohar*, quoted p.291, treating the world as an organism, rather than the more standard "there is no place/*atar* empty of Him")... and there is nothing else besides Himself alone blessed be, truly, no thing at all in all the worlds, from the most high of the upper ones to the lowest abyss of the abysses in the earth, to the point that one can say that there is no [separate] creature or world, only that all is filled with the essence/`*atsmut* of His simple unity [...] this is the language of "He is the place of the world and the world is not His place"... He is the place of all places, for from His side, all of them are accounted as if they were not in existence at all... like before creation.
>
> (*Shaar* 3, chs.2–3 184–5)

Intermediate conclusions

From Midrash to Kabbalah

Even before Kabbalah, *tselem* had a tremendous range of meaning, which included aspects of the more-than-human world. *Tselem* was not limited to human beings, nor even to human beings and angels. For at least some schools, the beings and bodies of the heavens were created in the image. At the same time, the rabbis determined that only half of Creation is in God's image, dividing up the world into lower and upper creatures. This boundary was occasionally breached in aggadah, suggesting that it was a general description of how *Chazal* viewed the world, rather than a hard metaphysical division. As I will show in Part II, Kabbalah transformed this metaphorical boundary into a permeable and frequently crossed border.

The fact that the rabbis did not believe that humans alone are *b'tselem* differentiates their ideas from modernist-humanist interpretations of *tselem*. Their insistence that *tselem* was an attribute of our physical bodies also belies the modern and medieval philosophical interpretation of *tselem*. For the earliest *midrashim*, *tselem* was not any metaphysical or transcendental element, such as moral responsibility, free will, rationality, or the soul, that set humanity apart from and above all the creatures and Creation. In rabbinic hermeneutics, the realms of the physical and the spiritual or metaphysical, while sometimes distinct, were never separate. Moreover, the very great value they placed upon every individual human life was grounded in the value of Creation itself, more than in the value of God's image.

BETWEEN MIDRASH AND KABBALAH

The impact of philosophy on Judaism in the Geonic period and after led to an extraordinary diminishment in the variety of anthropologies found in Jewish theology, excluding all physical or embodied interpretations of *tselem*. But this same diminishment induced the reaction we know as the Kabbalah. In the words of Moshe Idel,

One of the heaviest prices of [the medieval] apologetic reinterpretation of Judaism was the further suppression of apocalyptic, magical, mythical, and mystical elements... [But] the rationalistic reconstructions of Judaism prompted, in turn, a powerful reaction wherein an amalgam of older traditions, including the same mystical, mythical, and magical elements, came to the surface in more overt and more crystallized forms.[555]

However, Idel also asserted in the same place that these "mythical elements" were already "excluded from the rabbinic universe and condemned to total oblivion". In contrast, in "De Natura Dei" Yehuda Liebes presents myth as an essential aspect of rabbinic interpretation, and Boyarin asserted that *"vis-à-vis* the earlier ancient traditions of biblical interpretation, rabbinic [personification of Nature] as actual sentient subject represents a reversal of conventional historical-cultural development..."[556] In other words, *Chazal* remythologized tradition, rather than demythologizing it.

This fits with what we have seen. Part II will explore the many ways that Kabbalah deepened these mythic elements and extended them far beyond what *Chazal* had imagined. This extension included seeing God's image in the detailed structure of the body, and in the totality of the world.

The modernist-humanist reading of tradition is utterly dependent on medieval Jewish philosophy, which, as we have seen, rejected both the mythos and the ethos of earlier rabbinic tradition. Neither modern nor medieval theologies are disproved by this fact. But paying close attention to it opens up a huge range of theological possibilities.

A HOLISTIC ANTHROPOLOGY

A whole complex of qualities and dimensions defines humanity within rabbinic literature; no dimension in isolation does this. The *Bavli* conveys this holistic sense in the following passage:

[At conception,] the Holy One puts in [a person] spirit/*ru'ach* and breath/soul/*n'shamah*, bright features, and eye-sight and ear-hearing, and speaking by mouth, and walking by legs / *hilukh raglayim* (perhaps: "bipedally"), and understanding and discernment; and when his time arrives to be released from the world, the Holy One takes His share and leaves the share of his father and mother before them.[557]

Together, these elements create the divine image of the human.

---

[555] "Infinities of Torah in Kabbalah" in *Midrash and Literature*, eds. Geoffrey Hartman and Sanford Budick (New Haven CT: Yale University Press, 1986), 143.

[556] "*De Natura Dei*: On the Development of Jewish Myth", *Studies in Jewish Myth and Messianism*, trans. Batya Stein (Albany NY: SUNY Press, 1993), 1–64, esp. 1–2 and 55–6; Boyarin, *Intertextuality and the Reading of Midrash* (Bloomington: Indiana University Press, 1990), 100. See also Goshen-Gottstein, "The Body".

[557] TB Nidah 31a, also quoted in Urbach, *The Sages*, 218. An odd aspect of this passage is that it presents a picture of a child dying before its parents. The anthropological elements here were reframed as cosmology in ZCh (see p.210).

One can readily see that some of the qualities mentioned here are also embodied in other creatures. Some may be attenuated in individual humans, or accentuated in individuals of other species. Constructive ecotheology can assert that there is a "portion from the Holy One" in these others, and that this portion is analogous to the image of God in humanity. Doing so would extend God's image, along with the sense of intrinsic moral and metaphysical standing it entails, to other creatures, and to the world beyond ourselves.

Beyond this, knowing God's goodness, as Maimonides taught (pp.71–2), means knowing the goodness called "very good", that is, the goodness of Creation. This means apprehending not just the nature of all creatures, but also "the way they are mutually connected". This is in essence what Kabbalah attempts to do. What the ancient rabbis would have made of this is an open question, but we can say what it would mean for us. The words of Rav Kook (quoted p.38) speak to this exact point: "Contemplate the wonders of Creation, the divine dimension of their being... as the reality in which you live... The love that is astir in you... extend it to all its dimensions, toward every manifestation of the soul that sustains the universe."

BIOPHILIA AND GOD'S IMAGE

The capacity to see the divine dimension of other creatures is readily imbricated or interwoven with biophilia, the sense of solidarity most people have with other creatures, and their love for the richness and diversity of the more-than-human world. The term "biophilia" was coined by E. O. Wilson, the great evolutionary biologist, to indicate, in part, that loving other creatures is not something that lifts human beings out of Nature, but is rather an instinct that comes from Nature, and from our nature. He writes, "Humanity is exalted not because we are so far above other living creatures, but because knowing [the other creatures] well elevates the very concept of life."[558] By understanding our desire for the more-than-human world, and binding ourselves to other creatures in this way, we are enriching the meaning of our own humanity. According to Wilson, who is in this point remarkably parallel to Rav Kook, our humanity is enriched because we are enriching the meaning of Life itself.

This provides a wonderful, holistic picture of humankind's uniqueness, one that complements the holistic anthropology of the rabbis and that helps us make sense of our purpose in relation to the whole of Creation. In this vein, biophilia may be understood as a uniquely human power that connects us to both the Creator and to Creation, and is part of God's image within us.

---

[558] See E. O. Wilson, *Biophilia* (Cambridge MA: Harvard University Press, 1984), 22.

FULL! TO THE PLACE WHERE THE RIVERS FLOW

PART II

KABBALAH

Floating Letters by Nikki Green
Etching over Relief Print (1/18), 22.5 × 15cm

6

Tselem Elohim in Kabbalah, part 1
The Sefirot, the soul and body, the hypostases, and the heavens

> R' Eliezer said: Father, how was Adam made in the image above, for we have heard many opinions about it?
>
> *Tiquney Zohar* 56

There is scarcely a more important theme than *tselem Elohim* in the Kabbalah; one could even say that the divine *tselem* or image is the primary topic of a huge proportion of Kabbalistic discourse. It is a touchstone not only for the Kabbalistic understanding of humanity and human potential, but also for the structure of reality and the process of divine emanation. The most important addition Kabbalah made to earlier conceptions of *tselem* is the idea that the image of God comprises the Sefirot (*s'firot*; sing. Sefirah, *s'firah*) – the ten divine potencies or vessels through which God created or emanated the world. These Sefirot, which mediate and describe God's ongoing interaction with the Creation, constitute a kind of map of divinity.[559] This map is also known as the Tree of Life. Not only did the Tree of Life describe *tselem* in the human body and soul, it also described and was embedded in the world and the other creatures. The Sefirot simultaneously represented the structure of divinity, of Creation, and of the human being; they were the template and means through which the Kabbalist could theurgically affect the flow of divine blessing into the world. They thus became a mechanism through which the meaning of *tselem* was expanded, effectively extending *tselem* to the entirety of Creation.

---

[559] The Sefirot can be imagined metaphorically as transformers that "step down" the voltage of divine energy, so that it can generate and flow into physical reality, and be received by creatures with more limited capacity. For a map of the Sefirot and brief explanation of their evolution, see the Appendix. Most texts mentioned in this book that deal with specific Sefirot refer to *Tif'eret* (Beauty) and *Malkhut/Shekhinah* (Presence), the "lower male" and "lower female", while a few also refer to *Chokhmah* (Wisdom) and *Binah* (Understanding), the "upper male" and "upper female", or to *Chesed* (Love) and *G'vurah* (Might).

176   6 *Tselem Elohim in Kabbalah*, part 1

This chapter and Chapter 7 will survey some of these many and varied interpretations of *tselem* in Kabbalah. While in Part I of this book I did a relatively exhaustive reading of most material on *tselem* from the earlier strata of rabbinic literature, in these chapters I will be looking at trends without trying to read all the relevant material from any work or set of works. This chapter will focus on texts that discuss themes already associated with God's image in Midrash (i.e., humanity, the heavens, etc.) and note the ways that the Kabbalistic interpretation of *tselem* differs from the Midrash. The next chapter will discuss themes and tropes that are not represented at all in Midrash. For Kabbalah scholars, these sections may seem overly schematic; I do not plumb any depths of how the texts mean what they mean, or how they were written, or why they say what they say. My narrower focus is in some ways reductionist, but it will allow me to highlight some salient features of Kabbalah, for ecotheology and for understanding Kabbalah in its own right.

FOUNDATIONS

Tselem and the body

Kabbalah boldly asserted, in contrast with earlier midrashic and philosophical literature, that the detailed structure of the body was itself an image of God. This structure reflected the structure of the *Sefirot* (see diagram in Appendix). This concept is at the very heart of *Sefer Habahir* ("The Book of Brightness", also called "the *Bahir*"), the first work that can be distinguished as Kabbalah proper,[560] which states, "'In the image of God He created him'—in all of his limbs and parts."[561] Some of those limbs and parts will be discussed further on.

While the normative texts of rabbinic literature accepted the idea that the physical body was "in God's image", they did not specify many ways in which the body reflected that image beyond upright stature and circumcision. These physical characteristics were chiefly symbolic of spiritual ideas. Leaving aside the *Shi`ur Qomah* teachings, which we will discuss presently, rabbinic literature also distanced the body from God by referring the idea of *tselem* not to God but to the angels or the heavens.

The philosophical interpretation of *tselem* which became dominant after the Geonic period, went many steps further, completely severing the image of God from the body. By the time Kabbalah penetrated Iberia, Jewish philosophy had largely banished any remnants of the idea that the physical body was created

---

[560] Though there is a long tradition of mysticism before *Sefer Bahir*, the *Bahir* introduced three themes that characterized Kabbalah from the twelfth century on: (1) the concept of the Sefirot and their interrelations (though the term "Sefirot" is already found in the much earlier *Sefer Y'tsirah*), (2) the idea that human beings can increase the flow of blessing into the world (see §119, quoted in n.713), and (3) the doctrine of reincarnation. See Appendix.

[561] §82 (ed. Reuven Margaliot, publ. in one vol. with *Tiquney Hazohar*).

in God's image. Part of the Kabbalists' mission was to recover the body as an image of God.⁵⁶² This rejection of philosophical dualism was of a whole with other ways in which Kabbalah rejected philosophy. Most importantly, philosophy valued the ideas taught by the *mitsvot* and the reasons behind them. Kabbalah responded by asserting that the embodied, physical aspect of ritual was most essential, because it fulfilled *tsorekh gavoha*, divine need, and that blessing was drawn into the world specifically because ritual united the physical with the spiritual. The body's God-likeness was necessary in order for this to happen.

Shi`ur Qomah and ancient Jewish mysticsm

The textual roots for Kabbalah's embrace of the body are found, most importantly, in ancient Jewish mysticism. The more mystical strands of Jewish thought, even (or especially) from the earliest times, were not circumspect about defining God's image in physical terms, the way most Midrash was. The most extreme expression of a physical conception of God's body is found in the esoteric text *Shi`ur Qomah*, which means "The Measure of Stature" or "The Measure of the Body".⁵⁶³ This ancient work purports to give measurements for God's humanly limbed body, using a scale on the order of light-years. The height and width of each body part, and its "secret name", are revealed.⁵⁶⁴ While many medieval philosophers rejected this text as heretical or spurious, *Shi`ur Qomah* continued to invigorate the idea that the physical structure and shape of the human body is itself an image of God, centuries after its teachings ceased to be the focus of an active mystical discipline.⁵⁶⁵ Scholem wrote, "Unlike the philosophers, the Kabbalists were not ashamed of these images

---

562 This is true even in Kabbalistic works where a sharp distinction is made between soul/spirit and body/physicality.
563 Scholem says, "'[H]eight' or 'stature' is valid... Nevertheless, komah [sic] most likely has the precise significance here that it has in Aramaic, where it means quite simply 'body'" (*OMG* 21; see also *Major Trends in Jewish Mysticism* [New York: Schocken Books, 1974], 364, n.81 – cited hereafter as *MTJM*). Despite the correctness of Scholem's point, I am using the more literal translation of "stature" in order to emphasize linguistic connections between *Shi`ur Qomah* and the midrashic phrase *qomah z'qufah*, which means erect stature.
564 The form of this human-shaped body, which was the imaginative canvas for God's *qomah*, is male. See "Circumcision/the gendered body", p.190ff.
565 On the variety of responses to *Shi`ur Qomah*, see Alexander Altmann, "Moses Narboni's 'Epistle on Shi`ur Qoma'" in *Von der mittelalterlichen zur modernen Aufklärung: Studien zur jüdischen Geistesgeschichte* (Tubingen: Mohr, 1987), 130–54; on Maimonides, see 135–6. See also Scholem's discussion in *OMG* 35–7 and in "Anthropomorphism" (*EJ* 2:188–92; 191). Maimonides said, "All in all, it would be a meritorious deed to snuff out this book and to destroy all memory of it" (*OMG* 37). In contrast with the mainstream of Jewish philosophy, many of the early Kabbalists wrote commentaries on *Shi`ur Qomah*. Along with Altmann, Saul Lieberman finds evidence that Maimonides held *Shi`ur Qomah* in high esteem in his early days (Appendix D to *Jewish Gnosticism*, 124). Lieberman also suggests that the vehemence of the later Maimonides against *Shi`ur Qomah* may reflect Maimonides' approach to all ideas he rejected from his earlier works.

[in *Shi`ur Qomah*], on the contrary, they saw in them the repositories of divine mysteries."[566]

The Kabbalah inherited *Shi`ur Qomah*'s way of seeing the human body and interpreted and transformed it into a way of seeing the spiritual within the physical. By reinterpreting *Shi`ur Qomah* in a theosophical fashion, so that its physical images or metaphors became pure symbols, the early Kabbalists found ways to integrate *Shi`ur Qomah*, alongside philosophical and midrashic ways of understanding *tselem*, into their mystical speculations and practices.

The phrase *shi`ur qomah* itself became reserved terminology standing for the image of God in Kabbalah after the *Zohar* ("The Book of Splendor", end of the thirteenth century), and it appears in many texts as an analogue for the Sefirot. In the following passage from *Tiquney Hazohar* (also called *Tikkunei* or *Tiquney Zohar*), *shi`ur qomah* also stands for the "body" of the Shekhinah, the immanent, feminine dimension of the Sefirot; and for *Tif'eret-Y'sod*, the "Righteous One", which is the phallic principle of the Tree of Life's central column that connects masculine with feminine.[567] This passage also shows the complex wordplay and concatenation of images common in Zoharic texts:

> The praise of the body / *sh'vacha d'gufa*: "This *qomah* of yours is likened to a date palm / *zo't qomateikh damtah l'tamar*" [So 7:8]. And one that knows the measure of Her[568] stature/body / *shi`ur qomah dilah* (symbolized by the upright palm) will inherit the world that is coming... about which it says: "Israel's purifying pool / *miqveh Yisra'el* is YHVH" [Je 17:13]—*miqveh*/MQVH מקוה, which is Her body/*qomah*/QVMH קומה, Her *shi`ur*. *Sh`iur qomah* – this is the Righteous One /*Tsadiq*, about whom it says: "*Tsadiq* like a date palm will bloom" [Ps 92:13].[569]

The idea that one who knows the *shi`ur qomah* or measurements of God's body will inherit the coming world is at the heart of *Shi`ur Qomah*. But here, *Tiquney Hazohar* has transmuted the term *shi`ur qomah*, so that the one who inherits the coming world is the person who knows the structure of the Shekhinah and the Sefirotic tree. The feminine aspect of the Shekhinah, represented by the female lover in Song of Songs, is far more pronounced in the Kabbalah than in Midrash. *Tsadiq*, as Shekhinah's lover, is described here as "Her body", that is, the body of the one whom she embraces.[570]

---

[566] OMG 38. See Joseph Dan, "Imago Dei" in *20th Century Jewish Religious Thought: Original Essays on Critical Concepts*, eds. Arthur Cohen and Paul Mendes-Flohr (Philadelphia: Free Press, 2009), 473–8; 474–7. For examples see Altmann, "Moses Narboni", 138–41.

[567] See Appendix on the names of the Sefirot and the structure of the Tree of Life.

[568] Here and elsewhere I capitalize pronouns that unambiguously refer to *Sefirot*.

[569] *Tiquney Hazohar*, ed. Reuven Margaliot (Jerusalem: Mossad Harav Kook, 1994), addenda 6, 146a (cited hereafter as TZ). This passage is further explained on p.287; see pp.188–9 for its continuation and pp.199–200 for context. Since a *miqveh* must hold enough water to immerse the whole body, it quite tangibly corresponds to body or *qomah*. *Sh'vacha d'gufa* is a legal term derived from *TB Bava M'tsiy`a* 34a that TZ has repurposed; it refers to things of value that began as an essential part of something else, like the fleece of an animal.

[570] "Bloom" in this context is also an erotic image.

Foundations

The passage is essentially a series of analogues that flow one into the next. By using antecedents from sources like *Shi'ur Qomah*, and by developing chains of such analogues, Kabbalah was able to talk about *tselem Elohim* at several removes, often, as in this passage, without even mentioning *tselem*, thereby creating a sense of mystery and concealing its more radical intentions.[571] We will examine this in detail further on.

Tselem as YHVH and the Sefirot

The Sefirot are the underlying basis of every analogue for *tselem*, while the trope of YHVH is perhaps the most important device for talking about *tselem*. In Kabbalah, the letters of the explicit name of God, *YHVH*, correspond to specific parts of the Sefirotic Tree of Life, which means that humans are created literally in the *tselem* of YHVH. This was expressed directly. For example, *Tiquney Zohar* states: "What is Adam? *Yud He' Va'v He'*."[572] Adam is not just in the image of YHVH, Adam *is* YHVH.

In the following passage from *Sh'ney Luchot Hab'rit*, a distinction is made between God's *d'mut* or likeness, associated with the body, and God's *tselem* or image, associated with the soul, though both have one root in the name *YHVH*:

The human being, his soul is from the extension/expansion of the name *YHVH*, and even the likeness/*d'mut* of his body is stamped/impressed and made [full of] signs from the name *YHVH*. And through this, one can explain the matter of the image and the likeness in which the human being is created and made [...] The *tselem* is the secret of the soul, and the *d'mut* is the secret of the body.[573]

The holistic bent of Kabbalistic thought focused the Kabbalists' attention on the entire body and soul as images of the divine, each in their own way.

Kabbalah was not innovative in connecting *tselem* almost exclusively with YHVH. Though in the Torah God's image is only associated with the name *Elohim*, in rabbinic tradition *tselem* was already strongly connected with the name *YHVH*. The origins of this shift may be untraceable, since even the earliest rabbinic texts assume it to be the case. Certainly, while the Midrash did take notice of the different names of God in a more general way,[574] the *targumim*

---

[571] See Pinchas Giller on the structure of *kinuyim*, which he translates as "euphemisms", used in place of other terms (*The Enlightened Will Shine: Symbolization and Theurgy in the Later Strata of the Zohar* [Albany NY: SUNY Press, 1993], 13–20). "The *kinnui* signifies the hidden Divinity in the profane world... *Kinnui* is the device that hides the essential reality of the divine from all but the cognoscenti" (18, 20).

[572] TZ 70, 121a (cf. 13b, 52b, 66b, 106b). See n.576 on this spelling.

[573] *Toldot Adam*, vol.1:1, *Beyt Yisra'el* I, 5b and *Beyt Yisra'el* II, 10b; *The Generations of Adam*, trans. Miles Krassen (New York: Paulist Press, 1996), 99, 156. *Generations of Adam* is a translation just of *Toldot Adam*, which is the introduction to *Sh'ney Luchot Habrit*. All quotes from *Toldot Adam* are from vol.1:1.

[574] For example, "When the Holy One created His world, He created it with the measure/quality/*midah* of judgment, as it is said, 'In beginning *Elohim* created', and [the world]

(early Aramaic translations of the Torah) did not. In fact, the name *Elohim* is already "translated" as *YY* (an abbreviation for *YHVH*), starting from the very first verse of Genesis.[575]

The shift of *tselem*'s association from *Elohim* to *YHVH* is occasionally made a topic of inquiry in Kabbalah. One example is found in the same passage from *Tiquney Zohar*, which asks, "'Let us make Adam/ a human'—to whom did the Cause of causes say this to? The Cause of causes said [it] to none other than *Yud He' Va'v He'*, which is [drawn] from out of ten Sefirot."[576] The Kabbalistic framework allowed such hermeneutical operations to be performed consciously and explicitly because the various names of God were treated as hypostases, as specific entities or dimensions of God within a greater "ecosystem" of divinity.

Here, the name YHVH stands for both the whole and the essence of the Sefirot. In another instance, from the teachings of Isaac (Yitshak) Luria (1534–1572, Egypt, Palestine), the *tselem Elohim* is described as coming from *Imma* (Mother or *Binah*) and the "*tselem YHVH*" as coming from *Abba* (Father or *Chokhmah*).[577] In that case, YHVH stands for a particular (and particularly exalted) level within the Sefirot.

There are relatively few commentators who actually read the Torah text as it stands, to say that the human is created in Elohim's image, rather than in

---

didn't stand until He joined/*shataf* the quality of mercy with it, as it is said, 'In the day when YHVH Elohim made earth and heavens' [Gn 2:4]" (*BM*, vol.1, *Midrash Y'lamdeynu*, 141). Another example reads:

"*YHVH Elohim*" – a parable to a king ... who poured hot and cold mixed into his [glass] cups and they withstood (didn't break). Thus says the Holy One: If I create with the quality of judgment (Elohim), how will the world stand? With the quality of mercy (YHVH), then won't sin spread? Rather here I will create it with the quality of judgment and the quality of mercy – may it only be that the world will stand! (*YSh* 1:19)

Even though God is considering Creation as a whole in this midrash, it is the problematic of sin, that is, humanity, that necessitates the mixing in of mercy.

[575] On the verses about the creation of Adam, one finds: "And YHVH said: let us make a human in the image... and YHVH created Adam in His image / *Va'amar YY na`avid enasha b'tsalmana... Uv'ra' YY yat Adam b'tsalmeyh*" (*Onkelos*); "And YHVH created Adam in His image / *Uv'ra' YY yat Adam bid'yoqneyh*" (*Pseudo-Yonatan*); "And YHVH's word/speech created Adam in His image / *Uv'ra' meimra d'YY yat Adam bid'muteyh*" (*Y'rushalmi*). Note that *tselem* is translated a different way in each. On other aspects of the *targumim* on this verse, see Altmann, "*Homo Imago Dei*", 235–59; 234–8. By rendering *Elohim* as *YHVH*, the *targumim* gloss over the switch in God's names in Gn 2.

[576] *TZ* 70, 120a. *Vav* can be spelled three different ways: *VV* וו, *V'V* ואו, or *VYV* ויו. Using a longer spelling (here, *V'V*) yields ten letters, יודהאואהא *YVDH'V'VH'*, corresponding to the ten Sefirot. The total of the numerical values for these letters is 45, the same as the *gematria* (numerology) of *Adam* (cf. *TZ* 47, 83b).

[577] Chayyim Vital, `*Ets Chayyim*, vol.1 (Jerusalem: D'fus Levi, 1910), *Heykhal* 5 22:1, 206 (hereafter *ECh*), quoted in Magid, "Nature, Exile", 210.

YHVH's image. Yosef ben Shalom Ashkenazi (late thirteenth century, Spain) is one of them.[578] He wrote,

[S]ince all the existences from the upper and lower ones are all of them tied into His great, mighty and awesome name, therefore He warned [Israel] to not worship them, [not] to separate [them] from His name, only to [worship] the name *YY Echad* (*YHVH* – one)... And you must know that [for this reason] it is not said about Adam that he was made or created or formed in the *d'mut* of *YHV"H* or the *tselem* of *YHV"H*, but in every place that mentions *tselem* and *d'mut* it mentions the seal/*chotam* of Elohim, blessed be His name and recollection, amen, selah.[579]

For Ashkenazi, YHVH stands not just for the whole of the Sefirot, but for the totality of all Being. He also seems to be implying that if humans were created in the image of YHVH, then a human or an image/*t'munah* of a human would have been a valid object of worship. For this reason, scripture teaches that we are not in YHVH's image, but rather in Elohim's image – representing a level of God that is not the direct focus of worship.

In another example, again from *Tiquney Zohar*, it is explained, "[T]here would have been [good reason] to say, 'And *H*' (*YHVH*) created the human'. What is *Elohim*? Rather, the Shekhinah is called *Elohim*. And about this soul/*n'shamah* that is in the human, it says... '*b'tsalmo*' – in the image of the Shekhinah".[580] Here again, Elohim stands for a particular level of the Sefirot.

As we will see further on, YHVH, because it represents the whole Tree of Life, functions as the primary analogue for *tselem* in Kabbalah.[581] Often it appears without the term *tselem*, as a way of alluding to God's image in a more recondite manner. For Jewish mysticism, the name *YHVH*, along with its form, sounds, and numerology, became the pattern for God's image as expressed in

---

[578] Some scholars date Ashkenazi to the early fourteenth century. However, Ashkenazi does not quote the *Zohar*, which was extant among the Spanish Kabbalists near the beginning of the fourteenth century. Liebes discusses Ashkenazi's relationship to the *Zohar*, even speculating that Ashkenazi was one of its authors, though he also notes that Ashkenazi's Kabbalah was "completely different in nature and tendency" from the *Zohar* ("How the *Zohar* Was Written", *Studies in the Zohar* [Albany NY: SUNY Press, 1993], 93–5). Ashkenazi's theology is so radically different from the *Zohar* that I cannot imagine him having any hand in its composition.

[579] *Peyrush L'parshat B'rei'shit*, ed. Moshe Hallamish (Jerusalem: Magnes, 1984), 148, 41b, cited hereafter as "Ashkenazi". The passage is discussed further on p.238. Menachem Recanati (1250–1310, Italy) also remarked on the fact that only the name Elohim is mentioned in connection with the image in his *Bi'ur `al Hatorah `al Derekh Ha'emet* (Venice, 1545), 13b–14a. See also ECh 2, *Heykhal* 5 26:3, n.635; cf. Sforno, n.332.

[580] 62, 94b. TZ 121a also states that Shekhinah is called "the likeness of Adam". This trope occurs frequently; see e.g. 23a, 116b, 133b, 140a.

[581] In such cases, *YHVH* represents the Tree of Life as a whole. Sometimes *YHVH* may be considered one of numerous divine names standing for particular Sefirot.

human beings. As I go through spiritual, ethical, and physical interpretations of *tselem* in Kabbalah, I hope to show how this trope is central to almost everything Kabbalah has to say.

THE HUMAN TSELEM

I. Spiritual and ethical meanings *of tselem*

Tselem *as soul*

The Kabbalah is generally explicit about the connection between *tselem* and soul. In a passage from the *Zohar*, for example, we read, "And He blew in his nostrils life's breath / a living soul / *nishmat chayyim*" [Gn 2:7]—this is the image/*d'yoqna* upon human beings... [582] The next passage, from *Tiquney Zohar*, draws clear theological ideas out of the more obscure and multivalent formulations of earlier works. The passage reports a dialogue between R' Shimon and his son:

R' Eliezer said: Father, how was [Adam] made in the image above / *d'yoqna dil`eyla*, for we have heard many opinions about it? He said to him: My son, when all the *s'firot* were made, they were included in the image of the soul/*n'shamah*, and the soul was their chariot.[583]

The *n'shamah* is in God's image by virtue of including the Sefirot.

This short passage includes two important Kabbalistic tropes. First, it shows how the image of the Sefirot was equated with God's image. This foundation informs almost everything in Kabbalah. We will see how Kabbalah applied this trope independently of Adam to other creatures and dimensions of being. Second, the Aramaic terminology used here and in the previous text for "image", *d'yoqna*,[584] may also be used elsewhere to extend *tselem* beyond humanity to other creatures (see p.224).

While the influence of philosophy is important here, Kabbalah often did not adopt the philosophical conception of soul. This was congruent with Kabbalah rejecting the philosophical definition of *tselem* as intellect or contemplative capacity. In fact, the need to polemicize against this idea drove much of Kabbalistic literature. In most Kabbalistic texts, this rejection was expressed by affirming that the physical body, along with the soul and intellect, was also an

---

[582] *Ra`ya Mehemna* 3:123b. This passage is discussed further pp.198–9, 205, 228, 312.
[583] *TZ* 56, 90b, quoted in Giller, *Enlightened*, 94.
[584] This term is already used by the *targumim* to translate *tselem* and functions as a synonym for *tselem* in TB Mo`ed Qatan 15b ("*d'mut d'yoqni natati bahen*") and Bava Bat'ra 58a (n.152). See also Rashi, next note. The phrase "*d'yoqna dil`eyla*" is standardly translated as "supernal image" or "high image". I have used the terms "above" or "upper" instead of "supernal" or "high" here and elsewhere in order to keep intact the connection between the language of the Kabbalah and the *midrashim* discussed previously.

The human tselem

image of God.⁵⁸⁵ Some texts went further in their opposition to philosophy, however, as one finds in this passage from *Zohar Chadash*, which rejects the idea that either intellect or body are in God's image:

> "And You would make him lacking little from *Elohim*" [Ps 8:6]. Said R' Abahu: [Lacking little] in his soul, which is holy, and resembles/*damey* Him. But what is his defect (i.e., his lacking)? That there was the body, and it was taken from the earth! And if you say [that the human resembles God] in knowledge and wisdom, it's not possible, for the human is far from the upper ones... But then in what does the human resemble Him? R' Abahu said: Through the soul/*n'shamah*, which is holy and will never be consumed, for it is taken from [God], from His power and from His might.⁵⁸⁶

By rejecting the body as God's image, this passage differs from most of Kabbalah.⁵⁸⁷ And by stating that our wisdom is not like "the upper ones", this passage teaches that the intellect is *davqa*, specifically, **not** in God's image. In doing so, it rejected a philosophical perspective that was solidly rooted in midrashic tradition and was often accepted by the Kabbalists.⁵⁸⁸ In this instance, *Zohar Chadash* is emphasizing the distance between human and divine realms, not because of any aversion to anthropomorphism, but in order to polemicize against philosophy.

This *Zohar Chadash* text represents a strong thread in Kabbalah that rejects the connection between divine image and the lower realms, which are the realms where one can speak of ecology. Often, Kabbalah envisions the highest world or heavens as *Adam Ha`elyon* or the upper human (usually translated as "supernal Adam").⁵⁸⁹ These motifs posit a vast distance between God's image and the Earthly realm. Most of our discussion from here on will focus on texts that point in the opposite direction.

Tselem *clothes the soul*

One important function of *tselem* in Kabbalah is to act as an intermediary between the soul and the body. Scholem equates this with the concept of astral body.⁵⁹⁰ In passages that share this trope, the soul is completely distinct

---

[585] The Kabbalah in essence restored Judaism to its pre-philosophical position. Rashi, as good a barometer as any for Jewish thought before philosophy, states in his comment on Gn 1:27, "'Elohim created the human in his (Adam's) image, in Elohim's image He created him...'— with the mold made for him (the human)... [for] he was created with [God's] hands... and [the verse] explains to you that this same image set up for him is the image of the icon of the One who formed him / *tselem d'yoqan yotsro*."

[586] *Midrash Hane`elam* 16c; WZ 782. ZCh here delineates a hierarchy in which the hosts of heaven are closer to God's image in intellect than are human beings, and the angels all the more so.

[587] But see p.277ff.

[588] ZCh elswhere appears to affirm the association between God's image and other qualities in the Midrash, particularly standing and speaking (*Midrash Hane`elam* 10d, discussed p.319).

[589] See p.206 and n.815.

[590] "[T]he *tselem* is the mediating element between the life soul, *nefesh*, which is the lowest sphere of the human psyche, and the body itself. It follows from this that the *Zohar* regards the *tselem*

from *tselem*. Two Lurianic passages may suffice as examples.[591] In the first, Chayyim Vital (1542–1620, Palestine), Yitshak Luria's preeminent student and interpreter, explains a difficulty in the Torah's text that is not resolved in the Midrash: What is the relationship between *tselem*, *n'shamah*, and *nefesh*?

> [I]n the upper Adam / *Adam Ha`elyon* there are five dimensions of forms, this one inside this one. They are *nefesh*, *ru'ach*, *n'shamah*, *chayah*, *y'chidah*. And they have a dimension of matter clothing them, and it is called body/*guf* and vessels/*keilim*. And this body also is divided up into so many divisions: brain, bones, and sinews, flesh and skin. However, it is impossible for form to clothe itself in matter except by means of an intermediary/*em'tsa`i*. One finds that there are five kinds of clothing [corresponding] to five kinds of forms... called images/*ts'lamim*... And it is impossible for any form of these five forms to clothe itself inside the body until [it is] clothed within its own particular *tselem*.[592]

While this part of the passage speaks specifically about *Adam Ha`elyon*, Vital explains subsequently that the same structure is found in each of the four worlds, all of which are present in the lower Adam, which is inclusive of physical human beings.[593]

The tension between *tselem* and *n'shamah* is emphasized by Vital, rather than glossed over. Because *tselem* is more substantial than soul but less substantial than the body, it can act as a bridge between them. There are five

---

as the astral body" (*OMG* 266. See also "Tselem: The Concept of the Astral Body", esp. 260–70). Scholem also calls the *tselem* the *principium individuationis* (individuating principle), citing Shem Tov ibn Shem Tov (c.1380–1441, Spain), who states, "[the *tselem*] is a spiritual body, in which all the powers [of the soul] are imprinted in a physical but hidden manner, and upon it is built the body... This is [what is meant by] 'And *Elohim* created the human in his image'—that is, in the *tselem* unique to him, which connects the body and the soul" (*Sefer Ha'emunot*, 62a, quoted in *OMG* 270; see also 317, n.40).

[591] The complex Lurianic vision of *tselem*, which occupies chapters and volumes within *`Ets Chayyim*, is beyond the scope of this work. My goal is only to demonstrate that *tselem* and soul are regarded as different entities.

[592] *ECh* 2, *Heykhal* 5 26:1, 27–8. The *tselem* is formed from recycled material, as it were, unlike the soul: "However, the secret [of the images] is from the 288 sparks that were left in the midst of the vessels that were broken."

[593] He writes,

> For in *Atsilut* (the highest world), all the lights and all the images and all the vessels, [all] is called complete divinity, one, together, and united / *echad yachid um'yuchad*... up to the dimension of *n'shamah*, and from *ru'ach* on... it separates [into the lower three worlds, dividing] in the lower Adam / *Adam Hatachton*, who includes all [four] worlds... and behold, his vessel (i.e., body), before *Adam Harishon* sinned, was from holiness, from the best-chosen of *`Asiyah* that is from the dirt of the earth of *Gan Eden*, and after he sinned [his body] was [made] from the dirt of this world.

> On the level of *Atsilut*, even the vessels of the body are completely divinity, whereas on the physical level there is separation between soul, image, and body. See "Anti-Gaia" (p.277ff.) for further discussion about the metaphysical division between *Gan Eden* and the physical world in Zoharic and Lurianic Kabbalah.

ts'lamim or images that mediate between the physical vessels of the body and the five levels of the soul's spiritual forms. This passage also gives an implicit rationale for why *tselem* is created in the first chapter of Genesis, and *n'shamah* in the second chapter. Even though the soul exists prior to *tselem*, it cannot be manifest in Creation until the scaffold of the *tselem* is in place.

Vital explains that the five images should be regarded as a single *tselem*: "And the principles of the five images are called '*tselem Adam*', and this is not Adam himself, and the five forms are called the *n'shamah* of Adam himself, and the principles of the vessels, bones and sinews etc., are called the body/*guf* of Adam." The combination of all the images is called *tselem Adam* (rather than *tselem Elohim*).[594] Because of the intermediate position that *tselem* occupies, being neither soul nor body, the *tselem* is "not Adam himself", whereas the soul is of "Adam himself".

Another interpretation that envisions *tselem* as separate from soul is found in *Shulchan `Arukh Ha'ari* (also found in *Sefer Haliqutim*).[595] This passage explicates the punishment of *karet* or excision, described in Torah as the *nefesh* (soul or person) becoming "cut off from its people".[596]

[A person] has two souls/*n'shamot*... she (the lower soul) is in the body, and... she (the upper soul) is in the secret of *tselem*, encompassing [a person's] head... And according to the [divine] decree [resulting from the person's sin], his [lower] soul descends down below his feet. According to that very manner, the upper soul enters into him [through] the secret of *tselem* that is upon his head. And when his soul finishes descending down to *Gehinom* (Hell), then the *tselem* finishes entering him [from above], and if he sins more, even this *tselem* descends down below his feet and goes out from under his feet. And when she is compelled to go out, it's written about her "and that soul/*nefesh* will be cut off". For all dimensions of his soul are cut off and have descended below, and there remains for him no root or grasp above. But the righteous do not let their soul descend... and so the upper soul remains for him, which is the secret of the *tselem* standing over him, and she draws life down to him from above.[597]

The metaphysics of this passage is fairly impenetrable. The *tselem* fully enters the body only because sin forces it down from the head. This picture contrasts with what one finds in other Kabbalistic works (e.g., Cordovero), where a

---

[594] At the level of *Adam Ha`elyon*, there is no hierarchy between Elohim and Adam, which exist as different facets of the divine related through the Sefirot and the `olamot (worlds).

[595] *Ha'ari*, meaning "the lion", is an acronym standing for *Adoneynu Rabeynu Yits'chaq*, our lord our teacher Isaac.

[596] This phrase appears frequently – see Gn 17:4; Ex 12:19, 31:14; Lv 7:20,21,27, 22:23; Nu 15:30, 19:13,20.

[597] (Jerusalem: Makhon Chatam Sofer, 1987), 154, from the section titled "*Kavanat Malqot*". Some of the motifs here are addressed by Shaul Magid in "Deuteronomy: The Human and/as God: Divine Incarnation and the 'Image of God'", ch.5 in *From Metaphysics to Midrash: Myth, History, and the Interpretation of Scripture in Lurianic Kabbala* (Bloomington, 2008), 206–7. Magid's chapter, which deals with the incarnation of the divine in the human, also includes Lurianic material about the departure of the *tselem* thirty days before a person's death (206–9).

greater degree of embodiment of the divine image is positive. The idea is that serious sins can impinge first on the lower soul, and then even on the upper soul, which is "in the secret of *tselem*", forcing both of them down and out of a person's body, to be cut off in *Gehinom*. More generally, the *tselem* is, as in the previous text, a kind of link between realms.

Tselem *as* imitatio Dei *in Kabbalah*

Like the *m'forshim* (commentators) and the philosophers, Kabbalistic tradition also gave a transformational meaning to the idea of God's image, especially in ethical works. Cordovero's *Tomer D'vorah*, one of the most important of these works, states:

> [T]he thirteen qualities in which a human being may be like unto his Possessor (God)... are the qualities of higher mercies, and their gift/*s'gulah* is that just as a person would conduct himself below, so will he merit opening that higher/upper quality from above, truly... thus will he make [that quality] flow from above, and he causes that quality to shine in the world.[598]

As in much of Kabbalah, Cordovero stresses that becoming like the Creator means bringing beneficence upon the Creation. He particularly focuses on the expression of mercy or compassion toward the other creatures, including within this even the way we treat objects: "[A person's] mercies need to be distributed to all the creatures, not despising them and not destroying them, for so is the upper/highest wisdom distributed to all the creatures, silent and growing and moving and speaking (i.e., rocks, plants, animals and humans)."[599]

Cordovero also explains that becoming like God can be a preparation for uniting with God: "The Shekhinah does not come to him if he does not resemble/*y'dumeh* the upper reality / *m'tsi'ut ha`elyon*."[600] The union between different Sefirot within divinity is acted out in the being of the Kabbalist, who must become like the one who gives, the male, which is above, in order to unite with the one who receives, the Shekhinah (also called *Malkhut*, Realm, or Kingdom), which is the receptive Sefirah, the feminine or female, as well as

---

[598] Ch.1, §13, 16; *Palm Tree of Deborah*, 69 (above, my trans.). Since each quality is represented within one or more of the Sefirot, every action has the potential to make a person both in the image of God and in the image of a particular Sefirah. Here, Cordovero emphasizes mercy and the Sefirah of *Chokhmah* by enumerating thirteen ways of mercy, corresponding both to the thirteen attributes derived from God's revelation to Moshe and to the thirteen attributes of mercy described in Micah, as well as to the thirteen "paths of the beard" described in *Idra Rabba* of the *Zohar* and elsewhere. More simply: "His thoughts should resemble the thoughts of the Crown, just as that wisdom (of *Keter*) never ceases from thinking good thoughts... for it is completely mercy" (ch.2, 17; *Palm Tree of Deborah*, 71).

[599] See p.164. The formulation that God's image in a person is constituted as compassion for all creatures is found in Christianity as well. Isaac of Syria writes that the saint "offers tearful prayer at every hour, even for [the animals,] out of the great mercy that is aroused in his heart boundlessly, in the likeness of God" (quoted from *Orthodox Tradition* 13:1 [1995], 38–40). This translation differs from a translation of the same text quoted in n.540.

[600] *Tomer D'vorah*, ch.9, 29; *Palm Tree of Deborah*, 117.

the lowest Sefirah.[601] (See further discussion on Cordovero and *imitatio Dei* on pp.189–90.)

II. The physical image equals the spiritual image

Fundamentally, Kabbalah saw the structure and meaning of the spiritual world in the structure and details of the physical world.

The human body

First and foremost, this meant seeing the image of God in the human body, as we have already seen. The whole human *in all the body's aspects and details* corresponded to God's image and to the Sefirot. This is the strongest dividing line between the Kabbalistic and midrashic or philosophical approaches to the interpretation of *tselem*. Throughout Kabbalah, even in texts where body–soul dualism predominates, the body is understood as being built on the plan of the Sefirot, in the divine image.

The foundations for this leap in the oldest Jewish mystical literature are clear. *Sefer Y'tsirah* already aligns the limbs and organs of the body with the letters of creation, and *Shi`ur Qomah* analogizes the divine body to all the parts of the human body. Both works may date back to the early rabbinic period. *Sefer Bahir* enumerates the seven parts of the body that correspond to the parts of God's image.[602] In other sources, the image of God maps the details of the upper worlds and the heavens onto the human body.[603] The Kabbalah in all eras drew out the idea that Adam comprises the Sefirot or the four letters of God's name in a series of correspondences between specific parts of the body and the Sefirot or the letters.

For example, *Zohar Chadash* teaches that there are "four *tiqunin* (preparations/embodiments/ divine structures[604]) below, [corresponding to the four

---

[601] Shekhinah unites with the masculine *Tif'eret-Y'sod*. Since the Earth is also a symbol and a manifestation of the Shekhinah, this too may be reinterpreted for its ecological implications, though it would be hard to claim that that was in Cordovero's thought.

[602] §82, quoted p.176 and n.674. They are: "a person's *b'rit milah* and his partner /*zugo* counting [as] one", plus two hands, head, body, and two thighs. §172 (cf. §168), in its enumeration, counts thighs, hands, body-*b'rit* (trunk, including genitals, counting as one), and head – to which the interlocutor says, "But you said seven!" The answer given is, "Seven would be with his woman." Incidentally, these passages clearly reflect Wolfson's thesis that the redemption of the feminine in Kabbalah comes through its absorption into the masculine. However, there is much debate about whether this thesis applies to all of Kabbalah. (See nn.620, 624, 971, as well as the section on Wolfson in *Methods*.) Wolfson's analysis of this and other *Bahir* passages can be found in *Language, Eros, Being: Kabbalistic Hermeneutics and Poetic Imagination* (New York: Fordham University Press, 2005), 147–51.

[603] While this symbolic mapping may be inscribing *tselem* onto the body as a kind of externalized object, it was also the basis for meditations that were intended to transform the Kabbalist's own body into the image of the divine name, and to complete the meditator's divine *tselem*. See Magid, "Deuteronomy", esp. 200, 216–7.

[604] There is no real English equivalent. Giller, *Enlightened*, 4, renders *tiqunim* as "infrastructures".

letters of] *Adonai*, and these are: making with hands, swaying with the body (prayer?), using [the bed] with the *b'rit milah* (sex), walking with legs, and that [altogether is] a *shi`ur qomah*."[605] *Shi`ur qomah* and the name *Adonai* (a kind of lower reflection of YHVH) are both analogues for *tselem*. A later example comes from *Sh'ney Luchot Hab'rit*, which states that "there is another hint of the name YHVH in the full body of the human / *shi`ur qomat adam* from above to below and from below to above", explaining that in the upper body, the head corresponds with *Yud* (י) the trunk with the elongated shape of the letter *Vav* (ו), and the hands with two letter *Heh*s (the five fingers on each hand, "five against five", representing the numerical value of *Heh*). Thus, the upper body spells out God's name. Similarly, the feet are equated with the two letter *Heh*s ("like a shadow of fingers of the hand"), the length of the penis with *Vav*, and the corona with *Yud*, spelling out the name with the lower (male) body.[606]

An even more complex mapping from God's name to the body is found in the passage from *Tiquney Zohar* quoted on p.178. The continuation of this passage uses several numerologies related to God's name and the Sefirot:

The praise of the body: "This *qomah* of yours is likened to a date palm" . . . for it says about her/Her: "And they came *Elim*-ward, and there [were] twelve springs of water and seventy date palms" [Ex 15:27]. "Twelve springs"—these are twelve joints/sections, which are: six in the arms (right and left shoulder, elbow, and wrist, or upper arm, lower arm, and hand) and six in two legs/*shoqin* (right and left hip, knee, and ankle, etc.). That is what's written: "His hands [are] rolls of gold filled in *Tarshish* (or: with beryl)" [So 5:14]. What is "in *Tarshish* (תרשיש)"? "In two, six / *t'rey shesh* (תרי שש)"—in two arms [are] six joints; and so [are there] six/*shesh* others in two legs, [as it says:] "His [two] thighs are pillars of marble/*shesh* (שש)" [So 5:15]. These are twelve springs.[607]

---

[605] *Yitro* 31c, *Ma'amar V'atah T'chazeh*.

[606] *Toldot Adam, Beyt Yisra'el*, 6b; Krassen, "House of Israel I", 114. On gender issues, see next sections. Other texts equate the clitoris with *Y'sod* (the "point of Zion" – see Daniel Abrams, *The Female Body of God in Kabbalistic Literature* [Jerusalem: Magnes, 2004], 46–53; *Zohar* 1:229a–b). Applied to the Shlah's schema, *Yud* would be the clitoris and *Vav* the vagina or erect clitoris. The Shlah's description is the closest I have found to the Jewish Renewal mapping of the divine name onto the body, which connects *Yud* י with the head, the first *Heh* ה with the frame of arms and shoulders, *Vav* ו with the trunk or spine, and the final *Heh* ה with the frame of the two legs and pelvis. This image, of recent origin, has become the Jewish Renewal *Sh'viti*, or meditation "mandala". See Zalman Schachter-Shalomi, *Gate to the Heart* (Boulder CO: Albion-Andalus, 2013), 37. It is more overtly anthropocentric than images from Kabbalah, despite the fact that the Jewish Renewal world tends to be committed to environmentalism. This shift in pictures corresponds to looking at Kabbalah as a symbolic system, rather than a textual hermeneutic. See Seidenberg, "The Body in Kabbalah". Traditional *Sh'viti* figures, often set in synagogues before the `amud (the prayer leader's stand), include names of God, angelic inscriptions, and the verses of Psalm 16 (the name *Sh'viti* derives from v.8) laid out in the shape of a menorah.

[607] TZ 146a. Here the pattern of arms and legs is in the pattern of God's image (more precisely, Shekhinah's image), while the human body as a whole is included with the extremities. The number twelve is frequently connected with the image, specifically through the constellations and the tribes (see p.224). The passage continues:

The human tselem

This passage shows the level of physical detail that some Kabbalists were willing to associate with God's name and image. The body in this passage refers to the supernal body comprising the Sefirot, but the pattern is very literally the human body. More examples that map God's image to individual body parts are explored further on.

This passage and the verse from *Shir Hashirim* on which it is based have at root the upright stature of the human being, alluded to with the word *qomah*, which is also an aspect of *tselem*.[608] *Tiquney Zohar*'s esoteric calculations add up to something very simple: "the praise of the body", which represents the *qomah* or *tselem* of the Righteous One, the cosmic image of God, the Tree of Life, and *Adam Qadmon* (the primordial human), all bundled together as one.

Tiquney Zohar also connected the perfection of the body in God's image with reincarnation (see p.291). By the time of Cordovero, this understanding of the body was finely integrated into Kabbalistic ethics. Cordovero explains that the body is in God's image even when the soul or personality is not:

> [Concerning] the human being, it is proper/worthy/*ra'uy* that he should make himself resemble /*yitdameh* his Possessor /*qono*, and then he will be [configured] in the secret of the upper/exalted (supernal) form/*tsurah*, *tselem* and *d'mut*. For if he is alike in his body and not in his actions, he makes the form [in which he was created] a lie. And they will say of him: "A lovely form and (but) ugly deeds". For the essence of the exalted/`*elyon* image and likeness is his actions. And what use would it be to him to be like the higher form [in] the image of the structure of his limbs / *d'mut tavnit eivarav*, while in his actions he does not make himself like his Creator? Therefore it is proper that he should make [his actions] resemble the actions of *Keter*, the thirteen qualities of upper (divine) compassion.[609]

Though Cordovero rejects the philosophical understanding that *tselem* applies only to the intellect, his emphasis on right action is nevertheless congruent with Maimonides' position, and that of most other medieval philosophers,

---

"Seventy date palms"—because through [the twelve springs] "*Tsadiq* like a date palm will bloom" [Ps 92:13]. Here, [if you count all the sections of the hand,] these are: five fingers, and in them thirteen joints – that's 18. (The thumb is counted as one.) And so [in the other hand and in the two feet, making 18 times 4] – here's 72. Seventy of them are seventy palm trees. Two [more are the] "righteous [who] like a date palm will bloom".

Seventy-two corresponds to the *gematria* of YHVH if one spells out the names of the letters as YVD HY VYV HY. The final two added to the seventy are "*Tsadiq*", (Righteous One, here meaning Y'*sod*), which represents the phallus, indicating the energy drawn into the phallus from the two testicles as semen. So this is also a male image, while the first part of the passage, discussed p.200, focuses on the female image of the Shekhinah's body.

608 Other Kabbalistic texts on stature can be found on pp.210, 223–4, 319. See also the discussion of kissing in Kabbalah, pp.200–201.

609 *Tomer D'vorah*, ch.1, introduction; *Palm Tree of Deborah*, 46. See also Matt's translation, *The Essential Kabbalah*, 83. There is an implicit aesthetic theory in Cordovero's words, which suggests that ugliness exists only in a place where God's image should be present but is found absent.

that a person reflects God's image only when they have developed their spiritual/intellectual capacity. For Cordovero, however, the very separation between soul and body enables the body to retain the image even when a person's soul does not.

Thus, the counterpoint for the body is not the soul but action, which is "the essence of the higher image and likeness", and which unites soul and body. This step away from dualist metaphysics characterizes many of the ethical works of Kabbalah.

Circumcision/the gendered body

We have seen that *Sh'ney Luchot Hab'rit* understands the male body specifically to be spelling out God's name. This section will focus on passages that appear to presume that God's image is gendered male, while the next section will focus on passages that present God's image as the union of male and female.[610] These are among the most commented-on themes in the study of Kabbalah, so my explanations here may seem superfluous to Kabbalah scholars, though I hope they are sufficient for others.

Already in earlier Jewish mysticism, *Shi'ur Qomah* presented the divine body as male,[611] and *Sefer Y'tsirah* implied that the circumcision (*b'rit*) itself is God's image: "Ten *s'firot*, intangible... and a single covenant/*b'rit* directed in the middle, in the circumcision of the tongue and in the circumcision of the [fore]skin."[612] *Sefer Y'tsirah* does not use the term or figure of God's image anywhere (and in this it is radically different from the *Bahir* and the rest of the Kabbalah) – this is the closest it comes to defining the image.

Later Kabbalistic texts frequently play on the midrashic idea that *tselem* equals or depends on physical circumcision. For example, *Tiquney Zohar* teaches,

> "Let us make a human"—this is the command to circumcise the convert to become "in our image" through the cutting of the foreskin, "as our likeness" through tearing back [the foreskin], and if they freed the sign of the covenant through these two [actions] then he is "in our image as our likeness", and if not, not.[613]

Freeing the sign of the covenant of course means freeing the corona of the penis from being covered by the foreskin. The passage continues by enumerating

---

[610] Though these two ideas are in tension, normative Kabbalah often resolved this tension by imagining a male body with a female limb, as it were. See n.602.

[611] See Martin S. Cohen, *Shiur Qomah: Liturgy and Theurgy in Pre-Kabbalistic Jewish Mysticism* (Lanham MD: University Press, 1983), 217, n.6.

[612] (Jerusalem, 1961), 1:3. The "Gra" version (12, addendum) has "in the circumcision", while the standard version has "like the circumcision", which could refer to the circumcision of the heart "in the middle", that is, between the tongue and genitals (41).

[613] *TZ* 47, 84b.

The human tselem

various other *mitsvot* the convert must perform in order to be in God's image.[614]

A similar passage can be found in the earlier writings of Elazar of Worms:

"And Elohim created the human in His image, in Elohim's image He created him" — this was spoken of Israel and not of the uncircumcised... Behold anyone who is not circumcised and who does not keep Shabbat is not called *Adam*/human... And the Holy One keeps Shabbat, and He commanded circumcision in order to make known that there is no foreskin/`*orlah* | nakedness/`*eirvah* above.[615]

Note that for *Cha̱sidey Ashkenaz*, characteristically, there is no compunction about saying that only Israel are in God's image, and that only Israel are fully human.[616]

But what does Elazar of Worms mean when he says that circumcision "makes known that there is no nakedness/foreskin above"? This might sound like a simple statement that God's form is, as it were, circumcised. However, *Tiquney Zohar* explains the idea that there is no nakedness or "foreskin" above in a different way, as referring to the unification of male and female in the divine body:

[The Holy One wanted to create the human] like the form of His image/*d'yoqna*, without nakedness and without rupture or division, as it said: "Let us make a human in our image as our likeness", to have all the Sefirot included in him... and to unite Son and Daughter (*Tif'eret* and *Malkhut*), who are siblings.[617]

"Nakedness" here is shorthand for "uncovering nakedness", the Torah's term for incest and other forbidden sexual relationships. *Tiquney Zohar* is explaining that even though the hypostases of "Son" and "Daughter" are "siblings", it is

---

[614] The expansion of what is required to be in God's image represents a progression that is perhaps characteristic of the mystical way of thinking:

And if he upholds "remember and keep [Shabbat]" then he is in our image... and if not, not. And [this is so] if he puts on *t'filin* (etc.)... and if he upholds the *mitsvot* of *chalitsah* and *yibum* (etc.)... and all [is done] in fear and trembling of the Holy One. And if it is not done with fear and trembling, then he is not "in our image".

[615] *Sefer Sodey Razaya*, Ot Alef, 145. The two versions of this text, one using "`*orlah*", the other "`*eirvah*", are discussed n.618.

[616] It is ironic that the trope of God's image – which according to so many scholars and theologians was one of the Torah's greatest teachings, inculcating a notion of universal humanity – is used here for the opposite purpose. See Magid's discussion of this motif in "Deuteronomy", nn.18, 126, 131. Note Magid's speculation, however, that in Lurianic Kabbalah, redemption entails the recovery of *tselem*, and that "the recovery of *zelem* [sic] is the expansion of *zelem*, from the Jew to the human..." (221).

[617] TZ 56, 90b; cf. 69, 99a. TZ is here interpreting a verse describing how the boards of the *mishkan* are joined by a ring: "And they will be twinned from below, and together they will be whole/*tamim* on its head (on top) unto the ring/*taba`at*" [Ex 26:24]. *Tamim* is already strongly associated with circumcision in Midrash (see p.88), while the ring is "the sign of the circumcision covenant", standing for the phallus, (or more specifically, the corona), which joins masculine and feminine when they are coupled.

not "nakedness", that is, it is not incest, for them to be in "sexual" conjunction. Physical circumcision, which reveals the corona of the penis, is read as a symbol of this conjunction because the permanent uncovering of the corona resembles the continual state of arousal and unification that reigns above.[618]

A related but more human-centered point is made in a parallel *Tiquney Zohar* passage: "One who guards/protects [circumcision], he is compared as partner to Me, in My image. About him it is said: 'And Elohim created the human in His image', because a person who guards the *b'rit* merits [receiving] *Malkhut*".[619] Here, the man who protects his circumcision, that is, who exercises sexual propriety by being with his wife in a holy manner, becomes God's image *because* he receives the feminine divine potency and becomes male and female.

What do these texts teach us about women's bodies, which are neither circumcised nor uncircumcised? For one thing, the (male) Kabbalist cannot be truly in God's image unless he can be in proper sexual conjunction with his wife (thus "meriting *Malkhut*"). Other passages clearly teach that women are contained in God's image, as in this example: "The statement 'they felt no shame' [Gn 3:1] was before the sin, because they were in the pattern above 'for in the image of God He created them, male and female He created them.'"[620] Male and female bodies are equally part of God's image (see next section).

---

[618] Thus, there is a paradoxical understanding of nakedness here, in that the foreskin, which covers the penis, is equated with nakedness or *giluy 'ervah*, "uncovering nakedness". The two versions of the *Sodey Razaya* passage point to the same paradox. The foreskin can just as readily (or more readily) be thought of as something that clothes nakedness. From a structuralist perspective, removing the foreskin removes nakedness by removing the difference between being naked and being covered, perhaps with the sense of symbolically creating uninterrupted virility by exposing the glans (*atarah*/crown in rabbinic Hebrew). (On both points, see n.275.) Kabbalah may be seen as expanding on this originary purpose of circumcision. Note also Michaelson's description of circumcision as the inscribing of (feminine) negative space upon the phallus, which becomes completed by becoming less ("I'm Just Not that Kind of God: Queering Kabbalistic Gender Play" in *Queer Religion*, vol.1, eds. Donald Boisvert and Jay Emerson Johnson [Denver: Prager, 2012], 51–68; 59–61). The equation between foreskin and nakedness can also be understood midrashically in relation to the first humans' response to knowing their nakedness, which was to sew together fig leaves and cover themselves. The Midrash tells us that the first humans were "naked of *mitsvot*" (BR 19:6) after eating from the tree of knowing, implying that mitsvah can clothe nakedness. From this perspective, uncovering of the glans through the mitsvah of circumcision clothes the body, restoring it to some primordial state that existed before eating the fruit of the tree.

[619] TZ 69, 99a. "Guarding/observing the *b'rit*" refers both to performing circumcision and to sexual restraint.

[620] Reuven Tsarfati (fourteenth century, Italy), ms.Oxford, Bodleian Library 1923, 93a, quoted in Wolfson, *Circle in the Square*, 84–5. The passage continues, in Wolfson's translation, "The allusion is to the androgyne (*du-par'tsufim*). The moon was not yet diminished and there was none to give or receive for the chain was doubled in itself (*hashalshelet haytah k'fulah b'atsmo*)." Wolfson adds, "The locus of masculinity and femininity was in the phallus, a point alluded to by the statement that the 'chain was doubled in itself.'" However, equating the androgyne and *du-par'tsufim* may not be correct. In the Midrash, *androginos* and *du-par'tsufim* can have different implications (see p.80); the same may be true here. *Du-par'tsufim*, Moshe Idel

The human tselem

Kabbalah devotes volumes to the rectification of the male body through circumcision, but there are few texts that describe whether or how the female body is to be rectified.[621] This question might have led to extensive consideration of traditional women's rituals of *nidah* and *miqveh* (*mikveh*), that is, sexual separation during menstruation and immersion, respectively, but the common Kabbalistic understanding that the female was dependent upon the male for rectification seems to have closed most of Kabbalah to this developmental path.[622] We should also not ignore the importance of *miqveh* as a symbol or image of God in some Kabbalistic texts,[623] which is based on the explicit statement in Jeremiah that "Israel's *miqveh* is YHVH" [Je 17:13]. But this represents a site for constructive theology to work out new interpretations, as opposed to an idea about the female body that can already be found in Kabbalah.

Male and female

Looking at male and female as separate valences, especially through the lens of circumcision, yields an imbalanced and fragmentary picture of what Kabbalah says about gender. Kabbalah also presents the complementarity of male and

---

argues, is connected with the idea that the female is or will become fully embodied in a manner equal to the male ("Du-Partzufin: Interpretations of Androgeneity in Jewish Mysticism", ch.2 in *Kabbalah and Eros* [New Haven CT: Yale University Press, 2005], 53–103). See further discussion, nn.624, 947, 971.

[621] It might be argued that women's bodies wholly image God already, and that circumcision of the male body meets a need that has no correlate for women. This does not reflect the tone of many Kabbalistic texts, nor the fact that women's bodies in traditional Judaism are circumscribed by the rituals of *nidah* (menstrual purification) (see Perle Besserman, *A New Kabbalah for Women* [New York, 2005], 135). This is also a general question in Jewish practice and ritual. It has been suggested that *taharah* – the immersion ritual following menstruation/*nidah* – be treated as a covenanting ritual; in light of this discussion, that would mean seeing *taharah* as a ritual completion of God's image in the female body on a par with circumcision. See Seidenberg, "Brit Taharah"; Zoë Klein, "Growing Girls Whole", *The Jewish Journal* (Nov. 24, 2005); and David Biale, *Blood and Belief: The Circulation of a Symbol Between Jews and Christians* (Berkeley: University of California Press, 2007), 103–7.

[622] Menstruation was also considered to be in tension with God's image, associated with the "pollution of the snake" that damaged or expunged the image from humanity, as one finds in *TZ*: "'[God said to Qayin: you will be] shaken off and thrust out / na` v'nad נע ונד' [Gn 4:12]—because you [are the result of] the sin/`avon עון of *nidah* נדה (`avon is an anagram of na` v', while *nidah* corresponds to *nad*)... which is the filth that [the] snake cast into Chavah... because you are from the side of the snake" (69, 118b). Cf. *ShLH*, *Toldot Adam, Beyt Yisra'el*, 14d; Krassen, "House of Israel I", 213. For a more positive but still ambivalent depiction of the blood that issues from the womb, see *Zohar* 3:249b (WZ 395–6), based on TB *Bava Bat'ra* 16b.

[623] See p.178. While *miqveh* was (and is) of paramount importance in the ritual practice of Kabbalists, it has mostly been used as a ritual for men's spiritual elevation; for women, the purpose is still mostly to restore the "purity/*taharah*" that allows a (heterosexual) couple to resume sex after the woman's period. One might even say that the Kabbalistic use of *miqveh* by men to access higher or esoteric spirituality in some sense displaces the female body by the male.

female as the image of God, and it does so widely and consistently. The relationship between these two gender models in Kabbalah is hotly contested.[624] In this section I will focus on the second model, independent of the first.

In Chapter 1 we saw that for classical Midrash, "male and female" in Genesis 1:27 either indicates man and woman in the biological sense, or refers to the conjunction of male and female in the double-body of the first human being(s). In *B'rei'shit Rabbah* 8:11, "male and female" stands for aspects of humanity not connected to God's image, while in most other places, "male and female" is associated with expanding God's image through procreation.

In Kabbalah, however, male and female together are God's image, even the essence of God's image, and this image is limited neither to humanity nor to biology. Rather, gender is projected onto all levels of reality. Yosef ben Shalom Ashkenazi explains, "[E]verything that the Holy One created in His world, they are all of them male and female, even up to the ten *s'firot* they are male and female."[625] The *Zohar* similarly teaches:

"Male and female He created them"—From here [we learn that] any image/*d'yoqna* where male and female are not found is not a high image... Come see: In any place where male and female are not found as one, The Holy One does not rest His dwelling /*madureyh* in that place. And blessings are not found except in a place where male and female are found, as it's written: "He blessed *them* and called their name Adam in the day of their being created" [Gn 5:2]. It's not written: "And He blessed him and called his name Adam"—for [a human being] is not even called Adam except [when] male and female are as one.[626]

---

[624] The question is how one integrates these two pictures. According to Wolfson, the Kabbalists understood redemption to come only when the female is masculinized and absorbed by the male, or in his words, "obliterated in the identity of sameness" (*Circle in the Square*, 116). If Wolfson is right, this aspect of Kabbalah is problematic for contemporary feminists who want to make use of Shekhinah imagery. However, some scholars understand Kabbalistic redemption differently. See Idel's critique of Wolfson in *Kabbalah and Eros* (128–34), and Wolfson's response to Idel in *Language, Eros, Being*. Daniel Abrams has demonstrated that Kabbalists also depict a female androgyne that includes the male within herself (*The Female Body of God in Kabbalistic Literature*, 68–74). See also Shifra Asulin, "Hahavaneha Hak'fulah shel D'mut Hash'khinah" in *Ma`ayan Eyn Yaakov L'Rabi Moshe Qordovero*, ed. Bracha Sack (Beersheva: Ben Gurion University, 2008), 61–111. Michaelson also raises important issues concerning Wolfson ("I'm Just Not That Kind of God", 59–62), as does Ellen Davina Haskell, who critiques Wolfson's exclusive focus on sexual interpretations in *Suckling at My Mother's Breasts: The Image of a Nursing God in Jewish Mysticism* (Albany NY: SUNY Press, 2012), 101–6. See also Hava Tirosh-Samuelson, "Gender in Jewish Mysticism" in *Jewish Mysticism and Kabbalah: New Insights and Scholarship*, ed. Frederick Greenspahn (New York: New York University Press, 2011), 191–231, esp. 193–215. A different approach that sidesteps the debate is to thematize those Kabbalists who believed that redemption comes when the female becomes both independent from and equal to the male, as Sarah Schneider does in *Kabbalistic Writings on the Nature of Masculine and Feminine* (Northvale NJ: Jason Aronson, 2002). I discuss this and related issues from the perspective of constructive theology in nn.945 and 971 and in *Methods*.

[625] Ashkenazi, 133.

[626] 1:55b. There are literally thousands of passages in Zoharic literature that make or assume this same point. Note that here and throughout, I use a "literal" (or concordant) style of

The human tselem

The *Zohar* does not need to use the term *tselem* to express the idea that male and female together are in God's image. This is an important hermeneutical difference between midrashic and Kabbalistic texts.

A more explicit relationship between gender complementarity and the image of God is found in the next passage about the divine masculine, known as *Tif'eret* or "the Holy One", and the divine feminine, known as *Malkhut* or Shekhinah:

> "Let us make Adam (in our image)"—The Shekhinah below took up advice from the Holy One... For [concerning] the central pillar (*Tif'eret*) and the Shekhinah, it says about them: "Male and female He created them" and they are called Adam, and according to [this] pattern, it was said below about Adam and Chavah, "male and female He created them... and called their name Adam".[627]

The first humans were created in the image of the divine masculine and feminine.

This image of God includes both genders, both in and of themselves and in their sexual union, as we saw in the previous section. In Wolfson's words: "Coitus is considered a form of *imitatio Dei* insofar as the unity of the divine anthropos is imaged as the coupling of the masculine and feminine."[628]

What is even more important is the Kabbalistic idea that gender is also introjected onto all the levels of the human individual, rather than only being found in the conjunction of biological male and female.[629] Ashkenazi describes this idea in the passage we began with:

> "Male and female He created them"—And the secret is that from the secret of male and female they were created, and therefore they are in the image of Elohim. And know that the power of the crown/ *`atarah* (Shekhinah) is called female, for she receives power from the upper power / *koach ha`elyon* called male... and therefore "He created him *androginos*"[630]... For in the image of the human there is image/*tselem* and

---

translation for the sake of doing terminological analysis. I commend to the reader Daniel Matt's translations of the *Zohar*, which are mellifluous and lyrical, for further study. (This passage can be found in Daniel Matt, *Zohar: The Book of Enlightenment* [New York: Paulist Press, 1983], 55–6, and in Matt's translation of the entire *Zohar*, *The Zohar: Pritzker Edition*, vol.1 [Stanford CA: Stanford University Press, 2004–], 314. The eight volumes already printed go through 3:156a.)

[627] TZ 47, 83b. Note that the Shekhinah receives advice from the Holy One, meaning She is the one who creates the human! This structure could be compared to the relationship between the Demiurge and God in Gnostic thought, but without the negative overtones.

[628] *Language, Eros, Being*, 312.

[629] This is one way in which the heteronormativity of Kabbalah is overcome within Kabbalah itself. On the "queering of Kabbalah" more generally, see Jay Michaelson, "On the Religious Significance of Homosexuality; or, Queering God, Torah, and Israel" in *The Passionate Torah: Sex and Judaism*, ed. Danya Ruttenberg (New York: New York University Press, 2009), 212–28; as well as "I'm Just Not That Kind of God".

[630] BR 8:1, quoted p.79.

likeness/*d'mut*, meaning that all the courts above, [whether] they are male [or] they are female, all of them were created in him.⁶³¹

The "courts above", both male and female, are created within the human, who includes all the realms of divinity within. Even though the *androginos* that was the union of male and female was separated into a man and a woman in Eden, the quality of the *androginos* is not completely lost from our nature.

The theme of wholeness is interwoven with gender in a manuscript quoted by Wolfson, which imagines the two cherubs, the winged figures atop the ark of the covenant, to be *Tif'eret* and *Malkhut*:

> These two cherubim/*k'ruvim* are *Tif'eret Yisra'el* and his *Malkhut*, and they are *du-par'tsufim* (i.e., two faces in one body). Concerning them it is said, according to the hidden meaning /*nistar*, "Male and female He created them". This is the perfect (or: whole) human / *ha'adam hashalem*, and the cherubim depicted in the Sanctuary were in their pattern. They were made of one hammered work to indicate the perfect (whole) unity. In their pattern Adam and Eve (Chavah) were created, and this is the secret of "Let us make Adam in our image and in [sic] our likeness".⁶³²

The *k'ruvim* are made from a single piece of gold according to this passage,⁶³³ reflecting the unification of male and female.⁶³⁴

Lurianic Kabbalah gives an even more complicated reading of gender and God's image. In one typical passage, Vital applies the verses about the creation of *adam* to the Sefirot themselves, so that instead of describing anything in the physical realm, they describe how the upper divine feminine (called *Imma*/Mother) and masculine (*Abba*/Father) were both needed to create the lower divine feminine (*Malkhut*, or in Lurianic Kabbalah, *Nuqva*, "the Female"), while *Imma* by herself was sufficient to create the lower divine masculine (*Tif'eret*, or *Z`eyr Anpin*, lit. "the Small/Short Face").⁶³⁵ In this reading, the entire creation story takes place *within* God. To the non-Kabbalist this

---

⁶³¹ 36a, 132–3. It is possible to interpret this passage along the lines of Recanati, who states that *tselem* means the male and *d'mut* means the female (*Bi'ur `al Hatorah*, 14a). `Atarah generally means Shekhinah/*Malkhut*.

⁶³² ms.Vatican, Biblioteca Apostolica ebr. 504, 312b, in *Circle in the Square*, 83 (punct. and translit. modified). The text continues: "You already know that these two countenances are the Written and Oral Torah."

⁶³³ Ex 25:17–21 does not specify that they are made from one piece of gold.

⁶³⁴ Already in the *Bavli*, Rav Qatina says that the two *k'ruvim* were male and female in sexual embrace (*Yoma* 54a), while the *stam* in *Bava Bat'ra* says that in times of divine favor they faced each other, but in times of divine anger they would face away from each other (99a).

⁶³⁵ *ECh* 2, *Heykhal* 5 26:3, 30. *Z`eyr Anpin* and *Nuqva* are the *par'tsufim*, or Lurianic reconstructions, of *Tif'eret* and *Malkhut*, while *Imma*/Mother and *Abba*/Father are the *par'tsufim* or reconstructions of *Binah*/Understanding and *Chokhmah*/Wisdom (see Appendix). According to this passage, the initiative to create the lower divine levels comes from *Imma*, which is also called *Elohim*. But paradoxically, *Imma* needs *Abba* in order to generate the lower feminine, and "this is [why] 'let us make /*na`aseh*' is in the plural." Consequently, Gn 1:27 means "in Elohim's image *Imma* created **him**", that is, *Z`eyr Anpin*, but "male and female, *Abba* and *Imma* created **them**", that is, *Z`eyr Anpin* and *Nuqva* together.

The human tselem

may sound impossibly dense and almost polytheistic. Here my interest is only to illustrate the depth of gender in the divine reality according to Luria.

Running through all these examples is the thread that the union of male and female, in and of itself, is the image of God.

The human face, hand, and parts of the body

If the whole body as a unity is an image of God, this is paralleled by the idea that every limb is an image. Ashkenazi talks about this fractal dimension of the human body not only in terms of the image but also in terms of the explicit presence of the Sefirot, writing that "each and every limb has an indwelling presence /sanctuary/*mishkan* in the ten *s'firot*, and this is the secret of 'Back and before You formed me' [Ps 139:5]."[636] The turn of phrase "the secret/*sod* of...", or the synonymous phrase "the mystery/*raza* of...", usually indicates that what follows is an analogue for *tselem*, particularly when reference is to some hypostatic phrase from scripture that stands in for an abstract divine quality or realm.[637] Here, the phrase "the secret of 'Back and before You formed me'" means the secret of *du-par'tsufim*, that is, male and female, which is equivalent to *tselem*.

Tishby declares, "There is hardly one part of the human body, whether internal or external, that is not pressed into service for symbolic purposes. Sometimes a minute anatomical analysis is offered in order to symbolize the Godhead; the parts of the skull, the hair, facial features, and the beard are especially subject to detailed exposition."[638] There are many passages throughout the history of Kabbalah that carry out this idea literally, describing the map of the Sefirot or the name YHVH that can be found in the lines on the forehead or the corner of the eye, the shape of the ear or hand, the arrangement of the organs, and so on. Each part or group of features is a kind of fractal representation of the image of God in the whole human body.

The human face especially is an image of God. The continuation of the passage from *Tiquney Zohar* that says that Adam is *Yud He' Va'v He'* talks about the Shekhinah and the human face together as being in the image:

This is the Shekhinah that is called "the human likeness / *d'mut Adam*" [Ez 1:5], for every likeness/*dimyon* and face/*par'tsuf* of human beings are recognized in her, and every form above and below; and because of her it is said, "and through the hand of (by) the prophets I will be imaged /*adameh*" [Ho 12:11].[639]

---

[636] Ashkenazi, 132, 36a.

[637] There is no difference in meaning or usage between these two terms; the first is Hebrew and the second Aramaic. I have translated them differently throughout simply to help the reader access the original text.

[638] WZ 296.

[639] TZ 70, 121a. Note *adameh* (אדמה) is spelled like *adamah* (אדמה), meaning earth or ground, which is also sometimes an analogue for the Shekhinah; *adamah* can be read as the feminine form of *Adam*/human. Thus, the connection between human and Shekhinah can be made on multiple levels. This double reading of *'DMH* is sometimes used to connect God's image and

Here the "earthly" aspect of God, Shekhinah, is analogized to a part of the human body, the face. Both are synecdoches for the whole image of God, with the part not only standing for the whole but containing the whole within itself. In this passage, the words *par'tsuf* and *dimyon* are analogues for *d'mut* and *tselem*. Likewise, "every form above and below" is an analogue for *tselem*. Because the human face stands for the whole body and hence for the full image of God, it too can sometimes function as an analogue for *tselem*.

D'mut Adam stands in for *tselem Elohim*; the distinction between the human image and God's image is here erased. This tendency is characteristic of Kabbalistic texts. One important example is the *Idra Rabba* section of the *Zohar*, which describes God's thirteen attributes of mercy in terms of the thirteen "pathways of the beard".[640] The normal conceptual understanding of *tselem* would be that an image is derived from a more "real" original, but *tselem* and *d'mut* in Kabbalah begin to mean something more: a process of mutual reflection between human and divine in which the human is in some sense commensurable with the divine.

A much more literal connection between the face and God's image is made by Yishayah Horowitz:

> You find in the likeness of the face two eyes and a nose. This is in the likeness of two *Yuds* [and a] *Vav* (like this: ייו), corresponding to the name *HVY"H*, [because both] add up to 26 (in gematria). The great level in a human being is when he lowers his eyes. Then they remain in one union.[641]

Here it is specific parts of the face, the eyes and nose, which "spell out" the gematria of God's name, and which are, in union, a fractal image of God's name, that is, God's image.

A different way of relating the face or the head to the image of God is found in this passage from the *Zohar* about Jacob's ladder:

> "And He blew in his nostrils life's breath / a living soul / *nishmat chayyim*" [Gn 2:7]— this is the image/*d'yoqna* upon human beings, about which it says: "And he dreamed and here, a ladder" [Gn 28:12]. "Ladder" certainly is *nishmat chayyim*, the throne for

---

the earth. It is also sometimes used to express disjunction between them; that is, if a person merits, they are likened to God, and if not, they are like *adamah*. See, e.g., ShLH, *Toldot Adam, Beyt David*, 15b; Krassen, "House of David I", 222 or *Sefer Ha'arakhim*, vol.1 [New York: Otsar Hachasidim/Kehot, 1987], col.149.

[640] 3:130b–134b. Also *Sifra d'Ts'ni`uta*, *Zohar* 2:177a–b. Here is a decidedly male image of God.

[641] ShLH, *Toldot Adam, Beyt Yisra'el* 6b; trans. adapted from Krassen, "House of Israel I", 115. "But when he raises his eyes, then the eyes look out (away from) the nose and then YHVH does not rest on the throne of compassion. Only the nose remains. And then there is 'anger/burning of the nose / *charon af*' (divine anger) in the world." If eyes and nose are divided, then the nose by itself becomes the image of God's anger, and is no longer a full image and likeness. This is founded on the Torah's description of God's mercy as *"erekh apayim"*, which idiomatically means "patient" but can be translated "long-nosed", and God's judgment as *"charon af"* or *"chari af"* (Ex 32:12, Dt 29:23, etc.), which means "burning anger" but can be translated over-literally as "burning-nosed".

The human tselem

the name *YHV"H*, which is the awe and the love, the Torah and the mitsvah, and upon her (the soul) they dwell. And from this throne are hewn all the souls of Israel. Its image is upon the head of a human being. (Giller: "Its image is the human face".)[642]

Here, *nishmat chayyim* is equated with "the image/*d'yoqna* upon human beings", which is the image of God. One can glean several analogues for *tselem* – throne, ladder, and the human head (or face) – from this passage.[643]

Another analysis of God's image in the human face is found in *Tiquney Zohar*:

And it is the form of the lines in the forehead as the form of YHVH, and these are impressions/tracings of lines, which are "depth of height and depth of below and depth of east and depth of west".[644] Short lines from the eye, from the side of the letter *Y*; lines along the length of the mouth in height, from the side of the three letters that are HVH; all of them are made known in the *shi`ur qomah* of the human/ *bar nash*.[645]

Not only is the human face an image of God, but its creases actually spell out the letters of God's name. The cardinal directions, discussed further on, are also an analogue for *tselem*. *Shi`ur qomah* can also function as an analogue through which a new concept may be joined to God's image.[646]

Sefer Y'tsirah makes its strongest claims related to the body in passages about the human hand. "Ten *s'firot*, intangible/*b'limah* (lit. 'without-what') – the number of ten fingers, five corresponding to five".[647] The *Zohar* teaches that "in the image of God is the secret of the palm [of the hand]".[648] "Secret of the palm" is thus defined as an analogue for *tselem Elohim*.

We saw in *Tiquney Zohar* and *Bahir* that the limbs altogether represent the image of God in the body. The next two examples, from the same passage in *Tiquney Zohar*, recognize in different limbs and parts of the body a literal depiction of God's name. In the first passage, the name of God is imaged in the arm of the Shekhinah (called here *matronita*), which is like a human arm:

And the hands of the *matronita*, are all of Her holy. All of them are tracings in (of) the name YHVH, like this: in the palm *Y* י, in the five fingers *H* ה, in Her arm *V* ו and in Her shoulder *H* ה. In Her palm are formed so many lines, like branches of the Tree of Life ... That is what's written: "A tree of life she is for the ones holding her (i.e. the arms) and her supporters are happy" [Pr 3:18].[649]

---

[642] *Ra`ya Mehemna* 3:123b; Giller, *Enlightened*, 95. What follows is one of the most important passages from the *Zohar* concerning the question of this book. See p.228.

[643] The first two elements are discussed on p.205.   [644] Quoting *Y'tsirah* 1:5, 49.

[645] TZ 70, 125a. Except where it is specifically relevant, no distinction in translation is made between *bar nash* (*ben enosh*) and *adam*/*ha'adam*.

[646] See Chapter 11.   [647] 1:3, 41.

[648] 2:76a. This and related texts are discussed in Yakov Travis's paper "Zoharic Conceptions of Humanity's Divine Image", Association for Jewish Studies Conference, 1994.

[649] TZ 146a. *Heh* is the fifth letter of the alphabet. Thanks to Raquel S. Kosovske for help interpreting this and the following passage.

YHVH is an analogue for *tselem*, as is the Tree of Life. This passage illustrates how various images are nested within one another. The hand, which is a complete image of God on its own, also comprises the first two letters of YHVH in the palm and fingers, becoming one half of the image that is the whole arm, while the arm again is one element in the greater image that is the body.

In the continuation of this passage, the abbreviation of God's name, YY, is found in the image of a woman's breasts, which are compared to the stone tablets of the covenant on which were written the ten commandments. Moshe's breaking of the tablets after the incident of the golden calf symbolizes both breaking the hymen and initiation of the flow of breast milk:

> V is the written Torah, which is given in two arms ... and with them the two tablets are given, which are "two breasts" [So 4:5]. And these are YY ״, (i.e., two dots, perhaps the areolae or nipples), and in (i.e., between) them is the form of a *Zayin*, and in (between) them it is narrow/*tsar*. That is why it's written: "And [God] formed/*Vayyitsar*/ VYYTsR [the human]"[650] [Gn 2:7], and they are the virginity-signs/*b'tulim* of the maiden [which signify] the Torah by mouth (oral Torah).[651]

The two *Yuds* are a symbol of God's name and the breasts or cleavage a *Zayin* ז, connected here also with the female genitals, which stands in other places for the phallus.[652] Both name and phallus are analogues for *tselem*; in this passage, so too is the vulva, as are the breasts.[653] Both passages are examples of the manifold ways Kabbalah projects the image of God onto the human body.

In Kabbalah, the act of kissing is also given special significance. The human kiss on a profound level unifies many qualities that Midrash and Kabbalah identify as aspects of God's image: upright stature and face-to-face sexuality, the union of male and female, the human face and human individuality, and, according to Lurianic Kabbalah, human speech.[654] The kiss itself comprises four breaths, which are the "mystery of faith" (a homologue for *tselem*), and

---

[650] TZ is explaining why VYYTsR, referring to the creation of Adam, is spelled with two *Yuds* instead of one. (Cf. n.245.) According to TZ, arms, breasts, and vulva spell out VYYTsR. Thus Shekhinah, the woman, and the revelation at Sinai are inherent aspects of Adam.

[651] TZ 146a. The narrowness of the eroticized virgin refers to Israel, while its derivation from Gn 2:7 transfers God's creative process from the male to the female body.

[652] e.g. TZ 27b. *Zayin* ז would refer both to the cleavage between the breasts, and also to the vulva, "which is narrow". One could also imagine two *Yuds* combining to form a *Zayin* Elsewhere, *Zayin* is resolved as *Yud* י on top of *Vav* ו, which can represent the phallus (cf. *Sh'lah*, quoted p.188) or the union of male and female (see, e.g., TZ 25b and 29b).

[653] The oral Torah is connected with virginity because the mouth and vulva can be regarded as similar. According to TZ, the breaking of the stone tablets, as of the hymen, is necessary for the fructification of the oral law. The passage also claims that God is really the one who broke the tablets, which are the *b'tulim* of Israel. By analogy with Dt 22:19, God is imagined to be like the bridegroom who falsely accuses his bride of not being a virgin, and who is therefore penalized by being fined and losing the right to divorce (i.e., exile) her.

[654] ECh 1, Sha`ar Haklalim 2, 11; *Kabbalah of Creation: Isaac Luria's Earlier Mysticism*, trans. Eliahu Klein (Northvale NJ: Jason Aronson, 2000), 64–6. Speech is part of this hypostatic kiss by virtue of the mouth of *Abba*, which includes the five "issuances of the mouth".

these ascend through four letters "on which the Holy Name depends".[655] It is not just the parts of the body viewed statically that are in God's image; the way the body is used also traces that image.

There are many other passages equating the name YHVH or the Sefirot with other body parts and organs and other aspects of the body, which suggests that the divine name appeared to the Kabbalists whenever they wanted to see a kind of fractal image of God. The much later-developed concept that a complete *qomah* (cosmic structure or divine image) inheres within each limb (see p.288ff.) is based on this trope.

Torah and mishkan *as bodies in the divine (and human) image*

While the Torah and the *mishkan* (the desert sanctuary or Tabernacle), might be placed in the next chapter on *"Tselem* in the More-Than-Human World", it is proper to consider them as extensions of or patterns for the conjunction between divinity and the human body, because this is how they are understood in Kabbalah. The following passage, for example, understands the Torah to be a complete name and body. The passage is structured around the fact that *pereq* means both "joint" and "chapter".

[S]ince the Torah is called "name" and she restores the soul, she has portions and chapters/*p'raqim* and passages that are open and closed portions, a model of a complete structure / *dugmat binyan shalem*, [just] as there are in a person ligaments/*qish'rey* of hand and foot and joints/*p'raqim*. And as there are limbs on which the soul/*nefesh* (life) depends, and there are limbs on which the soul does not depend... so there are portions in the Torah and scriptures that appear, to one who does not know the reasons that explain them, to be worthy of being burned, and [yet] to the one who attains knowledge/*da`at* of their explanation, they appear like the embodiment/ essential parts of the Torah / *gufey hatorah*, and one who deletes/ leaves out one letter or one [vowel] point from them, [it] is as if he leaves out the complete body / *guf hashalem*, and there is no difference between [leaving out] the chieftains of Esav[656] and the ten commandments, for all is one thing and one structure.[657]

Here the complete structure of the Torah corresponds to the structure of the soul and the body.[658] This body is a human body, with "hands and feet".

---

[655] 2:146a–b. The four spirits/*ruchin* are the breaths of each person coming from inside him/ herself, and the breaths of each of them inside the other. The four letters, upon which depend YHVH and the upper and lower ones, are the letters of the word love, *aha̱vah* אהבה. See Joel Hecker, "Kissing Kabbalists: Hierarchy, Reciprocity, and Equality", *Studies in Jewish Civilization* 18 (2008), 189–95.

[656] This refers to the verses that recount the genealogy and succession of the rulers of Esav/Edom, which become the paradigmatic example of a section of Torah that can only be made meaningful when read through a mystical lens.

[657] *Peyrush Ha'agadot L'Rabi Azri'el*, ed. Isaiah Tishby (Jerusalem: M'qitsey Nirdamim, 1945), 15b–16a, 37–8; also in Scholem, *On the Kabbalah and Its Symbolism*, trans. Ralph Manheim (New York: Schocken Books, 1965), 45.

[658] The letters of the Torah themselves are also seen as the shape of God. See p.204.

Binyan shalem is used here as another analogue for *tselem*. One who leaves out a part of the name leaves out a part of the body, rendering the whole incomplete.

The Torah is equated with "the mystery of Adam" and with the union of male and female in the next passage, from the *Zohar*. All of these tropes, along with the Torah herself, are used as templates through which to understand the divine image present in the *mishkan*.

"And with the *mishkan* you will make ten curtains"—here, this is the mystery of unification, which is fixing/arrangement of the *mishkan* from so many levels, as it's written, "and the *mishkan* was one" [Ex 26:6; 36:13]... In a person there are so many parts, upper and lower ones, those that are innermost within, and those that are revealed outside, and all of them are called one body. So also... the mystery/*raza* of the *mishkan*, which is [made of] limbs and parts / *eivarin v'shayyfin* – they all go/add up to the mystery of Adam, like the pattern/*k'gavna* of the commandments in the Torah, for the commandments in the Torah are all of them in the mystery of Adam, male and female, for when they are joined together as one they are one, the mystery of Adam.[659]

The ten curtains, of course, symbolize the ten Sefirot. "The mystery of Adam" is an analogue for *tselem*, as is "male and female". The "mystery of the *mishkan*" and its unity are thus defined as analogues of *tselem*. Elsewhere, parts of the *mishkan*, such as the menorah or the Holy of Holies, are also treated as images of God, while the *k'ruvim* (cherubim on top of the gold cover of the ark in the *mishkan*), representing the sexual embrace of male and female, are an especially important image (see p.196.)[660]

As I will discuss in Chapter 11, the commandments themselves are what perfect the image of God in the human body. That the *mishkan* is essentially a perfected image of the human body, as well as an image of the body of the entire Creation, was already described in the Midrash, in *Tanchuma P'qudey* and elsewhere.[661] Here, the *Zohar* overlays the image of God upon the *mishkan*

---

[659] 2:162b; WZ 1086. Cf. TZ 13b, which equates the *mishkan* with the Sefirot.
[660] See, e.g., *Zohar Ra`ya Mehemna* 2:157b–158a. On the *k'ruvim*, see also *Zohar* 3:59a and the Talmudic precedent at TB Yoma 54a.
[661] *P'qudey* 3, quoted p.245. The motif of *mishkan* as cosmos is also expressed in *Midrash Tadshe'* (date unknown). Jonathan Klawans explores the lineage of this motif in *Purity, Sacrifice, and the Temple* (Oxford: Oxford University Press, 2006), 113–28. Cf. Josephus, *Antiquities of the Jews* 3.7.7: "[F]or if any one do... look upon these things [of the Tabernacle], he will find they were every one made in way of imitation and representation of the universe" (trans. William Whiston, www.earlyjewishwritings.com/text/josephus/ant3.html [Apr. 2010]). See also *Antiquities* 3.6.4 and *The Wars of the Jews* 5.5.4 (trans. William Whiston, www.earlyjewishwritings.com/text/josephus/war5.html [Dec. 2011]). Also compare *BmR Naso'* 12:4 (which is later than *Tanch*), where the *mishkan*, equated with Solomon's *apiryon* (palanquin), is compared to the world:

"And it was in the day of completing [the *mishkan*]" [Nu 7:1]—that is what's written: "An *apiryon* he made for himself" [So 3:9]—this is the world, which is made like a kind of canopy; "...Shlomo (Solomon) the king"—this is the Holy One who set peace/*shalom* between fire and water and kneaded them, this with this, and made from them the firmament... which is fire and water; "... from the trees of *L'vanon*"—for [the world] was built from the place of the

directly. As the site where God's presence is manifest, the *mishkan* stands in relation to divinity as body stands in relation to soul. In this passage, the *mishkan* and "the commandments in the Torah" are both read as analogues for *tselem*. In both cases, the vessel must parallel what it manifests/contains in order to fulfill its function. The imbrication of these patterns one upon the other adds its own layer of meaning, serving to reinforce the mystical potency of every mitsvah.

Similar to the *mishkan*, the Torah also represents the body of Creation as a whole, as well as the body of the human, in the following passage:

> Come see: Anyone who strives in/with the Torah sustains the world and sustains each and every thing according to its redeemed-order /`al tiquneyh as it properly should be. And you have no part/organ/*shayyfa* that exists in a person that does not have a creature/*b'riyah* in the world to parallel/receive it. For behold, just as a person is divided into parts... and all of them are one body, so also is the world: all these creatures are all of them many many parts / *shayyfin shayyfin* [of the world], and they are sustained, these upon these, and when all of them are righted/redeemed/*mit'taqnin*, behold all of them are really/*mamash* one body. And all is like the pattern /*k'gavna* of the Torah, for the whole Torah is parts and joints (also meaning "chapters") / *shayyfin uf'raqim*, and they are sustained, these upon these, and when all of them are repaired/redeemed they are made into one body. When David gazed upon this thing he opened and said, "How diverse are Your works YHVH, all of them with wisdom You made, what fills the earth are Your possessions" [Ps 104:24].[662]

The body here is primarily an image for wholeness, a wholeness that embraces the diversity of many parts. The pattern (*gavna*) marking the body, whether the body of Creation or human, is the image of God. Thus, the diversity of creatures and the complexity of the body are equally the structure of divinity. This

> Temple/*Beyt Hamiqdash* (which was made of cedar from Lebanon)... Why is [the Temple] called foundation stone / *even sh'tiyah*? Because from it the world was founded /*hushetet*. "Its pillars he made silver" [So 3:10]—this is the firmament, as you would say, "the pillars of the heavens would shake loose /*y'rof'fu*" [Jb 26:11]—and why is it called silver/*kesef*? Because it covers/*m'khasef* over all the work of Creation...; "... its back /*r'fidato* gold" [So 3:10]—this is the earth, that raises fruits of the earth and fruits of the tree, which are like gold – as gold has many kinds and many colors, even so the fruits of the earth, some of them are green, some of them are red; "... its chariot-seat /*merkavo* purple" [So 3:10]—this is the sun, who is placed above and who rides in a chariot and lights up the world, like what it says, "and he is like a bridegroom going out from his wedding-canopy/*chuppah*" [Ps 19:6], and from the power of the sun, the rains come down... and the earth raises fruits, and therefore they call [the sun] purple/*argaman*, for the Holy One formed him to weave /*la'arog* manna for the creatures, and there is no manna except for fruits and grains.

> This passage, while greatly expanded, parallels *Shir Hashirim Rabbah* 3:8:4; cf. *PRK* 1:2, 3. (The continuation of the passage takes a very different tack. See end of n.318.) The *mishkan* is also implicitly taken to be the model for the universe in *P'ri `Ets Hadar*. See p.212.

[662] *Zohar* 1:134b; WZ 1123–4; discussed further p.250. Matt (*The Zohar*, vol.2 [Stanford CA: Stanford University Press, 2004], 258) translates `al tiquneyh as "fittingly" and *mit'taqnin* as "arrayed". The range of meanings for *tiqun* is difficult to translate concordantly (see n.604). *Pereq* means joint or section, as well as chapter.

passage also includes a theme I will return to in Chapters 7 and 9 that is fundamental for ecotheology: because the world is an image of Adam, it is also an image of God.

Just as the Torah as a whole is a complete body, in the following text, the letters of the Torah are in themselves complete bodies and complete names:

All the letters of the Torah, in their shapes/forms and in their joining and in their separation, and in the letters [that are] spiral, embellished and twisted, and missing and extra, and smaller and enlarged and backwards... and the closed and open sections and their orders (Torah portions) – these are the shapes/*tsurot* of God.[663]

There is no ambiguity here; the letters themselves are the shape of God. Each is a body unique in itself, as well as an element in the body of the Torah and in God's image. This idea is ultimately rooted in seeing the letters of the Torah as the substance of Creation.

TSELEM IN THE MORE-THAN-HUMAN: THE TRANS-HUMAN

III. *Tselem* in the upper worlds

In the remainder of this chapter, I will detail a few examples from Kabbalah of God's image in the `*elyonim* – the realms where Midrash already sees God's image. One might call these realms the "trans-human". For Kabbalah, this includes not only the angels and the heavens, and of course the Sefirot, but also the throne and the chariot, which function as divine hypostases.

The angels and the divine hypostases

The extension of God's image to the upper ones, that is, heavenly bodies and angels, was an accepted trope within the world of midrashic discourse, as discussed at length in Part I. *Heykhalot* mysticism also connected God's image with the names of God in themselves, in their own right or transformed into the names and essences of angels, centuries before the development of what we call Kabbalah. One finds rabbinic catalogs of angels in which the letters of God's names in themselves constitute a tracing of God's image. Scholem notes:

Several aggadic sayings state that the angels bear the name of God imprinted on their hearts, and this may explain the custom of the Merkavah mystics to add the Tetragrammaton or one of its many substitutes to the names of the angels. In the *Midrash Tehillim*, R. Levi says: "A tablet with the name of the Holy One, blessed be He, is engraved on the hearts of the angels as a sort of mark (*asteriscus*)."[664]

---

[663] *Sefer Hayichud*, ms.Milano-Ambrosiana 62, f.113b, quoted in Idel, Kabbalah: New Perspectives (New Haven CT: Yale University Press, 1988), 370. The passage lists decorative and non-orthographic scribal variations. Some are required, others Kabbalistic. The modern (Orthodox) rabbinate has repressed the latter – a facet of the homogenization of modernity.

[664] Scholem, *Jewish Gnosticism*, 71; Hebr. text, 125. Brackets in original changed to parentheses.

Tselem *in the more-than-human: the trans-human*

An angel manifests its divinity by virtue of having a name of divine origin, that is, a name that incorporates one of God's holy names.[665] As one looks to the margins of rabbinic tradition, one can see that the idea of God's image becomes more concrete, defined by letters rather than qualities. This trope becomes the norm in Kabbalah.

Other mystical or metaphysical entities, such as the throne and the chariot, are also described as imaging God in pre-Kabbalistic literature. The throne appears not only in Ezekiel but also in Jeremiah and Isaiah.[666] In Midrash, the throne of glory is already given an exalted ontological status similar to the status of the Torah.[667] It is also equated with seeing God,[668] and it receives praises from the angels.[669] The chariot of Ezekiel 1 is one of the most important images of God for the early Jewish mystics (called *yordey hamerkavah*, those who "descend to the chariot"). They aspired to behold the chariot through spiritual visions, along with the throne of glory, which figures as a goal of mystical vision in all *Heykhalot* literature, most especially *Shi`ur Qomah*. Kabbalistic texts on these same subjects are not theologically innovative, but they are innovative hermeneutically, demonstrating how the Kabbalah uses analogues and metonymy to say that something is in God's image. On the subject of the throne, for example, we have already quoted the following:

"And He blew in his nostrils a *nishmat chayyim*" [Gn 2:7]—this is the image/*d'yoqna* upon human beings, about which it says: "And he dreamed and here, a ladder" [Gn 28:12]. "Ladder" certainly is *nishmat chayyim*, the throne for the name YHV"H.[670]

"Throne" or *kursayya* is here used as an analogue for *tselem*. *N'shamah* is equated with *d'yoqna*, that is, *tselem*, while the ladder, which is a symbol of the unity of heavens and earth, is equated with the soul that unifies the divine realm and the human body. For this reason, the ladder becomes the throne for God's name.

Similarly, the chariot is an image of God. Writes the Shlah: "the limbs of sections of the Chariot, their names are in Him blessed be, in essence, and He is the upper Adam / *Adam Ha`elyon*."[671] Yosef Gikatilla (1248–c.1310, Spain) lists "*qomat hamerkavah* / the stature/form of the chariot" as one of the *kinuyim* for Shekhinah, and he also describes the parts of the body as a sign for "the work of the chariot".[672] There are many similar correspondences between the image and the `*elyonim*, whether they be planets and stars, angels,

---

[665] See *Sefer Sodey Razaya, Ot Resh* (esp. §§4, 6, 7).
[666] Je 14:21, 17:12 and Is 6:1.   [667] *PRE* ch.4, 7.
[668] *Sifrey B'midbar, pisqa* 115; 126. Page numbers refer to Chayyim Shaul Horowitz's edition, *Sifrey d'Vey Rav: Sifrey `al Sefer B'midbar v'Sifrey Zuta* (Frankfurt-am-Main: J. Kauffman Verlag, n.d.).
[669] *BR* 1:4.   [670] *Ra`ya Mehemna* 3:123b.
[671] *ShLH, Toldot Adam, Bayit Ne'eman*, 10b; Krassen, "Faithful House II", 153.
[672] *Sha`arey Orah* (Warsaw: Argelbrand, 1883), 4, 28. Note also 115, where Gikatilla says that all of the sections of the chariot and the supernal (upper) ministers are together called "Adam".

divine instruments, or potencies. And the anchor for any such chain of symbols in Kabbalah is the Sefirot, which are the primary articulation of the image of God.

The heavens

The heavenly bodies themselves were already elaborated as part of the system of *t'murot* and divine names in *Sefer Y'tsirah*, which aligns the planets with the seven "double" letters (ב ג ד כ פ ר ת), and the constellations with the twelve "simple" letters.[673] In the *Bahir*, one celestial feature, the *t'li* (dragon, or axis, possibly meaning the Milky Way or the circumpolar constellation called Draco), is identified as "the *d'mut* before the Holy One, as is written, 'his (i.e., God's) locks (of hair) are *taltalim*' [So 5:11]".[674] In Zoharic literature, the full potential of *Sefer Yetsirah*'s correspondences is realized. The image of the upper (or supernal) human is the seal of the divine image in the heavens. *Tiquney Zohar* teaches, "'This/*Zeh* is the book of Adam's generations'—*Zeh* literally (i.e., in *gematria*, where Z + H is 12), including the twelve constellations of Adam dil`eyla (Adam Ha`elyon)."[675]

An example from early Hasidic literature shows how the Kabbalistic way of seeing the celestial bodies played an important part in the development of later theological traditions. The Besht (Yisrael Baal Shem Tov, founder of Hasidism, 1698–1760, Poland/Ukraine), taught:

It's written: "Sun and Shield are YHVH Elohim" [Ps 84:11]. It's explained: for the name *HVYH* (YHVH) is called sun/*shemesh*... and what's written, "sun and shield", [indicates that this "shield"] is like a barrier protecting against the light of the sun. He (the sun) [has] an image/*dimyon* like *Hashem* (YHVH) Elohim, meaning to say, that it is impossible to look on the sun, because of the greatness of his light's brightness... So is [the brightness of] the name *HVYH*: its light is very great... therefore it was necessary to contract it and limit it within the name Elohim – [which] *gematria* (numerology) [reveals to be] Nature/*Hateva`* (= 86) – which is the shield.[676]

---

[673] 4:5–11, 102–6; 5:2, 113–5. This is not the same as the heavenly bodies being in God's image; on the contrary, each letter *rules* over one of the celestial beings. The three other letters are the "mothers", א מ ש, the elementals.

[674] §106; see also §95; cf. *Y'tsirah* 6:2, 118: "*T'li* in the world is like a king on his throne." "*D'mut* before the Holy One" is simply a more circumspect way of saying "*d'mut* of the Holy One". *Taltalim*, usu. trans. "curly", is here understood as "twisting like a dragon". More generally, §82 equates the "seven limbs" of the body with "their powers in the heavens" (§172 equates them with the Holy One's "seven holy forms"). On *t'li* as the Milky Way, see Donnolo, *Sefer Chakhmoni*, 129, which analogizes it to the spinal cord. But see Marc Epstein, *Dreams of Subversion in Medieval Jewish Art and Literature* (University Park PA: Penn State University Press), 79–82, for a different and more thorough examination of this motif.

[675] TZ 70, 121a, further discussed on p.224.

[676] *Sefer Ba`al Shem Tov* (*Ba`al Shem Tov `al Hatorah*), ed. Shimon Menachem Mendel (Israel: Book Export Enterprises), 43 (hereafter *SBST*). *Keter Shem Tov* 2:24d is cited, but the correct source seems to be vol.1, §246.

Also, the connection made between Elohim and Nature (distinguished in Hebrew from "nature/*teva*̀" by the definite article) in this passage is very important as a next step in this theological work, though it will only be touched on here. The quote itself shows how Hasidic thinkers were unafraid to assign divine qualities to created beings. In many passages such as this one, the framework of *tselem* or *dimyon* and the projection of the name YHVH are used to accomplish this, just as they are in Kabbalah.

Kabbalistic anthropology
Like Midrash, the Kabbalah includes a wide range of interpretations of how *tselem*, soul, and body interrelate. Kabbalah, unlike early midrash, universally accepted the idea that body and soul were divisible. But because both body and soul were explicitly images of God, there was still a tendency in Kabbalah to reject the metaphysical opposition of spirit and matter.[677]

This anthropology also led to a kind of unification of culture and the natural world. Starting from the relationship between divinity and the human body, Kabbalah included details upon details within the divine image, progressing to include Nature via the bridge of the body.[678] In this chapter we have sampled the beginnings of this progression, from the body to the details of the body, and from the body to the bodies of the Torah, the heavens, and so on. In the next, we will see how this led Kabbalah to embrace many other dimensions of the more-than-human world, ultimately including all of Being within divinity and uniting Nature with divinity.

This relates directly to the core question of the "more-than-human". The term "more-than-human" was coined by David Abram specifically to avoid separating human culture from what we call "Nature". It reminds us that our humanity is part of the landscape of Nature, and that the non-human Other is a vital part of our lived consciousness. But "more-than-human" should equally include souls, divinity, and worlds, both physical and spiritual, just as it should include all beings, upper and lower. As such, when we seek the more-than-human we are also led in a natural progression, beyond a narrower view of the phenomena of Nature, toward a view that unites divinity and Nature.

---

[677] Nevertheless, dualism is also present in many Kabbalistic texts. See p.277ff.
[678] For the Kabbalists, this was a journey that unfolded through mystical experience, rather than just a philosophical insight.

7

Tselem Elohim in Kabbalah, part 2

The more-than-human world – holism and unifications, trees, birds, animals, and colors

> *Mah adir shimkha b'khol ha'arets* – How great is Your name in all the earth!
> Psalms 8:2,10

This chapter will focus on Kabbalistic texts that project the image of God, either directly or through various analogues, onto the earthly creatures or *tachtonim*. These texts, which run counter to the midrashic trope of radical separation between the upper and lower realms, represent a thread that is thoroughly woven into Kabbalistic symbolism and is continually alluded to as a great mystery. One way to study this thread in Kabbalah is to thematize it by connecting the texts in which it appears, independent of their historical contexts.[679] In the words of Sarah Schneider, one can build up such redemptive texts into a "complete *par'tsuf*", that is, a complete theological pattern that reveals what was hidden in fragments of texts.[680]

As these teachings are strung together, one valid question is whether they were meant as theological or metaphysical truths, or simply as poetry and metaphor. The rule in Kabbalah, however, is to insist upon metonym and to equate every image with a hypostatic reality, so that the image itself is treated as more real than what it refers to in the sensory world.[681] In other words,

---

[679] See nn.105, 945. Connecting texts from different periods in this way can lead to unfactual statements about what the rabbis, "Judaism", or Kabbalah say about a topic. Considerations about how to do this in a way that attends to differences across time and between texts are dealt with in *Methods*. Most importantly, I connect different texts not because they have the same meaning, but because they use the same terminology.

[680] Lecture, Berkeley CA, Oct. 17, 2002. Schneider was referring to her own work, *Kabbalistic Writings on the Nature of Masculine and Feminine* (Northvale NJ: Jason Aronson, 2002), which presents Kabbalistic texts in which female autonomy (what we would call gender equality) is the redemptive, messianic ideal. Schneider repurposes the term *par'tsuf*, which has the sense of building a whole out of interrelated parts. See n.635.

[681] See n.717.

there are very few parables in which one half of a comparison may be said to be symbolic or literary, and the other said to be real. The process of turning metaphors into metonyms and parables into hypostases is one of the things that defines Kabbalah as Kabbalah.

An explicit example of this process can be found in the *Bahir*, which compares the process of creation as the planting of a garden:

> A parable, to what does the thing compare? To a king that wanted to build a palace... He cut [through] rock... and a great spring of water emerged for him, living water. The king said: Since I have flowing water, I will plant a garden, and I will delight in it, I and all the world.[682]

Suddenly, in a later passage, the narrative frame shifts from a parable about a king planting a garden, into a direct speech from God about the Cosmic Tree:

> I am the one that planted this tree/*ilan*, [for] all the world to delight in, and I hammered out all/*kol* with him (the tree), and I called his name "the Whole/All /*hakol*", for all depends on him, and all comes out from him. And all are needing him, and through/to him they gaze and for him they wait. And from there bloom/grow the souls in joy. Alone was I when I made him ... for in the time when I hammered out my earth, I planted and rooted this tree in her, and I rejoiced together [with him] and I rejoiced in them.[683]

I will return to the theme of the Cosmic Tree further on. What is important here is how the *Bahir* shifts from the language of midrash and parable into a more mystical idiom, opening God's "inner life" to us using images of the created world. In most cases, I will take it as given that Kabbalistic texts are metonymic in this way, unless they are explicitly described as parable. Here then are some of the teachings that extended *tselem* beyond humanity, long before our ecological concerns would bring these issues to the fore.

TSELEM IN THE MORE-THAN-HUMAN: THE EARTHLY REALM

IV. *Tselem* in the whole of Creation

Upper and lower

The critical issue for this book is whether Kabbalah does imagine the boundaries between upper and lower being crossed. On a most basic level, the statement found in *Tiquney Zohar* that "there is no place empty of Him, not in the upper ones and not in the lower ones / *la b'ila'in v'la b'tata'in*" intimates that it does.[684] However, this statement is hardly specific enough to derive any ideas about God's image.

---

[682] §5. In the very next section, the *Bahir* shifts back into parable, comparing God with "[a] king that sought to plant a tree in his garden".
[683] §22. [684] *TZ* 57, 91b; cf. *TZ* 70, 122b. For midrashic parallels, see n.1002.

This section will focus on texts whose theological significance is clearer. In the following passage, the totality of Creation represents the ten Sefirot, without distinction between upper and lower realms: "The ten s'firot... are clothed in ten things that were created on the first day, and these are: heavens and earth, light and darkness, abyss and chaos, wind and water, the measure of day and the measure of night."[685] If the physical elements of Creation in their entirety embody the Sefirot, this means that they represent God's image.

In *Zohar Chadash*, midrashic ideas about upper and lower beings combine in a passage that conjoins several *midrashim*:

When [the Holy One] created the *adam*, He united with [the earth, the heavens, and the waters] in making him, and said, "Let us make a human". And He put in him bright features, sight, smell, stature/*qomah*, walking/*halikhah*, rejoicing/*m'sos*, speech, doing. He made him rule /*hamshilo* over the work of His hands. That is what's written: "You made him rule over the works of Your hands; all You set under his feet" [Ps 8:7]. And when He threw breath into him, he stood on his feet and resembled/*nidmeh* the lower ones and the upper ones. His body became like the earth and his *n'shamah* like the upper ones, in form/*to'ar* and majesty and glory, in fear and in awe. That is what's written: "You crowned him with glory and majesty" [Ps 8:6].[686]

The phrase "resembled the lower ones and the upper ones" is equated with God standing Adam on his feet, which is specifically connected with God's image, embracing an idea of the image that specifically emerges when the lower ones support the upper ones. While it is the *n'shamah* that represents *tselem* (or here, *to'ar*) and not the body, the image becomes manifest through the integration of upper and lower into one living being. This integration is what gives the first human its metaphysical "height".[687]

---

[685] TZ 70, 120a–b.

[686] *Midrash Hane'elam* 16c (WZ 782), based on BR 14:8 (p.247) and TB Nidah 31a (pp.170–71). See connected ZCh passage on pp.272–3. ZCh transposes the partnership in reproduction of man, woman, and God described by the *Bavli* to the time of the creation of the world, with earth and water (or, as it says elsewhere in the same passage, earth and heavens) acting in the place of mother and father. Note that ZCh has substituted *qomah* or stature along with *halikhah* in place of the Talmud's "*hilukh raglayim*", using terminology found in *midrashim* about *Adam Harishon*. Tishby's translator translates *qomah* here as "the ability to get up", but the idea of erect stature is certainly what was intended. (Tishby also cites TB B'rakhot 30b [WZ 780], which is not correct, though he may have had in mind Qidushin 30b, which mentions the three partners that join in conception. However, only Nidah 31a describes "the portion that the Holy One gives him".)

[687] This raises a subtle point about the substantive interpretation of *tselem*. The divine image can be thought of as a quality found in the upper realms, which is extended to the lower realms – that is, a characteristic from the upper realms that, once placed into human beings, becomes a kind of image of the upper realms. The divine image can also be more like a literal image – a "momento" of what is not there, so that a momento of God and the upper realms is present in human beings. (On image as momento, see McLeod, *Theodore of Mopsuestia* [New York, 2009], 30.) A third possibility is presented here: the divine image is constituted from out of the *unification* of upper and lower realms, and it is this unity that points to the divine.

Another Zoharic example goes beyond the language of aggadah to make a direct theosophical claim. Discussing the process of emanation from the beginning of the *Yud* through to the final *He'* of God's name, *Zohar Chadash*, in a section called "The Secrets of the Letters", states:

> In the secret of the ten Sefirot... all is included in this image of *He'* ה ... [I]n this secret were created and affixed/ordered/*it'taqnu* all these lower ones. For this [reason] it's written: "Elohim said: Let us make /*na`aseh* Adam in our image as our likeness..." "*Na`aseh/N`SH*"—certainly this [means the letter] *He'* ה, literally, and (i.e., along with) all these that are existing below and are united in her, in her image, truly/*mamash*.[688]

"The secret of the ten *s'firot*" is *tselem*, of course, and "this image of *He'*" is also an analogue of *tselem*, as well as a symbol of Shekhinah. The lower ones are united together in this image, *mamash* – really and truly, not just symbolically or metaphorically – and this image, which is also Adam, is the completion of God's name.[689]

The last letter of God's name is a fractal image of the whole name and all the Sefirot, and like Shekhinah it specifically includes and sustains all the lower beings, so God's image here comprises the union of all the lower ones, independently from the image created by the upper ones and the greater image created by the unification of both.

Shekhinah, the image of God that is closest to the earth, is also called "the image that includes all images", meaning the images of all creatures above and below.[690] She embraces and sustains all the lower creatures, like a mother, and embraces and unifies with the upper ones, that is, the Sefirot, like a lover. The diversity of worlds and beings unites to create and be created as the single name of God. Within this great whole is humanity or *Adam*, each individual of whom is a complete image and name of God. Unlike the Midrash, which foreclosed the possibility of ascribing God's image to the other creatures of the earthly realm, the Kabbalah avidly affirms it, and finds within that ascription the ground of our humanity.

In *Zohar Chadash*'s description, the unification of the lower realm comes through the mediation of the supernal Adam. For Yosef Ashkenazi, however, this is the unmediated state of all being: "[A]ll the existences from the upper ones and the lower ones are all of them tied into His great, mighty and awesome

---

[688] Sitrey Otiyot, "H' Achronah d'Havayah", 2a. See also Wald's translation in *The Doctrine of the Divine Name: An Introduction to Classical Kabbalistic Theology* (Atlanta GA: Scholars Press, 1988), 83.

[689] See further discussion, p.215ff.

[690] Some examples are: "*hat'munah hakolelet et kol hat'munot*" (David ben Yehudah Hechasid [fourteenth century?], *Mar'ot Hatsov'ot*, ed. Daniel Matt [Chico CA: Scholars Press, 1982], 152), "*d'yoqna dikh'lil kol d'yoqnin*" (Zohar 1:13a), and "*dimyona dikh'lil kol dimyonin*" (ZCh 59a). Thanks to Daniel Matt for these references. This trope appears frequently, e.g., TZ 18a, 140a; see also Scholem, *Von der Mystischen Gestalt* (Frankfurt am Main: Suhrkamp Verlag, 1973), 173–4. The more obvious meaning of this trope is that the Shekhinah receives the influence and effluence of all the other Sefirot, but the broader meaning is also understood.

name" (see p.238). One way in which these varied expressions can be understood is that the *telos* of Creation is to become unified or whole.

Many texts of Kabbalah relate this powerful idea. One of its most beautiful expressions is found in the blessing prayer from *P'ri `Ets Hadar* ("Fruit of the Majestic Tree"), the first published Tu Bish'vat seder (a Kabbalistic ritual meal in honor of the Mishnaic New Year for the Tree), which first appeared as part of the book *Chemdat Yamim* (seventeenth century):[691]

Please, God, the One who makes, and who forms, and who creates, and who emanates the upper worlds; And in their form/*tsurah* and in their design/*tsivyon* You created their model/*dugma*[692] on the earth below; You made all of them with wisdom, upper ones above and lower ones below, "to join [together] the tent to become one". [Ex 36:18][693]

According to this prayer, the Earth is a model of the upper worlds, and the *tachtonim* are created to be joined to the `*elyonim*. Since the term "upper worlds" also means here the Sefirot, that is, God's image, this would mean that the Earth is patterned in God's image.[694] The purpose of this doubled pattern above and below is itself twofold: "to join the tent together to become one", that is, to unify the disparate realms of Creation, and "to cause the children of Adam to know the wisdom and discernment that is in them, to reach what is hidden", that is, to allow people to understand the upper realms through what they can learn from the life they see in this realm.[695]

---

[691] Some scholars believe *Chemdat Yamim* (Livorno, 1763; repr. Jerusalem: Makor, 1970), first published in 1728, was written by Natan of Gaza (1643–80, Palestine), the prophet of the heretical messiah Shab'tai Tsvi, or by one of Natan's students. If Natan was the author, his connection to the book would have to have been suppressed in order for it to be published. This may be the reason why no author's name appears in any of the early printed editions. Miles Krassen ("*Peri Eitz Hadar*: A Kabbalist Tu B'shvat Seder", *Trees, Earth, and Torah*, 135) notes that the provenance of *P'ri `Ets Hadar* is far from clear, and that it could have been copied into *Chemdat Yamim* from an earlier source. In any case, the book remained popular for centuries, and if there were concerns about Sabbatean influence, there was enough love for the book for it to be preserved despite those doubts.

[692] *Dugma* or "model" may here be a synonym for *tselem*. Liebes interprets it to indicate a lesser ("symbolic" rather than "mythic") relationship between realms (*Studies in the Zohar*, 38 and 179, n.116), so we are only as close as the "model of the image" from his perspective. Wolfson, however, disagrees with this distinction (*Language, Eros, Being*, 35–7).

[693] Portions of this prayer will be referenced throughout *Kabbalah and Ecology*; see Excursus 2 for extended quote of the prayer.

[694] Cf. Plato, *Timaeus* 37c, which describes the physical world as the image/*agalma* of the divine world.

[695] This motif permeates Kabbalah. See *Zohar* 2:15b (quoted pp.219–20), a primary source text for *P'ri `Ets Hadar*, as well as 2:5a (p.216). An even earlier folkloric depiction of the idea of correspondence may have existed in a legend about Chanokh (Enoch), who in his work as a shoemaker was said to have connected the upper and lower worlds "with every stitch". See *MTJM* 365, n.101; also www.calba-savua.blogspot.com/2010/10/enoch-shoemaker-or-why-god-took-up.html (Aug. 2014). However, in *P'ri `Ets Hadar*, the joining comes prior to humanity.

Furthermore, the phrase "to join [together] the tent to become one / *l'chaber et ha'ohel lih'yot echad*" in Exodus describes the construction of the *mishkan* or Tabernacle in the desert. The message of *P'ri `Ets Hadar* is therefore that the entire Creation is a *mishkan*, a dwelling place of divinity, just as the desert *mishkan* was (cf. passages from *Tanchuma*, p.245, and *B'midbar Rabbah*, n.661).

The rhythm and rhetoric of the prayer also suggest that the purpose of unification is embedded in Creation, even before the advent of humanity, for the `*elyonim* and *tachtonim* are already destined to be joined the moment they receive their common pattern. I do claim that this pattern is equivalent to the image of God, but no matter how we interpret it, the pattern, presented here as form, design, model, and teacher of wisdom – however these be understood – unites the physical, spiritual, and divine levels of reality. It defines and conjures a world that is more-than-human, more-than-Nature, more-than-divinity, and that is at the same time deeply attuned to the human.

The image at all levels

Some Kabbalists not only saw those beings among the lower ones that effected the unification of the upper and lower realms as an image of God, they also saw each level of reality in and of itself as being an image of God.[696] For example, the following passage from *Sh'ney Luchot Hab'rit* describes the Sefirot, the angels, the animals of the chariot, and the four elements as manifestations of the same pattern (the divine image) at different levels:

Concerning [the four elements, fire, air, earth and water], the *Zohar* wrote at length that they are extensions of the supernal (upper) Chariot. *Che̲sed* is water, *G'vurah* is fire, *Tif'eret* is air, and *Malkhut* is earth. We call them, metaphorically, what is later manifested from them, "fire," "water," "air" and "earth", in the secret of the four animals. In the next stage, the manifestation of bands of angels, Michael is the element of water, Gavriel is the element of fire, Uriel is the element of air, and Rafael is the element of earth. This process continues through the manifestation of the orbs, until the elements are in their places.[697]

---

[696] This trope would lead directly to the conclusion that all is in God's image. However, the image in humanity also refers to the unique role that human beings play in manifesting God's image. As Wolfson explains:

> The import of the scriptural axiom that Adam is endowed with the image of God is that the [Kabbalist]...can prepare his being to be in the pattern of the supernal archetype. The construction of the imaginal body is critical to establishing the unity of the one in all things. In this respect, the human is accorded a distinguished ontic status even though all things are infused with and therefore can be said to mirror the divine reality.
>
> (*Language, Eros, Being*, 35–6)

The unifications that a human being effects are necessary for unifying Creation and for manifesting of God's unity in Creation.

[697] *Toldot Adam, Bayit Ne'eman*, 10b; Krassen, "Faithful House II", 152, Krassen's trans. (translit. modified). This passage will be examined in more detail further on.

The Sefirot at the highest level are the guarantor that each of the subsequent levels is actually an image of God. This is mediated not only through the fractal structure of the Sefirot at every level of Being, but also through language. Yishayah Horowitz explains:

> In saying that language is holy, I mean that what is called hand exists above in the place of holiness. Later, during the process of its manifestation through all of the worlds, from one stage to another, through myriad levels, the manifestation is called hand at every level, as a metaphor. That which properly bears the name is actually located above.[698]

Just as physical fire is really another name and a symbol of the real fire of *G'vurah*, so are both the physical hand and the word "hand" symbols of what is the divine hand above.

Most importantly, this passage contains two tropes that are the foundation of a large part of Kabbalistic hermeneutics: every level of Being is assimilated through the process of metonymy and symbolic concatenation to the highest levels of Being, and everything has within it the essence and image of those levels through its participation in the name of what is above. This is one of the clearest statements of what is happening everywhere in Kabbalistic theology.

YHVH and the image of God in the world

The name YHVH, comprising the Sefirot and so much more – the image of God in the human, the quality of compassion, and the union of Shekhinah and *Tif'eret* – is a primary facet of the holism that characterizes the Kabbalistic picture of the world. Earlier, I described this holism as inhering in each level of reality. Here I will briefly discuss how the name YHVH stood for the fourfold dimensionality of the world and the structure of the whole of Creation.

In simple terms, all beings were emanated through many stages of differentiation by the One that stands at the beginning of Creation. Like the Neoplatonists, the Kabbalists found God by tracing back the patterns of emanation, what is called *seder hishtalsh'lut*, but they made this process concrete, finding the levels in rituals and in God's names, and especially in the letters of God's explicit name. In the emanationist model of how the world was created, there is no one point where God stops and Creation begins.[699] Creation as such is both the object of God's munificence, what we might call Nature, and the manifesting of God's hidden process. At the level of the planet and the cosmos, Nature can be seen as a direct embodiment of *Elohim*, and this process continues down to the "lowliest" worm or bacterial cell.

---

[698] Krassen, "Faithful House II", 153.
[699] At the same time, there is no point where Creator and created are the same, nor are there two points in the chain of emanation in which the relationship between Creator and created is exactly the same. Every being and state occupies its own unique place in the flux of divine energy. Every transition reveals (and conceals) something more of God, as it reveals something more of Creation.

The four letters of God's name were seen as corresponding to this multi-level process of emanation, becoming well-defined in Cordoveran Kabbalah by four stages of being, also called the four worlds, which are Emanating/*Atsilut* (Y), Creating/*B'riyah* (H), Shaping/*Y'tsirah* (V), and Doing/`*Asiyah* (H).[700] From this perspective, the entirety of Creation, embracing all its levels, is God's image. In Arthur Green's words, "God is Being – Y-H-W-H – when existence is seen from a fully unitive, harmonic, and all-embracing point of view."[701] This correspondence between God and world is made explicit through the concept of *Adam Qadmon* (studied in detail in the next chapter). More than that, the interrelationships between the different levels are what form the name of God and hence the image of God.

Most importantly, the name also represents physical Creation directly: "It is known that the heavens/sky is [sic] YH"V and earth is the final H'".[702] The most physical level, the earth or the *tachtonim*, must be in conjunction with the higher levels so that, as *Zohar Chadash* taught, "all is included in this image of He'".[703] Without the *tachtonim*, without the final H, as it were, God's image is incomplete.

The Earth and Nature as tselem

Seeing the whole of the cosmic order, from the Sefirot to the *tachtonim*, as an image of God was a short step away from seeing Nature as God's image. In fact, many teachers equated Nature directly with Elohim based on the *gematria* (numerology) they share, 86, as did the Besht (p.206), and Yosef Ashkenazi explains that what the non-Jewish philosophers call Nature is what "we call Elohim".[704] Also, the thirteenth-century text on sacred sexuality called *Igeret Haqodesh* uses a synonym for Nature, *seder `olam*, "the order of the world", as an analogue for God's image, describing Jacob's sons as being "completely righteous... all of them were worthy of being in the image of the order of the world / *b'dimyon seder `olam*".[705] *Seder `olam* can also be read as a synonym for the Sefirot here, but its earliest meaning is Nature.[706]

---

[700] Generally, these levels are mapped onto the Sefirot in this way: *Yud* corresponds to *Chokhmah* (plus *Keter*), *Heh* to *Binah*, *Vav* to *Tif'eret* and the five Sefirot surrounding *Tif'eret*, and the final *Heh* to *Malkhut/Shekhinah*. See the map of the Sefirot in the Appendix, p.361.

[701] "A Kabbalah for the Environmental Age", *Tikkun* (14:5): 33–40; 34.

[702] Eliyahu ben Shlomo (the Vilna Gaon, 1720–97, Lithuania), *Siddur Hagra* (Jerusalem: Yits'chaq Nachum Levi, 1926), 18a.

[703] See p.211.   [704] See p.275.

[705] *Kitvey Ramban*, ed. Chayyim Dov Chavel (Jerusalem: Mossad Harav Kook, 1963), 334. *Midrash Y'lamdeynu* (BM, vol.1, 161) similarly describes the twelve tribes as representing *siduro shel `olam*, comparing them to the twelve constellations, the twelve hours of day and of night, and the twelve months of the year. Cf. TZ 121a, quoted p.224, which compares the tribes to the constellations, i.e. the heavens, but not to the whole world.

[706] See BR 12:1: "If you cannot stand on (understand) the order (law/nature) of thunder, the order of the world / *seder shel `olam* all the more so." See also *Y'lamdeynu*, previous note.

Sefer Bahir goes one step further, specifically locating the image of God in the Earth itself, explaining that the Earth (or the hypostasis called "earth") is the source of the heavens or skies, and at the same time is itself the throne of glory. While the passage itself is difficult to parse, the chain of associations is relatively straightforward:

"The advantage/profit/surplus/*yitron* of the land/*arets* over All /*bakol* is a king" [Ec 5:8] – And what is *yitron*? A place from which is carved out the earth/*arets*... And what is this "earth"? That from her was carved out the Whole /*hakol*, and from him (*hakol*) was carved out heavens, and he is the throne of the Holy One, and he is a precious stone, and he is the sea of wisdom. And corresponding to her (the earth) is the deep-blue/*t'cheilet* of the *tsitsit* (the corner fringes on a prayer shawl). For R' Meir said: How is *t'cheilet* different from all kinds of colors? Because *t'cheilet* resembles the sea and the sea resembles the firmament and the firmament resembles the throne of glory, as it is said, "And they saw Israel's God and under His feet [was something] like sapphire brick-work and like the essence of the heavens for purity" [Ex 24:10] and it says, "like the appearance/*mar'eh* of sapphire stone, a likeness of a throne / *d'mut kisei*'" [Ez 1:26].[707]

The teaching from R' Meir used by the *Bahir* is first found in *Sifrey B'midbar*, where it is prefaced with the statement that looking at the *tsitsit* means *seeing God*.[708] The throne of glory is an analogue for God's image, while the "sea of wisdom", a synonym for the Torah in *Sefer Bahir* (see §3), is another analogue. This chain of likenesses from *t'cheilet* to sea to firmament to divine throne is completed in Ezekiel 1:26 by the "human likeness" that sits upon the throne. The *Bahir* makes its radical statement by placing the Earth at the beginning of this chain of likenesses, where R' Meir's statement in the Midrash begins with the sea, and by identifying the Earth with the throne at the end of this chain.

In general, the Earth's image already comprises the body of Adam (and vice versa) in the Midrash (see p.243ff.). Kabbalah adds to this image, elaborates it, and connects it with *tselem*. The Kabbalah also projects the image of God onto the Earth without the mediation of Adam. For example, the *Zohar* states, "According [to] the pattern of the firmament / *k'gavna d'raqi`a* did the Holy One make the earth", where *gavna d'raqi`a* is an analogue for *tselem*.[709]

---

[707] §§95–6. I am using the standard published text (given in n.1), rather than the one given by Margaliot. (Margaliot seems to be pushed to his selection, even though the pronouns make no sense, by Ramban's interpretation, which comes as much as several centuries after the original text.) The *Bahir* repeatedly uses the sea as one of its images for God (e.g., §§3, 7), along with the image of "great living water". Cf. *PRK* 1:2, 4 (|| *BmR* 12:4), which analogizes the way the Shekhinah or divine presence would fill the *mishkan* with the way the sea would fill a cave by the shore without being thereby lessened.

[708] *Pisqa* 115; 126. According to R' Meir, "you will see it/*oto*" [Nu 15:39] (that is, the thread of *t'cheilet*) means "you will see Him/*oto*" (that is, God), because "the one who upholds the commandment of *tsitsit*, it is as if he received the face of Shekhinah". (See also parallels at *TB M'nachot* 43b, *Chulin* 89a, and *Sotah* 17a, as well as *BmR* 17:5, which may be later than the *Bahir*.)

[709] 2:5a. See p.237.

Kabbalah also expands the midrashic image of the Earth as ruler concretely into the realm of *tselem*. In *Zohar Chadash*, R' Shimon explains that the phrase "Let us / We will make a human" indicates that God invited the earth, the heavens and the waters, the elements present at the start of the creation story, to participate in making the human:

[B]y the hands (means) of these three was all the work of creation done, each and every according to its nature. When the sixth day came all of them were prepared to create, like the rest of the days. The Holy One said to them: No one of you can make this creature itself... Rather, all of you must join together, and I with you, and we will make the human... [T]he body will be the three of yours, and the soul mine. Therefore the Holy One called to them and said to them, "Let us make a human / *na`aseh Adam*"... I the soul and you the body... R' Elazar son of R' Shimon said: That's right, but the earth took up the power of the three of them by herself, until it was through her that the four elements existed/ were sustained.[710]

In these stories, Earth acts with the status of a person and is represented as God's partner and co-ruler. In the Zoharic passage, the human body is in the Earth's image, which comprises in its power not only heavens and waters but also "the four elements", taking on the power of the heavens (i.e., fire and air) and of the waters. We already know that the four elements together are an aspect of YHVH's image, so this passage represents the Earth as a kind of image of God. In Chapter 9, I will further discuss the way that the Earth was conceptualized as a person in Torah, Midrash, and Kabbalah.

V. *Tselem* in the *tachtonim*

For the remainder of this chapter, I will focus on the lower ones, that is, dimensions, creatures, species, and phenomena we can point to within the earthly realm, that Kabbalah describes as expressions of God's image or of an analogue of God's image. Of course, the significance of the natural world has long been noted.[711] But we will see that all creatures and creations that bridge upper and lower realms (such as the vegetal world in *P'ri `Ets Hadar*) are understood not only as signs of divinity but as images of God. In Midrash, the creature that primarily effects unification is the human being. By extension, this category in Midrash also included the Torah and the *mishkan*, which became explicit images of God in Kabbalah, as discussed. But in Kabbalah, this category expands to include fruit trees, birds, and many other created beings.

---

[710] *Midrash Hane`elam* 16b; WZ 779–80. See further discussion, p.273.
[711] See, e.g., Arthur Green, quoted p.231, or more recently, Melila Hellner Eshed, *A River Flows from Eden* (Stanford CA: Stanford University Press, 2009), 43–5, 103, 111, 113, 150. She writes about the *Zohar*, "[N]ature itself – animal, vegetable, and mineral – is brimming with hints of the divine" (113).

Trees

One of the most important examples in which *tselem* is extended beyond humanity is the fruit tree, which is the image of the Cosmic Tree that unites the upper and lower worlds. This image is at the heart and the origin of Kabbalah. The *Bahir* is the most important source for this image, as one finds in this passage: "I am the One that planted this tree, all the world to delight in him; and I hammered out all/*kol* with him, and I called his name 'the Whole/*hakol*', for all depends on him, and all comes out from him."[712] This tree is more specifically related to the image of God in the following passage:

> And what would the tree be that you spoke of? He said to him: [It is] the powers/*kochot* of the Holy One, this on back of this, and they resemble/*domin* a tree: just as this tree, by means of the waters, brings out fruit, even so the Holy One by means of the waters increases the powers of the tree.[713]

Kochot or "powers" is an analogue to *tselem*, as is stated elsewhere in the *Bahir* (§82), where the limbs of the body, which are arranged *b'tselem Elohim*, are said to be in the pattern of "the powers of the heavens". The image is not of any tree, but specifically of a tree that bears fruit. Using the terminology I will develop in Chapter 11 (p.288ff.), a fruit tree in Kabbalah is seen as a *qomah sh'leymah* or complete form comprising God's image, like the human being.[714]

Explicit statements about the relationship between YHVH, the image of God, and the fruit tree abound in Kabbalistic texts, fueled also by the motif of the Tree of Life. This is a clear break from the midrashic idea that the upper

---

[712] §22, quoted further p.209. See also §§81, 95, 99, and others.
[713] *Bahir*, §119. The passage continues,

> And what are these waters of the Holy One? They are wisdom, and they are the souls/*n'shamot* of the righteous that bloom/grow/fly/*por'chin* from the spring unto the great channel. And he goes up and joins with the tree, and by what means does [the tree] bloom/grow? By means of Israel, [for] when they are righteous and good, Shekhinah rests among them, and through their deeds she rests in the bosom of the Holy One, and makes them fruitful and increases them.

This passage is the locus of the idea that the mystic (*tsadiq* or righteous one) can increase the flow of blessing into the world.

[714] Trees that do not bear fruit might perhaps be regarded similarly to other animals, as a partial *qomah*. An exception to this may be the cedars of Lebanon, which though they bear no (humanly edible) fruit, were also treated with the same reverence as fruit trees, because they were used to build the Temple. (By extension, we might include redwoods and sequoias.) The holiness of the cedars was already a theme in the Midrash: "R' Yochanan said: The world was not worthy to make use of the cedars, for they were not created except for the needs of the *Beyt Hamiqdash* (the Temple)" (*BR* 15:1). We learn from one midrash that cedar trees were used to build Noach's ark, but that Noach did not cut down any old-growth cedars (so to speak), instead using only those he planted: "For one hundred and twenty years Noach planted cedars and cut them down" (*BR* 30:7). The main thrust of this passage is that Noach started to build the ark by planting cedar trees rather than harvesting timber, so that during the long time they took to grow, people would have a chance to do *t'shuvah* (to "return" or repent). But it also signifies that Noach did not have the right to use the cedars planted by God for the Temple, but only those that were domesticated by his own planting.

Tselem in the more-than-human: the earthly realm

ones are in the divine image but the lower ones are not, and it is the clearest case we will encounter. Here is an example from *Sh'ney Luchot Hab'rit*:

The Kabbalists refer to the extension of the worlds as a tree/*ilan*. And this tree... is the true Tree of Life, the soul of all life. The name YHVH is alluded to in the word tree/`*ets*, when certain mathematical functions are performed on the first two and last two letters. [How so? *Yud* (10), *Heh* (5): $(Y \times H) + (H \times Y) = 100$. Then, *Vav* (6), *Heh* (5): $(V \times H) + (H \times V) = 60$, totaling 160. Thus the total equals `*Ets*, which is `*Ayin* + *Tsadi*, 70 + 90, also 160.] Concerning this, there is an allusion in the verse, "Is there a tree in it (the land) or not?" [Nu 13:20]... It is as if the verse said, "Is YHVH in its midst, or not?"... *TsLM* (= 90 + 30 + 40) has the same numerical value as `*Ts* (tree). And the Torah is also called `*ets*... both are connected with the name YHVH. Thus the verse said, "Let us make a human in our *tselem*".[715]

Tselem is tree according to this passage, and "tree" is literally a function of the name YHVH.[716] The Tree of Life, representing the Sefirot, stands above other images of God, even Adam. The nature of the tree is that it images God.[717]

While in the *Bahir* it is the fruit tree which bears souls that is a primary image of God, all the plants are symbolically significant according to the *Zohar*:

R' Yehudah said: Why is it written: "Also this corresponding to this did *Ha'elohim* make" [Ec 7:14]? Like the pattern of the firmament / *k'gavna d'raqi`a*, the Holy One made [everything] in the earth, and all of it is a hint about what is above... Like what R' Yosi said: These trees through which wisdom is shown, like the carob, the palm, the pistachio, and what is like them, in one (from the same) combination/*r'khiva* all

---

[715] *Toldot Adam, Beyt Yisra'el*, 6b; Krassen, "House of Israel I", 111–12 (modified from Krassen and parens. added).

[716] Actually, something like the scalar product of the four letters of the name.

[717] One of the difficulties in reading these texts is discerning when a term meaning "image" is being used as a substantive category, and when it simply means "metaphor". In more philosophical works of Kabbalah, the fruit tree may be used as a metaphor rather than an actual image of God. For example, Gikatilla writes:

> Know that all the holy names mentioned in the Torah are all of them hanging on the name of four letters which are *YHVH*. And if you would say, isn't the name *'HYH* (*Ehyeh*) the root and the source, know that the name of four letters is like the image/*dimyon* of the body (trunk) of the tree and the name *'HYH* is the essence/root of this tree, and from him the other roots root themselves and the branches spread to every side. And the rest of the holy names are in the image of branches and fronds extending/ drawn out from the body of the tree, and every one among these branches makes fruit by its species (after Gn 1:11,12).
> (*Sha`arey Orah*, 3; also *Gates of Light: Sha'are Orah*, trans. Avi Weinstein [New York: HarperCollins, 1994], 6; my translation)

In this passage, the word for image, *dimyon*, is not necessarily a synonym for *tselem*. In *Eden Miqedem* (Jerusalem: Makhon Yismach Lev, 1996), Refael Moshe Albaz (1823–96, Morocco) similarly states that "[YHVH] is the name standing like the image/*dimyon* of the body of the tree, and all the rest of the holy names are like an image/*dimyon* of the branches of the tree" (*Ot Chet*, 118). Both passages use *dimyon* to mean that God can be understood through the metaphor of a tree, rather than that a tree is an image of God. I focus in this work on texts that unambiguously use image in the metaphysical rather than metaphorical sense.

of them were combined. And all those that make fruit, except apples, they are one mystery, except the paths that separate. And all those that do not bear fruit and are great, except the river willows that have a mystery alone (of their own) like the pattern above / *k'gavna dil`eyla*, from one [breast] they suck. And every one from those that are small, except the hyssop, from one mother they are born. All the plants in the earth, which have placed over them great forces in the heavens, each and every one is a mystery alone/ of its own like the pattern above, and because of this it's written: "Your field you will not sow [with] mixtures/*kilayim*" [Lv 19:19], for each and every one goes up alone and emerges alone.[718]

The *Zohar* goes beyond the affirmation of God's image in the fruit tree, making every single plant a model of what is above. Since the heavens are an image of God, this passage informs us that the Earth, modeled on "the pattern of the firmament", is an image as well. Like the expression "pattern of the firmament", "pattern above" is also an analogue for *tselem*.[719] Concerning the plants, if "each one is a mystery of its own like the pattern above", this implies that each plant (or plant species) is itself an image, and not just the diversity of the plant world altogether.

P'ri `Ets Hadar also describes all the vegetation of the world using terms that are connected with *tselem*:

[T]rees and grasses You made bloom from the ground, with their stature/structure /*qomatam* and with their design /*tsivyonam* [according to what is] above, to cause the children of Adam to know the wisdom and discernment that is in them... And upon them You will drop the flow and strength of Your highest (upper) powers / *shefa` v'koach midotekha ha`elyonot*.[720]

Here, the pattern of the trees and plants has a specifically anthropic purpose, to teach humanity about the pattern of what is above by being "*b'qomah shel ma`lah*". This phrase is specifically a synonym for *tselem*.[721] Here, the entire world of the trees and plants is described as being *b'tselem Elohim*, rather than each species of tree or plant.

Birds

In addition to the fruit tree being an image of God, one also finds that the bird represents YHVH, in a manner similar to what we encountered in one of the passages about the human body discussed previously:

"For the bird of the skies will lead/bring the voice, and the masters of wings will tell a word" [Ec 10:20]. Here this [word] is *YHVH*, the central pillar... *Y'* י is the head of the bird. *V'* ו is his body. *H"H* ה ה are the two wings, through which he flies upward and comes to rest below. And these two wings are two breaths, *H"H*, and concerning them it

---

[718] 2:15b–16a; WZ 671–2.
[719] For example, for the union of male and female (1:50a), for Solomon's throne (1:27b), for the circumcised body or circumcision/*b'rit* (1:181a), and for the twelve tribes (1:155b, 246a). Other phrases with "*k'gavna*" can also mean *tselem*, such as "the pattern of the commandments" (see p.202). "The pattern of the firmament" is also applied to the Earth (see p.219).
[720] See Excursus 2. [721] See Chapter 11.

Tselem *in the more-than-human: the earthly realm*

is said, "And the animals/*chayot* [bearing the divine chariot] ran and returned" [Ez 1:14], for these are Y"V: a breath leaves through Y' י – a breath returns through V' ו.[722]

Though this text is about the body of Metatron (the archangel) and the nature of the soul that Torah scholars inherit, both of which are envisioned as birds, it teaches us equally about birds as creatures. While *Tiquney Zohar* explains that the creation from the sea of fish and birds ("swarming living *nefesh*; and fliers flying" [Gn 1:20]) is a description of the soul and breath that come from Shekhinah,[723] it maps the letters of God's name onto a bird's physical body. These are real birds flying, so to speak.

The end of the passage delineates another image of God in the breath. The two wings, which are *HH*, are also exhalation and inhalation. Since breath "runs and returns", like the animals of the chariot, it comprises an image of God (see further on). This cycle is represented by *Y* and *V*, which combined with the two *Hehs* complete the name YHVH.[724] Since we are talking about birds and animals, this could mean the breath of all creatures, not just human breath. It is not coincidental that the two earthly archetypes most clearly invested with the image of God, birds and trees, are beings that bridge heaven and earth and, like humans, in some sense unite them.

The play of fours: colors, directions, elements
Other passages conceptualize various spectrums of reality mapped onto the name YHVH or directly connected to *tselem*. The next passage connects God's image with the colors.

---

[722] *TZ* 45, 82b; cf. 5, 20a; 13, 30a. The letters literally make a picture of a bird. This image is more one-dimensional than the mapping of YHVH onto the human body, where every part of the human body is also a representation of YHVH, not just the body as a whole. Such "fractal" descriptions of birds' (or other animals') bodies are not found.

[723] The beginning of this passage reads:

"In beginning created אלהים '*LHYM/Elohim*" [Gn 1:1] – [this means] אל הים '*L HYM* / God of the sea /*El Hayam* (i.e., the sea of Torah). And concerning that (him) it says: "Elohim said: The waters will swarm with swarming living beings / *nefesh chayah*, and fliers (birds) will fly over the land" [Gn 1:20]...—those that are immersed in Torah will inherit a living soul / *nefesh chayah* from the Shekhinah, as it's written, "swarming *nefesh chayah*"; "and fliers flying"—this is *ru'ach*, about which it says: "For the bird of the skies..."

Based only on this introduction, one would read "bird" as a purely spiritual symbol, similar to other Kabbalistic texts, but the passage insists on the image of a real physical bird. Thanks to Zalman Schachter-Shalomi, who alerted me to this text. Note the introduction to the *Zohar* passage about fruit trees quoted p.219, which also connects birds with *tselem* via the intermediary of the fruit tree: "When R' Abba saw this one tree whose fruit turned into a bird and flew away, he wept and said: If people only knew what [these things] hinted at, they would rend their garments... because this wisdom is now forgotten" (2:15b).

[724] The breath is visualized as ו emptying to become י, followed by י filling to become ו – like the lungs breathing out and in. Connecting the breath with the letters of *YHVH* is also a frequent trope of Jewish Renewal teaching (see Seidenberg, "The Body in Kabbalah") and a central point of Waskow's theology (see n.58).

"My Beloved is clear and red" [So 5:10]—His likeness/*d'mut* is from redness, from black, from green, from white; **such is the likeness of the Holy One,** "Like the appearance of the bow which would be in the cloud" [Ez 1:28].[725]

By using the Biblical term *d'mut*, this passage makes clear its theological intent. Most literally, the spectrum of the rainbow is also mapped onto God's name by *Tiquney Zohar*: "Four letters are clothed in these four colors: *Y* in the color white, *H* in the color red, *V* in the color green, *H* in the color black."[726] (These colors characterized the full spectrum of visible light in medieval literature.) As we've seen, mapping something to YHVH makes it an analogue for the image of God.

This trope is applied to other instances of a spectrum or array that covers some whole aspect of reality. A common motif is the four or six directions (depending on whether one includes up and down). In *Sefer Y'tsirah*, the letters *YHV* are permuted by the Creator to "seal" each of the six directions.[727] In the *Zohar*, we read:

"Let us make Adam in our image as our likeness"—in order for him to be like this pattern in the four directions, and upper and lower, and east [would] cleave to west and go out to him. And concerning this they taught, "Adam was taken from the place of the Temple/ *beyt hamiqdash*".[728]

The image of Adam is derived from the pattern of the directions, which is alluded to by the Temple, because it is the center and foundation stone of the world. All space, drawn together through the letters of God's name and the creation of Adam, is unified through its relation to God's image. The directions thus become an analogue for *tselem*.

We have already encountered another common mapping that reflects this "play of the four" (to steal a Heideggerian phrase) in *Sh'ney Luchot Hab'rit*: "*Che̱sed* is water, *G'vurah* is fire, *Tif'eret* is air, and *Malkhut* is earth".[729] The correspondence between the Sefirot and the "elements" of earth, air, fire, and water is one of the most important, since it truly embraces all of physical Being in all its forms. Any time all four are present, there also, independent of the status of any particular creature or class of beings, is an image of the Sefirot, and hence, an image of God.[730]

---

[725] *Mishnat Shir Hashirim*, ed. Saul Lieberman, Appendix D to Scholem, *Jewish Gnosticism*, 123. The midrash reads the verse from Song of Songs as "my beloved is, at the same time, both white and red".

[726] TZ 70, 125a. These four colors are of course *Che̱sed*, *G'vurah*, *Tif'eret*, and *Malkhut*. In other passages the image of God is found in the three colors of white, red, and green, which are "*k'gavna dil`eyla*", representing the three columns of the Sefirot that pour into *Malkhut* (ZCh, Sitrey Torah 1:98b).

[727] 1:13, 69.   [728] 1:34b, west being the Shekhinah/*Malkhut*.   [729] 10b, quoted p.213.

[730] According to medieval understanding, all four elements are included in virtually every compound object and creature. An idiosyncratic parallel can be found in the thinking of one

In each of these cases, the spectrum under discussion can be understood with reference to its real-world content, or it can be understood as an array of symbols, referring primarily to the Sefirot. Some people might read these texts purely symbolically, assuming that these teachings interpret words in scripture rather than phenomena in Nature. However, while the intent of certain texts may be purely theosophical, others indicate that they are meant to be read in a literal or "real" way. For example, according to the text just quoted from *Sh'ney Luchot Hab'rit*, the Sefirot become enclothed in the real physical elements, making up the whole body of Creation.

Each of these examples defines a continuum that embraces an entire reality. Each continuum symbolizes the unification of the Sefirot. At the same time, each is a synecdoche for the unification of all creatures in the wholeness of Creation.

The animals, above and below

The play of fours also applies to the "spectrum" represented by the four *chayot* or animals of Ezekiel's chariot – human, ox, lion, and eagle – which already places humanity in a continuum with all the animals. The *chayot* were naturally a subject of intense speculation in Kabbalah. Even on the most superficial level, the *chayot* as angelic creatures suggest a connection between animals and the image of God. This connection is made in various ways in Kabbalistic texts. In the following passage from Elazar ben Yehudah of Worms' *Sefer Sodey Razaya*, the *chayot* are described as a kind of hybrid between human and animal:

> And the animals [of the chariot] are huge/*ramim* in stature/*qomah* ... Here the *Lamed* (ל) without the head (stem) is *Kaf* (כ), "like the sole/*kaf* of a calf's foot" [Ez 1:7].[731] And the neck thus [added on top makes it a] *Lamed*, [symbolizing] that [the animals] go with upright stature / *qomah z'qufah*, yet the *Lamed* is bent [at the very top] for their *qomah* is upright and their heads are bent.[732]

In Ezekiel, the *chayot* are compound creatures that bridge the anatomy of the animal and the anatomy of the human. Elazar of Worms emphasizes the quality of uprightness, which the Midrash teaches is one of the marks of God's image, to depict how the image is reflected in the animal-angels of Ezekiel's

---

peasant, Menocchio (1532–99, Italy), who was put to death for heresy by the Catholic Church. In his testimony before his inquisitors, he stated,

> I believe that the whole world, that is, air, earth, and all the beauties of this world are God ... because we say that man is made in the image and likeness of God, and in man there is air, fire, earth, and water, and it follows from this that air, earth, fire, and water are God. (Carlo Ginsburg, *The Cheese and the Worms: The Cosmos of a Sixteenth Century Miller*, trans. John and Anne Tedeschi [New York: Penguin Books, 1982], 124)

[731] Since calves are cloven-hoofed, it must be that Elazar imagines the two sides of the hoof being joined together as the top and bottom half of a *Kaf*.

[732] *Ot Lamed*, 148.

vision.733 Unlike earthly, four-legged animals, the *chayot* are upright, yet their heads are bent – possibly indicating that the *chayot* are both in God's image and not in God's image.

We also saw in *Sh'ney Luchot Hab'rit* (see p.213) that the four animals together represented the dimensions of the Sefirot: "*Chesed* is water, *G'vurah* is fire, *Tif'eret* is air, and *Malkhut* is earth. We call what is later manifested from [*Chesed*, *G'vurah*, *Tif'eret*, and *Malkhut*], metaphorically, 'fire', 'water', 'air', and 'earth', in the secret of the four animals." Together with the human, the three non-human *chayot* constitute "the secret of the four animals", representing the Sefirot, and therefore also *tselem*.

In the *Zohar*, the other animals comprise an image of God separate from the human, while the image of Adam comprises them all:

[The] human gazes at them all (ox, eagle, and lion), while all of them ascend and gaze at him. Then they all are traced in their engravings... in the mystery of one name called awesome/*nora'*. So it is written of them: "The likeness/*d'mut* of their faces was a human face" [Ez 1:10]. All of them include this image/*d'yoqna*, and this image includes them.734

The image that comprises all the animals is itself contained within the image that is human alone. Elsewhere, the *Zohar* states: "The image of the human includes all of them, and they face to the four sides of the world, and are separated by their images, and all of them are included in the human."735 The human is part of the spectrum even as it contains the spectrum; this is one dimension of seeing humans as microcosms of the world.

The following text from *Tiquney Zohar* also connects the image of God to the diversity of the animals represented in the *chayot*, in a slightly different way:

"This/*Zeh* is the book of the generations of Adam". "ZH" (7 + 5) literally/*vad'ay*, comprising the twelve constellations of Adam that is above / *Adam dil`eyla*, about which it says concerning them, "tribes of Yah, testimonies of Israel" [Ps 122:4]. "*Zeh*" literally are the four faces of the lion, four faces of the ox, four faces of the eagle, that in them are recognized the faces/*par'tsufin* of human beings. And all of these faces are impressed in the four letters of YHV"H.736

Just as Israel is a complete image of God – its twelve tribes an image of the constellations, which are an image of *Adam Ha`elyon*, the upper or celestial

---

733 He also describes each animal as "king" among its class of creatures; see end of n.323.
734 1:19a, quoted in Matt, *The Essential Kabbalah*, 145. Here, each of the four animals, including the human, corresponds to one of the words in the liturgical phrase taken from Dt 10:17: "*ha'el hagadol hagibor v'hanora'* / God, the great, the mighty, and the awesome".
735 3:118b.
736 70, 121a. This passage is possibly based on the preceding *Zohar* passage, which quotes the same verse.

Tselem in the more-than-human: the earthly realm

Adam – so too is the spectrum of animals embodied in lion, ox, and eagle understood to be an image of *Adam Ha`elyon*, "impressed in the four letters" of God's name. The three non-human *chayot* divide the land animals into the realms of the domesticated (or herbivorous), represented by the ox, the wild (or carnivorous), represented by the lion, and the birds, which are a single class, represented by the eagle.[737] Here, these three classes of the animal world, represented by their faces – that is, by the parts of the *chayot* that are wholly animal – construct a divine image on their own, completing together one figure of *Adam Ha`elyon*.

All twelve faces of the other animals together correspond to the single spectrum of human faces, which comprises in itself a full and complete image of the twelve constellations that are the celestial Adam. While each human being is generally understood to be a complete image by itself, here the full diversity of humanity is what completes the image. Together, all human beings constitute a sacred and complete name and image of God.

No single human individual can completely represent the image of God; in the same way, no one species is the full image of God. But the image of God comprises the whole array of individuals or of animal species, in all their interrelationships.[738] Even though the human image remains the primary image, this primacy does not conflict with an ecological interpretation, and in fact the scriptural trope becomes the basis for extending God's image.

This extension has several limitations with respect to the goals of this work: (1) The faces of the animals in this passage may be read as mere symbols of the diversity of human faces. (2) *Tiquney Zohar* is not concerned with the "lower ones" or real earthly animals but rather with the "upper ones", the *chayot* that exist in the heavens of Ezekiel's vision. (3) Even if the *chayot* teach us about earthly animals, each class of animals on its own is specifically *not* in God's image, because the only full image is *Adam Ha`elyon*, which includes all the faces of the lion, ox, and eagle.[739] These issues will be dealt with in the following paragraphs.

On the first point, one may ask, does the *Tiquney Zohar* passage imply that the true image is the human and the *chayot* are merely a kind of symbol of humanity? Such an interpretation would parallel Maimonides, for example,

---

[737] It must be pointed out that this animal spectrum does not include reptiles or insects, *sh'ratsim* in Hebrew. From the perspective of emotions and intelligence, birds and mammals indeed share the most with us.

[738] Contrasting passages in Kabbalah see God's image or the Sefirot specifically in the "ten kosher animals", while denying the presence of God's image in the animals that only non-Jews eat (e.g., *Zohar* 1:20a).

[739] If one interprets "all of these faces are impressed in the four letters of YHVH" to mean that the four faces of each class are equated with four letters, then each class of animals will be implicitly represented as an image of God in and of itself.

who says that the faces of the chariot that **resemble** ox, eagle, and lion are simply human faces that have a certain cast to them, the way one might say that someone with a very long face looks like a horse.[740] However, the differences between Maimonides and *Tiquney Zohar* are clear. Though both relate the animal faces of the chariot to the faces of human beings, in Maimonides there is a *mashal* and a *nimshal*, a metaphor and what it stands for. The hierarchical relationship between the two applies in only one direction: the animals are images for what is not really animal but rather human (as it were – we are still speaking about the divine chariot).

This hermeneutic is typical of philosophy, as well as of the more philosophical texts of Kabbalah. But in Zoharic literature, as discussed at the beginning of this chapter, when a connection is made, it generally goes both ways; one side of the equation is not a more "real" image than the other. Saying that the faces of the animals are the faces of the human *is Tiquney Zohar*'s way of saying that they are in God's image.

On the second point, while it is true that the *chayot* are of the heavens, corresponding to the constellations, a connection to the lower or earthly animals is what underlies the vitality of the entire trope. This is not only true in the obvious sense that symbolic meaning is derived from our experience. It is also true that within the framework of Kabbalah, corresponding images above and below are understood to create a bridge or unification between heaven and earth.[741] This trope is in fact fundamental to the entire concept of God's image in Kabbalah.

On the third point, if we were able to say that the animal kingdom in its totality was an image of God, and that therefore every species participates in the image, this would accomplish much, establishing a theological basis for the moral standing of all species.

Nevertheless, all images are not equal. In this case, for example, if the earthly animals are associated with the heavenly *chayot* and the *chayot* are associated with the four letters of the divine name, the earthly animals are like the image of an image. Moreover, the image created by all of the animals together is not something one simply encounters in the world, but rather something that must be synthesized by prophetic vision or human cognition. (Alternatively, one might say that this image is already synthesized by Nature itself, but that ecological science allows us to see it.) In contrast, the image of God in humanity according to Midrash and Kabbalah is so immanent that even the other animals are able to directly perceive it.

---

[740] *MN* 3:1, 417. Thanks to Shaul Magid for pointing out this text. Magid interprets the passage in *TZ* to be saying the same thing as Maimonides.

[741] The origins of this trope predate Kabbalah; their rudiments can be found in the Midrash, not only in the idea that humans below are in the image of the upper beings or heavens, but also in the idea that there is a Temple above corresponding to the Temple below.

Tselem *in the more-than-human: the earthly realm*

The *chayot* remain a potent symbol in *Chasidut*. One particular example, from the commentary of Yaakov Lainer (1828–78, Poland, son of Mordechai Yosef of Izhbitz), reconfigures Kabbalah in a way that is especially important for our purposes, because it "gets real", that is, it explicitly brings in physical animals. Here, Lainer explains the connection between the heavenly and earthly *chayot*, between the angels above and the creatures below, in terms of the principle that "[i]n this world, what is further below branches off from a higher place."[742] He writes:

> The beast branches from the ox that is in the chariot, where [the *chayot*] stand in brightness/radiance always, without any forgetting [of God], and they do not remember anything in (about) themselves ... and from the ox above branches off beasts of the field, which in this world are completely without awareness/*da`at* and do not have erect posture / *qomah z'qufah*.[743]

Lainer connects the animals of the chariot and the real animals that live in this world – something rarely done in earlier texts. Both stem from a place where they have awareness only of God, not of themselves. The immanence of God's presence that the animals' archetypes enjoy is the reason that they are without consciousness or erect stature. In this case, the *chayot* are not mapped onto God's image as a continuum. Rather, each animal, tethered as it were to its heavenly *chayah*, represents a potential unification of the divine world and the physical world.

The immanence of God's image

The divine image in the lower ones is an idea that presents itself unsystematically. We can establish the foundation for a theology of Nature by thematizing this trope in diverse texts over many centuries of Kabbalistic writing. But we can also thematize the ways that this image differs from the image in human beings. The image of God is something we, as images of God, can actively recognize, or even bestow, on other creatures. But the image of God in humanity is understood even in Midrash, as well as in the *Zohar*,[744] to be recognized by the other animals.

One might imagine that if God's image in human beings is so immanent as to be recognized by them, then the other animals must have some element of that

---

[742] Because what was higher in the root of the Creation fell further when the vessels for creating the universe broke (see Appendix).
[743] *Beyt Ya`aqov `al Sefer Vayiqra'* (New York: Rabbi M. J. Lainer, 1991), *Vayiqra'* 18. The reference to erect stature probably means not only that oxen do not stand erect, but also that they do not have "complete being" here in this world. Thanks to Sarah (Susan) Schneider, who quotes this text and the following one in her pamphlet *Eating as Tikkun* (Jerusalem). Lainer is explaining why sacrifices are effective.
[744] The animals "look and see in [the human] that image and the soul in him" (1:191a), discussed p.160.

image in themselves. In fact, the *Zohar* teaches exactly this. In the following passage, which we have had several occasions to cite, the creatures recognize God's image in human beings **because** they are created in God's image:

"And He blew in his nostrils life's *nishmat chayyim*" [Gn 2:7]—this is the image/*d'yoqna* upon human beings, about which it says: "And he dreamed and here, a ladder... And here angels of Elohim going up and down it" [Gn 28:12]—these [angels] are the breaths/*havelim* that leave and go out through the body by means of that ladder (equated here with the soul)... and they are seven,[745] to receive seven days of creation. **They are all the creatures of heavens and sea and land**, that is, wild animals, birds, domestic animals, fish, and whatever generations depend upon them. And because **all was created in that image/*tsolma*** which is upon all Israel, which is the Righteous One, it was said about them: "And a terror of you and dread of you will be over every animal of the earth and over every bird of the heavens" [Gn 9:2]... And all these, why are they afraid of this image from which they were created? Only because the name YHV"H rests on [Israel].[746]

This passage represents one of the most radical statements about God's image in all of Zoharic literature: all was created in the image of God! Just as we may be able to see the image of God in the other creatures because we are created in God's image, so too here can the animals recognize the image in humanity because they are created in the image. However, the image of God in which they are created does not fully manifest the name *YHVH*, and so they respond to that manifestation in human beings (or rather, Israel) with fear.

Though this passage is astonishing, its use as a precedent is limited, because it is explicitly described by the *Zohar* as a *mashal* or parable, in which the animals represent non-Jews in comparison with Israel.[747] The animals in this *mashal* are thus lifted up to the level of human beings, while the humans (with the exception of Israel) are "lowered" to the level of animals. Therefore, while the existence of this passage is important, its theological implications must be bracketed.

The case is much clearer with respect to the plant world. To return to the prayer in *P'ri 'Ets Hadar*, plants are made "in the stature and in the

---

[745] Seven breaths, meaning the seven lower Sefirot, based on Ec 1:2 (*"havel havelim... havel havelim, hakol havel"* – where each *havel* equals one, each *havelim* equals two). Cf. *Zohar, Sitrey Torah*, 146b.

[746] *Ra`ya Mehemna* 3:123b. This passage can be interpreted as saying that other creatures are in Elohim's image only, and hence afraid/overawed by the name YHVH. Alternatively, it could be distinguishing between image and name, with name representing a higher ontology.

[747] The sentence belonging to the third ellipsis reads: "And this was spoken about all human beings, for they are **compared**/*m'tilin* to wild animals and to the beast and to birds and to fish of the sea..."; cf. *TZ* 69, 118b, "I said to Adam, 'Have dominion over the fish of the sea and the bird of the sky and the animal'—for these are the human beings that depend on the constellations (i.e., everyone but Israel) that are likened to wild animals and domestic animals and birds." It is unusual for the *Zohar* to specify that a relationship between two symbols is parabolic.

pattern of what is above, to cause the children of Adam to know the wisdom and discernment that is in them", that is, a *tselem* of the upper realms. This means the pattern of the Sefirot, and this is God's image. The prayer continues:

May the will [come] from before You... through the strength of the merit of eating the fruit... and our meditating upon the secret of their roots above... to cause [divine] flow/*shefa`* to flow... over them... And from there [divine] flow will flow over us... And may the Whole /*Hakol* return now to his original strength... for You are the one who will bless the Righteous One.[748]

"Returning the Whole to his original strength" means restoring the cosmic *tselem* that embraces and comprises all Creation.[749]

The texts examined in this chapter can be thought of as dialogues between mystics, inviting each other to see the pattern of God's image in this or that being or dimension of reality. The divine image exists below to teach human beings what is above. But the reason is not only anthropocentric. By teaching us, the trees empower us to bring blessing to them and to all Creation. By doing so, we reciprocally bring blessing to ourselves. According to *P'ri `Ets Hadar*, when humans understand "their roots above" by contemplating trees and plants, we become more able to restore the full *qomah* or body of the cosmos to a state of blessing. Thus, the trees exist both as subjects and objects in this paradigm. According to Kabbalah, however, the subjecthood of human beings translates the image of God, whether in trees or in humans, into a kind of living force.

FIRST CONCLUSIONS

Kabbalah extends the meaning of *tselem* through a number of avenues. The Sefirot define or allude to wholeness, and at the same time define God's image. The structure of the Sefirot in themselves and through the name *YHVH* is used to extend *tselem* beyond the human realm in an allusive way, and this extension is treated as a privileged kind of mystical awareness. Since the Torah only teaches us that human beings are in God's image, and the rabbis explicitly did not extend this idea to the *tachtonim*, the earthly realm, the Kabbalah did not openly contradict midrash by stating that other earthly creatures are in God's image. The development of this new perspective proceeded under a veil of esotericism, using frameworks and terms that were isomorphic and homologous with the idea of *tselem*, often without explicitly referencing God's

---

[748] See Excursus 2.
[749] *Hakol* also indicates the Sefirah of *Y'sod*, which is called *Tsadiq*, Righteous One, corresponding both to the male genitals or phallus and to the Sefirotic principle that bestows blessing.

image.[750] The concept of *tselem* was applied in this way to many dimensions of being and particular beings or classes of being.

We can also identify four tropes that *describe* how the idea of God's image functions in most of the examples in this chapter. The first two are wholeness and holographism (the part containing the structure of the whole). Wherever the Kabbalah identified a continuum representing one whole dimension of reality, there was an image of God. Wherever the Kabbalah identified an ʽolam qaṯan, a "small world", this by analogy with *Adam* can be represented as an image of God. These images may be interlocking, nested within each other, or repeated at many levels. As we have seen, *Tiquney Zohar* regards a human being as an image of YHVH on all the following levels: not only is each human being as a whole person an image, but each limb of the human body is or can become an image, the diversity of humanity is also an image, and the species as a whole can be seen as one letter of a greater spectrum of all the animals that forms another divine image.

The third and most consistent trope is unification: every element, structure, or being in Creation that unifies the upper and lower realms is an image of God. This is the function of the *mishkan*, and it is fundamentally why a tree is understood to be an image of God. It is also why birds and Jacob's ladder are described as images of God. The *talit* (prayer shawl) and *tsitsit* (fringes) are described in such terms,[751] and the rainbow can be included in this category as well.[752] This is one reason for the common Kabbalistic belief that one should not gaze at a rainbow.[753] This same trope also signifies the unification of male and female. The fourth trope, which may be regarded in most instances as an aspect of unification, is mirroring – when there is a creature or thing below that is connected to a presence above (such as an angel or soul), then that creature

---

[750] Given the conserving nature of textual reinterpretation in Judaism, it would in fact be surprising to find texts that do this explicitly. Rather, Kabbalah accomplished its goals through *remez* and *has'tarah*, through hints and concealed meanings. The hermeneutics of this trope are a normative part of Judaism's textual tradition, which depends on "creative betrayal" and midrashic reading to further its evolution, while at the same time saving the appearance of continuity.

[751] See the Vilna Gaon, *Siddur Hagra*, 18a: "Making the *tsitsit* [effects] tying [together] the heavens and the earth, as it says, '[*t'cheilet* (the blue thread of the *tsitsit*)] resembles the firmament' etc. And it is a complete being / *qomah sh'leymah*" (quoting *Bahir*, see p.216). On *qomah sh'leymah*, see Chapter 11, p.288ff.

[752] See p.222, also *Zohar* 1:117b. Dew as a symbol of *shefaʽ* can also be related to this trope. (*Zohar* 1:88a, *TZ* 17a; also *Siddur Hagra*, 18a.)

[753] See Elliot Wolfson, *Through a Speculum That Shines: Vision and Imagination in Medieval Jewish Mysticism* (Princeton NJ: Princeton University Press, 1994), 340–41 and n.48; and Martin S. Cohen, *Shiur Qomah: Liturgy and Theurgy*, 225, ll.132, and nn.1–2. The practice of not staring at a rainbow is rooted in *TB Chagigah* 16a. More specific reasons are that the rainbow represents the phallus, or is the union of *Tif'eret* and Shekhinah, or manifests the Shekhinah herself (Rashi *ad Chagigah* 16a calls the rainbow "the Shekhinah's image / d'mut hash'khinah"). The *P'ri ʽEts Hadar*, however, did not eschew gazing at the rainbow (see p.358), and in our time, one could argue that bearing witness to such beauty is almost an obligation.

or thing below is a kind of image of God, and its connection above creates a unification.

While in midrash the quality of uniting Creation made *Adam Harishon* unique in Creation, in Kabbalah all kinds of creatures, realities, senses, spectrums, and dimensions are seen as corresponding to YHVH, to the Sefirot, and to the unification of Creation, so that the structure of the whole and each whole within the structure bears witness to the image of God.

The meaning of Kabbalistic imagery for contemporary theology

In this sense, homiletically speaking, every aspect of reality that represents wholeness to us can also be seen as an image of God. Also, our understanding of the heavens affords us a broader perspective on the ways that the earthly and heavenly realms are unified, expanding those aspects of the earthly realm that represent unification and that can therefore be represented as an image of God. Any element of Creation that represents the wholeness of Creation or the flow of energy and life between realms, and any element, species, or object that unites or ties together the heavens and the Earth, can be seen as an image.

What does the panoply of images in Kabbalah mean? Arthur Green explains the surfeit of images to be a way of avoiding idolatry by overwhelming our senses:

The Kabbalist knows well that metaphors can become idolatrous. Surely this is the reason why our mystics' writings are filled with such a great and ever-changing wealth of images. The God who in one moment was seen as light quickly turns into water, then into Temple, Moon, Father, Daughter, Mother, Sabbath, Jubilee, Covenant, Land, Sea, and a host of others. The worlds of both Judaism and nature serve as sources for this seemingly infinite flow of symbolic speech... So long as the metaphors are kept flowing, the mystics tell us, none of them will be frozen.[754]

Though few Kabbalists might have articulated what they were doing in this way, there is a deeper phenomenological truth in what Green says. The diversity of images of God in Kabbalah turns our attention to each and every detail in Creation, so that we do not settle upon a static idea of the divine image, or imagine that it is just in human beings, or even in a bigger subset of beings that is limited to the angels or the heavens.[755]

---

754 "Keeping Feminist Creativity Jewish", *Sh'ma* 16/305 (Jan. 10, 1986): 33–5; 33.
755 Moreover, in Judaism, the mystic's quest was almost always clothed in physical and sensual metaphors. Though *Ayin* (Nothingness) meditation exists in Kabbalah, there was no stage characterized by a "dark night of the soul", as one finds in Christianity, *viz.* John of the Cross's *The Ascent of Mount Carmel*, Marguerite Porete's *The Mirror of Simple Souls*, or *The Cloud of Unknowing*. (I do not mean to suggest that this form of Christian mysticism is inharmonious with ecological concerns. The kenosis, self-emptying, of the Christian mystics is a powerful antidote to human arrogance, and it can be a vital element in ecospirituality.)

Kabbalah's readiness to draw each new thing into relation with God's image models a way we can embrace the diversity of the more-than-human world and expand our imaginations beyond the narrow vision of contemporary culture. And it demonstrates that other imaginations over many centuries also sought this embrace. If such approaches are immediately censored as "pagan" by contemporary sermonizers, this only shows how Judaism has become disconnected from its roots in the process of conforming to modernity. Personifying or extolling the image of God in the created beings of the world can hardly be called antithetical to Judaism when there are centuries of evidence that doing so was an accepted expression of Judaism.

8

Of rocks, names, and codes

The letters of Creation

The previous chapter surveyed correspondences in Kabbalah between YHVH, the Sefirot, and the beings and dimensions of the world, outlining four tropes that characterize these correspondences: wholeness, holographism, unification, and mirroring. One could scour Kabbalistic literature to collect more correspondences between the name YHVH or the Sefirot and the more-than-human world. However, this would only bring one marginally closer to a theology of how all the particulars of Creation might participate in God's image.

In this brief chapter, I will look at a class of being – the *dom'mim*, "silent ones", that is, rocks and stones and such – that does not fit well into any of those four tropes. Of course, Kabbalah does pay attention to special stones, such as the precious stones used for the High Priest's breastplate, the *even sapir* beneath God's throne, and the foundation stone or *even sh'tiyah* of the world, and there are passages that use rock or stone as a metaphor for God.[756] The *Zohar* also talks about about the "upper rock / *tsur dil`eyla*", and it often takes *tsur* as a symbol of *G'vurah*/Might.[757]

But what I want to explore here are two Hasidic theologies about the *chiyut* or lifeforce (sometimes pronounced "*chayut*") that is present in the silent/inanimate beings (rocks), and in the *tachtonim* in general, one from Shneur Zalman of Liady, and one from Yaakov Lainer. Because Shneur Zalman's theology is based on how the letters of creation through the process of *hishtalsh'lut* or emanation encode the essence of each being, I will also discuss

---

[756] *Seder Rabbah d'B'rei'shit*, for example, explains the divine epithet *Tsur `Olamim* ("Rock of the worlds") thus: "for He is likened/*domeh* to a rock that bears all the pillars of the house, even so does the Holy One bear 196,000 worlds under His arm" (*BM*, vol.1, 8). Gikatilla similarly explains that "sometimes the name *Adonai* is called by the *kinui* 'stone/*even*', because He is the foundation of all the structures of the world, and all the existences in the world lean on Her and are supported by Her" (*Sha`arey Orah*, 13 – see also rest of passage).

[757] 2:64b.

letter mysticism, as well as parallels contemporary thinkers draw between the letters of creation in Kabbalah and the "letters" of the genetic code.

LETTER MYSTICISM AND THE WORLD'S CREATION

One of the most important dimensions of early Jewish mysticism that Kabbalah draws on is the idea that the letters of the Hebrew alphabet contain the power of creation and express this power in their shapes, order, and numerology, and that God permutates and recombines them in order to bring the creatures into being – a process called *tseruf ha'otiyot*.[758] While this belief is most prominent in *Sefer Y'tsirah*, where each letter is associated with specific potencies and dimensions, it also grounds mystical *midrashim* like *Midrash Otiyot d'Rabi Aqiva*, as well as the *Bahir*, which is also the earliest text to explore the mystical meaning of the vowels.

In a commentary on *Sefer Y'tsirah* now known to be the work of Yosef Ashkenazi, we find the idea that the letters that form each created being are derived from God and are carriers of the image of God:

All the existences, which all have in them the ten Sefirot, are constructed through the joining of letters, whether silent, whether growing, whether moving, whether speaking, and thus each one is in the structure of the seal belonging to God.[759]

"The seal belonging to God" is of course *tselem*. Here as elsewhere, Ashkenazi takes the most radical stance with respect to extending the image of God to all levels of the more-than-human world.

One of the most powerful statements about the letters of creation is found in *Sha`ar Hayichud v'Ha'emunah* by Shneur Zalman of Liady (1745–1813, Russia, also called Baal Hatanya or the Alter Rebbe), the founder of Lubavitcher or Chabad Hasidism.[760] Shneur Zalman wrote:

[T]he power of the One who acts /*hapo`el* must be in what is acted upon /*nif`al*, always/continually, to give it life and sustain it. And [the elements that transmit this lifeforce] are of the dimension of the letters of speech from the ten speech-acts[761] [in Genesis], through which [all beings] were created[...][F]or the Holy One contracted

---

[758] Apropos of the present subject, *Sefer Y'tsirah* describes the letters of creation as stones: "three stones build six houses, four stones build 24 houses... seven stones build 5040 houses" (4:12, 107–8). The number of houses is the number of permutations that can be made from that number of letters (equal to the factorial of that number). It adds, "from here and beyond, go out and calculate what the mouth cannot speak and the ear cannot hear."

[759] *Sefer Y'tsirah, Peyrush Hara'vad ad* 1:12, 67–8. This commentary was attributed to R' Avraham ben David of Provence and Posquières (Hara'vad). See further discussion p.238.

[760] Chabad stands for *Chokhmah, Binah*, and *Da`at* (*ChB"D*), where *Da`at* is a lower reflection of *Keter*, the highest Sefirah. These Sefirot represent the intellect (the "three brains"). Chabad adherents contrast their sect's intellectual intensity with the approach of other Hasidic sects, which they label *Chagas* ("*ChaGaT*") Hasidism, that is, *Chasidut* based on "*Chesed, G'vurah, Tif'eret* / Love, Judgment, and Beauty" – the emotional Sefirot.

[761] See n.371.

The divine reality of stones

the light and lifeforce/*chiyut*... and clothed it within the combinations of letters... For every exchange and transposition [of the letters] points to the descent of the light and lifeforce from level to level, for thus is it possible to create and give life to creatures... and after all these contractions... it would be possible for the light and lifeforce to clothe even the *tachtonim*, like stones and dirt.[762]

This chain of reactions and constrictions is a depiction of *seder hishtalsh'lut*, the process of emanation, which was discussed on p.214.

THE DIVINE REALITY OF STONES

Shneur Zalman uses the specific example of a stone to illustrate how this process of unfolding works:

Stone/*even*/'BN אבן, by way of example, her name points out that her root is in the exalted name whose number is *B"N* ב"ן,[763] and a further *Alef* א is added to her from another name, for a reason known to the One who formed her. And behold, the name *B"N* in itself is in very high worlds / `olamot `elyonim m'od, but by means of numerous and powerful contractions, from level to level, there descended from him a lifeforce concentrated very very much, until it could clothe itself in a stone. And this is the soul of the silent one /*domem*, which makes it live and brings it into being from nothing to something in every moment.

What does it mean to say that a stone has lifeforce? For one thing, it means that a stone is alive. For Shneur Zalman, it also meant that the stone had a soul. The stone's soul is an expression of divine names, some whole and some fragmentary. This elemental animism may have laid the foundation for Shneur Zalman's radical description of the radiance of the Earth (see p.255ff.).

Yaakov Lainer articulates an equally exalted understanding of the silent ones. Like the animals below, which "branch off" from the *chayot* angels of the chariot (see Chapter 7, p.227), the *dom'mim* are also derive from above:

And the silent ones (rocks, minerals) from this world branch off from a high place, even more so [than the animals]. A parable/*mashal*:... one who stands before the king voids himself completely from existence because of the awe [he feels] – for this [reason] there is no movement in him. And one who looks upon him from behind, it appears to him that there is no life in this person, but in truth there is true life there.[764]

---

[762] This work is published with *Liqutey Amarim*, also called *Tanya*, trans. Nissan Mindel et al. (London: Otsar Hachasidim, 1972); passage selected from ch.2, 292, and ch.7, 320.

[763] *B"N* equals 52, which is the *gematria*, or numerological sum, of all the letters when one spells out the names of the letters YHVH in a certain way. Four different sums are derived from different spellings of the letters; the other three are *M"H* (45 – see n.576), *S"G* (63), and `"B (72 – see n.607). Each one is important in Lurianic Kabbalah.

[764] *Beyt Ya`aqov `al Sefer Vayiqra'*, *Vayiqra'* 18. Cf. Meister Eckhart (1260–1328, Germany): "All creatures are words of God. My mouth expresses and reveals God but the existence of a stone does the same" (Matthew Fox, *Passion for Creation* [Rochester VT: Inner Traditions 1980/2000], 58–9).

It is a commonplace in Hasidic thought that there is life and presence in everything, even stones. But Lainer goes a step further, teaching us that the stone is analogous to a person, even if "it appears that there is no life in him" – because we see the *dom'mim* from behind, as it were, without a face. The reason why, Lainer explains, is that "whoever is closer to God, his back is seen" by those farther away. But seeing the face of the rock from "the front" – from God's perspective – means seeing that there is "true life there" – individuated life. Thus, for Lainer, the divine power in the rock is more than "mere" *mana* or lifeforce, more than the unfolding of God's presence (though to see that would itself be a powerful mystical experience). Moreover, for Lainer, the soul of the *domem* is not mediated by the descent of letters; rather, that soul is, in this very moment, attached to the highest place before God's throne.

In other contexts, such as the animals of the chariot, or the Temple below corresponding to the Temple above, when a lower being is connected to a higher angelic or hypostatic being, this means it represents a facet of God's image. By applying this trope to the *dom'mim*, Lainer extended the paradigm of God's image from the animals of the chariot, where there was a strong foundation in scripture and early Kabbalah, to rocks and stones, where there was much less precedent. At the same time, this was not just an intellectual exercise, for it meant *truly seeing* the silent ones in their divine transfiguration.

What did it mean for both Shneur Zalman and Yaakov Lainer to see life in a stone? For both, stones evinced more than just God's presence. Rather, a stone calls us to look closely and see that "there is true life there". What does it mean *for us* to say that a stone has a lifeforce? We can begin to answer that question through textual reasoning and theology. The work of this book is a kind of preparation to help us do this. But the real answers lie within our lived experience, as it emerges in our encounters with the world, in our *meeting* the world.

NAMING AND THE EARTH

According to Shneur Zalman in *Sha'ar Hayichud*, the fundamental principle of the creative process is that God's names are equally in all things, even the lowest of the *tachtonim*. However, if we look at earlier Kabbalistic ideas about names, we find that the Earth itself was not just an equal recipient of divine names, but was also a special locus of divine naming. For example, according to the *Bahir*, naming was a special act in the creation of the Earth. R' Yanai, who asserts that the Earth was created *before* the heavens even though the Earth is first named only *after* the heavens, explains why naming was the last act in the Earth's creation:

To what does the thing resemble? To a king who took possession of a beautiful, precious thing, and it was not complete, and [so] he did not name it by name. He said: I will complete it and prepare its mounting and its setting, and then I will call out its name over it.⁷⁶⁵

The Earth is like a jewel set in the heavens; its status is higher than the heavens. Since it is the final goal of this creative process, it waits the longest to get a name. The *Bahir*'s focus on the Earth as the locus of naming continues in the *Zohar*:

R' Aba opened and said: "Go, see YHVH's workings, that placed desolations/*shamot* in the earth/land /*ba'arets*" [Ps 46:9] – don't read *shamot* but rather names/*sheimot*. And this goes like what R' Chiyya said: According [to] the pattern of the firmament / *k'gavna d'raqi`a* the Holy One made the earth. In the firmament are holy names; in the earth are holy names.⁷⁶⁶

The holy names constitute the image of God, which is the pattern of the firmament above in the heavens, and below, in the Earth.

HOMILETICAL AND THEOLOGICAL QUESTIONS AND IMPLICATIONS

DNA and God's names

This section will focus exclusively on Shneur Zalman's ideas. Many contemporary Jewish thinkers draw a connection from DNA to the teaching that the world is created through permutating the letters. In a time when the trope of the "code", derived from both genetics and computer science, has become dominant in so many areas, its connection to letter mysticism, where letters are also treated as a kind of code, flows naturally. Both models describe, even if in fundamentally different ways, how miraculous complexity can be derived from a simple code.⁷⁶⁷ Kocku von Stuckrad even suggests that biology borrowed its language from Kabbalah.⁷⁶⁸ Shlomo Blickstein, writing about the doctrine of emanation in Gikatilla's *Ginat Ha'egoz*, refers to this similarity when he explains, "Every created thing has its unique numerical and alphabetic constitution, a kind of mystical 'genetic code', which is the ground of its being."⁷⁶⁹

---

[765] §24, quoted more fully n.912; see also §§95–6, p.216.   [766] 2:5a.
[767] Cf. Shneur Zalman on *ribui*, n.838. Structurally, the model presented by Chayyim Vital (*ECh*, vol.2, *Heykhal* 6 6:15, 156), in which there are two codes, one pairing the letters of *YHVH* with *HVHY*, and the other pairing *HVHY* and *'DNY*, could even be "mapped", respectively, onto DNA and RNA "language".
[768] "Rewriting the Book of Nature: Kabbalah and the Metaphors of Contemporary Life Sciences", *Journal for the Study of Religion, Nature and Culture* 2:4 (2008): 419–42.
[769] "Between Philosophy and Mysticism: A Study of the Philosophical-Qabbalistic Writings of Joseph Giqatila (1248–c.1322)" (Jewish Theological Seminary, PhD dissertation, 1983), 76, citing *Ginat Ha'egoz* 54c and 46b.

While Blickstein uses the image of a genetic code as a metaphor to help us understand Kabbalah, Arthur Green, writing as a theologian, interprets the meaning of DNA through Kabbalah, and Kabbalah through his understanding of DNA:

For the initiate, the sefirot... serve as rungs or marking points of the mystic's inward journey... All the rungs of descent (and potential ascent) are contained in each soul. But that is true, even in de-mythologized form: all of our ancestors, each stage and mini-step in the evolution of life that brought us to where we are today, are present within us. The DNA that constitutes the life-identity of each of us exists indeed *zekher l'ma`aseh b'rei'shit*, "in memory of the act of Creation", linking us back to our most remote origins.[770]

For Green, DNA is a kind of sacred story or memory. Arthur Waskow also finds the inner sacred meaning of DNA in Kabbalah's understanding of names. It is in this tenor that Waskow reads the phrase from the Kaddish, "May the great name be blessed", as referring to the name that includes all the "names" of all the creatures, represented by their DNA.[771]

Yosef Ashkenazi explained the prohibition against idolatry in a way that resonates deeply with these formulations. As already cited (pp.211–2), he wrote:

[A]ll the existences from the upper ones and the lower ones are all of them tied into His great, mighty and awesome name... therefore He warned [Israel] to not worship them, [not] to separate [them] from His name, only to [worship] the name YHVH – one / *YY Echad*.[772]

According to Ashkenazi, when one worships something in an idolatrous way, this separates that thing from the name of God, taking it out of divinity and detaching it from God's image. The only true relationship we can have to the "mighty and awesome name" is one that embraces the whole that unites all creatures and unifies God's name, co-creating or affirming the fullness of God's image in the world.

In this light, one could read the verse, "How mighty is Your name throughout all the earth / *Mah adir shimkha b'khol ha'arets*" [Ps 8:2] as a meditation on the nature of the divine name in all things. Nothing in this sense is outside God, and ultimately, nothing is outside God's image. As Shneur Zalman taught, every being in the world is filled with divine names. Applying these perspectives to our world, one might think of each species as a particular letter or syllable of God's name, in the same way that Kabbalistic midrash on the chariot elaborated the idea that classes of species were parts of God's name.

If one starts from these premises, then it would be right to conclude that the image of God is diminished every time a species becomes extinct. But extinctions have happened throughout Earth's history. Moreover, there would be no human beings to perceive God's image if the great extinctions of the past

---

[770] "A Kabbalah for the Environmental Age", 34, translit. modified. See further discussion p.333.
[771] Discussion, Shalom Center retreat, May 28, 2001.   [772] Ashkenazi, 148, 41b.

had not repeatedly transformed life on this planet. One might even say that the great extinctions are necessary steps in the expression of all possible life forms. If that is the case, and if "the entire purpose consists in bringing into existence... everything whose existence is possible",[773] then the image of God is not a static thing to be expressed by the sum of all life in a particular epoch or climactic moment, but rather something dynamic that reveals itself over vast periods of time. The unfolding of Creation is an unfolding of God's names.

However, while previous extinctions can be imagined as a kind of divine reshaping of life on this planet, human beings acting as the primary agents of extinction is surely not what it means for us to be in God's image. To the extent that the image of God is especially found in the diversity of Life and the Cosmic Tree of Life, in the letters of Creation and the genetic codes of evolution, we who are destroying so many species also become destroyers of divinity. If human beings have inside themselves the capacity to embody the image of God, then we become destroyers of this divinity as well, on the spiritual level and not just the ecological level.

Is the text the world?

Interpreting science and Nature in terms of Kabbalah raises a number of issues, which are discussed in Chapter 13. Here I want to address one specific problem that is endemic to Kabbalah, whether it is applied to science or Nature: the tendency to reduce everything to letters.

It seems probable to me that Shneur Zalman and Yaakov Lainer had in common some kind of lived experience of the lifeforce inhering in what we define as inanimate, even though one of them used letters to express this experience and one did not. However, it is hard to escape the impression that, at least for some Kabbalists, the idea that Creation was formed out of letters, and the process of transducing various images or creatures into various combinations of divine names was an intellectual exercise, without consequence beyond one's interior sense of relationship with God. As Tirosh-Samuelson summarized, "All created things were various manifestations of linguistic information. Nature itself was viewed as a text that could be decoded and manipulated by anyone who grasped its grammar, so to speak."[774] This may in fact be the reality of *Tiquney Zohar*, which was the source in Chapter 7 for so many correlations between God and the more-than-human world.

Because of this, some scholars question whether any aspect of Kabbalah truly represents an opening to the natural world. Elliot Wolfson, for example, sees in Kabbalah's imagery of Nature a form of control and domination, and Ari Elon criticizes the tendency in Kabbalah for the text to replace the world. Elon writes,

---

[773] MN 3:25, 504, discussed pp.20, 28.   [774] "Nature in the Sources of Judaism", 121.

The *talmidey chakhamim* (students of the sages) and kabbalists are the letter-elite of the people of the Book. It is a lonely elite who lives the life of eternity in the kabbalists' cave and gives itself the challenge of changing all the world's objects into letters, which will become part of the express name of God. They do not allow themselves to go outside the cave to see nature and trees as they are in themselves. All those trees and hills are, according to them, nothing more than a foggy and dull copy of the transparent Torah, which is a magical combination of flowering letters.[775]

Can there be a synthesis between the letters and the creatures of the world, rather than a reduction of the world to its letters? Can we get from a consciousness of the "letters of creation" and the patterns of God's names, to a lived understanding that the whole of Creation is God's name, as described by Waskow? Is there a libertory practice embedded in Shneur Zalman's interpretation of the soul of a stone?

I believe the answer is yes. Tirosh-Samuelson gives qualified support to such an outlook, stating that "[t]he very fact that for the Kabbalists everything in the world was a symbol of divine reality facilitated the creation of new rituals and endowed natural objects with a new spiritual meaning. Nature was absorbed into the sacred narrative of Judaism."[776] The truth is, one cannot make a singular historical judgment about the many varieties of Kabbalah. But we can be certain that these Kabbalistic tropes represent tools that *we* can use to become open to the more-than-human world, even as they describe how some Kabbalists might have opened themselves to that world.

---

[775] "Through Tu B'Shvat to Yah B'Shvat", in *Trees, Earth, and Torah*, 306 (translit. modified).
[776] "Nature in the Sources of Judaism", 108.

9

Adam Qadmon
The universe as God's image

If the emanation of the universe, unfolding through the order of *hishtalsh'lut*, is an embodiment of YHVH, as we have seen, then this implies that the universe is in God's image. We can reach the same conclusion more explicitly through the Kabbalistic myth of *Adam Qadmon*, the primordial human. According to this myth, rooted in the midrashic correspondence between human microcosm and cosmos or macrocosm, Creation was originally configured in the body of a human, *Adam Qadmon*, who spanned the height and breadth of the universe. Though this universe, which would include all the "upper worlds", the Sefirot, and so on, might only tangentially include the physical world and the *tachtonim* or earthly creatures, we will see that some Kabbalistic and Hasidic texts understood this trope to mean that the physical universe, like the human, was created in God's image. The idea that the universe as a whole is in the divine image of course has profound ecological and theological ramifications, as I will explore.

In this chapter, I will trace some of the midrashic precedents for *Adam Qadmon*, discuss how they were incorporated into Kabbalistic theory, and identify several Kabbalists that drew from *Adam Qadmon* the conclusion that Creation itself is the image of God. I will also explore two specific aspects of *Adam Qadmon* that have a great impact on ecotheology. The first is that *Adam Qadmon* is structured hierarchically, in a way that diminishes the significance of the earthly realm, the *tachtonim*. We will see how Shneur Zalman's concept of *Or Chozer* or reflected light mitigates or "sweetens" this hierarchy by identifying the *tachtonim* as the source of the greatest light, and so redeems *Adam Qadmon* for ecotheology. The second aspect, which is the focus of Chapter 10, is that *Adam Qadmon* can be seen as a representation of the idea that the universe as a whole is alive. This interpretation shares important elements with the scientific idea called Gaia theory, which posits that the Earth can be interpreted to be a living organism.

THE MIDRASHIC BACKGROUND OF ADAM QADMON

In this section, I will look at three necessary elements for the evolution of the idea of *Adam Qadmon*: the concept of a universe (`olam`), which is pre-rabbinic, and the midrashic ideas that a person is a microcosm (`olam qaṯan`), and that *Adam Harishon*, the first human, was gigantic.

`Olam as cosmos

The evolution of a concept of cosmos or world was obviously a necessity before any concept of the human as a microcosm could develop. Scripture approached the totality of Creation in two ways: through the hendiadys of "*shamayim va'arets*" ("skies and land" or "heavens and earth"), and through the unity of the Creator, especially reflected in the name *Elohim*. The Midrash developed its own terminology that paralleled *shamayim va'arets*: "upper ones and lower ones". `Olam`, without the definite article, means "eternity" or "all-time" in the Torah; there is no name for cosmos or for the unified Creation. But somewhere between the Bible and the rabbis, ancient Jewish culture, possibly under the influence of Hellenism, developed its own terminology for cosmos, adapting `olam` to mean "all-space".[777] Rabbinic culture created or elaborated new dimensions for this idea by asserting the duality of "this world / `olam hazeh`" and "the coming world / `olam haba'`".[778]

Furthermore, in Jewish liturgy and theology, the term `olam` was used both for the universe and for the idea of many universes.[779] This idea, as it evolved in Kabbalah, meant much more than what we mean by Nature, though it also includes that meaning.[780] "Worlds" includes all the levels or gradations of

---

[777] Arguably, Ec 3:11 ("*natan ha`olam b'libam*") or Da 12:7 ("*vayishava` b'chey ha`olam*") could represent steps in this evolution.

[778] Kadushin considers the term `olam` in the sense of world to have originated with rabbinic culture. But given the ubiquitous and consistent use of the term in rabbinic sources, both midrashic and liturgical, it seems more plausible that its use in this sense was coined earlier (*The Rabbinic Mind*, 293–5; see also 151). If the idea of `olam` as world was fully formed before the recording of rabbinic traditions, it may not be possible to trace its evolution. However, an evolution internal to rabbinic Judaism is also imaginable. The idea of `olam` as world could have developed out of the idea of `olam haba'` (usually translated as "the world-to-come") or the afterlife, and this world, `olam hazeh`, which essentially bifurcates all-time/eternity, `olam`, into two realms. The term `olam hazeh` could have easily evolved into a more spatial concept of this universe.

[779] As in the statement that God "created worlds and destroyed them" before this one was created (*BR* 9:2; *YSh* 1:16), or in the ending of the *borei' n'fashot* blessing after eating, "Blessed be the life of the worlds / *barukh chey ha`olamim*". Both are reminders that the only true singularity is that of God. From an ecological perspective, the idea that the world is contingent might engender a feeling of humility about our power.

[780] We do not find a term for Nature *per se* until the Middle Ages, when *teva`* transitions from meaning the nature or character of individuals and species to Nature as a whole, *Haṭeva`*. Even in the Christian scriptures, which use the vocabulary of Greek philosophy, the term *physis* is only used in its narrower sense to denote the nature of a particular species or individual.

The midrashic background of Adam Qadmon

divinity, which become more physically manifest as the process of emanation unfolds. All these levels together are found in the whole of Creation.

The evolution of `olam qatan

The idea that the human body is a microcosm that reflects the macrocosm of the universe is a fundamental piece of the mythologoumenon of *Adam Qadmon*, which in essence says that the universe, inclusive of all the spiritual and physical worlds, is or was in the figure of a great human. The microcosmic idea has ancient roots in many cultures and civilizations, from Manichaeism to early Christian thought to the metaphysical systems of later Taoism, and was important in Platonism as well.[781] It also played an important role in the development of healing systems like Ayurvedic medicine and acupuncture, and in the growth of Renaissance science.

In the Midrash, extended physical comparisons between the human body and the earth are found in *Avot d'Rabi Natan* and *Kohelet Rabbah*. In *Kohelet Rabbah*, we read:

R' B'rakhyah said in the name of R' Shimon ben Lakish: Whatever the Holy One created in the human, He created in the earth as a model for him / *l'dugma lo*. A person/*adam* has a head and so does the earth, as it is said, "and the head of the dirt/ `afar of the world/*teivel*" [Pr 8:26]. A person has eyes and so does the earth, as it is said, "And they will cover the eye of the earth" [Ex 10:5], etc.[782]

---

[781] See Altmann's summary in "The Delphic Maxim", 211-12. One significant citation in Altmann comes from *Photii Bibliotheca* (ninth century, quoted in the name of Pythagoras): "Man is called *micros cosmos* not because he consists of the four elements – this applies also to the animals, even to the lowest – but because he possesses all potencies of the cosmos. For in the cosmos are the gods and also the four elements, and [in it] are also the irrational animals and the plants. All these potencies man possesses." Cf. Maimonides on `olam qatan, MN 1:72, quoted p.269.

[782] ad Ec 1:4, "and the earth is standing forever / *v'ha'arets l`olam `omadet*"; also YSh 1:186, in the name of Resh Lakish. Both passages list correspondences between humanity and the earth, including head, eyes, ears, and mouth, hands, arms, and legs, a navel, as well as eating, drinking, and vomiting. *Kohelet Rabbah* adds nakedness or genitals; YSh adds quaking, getting drunk, and giving birth. The last shows clearly that *ha'adam* in this passage means both men and women. Concerning birth, YSh says, "Just as woman gives birth so does the land, as it is said: 'Has the earth [gone into] labor for a single day, even birthing a nation in a moment?' [Is 66:8]", reading the passage against the grain to say that "[t]hese are Israel, for the Holy One will bring them into Jerusalem in a single moment [at the time of the Messiah]."

The quoted verse, Ec 1:4, serves to establish the correspondence, "the human has legs, and the earth has legs". *Kohelet Rabbah* adds important commentary here: "What is 'she is standing / `omadet'? (How can one say the earth stands?) She keeps/preserves/*m`amedet*. R' Acha and the sages – R' Acha says: [Keeps] her appointed tasks/commands /*taf'qideha*, and the rabbis say: [Preserves] her sustenance/foodstuffs /*m'zonoteha*." One could synthesize the interpretations of Acha and the sages to say that God gave the earth a command to sustain the plants along with their fruits. Such a homiletical reading would imply a criticism of human beings, who could not keep their command to preserve (i.e., not eat) the fruit of the tree in *Gan Eden*. Along these lines, the first teaching in this section, from R' Yehoshua ben Qorchah, notes that "the earth stands in (fulfills) the tasks of the Holy One, therefore she does not wear out,"

Avot d'Rabi Natan inverts this framework: "R' Yosi Haglili says: All that the Holy One created in the earth/*arets* He created in the human... In the world/`olam* He created forests, and in the human He created forests – this is human hair", and so on, comparing natural phenomena with parts of the human body.[783] The fact that there are *midrashim* drawing parallels in both directions suggests that the analogy between human and earth was seen as one-to-one.

Significantly, the analogy in *Kohelet Rabbah* is strictly between the physical earth/*arets* and the physical body. While the Midrash in other places asserted that the heavens and human beings were both in God's image, *Kohelet Rabbah* views the Earth and human bodies as sharing the same structure. Just as the relation between heavens and humanity indicated something unique about humanity, this analogy must also indicate something unique, but there is no early passage that explicates this. It remained for later authors and texts to work out the significance of this relation.

Avot d'Rabi Natan compares both *arets* (earth or land) and the `olam* (world or cosmos) to the human being.[784] *Ha`olam*, like "world", can refer primarily to the earthly realm (e.g., forests, etc.), or to the entire cosmos. The first meaning appears in the part of the passage just quoted. The second meaning appears in the continuation of the passage, which also uses `olam* to mean eternity or all-time:

All that the Holy One created in the earth/*arets* He created in the human... [T]he Holy One, may His great name be blessed for all-time/eternity/`olam* and for

while "a generation [of human beings] does not stand in the tasks (keep the commandments) of the Holy One, therefore it wears out."

[783] *ARNA* ch.31, 91–2. Though most analogies are to features of the Earth, three are to the heavens: the sun is Adam's forehead, the firmaments are Adam's tongue, the stars are the jaws (or cheeks, according to Schechter's suggestion, n.21; cf. *TB Shabbat* 151b). Therefore, this is really a correspondence with the cosmos, even though from this midrash's terrestrial perspective the sun and other heavenly bodies are like a part of the earth's atmosphere/clothing. There are also three analogies to what appear to be phenomena of human civilization: "Walls/*chomot* in the world, walls in the human – these are his lips... Doors in the world, doors in the human – this is his teeth... A king in the world, a king in the human – his head." The first may be read "seals/*chotmot*", which better fits the function of lips (see Schechter, n.18). The second may refer to openings, rather than architecture. The third is more difficult – does it refer to God as king of the world or does it have in mind human kings as a kind of natural phenomenon (as in Ps 148)? Jonathan Schofer compares the whole passage with similar ones in Christian, Zoroastrian, and Hippocratic texts in "The Image of God: A Study of an Ancient Sensibility", *Journal of the Society for Textual Reasoning* 4:3 (May 2006), jtr.lib.virginia.edu/volume4/number3/TR04_03_r02.html.

[784] Some *midrashim* about the microcosm shift the focus away from earthly parallels. For example, one text published by Adolf Jellinek draws extended analogies with the firmament, sun, moon, constellations, fire, and weather (which is understood as an extension of the heavens) (*Aggadat `Olam Qatan*, in *Beyt Hamidrash*, vol.5 [Vienna: Bruder Winter, 1873], 57–9). Though it also draws a very few analogies from the Earth to the body, these analogies are to postures and fluids, rather than organs or parts, hence one step removed from concrete physicality. Note that the title was created by Jellinek (intro., xxv); the term `olam qatan* does not appear in the text.

The midrashic background of Adam Qadmon

eternities of eternities / *l`olmey `olamim*, in wisdom and understanding created the whole world / *kol ha`olam* entirely, and He created the **heavens** and the earth, upper ones and lower ones, and He formed in the human whatever He created in the **world** /*ba`olam*.[785]

In this part of the passage, one witnesses a transition from the idea that the human being is created in the image of the Earth (a relatively small midrashic leap, given the close etymological relationship between Adam and *adamah* or ground), to the idea that the human being is created in the image of the whole cosmos, both heavens and Earth, upper and lower.

What may be the earliest tradition expressing an idea of correspondence between a human being and the universe is found both in *Avot d'Rabi Natan* and in *Mishnah Sanhedrin*: "Anyone who destroys one soul, the scripture lays it upon him as if he destroyed a full/complete world / *`olam malei'*, and anyone who sustains one soul, the scripture lays it upon him as if he sustained a full world."[786] While the significance of *malei'* is not defined, there is no reason to assume otherwise than that it includes heavens and Earth, as well as the species or "hosts" of the heavens and the Earth.[787]

The term *`olam malei'* appears only in the early *midrashim* and in the Mishnah. The later rabbis expressed this idea as "*Adam `olam qaṯan*", meaning "A human is a small world".[788] The term *`olam qaṯan* is not used any earlier than the source documents for *Tanchuma*, which states, "The *mishkan* weighs equal to the whole world, and equal to the formation/structure of the human, who is a small world / *k'neged kol ha`olam uk'neged y'tsirat ha'adam shehu `olam qaṯan*".[789] *`Olam qaṯan* became the standard terminology in all later rabbinic literature.[790]

---

[785] *ARNA*, ch.31. The ellipsed part of this passage is discussed p.307.

[786] *Mishnah Sanhedrin* 4:5, *ARNA*, ch.31, *ARNB* ch.36. The moral dimension of these teachings was explored in Chapter 3. According to Lorberbaum, they already indicate that *`olam malei'* is synonymous with *tselem* (see n.367), which would prove the point that the world was seen as being in God's image. However, I would argue for a much longer period during which this connection slowly evolved. Note also Hechel's perspective (see n.373) that the concepts of *tselem* and *`olam* as applied to human beings represent two separate schools of rabbinic thought.

[787] Another connection is made in *ARNB*, where two different manuscripts use *adam* and *`olam* (in the sense of universe) interchangeably. One version reads, "Through ten things the world was created..." and the other, "Through ten things the human was created..." (ch.43, 119).

[788] For a bibliography of references, see Margaliot, *SCh* 103, n.8; Hallamish, Ashkenazi, 136, nn.95–6; and Kafich (*MN*), 130, n.72.

[789] *P'qudey* 3. The passage also includes a well-developed female image of God: "When the Holy One created His world, like the child/gestation/*yalud* of a woman He created it. As the child begins from the navel and stretches...to four sides, so did the Holy One begin from the foundation stone..."

[790] There is little consciousness in later texts that the term "small world" is not found in the early *midrashim*. For example, in *Sefer Ha'emunot*, Shem Tov ibn Shem Tov states, "Men of science called Adam a small world... And *so did the prophets of Israel and its sages*" (Hallamish, Ashkenazi, 136, n.95, my emphasis). See further discussion of this passage, n.815.

From the perspective of some of these *midrashim*, humanity in a primary sense resembles the Earth, rather than the heavens,[791] but in most cases this resemblance was also extended to the physical universe. In Kabbalah, the structure of the human body, as a "small world", became the symbol of an infinitely greater structure of divinity, imaged also as the many-dimensional body of the cosmos.

Adam Harishon – the first human

The third important midrashic element behind *Adam Qadmon* is the idea that *Adam Harishon*, the first human, was as great as the universe. This element too is widespread throughout the world's civilizations. In one of the Upanishads, for example, one finds: "In the beginning this [universe] was the Self alone, – in the likeness of a man," and there are many more examples one could give.[792]

---

[791] Note the contrast with Philo's interpretation, rooted in Greek conceptions: "Philo declares that first among the created beings God set up the heavens, the most perfect among the imperishable things, and at the end of Creation He formed the most perfect being among the transient entities, who is, as it is said in truth, 'a miniature heaven' (*brachun ouranon*)" (Urbach, *The Sages*, 785, n.8). Urbach notes that Philo polemicized against the idea stated in several midrashic passages that humans were created last so that, should a person be haughty, people can say to him, the mosquito came before you (see n.318). Philo's non-dialectical way of thinking could not entertain the simultaneous reality of opposite perspectives that the Midrash insists upon.

Urbach also cites as a parallel text to Philo a passage in *Midrash Hagadol* comparing Adam to the heavens, even though *Midrash Hagadol* does not share Philo's metaphysical framework. Nonetheless, the fact that such a trope is found at all in this late midrash does correlate with the more dualistic metaphysics found therein (see n.229). Such tropes are not absent from other texts (see nn.152, 784), but the earliest texts only present a comparison between human and Earth. Only in Kabbalah does one find a full-on equation between the human and the heavens, especially with respect to *Adam Ha`elyon*, as in the TZ text discussed pp.224–5. On the dualistic aspects of this motif, see the end of Chapter 10.

[792] *Brhadranyaka Upanishad* 1:4, in *Hindu Scriptures*, ed. Dominic Goodall (Berkeley: University of California Press, 1996), 48. The Upanishads are dated from 1400 to 800 BCE, and provide a plausible origin for the later appearance of this motif in various cultures, though the idea may have originated independently more than once. Similarly to Kabbalah and Midrash, this Upanishad proceeds to the idea of *du-par'tsufim*: "Now he was of the size of a man and woman in close embrace. He split (*pat-*) this Self in two: and from this arose husband (*pati*) and wife (*patni*)." However, what follows differs radically from the Midrash: every time the female escapes by taking on the female form of various other animals, the male pursues her by taking on the male form of the same animal, copulating with her to produce another species.

See also *Atharva-Veda* 10:7: "Whose measure is the earth, whose belly the atmosphere, Who made the sky his head – to him be homage – Brahman, best! Whose eye is the sun, and the moon forever new, Who made the fire his mouth – to him be homage – Brahman, best!" (Goodall, *Hindu Scriptures*, 28); and *Rg-Veda* 10:90, "A thousand heads had [primal] Man, A thousand eyes, a thousand feet: Encompassing the earth on every side, He exceeded it by ten fingers' [breadth]. Man is this whole universe – What was and what is yet to be... All beings form a quarter of him, three-quarters are the immortal in heaven... A quarter of him came to be again [down] here: From this he spread in all directions, Into all that eats and does not eat"

The midrashic background of Adam Qadmon

Many of these *midrashim* about *Adam Harishon* focus on explaining why contemporary human beings do not have the same stature. According to Urbach, "Dicta that describe the first man in a manner... representing him as a kind of 'macroanthropos', are enunciated by the Amoraim only from the beginning of the third century."[793]

Some of these passages emphasize that Adam reached from earth to heaven, thus underlining the connection between the two: "'And He blew into his nostrils'—This teaches that He stood him up as a *golem* stretching from earth to the firmament and then threw breath/*n'shamah* into him."[794] Though the *golem* here is less than the height of the universe, reaching only to the firmament that divides the upper and lower waters, it is comparable in scale to the universe. Urbach speculates that these stories might have been intended to contradict the idea of a radical division between heaven and earth.[795]

Other texts emphasize that *Adam Harishon* encompassed the Earth:

R' Tanchuma in the name of R' Banayah and R' B'rakhyah in the name of R' Elazar said: In the time that the Holy One created *Adam Harishon*, [as] a *golem* He created him and he was set up from [one] end of the world and unto its [other] end – that's what is written: "Your eyes saw my *golem*" [Ps 139:16]. R' Yehoshua bar Nechemyah and R' Yehudah bar Simon in R' Elazar's name said: He created him filling the whole world. From where [do we know he extended] from the East to West? That it's said: "Back/*achor* (i.e., after, the place of sunset) and before/East/*qedem* You formed/enclosed me /*tsartani*" [Ps 139:5]. From where [that he went] from North to South? That it's said: "and from the edge of the heavens and until the edge of the heavens" [Dt 4:32]. And from where [that he filled] even the world's hollow-space? That it's said: "...and You laid Your palm upon me" [Ps 139:5].[796]

Even the heavens are understood to indicate cardinal directions in the earth. In both texts, what is important for this discussion is that the human being fills or encompasses, or in some sense *is*, the world.[797]

If the first human was gigantic, then the midrashic literature must also explain how the stature of Adam became diminished. One midrash reads:

(ibid., 13). In *Rg-Veda*, primal man is offered up by the gods as a sacrifice, and his various parts distributed to become the elements, bodies, and species that found in the cosmos. Again, the differences are as striking as the parallels.

[793] *The Sages*, 228.
[794] BR 14:8. Porton (*Understanding*, 172) discusses whether this means that the human encompassed the entire universe or merely reached the dome of heaven.
[795] He writes, "Even the homiletical expositions of the *Amoraim* that speak of the enormous proportions of the first man and thus resemble the statements of Philo lack the differentiation... between the heavenly man (*ouranios anthropos*), who was not fashioned but stamped with the likeness and image of God... and Adam who was formed out of the dust of the ground. On the contrary, it appears that they actually seek to contradict this conception" (*The Sages*, 229). This conception does appear in later Kabbalah (see p.278).
[796] BR 8:1 ‖ 21:3, 24:2; VR 14:1, 18:2.
[797] See Aaron, "Imagery of the Divine and the Human", 53-4.

What is "and You laid Your palm upon me"? At first the human was created from the earth to the firmament, and since (when) the ministering angels saw him... they said before [the Holy One]: There are two dominions, one in the heavens and one in the earth. What did the Holy One do? In that same moment He set His hand upon him and diminished him and he stood [only] 100 cubits.[798]

Here the human stature is diminished in order to stop the angels from sinning.[799] A more obvious explanation is that Adam's diminished stature resulted from the sin of eating from the tree: "Since he was spoiled [by sinning] the Holy One set His hand upon him and diminished him, for it is said, 'and You laid Your palm upon me'."[800] Whether because of human sin or because of angelic sin (or error), it became necessary for God to diminish God's own image in the world (or upon the Earth). On the simplest level, the idea that God diminished the stature of Adam means that God became distanced from the original human, but it parallels the idea that human actions can "diminish the image of God".

Some of these *midrashim* refer both to the diminution of Adam's stature in the garden, and to the restoration of Adam's stature at the time of redemption, and so provide a seedbed for the development of the Kabbalistic idea of *Adam Qadmon*.[801] Similar ideas about the restoration of the cosmic human body are associated with the apotheosis of Enoch in pre-rabbinic literature.[802]

Homiletically, one could define the human mission as the restoration of Adam's stature/*qomah* that God reduced. One simplistic way to imagine this happening is to increase the number of human beings in the world, as suggested by some *midrashim*.[803] Kabbalah suggests its own methods for accomplishing this restoration, including developing the image of God in the body, and uniting masculine and feminine. Yet other ways humanity can expand the image

---

[798] *Midrash Otiyot d'Rabi Aqiva B*, in *BM*, vol.2, 413.

[799] Similarly, some versions of *Avot d'Rabi Natan* teach: "The ministering angels went down to serve (i.e., worship) him /*l'sharto* and the Holy One picked him up and put him under His wings, as it says: 'And You laid Your palm upon me'" (*ARNA* ch.1, 8, n.97). This interpretation of Ps 139:5, also found in *BR* 8:1, strongly differs from the interpretation that God diminished Adam, and it implies a unique intimacy between the first human and God. Note Schechter chooses as his primary text a manuscript that reads: "The ministering angels went down to corrupt him /*l'shachato*", that is, because they were jealous.

[800] TB *Chagigah* 12a and *Sanhedrin* 38b. *ARNA* ch.1 interprets the same verse to mean that God diminished Adam by *removing* God's hand: "Another teaching: 'And You laid Your palm upon me'—Since [the human] was spoiled (by eating the fruit), the Holy One lifted one of [His hands]". (The passage begins with the idea that the human was created by God's *two* hands; see n.291.) *BR* 12:6 ‖ 14:8 also sees Adam's diminished stature as a sign of the fall: "'And he hid, the human and his woman /*ishto*' [Gn 3:8] —Said R' Abahu: In that same moment [that he sinned and wished to hide], the *qomah* of *Adam Harishon* was pared down and became 100 cubits."

[801] See esp. *BR* 12:6 and parallels in *Midrash Chaseirot Viyteirot* 11, *BM*, vol.1, 226.

[802] See Andrei Orlov, "Without Measure and Without Analogy: The Tradition of the Divine Body in 2 (Slavonic) Enoch", *Journal of Jewish Studies* 56:2 (2005): 224–44, www.marquette.edu/maqom/objatie.html (June 2013).

[803] e.g., *BR* 17:2.

Adam Qadmon – *the primordial human*

of God are described in Kabbalah and *Chasidut* (Hasidism), as explored later in this chapter and in Chapters 10–11. As we will see, "raising the sparks", whether through the holy use of things that come into our hands, or through our consciousness of God's presence in them, entails restoring their *qomah* (the manifestation of God's image or imprint that is already in them), as well as restoring our own (p.292ff.). What is suggested by the need of Creation – by *tsorekh gavoha* (p.164), as it might be defined for our own time? We may think of our task as one of finding and magnifying the image of God in all places, not only through our use of other things and other species, but through our contemplative appreciation of all species and of the weave of their relationships,[804] and our service in behalf of the greater whole created from this weave.

On the level of constructive theology, this process itself can be imagined as a way of restoring the divine image of *Adam Harishon* to its original cosmic proportions. "Finding" God's image in this sense would require us to actively open our minds to perceive and value God's image in every being and "holon" (to use Wilber's term for a part that includes the whole – see p.309). The outline of such a practice is something I will continue to explore further on.

The implications of the idea that the body of *Adam Harishon* encompassed the Earth or the cosmos were not explored more fully in the Midrash. Nor did rabbinic literature explain the metaphysical significance of its extended analogies between the structure of the human body and the structure of the Earth or cosmos. One might project that an analogy was made between the human body in its structure and the image of God, but no text hints at that. On the contrary, it is more reasonable to read these *midrashim* as saying that the image of the Earth and the image of God are separate images that overlap within the human being. In *Shi`ur Qomah* too, where the structure of the human body described God's body, no connection was made to the structure of the world.[805]

Yet it seems almost obvious that, if the human is in God's image, and the human is in the Earth's image or the world's image, then the world or the Earth must also be in God's image. While Midrash did not make this leap, certain Kabbalists did.

ADAM QADMON – THE PRIMORDIAL HUMAN

The earlier picture of the human being as microcosm was only given theological significance in later Kabbalistic and philosophical literature.[806] The *Zohar*, for

---

[804] See pp.171, 274.
[805] Note, however, that according to Scholem, Shimon ben Tsemach Duran thought *Shi`ur Qomah* could be given a "pantheistic interpretation" in which "reality itself as a whole is the mystical shape of the deity" (*OMG* 37). See also the related example of Moshe Narboni, p.254.
[806] Nevertheless, Scholem and Idel claim that the Kabbalistic idea that the world was included in *Adam Harishon* is already referred to in *Midrash Avkir* (preserved in *YSh* 1:3), which states, "*v'khileil bo ha`olam*" (Idel: "He concentrated the whole world in [Adam]"). Aaron rejects their interpretation, instead reading the phrase as "He completed the world with him" ("Imagery", 54–6).

example, taught that "the image/*d'yoqna* of Adam would be the image of the upper ones and lower ones that are included in him"[807] and that there is "no part/organ that exists in a person that does not have a creature in the world to parallel it. For behold, just as a person is divided into parts... and all of them are one body, so also is the world: all these creatures... are really one body."[808] In Kabbalah, which had assimilated the framework of *Shi`ur Qomah* into its cosmology, the connection between human and world was also expressed using the terminology of this ancient mystical work.[809]

Kabbalah, through the concept of *Adam Qadmon*, drew the connection between the form of the human body, the universe, and the divine image, thereby connecting *tselem Elohim* and Creation on multiple levels. Pinchas Giller writes, "The paradigm for the most transcendent levels of Divinity is the primordial man, *Adam Qadmon*. This anthropos serves as a metaphor for God, the Cosmos, the Torah, and by association, the Temple and its sacrificial cult."[810] The human body served as an imaginative bridge linking God and Creation.[811]

The world as God's image

That "the world was created in God's image" is implied in many or even most Kabbalistic systems, though only a few texts state this explicitly. *Peyrush L'parshat B'rei'shit*, a commentary on *B'rei'shit Rabbah* by Yosef ben Shalom Ashkenazi, is the earliest work I have found to do so. Ashkenazi writes:

And [in order] for Adam to be ordered within and without in the image/*dimyon* of the whole world and its guide in the absolute intellect / *seikhel nivdal*, [scripture] said "in Our image / *b'tsalmeinu*", to hint at the *dimyon* of the One who guides through individual providence, and it said "as our likenesses / *kid'muteynu*" (spelled with a Yud, perhaps intending a plural reading of *d'mut*) for the *dimyon* of the structure of

---

[807] *Zohar* 3:141b, quoted in Moshe Idel, *Kabbalah: New Perspectives* (New Haven CT: Yale University Press, 1988), 119, 332.

[808] *Zohar* 1:134b; for context, see p.203.   [809] See "The History of *Qomah*", p.285ff.

[810] *The Enlightened Will Shine* (Albany NY: SUNY Press, 1993), 94. See also Idel, *Kabbalah*, 118–20. The pattern of identifying *Adam* in all things, so characteristic of *TZ*, is the focus of Giller's book, but it is also found at every stage of the evolution of Kabbalah.

[811] Anglican Bishop John Habgood draws a similar insight from Christian thought. He quotes Orthodox Bishop Kallistos Ware, who writes,

> The human person is not only microcosm, the universe in miniature, but also *microtheos*, God in miniature. Each of us is not simply *imago mundi*, image of the world, but also *imago Dei*, image of God. Each is a reflection of the uncreated Deity, a finite expression of God's infinite expression. That is why Gregory of Nazianus states that "man is a second cosmos".
>
> ("A Sacramental Approach to Environmental Issues", in *Liberating Life*, eds. Charles Birch et al. [Maryknoll NY: Orbis, 1990], 46–7, my emphasis)

> Habgood adds, "If this [*imago Dei*] is true of humanity then *it must in some sense extend to the whole cosmos* because Christ, the perfect image of God, is also in St. Paul's thought the agent and fulfillment of creation."

Adam Qadmon – *the primordial human*

the worlds and ten *s'firot* and their details and principles, which are truly made similar to him. And therefore Adam is called a small world / *'olam qaṯan*.[812]

Ashkenazi conjoins Adam being in God's image with Adam being in the world's image. Adam is called a small world because he is in the image and likeness, because he is "ordered within and without in the image of the whole world and its guide".[813] Here Ashkenazi understands the verses that describe human creation as referring to the image of the *'olam*, as well as the image of the Creator and the Sefirot.

That this image includes the physical Creation and not just its deep structure in a spiritual sense is made clearer in the following passage:

> [T]he *adam/Adam* should be called *'olam qaṯan*, for in his form/*y'tsirah* he resembles all [the existences] (i.e., all the creatures of the universe) – if so, the human, formed of the dirt of the ground, included in him, to become him, seal/*chotam* and structure/*taṿnit* and *d'mut* and *tselem* for all ten *s'firot* and **for all that is created and formed and made from them**.[814]

Ashkenazi emphasizes that the dirt of the ground in itself includes the seal and structure of Adam, and that this structure is connected both with the *d'mut* and *tselem* of the Sefirot, that is, with God's image, and with the creatures. He describes this as "the secret of *Adam hagadol*"—the universe is the great Adam, just as the human is a small world.[815] Not only does this passage complete the connection between the world and God's image through the mediation of Adam, it also includes the diversity of Creation. And this totality, in all its complexity, is an image of God, even *the* image of God.

We find an even clearer statement of this thesis in a commentary on *Sefer Y'tsirah* that scholars have established as being written by Ashkenazi:

> This is the principle that should be [grasped] in your hand: All the existences, which all have in them the ten Sefirot, are constructed / become ordered through the joining of

---

[812] Ashkenazi, 147, 41a.

[813] Ashkenazi's formulation of *'olam qaṯan* is not far from that of Maimonides (see p.269ff. and notes). Where Ashkenazi goes with his interpretation is completely different, however. Note also that many philosophical interpretations of *'olam qaṯan* (e.g., ibn Ezra and Shabtai Donnolo, n.879) are in direct opposition to Ashkenazi and Kabbalah (and to a more ecological interpretation).

[814] Ashkenazi, 136, 37a, my emphasis. In this passage, Ashkenazi is explaining the BR passage that describes the *golem* as stretching across the whole universe, which was the *locus classicus* for the idea of the cosmic Adam.

[815] Ibid. Applying the phrase *Adam Hagadol* to the world is somewhat unusual; here it underscores a relationship between the physical world and God's image. Hallamish records the following parallel from *Sefer Ha'emunot* of Shem Tov ibn Shem Tov: "Men of science called Adam '*olam qaṯan* /a small world', and the world '*ha'adam hagadol* / the great human' because of the joining of its parts" (Ashkenazi, 136, n.95; cf. al-Shahrastani on Pythagoras, and Philo, quoted in Altmann, "The Delphic Maxim", 17). In general, Kabbalah connects the cosmic anthropos with the concept of *Adam Ha'elyon*, which would exclude the lower orders of Creation. Shem Tov's statement is important because of its clarity, though Ashkenazi goes far beyond it in connecting God's image directly with the world.

letters, whether silent, or growing, or moving, or speaking, and thus each one is in the structure of His seal which is His. Understand this, for it is a hint towards the truth, as it is said, "Let us make Adam in our image, as our likeness", and it is said, "The heavens rejoiced and the earth sang out / *Yism'chU* ישמחו *HashamayiM* השמים *V'tageL* ותגל *Ha'areTs* הארץ" [Ps 96:11]—the first letters (of these words) spell out YHVH, and the last letters of the words spell צלמו "His image/*tsalmo*", and this is why the rabbis said (about the name of God used in Genesis 2): "A full name for a full world".[816]

This remarkable passage claims that the animate heavens and earth together are God's image – more than this, they are the full name of God – and that the human is created in *their* image. It is God's image that completes both the world and the human.[817] Moreover, in *Peyrush L'parshat B'rei'shit*, Ashkenazi brings the same interpretation of Psalms 96:11 as the preface to his argument that the problem with idolatry is that it separates the creature worshipped from the rest of Creation and from the divine name (see p.238).[818] Since every being is "in the structure of the seal belonging to God", every being is a part of the divine image of Creation.

Moshe Cordovero also makes the point that Adam's image includes the diversity of creation, in more simple language:

[T]he human is not at all like any creation by itself, but he is like all of them together, and that is the reason it is saying "Let *us* make a human", because [from] each and every one, [God] placed a part in him, and for this he was created last, so that he could include a part from each creature.[819]

---

[816] *Sefer Y'tsirah, Peyrush Hara'vad ad* 1:12, 67–8. This and the previous passage also appear to contradict Idel's claim, if I have understood him correctly, that the *Zohar* is the first work that "implies that divine structures in human shape compose the higher and lower entities" (*Kabbalah*, 119).

[817] Ashkenazi does not explicitly connect this with the statement that a person is a "full/complete world", but it is reasonable to assume that he had this in mind.

[818] Ashkenazi, 147, 41b.

[819] *Shi'ur Qomah* (Jerusalem: Dov Ze'ev ben Yosef, 1966), *Torah* 13:4, 21. Gershon Winkler quotes this passage in *Magic of the Ordinary* (Berkeley CA: North Atlantic Books, 2003), 17–18, though his translation is radically different. This interpretation of *na`aseh adam* is reflected in the popular work of some contemporary authors, such as in Harold Kushner's *When Bad Things Happen to Good People* (New York: Anchor Books, 2004), 81–2, quoted in Sicker, *Between Man and God*, 93, and in Nancy Sohn Swartz's children's book, *In Our Image: God's First Creatures* (Woodstock VT: Jewish Lights, 1998). Note also the Vilna Gaon, who like Cordovero imagines God to be addressing the creatures:

"Let us make Adam"—Its explanation is that since Adam was created last of all creatures, therefore the Holy One said to all the creatures that they should give a portion from their character to the body of the human: for might is related to the lion, speed to the deer, agility to the eagle, cleverness to the fox ... and this is the meaning of "in our image", that the form of every species became united in the human species.

(*Aderet Eliyahu* [New York: Shulzinger Bros., 1950], *ad* Gn 1:26)

However, according to the Vilna Gaon, the purpose for the unification of all species in the human contradicts the gentler (and more ecological) interpretation found in Cordovero and in Kushner and Swartz, as one sees in the continuation of this passage:

Adam Qadmon – *the primordial human*

Cordovero includes all the lower creations in the image in which Adam is made, though of course, as he explains, God is addressing all levels of Creation, from the creatures to the elements to the angels. Cordovero also says in the same section that the creatures were not "tied together", and the Creation was not whole, until all was united within the human being, who is the "the embryonic axis between (i.e., uniting) all of them / *t'li ha`ubar bein kulam*".

The Shlah similarly teaches that the purpose of the human was to unite the diversity of Creation within one being. "'The end of the matter/thing' [Ec 12:13] is Adam, who was created last. And the beginning of the thought is the end of the deed. He was created at the end so that he would include everything in his image and his likeness."[820] Horowitz turns on its head the traditional idea that Adam was created last because humanity was the purpose of creation. The converse, he says, is true: Adam was created last because the purpose of humanity was to fulfill the need of Creation.

Ashkenazi adds one more turn to this motif, in which he bridges two important interpretations of Genesis 1:31. Commenting on the teaching in *B'rei'shit Rabbah*, "'And here very good / *tov m'od*'—'very' מאד M'D, this [means] Adam אדם 'DM",[821] he writes:

> Its explanation is: the principle of all [things] formed / *hay'tsurim* is Adam, and in Adam is the whole, and all of them are called Adam, and Adam is called by the name of all of them, as it says: "Ask please the first days which were before you, from the day when Elohim created the Adam on the earth, and from the edge of the heavens and until the edge of the heavens" [Dt 4:32].[822]

The teaching "'very/*m'od*' means Adam" implies that the final or ultimate good in Creation, that which makes it very good, is the human being.[823] Ashkenazi, like the Shlah in the previous quote, turns this idea upside down. Adam and all

> ...the form of every species became united in the human species in order that they would all of them be occupied/conquered/*yichboshu* under his hand – silent, growing, moving, speaking/*DTsCh"M*...so that he would dominate/*rodeh* over all. And He placed in him "a portion of God from above" so that he would serve *Hashem*.

> There is some incoherence here in that the "speaking ones", that is, humanity, are included in the list of beings that should be conquered, but there is a clear division between what the other creatures contribute to the "body of the human" and the divine contribution of soul. In contrast, for Cordovero, the human is regarded *in toto* as a whole being in God's image. Either interpretation can make sense hermeneutically, but the preponderance of texts that use this trope leans toward the more ecologically meaningful interpretation.

[820] *ShLH, Toldot Adam, Beyt Yisra'el*, 15a; Krassen, "House of Israel III", 216.
[821] 9:12; the words are anagrams.
[822] Ashkenazi, 140, 38b. The *p'shat* of the verse is that Israel should inquire whether anything as great as Sinai and the redemption from Egypt has ever happened since the beginning of time, anywhere under the heavens, but Ashkenazi, following *midrashim* about the cosmic dimensions of *Adam Harishon*, understands the verse to mean, "Elohim created Adam from one end of heaven to the other".
[823] Most commentators, unlike Ashkenazi and Horowitz, readily accept this idea. But even accepting that humanity is the goal of Creation, one need not affirm the potentially tyrannical and self-centered dimension of this idea. We have already seen what Rebbe Nachman did with the

the creatures share the same names. Adam is the "very-ness" of what is good in Creation, because Adam is the principle of interrelationship between every being in Creation. Ashkenazi also states:

You should know that in the *golem* of Adam/ a human being and in his *nefesh* the Blessed Name incorporated/ caused to participate [every creature] from all species of creatures and forms and works, whether those that are in the ten *s'firot*, [or] those in the *t'murot* (transformations), [or] those in the chariots, whether those from `olam and shanah and nefesh (world, year, and person[824]), those from [among the] silent, from growing, from moving, from speaking (mineral, vegetable, animal, and human), for in/with all of them he (Adam) participates/ is joined.[825]

The primary meaning of the image of God in the human is that we participate in every being and every level of Being. If so, then all the other creatures also participate in us.[826] Each is somehow part of our humanity, just as each is part of God's name. (see pp.181, 238). Cutting ourselves off from the other creatures means cutting off these parts of ourselves, parts of the image of God, just as it means cutting off part of God's name.

To give three more examples of this pattern, in the realm of philosophy, Moshe Narboni (c.1300–62, France, Spain), who was heavily influenced by Kabbalah, wrote that the dimensions of God's "body" or *qomah* described in *Shi`ur Qomah* represent the levels of Creation (e.g., the sublunar sphere is the divine body below the knees), that all existents are part of "the image of God", and that the world itself is the *qomah* and the "image/*t'munah*" of God.[827] In later *Chasidut*, Tsadok Hakohen of Lublin (1823–1900, Lithuania, Poland), wrote that "the human is called `olam qatan, for he includes all the creation and all the world entirely... and therefore it is said about him, 'in our image as our likeness'".[828] And in the non-Hasidic Haredi ultra-Orthodox) world, an astonishing presentation of this idea is found in the commentary of Naftali Tsvi Yehudah Berlin ("The Netsiv", 1817–1893, Russia). He explains:

[F]rom the moment that it arose in thought and speech that there would be Nature, then was the Place/*Hamaqom* (i.e., the Creator) called Elohim. And since all of Nature is included in Adam, behold, he is in Elohim's image.[829]

idea that "the whole world was created for me". Maharal similarly transforms this passage from *BR* into a deeply ethical teaching:

[T]he creatures, all of them, depend on the human, for they were created for the sake of the human... And this is not found explicitly in scripture... [but] only by a hint: 'and here it is very good' – and they said in the midrash '*very/m'od* – this is the letters of *adam*'... And [so] it is necessary that humanity be good (i.e., virtuous)".   (*Derekh Chayyim*, ch.1, 25)

He enumerates three dimensions in which virtue is good: for the person himself, for the heavens (God), and for the people who are with him. But the dimension of Creation itself appears to be the ground for the other dimensions.

[824] These are ontological categories derived from *Sefer Y'tsirah* 3:4–6.
[825] Ashkenazi, 137, 38a.   [826] See n.18.   [827] Altmann, "Moses Narboni", 150–54.
[828] *Sefer Machsh'vot Charuts* (Pieterkov: Yachdut, 1911, repr.), 83.
[829] *Ha`emeq Davar* (New York: Friedman Press, n.d), *s.v. b'tselem Elohim*, 6.

In short, the motif of the world being in God's image is woven throughout the history of Jewish thought and Kabbalah. Lastly, some texts connect the world with God's image directly, without the mediation of Adam, as we saw in *Igeret Haqodesh*, where *seder ʽolam* or "the universal order" – that is, Nature – is a synonym for God's image.[830]

Between Horowitz, Ashkenazi, and the concept of *seder ʽolam*, one can synthesize a well-developed theology of Nature with relatively few gaps. This leads to what is one of our most important conclusions from the perspective of ecology: It is completely consonant with the rabbinic tradition and Kabbalah to regard both the whole universe and the Earth as being created in God's image.

ADAM QADMON AND THE TACHTONIM

There is one more important step toward creating a powerful ecotheology. From the perspective of emanation, the divine flux travels in one direction. In most Kabbalistic systems, this flux becomes attenuated the farther one gets from the source, so that the "lower ones" are a much weaker manifestation of the light of *Adam Qadmon*. Though they are a part of the entire image of God, when viewed as a separate realm, they do not suggest God's image.

Homiletically speaking, since the Midrash already notes that even the heel of *Adam Harishon* shone like the sun,[831] one could easily extemporize an ecotheology about light manifest in the lower beings, that is, in the language of *Adam Qadmon*, at the level of the soles of *Adam Qadmon*'s feet. But this interpretation, though homiletically interesting, would not have any internal or historical connection with the idea that Creation as a whole is in God's image. There is a much stronger foundation that fully resolves this question.

OR CHOZER – REFLECTED LIGHT AND THE POWER OF THE EARTH

To go beyond these hierarchies of emanation and *Adam Qadmon*, I will turn again to the Kabbalah of Shneur Zalman of Liady. In *Igeret Haqodesh* 20, the last thing Shneur Zalman wrote before he died,[832] he describes the immense

---

[830] See p.215. *Seder ʽolam* can also be read as a synonym for the Sefirot, but its earliest meaning is Nature (see *BR* 12:1). One might understand *seder ʽolam* in this sense as "the orderliness of the world". Cf. the Zoharic comparison between the twelve tribes and the constellations, p.224.
[831] See n.152.
[832] *Igeret Haqodesh* 20 is found in *Tanya*, 497–513. At the end of *Igeret Haqodesh* 20, the editor adds: "Until here we found his holy writing" (*Tanya*, 513). See *Tanya*, 514, n.135: "R. Menachem Mendel of Lubavitch...writes that his grandfather wrote this discourse a few days before his passing." Shneur Zalman was a refugee at this time, having fled with his court before Napoleon's advancing army. We cannot know whether Shneur Zalman saw something new in his last days that needed expression, though the possibility is tantalizing.

manifestation of divine power in the soil, which he describes as a process of "*Or Chozer*", reflected or returning light. The radiance of this light, he says, "shows her power and her ability in the element of physical earth in a mighty revelation, with immense strength beyond the elements higher than it, even the host of the heavens."[833] The power of this revelation comes from the very fact that it is at that bottom, at the level of "the soles of the feet of *Adam Qadmon*", as Shneur Zalman will explain.[834]

The workings of the universe that create the *Or Chozer* are complex; I will skim through the passage here in order to glimpse the bigger cosmological picture. First, Shneur Zalman explains that the manifestation of divinity in the heavens is not greater than on earth, as people might erroneously think:

> [T]he existence and being of the light of *Eyn Sof* has no limit of place at all and encompasses all worlds equally, and [so it says,] "the heavens and the earth I fill" [Je 23:24] with one equal-measure/*hashva'ah*,[835] and, "There is no place empty of Him" even in this material earth/*arets*.[836]

He next describes the difference between the circular light, which maintains the same strength at all levels of being, and the straight light of emanation, which contracts as it descends:

> But this is in the dimension of encircling and encompassing / *maqif v'sovev*... and not [the dimension of] extension and enclothing the lifeforce / *hitpashtut v'hitlabshut hachiyut*, which gives life [to the creatures and worlds] and brings them into being from nothing to something, each one by means of the radiance/*he'arah* of the radiance of the radiance, etc., from the ray/*kav* [that extends downward by way of contraction/*tsimtsum*][837]... and through His (*Eyn Sof*'s) radiance inside the vessels, He puts in them the power and strength to create something from nothing / *yesh mei'ayin*.[838]

---

[833] *Tanya*, 508–10.

[834] Cf. Narboni, who described the lowest level of materiality as the soles of the feet of God's *qomah* (Altmann, "Moses Narboni", 151).

[835] Rachel Elior, in *The Paradoxical Ascent to God: The Kabbalistic Theosophy of Habad Hasidism* (Albany NY: SUNY Press, 1993), uses the beginning of this passage as prooftext for the principle of *hashva'ah*, "equalization", which she equates with the principle underlying acosmism: that all is God (68). Certainly this is an important principle in *Tanya*, but the very point of what follows in *Igeret Haqodesh* 20 is that the heavens are not equal to, and cannot compare with, the Earth.

[836] *Tanya*, 508.

[837] This radiance is the contracted light that comes by way of the *keilim* from "top" to "bottom". Elsewhere, Shneur Zalman describes this light as being present in the earth only in the most minute quantity (Ibid., 254, quoted n.853).

[838] Ibid., 508. Shneur Zalman explains here that creation by means of the vessels or Sefirot is the source of what we might call biodiversity:

> And also from the light of *Eyn Sof* that encircles and encompasses the four worlds of *Atsilut*, *B'riyah*, *Y'tsirah*, `*Asiyah* equally, He illuminates unto the inner ray by way of the vessels of the ten *s'firot* [of each of the three lower worlds] of *B'riyah*, *Y'tsirah*, `*Asiyah*, and through His radiance inside the vessels, He puts in them the power and strength to create *yesh mei'ayin*. And since creation is by means of the vessels, because of this they, the created beings, [are]

Or Chozer – *reflected light and the power of the Earth*

From this perspective, the apparent light at the bottom of the chain of emanation, that is, at the level of the Earth, should be much much less than the light above. But in fact, Shneur Zalman states, the light at the bottom is immensely more powerful:

> And furthermore, so much beyond all that, ... [the radiance of the encompassing light] shows her[839] power and her ability in the element of physical earth/ `afar* in a mighty revelation with so much strength / *b'giluy `atsum b'yeter `oz*, beyond the elements higher than [earth], even [beyond] the host of the heavens. For it is not in their power and their ability to bring forth *yesh mei'ayin* continually like the element of earth, which constantly makes grow something from nothing – these are the plants and trees – ... from the growing/vegetative power in [the earth], which is no-thing/*ayin* and spiritual, [even though the creatures] are material.[840]

The light of *Or Chozer* in the physical earth is greater than the light of the whole host of the heavens, which cannot "bring forth something from nothing continually". (From Shneur Zalman's perspective, the light of the sun is constant, not continuously brought into existence through nuclear processes.) The reason for this has to do with the structure of *Adam Qadmon*:

> And this is only because the feet of *Adam Qadmon* end/close at the bottom of /below/*b'tachtit `Asiyah*, and below his/His feet[841] shines the light of *Eyn Sof*, blessed be, that encompasses all worlds... and also the ray/*qav* from the light of *Eyn Sof*, which closes/*mis'tayem* in the end/*siyum* (soles) of the feet of *Adam Qadmon*, shines from below to above, in the dimension of *Or Chozer*.[842]

Adam Qadmon encompasses the whole world system, extending to include the end of the Sefirotic tree, the *Malkhut* of the *Malkhut* of `*Asiyah*. Below that point, the world is directly immersed in and sucking from the *Or Maqif* or the encompassing light of *Eyn Sof*, which is originary light, unrestricted by the contractions that took place at each level of emanation. At the same time, the straight light that did undergo contraction is reflected back, with greater strength.

Together, these lights combine, so that the radiance "reveals herself with so much strength, from the light of *Eyn Sof* that surrounds all worlds, and from the ray of the light of *Eyn Sof* that is in the end of the feet of the *yosher* (straight

---

in the dimension of multiplicity/diversity/*ribui* and division and limit and end/*takhlit*, and in particular [this happens] by means of the letters.

[839] The gender of the pronouns indicates that this refers to "radiance" (*he'arah*).

[840] Ibid., 508.

[841] Echoing Ex 24:10: "they saw the God of Israel, and under His feet [what was] like the appearance of sapphire brick".

[842] *Tanya*, 510. Parallels to this segment are found in Lurianic Kabbalah, but no connection is made between the feet of *Adam Qadmon* and the physical realm or *Or Chozer*. See ECh 1, *Heykhal* 1 1:4, 27 and *Heykhal* 2 10:3, 96.

path)[843] of *Adam Qadmon*".[844] One, the "straight" light, evolves through the body of *Adam Qadmon* and reaches the feet or bottom of the cosmos, where it reflects again upwards, and the other, the encircling light, upwells through the soles of the feet of *Adam Qadmon*.[845] As in a laser, the lights become entangled and intertwined, the reflected light from within becoming magnified and the unmediated light from without becoming focused.

This creative principle embedded in the Earth is hinted at in the creation story itself, where the meaning of "the saying 'Let the earth/*arets* sprout [herbage]' [Gn 1:11] [is that] it would be a potential within the earth/*arets* always for all-time and beyond, of the dimension of *Eyn Sof*, and not only during the six days of the beginning/creation."[846] Here Shneur Zalman is alluding to the fact that this is the only verse in Genesis 1 where the medium of creation actively carries out God's command.[847]

The growth of plants and trees is therefore as dramatic as their first appearance on the third day of creation. Shneur Zalman identifies this power and radiance, manifest in the physical growth of plant life from the soil, as "pure Love / *Chesed chinam*" – the one remnant of the original *Chesed* that created the world which we can access directly:

For during the seven days of the beginning, there shone in this world a radiance from the light of the *Eyn Sof* in pure/freely-given Love/loving kindness / *Chesed chinam*... to make plants and trees and fruits grow from nothing to something continually, more than enough year by year, which is an essence of the dimension of *Eyn Sof*[848]... [By means of these] the living (animal) is nurtured and lives by the growing (plant), and the speaking (human) receives his lifeforce/*chiyut* from both, even wisdom and knowledge.[849]

While it would be possible to look at all this as a complicated theoretical construction, I would not make light of (and we ought to "make light from")

---

[843] *Yosher* here is used in a way that parallels *qomah*, with the feet standing (figuratively and metonymically) for the upright stature of *Adam Qadmon*.

[844] *Tanya*, 512.

[845] The two lights are also thus a union of male and female, though Shneur Zalman does not call attention to this.

[846] Ibid., 510–12.

[847] As it says: "And the earth brought forth herbage / *vatotsei' ha'arets deshe'*" [Gn 1:12].

[848] The phrase "the dimension of *Eyn Sof*" means both having the quality of the originary light before it was contracted into *l'vushim* (the "clothing" or trappings that shield Creation from being overwhelmed by Divinity), and literally being "without end" or infinite, as is clear from the next phrase: "for if this world would stand for myriads of myriads of years, they would [still] grow abundantly, year by year". Shneur Zalman adds that those fruits that grow from the raising of *mayin nuqvin* (female waters) or arousal from below – that is, through sowing and planting – are to be praised "very very much" beyond what grows of itself from the earth. So his schema still assumes an important role for the human presence.

[849] *Tanya*, 512.

the possibility that Shneur Zalman is describing a lived and living experience of the Earth.[850]

Or Chozer is a direct consequence of the hierarchy that stuctures *Adam Qadmon*, and at the same time, it overturns that hierarchy. The light's reflection, which is an intensification and magnification, manifests "in a mighty revelation" the original power that created the world. Its radiance emerges from within the physical earth, in real time; yet it is "of the dimension of *Eyn Sof*", that is, infinite, at the level of *yesh mei'ayin*, "creation out of nothing" or *creatio ex nihilo*, beyond even the limitations of the Sefirot.

Compare this perspective with a different vision of the earth, described by one of Shneur Zalman's contemporaries, Meshullam Feibush of Zbarazh (d.1795, Galicia): "After everything was finished on the sixth day, if the world had remained in [the state of] creation, it could not have continued because of the **small quantity of vitality** (lifeforce/*chiyut*) that was in it / that it contained."[851] The physical world could neither contain nor express anything "of the dimension of *Eyn Sof*" according to this cosmogony. Rather than an upwelling of light from within or from below, the Earth or material world requires a transfusion of light from above:

For this [reason], after finishing all the work of Creation, God made shine /*hivhiq* an illumination/*b'hirut* from the hidden creation. It emanated from what caused the creatures to come into being in His thought, a very spiritualized state of being/*havayah* and this is really [of] the divine essence itself.[852]

The illumination functions in some ways like *Or Chozer*, bringing completion and unity to Creation. However, it is unlike *Or Chozer* in numerous ways, as one can see in the continuation of the passage:

And He made shine the splendor/*ziv* of His glory from the end of the world to its other end, throughout all the work of Creation, and most especially/essentially, in the human, which is the most chosen of God's creatures, He made shine unto him illumination from the hidden root in God's thought.

This illumination emanates from the highest levels, illuminating the divine work without making Creation itself luminous. Though God's splendor appears to include the earth within its cycle, going "from one end of the world to the other", *b'hirut* flows directly between the human and the divine realm.

---

[850] It is worth mentioning here that there is a tradition in Chabad that the Alter Rebbe spent his youth working for a gardener. I was told he declaimed it to be a taste of *Gan Eden*. (Rabbi Dovid Edelman of Springfield MA, personal communication, Sep. 2008).

[851] *Liqutim Y'qarim* 137a, *Yosher Divrey Emet* §45; quoted in Miles Krassen's *Uniter of Heaven and Earth: Rabbi Meshullam Feibush Heller of Zbarazh and the Rise of Hasidism in Eastern Galicia* (Albany NY: SUNY Press, 1998), 149, trans. based on Krassen.

[852] Ibid.

Most of Kabbalah and *Chasidut* follows the path of Meshullam Feibush, looking for the original light of creation only in the most recondite mysteries. Even Shneur Zalman, elsewhere in *Tanya*, teaches that the original light can only be found in minute quantity in the physical elements.[853] In *Igeret Haqodesh* 20, however, Shneur Zalman uniquely tells us to look to the physical earth to see this light.

Or Chozer in Lurianic and pre-Lurianic Kabbalah

While Shneur Zalman's conception of *Or Chozer* is consonant with his description of the way stones manifest God's name (p.235ff.), it goes much further. What are the roots of his conception? Shneur Zalman cites the Ari (Yitshak Luria) as a source for *Or Chozer* in *Igeret Haqodesh* 31,[854] but a comparison with Lurianic texts shows that his understanding of *Or Chozer* is only loosely related.

Frequently, the Lurianic concept of *Or Chozer* is one of withholding light, an expression of divine or sefirotic anger: "The light that comes directly/*b'yosher* is mercy, and the light that comes by way of return upward is *Or Chozer*

---

[853] For example, in *Tanya* ch.48, Shneur Zalman writes:

> [S]ince the worlds are on the level of the bounded and finite, one finds that there is no revelation of the flow of light of the blessed *Eyn Sof* in them except only a tiny limited radiance/*he'arah*, very, very minute and contracted... But the essence of the light without such contraction is called encircling and encompassing / *makif v'sovev*... And the analogy for [understanding] this is this earth of materiality / *ha'arets haleizu hagashmiyut* (possibly: "this material earth / *ha'arets haleizu hagashmit*"): even though "the fullness of the whole earth is His glory" [Is 6:3] – and this means the light of *Eyn Sof* blessed be, as it is written: "Do I not fill the heavens and the earth? swears *Hashem*" [Je 23:24] – even so, [the glory/ *Eyn Sof*] does not clothe itself in her (the earth) in the manner of revealing the [divine] flow / *giluy hahashpa'ah*, but only [as] a limited, tiny [amount of] lifeforce/*chiyut*, at the level of silent/*domem* and growing/*tsomei'ach* [beings] alone. (254)

> See also ch.23, 100: "all the worlds upper and lower are as if they did not count before him, like nothing and emptiness really, to the point that that none of [the light of *Eyn Sof*] is really clothed in them; rather it encircles all the worlds... to give them life; only some (i.e., a small amount of) radiance (Schochet: 'glow') is clothed in them"; ch.51, 270: "[T]he lower ones, even the spiritual ones, do not receive [the light] on the level of revelation so much, [but] only through many garments... and the light or lifeforce is hidden in them..."; and ch.6, 24.

[854] *Tanya*, 590. Shneur Zalman, in the course of explaining that the souls of Israel are related to the Shekhinah as limbs of the body to the heart, says that the circulation of the blood is referred to as *Or Yashar* and *Or Chozer* in Lurianic writings. Here, *Or Chozer* emerges only at the level of the souls of Israel, not at the level of the earth. The analogy Shneur Zalman makes is that if any limb blocks the circulation/*sivuv* of blood, it will not return/*chozer* properly to the heart, and the whole body will sicken. Connecting the idea of completing the divine body of Shekhinah found here with the Talmudic saying that "Ben David will not come until the souls in the body are completed/finished" (TB *Y'vamot* 62a, 63b; *Avodah Zarah* 5a; *Nidah* 13b), a new meaning emerges: *Or Chozer* is the process that leads to the completion and redemption of the Shekhinah.

Or Chozer – *reflected light and the power of the Earth*

and it is judgment."[855] *Or Chozer* is connected with *"his'talqut ha'orot"*, the fleeing/removal of the lights, a highly negative dynamic within the process of emanation:

> When there is desire and strength in the lower ones and wholeness to be able to receive the supernal (upper) light of the One who emanates, then the upper lights yearn and desire to shine below, and in this manner they turn their faces below to the ones receiving, to go down to shine in them. They shine by way of "face to face". But when there is no wholeness in the lower ones, and the lights flee, they turn [their] faces toward the One who emanates, for their intention is to go up to there, and they turn/*mach'zirin* their backs upon the ones that receive below. And then the radiance that shines on the lower ones at that time is by way of their backs, and from their backs the lower ones receive the radiance that is necessary for them to remain living, and no more.[856]

Rivka Schatz Uffenheimer understands the Lurianic conception of *Or Chozer* "in terms of Divine contraction and the attempt of the light which remains within space to return specifically to its own essence. This is the 'reflected light', which is the carrier of the Attribute of Judgment, which is **the opposite of Creation** outside the Godhead."[857] According to Uffenheimer, the returning light symbolizes the reversal of creation.

In contrast, Shneur Zalman's description of *Or Chozer* as *Che̲sed chinam*, and as an echo of the original light of creation, has no hint of judgment. Rather, it is a full-throated expression of exuberant wonder.

Not all explanations of *Or Chozer* in Lurianic Kabbalah focus on the element of judgment, however. The following example offers a neutral conception of *Or Chozer*:

> The *s'firot* are [both] direct light / *Or Yashar* and *Or Chozer* and this [means]: when the *Eyn So̲f* emanated ten *s'firot* from above to below, which are *Keter* through *Malkhut*, and then returned, he (the light) illuminated again and emanated again ten other *s'firot* at the time of his returning to his source, from below to above: *Keter* in *Malkhut* and *Chokhmah* in *Y'so̲d*, etc., through *Malkhut* in *Keter*... And there is a distinction [between the two kinds of light], for *Or Yashar* is the essence of the light of pure emanation/*Atsilut*, like the appearance of the light of the sun that strikes upon a lantern/*ashashit* (thereby nullifying the light of the lantern). But *Or Chozer* is not similar to this, [but] only an extremely weak light, like the light of the sun that strikes [upon a thing] and is turned/reflected/*mit'hapeikh* from it.[858]

---

[855] *ECh* 1, *Heykhal* 1 6:5, 53. [856] Ibid., 6:7, 56–7. Cf. 6:6, 7:1.
[857] *Hasidism as Mysticism* (Jerusalem: The Magnes Press, 1993), 264, my emphasis.
[858] *ECh* 2, *Heykhal* 6 39:15, 156. In Shneur Zalman's writings one finds a similar parable. Explaining the soul's descent and return to God, he describes how "the light of the sun that falls on the earth strikes with power and returns and rises, from below to above, and therefore the lower air is hotter" (*Liqutey Torah* [Brooklyn NY: Kehot, 1973], *Shir Hashirim* 17c). He uses the same parable for *Or Chozer* in *V'etchanan* 10c. In both cases, however, heat below is a symbol of power.

The passage continues with a positive image of *Or Chozer*, equating it with the *mayin nuqvin* or feminine waters that flow at the beginning of intercourse and prepare the divine unification.[859] However, this still differs radically from Shneur Zalman's teaching, since *Or Chozer*, rather than being an intensification of light and a "mighty revelation", is only "an extremely weak light".

This last passage from `*Ets Chayyim* closely parallels descriptions of *Or Chozer* found in Moshe Cordovero, and its two halves are almost identical to two separate passages from *Sefer Pardes Harimonim*.[860] Cordovero does explain that the light returning from *Malkhut* has an aspect of the status of *Keter*. Nonetheless, while this seems to parallel the *Tanya*'s lifting up of the earth in *Igeret Haqodesh* 20, the remainder of the passage describes how *Or Chozer* is manifest at every single level of divine reality ("from *Keter* through *Binah* and from *Binah* to *Keter*; also from *Chokhmah* to *Binah* and from *Binah* to *Chokhmah*", etc.), producing an infinite series of reflections and interactions within and between the Sefirot.

Neither `*Ets Chayyim* nor the earlier Kabbalistic sources it drew on privileged the lowest manifestation of *Or Chozer* in *Malkhut*, nor was physical matter, `*afar*, represented as participating in this process.[861] In contrast, Shneur Zalman emphasized that *Or Chozer* is a manifestation of divinity in the earth and the "lowest" creatures, through which the body of Creation and of *Adam Qadmon* becomes complete. Unlike in Lurianic Kabbalah, where *Or Chozer* may be the opposite of *Or Yashar*, "straight" or direct light, in *Tanya*, *Or Chozer* is its fulfillment.

Though Shneur Zalman only cites Luria, with respect to both Luria and Cordovero, Shneur Zalman made theologically and ecologically significant leaps. In the aspect of *Or Chozer* being the lowest but the most intense manifestation of divine light, and in its being the one remnant of the light of pure *Chesed*, and in its beginning from the level of the *domem*, that is, the element of the physical earth, *Igeret Haqodesh* 20 radically revises the concept of returning/reflected light. The divine light becomes transfigured by Creation, which thereby generates its own redemptive energy, independent of human beings. This energy nurtures the whole chain of biological life, while the chain of life enables the light to complete its cycle and return to its source.[862]

---

[859] Cf. Sha`ar Haklalim 1. Tremendous thanks to Menachem Kallus for pointing out this trope to me here and in other texts.

[860] The passage found at 89b (quoted in Yosef Ben-Shlomo, *Torat Ha'elohut shel Rabi Moshe Qordovero* [Jerusalem: Bialik Institute, 1965], 273) includes the metaphor of the sun and the lantern; 91a (*Torat Ha'elohut*, 270) includes the first half of the teaching. Ben-Shlomo notes that the term *or mit'hapeikh* comes from Alkabets, who sees it as an aspect of judgment.

[861] Instead, `*afar* is used *symbolically* to refer to *Malkhut*; or, where `*afar* is described as having ontology, as for example in *Pardes Rimonim* 9:3, it is *ha`afar ha`elyon* ("supernal earth").

[862] *Or Chozer* is the reason why the higher creatures are nourished from those below: "And from this understand well the matter of the order of levels of silent, growing, moving and speaking, which are aspects of earth, water, fire, and air. For even though the moving (animal) is higher than the growing (plant), and the speaking (human) is higher than the moving, the moving

Or Chozer in Lubavitch *Chasidut* – other texts

We already noted that the presentation of *Or Chozer* elsewhere in *Tanya* is radically different from *Igeret Haqodesh* 20. Comparing this teaching with other passages in Lubavitcher *Chasidut*, and even in *Tanya* itself, there seem to be no clear precedents for Shneur Zalman's description of the manifestation of light in and by the earth itself. Other passages that talk about the illumination of the earth describe a human-centered process, initiated at the level of soul or thought, and encompassing the earth through the physicality of mitsvah, rather than starting from the physical level of the earth.

For example, the special role humanity plays in the dynamics of completing and restoring Creation is expressed in the following passage:

> [O]ne does not fulfill one's duty [to concentrate on Torah] by meditation and deliberation alone, until one expresses the words with his lips, in order to draw the light of *Eyn Sof*, blessed be, downwards to the vital soul / *nefesh hachiyonit* that dwells in human blood, which in its being is from the silent, growing, moving [creatures], in order to raise them all to *Hashem* along with the whole entire world, and to include them in His unity and His light that will illumine the land and the ones dwelling [on her]... For this is the purpose of the evolution/entwining/*hishtalsh'lut* of all the worlds, that the glory of *Hashem* fill all the earth.[863]

There are three dimensions to completion and rectification in this passage: drawing down, raising up, and unifying. Each is suggestive of an approach to environmental and Kabbalistic practice. However, while this passage emphasizes a particularly positive view of Creation, the source for light comes through human agency, in the mode of *Or Yashar*, not *Or Chozer*.

Similarly, "the Rabbis declared, 'Not learning but doing is the essential thing'... For 'this is the whole human' [Ec 12:13] and the purpose of his creation... in order to be for [God] a dwelling place among the lower ones / *dirah batachtonim* especially, to turn the darkness into light."[864] In this passage, the human being becomes, as it were, the lamp that lights Creation. In none of these passages do we find language comparable to *Igeret Haqodesh* 20.

Lastly, two passages in *Tanya* about the revelation of the light of *Eyn Sof* are clearly parallel to *Igeret Haqodesh* 20. The first describes the revelation of "this lowest world" in the time of the Messiah, when the light of *Eyn Sof* will be shining in the darkness "with so much uplifting and so much strength / *b'yeter s'eit v'yeter 'oz*".[865] The second describes the revelation in the Holy of Holies of the first Temple. There, Shneur Zalman says that the light of *Eyn Sof* (in this instance coming from the level of *Malkhut* of *Atsilut*, the highest world of emanation, as opposed to the *Malkhut* of *`Asiyah*, the lowest world[866]) dwelled

---

is nourished and lives from the growing and the speaking receives its lifeforce from both of them" (*Tanya*, 512).
[863] Ibid. ch.49, 262. [864] Ibid., ch.37, 178. [865] Ibid., ch.36, 166.
[866] According to this schema, each level or world has its own set of Sefirot.

within the *luchot* (the tables of the ten commandments) "with so much uplifting and so much strength, in a revelation great and mighty / *b'yeter s'eit v'yeter `oz b'giluy rav v`atsum*, more than the revelation of the palaces of the Holy of Holies above in the upper worlds"[867] – using language almost identical to how he describes the *Or Chozer* revealed in the earth. Both of these revelations, like the *Or Chozer*, come from the bottom up. But both are mediated by human beings, not by the earth.[868]

Even though the anthropology of the *Tanya* emphasizes our responsibility to the physical Creation, only in *Igeret Haqodesh* 20 are the lower or more "primitive" levels conceived as being able to manifest the divine light from their own essence. Shneur Zalman's teaching speaks about the extraordinary diversity and intensity of all life at all levels, while emphasizing most especially the "lowest" level, the transition from silent to growing, from rock or soil to living plant.[869] I conclude from this that the concept of *Or Chozer* in *Igeret Haqodesh* 20 is unique not only compared to the rest of Kabbalah, but even compared to the rest of Shneur Zalman's work. It seems no coincidence that this letter was the very last thing that Shneur Zalman wrote.

The essential aspect of *Or Chozer* in *Igeret Haqodesh* 20 is that the completion and perfection of Creation brought about by the returning light is effected through the agency of the earth itself, and not just through human agency. Human beings are primarily witnesses and beneficiaries of the returning light, and only secondarily agents for transmitting that light. What Shneur Zalman describes is a kind of ecosystem of divine energy, one that overturns hierarchies and affirms wholeness and complexity. The "*sovev kol `almin*" that encompasses all creatures and worlds enters through "the feet of *Adam Qadmon*" into the life of all creatures. As part of a "theo-ecology" (and not just an ecotheology), the concept of *Or Chozer* suggests a deep connection between ideas about God and ideas about ecosystems. As such, *Or Chozer*, as conceived by Shneur Zalman, provides a foundation for an ecological understanding of the dynamics of divine energy that could be part of any constructive theology based on Kabbalah.

---

[867] *Tanya*, ch.53, 278.

[868] Other works where Shneur Zalman discusses *Or Chozer* are also dissimilar from *Igeret Haqodesh* 20. Some passages clearly see *Or Chozer* as an expression of *Din* or Judgment, such as *Liqutey Torah, R'eih* 27d, *Chukat* 58c, *Drushim LiSh'mini `Atseret* 92b–c. Others do emphasize mercy or blessing, such as *V'etchanan* 10c, *Shir Hashirim* 19a, and in *Torah Or* (Brooklyn NY: Kehot, 1996), *B'rei'shit* 5a–b. *Liqutey Torah, Shir Hashirim* 16b even uses the metaphor of the growth of seeds. Nevertheless, even these positive images of *Or Chozer* describe the point of reflection as manifest only within the Sefirot or through human action. Immanuel Schochet graciously provided me with some of these citations, though in his opinion, "the Alter Rebbe consistently follows the Ari in regarding *Or Yashar* as *Chesed* and *Or Chozer* as *Din*" (personal communication, Aug. 2002).

[869] A true theology of Nature must also incorporate the fact that soil is very much alive, beyond what could have been imagined prior to discovery of the role of bacteria and mycelia.

Shneur Zalman's Kabbalah outlines two complementary perspectives from which we can imagine this divine ecology. We can contemplate the divine flow from the top down, so to speak, focusing on the descent of the letters from the holy names to the instantiation of each creature, following *Sha`ar Hayichud*'s interpretation of how the letters of divine speech combine to create reality, or we can contemplate the flow of divine energy through physical reality, from the bottom up, tracing the course of the *Or Chozer*, the light of creation that is manifest in the most basic element of earth, which is *Chesed chinam*.

Shneur Zalman suggests elsewhere that we participate in the flow of light directly through contemplation.[870] One of the primary ways we can act to strengthen this flow is by recognizing its presence and acting in a way that subtends and nurtures it. If this is our divine purpose, as Shneur Zalman states,[871] then it becomes one more aspect of what it means to be in God's image. Again, this provides one more path to the idea that being in the divine image means seeing the image reflected in the more-than-human world, specifically in the Earth itself.

---

[870] See *Tanya*, ch.41, 208, where Shneur Zalman describes how one should reflect on the light of *Eyn Sof* in order to drawn down this light into the material world whenever one uses a physical implement to do a mitsvah. See also ch.49, quoted p.263. Though both of these passages elaborate the normative framework of the rest of *Tanya*, rather than the perspective of *Igeret Haqodesh* 20, it is not unreasonable to extrapolate that human contemplation would also strengthen the flow of light upward. Cf. *Liqutey Torah, Shir Hashirim* 16b.

[871] *Tanya*, 212.

10

Gaia, *Adam Qadmon*, and Maimonides

> The body of this world is the Shekhinah below.
>
> *Tiquney Zohar*, §70

This chapter will examine resonances and parallels between the Gaia hypothesis, *Adam Qadmon*, and Maimonides' cosmology. All three conceptualize the world system – whether that be the cosmos or the spheres or the planet – as a kind of living individual. While the differences between these ideas are significant,[872] the affinities between them are extraordinarily powerful for ecotheology.

THE GAIA HYPOTHESIS AND ADAM QADMON

Ecotheologians have been deeply influenced by the scientific idea known as the "Gaia hypothesis" or "Gaia theory", which teaches that the Earth as a self-regulating system can be best understood by viewing it holistically as if it were a living organism.[873] For some ecofeminists, the idea of Gaia means that

---

[872] *Adam Qadmon* and Maimonides' theory concern the whole universe (and for Kabbalah, much more than the physical universe) rather than just the Earth and its relation to divinity. Conversely, the scientific understanding of Gaia is focused on the planet, and God or theism does not (and cannot) play any descriptive role.

[873] The Gaia hypothesis was first articulated by James Lovelock and Lynn Margulis in "Atmospheric Homeostasis By and For the Biosphere: The Gaia Hypothesis", *Tellus* 26:1 (1974): 2–10. See Lovelock, *Gaia: A New Look at Life on Earth* (Oxford: Oxford University Press, 1979). "Atmospheric homeostasis" refers to the fact that the oxygen component of the atmosphere that we live in and breathe is not simply intrinsic to the planet Earth, a precondition that allowed life as we know it to have evolved, as if by accident. Rather, the level of free oxygen is created and sustained by life itself (this is called "autopoiesis"). For this reason, one can regard the atmosphere, and the living things that create it, as organs of one whole living system, Earth. Lovelock came to this realization through his efforts to imagine what

the Earth is a spiritual being (and for neopagans, this may entail the mythic idea that the Earth is "the Goddess"); for others, like Creation theologians, it may be closely connected with the anthropic principle, which proposes that the universe is designed to evolve conscious beings. More conservative ecotheology applies the idea of Gaia in consonance with its scientific meaning, as a hermeneutic for understanding the Earth as a place that is alive and not just a place where life exists. (Except where noted, I am referring in this chapter to Gaia's scientific meaning.)

Gaia and *Adam Qadmon* comprehend the universe at different scales. *Adam Qadmon* includes the heavens, spheres, spiritual worlds, and Sefirot, along with the earth; for Kabbalists, the upper spiritual realms within *Adam Qadmon* are prioritized over the physical, and for most Kabbalists, the heavens are prioritized over the earth. For this reason, Shneur Zalman's unique understanding of *Or Chozer* and "the feet of *Adam Qadmon*", which brings back into view the primacy of the Earth and the land, is a critical element for relating *Adam Qadmon* to ecotheology and to Gaia. But the large-scale picture of a macroanthropic cosmos is also an essential step in the theological argument that Creation is in God's image, as we will see.

In applying the analogy between world and human being to a theology of Nature, the concatenation of these two ideas, of human as Earth, and of human as cosmos, is very rich, and the overlapping dimensions of person, planet, and universe resonate with the deep fractal structure of Creation. The life of Planet Earth is in fact part of the unfolding of the cosmos in its entirety, and the life of the whole universe is, as it were, made manifest through life on Earth. The Earth may be viewed as one of many planets and celestial bodies participating in a very large and unbelievably complex system that has engendered life (an *Adam Qadmon* perspective), or as the home and center of life, that is, as the mother of Life, *eim kol chai*, as we understand it (the spiritual Gaian perspective). Gaia then limns an idea about the force that makes for evolution and Life both on the Earth and in the cosmos, as well as being the personification of that force in the unique system of the Earth.

With this conceptual expansion of Gaia, and with the grounding of *Adam Qadmon*, we have two pictures of the universe, a mystical-scientific one (if one may call it that) and a mystical-Jewish one, which are in harmony with each other, even while they provide different information and different hermeneutics for comprehending reality.

> characteristics one would look for in a planet to know *if* it had life, while Margulis contributed her understanding of microbiology and symbiosis to Gaia theory to explain *how* life on the planet regulated Earth's atmosphere. Many other cycles upon which life depends similarly evolved through "biogenesis". For a wonderful and literary exposition of Gaia theory, see Eisenberg, *The Ecology of Eden*, ch.21, esp. 262–5, 274–7. For a useful introduction from a Jewish perspective, see Troster, "Created in the Image", 176–7. There, Troster also explores the idea that human consciousness is the expression of Gaia's "awakening", which may "lead us out of our childhood into the divine image that awaits us" (181).

GAIA AND MAIMONIDEAN COSMOLOGY

Kabbalah is just one basis for arriving at a Jewish conception of Gaia. In Kabbalah, the universe is a direct extension and manifestation of God. A very different but equally powerful way of seeing the universe holistically can be found in Maimonides, for whom Creation is a single being that stands in relation to its Creator.

Maimonides strongly emphasizes the idea that the universe is an organic whole: "Know that this whole of being is one individual and nothing else". The whole of Creation is "a single being which has the same status as Zayid or Omar", in other words, a person, endowed with a heart and a soul.[874] He sums up: "Accordingly, it behooves you to represent to yourself the whole of this sphere as one living individual in motion and possessing a soul," or (in another translation), "You must therefore consider the entire globe (universe) as one individual being endowed with life, motion, and a soul."[875] Maimonides claimed to know the universe in this manner through direct or empirical perception; looking at Maimonides' holism from a modern or postmodern perspective, it appears to be a hermeneutic that constitutes and organizes perception.

---

[874] MN 1:72, 184. The importance of this perspective for Maimonides' scientific and theological method is discussed in n.221. Josef Stern, *The Matter and Form of Maimonides' Guide* (Cambridge MA: Harvard University Press, 2013), reads this chapter as focused on divine governance and theodicy (ch.7, esp. 257–63). While this is certainly true, I think the identification of the Creation with the Creator, on both the ontological and the teleological level, is paramount.

[875] MN 1:72, 187. To my mind, Friedländer's translation (113–15) better conveys the intensity of this passage:

> Know that this universe, in its entirety, is nothing else but one individual being; that is to say, the outermost heavenly sphere, together with all included therein, is as regards individuality beyond all question a single being... The living being as such is one through the action of its heart, although some parts of the body are devoid of motion and sensation, as e.g., the bones, the cartilage, and similar parts. The same is the case with the entire universe; although it includes many beings without motion and without life, it is a single being living through the motion of the sphere, which may be compared to the heart of an animated being. You must therefore consider the entire globe (meaning, "universe") as one individual being endowed with life, motion, and a soul.

Maimonides also delineates the relationship between the parts of the body and parts of the world at great length (1:72, 186–90). Cf. Plato: "Therefore, we may consequently state that: this world is indeed a living being endowed with a soul and intelligence... a single visible living entity containing all other living entities, which by their nature are all related" (*Timaeus*, 30b–d). Note that this translation is widely dispersed on the Internet and in print without attribution. Here is Benjamin Jowett's translation:

> [T]he world became a living creature truly endowed with soul and intelligence by the providence of God... For the Deity... framed one visible living creature comprehending within itself all other animals of a kindred nature.
> (*The Dialogues of Plato* [London: Oxford University Press, 1892], 450ff.)

Gaia and Maimonidean cosmology

The unity of Creation is not only important in itself, it is also the way to know God's unity: "For this way of representing the matter to oneself is most necessary... for the demonstration that the deity is one... By means of this representation it will also be made clear that the One has created one being."[876] This wholeness is also wholly good, as Maimonides makes clear in his interpretation of Genesis 1:31: "About the whole, it says: '... it was very good.'"[877]

Maimonides uses the concept of ʽolam qaṯan to frame this belief in traditional terms:

Know that it is not because of all that we have mentioned (about organs and such) in comparing the world to a human individual that it has been said about humanity that [each person] is a small world. For this whole comparison can be consistently applied to every individual animal that has perfect limbs but you never hear that one of the ancients has said that an ass or a horse is a small world.[878] This has been said only about a human being. This is because of that which [belongs to humanity] only, namely, the rational faculty – I mean the intellect, which is the hylic intellect.[879]

Though Maimonides explicitly states that the thing that operates like the rational faculty in the world is "the deity"(see continuation of this passage, p.275), he imposes several restrictions on this analogy, all of which suggest that its proper referent is not most importantly the deity, but rather the outermost

---

[876] MN 1:72, 187. Cf. 2:1, 250 and 1:71, 183 (quoted p.72). Thus, perceiving the unity of Creation seems to provide positive knowledge about God's nature, in contradistinction to the apophatic (negative) theology that is considered Maimonides' hallmark. See also n.64.

[877] MN 3:13. See Introduction, p.15–16.

[878] See n.781. Maimonides' claim notwithstanding, in Hindu scriptures one finds exactly this analogy between a horse and the world: "Verily, the dawn is the head of the sacrificial horse; the sun his eye; the wind, his breath; universal fire..., his open mouth. The year is the body...; the sky, his back; the atmosphere, his belly; the earth, the under part of his belly... Sand is the food of his stomach; rivers are his entrails. His liver and lungs are the mountains; plants and trees, his hair... " (Brhadarnyaka Upanishad, Goodall 1:1, 41–2). This bears some relation to the locus classicus of ʽolam qaṯan, where the world is analogized not to a particular sacrifice, but to the place of sacrifice, the mishkan. See pp.202, 245.

[879] MN 1:72, 190. Ibn Ezra's interpretation of ʽolam qaṯan is congruent with Maimonides, though in his analysis the soul stands in the place of the intellect: "[T]he exalted human soul / nishmat ha'adam ha'elyonah that doesn't die is compared in her lifeforce to Hashem (God), and she has no body and she fills all of [the body], and the human body is like a small world / ʽolam qaṯan" (ad Gn 1:26). Shabtai Donnolo gives a similar explanation of ʽolam qaṯan in Sefer Chakhmoni (124–31). Yehudah Halevi's understanding is also parallel – Howard Kreisel even speculates that MN 1:72 could have been influenced by Halevi ("Judah Halevi's Influence on Maimonides: A Preliminary Appraisal", in Maimonidean Studies, ed. Arthur Hyman [New York: Yeshiva University, 1992], 95–122; 113–15). All three predate Maimonides, and the overt interpretation of the parable given by Maimonides is closer to what they taught. However, my claim is that Maimonides' understanding actually and substantively differed from this analogy, despite the fact that he found it to be a useful first approximation.

sphere, which he compares to the heart in a person.[880] Moreover, this analogy would imply that the world is God's body, but this is diametrically opposed to Maimonides' understanding that the universe is one whole individual that stands *in relationship* to God.

These principles had profound ethical implications for how Maimonides understood morality and meaning in the natural world. This holism entailed three propositions. The first is that "all the existent individuals of the human species... are things of no value at all in comparison with the whole [of Creation] that exists and endures".[881] Second, "all the beings have been intended for their own sakes and not for the sake of something else", nor "for the sake of the existence of man".[882] Third, holism is the foundation that enables us to know God's unity, because "the One has created [only] one being".[883] These propositions are clear, and they led Maimonides to reject the idea that humanity was the final end of Creation. A fourth consequence of this holism, I would argue, is that for Maimonides, the metaphysical distance between other animals and human beings was not great. This dovetailed with his belief that animals have feelings equal to what humans feel (see p.148).

In Maimonides' time, apprehending the living unity of the universe was one of the highest philosophical goals, completely consonant with metaphysics and physics. In modern times, *Wissenschaft*-influenced scholars (many coming from a rationalist *Torah u-Mada`* perspective) virtually ignore this element of his thought.[884] David Novak, one of the few who attends to it, argues that Maimonides' "cosmic teleology" is no longer relevant: "[W]ith the shift in

---

[880] These restrictions are three: (1) The proper target of this analogy does not profit from its governance over the body of Creation – this is a characteristic that Maimonides applies to the spheres as well as God. (2) Unlike the heart, which is at the center of the body, the "nobler part" of the world (that is, the outermost sphere) surrounds the other parts, because it is "secure against receiving an influence from what is other than itself" and therefore does not need to be protected. (3) The rational faculty, because it subsists in the body, is more like the intellects of the spheres (192–3; see n.296). For Stern's interpretation, see *Matter and Form*, 271–87. Maimonides also states that all the spheres have souls and apprehend God (1:72, 193; 2:5, 259–60; 2:7, 266, *contra* Stern, *Matter and Form*, 257–63).

[881] MN 3:12, 442. Maimonides adds, "and, all the more, those of the other species" (Schwartz: "other animals"). So a hierarchy of humanity over other species exists according to Maimonides. However, Maimonides subordinates the *significance* of humanity to the *existence* of the other species (see p.27ff.).

[882] MN 3:13, 452.   [883] MN 1:72, 187.

[884] *Torah u-Mada`* ("Torah and Science") is the motto of Yeshiva University, the flagship of modern Orthodoxy. Neither Dan Fink ("Between Dust and Divinity: Maimonides and Jewish Environmental Ethics" in Bernstein, 230–39), nor George Gittelman ("Maimonides and *The Guide to the Perplexed*: An Environmental Ethic for Our Time", *CCAR Journal* [Fall 2010]: 42–53) address this point, though Gittelman does mention Gaia in relation to MN 3:13 (48). Jeremy Benstein's *The Way Into Judaism and the Environment* (Woodstock VT: Jewish Lights, 2006) does briefly discuss Maimonides' position, describing it as biocentric and comparing it to the Gaia hypothesis (81–2). The only discussion on Maimonides from an environmental perspective prior to this book that fully incorporates MN 1:72 I am aware of is my article in *ERN* ("Maimonides", 1026–7), online at www.neohasid.org/torah/rambam (Jan. 2014).

scientific paradigms after Galileo and Newton, the earlier paradigm seems to be irretrievable. That is certainly so in astrophysics, where all Aristotelians have located the teleology *towards* which the human intelligences aspire."[885]

While Novak is right that the astrophysics underlying the motion of the spheres is "irretrievable" (in truth, an average eight-year-old has a clearer picture of the structure of the universe than the greatest astronomer of Maimonides' era), the shifts in science related to Gaia make the organicism and intelligence of the cosmos a "retrievable" and usable idea.[886] It is seeing the universe as whole and alive that makes sense again in our time, as opposed to any details or postulates of the ancient theories. From a neo-Maimonidean perspective, Gaia can be represented as a kind of super- or meta-intelligence that functions in a way similar to the spheres.

We should remain cognizant that, for Maimonides, the whole is the entire cosmos and not just the planet. Medieval Jewish philosophy drew on the idea of the macroanthropos in order to ground the Aristotelian idea of a living universe in the Jewish tradition, while leaving behind the midrashic idea of the Earth itself as the macroanthropos. This is not a problem for ecotheology, but rather a corrective to a naïve apprehension of Gaia that ignores the far greater dependence of this planet and all its creatures upon the generation of its elements through stellar evolution.[887]

GAIA AND TSELEM IN MIDRASH AND KABBALAH

While Maimonides spoke about the unique status of the cosmos as a living whole, there is a strong midrashic basis for attributing this status to the Earth as such. The many midrashic and Kabbalistic texts that view the Earth as an active subject participating in creation provide a foundation for seeing the Earth in Gaian terms, that is, as having the standing of a person. This perspective is

---

[885] *Natural Law in Judaism*, 165–6, Novak's emphasis. For a brief summary of Aristotelian cosmology, see Tamar Rudavsky, *Time Matters: Time, Creation, and Cosmology in Medieval Jewish Philosophy* (Albany NY: SUNY Press, 2000), 16ff. Maimonides' understanding of the teleology of the cosmos, of humanity, and of the spheres, differs somewhat from that found in standard Aristotelianism. On Maimonides' specific version of Aristotelian cosmology, see Rudavsky, 25ff., and *MN* 3:13, 449–50.

[886] This would be at least the second time in intellectual history that the idea of the universe as an organic living being has come back into relevance since Maimonides. It was also current in the Renaissance: Leone Ebreo (Yehudah Leon Abravanel, c.1465–c.1523, Portugal, Italy) wrote in *Dialoghi d'Amore*, "The entire universe is like an individual or person, and each of these corporeal and spiritual or eternal and corruptible things is a member or part of this great individual" (quoted in Hubert Dethier, "Love and Intellect in Leone Ebreo: The Joys and Pains of Human Passion: Reflections on his Critical Panpsychism and Theory of 'Extraordinary Reason'", in *Neoplatonism and Jewish Thought*, ed. Lenn Goodman [New York: SUNY Press, 1992], 359).

[887] See discussion p.60.

also strongly rooted in Torah, for example in Leviticus 25 and 26, where the land is treated as a kind of person with rights.[888]

An important midrash already quoted that takes this perspective, which I repeat here, teaches that the Earth (or earth/land) ran to do the will of God in creation:

She is called "*arets*" because she ran /*rats'tah*. A parable, to what does the thing compare? To a king that called to his retinue, and one ran and stood before him, and [so] the king made him ruler/*shilton*. So did the Holy One call to all that came into the world, and the *arets* ran and stood before him.[889]

The Earth here is a person or subject, a member of the divine court, and finally a ruler and co-creator with God – with all that implies.

The special status of the Earth in Midrash, and the idea that the first human was created specifically in the Earth's image, also imply on a homiletical level that the Earth reflects the divine images of cosmos and human. Though some contemporary Jewish thinkers might protest that such a description of the Earth is "pagan" rather than Judaic, this way of seeing the Earth is already well-established in Kabbalistic sources, as discussed already (p.215ff.).[890]

We also saw that Kabbalah represented the Earth as co-ruler with God in the creation of humanity. When God invited the earth, the heavens, and the waters to help make the human,

[T]he earth took up the power of [earth, heavens, and waters] by herself, until it was through her that the four elements were sustained... This is the meaning of "And YHVH Elohim formed the human, dirt/`*afar* from the ground/*adamah*"... Behold the two of them, the earth and the Holy One, that participated/partnered as one to make

---

[888] See further discussion pp.126–7, 166–7 and notes. Most importantly, the covenantal rights of the land to rest in the *Sh'mitah* or sabbatical year trump any human claims to God's protection or to possession of the land. Living in the "promised land" is not a right but a privilege, which can be revoked if humans refuse to submit themselves to the land's needs. Rashi's famous comment on Gn 1:1 that the Creation story proves God has the right and power to take the land from one people and give it to another is a double-edged sword.

[889] *ARNB* ch.43, 119, cited p.101.

[890] This is not to say that these sources conform to modern "neopagan" ideas. Neopagans often direct their worship of "the Goddess" toward the Earth, which ignores the coming into being of the heavens, as well as the coming into being of the substance of Earth inside the stars themselves. While some interpretations of neopaganism espouse a monistic conception of the Goddess that is more compatible with Judaism, the stars attest to a Creation far greater than what Gaia encompasses. In Jewish terms, when people equate Gaia and the Goddess, they ignore Isaiah's exhortation, "Lift up your eyes above and see. Come ask, Who created these?" [Is 40:26]. From a Jewish perspective, the Creator is not only greater than the Earth, but is necessarily greater than the whole of Creation (see discussion p.276).

[the human], and it was because of her (the earth) that He said "Let us make a human [in our image]", for the Holy One said to her: You make the body and I the soul.[891]

While this passage explicitly separates the Earth's contribution of the elements that constitute the body from God's contribution of the soul, the body too is known as an image of God, here and throughout most of Kabbalah.[892] The Earth can be known as the image of God through the same trope. By seeing God's image in the Earth, this passage runs contrary to ancient and medieval cosmologies in which the heavens were divinized because of their (apparent) eternality, while the Earth or sublunar sphere, subject to corruption and decay, was not divine and was of lesser value.[893]

From a theological perspective, our "microcosmic" relationship to both the Earth and the cosmos, as the children of the first *adam*, is fundamental. On both the deepest spiritual level and the level of straightforward science, the extraordinary diversity of the heavens reflects at different scales of time and space the extraordinary diversity of the Earth. To disconnect the two realms undermines an accurate conception of the unity of Creation, which is the hermeneutical foundation of modern science. This dualism, as much as any other idea about humanity or Creation, is a root of the ecological crisis.[894]

THE MEANING OF GAIA

Gaia, microcosm, and ecosystems

The Earth exists as a whole within the greater whole of the universe, an `olam qatan within an `olam gadol. So too does the human species exist as its own smaller world within the greater circle of the Earth. "Ecosystem" is similarly a concept that outlines a small world within a larger world. These gradations and levels of worlds allow `olam to be a term that is important for ecotheology as well, giving us another native category with which to speak about the fractal symmetry of Nature; that is, an individual ecosystem can be termed an `olam, and the many levels into which life is organized can be termed

---

[891] ZCh, Midrash Hane`elam 16b; WZ 779–80. The beginning of this passage is quoted on p.217.
[892] In the continuation of this passage, however, the opposite view is expressed – see p.277.
[893] This generalized picture does not reflect all the nuances of ancient philosophy. For example, in *On the Universe*, attributed to Aristotle, one reads:

> The universe is a system made up of heaven and earth and the natural things which are contained in them. But the word is also used in another sense of the ordering and arrangement of all things preserved by and through God. Of this universe, the center which is immovable and fixed is occupied by the life-bearing earth, the home and mother of diverse creatures.
> (II, 391b, trans. E. J. Forster, Barnes, vol.1, 627)

[894] Of course, Maimonides accepted this dualism, even though he asserted that the unity of Creation was the bedrock of theology. We are in a position to apply Maimonides' holism at an even deeper level of understanding and in a different way than he could have imagined.

"worlds/ `olamim"*, even while the entire Earth is one system, one `olam*. This interweaving of complexity and unity is reflected in the *borei' n'fashot* blessing after eating,[895] which extols God for creating a complex system of beings whose interactions weave the web of life:[896]

> Blessed be You YHVH our Elohim ruler of the world/ `olam who creates many souls (i.e., beings) / *borei' n'fashot rabot* and all of their lacks /*che̱sronan* (needs or deficiencies), for everything that You created, to give life through them to the being/soul of all (or: every) life / *l'hachayot bahem nefesh kol chai*. Blessed be the Life of the worlds / *barukh chey ha`olamim*.

In this blessing, all life gives life to all other life, through the process of *che̱sronan*, that is, not through meeting needs *per se* but through having them. God is not only "the Life" that creates and sustains this system; God may even be thought of as the essence or "substance" (in the Spinozan sense) of this system.

Gaia or World as the body of God

In this section, I want to explore the spiritual interpretation of Gaia. Sallie McFague's work *The Body of God* focuses on the philosophical and theological aspects of this idea in Christianity, especially as it relates to organicism, something that was explored earlier.[897] In popular theology, this idea often amounts to personifying the Earth and identifying with "her" as mother or (in neopaganism) as Goddess. The whole of Creation in this sense may be imagined as something akin to a divine body, and the Earth as the mother of all the creatures. Even this interpretation, though far from normative, is not entirely foreign to Judaism. In Jewish terms, Gaia in this sense translates as the Shekhinah, as for example in this passage from *Tiquney Zohar*:

> R' Eliezer said to him: Father, is it so above that they learned that there is no body/*guf* and no substance/*g'viyah?* He said to him: My son, about the coming world was it said, for that is an upper (i.e., purely immaterial) mother, but below there is the body of this world, which is the Shekhinah below.[898]

The Shekhinah in some sense represents Nature in this passage, but Shekhinah is a divinized Nature that is potentially free and self-willing through its integration with the worlds above it.

---

[895] This blessing is used for any non-specific foods, that is, any food that is not wine, bread, a grain product, or one of the seven archetypal fruits of the land of Israel.
[896] Though this might be viewed as a homiletical reading of the blessing, I think it is also closely related to its original meaning.
[897] (Minneapolis MN: Fortress, 1993). See esp. ch.1, as well as 151–7 and ch.6, for an exploration of Christian thought along these lines. Robert S. Corrington's very difficult but important work, *Nature and Spirit* (New York: Fordham University Press, 1992) explores these issues from a radically different perspective that has significant parallels to Lurianic Kabbalah.
[898] TZ 70, 131a, quoted in Giller, *Enlightened*, 95.

The Meaning of Gaia

The oft-cited *gematria* equating Elohim and Nature/*Hateva*̀ (the letters of both words numerologically add up to 86) is an important trope that is rooted in a deeper understanding of the relationship between these concepts. Ashkenazi wrote,

And just as there is in the human the power that ties together all the limbs end in/to end and preserves him... **which the doctors call Nature, and which we call Elohim**, so in the world there is a power that will tie it together end in/to end, and will preserve the *ishim* (i.e., people) and the [many] species.[899]

This passage does not fall back on the more normative analogy that God is to the universe as the soul is to the body. Rather, God is like a force within the body of the universe that unifies and sustains it. There is a tension within Jewish mysticism, present in this passage, between understanding Nature at some level to be willing and creative (similar to what Spinoza called "Nature naturing / *Natura naturans*"), and rejecting the idea of Nature altogether by interpreting every change as something expressly created through the divine will.[900]

There is no need here to delve into these tensions; it is enough to show that a number of important and diverse perspectives exist. The last example I will touch upon is the explanation Maimonides gives for the epithet from Daniel 12:7 that God is the "Life of the world":

[T]here exists in being something that rules it as a whole and puts into motion its principal part... [I]t is in virtue of this thing that the existence of the sphere and of every part endured. This thing is the deity, may its name be exalted. It is only with a view to this that it is said specifically about a human being that he is a small world, inasmuch as there subsists in him a certain principle (the intellect) that governs the whole of him. And because of this, *Hashem*, may he be exalted, is called in our language the life (lifeforce) of the world / *chiyut ha`olam*.[901]

Just as the intellect governs the whole of the body, God governs the world, and so the world is, as it were, the body of God. Though this was not Maimonides'

---

[899] Ashkenazi, 131, 35b. Ashkenazi is very nearly quoting Maimonides, but Maimonides stops short of equating this power (translated as "force" in Pines) with God (*MN* 1:72, 187–8). Maimonides does identify the forces of Nature with the angels in 2:6. (263–4). However, only those forces that derive from the spheres and intellects "apprehend their acts" (2:7, 266). Of course, that would include the unifying force of all the cosmos, whose source is the highest sphere.

[900] See n.65.

[901] *MN* 1:72, 191–2; Kafich, 141. Maimonides cites Da 12:7. See also 1:69, 169, Kafich, 131, where Maimonides says that "God has... with reference to the world, the status of a form with regard to a thing possessing a form... He is that upon which the existence and stability of every form in the world ultimately reposes and by which they are constituted... Because of this notion, God is called in our language the *Living of the Worlds / Chey Ha`olamim*". See Stern, *Matter and Form*, 288.

final position,[902] it was the position of a number of Jewish thinkers before him.[903]

The image of the world as God's body may fill the hearts of Nature lovers and ecotheologians with joy, but if we take it as a metaphysical truth, rather than as one of many images of Creation, it presents certain challenges. If Judaism is to preserve a sense of relationship to God as Creator, which one can argue is essential to Jewish belief, then it must imagine a God that is more than Creation (panentheism, rather than pantheism).[904] Maimonides recognizes this problem, explaining that while he drew on the rational intellect as a parable for God, the rational intellect is bounded by the body, but God is not bounded by the universe.[905] From a modern religious perspective, it makes more sense to use the metaphor of the body–soul relation, where the soul is thought of as not being contained within the body; similarly, the created order, even if fully invested by God, cannot contain God.

A further metaphor related to the world as God's body is the idea of the world as God's child. One finds this metaphor in Lurianic Kabbalah, which uses terms like embryo/`ubar*, gestation/`ibur*, birth/*leydah*, suckling/*y'niqah*, and *qaṯnut* and *gadlut*, which can mean smallness and largeness, or childhood and adulthood. The primary image of the process of creation is *tsimtsum* or contraction, which is an exact analogue to labor contractions.[906] Scholem relates

---

[902] See pp.269–70.
[903] See n.879. Incidentally, Leibniz criticizes as a category mistake the idea that the world is a unified body. He explains,

> What can be said of a creature or a particular substance, which can always be surpassed by another, is not to be applied to the universe, which, since it must extend through all future eternity, is an infinity... That is just what serves to confute those who make of the world a God, or who think of God as the Soul of the world; for the world or the universe cannot be regarded as an animal or a substance.
>
> (*Theodicy*, trans. E. M. Huggard [La Salle IL: Open Court, 1985], 249)

In other words, a body must exist in relation to other bodies, with respect to which it becomes delimited, but the world has no other "body" in relation to which it can be delimited.

[904] This is a fundamental point of divergence between any Jewish theology of Nature and Spinoza. Note, however, Shlomo Maimon's evaluation of Kabbalah: "[T]he Kabbalah is nothing but an expanded form of Spinozism, in which not only is the origin of the world explained by the limitation of the divine being, but also the origin of every kind of being and its relation to the rest, are derived from a separate attribute of God" (quoted in Idel, *Hasidism: Between Ecstasy and Magic* [Albany NY: SUNY Press, 1995], 40).

[905] Maimonides also says that the acquired intellect (that which contemplates God) would be a more accurate metaphor for God, because it is not bounded by the body, but is rather the consequence of divine overflow. However, he states, using this metaphor would create other confusions (*MN* 1:72, 193).

[906] That is to say, God contracts away from a central point in order to create a space within which the world can be born, the way the cervix contracts away from itself in order to create space through which a baby can be born. Unlike birth, creation unfolds within this empty space: God penetrates the space with a ray of light, causing the emanation of the vessels of light that create the world. The first image is female, the second male; the union of the two conflates conception and birth. Note the world is born into this space which encloses the whole of Being,

a different aspect of Lurianic cosmogony to birth: "the *Zohar*'s organological imagery is developed to its logical conclusion: the *Shevirah* [sic] (breaking of the Vessels) is compared to the 'breakthrough' of birth..."[907] He adds that God is, as it were, giving birth to God's self:

> The origin of Zeir Anpin [sic] in the womb of the "celestial mother," his birth and development, as well as the laws in accordance with which all the "upper" potencies are organized in him, form the subject of detailed exposition... Luria is driven to something very much like a mythos of God giving birth to Himself; indeed, this seems to me to be the focal point of this whole... description.[908]

This birth is not the birth of what we generally think of as the world, that is, the physical universe, though it is sometimes taken that way by people who reinterpret Lurianic Kabbalah (including some Hasidic thinkers). It is rather the birth of the world system, of which our physical world is a very small, though sustained, part. Whether this image provides a useful metaphor for contemporary ecotheology is a question to return to in future work.

GNOSTIC ELEMENTS IN KABBALAH – ANTI-GAIA

Many Kabbalistic systems, especially those rooted in Luria's teachings, emphasize that the cosmic body of *Adam Qadmon* was shattered or diminished through the sin or imperfection of Creation itself. The cosmos that is fully in God's image is the world as it existed before the first word of the Torah's creation story. In that primeval state, *Adam Qadmon* was the cosmos itself. The *sh'virah* or breaking that occurred in the process of creating the universe also broke the identity of cosmos and Adam.

Since the human of the Genesis story is born into an already shattered universe, this perspective leads to a different understanding of the image of God in Creation. For some Kabbalists, this shattering ultimately produced a physical earth that was removed from the divine pattern, so that the connection between God's image and the Earth, as well as between God's image and the body, was radically attenuated. In a passage from *Midrash Hane`elam* already quoted (p.183), one reads, "what is [Adam's] defect? That there was the body, and it was taken from the earth."[909] Another example, from *Ra`ya Mehemna*,

---

rather than from out of it. Midrash also hints at God birthing the world. See n.789, and see Raquel S. Kosovske, "The Sacred Placenta in Rabbinic Literature and Consciousness: Towards a Jewish, Feminist Placenta-inspired Theology" (thesis, HUC-JIR, 2007), 82–3, 120–21.

[907] MTJM 267. He explains this breakthrough as "the deepest convulsion of the organism which... is also accompanied by the externalization of waste products. In this manner, the mystical 'death of the primordial kings' is transformed into... a mystical 'birth' of the pure new vessels." The "death of the kings" means *Sh'virat Hakeilim*, the breaking of the primordial vessels. See Appendix. Scholem here cites Vital, *Sefer Haliqutim*, 21b.

[908] MTJM 271. Perhaps it would be appropriate for Scholem to refer to God as "Herself" here.

[909] ZCh 16c. This perspective of R' Abahu contradicts R' Elazar's (though of course they are both views of the authors). See pp.217, 272. For other examples, see Tishby, WZ 681, 683.

reads, "*Adam Qadmon*, even though his body is made from dirt/`afar, it's not from the dirt here...*Adam Qadmon* has nothing from this world at all."[910] This path of interpretation could be characterized as the "two earths" theory, where the element from which the primordial human is created is entirely derived from the "anti-physical" (or "ante-physical") earth.[911]

These texts represent a strong vein within Zoharic literature, even though many passages from the same corpus present the opposite perspective. They also represent a break with *Sefer Bahir*.[912] Such dualistic texts may be seen

---

[910] *Zohar* 3:83a. Cf. *ECh* 2, *Heykhal* 5 26:1, quoted n.593.

[911] The theme of two earths is alien to classical midrash but similar to Gnostic motifs related to the primordial human. The division between *Adam Qadmon* and human beings, and hence rejection of the physical earth, tends to be much deeper in Gnosticism than even in the most dualistic texts of the Kabbalah. See Urbach's discussion in *The Sages*, 227–31. On Lurianic Kabbalah and Gnosticism, see Lawrence Fine, *Physician of the Soul, Healer of the Cosmos: Isaac Luria and His Kabbalistic Fellowship* (Stanford CA: Stanford University Press, 2003), 144–9.

[912] The following passages are typical of the *Bahir*:

> §23 R' R'chumai said: From your word we learn that the Holy One created the need of this world before the heavens. He said to him: Thus so. §24 R' Yanai said: The earth was created before the heavens, as it says, "[in the day of YHVH Elohim's making] earth and heavens" [Gn 2:4]. They said to him: But isn't it written, "[Elohim created] the heavens (first) and the earth"? He said to them: To what does the thing compare? To a king who took possession of a beautiful, precious thing, and it wasn't complete...He said, "I will complete it...and then I will call out its name over it..." §31 R' Amorai said: *Gan Eden*, where is it? He said to them: In the earth.

The earth is "beautiful, precious". In the broadest sense (according to which the process of creation is divided up into only two or three acts, that is, heavens and earth, or, waters, heavens, and land), the earth is "first in thought, last in deed", just as Shabbat and Adam are described in other *midrashim*. §31 moreover pointedly contradicts a more dualistic cosmology in which *Gan Eden* is somewhere else besides the earth. (On §24 and the idea of naming, see pp.236–7.)

Scholem, and other scholars who follow his lead, read the Kabbalistic tradition as a Gnostic phenomenon (*Origins of the Kabbalah* [Philadelphia: JPS, 1987], esp. 69–105). This claim has not been proven in terms of direct historical influence, however, and scholars such as Moshe Idel (*Hasidism*, 7–8 and 254, n.33; *Kabbalah: New Perspectives*, 30–32) and Joseph Dan (*The Ancient Jewish Mysticism* [Tel Aviv: MOD Books, 1993], 42–62) have raised serious questions about it. (David Biale also notes that Scholem's definition of Gnosticism was highly variable [Gershom Scholem: Kabbalah and Counter History, 52].) The *Bahir* in particular, which according to Scholem was the Gnostic seed around which Kabbalah crystallized, must be seen as anti-Gnostic. In fact, where one can compare parallels between the *Bahir*, the *Zohar*, and the extant Gnostic writings, only the *Zohar* shows any literary similarity with Gnosticism. On the other hand, a consciously anti-Gnostic tendency is part of the origins of Kabbalah, and can be traced from the *Bahir* to Cordovero to Hasidism. To the extent that we can trace Gnostic tendencies in Kabbalah, these tendencies *increase* with time, from the *Zohar* to Lurianic Kabbalah to the antinomian schools of Shabtai Tsvi and then Yaakov (Jacob) Frank, becoming at the extreme sectarian and isolated from the main evolutionary stream of Kabbalistic literature.

as contradictory to the ecotheology outlined here. However, they may also simply be seen as alternative voices that stand in tension with this theology. Despite the separation of the physical earth from the "earth" of creation, this earth remains an image of the metaphysical earth, just as the physical human remains an image of God and an image of the primordial human. The pattern of the cosmic human has not disappeared entirely. Rather, it has left its traces in the earthly human, as well as in other aspects and dimensions of Creation.

The tension that exists within Kabbalah can help us to remain open to diverse ways of seeing the human place in Creation, even those that do not fit in with our political and spiritual ideologies. A theology that extends *tselem Elohim* beyond the human is not the only interpretation of the tradition; rather, it is a valid and enriching one. The choice between one or another interpretation is guided both by the internal hermeneutic of how we read the traditional texts, and the external hermeneutic of how we relate to the world.[913]

A dualistic cosmology, while less connected to Nature, can still be empowering for an ecological Judaism. Lawrence Fine, discussing dualism in Luria, explains:

On the one hand, [Luria's] cosmogonic teachings exhibit an anticosmic dualism in which the material world is deprecated in favor of a divine one... Nevertheless, these views did not translate into an utter devaluation of the natural world. On the contrary, the natural world for Luria was a means by which to encounter the divine.[914]

Moreover, the connection between the cosmic human and the earthly human remains. Since our bodies have the potential to express the divine pattern in its completeness, our physical actions can bring *tiqun*, the repair of the breaking of Creation that occurred at its origin.

INTEGRATING THE COSMOS

Whether one is looking at the more dualistic face of Kabbalah or the more holistic one, the purpose of human endeavor is to bring *tiqun* to the cosmos. Either the universe is already the most magnificent image of God we can know, and our human task is to cause that truth to be revealed, or it is the work of redemption to reconstruct the universe so that it once again becomes the fullest image of God. From Maimonides' perspective, too, the universe as a whole is the greatest being, the one being that most reveals God. There may be no other area of Jewish thought where one can so deeply unify Maimonides and Kabbalah.

---

[913] These hermeneutics also determine and depend upon our relationship to God, which is both internal and external.
[914] *Physician of the Soul*, 356.

Not only is this a spiritually meaningful way of seeing the universe. Gaia theory also teaches us that it is a scientifically significant one. As we come to appreciate in more and more ways how Life itself creates the possibility of Life, and how the emergent properties of the universe and the emergent properties of Life are one and the same, we come closer to seeing the living unity of Creation. And as we do, from a theistic perspective, we also come closer to reconstructing and revealing the image of God in Creation.

11

Qomah
The stature of all beings

THEOLOGICAL TERMS

In Chapters 9 and 10, we encountered many ways that Creation or the Earth as wholes could be understood to be in the divine image. There are also many texts discussed in earlier chapters through which one can behold the idea that particular animals or species are imbued with the divine image. Kabbalah, more than Midrash, broadly sees God's image embodied in kinds of species or categories, like birds or fruit trees. But is there a vantage point from which to discern God's image in every species or living being, one that would stand halfway between specific cases that embody the image, and the expansive idea that the whole of Creation is God's image? Can we develop a broad metaphysical framework that would help us to find or elicit or subtend the *tselem* in any living being, a kind of *tselem in potentia*?

The frameworks we have already examined cannot quite accomplish this, for varied reasons. For example, the idea of *sheimot*, the divine letters and names embedded in every existent thing and creature, implies that anything that can be named, from an ancient redwood to an iPod to a toxic waste dump, must result from the declension of these names, which are the sustenance and even the essence of each thing. However, we want to be able to distinguish between organic, living wholes on the one hand, and on the other, artifacts of human culture, as well as the broken-down ecosystems damaged by human consumption and waste (which in some sense also become human artifacts).

The idea of *Or Chozer* is also insufficient. Even though it provides an extraordinary valorization of the infinity and diversity of the Earth and the flora it grows, and even though it could readily be applied to the fertility of the ground and the species in a specific place or ecosystem, it has nothing to say about the "smaller infinity" that constitutes the being of each individual creature or species.⁹¹⁵ The midrashic idea of `olam malei' or `olam qatan, a full, complete world or microcosm, which was applied only to human beings, could also be used *constructively* for this purpose, but its history and the trajectory of its evolution do not point in this direction.

And so for Jewish ecotheology, we still need a vocabulary that lifts up the complexity and meaning of individual beings and aggregates embedded in greater systems. Since the Sefirot already represent the structure of Being at every level, from the entirety of the universe to the most infinitesimal, finding a vocabulary that builds upon that framework is a desideratum. Such a vocabulary would also correlate with ideas of complexity and fractal symmetry or self-similiarity, which are concepts that science uses to make distinctions between Life and mere chemistry, or between healthy ecosystems and endangered or damaged ones.⁹¹⁶

In the bulk of this chapter, I will trace the evolution in Midrash and Kabbalah of a concept of structure and wholeness, rooted in the term *qomah*, that can serve this exact purpose. The terminology of *qomah* shows a meaningful development that goes back to the *Tanakh* (Hebrew Bible) and forward through all of Jewish intellectual history. The trajectory of its development also points toward the ecological meaning I am seeking, specifically in the terminology *qomah sh'leymah*, which developed in later Kabbalah and *Chasidut*.⁹¹⁷ (See pp.292, 296ff.) I will also examine other candidate terms that can mean God's image *in potentia*, as well as one more term, *golem*, that means the opposite: the appearance of wholeness without real wholeness and without God's image. The discussion will turn to the broader theme of the Sefirot and self-similarity at the chapter's end.

THE HISTORY OF QOMAH

Qomah in *Tanakh* can refer to height as a dimension of measurement (e.g. Gn 6:15, Ex 27:18), or to the stature of a living creature, whether human (e.g., 1Sa 16:7 and 28:20), or plant, as in the parable of Ezekiel: "Here, Ashur (Assyria) is a cedar in the Levanon, beautiful of branch...and of highest *qomah*...Cedars of the garden of God did not mob/obscure it" [Ez 31:3–8].⁹¹⁸ *Qomah* signifies more than physical height in this passage;

---

⁹¹⁵ Another useful valorization of ecosystem and land, with similar limitations, is found in Nachman of Breslov – see p.331.

⁹¹⁶ These and related concepts such as systems theory are what make ecology more than just natural history and the classification of species.

⁹¹⁷ I am seeking with this terminology to recreate what *poskim* do with halakhic precedent when applying Jewish law to new or untested situations. The reason for focusing on terminology, rather than ideas, is because that is the unit of evolution in Jewish tradition. New ideas are compounded out of a relatively constant formulary. Conserving theological terminology allows radical change to take place within a stable framework, which maintains cultural continuity "all the way back to Sinai". See n.750 and *Methods*.

⁹¹⁸ Eight of eleven instances in *Tanakh* where *qomah* means something other than physical measurement are found in Ezekiel, four in this chapter.

it is also a metaphor for being distinctive. Similarly, "This *qomah* of yours / *zot qomateikh* is likened to a date palm" [So 7:8] indicates the special beauty of a lover's posture or body.

Qomah also refers to the first human's height in traditions about the gigantic size of *Adam Harishon*. *B'rei'shit Rabbah* states that seven things were taken away from *Adam Harishon* after he ate from the tree of knowing, including among them "his brilliance, his life, and his stature / *zivo v'chayyav v'qomato*".[919] The *Avot d'Rabi Natan* version of the tradition that humans stand like angels also uses the term *qomah*: "The sages said: Six things were said about the children of Adam... They walk with erect posture / *b'qomah z'qufah* like the ministering angels."[920] Both these tropes are connected with *tselem*.[921]

In *Midrash Otiyot d'Rabi Aqiva A*, the term *qomah* is applied to the lower creatures in order to contrast them with the upper ones:

> *Samekh* [stands for] the One who supports/*someikh*... supporting the upper ones and supporting the lower ones... as it is said, "supporting the fallen" and there are no fallen except the lower ones that are brought low /*mashpilin* because of their *qomah* that is made low /*nimeikh* in this world.[922]

Here the midrash explains the difference between the *qomah* of the creatures and the *qomah* of Adam or *Adam Harishon*. The significance of this separation for the author is not that the lower ones are disconnected from God; on the contrary, it means that God makes a special effort, as it were, to connect to them and support them.

The Midrash and Talmud broadened the idea of *qomah* in another way as well, to mean a creature developed to its adult shape or fullest potential. In this use, *qomah* includes all the creatures equally. The *Bavli* teaches: "Said R' Yehoshua ben Levi: All the work[s] of creation / *ma`aseh v'rei'shit*, in/with their *qomah* /*b'qomatam* they were created, with their knowledge /*b'da`atam* they were created, with their desire (or: pattern, design) /*b'tsivyonam* they were created, as it is said, 'And they were completed, the heavens and the earth and all their hosts/*ts'va'am*' [Gn 2:1]—don't read *ts'va'am* but *tsivyonam*."[923]

---

[919] BR 12:6.   [920] ARNA ch.37, quoted p.58.

[921] In Talmudic sources, *qomah* also means posture or an individual person's way of standing, that is, one can walk "*b'qomah z'qufah*", with erect posture, or "*b'qomah k'fufah*", with bent posture. See, e.g., TB B'rakhot 43b: "One who walks with erect posture / *b'qomah z'qufah* even four cubits, it is as if he pushed away the feet of the Shekhinah, as it says: 'The fullness of the whole earth is His glory' [Is 6:3]."

[922] BM, vol.2, 383. This text refers to both meanings of *qomah* in early midrash – *qomah* as a person's stature, and *qomah* as the metaphysical height of each creature.

[923] Chulin 60a, also Rosh Hashanah 11a. Jastrow translates: "All the works (animals) of creation were created in their full-grown stature, with their consent, with their pleasure (in their mission...)" (s.v. *tsivyon*, 1258, Jastrow's parens.). His gloss of "animals" for "work/*ma`aseh*" fits the *Chulin* passage, where the rabbis are explaining how a full-grown bull with horns could have been found by Adam. However, *ma`aseh* or *ma`asim* ("work/works") may also

B'qomah here means full-grown or mature, so that everything was created at the peak of its growth. The *B'midbar Rabbah* version explains more fully that God "created His creatures complete/*sh'leimim . . . b'qomatam* they were created".[924] According to some commentaries, the phrase *b'da`atam* also means that the creatures came into being by their own consent and in their own chosen raiment.[925] Rashi similarly explains *b'tsivyonam* to mean "in the likeness/*d'mut* that they chose for them[selves]".[926]

For the remainder of the chapter I will focus on the evolution of the association between *qomah* and *tselem*. In the *Hoshana Rabbah* prayers for Sukkot, the connection between *qomah* and the image is already made. The phrase "*Hosha` na' ziv v'to'ar v'qomah* – Please save brilliance and form and stature" is given as a parallel to "*Hosha` na' d'mut v'tselem v'riqmah* – Please save likeness and image and weave".[927] *Qomah* could mean several things in this

---

refer specifically to plants, as it does in the parallel text in *Rosh Hashanah*. There, *l'qomatam* is understood to mean that the trees were created mature and full of fruit (and that therefore creation happened in the harvest month of Tishrei – cf. *P'ri `Ets Hadar*, quoted further on). Even on the same page of *Chulin*, the verse "YHVH rejoices in His works / *b'ma`asav*" [Ps 104:31] is recited in wonderment by "*Sar Ha`olam*", the (angelic) minister of the world, when the grasses emerge "by their species / *l'mineyhu*", even though they have not been commanded to do so. Thus, interpreting the term "works" more narrowly to mean only animals, like interpreting *b'riyot* (creatures) more narrowly to mean human beings, is inaccurate and can sometimes impose modernity's myopia on the universe of God's concern.

[924] 12:8. "*B'qomatan*" parallels two other phrases here: the sun and moon were created "at their fullness / `*al m'li'atan*", and the first humans were created "as twenty-year-olds". Cf. *BR* 14:7, which does not use *qomah*. The same meaning is found in Rashi *ad* Gn 4:24, paraphrasing Lamekh's speech: "Have I killed Hevel, who was a full-grown man / *ish b'qomah*?"

[925] See n.934. Generally speaking, *Chazal* assume that every creature has a kind of "soul" consciousness antedating its creation, and the heavens and the earth, all the more so, have consciousness and will. The desire of the other creatures to be incarnated contrasts sharply with *midrashim* about human beings' desire to stay in the pre-material world. *Tanch* (possibly elaborating on *Mishnah Avot* 4:22, "against your will / `*al korch'kha* were you formed") imagines the following conversation between the Holy One and a human soul about to be conceived. God says,

Enter this drop [of semen] . . . The *ru'ach* opens his mouth and says: Master of the world, the world that I have been living in from the day you created me is enough for me . . . The Holy One immediately says to the *n'shamah* (note change in terminology from *ru'ach* to *n'shamah* as the soul prepares to enter the body – see Excursus 1): The world I am making you enter is better for you than the one you've lived in, and in the moment that I formed you, you were formed only for this drop. Immediately the Holy One makes him enter there by force / *l'shem b`al korcho*. (*P'qudey* 3)

On the basis of these *midrashim*, one could say that humanity's uniqueness is that we, of all the creatures, do not have free will in choosing this form and this life!

[926] *Chulin* 60a, *s.v. l'tsivyonam*. Jastrow (*s.v. tsivyon*, 1258) adds his own gloss on Rashi's comment: "according to the shape of their own choice".

[927] From the fifth *haqafah* or cycle of the *Hosha`not* in the Ashkenazi *nusach*, which begins "*Adam uv'heimah*" ("Human and beast"), found for example in *Siddur Sim Shalom*, 541. The phrase "*ziv v'to'ar v'qomah*" parallels *BR* 12:6, which describes Adam in terms of "*zivo v'chayyav v'qomato*". See p.303 on *to'ar*. The prayer reads,

densely poetic passage, including *qiyumah*, which means both existence and sustenance, as well as the upright one, or humanity. For our purposes, what is important about this passage is that *qomah* is equated with *tselem*, even if the connection is poetic rather than theological.[928]

In the esoteric tradition, dating back at least to *Shi'ur Qomah*, the term *qomah* is used in a radically different way. It refers to the configuration of God's body, and specifically the measurements of God's body, which were the object of meditative experience (see p.205). *Sefer Bahir* also talks about "seventy *qomot*", which means something like angelic forces, represented by the seventy date trees at *Elim*, each one unique.[929] The range of meaning for *qomah* expanded radically as the Kabbalah began applying the terminology and concept of *shi`ur qomah* to the Sefirot, the "mystical shape of the Godhead", to use Scholem's phrase.

One can see *qomah* used in this way in *Peyrush L'Shir Hashirim* ("Commentary to the Song of Songs"), composed in the early thirteenth century.[930] Quoting the *Bavli* passage, the author explains that the *midot*, which are the Sefirot, were made whole and complete in their *qomah* on "the sixth day".[931]

And this is "and the heavens and the earth and all their hosts were completed"— the measures/*midot* were whole and were made complete vessels / *keilim sh'leymim* in their *qomah* and in their structure and in their design / *b'qomatan uv'tavnitam uv'tsivyonam*.[932]

> Please save human and beast! Please save flesh and spirit-wind/*ru'ach* and breath-soul/*n'shamah*! Please save sinew and bone and skin-covering/*qormah*! (Some versions read *qomah*.) Please save likeness and image and weave! Please save majesty, "compared to empty breath" [Ps 144:4]; and likened as the beasts to be silenced/*nidmah* (mortal)! (after Ps 49:21) Please save brilliance and form and stature! Please save, renew the face of the ground! Please save the planting of trees where desolate/breathing/*n'shamah* (depending on whether the root would be ShMM or NShM)... Please save undergrowth to strengthen her..., flowers to uphold her! Please save she who drinks (i.e., the Earth) – Exalt her!... Please save what is suspended upon nothingness/*b'limah* (lit. "without-what", meaning Earth; cf. Jb 26:7)! Please save!

> The prayer connects physical and spiritual, the realms of human, animals, and plants. The final salvation is for the Earth itself. On *ru'ach* and *n'shamah*, see Excursus 1.

[928] The other terms found here (*to'ar, riqmah*) may be poetic synonyms for God's image, and each one could be used to develop a terminology for talking about extending God's image beyond humanity. *Qomah*, however, is the most significant term because of how it evolved within Kabbalah and *Chasidut*.

[929] §§166-7, citing as a prooftext So 7:8: "This *qomah* of yours is likened to a date palm".

[930] This work, traditionally ascribed to Ramban, was written by either Ezra ben Shlomo of Gerona (d. c.1245) or Azriel ben Menachem of Gerona (1180-1238) (*Kitvey Ramban*, 474-5).

[931] In the Kabbalistic context, this does not refer to the physical days of creation, but rather to the stages of divine emanation before creation. The six Sefirot from *Chesed* to *Y'sod*, once complete, are able to manifest the "seventh day", the seventh of the lower Sefirot, *Malkhut* or *Shekhinah*, which completes the entire central column (see Appendix).

[932] *Kitvey Ramban*, 511. *Tavnitam* has been substituted for *da`atam*. *Tavnit* is another term for *tselem* (see pp.301-2). Brody's translation of this passage can be found in "Human Hands", 128.

The Sefirot, perfected at the beginning of creation, are necessary to allow the physical Creation to come into being. The completed Sefirot are unified in a single structure:

"In the crown that his mother crowned him" [So 3:11]—[this means] that the whole structure/*binyan* would cleave [together] and it becomes unified (in Keter) and raised up unto *Eyn Sof* (i.e., beyond *Keter*, the crown and beginning of emanation), and there is no gap/*siluq* of holy spirit there.[933]

This unification can happen only when the vessels become "complete in their *qomah*".

Yosef Gikatilla uses *qomah* in *Sha`arey Orah* as a stand-in for Shekhinah in the phrase "*qomat hamerkavah* / the stature/form of the chariot" (using So 7:8 as his prooftext).[934] The term *qomah* was also used by Yosef Ashkenazi in a description of *Keter* quoted by Moshe Idel: "He is emanated without time delay (i.e., instantaneously, as well as beyond time) from the cause of causes, the shadow from the *qomah* (Idel: standing form), and like the spark of the sun

---

[933] *Kitvey Ramban*, 494.
[934] 28. Gikatilla also gives a remarkable reading of *TB Chulim* 60a, which, though it does not refer to *tselem*, is relevant to ecotheology. Gikatilla exhorts his reader,

> Now open your eyes and see that in the great *beyt din* called "Elohim" were judged all the children of [the] world, upper ones and lower ones... [T]his is [the meaning of] what the sages said, "All the works of creation, with their knowledge they were created, in their *qomah* they were created, by their desire they were created", meaning, "with their knowledge"—understanding what they would be called; "in their *qomah*"—understanding the measure of their body and the structure of their limbs; by their desire—that they wanted with desire and yearned to receive all [of this] upon themselves... And every single creature who was created, He stood her up before Him and said: Know that you are in this shape, with these limbs, with this servitude and this rulership/authority/*memshalah*. Now, if you desire [to be] like this – say so. If not, you will be as if you were not created. [Each] responded and said: I desire this and rejoice in this great matter (endeavor)... If perhaps you would say that the creatures differing from each other received insult or injury in their being created so, the scripture says: "In beginning Elohim created..."—with the line of judgment and with a balance and with justice (139–40; *Gates of Light*, 250)

Gikatilla's interpretation of the *meimra* closely parallels (and may be dependent on) *SCh*, while underscoring the will and moral standing of every creature. Each creature, according to Gikatilla, had the right to say no, and each one had the right, so to speak, to be protected from insult or exploitation. Yehudah Hechasid's lengthy interpretation of the parallel passage from *TB Rosh Hashanah* begins:

> For all the works of the Holy One were created with two [kinds of] measures, measures of disability and measures of excellence, and each one of them chose, and he sorted/"specied" them according to what they chose, to equalize them /*l'hashvotam*... That is what's said: "And the heavens and the earth and all their hosts were finished" [Gn 2:1]—"by their knowledge and by their desire they were created / *l'da`atam ul'tsivyonam nivr'u*"
>
> (§530, 351; the phrase "*l'qomatan*" is left out)

The passage continues by elaborating the advantages and disadvantages of various creatures – see n.293.

emanated from the sun."[935] Idel notes that *qomah* is used here as a substitute for "cause of causes", adding, "It appears to me that the expressions *qomah* and *yad* are connected to *tselem*."

A characteristic example of how *qomah* is used in Zoharic literature is found in *Tiquney Zohar*, which admonishes those who weaken "their own image above", explaining that it is "as if they were weakening the orders of Creation / *sidrey v'rei'shit*,[936] and as if they diminished the *d'mut* that is [the] *shi`ur qomah* above".[937] *Qomah* here means the divine likeness, including all the Sefirot and worlds, which is divinity itself. In other words, those who harm their own divine image harm both the whole Creation and God's very being.

In the next passage, which we have already encountered (p.178), *qomah* means the completeness of the central column and the full system of the Sefirot, which is at the same time the fullness of YHVH:

"This *qomah* of yours is likened to a date palm" [So 7:8]. And one who knows the measure of Her stature/*qomah* will inherit the world that is coming/*`alma d'atey*, which is [the letter] V (ו), about which it says, "Israel's purifying-pool/*miqveh* is YHVH" [Je 17:13]— *miqveh*/MQVH is Her *qomah*/QVMH, which is Her *shi`ur*.[938]

In both passages, *qomah* is part of the phrase *shi`ur qomah*, which means the fullness of the divine stature, that is, its measure from top to bottom. In the latter quote, however, one also sees *qomah* separating from *shi'ur*, which is part of its development into an esoteric term standing for the image of God.

Later, Lurianic Kabbalah used *qomah* to indicate the fractal nature of divine reality – that is, to the way the whole Sefirotic structure was inscribed within each one of the Sefirot. *Qomah* therefore alluded to the structure of divinity as a whole, as in "*qomat Adam Qadmon*", as well as to the structure of the whole reflected in a single aspect or *par'tsuf* (sefirotic "face"), as in "*qomat Rachel*".[939]

Qomah thus took on a special meaning: it was the image of God as expressed through the Sefirot on a meta-cosmic level. We saw this meaning in *Peyrush L'Shir Hashirim*'s interpretation of the *Chulin* passage. *P'ri `Ets Hadar* also

---

[935] ms.Cambridge 671, 95a, quoted by Idel, "D'mut Ha'adam Shemei`al Has'firot" in Da`at 4 (1980): 41–55; 46.
[936] *Sidrey v'rei'shit* may include heavens and earth and all the creatures, or it may specifically refer to the *tachtonim*. A study of this phrase in *Chazal*, along with its halakhic and ethical implications, would be useful for ecotheology, environmental ethics, and bioethics. See p.347ff., esp. discussion of GMOs (genetically modified organisms) on pp.350–51 and notes.
[937] TZ 70, 125b; cf. 128b. This framework can be applied to ecotheology; see p.348ff.
[938] TZ 146a. Because *Vav* is a straight line, it is both like the spine (stature) and like a palm tree's trunk or the *lulav* (palm) branch used on sukkot (cf. TZ 134a). Here, *Vav* also stands for YHVH, and it symbolizes *Tif'eret-Y'sod* and the whole central column of the Sefirotic tree. "The world that is coming" usually refers to *Binah*, but it can also include *Tif'eret*, which is born from *Binah*. Cf. Zohar, Ra`ya Mehemna 3:252b.
[939] ECh 1, Heykhal 1 3:2, 33 and ECh 2, Heykhal 6 34:1, 89.

expressly expands the meaning of the term *qomah* by reconnecting this concept with the original phrasing of *Chulin*:

And in their form (of the upper worlds) and in their design You created their model on the earth below; You made all of them with wisdom, upper ones above and lower ones below, "to join [together] the tent to become one". And trees and grasses You made bloom from the ground, with their stature /*b'qomatam* and with their design /*uv'tsivyonam* of what is above, to cause the children of Adam to know the wisdom and discernment that is in them, to reach what is hidden.[940]

Here *qomah* refers not to the mature physical tree, but to the *qomah* and *tsivyon* of the upper world as reflected in the tree. The reference of the pronoun has shifted from the creatures back to the Sefirot. However, unlike the rarefied meaning found in *Peyrush L'Shir Hashirim*, the design of this supernal pattern remains connected in an integral way to the physical trees and plants; it is these lower ones that represent God's image and inculcate wisdom.

QOMAH SH'LEYMAH – COMPLETING THE BODY

The next stage in the development of *qomah* is marked by the appearance of the terminology "complete *qomah* / *qomah sh'leymah*". *Peyrush L'shir Hashirim* already began to shape this idea when it spoke of the vessels becoming "complete in their stature", though the actual terminology was not coined for several more centuries. The earliest use of the phrase *qomah sh'leymah* that I have found appears in the works of Chayyim Vital, where it occurs one time in `*Ets Chayyim*, closely connected to *tselem*.[941] The first work I found where *qomah sh'leymah* appears regularly is *Yonat Eilem* by Menachem Azaryah deFano (1548–1620, Italy). In one passage, which expounds on the `*Ets Chayyim*, deFano explains how the *par'tsuf Z`eyr Anpin* emerges from within *Binah* as a kind of embryo, with "his head between his knees", after which she develops his complete structure or *qomah sh'leymah* from herself.[942] In both works, the

---

[940] See Excursus 2. Note that *tsivyonam* can also mean "their desire".

[941] *ECh* 2, *Heykhal* 5 30:3, 54. This is the only occurrence I found searching all of the digitized texts available on the sites hebrewbooks.org and hebrew.grimoar.cz. Vital explains that "the back of *Binah*", comprising the lower triad of *Netsach-Hod-Y'sod*, is a complete *par'tsuf* (face /personality) in itself, so that this triad "become[s] one *tselem* toward the [completion of] *Z`eyr Anpin* ... and they [make the letter] *Tsadi* (צ) of *tselem*. They enter and are clothed alone in the entire *qomah sh'leymah* of the *par'tsuf* of the back of *Z`eyr Anpin*." The middle three Sefirot of the back of *Binah* make up the *Lamed* (ל) of *tselem*, and the three highest make up the *Mem* (ם) of *tselem*. These details are shared to illustrate the complexity of Lurianic Kabbalah (see Appendix) – they are not significant for the preceding discussion.

[942] (L'vov, 1858) ch.89, 69b. DeFano describes how the *qomah sh'leymah* of *Z`eyr Anpin* is made from the leg joints of *Binah*'s *Netsach-Hod-Y'sod* (where the upper third of *Z`eyr Anpin* comes from the hips of *Binah*, the middle third from the knees, and the lower third from the ankles). The image of the embryo reappears (with slightly different wording) in the Besht's most important teaching about *qomah sh'leymah* (p.298), where its meaning is

phrase *qomah sh'leymah* is used to emphasize that a particular configuration of the Sefirot forms a complete or fully elaborated pattern.

Qomah sh'leymah also appears in the pseudepigraphic work *Tsadiq Y'sod `Olam*,[943] with a somewhat evolved meaning. In a complicated analysis of the Ruth story, the author explains why Ruth (*Rut*) lies at Boaz's feet, instead of alongside or above him, on the night when when she comes to the threshing floor (Ru 3:6–8). According to the author, Ruth is taking on the aspect of *Malkhut*, the tenth and lowest Sefirah, sometimes called Lower Mother, when she puts herself at the feet of Boaz, while Boaz represents *Tif'eret* or Beauty, the sixth Sefirah, which is at the center of the sefirotic tree. However, according to *Tsadiq Y'sod `Olam*, Ruth is actually *Binah*, the third Sefirah, sometimes called Upper/Supernal Mother.

This is why Boaz asks Ruth, "Who are you?" [Ru 3:9] when he awakens to find her at his feet: he cannot tell whether she is *Binah* or *Malkhut*. By masquerading as *Malkhut*, while still drawing from the essence of *Binah*, Ruth is figuratively able to draw the power of the Sefirot from below and from above, multiplying, as it were, the power of the upper feminine and the lower feminine principles. This conjugation of the feminine with itself, which is a kind of prelude to the coupling with *Tif'eret*, is what produces the seminal drop that will bring the messiah into the world:

[F]rom the power of coupling, the secret of the drop is made from the hidden light, and she (the drop) is the secret of *Yud/YV"D*... [T]his would be the secret of *Quf* (= 100), and it is a *qomah sh'leymah* [made] from 10 by 10.[944]

"*Qomah sh'leymah*" here means the divine potency derived from the conjunction of every Sefirah within every other Sefirah, hence "ten squared". The

radically shifted, from the realm of the Sefirot to the physical realm. Two other examples are: "Leah (i.e., *Binah*) is face-to-face [with Jacob / *Z`eyr Anpin*] with a *qomah sh'leymah* before midnight" (ch.93, 73a), and "the great one (the sun or *Z`eyr Anpin*) [emerged] with a *qomah sh'leymah* and the small one's *qomah* (the moon or Shekhinah) was diminished" (ch.95, 75b, referencing the legend of the diminishment of the moon). *Qomah sh'leymah* also appears in ch.29, 24a, while *shi`ur qomah sh'leymah* appears in ch.24, 20b. Another term used by deFano, *kol haqomah/qomato/qomat*, is incorporated by Yishayah Horowitz (see further on), while a parallel expression, *m'lo' qomato/qomatah/qomatan*, meaning "the fullness of his/her/their *qomah*", which deFano uses four times more frequently, does not appear.

[943] This text circulated as the work of Yitshak Luria, but Liebes suggested it was a Sabbatean work, attributing it to Yehudah Leib Prossnitz (1670–1730) (*Studies in Jewish Myth and Messianism*, 103). If so, it is later than *Sh'ney Luchot Hab'rit*, discussed presently. However, the meaning of *qomah sh'leymah* in the passage from *Tsadiq Y'sod `Olam* is closer to earlier Kabbalah, so I have placed it first. In any case, Prossnitz has no other literary legacy to compare *Tsadiq Y'sod `Olam* with, unless one counts another putative Lurianic work also attributed to Prossnitz by Liebes, so its chronological place is uncertain. Whether or not *Tsadiq Y'sod `Olam* was Sabbatean, its vision of redemption and gender was understood by later readers who did not know the work's provenance to be normative.

[944] *Tsadiq Y'sod `Olam*, Yitshak Luria (attr.), (Jerusalem: Yeshivat Or Chozer, 1982), 47. The letter *Yud* evolves into *Quf* because spelled out it is imagined as $Y (= 10)$ times $V + D$ $(6 + 4 = 10)$.

multiplication of the Sefirot is what is necessary to produce the lineage of David, that is, the seed of redemption and messiah.

Tsadiq Y'sod `Olam's use of the term *qomah sh'leymah* is close to the meaning of *qomah* in Lurianic texts. *Qomah sh'leymah*, however, differs from *qomah* in that it includes every *qomah* of every *par'tsuf* and world; this is what makes it whole or complete.[945]

Yishayah Horowitz (the Shlah) takes the meaning of *qomah* in a radically new direction. *Sh'ney Luchot Hab'rit* uses a term related to *qomah sh'leymah*, "*shi`ur qomah sh'leymah*", alongside related formulations, including "*sh'leymut qomat ha'adam*", in the following passage, which I will go through piece by piece. In the first part, he explains that an advocate angel is created when one does a mitsvah:

> [I]n every mitsvah there is the trace of YHVH... and behold, YHVH comprises the whole body/stature / *kol haqomah*. But [even] in each and every limb/part there is also included the whole, and therefore the one who fulfills one mitsvah perfectly/*k'tiqunah*, it's as if he fulfilled all of them, as R' Shimon bar Yochai explained, and from [every mitsvah] one whole angel is made, with 248 limbs/*eivarim*,[946] which is his advocate/*s'neigor*.[947]

The body and power of this angel come from the power of the body used to perform the mitsvah.

In the continuation of the passage, the Shlah describes how an accusing angel is made from each sin. Here, he reformulates a Zoharic teaching, adding to it the phrase "*shi`ur qomah sh'leymah*":

> So it is with every [angelic] accuser/*katigor*, since it is made from the power of this person [when he or she sins]. In the power [that creates the accuser] there are 248 limbs [derived from the body of the person] and [each accuser] is part of such-and-such a limb from the *shi`ur qomah* (body) of Sama'el (Satan). And this is [the meaning of] "Don't say: I will repay evil /*ashalmah ra`*!" [Pr 20:22.] And it is explained in the *Zohar* that [this means] you should not say, I will **make whole** /*ashlim* the evil that is Sama'el through my sins, to make for him a complete body / *shi`ur qomah sh'leymah*, and it

---

[945] Elsewhere, *Tsadiq Y'sod `Olam* describes the same idea using *qomah*: "and since all ten vessels have been raised... [*Z`eyr Anpin* and *Nuqva*] can receive... the lights of *ChB"D* (the uppermost Sefirot – see n.760)... and they come to be 'face to face' with equal *qomah*" (75). This passage, and similar ones from *Or Hame'ir* and *`Ets Chayyim* quoted further on (p.295ff. and n.971), depict a relationship between male and female that transcends the common Kabbalistic understanding that the female becomes absorbed by the male. Redemption comes not through the integration of female into male but rather through the female attaining full stature, equal to the male. Such countertexts suggest a construction of the entire system of the Sefirot that correlates with feminist thought. See nn.105, 620, 624, 971, and p.208.

[946] According to tradition, 248 is the number of limbs/organs of the human body, corresponding to the number of positive (active) commandments.

[947] *Masekhet Yoma*, vol.1:2, 71b; cf. vol.1:1, 49a–b. The Shlah specifically praises *Yonat Eilem*, so it is reasonable to imagine that his use of the terms *shi`ur qomah sh'leymah* and *kol haqomah* derives from there, even though Horowitz employs these phrases differently.

Qomah Sh'leymah – *completing the body*

said, "for this disgusting one / *da m'nuvla* isn't made whole except through the sins of humanity."[948]

Each accusing angel becomes part of the body of Sama'el, the "anti-reflection" or negative image of the godhead, which comes closer to being a *shi`ur qomah sh'leymah* with every human sin.

The final section quotes *Tiquney Zohar*, which Horowitz uses to build a conceptual bridge between the just-mentioned *shi`ur qomah sh'leymah* of divine or angelic bodies, and the actual human body:

And also they said in the *Zohar*, "worthy is the one that makes [God] dwell in every one of his parts,... so that no limb/part/*eiver* should be empty of [God]. For if one part lacked serving the Holy One, because of this part he would return to the world through reincarnation, until his parts would be made whole, becoming all of them whole in the image/*d'yoqna* of the Holy One (etc.)",[949] as it says: "Elohim created the human in His image."

Tiquney Zohar postulates that intentionality and *mitsvot* configure the human body, part by part, to be in God's image.[950] The whole body does not acquire God's image until each part, after however many incarnations, is made whole in God's image.

It is only in a parallel passage, however, that the Shlah articulates his synthesis of these ideas, explicitly extending the language of *qomah* to the real human body:

[S]cripture said, "You will be holy for I am holy" [Lv 20:26], as if to say, you will be on the side of holiness, similar to (becoming like) Me, eye for eye, hand for hand, foot for foot, etc. Therefore a person needs to make holy /sanctify the entire measure of his body/*qomah* / *kol shi`ur qomato* from his head til his feet... so I will outline the [way of] wholeness of the human *qomah* / *sh'leymut qomat ha'adam*, how one can become holy.[951]

---

[948] The Shlah is quoting (with slight variations – the original says "*m'nuvla da*") *Zohar* 1:201a, which begins: "'Don't say: I will repay (make whole) evil / *Ashalmah ra*'—[because] if a person leans to the left (to sin), then he strengthens *yetser ra`* over *yetser tov*, and the one that is blemished (i.e., Sama'el) is made whole/*shalem* through [a person's] sins... " The Shlah combines this *Zohar* passage with the following one from *TZ* to create a new synthesis.

[949] *TZ* 70, 132a.

[950] Scholem argues that *Tiquney Zohar* is the origin of this theory of *imitatio Dei*, saying that it "made a deep impact on the Kabbalists". Scholem restates the theory thus:

[T]he primal shape of man corresponds to the mystical shape of the Godhead... [E]ach of [his limbs] corresponds to one of the supernal lights... Man's task is to bring his true shape to spiritual perfection, to develop the divine image within himself. This is done by observing [the commandments], each one of which is linked to one of the organs of the body. (*OMG* 220)

For a contemporary view of this passage, see David Cooper, *God is a Verb: Kabbalah and the Practice of Mystical Judaism* (New York: Riverhead Books, 1997), 267–9.

[951] vol.1:1, *Sha`ar Ha'otiyot, Ot Quf*, 52b. Horowitz also uses the phrase "*shi`ur kol haqomah*".

The connection the Shlah makes between the theosophical *qomah* and the physical, human *qomah* will come to provide a foundation for the Besht's use of *qomah sh'leymah*.[952]

To summarize thus far, *qomah* in Midrash meant bodily stature, height, and maturity, and the erect stature of a human being was described as an aspect of God's image. The use of the term in *Shi'ur Qomah* for the measure of God's dimensions evoked in Kabbalah the connection between *qomah* and the more-than-human world of the divine Sefirot. Through the mediation of the concept of *Adam Qadmon*, the primordial human, *qomah* came to be applied in Kabbalah to the entirety of the system of cosmos/divinity, coming to mean wholeness not just in height, stature, or enormity, but also in structure and complexity, and in Lurianic Kabbalah it came to mean the fractal structure of the divine reality. This idea was extended in *Tsadiq Y'sod 'Olam* to a kind of mega-universe of the Sefirot that is simultaneously the seed-ground and birth of redemption.

Yishayah Horowitz led this evolution in a new direction when he connected *qomah* with *sh'leymut* to mean not just the totality and dimensions of divinity, but also the connection of each of these multifarious dimensions with the idea of *tselem* in the human being, both in the body as a whole and in each of its limbs. The Shlah's understanding of *qomah* added a spiritual and transformational dimension to the connection between body and universe, thereby providing a theological basis for establishing through *qomah* a relationship between the human being and the more-than-human world. From this matrix, *Chasidut* grew a theology of interaction with the world and the beings and things we encounter in it.

Qomah Sh'leymah in *Chasidut*

The concept of *qomah sh'leymah* evolved in a new direction in the teachings of the Baal Shem Tov.[953] The Besht extrapolated from the humanistic interpretation of the Shlah, radically psychologizing *shi`ur qomah sh'leymah*.[954] He taught, "One who speaks without thought is like one who casts seed wastefully, for thought within the human being is a *shi`ur qomah*

---

[952] Note that Horowitz does not use the exact terminology of *qomah sh'leymah*, despite his dependence on *Yonat Eilem* and the close connection he makes between *qomah* and *sh'leymut*.

[953] *Qomah sh'leymah* also continued to evolve outside of *Chasidut*. See n.751, on the Vilna Gaon.

[954] The Beshtian understanding of *qomah sh'leymah* is almost certainly derived from Horowitz, whose work was influential in Hasidic circles. The Besht also restates Horowitz's idea that when intention, thought, and action are united, a complete angel's body is created (*Tsava'at Harivash* [Hebr.] 54, §116; *Tzava'at Harivash* [Engl.], 105; both ed. Immanuel Schochet [Brooklyn NY: Kehot, 1998]). Though the Besht does not associate that idea with *qomah*, as the Shlah does, he does connect a parallel idea from the Shlah with *qomah* – that a word uttered without intention would be "missing a limb" (see further on).

Qomah Sh'leymah – *completing the body*

sh'leymah."[955] In other teachings, he used *qomah sh'leymah*: "[E]very place that a person thinks of, he draws himself there, for thought is a *qomah sh'leymah.*"[956] The power of thought lies in the fact that it includes every dimension of the whole of reality, so that thought actually brings a person to the place of their imagination. This principle applies even to "strange thoughts" – thoughts about common or profane matters:

For a person is obligated to believe that the fullness of the whole earth is [God's] glory, blessed be. There is no place empty of Him, and every thought of a person has in it His existence, blessed be, and every thought is a *qomah sh'leymah*.[957]

The potential represented by *qomah sh'leymah* is also applied to language itself: "Know that every word/*teivah* is a *qomah sh'leymah*, and all of one's strength must be in it; for if not, it will be as though it were missing a limb."[958] The same framework is applied to desire:

For in truth in every desire of the world, there are sparks of the dimension of human beings / *b'ney adam*, [which are] a complete stature / *qomah sh'leymah*, and the *tsadiq* repairs them, [but] the one that goes after his heart's desires, he eats and destroys human beings.[959]

Here *qomah sh'leymah* also refers to the potential of the spark awaiting full redemption. This teaching makes a stronger connection between the idea of *qomah sh'leymah* and the idea of *tselem*, for what it means to say that sparks are of the dimension of "human beings" is that those sparks contain within themselves God's image.

Qomah sh'leymah is again the spiritual equivalent of a human being in the following passage: "[E]ven a bad or strange thought, when it comes to a person, it comes to be fixed and to be raised up, and if the person pushes the thought away from him, then he becomes like one that pushed away and killed a *qomah sh'leymah*".[960] The Ba`al Shem Tov teaches that every person has a profound responsibility to understand the depth of every thought. Thoughts

---

[955] Pinchas of Koretz, *Liqutim Y'qarim* 4b; SBST 132–3, §44. Note that scholars do not agree about how to determine which teachings in the name of the Besht are authentic, but the teachings cited here are unquestionably early and closely related.
[956] *Magid D'varav L'Ya`aqov* (New York: Otsar Hachasidim, 2003), 10b; SBST 76, §97. I first encountered the concept of *qomah sh'leymah* in this passage in 1995.
[957] Yaakov Yosef of Polnoye, *Ben Porat Yosef* (Pieterkov, Poland: Feivel Belchatovski, 1884), 50a; SBST 163, §116.
[958] *Tsava'at Harivash* §34, 14 (Hebr.), 26 (Engl.). Note the converse concept in §118 that "every letter is a complete world / `olam shalem*, so that when [a person] says the word/*teivah* with great attachment/*hitqashrut* he certainly awakens the upper worlds..." (54–5 [Hebr.], 108 [Engl.]). On the subject of this passage being *tselem Elohim*, see Dan, "Imago Dei", 477.
[959] Yitshak Isaac Safrin, *Notser Chesed `al Masechet Avot*, ch.3; SBST 100, §157.
[960] *Ben Porat Yosef*, 50a–b; SBST 166, §116.

have the status of persons here – the Besht even compares pushing a thought away and neglecting to redeem it with murder.[961]

Nachman of Breslov (1772–1810, Ukraine), the Besht's great-grandson, uses *qomah sh'leymah* not just in relation to thought or mitsvah or desire, but also in relation to feeling: "Joy is a *qomah sh'leymah*, including 248 limbs/parts and 365 sinews/connectors, and so [when a person] is rejoicing or dancing, he must see that he passes through all of the joy (Fishbane: 'activates the entirety of joy'), from head until heel."[962] This echoes both the teachings of the Besht, who identified *qomah sh'leymah* in the dimensions of human experience, and the Shlah, who understood *qomah* in relation to the symbolic limbs and parts of the body. In continuity with both, Nachman describes this happening through "many *mitsvot*, for the roots of the points of the *mitsvot* are in joy, and every one has a specific limb".[963]

Nachman of Breslov connects the trope of *qomah sh'leymah* to the very essence of feeling, the yearning of the heart, when he writes that the heart of the world is a complete *qomah*:

Know yourself that each and every thing in the world has a heart, and also the world in its entirety has a heart. And the heart of the world is a *qomah sh'leymah*, like *qomat Adam* / a human form, with face and with hands and legs. Except that even the nail of the small toe of the heart of the world is more "heartful"/*m'luvevet* than any other heart.[964]

Nachman defines *qomah sh'leymah* as the *qomah* of a human being. He continues (following the translation from the Yiddish):

There is a mountain, and on the mountain stands a rock from which flows a spring... This mountain with the rock and the spring stands at one end of the world, and the heart stands at the other end of the world. The heart stands facing the spring and continually longs and yearns very much to come to the spring, with very great yearning. It cries out greatly to the spring. The spring also yearns for the heart.[965]

Nachman relates that the heart is sustained by the "true man of kindness", who at the end of each day gives the heart another day to live, formed out of

---

[961] "[A thought] may come to void the person in his prayer and to confuse his thoughts, and then there is permission to push away that thought for 'the one who comes to kill you, rise up' [and kill him]" (ibid., quoting *TB B'rakhot* 58a).

[962] *LM* 1:178, 249, quoted in Fishbane, "To Jump for Joy", 375.

[963] Therefore, by fully embodying joy, one fulfills on a spiritual level all the *mitsvot*. Nachman also says that every mitsvah itself is a *qomah sh'leymah* (*LM* 1:277).

[964] *Sipurey Ma`asiyot Mishanim Qadmoniyot* (Jerusalem: Mossad Harav Kook, 1971), 189, from "The Tale of the Seven Beggars". I use the more heavily edited Hebrew version here in order to focus on the terminology. The continuation that follows, from the Yiddish version, is probably closer to the way Nachman told it.

[965] *The Thirteen Stories of Rebbe Nachman of Breslev* [sic], trans. Esther Koenig (Jerusalem: Hillel Press, 1978), 229.

human deeds of kindness. The heart then gives the day to the spring, which exists beyond time.

There are many ways to interpret this parable,[966] but what is most important for our discussion is the image itself. Nachman envisions the world as having a heart. Because the heart is a complete *qomah*, it also must have a heart; because it is the heart of the world, even its toe is more heart-like than the heart of any one being. (The translation from the Yiddish version reads, "the toe nail on the foot of the heart of the world is heartier than *the heart of any other heart*".[967]) For Nachman, *qomah sh'leymah* (which is ultimately the image of God) exists in its most intense and profound form neither within human beings, nor in *Adam Ha`elyon* or the Sefirot, but in the world itself.

Many other Hasidic teachers employ the term *qomah sh'leymah*. Zev (Z'ev) Wolf of Zhitomir (d. 1800, Ukraine), the author of *Or Hame'ir*, roots his whole theology in this concept. In explaining the encounter between Boaz and Ruth on the threshing floor (similar to *Tsadiq Y'sod `Olam*), he equates Boaz, who "awoke trembling" [Ru 3:8] when he realized Ruth was lying near him, with the Holy One/*Tif'eret*, "who trembles [with desire] to build the *qomah* of the Shekhinah to be *qomah* opposite *qomah*."[968] The Holy One desires this because as long as they are not body opposite body, the male and female dimensions of divinity cannot unite with each other, "[f]or now in the time of exile it is '*Alef* with all of them and all of them with *Alef*'[969] (i.e., they are unequal), but in the future they will be made equal, with one appearance, eye to eye". Therefore the Holy One asks the Shekhinah: "Who is with You in exile? Are there those searching for YHVH to seek Your unity, to raise up the limbs of the Shekhinah and to build Your *qomah*?"[970]

According to Zev Wolf, only in exile is Shekhinah or *Malkhut* like a kind of appendage of the Sefirot. In redemption, She will become a complete and independent body, able to join the Holy One.[971] He emphasizes that humanity

---

[966] See Magid, "Nature, Exile", 361–3, esp. nn.3, 8, 14, and 367–8, nn.38, 53.   [967] Ibid.
[968] *Or Hame'ir*, vol.4 (Warsaw: R' Meir Yechiel Halter, 1883), 27; also vol.3, 79–80, esp. "in the time of the days of *mashiach*, Her *qomah* will be equal to His *qomah* ... with a *qomah z'qufah* equal unto him". Cf. vol.1, 43; vol.2, 43; and many other places.
[969] In *Sefer Y'tsirah*, this quote refers to permutating Hebrew letters.
[970] *Or Hame'ir*, vol.4, 28.
[971] Though *Malkhut*'s independence can indicate exile and separation in Kabbalah, there are classical passages that describe the female uniting with the male only after becoming complete in herself. Vital, for example, wrote, "When [*Malkhut*] separates from [*Z'eyr Anpin*] and becomes an (Wolfson: autonomous) aspect by Herself, the two of them are in the secret of a husband and his wife, the male alone and the female alone" (*ECh* 1 *Heykhal* 2 10:3, vol.1, 97, quoted in Wolfson, *Circle in the Square*, 116). He also wrote, "The place of *Malkhut* was first [from] the root of crown/corona/`atarah in *Y'sod*, and after that, when She grew, She was uprooted from there and grew ... until She became a complete *par'tsuf* and turned face-to-face with *Z'eyr Anpin*" (*ECh* 2, *Heykhal* 6 35:1, 100). On Cordovero, see Asulin, "Hahavaneha Hak'fulah". Gender equality recurs as a redemptive theme throughout Kabbalah. See further discussion in *Methods*. See Sarah Schneider's important work on gender-redemptive

or Israel is responsible for raising up Shekhinah's limbs and building Her body:

And all this falls upon us, to bring near the time of redemption through means of good acts [so that] Her *qomah* will be built and established... [To become complete with God means] to know how to raise up, now in this day especially, the limbs of the Shekhinah, in order to redeem them from exile. For this is the essential drive of our soul in Torah and *mitsvot* [and prayer]... to be constant/assiduous in repairing Shekhinah, to build Her and to prepare Her with a *qomah sh'leymah*.[972]

We participate in completing the body of Shekhinah through our actions and intentions, and Her completion brings redemption.

Elsewhere in *Or Hame'ir*, Zev Wolf makes a strong connection between the Kabbalistic idea of *qomah* and midrashic ideas about *Adam Harishon*:

[At] the beginning of His blessed will, He wanted to reveal the might of His brilliance by means of the *qomah* of the first Adam, and since he sinned his *qomah* was diminished, and [so] the Holy One was unable to reveal openly His divinity by means of [Adam's] *qomah*.[973]

In other systems of Kabbalistic thought, God's hiddenness is connected primarily with *tsimtsum*, the contraction of God's infinite being in order to make a place for the world, and with *l'vush*, the concealment of God's presence in order for creatures to exist independently of God. Hiddenness is a necessary precondition for Adam to have been created. Here, however, the hiddenness of divinity in the world is a symptom of Adam's diminished *qomah*, whose original form was supposed to manifest God's image in a manner so great as to be called an "open revelation of divinity". Homiletically, we may ask: To whom would this revelation have been directed, when the only human was *Adam Harishon*? We may answer: It would have been directed toward Creation itself.

Zev Wolf also connects *qomah sh'leymah* to human nature in general. Explaining the rabbinic dictum "The whole world was not created except to join to this one/*l'zeh*,"[974] he says,

[A]ll that came into the totality of Creation and into *Havayah* (Being), their entirety is found to be *adam*... And this is what is hinted at in the verse, "For this/*zeh* is the whole human" etc. – for this points with a finger to the totality of the creatures and trees

---

interpretations of *mi'ut hayarei'ach* (the diminishment of the moon), *Kabbalistic Writings on the Nature of Masculine and Feminine* (Northvale NJ: Jason Aronson, 2002). On a theological level, redemption points toward what is unprecedented, so it is not surprising for mystics to imagine radical cosmic shifts taking place along side redemption's quickening.

[972] *Or Hame'ir*, vol.4, 27–8; also 72. Cf. vol.1, 20, where Zev Wolf explains that the purpose of Torah, prayer, and *mitsvot* is "to lift up the sparks", and vol.4, 76, where he explains that it is "to refine/*l'varer* the holy sparks and to lift them up".

[973] Ibid., vol.3, 14; cf. vol.4, 40, 60, and other places.   [974] *TB B'rakhot* 6b; see p.118.

and plants and all that came into the totality of *Havayah* – their totality is the *qomah sh'leymah* of *adam*, who also is a small world / `olam qatan*.[975]

Here again is the trope that all of Creation – with special emphasis on the *tachtonim* – is God's image.

The process of repairing the body or *qomah* of the Shekhinah also parallels the process of repairing our own *qomah*: "Certainly as one fixes his full *qomah* in wholeness... his example/*dugma* becomes also a *tiqun* (reparation/completion) of *qomah sh'leymah* in the Shekhinah".[976] We complete the *qomah* of the Shekhinah through Torah and *mitsvot*, we restore the *qomah* of *Adam Harishon*, reveal divinity, repair ourselves – and in doing so we repair Creation. The Holy One can only tremble and ask us to do this; the revelation depends on us.

But what are the limbs of the Shekhinah that we must raise up? Homiletically speaking, if our *qomah* in all its parts and limbs comprises all the creatures, and the *qomah* of the Shekhinah comprises the *qomah* of all humanity, then the creatures themselves are included in Her limbs. If we were to treat the forests, the species, the endangered habitats, as though they were limbs of the Shekhinah, as though our redemption and the redemption of Shekhinah depended on how we interact with them, this would indeed be enormous.

Returning to the roots of this concept, Yaakov Yosef of Polnoye (1710–84, Poland, Ukraine) quotes the Besht as describing "the totality/*k'lalot* of the world" as "a single unity, a *qomah sh'leymah*".[977] Avraham Yehoshua Heschel of Apt (1748–1825, Poland, Ukraine), echoing the Besht's teaching, similarly said that "Adam is a *qomah sh'leymah* of the dimension of `olam qatan*, and each and every world from the lower and upper worlds is a *qomah sh'leymah*, and so is the totality of the worlds a *qomah sh'leymah*."[978] It is these correspondences that enable a human being to effect *tiqun*, repair and redemption, in the world. Thus, embedded in the concept of *qomah sh'leymah* is a way of viewing redemption, cosmos, and divinity, as well as the depths of human psychology and spirit.

---

[975] *Or Hame'ir*, vol.4, 79; cf. vol.3, 56–7. In this section, Zev Wolf describes the human as having elements of the Side of Holiness, which must be strengthened, and elements of the Other Side, which must be purged. So, while the human contains the whole, Zev Wolf's is not simply a holistic view. Nevertheless, his overall perspective was one of affirming the divine presence in materiality – see Seth Brody, "Open to Me the Gates of Righteousness: The Pursuit of Holiness and Non-Duality in Early Hasidic Teachings", *Jewish Quarterly Review* 89:1–2 (July–Oct. 1998): 3–44, esp. 27–39.

[976] *Or Hame'ir*, vol.1, 36.

[977] *K'tonet Pasim*, ed. Gedaliah Nigal (Jerusalem: M'khon P'ri Ha'arets, 1985), *M'tsora`* 90. Here, the Besht explains that because the world is one organic body, when a righteous person returns (does *t'shuvah*, i.e., repents or fixes a flaw), it can cause ("force") another person, even one who had greatly sinned, to return.

[978] *Oheiv Yisrael* (Zhitomir, Ukraine: Nekhdei Harav Mislavita, 1863), 86; *cf.* 50, 127. *Qomah sh'leymah* is also equated with `olam qatan* in the works of later Chasidic masters (e.g., Dovid Twersky of Tolna [Ukraine, 180882], *Qohelet David* [Lublin, 1881], 17).

QOMAH AND REDEMPTION IN THE EVERYDAY WORLD

We saw that the Besht applied *qomah sh'leymah* not just to ultimate reality but also to everyday experience: words, thoughts, desires. According to Yaakov Yosef, the Besht's original teaching also demanded compassion toward the *qomah sh'leymah* existing in every thing we come in contact with:

> [I]t is known that every spark, from the silent, growing, living and speaking [beings], has in it a *qomah sh'leymah* [drawn] from 248 limbs and 365 sinews, and when it is within/*b'tokh* the silent or the growing being (rock/mineral or plant), it's in the prison house, for it cannot spread out its hands and its legs or speak, for "its head [is] on its knees and gut" [Ex 12:9]. And one who is able through the goodness of his thought to raise the holy spark to living or speaking, he brings it out to freedom, and there is no greater redeeming of captives / *pidyon sh'vuyim* for you than this, as I heard from my teacher (the Besht).[979]

Qomah sh'leymah means here not the completed *qomah*, but the potential *qomah* embedded within every being, from rock to plant to animal. This *qomah* is envisioned as yearning to develop into a full human body, in God's image, with hands and the power of speech.

This passage emphasizes the role of thought and intention, "the goodness of one's thought", in the process of redeeming the sparks. The sanctification of the sparks through our intentions was already suggested by the *P'ri 'Ets Hadar* prayer, which asks that the sparks be raised through our eating fruit and through "our meditating over the secret of their roots above upon which they hang/depend". Human contemplation and appreciation of each creature, in a form that honors the depth of being that sustains it, can reveal each creature's and each spark's *qomah*.

While redemption is often interpreted as occurring through consumption,[980] according to Yaakov Yosef, redeeming the sparks "is the purpose of a Jewish person's labor in Torah and *mitsvot*", not just in eating.[981] This universal purpose is reflected in the Besht's teaching that there are sparks in what we sit on and use in other ways:

---

[979] *Ben Porat Yosef* 74b; *SBST* 267–8, §116. This passage is almost assuredly derived from deFano (see n.942).

[980] For example, when Aharon Roth, rebbe of Shomer Emunim/Toldos Aharon (1894–1947, Hungary, Palestine), introduces this teaching, he writes:

> My brother, my beloved, the root of all [is that] when some kind of food is brought before you, or drink, you must imagine in your mind that there is here a spark crying out and seeking and pleading to you that you would have mercy on her to raise her through your good intentions and not push her away, God forbid / *chas v'shalom*.
> (*Shulchan Hatahor* [Jerusalem, 1966], ch.2, 165)

[981] As Yaakov Yosef describes at the beginning of this passage:

> [I]t is explained in the *kavanah* of the Ari (Yitshak Luria) concerning the sifting/separating/*beirur* of the holy sparks that fell at the time of shattering/*sh'virah*: a person needs to raise them and to separate them, from silent to growing, living and speaking, to separate the holy spark that is within the shell. And this is the purpose of a Jewish person's labor/service in Torah and *mitsvot*, and the intention of eating[.]

They eat humans/people/ *b'ney adam* and sit [on] people and use people, they are the sparks in those things. Therefore, a person must have pity/*chas* on his implements and on everything that is his, for these [implements come to him] from the side of (i.e., because of) sparks that are there.[982]

B'ney adam here refers to the same idea that each spark is a *qomah sh'leymah*, which, as we have seen, means that it is "of the dimension of *b'ney adam*" (p.293). Each spark, as a potential *qomah sh'leymah*, can manifest the full pattern of divinity that is also in humanity. Later Hasidic thinkers, as well as contemporary academics, interpreted this teaching in a much less radical fashion than it was originally intended.[983] According to the Besht, every action and interaction, through conscious compassion, has the potential to redeem sparks in the more-than-human world and to reveal image of God that is already in them.

Though these ideas are incredibly powerful for contemporary ecotheology, the image of the holy spark imprisoned in physical objects, as described by Yaakov Yosef, can be read as devaluing the natural world.[984] Moreover, whether or not Yaakov Yosef correctly interpreted the Besht's teaching, the Besht remains fixed on the idea that the sparks we encounter in the

---

Beirur, the refining and uplifting of sparks in the world and in other creatures, is generated by properly "harvesting" a thing's use-value, through actions done with a holy intention and purpose. I will detail further on how the concept of *qomah* transcends this limitation.

[982] *Tsava'at Harivash* (Hebr.) §109, 50, accepting Gellman's proposed version of the best text in "Early Hasidism and the Natural World" in *Judaism and Ecology: Created World and Revealed Word*, ed. Hava Tirosh-Samuelson (Cambridge MA: Harvard University Press, 2002), 382 (also found in "Buber's Blunder: Buber's Replies to Scholem and Schatz-Ufenheimer", *Modern Judaism* 20:1 [Feb. 2000] 20–40). Though Gellman's proposed text is good, I disagree with his interpretation – see next note.

[983] For example, *Tsava'at Harivash* reinterprets the Besht's radical statement about "eating people" to conform to the less radical idea of freeing imprisoned sparks in its preface to §109:

[W]hatever a person wears or eats, or [whenever] he uses an implement/tool/vessel/*k'li*, he takes pleasure from the lifeforce/*chiyut* that is in that thing, for were it not for that spiritual force there would be no existence/*qiyum* of that thing. And there are holy sparks there related to the root of his soul... And when he uses that *k'li* or eats that food, even [if only] for the need of his body, he repairs/*m'taqen* the sparks, for afterwards he works with that strength that came into his body from that clothing or food or whatever thing.

Both academics like Gellman and religious scholars like Immanuel Schochet accept this reinterpretation at face value. Schochet translates: "[when] people eat and sit with others and use others, it means that they are dealing with the 'sparks' in those things" (*Tsava'at Harivash*, 100). Scholem translates: "what a human being eats, and what he sits on, and what he uses are the sparks which are in those things" (*OMG* 246). Gellman, assuming "*b'ney adam*" refers to sparks coming from a previously incarnated human soul, states that "our mercy... should go out to the sparks of human souls, not to the objects themselves that hold them." This misunderstanding deeply colors Gellman's conclusions about the value of early *Chasidut* for ecotheology. It also leads him to dismiss Buber's impressionistic interpretation of *Chasidut*, though in this case I believe Buber correctly intuited the Besht's intent.

[984] On the debate about whether raising the sparks means nullifying the physical world or constructively engaging with it, see Seth Brody ("Open to Me"), who outlines the Buber–Scholem debate and related scholarship and gives his own, less polarizing interpretation.

world around us can only reach their potential through human intervention. In a fully realized ecotheology, we would seek to understand other avenues for expressing or realizating the *qomah* in every being – whether or not that being provides us with tools or food, whether or not we are the instruments for its redemption.

Such a model is already alluded to in the mystical *midrashim*, which teach that redemption will restore the stature of the lower creatures through the transformation of Nature itself. In a passage from *Midrash Alfa-Beitot* that echoes the restoration of Adam's *qomah*, one reads that every wheat and barley kernel, every grape, every fig, every olive, every date, every apple, every nut will reach fantastic proportions. Furthermore, "each and every tree is destined that they should put forth fruit... as it is said: 'And the land will give her produce and the tree of the field will give his fruit' [Lv 26:4]."[985] That every tree will produce fruit can mean, as shown earlier, that every tree will be in God's image.

This same passage also connects these motifs with the divine image when it asserts that the lower creatures are destined to become like the upper creatures:

Sh"T [stands] for the *Shevach* of His works, that He is destined to make the face of the heavens new, like the face of the sun, and the face of the earth new like the face of the moon, and the face of the fruit trees of the field like the face of the stars, the face of the fruits of the ground like the face of the constellations, and make sweet their scent like the scent of *Gan `Eden*.[986]

The heavenly bodies can be images of God, and their "faces" are images all the more so. If the faces of the lower creatures will become like the faces of the upper ones, this means they will be lifted up to the "height" of the upper ones, especially in terms of the image of God, which will shine in their faces. One could say that the *qomah* in every being becomes whole through this process. While here this trope is applied to fruit trees and fruit, which have a special relationship in Kabbalah to God's image, we could apply this pattern to all the creatures. How can human actions and intentions support each limb of the cosmic body of Creation, so that each reflects and embodies God's image, so that the fullness that was diminished by human sin at the beginning can be restored?

OTHER FRAMEWORKS FOR UNDERSTANDING TSELEM
AND WHOLENESS

We have focused on *qomah* because of its rich history in Kabbalah and *Chasidut*, but there are other analogues of *tselem* that also serve to broaden our

---

[985] BM, vol.2, 430. Every tree newly bearing fruit is also a restoration of what Eden was, and an indication that the curse of the land due to Adam's sin has been erased.

[986] Ibid. The text adds, "and all of [the fruits] prepared for the righteous", implying that even in "the coming world", humans will still in some sense be the measure of all things.

Other frameworks for understanding tselem *and wholeness* 301

picture of God's image in the world. Some terms function as simple synonyms for *tselem*, without extending the possibilities of what God's image might mean. *D'yoqan* or *d'yoqna*, which is used frequently in this manner in the *Zohar*, is the most significant example; *tsurah* is another term that appears in texts cited already. However, other terms, like *tavnit*, *chotam*, *r'shimu*, and *to'ar*, add to or extend the relationship between *tselem* and the more-than-human realms.[987] In this section, I will discuss each of these in turn.

Tavnit – structure

The most important term is perhaps *tavnit*. *Tavnit* is used similarly to *qomah*; it is closely connected with *tselem* but less defined in its meaning. In the Torah, it also has the specific meaning of "image that is worshipped", and can, like *tselem*, mean "idol"; this makes *tavnit* a less flexible term for constructive purposes.

Tavnit is directly connected to the image of God in the wedding liturgy: "Blessed be You who formed the human in His image /*b'tsalmo*, in the image of likeness of His structure / *b'tselem d'mut tavnito*".[988] An early Kabbalistic work that uses *tavnit* is the commentary to *Shir Hashirim* cited earlier, where *tavnit* is substituted for *da`at* in the *Bavli Rosh Hashanah* text: "the measures were made whole and became complete vessels, in their *qomah* and in their structure /*tavnitam* and in their design."[989] *Tavnit* refers here to a pattern that is complete or whole.

Tiquney Zohar uses *tavnit* as a synonym for image: "For there is no similarity/*dimyon* between Him blessed be and us from the side of essence/`*etsem* and structure/*tavnit*".[990] Yosef Ashkenazi also made use of the term *tavnit* as a parallel to both *qomah* and *tselem*: "[T]here is included in Adam's seal and *tavnit* and *d'mut* and *tselem* of all the ten *s'firot* and of all the creatures, and what is formed and what is made from them."[991] He specifically equates *d'mut* with *tavnit*: "[Elohim] said 'as our likenesses /*kid'muteynu*' for the image/*dimyon* of the *tavnit* of the worlds and ten *s'firot*".[992]

Moshe Cordovero, in his book *Shi`ur Qomah*, named after the ancient text, writes a strong approbation for *tavnit*, basing his teaching on the wedding formula:

Tavnit and *tselem*, *d'mut*, *t'munah*. These four words are names for *Hashem*: *Tavnit*, for they say [in the wedding blessings] "who formed the human in His image, in the *tselem d'mut* of His *tavnit*"—here it relates *tavnit* to the name and further it teaches about *tavnit* that it is greater than all of them, the *tselem* and the *d'mut* are related

---

[987] *Dugma* could also be included – see n.692.
[988] Neil Gillman discusses the relationship between *tavnit* and *tselem* in "Creation in the Bible and in the Liturgy", *Judaism and Ecology*, 137–8.
[989] *Kitvey Ramban*, quoted p.285.   [990] TZ 70, 120b–121a.
[991] Ashkenazi, 136, 37a, quoted p.251.   [992] Ibid., 147, 41a, quoted pp.250–51.

to the *tavnit*, and the *tavnit* is master... and one who said *tavnit* is not [an aspect of] Hashem and that the root [of the word *tavnit*] is "build/*BNH*" is not correct, for it is not [derived] from any root except [God's attribute] *Binah*.⁹⁹³

Tavnit is literally a name for YHVH according to Cordovero, connected to the Sefirah *Binah*. So *tavnit* refers both to structure and to *Binah*, understanding. A significance of this correspondence for constructive theology may be that we can limn the image of God in other creatures by understanding their structure.

Chotam – seal

Chotam or "seal" is used alongside *tavnit* as a synonym for *tselem* in the first Ashkenazi quote of the previous section, where it is applied specifically to the creatures. We encountered *chotam* in Mishnah as the seal with which God uniquely stamps each human being. "[T]he Holy One coins every *adam* with the seal/*chot'mo* of *Adam Harishon*, and one does not resemble his fellow, and therefore every single [person] must say 'For my sake the world was created'."⁹⁹⁴ This seal is the image of God in the human being, according to some interpretations.⁹⁹⁵ Scholem also remarked that "'great seal' (*chotam gadol*)... is another term meaning a secret name of God".⁹⁹⁶

The following passage from the *Zohar* portrays Shekhinah/*Malkhut* asking *Tif'eret* to affix Her image upon Him. The language used for Shekhinah is "the assembly of Israel":

Come and see. After they have clung one to the other, and She has received Her desire, She says: "Set me as a seal/*chotam* upon your heart" [So 8:6]. Why "as a seal"? When the seal is affixed to a certain place, then after it is taken away, a mark is left there, which is permanent; its whole impression/*r'shimu* and image/*d'yoqna* remain behind. So the assembly of Israel says: Behold, I have been attached to you. And now, even though I have become separated from you and have gone into exile, "set me as a seal upon your heart", so that my entire image / *kol d'yoqni* shall be in you – like the seal, whose image is left behind in its entirety at the place where it was affixed.⁹⁹⁷

In the *Zohar*, the *chotam* of God is also the image of human beings (and especially Israel) that becomes imprinted on God. And, just as our limbs hold the image of God, so to does God's arm, above, hold the image of the people. *Chotam* also can mean cervix, and in that context one finds in Lurianic Kabbalah the association of *chotam* with the divine name *Ehyeh*.⁹⁹⁸ Thus, in all these ways, *chotam* can also mean the inverse of God's image, the reflection of

---

⁹⁹³ (Jerusalem: Dov Ze'ev ben Yosef, 1966), §14, 52.   ⁹⁹⁴ *Sanhedrin* 4:5.
⁹⁹⁵ Cf. Rashi *ad* Gn 1:27, quoted in next section. See also n.336.
⁹⁹⁶ *Jewish Gnosticism*, 69. Scholem refers to a description of the name *Azbogah* found in Merkavah texts.
⁹⁹⁷ 1:244b; WZ 366.
⁹⁹⁸ *Sha'ar Hakavanot* 106d–107a, quoted in Magid, *From Metaphysics to Midrash*, 212.

Other frameworks for understanding tselem *and wholeness* 303

humanity in divinity. This is consonant with the actual image made by pressing a seal, which comes out as the reverse of the seal.

R'shimu – trace or impress

A midrash states that the *roshem*, tracing or impression, of human feet evinces the presence of God.[999] The *tselem* of Adam, marked in one way by our bipedal stature (our *qomah*), leaves its trace in the form of footprints. Just as *tselem Elohim* shows the divine presence in the human, so do footprints bespeak of a divine presence in a place.[1000] Rashi explicitly connects *roshem* with *tselem* when he explains the verse "Elohim created him in His image" thus: "made with a seal/*chotam*, like a coin made by means of a stamp/*roshem*".[1001]

There is a strong connection between *RShM* and the divine image in Kabbalah through the term *r'shimu*, meaning impression or trace, as we saw in the last quote from the *Zohar*. In Lurianic Kabbalah, *r'shimu* refers to the quality of divinity that remains in the void created by divine *tsimtsum*, which has been emptied (as it were) of God. While *r'shimu* has this important cosmogonic meaning, it also refers to the trace of divine presence dwelling within everything material. As such, *r'shimu* sometimes operates as a kind of democratized *tselem*, representing something more than the simple presence of God connoted by the idea that "there is no place empty of Shekhinah",[1002] but not quite embodying the level of image or its synonyms like *d'yoqna*.

To'ar – form

There is a close connection between *to'ar* and *tselem* found in the Merkavah literature. In the section "Upper and Lower Creations" (p.54), we saw the poetic line "*umito'aro nitazu sh'chaqim*", meaning "and from His form the constellations are shimmering", which continues: "and His form projects the exalted ones / *v'gei'im maf'lit to'aro*". In Scholem's analysis of this hymn, he notes, "I think it is obvious that the term *To'ar* (stature) here has the same meaning as *Komah* [sic] in *Shiur Komah*. The whole hymn describes the wonders of Creation stemming from God's majesty, His beauty, His stature,

---

[999] See p.90.
[1000] This trope could be used homiletically to include in God's image the earth itself, through the impression the human body makes upon it.
[1001] *ad* Gn 1:27.
[1002] The earliest expression of this idea seems to be *PRK* 1:2, 4 (∥ *ShmR* 2:5, *BmR* 12:4), where Rabban Gamliel, explaining why the Holy One spoke with Moshe from a bush, says that "there is no place in the earth empty from the Shekhinah / *eyn makom ba'arets panui min hash'khinah*." This is the source of the more generalized saying in Kabbalah and *Chasidut*, "There is no place empty of Him / *leyt atar panui mineyh*", first articulated in *TZ* 57, 91b and 70, 122b.

His crown, and His garment."[1003] *To'ar* is also paired with *qomah* and parallel to *tselem* in the *Hoshana Rabbah* prayers (see p.284). *To'ar* often relates to beauty as applied to the entirety of the body, though beauty is only discussed occasionally as being part of the divine image in rabbinic literature. A connection is also made between *tselem* and *to'ar* in *Pirqey d'Rabi Eli`ezer*, which states that upon becoming conscious, Adam Harishon saw all the animals, praised God, and then "stood on his feet and was described/proportioned/*m'to'ar* in the likeness of Elohim."[1004]

Golem as the inorganic

As we explore a coherent set of ideas about wholeness and image, the term *golem* provides an important counterpoint. In medieval legend, the *golem* is not simply a body without a soul; it is a form in the shape of a human body without the organization and complexity of a body, a body without organs, as it were. This interpretation can be related to one Talmudic passage, where an embryo is described in this way: "the rest of his limbs are contracted/*m'tsumtsamim* into him like a *golem*".[1005] In the passage "God stood Adam up as a *golem* stretching from earth to the firmament and then threw breath into him"(p.210), the breath that is missing from the *golem* can be understood as the organicity and patterning of Life, that which unites the whole through the growth of the parts and limbs. This interpretation is contiguous with the idea of breath as soul.

If *golem* means a body that is literally inorganic, without organs or breath, that is, the superficial appearance of a body without depth or inner structure, one could use the idea of *golem* homiletically as a metaphor for what has the appearance of being "in God's image" but is not in God's image. In relation to ecotheology, the concept of *golem* can work as a metaphor for what industrialized corporate civilization is creating out of the richness of the earth. All over the world, on land and in the seas, extraction-based economies are reducing the organicity and complexity of ecosystems to monocultures set up specifically for profit, using technologies that maximize the extraction of one resource at the expense of other uses or values that might be derived from or

---

[1003] *Jewish Gnosticism*, 62. The hymn continues: "And His crown blazes out the mighty, and His garment flows with the precious. And all trees shall rejoice in His word, and plants shall exult in His rejoicing, and His words shall drop as perfumes, flowing forth flames of fire, giving joy to those who search them, and quiet to those who fulfill them" (61–2). The emphasis on the vegetative world's response to the divine flow is unusual (and beautiful). This trope, which is more characteristic of medieval Kabbalah, would fit seamlessly with the prayer for Tu Bish'vat in *P'ri `Ets Hadar*.

[1004] Ch.11, 19, quoted p.65.

[1005] TB *Niddah* 25a. This could mean unextended in the sense of barely formed. One could alternatively interpret the concept of *golem* in line with *ARNA*, where *golem* is the opposite of sage (ch.37, 110). In that case, a *golem* lacks something like fully developed personhood.

Other frameworks for understanding tselem and wholeness 305

created by the ecosystem.[1006] So, for example, we replace old-growth forests, awesome entities filled with species sustained by millennia-old relationships of mutual aid, with *golem* forests,[1007] small farms with *golem* fields hundreds of times larger and filled with genetically modified soybeans,[1008] and villages with *golem* suburbs that have no gathering places or community centers other than malls[1009] and no class diversity, in a compartmentalized version of society which appears to be a whole body, but is actually missing most of the internal parts necessary for its survival, and is actively destroying, through a kind of parasitism, the organs (*viz.*, the organic ecosystems) outside of it, which are the source of its breath.[1010]

An example of this phenomenon that is of particular concern to the Jewish people is the forests planted by *Keren Kayemet L'Yisra'el* (the Jewish National

---

[1006] The problem is not created by localized and limited extraction for shorter periods of time, but by the globalization of that process, which leads to the colonization of all habitats and spheres of life, human and otherwise, under the regime of extraction.

[1007] A relatively new breed of *golem* forest has been developed in the maple-syrup industry, where corporate farms grow thousands of sugar-maple saplings that are cut off at the trunk and attached to vacuum pumps to suck out all the sap. Beyond the grotesqueness of that image, this technique turns one of the most sustainable and sustaining harvests – one which in its traditional form preserves thousands of acres of healthy forest – into a monoculture incapable of supporting a single bird's nest. (www.uvm.edu/~uvmpr/?Page=news&storyID=17209, Nov. 6, 2013)

[1008] On GMOs and *halakhah*, see nn.1120, 1122. The bulk of GMO crops are "Roundup Ready", that is, genetically modified so that they are not killed by the herbicide glyphosate. Planting "Roundup Ready" crops enables farmers to liberally apply glyphosate, thereby spurring the rapid evolution of glyphosate-resistant weeds. More importantly, these fields may end up with only a few genetically modified species; lacking a natural and diverse community (which, though it may compete with the planted crop, is also more disease- and catastrophe-resistant), they may truly be *golem*-like. Chemical-industry research shows glyphosate disappearing from the soil in less than thirty days, but according to some farmers it can take several years before the effects of glyphosate are mitigated (Ben Grosscup, Northeast Organic Farmers Association, personal communication, August 2012), and various remedial soil treatments have been developed to restore soil productivity after prolonged glyphosate use (www.nutritech.com.au/blog/2011/02/is-glyphosate-sustainable/ [Feb. 25, 2011]). These adverse effects may be due to changes in the composition of the soil's microbial community, rather than to persistence of the chemical (ibid.). Most industry literature and published studies ignore the possibility that adjuvants and surfactants used in various glyphosate formulations might increase the persistence of the herbicide, as well as its toxicity to aquatic species, to insects, or to animals ("Pesticide Profile – Glyphosate", American Bird Conservancy, www.abcbirds.org/abcprograms/policy/toxins/profiles/glyphosate.html [May 2014]).

[1009] Our attraction to smorgasbords of color and shape, which enables people to find satisfaction in synthetic environments like malls, may derive from an instinct for diverse ecological habitats that can sustain omnivores like ourselves (see end of n.235). For better or worse, our sense of well-being can be stimulated by the diversity of shops and goods in a mall just as well as by the diversity of species in a healthy forest.

[1010] Companies and economies cannot survive any more than civilization can outside the context of a healthy ecosystem – as it says, "No flour, no Torah" (*Mishnah Avot* 3:17 – the dictum is not "No money, no Torah", as it is often read). One could rewrite this, "No planet, no Torah".

Fund, also called KKL or the JNF) during the Zionist *yishuv* and the first 40 years of the state of Israel. These monocultural tree plantations were made up of the non-indigenous so-called "Jerusalem" pine or *oren*, and have less biodiversity than the more naked-seeming landscapes that in some places preceded them. They were not planted simply out of ignorance, though that surely played a role. According to the KKL representative to the first JNF-US Eco-Zionism conference, KKL got into planting forests because, under Turkish and British law, Arab tenants had the right to farm uncultivated land. These rights could be abnegated only if owners planted their own crops, so when KKL bought land from absentee Palestinian landlords, it would plant a "crop" of fast-growing *oren* trees to stake its claim.[1011] Created by an intention that was not whole – to plant a crop that was never going to be harvested – these old KKL forests are truly *golems*.[1012]

If we take *golem* to be body without a soul, and the "deformed angel" described by Horowitz as soul without a body, then we have a suggestion of what it truly means to divide body from soul: to create deficiency in all the worlds.

SELF-SIMILARITY, SELF-ORGANIZING SYSTEMS, AND THE
METAPHOR OF THE SEFIROT

In this section I will explore harmonies between Kabbalah and the sciences related to *qomah* that fall strictly within the framework of constructive theology. These harmonies suggest contours for a contemporary theology of Nature. One of the most important revolutions to consider in the natural sciences has been the wide-scale adoption of the mathematics and hermeneutics of self-similarity, fractal symmetry, self-organization, and complexity.[1013] Physical

---

[1011] Tuscon AZ, 1996. Later on, KKL forests served another purpose: to cover up the sites of former Arab villages that had been abandoned by their residents and then razed by the Israel Defense Forces. See "The Forest as a National Icon: Literature, Politics, and the Archaeology of Memory" by Yael Zerubavel in *Trees, Earth, and Torah*, 474, n.5. On the other side of the coin, the state of Israel still actively tears down fruit trees belonging to Palestinians, despite the very clear Torah prohibition at Dt 20:19 against doing so. Most recently (May 19, 2014), the IDF destroyed over a thousand trees belonging to the Tent of Nations, an educational farm dedicated to peace and reconciliation.

[1012] For the record, in the past 25 years KKL has changed its protocol and now plants native trees that can produce a healthy forest. However, there is still controversy over KKL's involvement in planting forests that dispossess the Bedouin.

[1013] Other important parallels between science and Kabbalah, especially cosmology, merit serious study. For example, the breaking of primordial symmetries theorized by physicists, which allows the various forces to emerge and propels the separation of matter from energy, is structurally similar to *sh'virat hakeilim*, the breaking of the primordial vessels. An analogy can also be drawn between the dark energy theorized to drive inflation of the early universe, and the hidden primordial light. Alternatively, the primordial light can be imagined as the light of the "Big Bang", before there were stars or matter, which we detect as the cosmic microwave background (CMB). See Matt, *God & The Big Bang*. See neohasid's script for

Self-similarity, self-organizing systems, and the metaphor of the Sefirot 307

science, in just half a century, has gone from being unable to analyze a simple system of three interacting bodies to being able to model the nature of real messy things and not just abstractions. A scientific and mathematical language now exists that can interpret the Earth and its immeasurable complexity in a meaningful way.

An object shows fractal symmetry or self-similarity when one can see the same pattern whether one looks at its parts up close or at the whole from farther away. Because a fractal pattern, at least on the level of theoretical mathematics, can repeat itself at every level of scale in an infinite regression or progression, no matter how small or large the frame, it directly provides a model for how the infinite can be contained in the finite. Fractal symmetry can be used to describe the difference between organic forms, which show complexity on multiple levels and scales, and inorganic forms, which do not. Fractal theory is also involved in understanding how complex order can be sustained within an anarchic (non-hierarchical) system. Complexity theory, catastrophe theory, and chaos theory are mathematical methods that describe the evolution of such self-organizing systems, which follow patterns without being predictable, and which can spontaneously develop self-sustaining structures.[1014] Most important is the idea of criticality, the moment when a system transitions between chaos or randomness and order or self-organization, which is involved in all the systems associated with Life.

These ideas can be translated into Kabbalistic terms quite readily. Even in Midrash, one can find a fairly accurate representation of fractal symmetry in primitive language, in a passage explaining the idea that everything in the world was also created in the human being:

A parable, to what does the thing compare? To one who takes wood and seeks to form/draw many forms [on it], and he has no room to make forms and he takes great pains/is pained. [It came to him] to draw upon the earth /ba'arets, for the one who makes forms in the earth, he can form and go on and delineate (i.e., create) many many [more, without limit]. But the Holy One, may His great name be blessed for

---

the "Cosmic Walk", which lines up the creation story with Kabbalah, cosmology, physics, and evolution. (Seidenberg, www.neohasid.org/ecohasid/cosmic_walk, Mar. 2011). In that script, I use the seven lower Sefirot, equated in Kabbalah with the seven days of creation, to structure the telling of the story of the universe. For example, the first day of Chesed/Love corresponds with the creation light in Genesis and with the Big Bang, inflationary expansion, and the CMB in physics. G'vurah/Might, which corresponds in Genesis to the division of the waters on the second day and in Kabbalah with destruction, is lined up with the supernova explosions that created and distributed the elements that make up the solar system, and with the great bombardment of the Earth that formed the moon and brought water to the planet. Tif'eret corresponds to the advent of Life, etc.

[1014] Complexity and chaos theory may already be familiar to readers; one introduction is Roger Lewin's *Complexity: Life at the Edge of Chaos* (Chicago: University of Chicago Press, 1999). Catastrophe theory concerns the conditions and mathematical modeling for when a system makes an abrupt and radical shift from one state of equilibrium or one developmental path to another.

eternity/`olam... in His wisdom and in His understanding He created the whole entire world/`olam, and created the heavens and the earth, upper ones and lower ones, [and He formed the human within it], and He formed in the human everything that He created in His world /`olamo.[1015]

God's creative pattern, as big as the universe, is expressed in all its detail within the human frame, in a kind of miracle. The infinite pattern within the finite signifies the hand of the divine artisan. The Kabbalists codified this pattern as the Sefirot, which underlie every entity, whether on the scale of the universe or on that of a grain of sand. This pattern is the divine image.

The essence of the doctrine of `olam qatan, and an essential aspect of God's image, is that the human being is a fractal image of everything contained within the world. If the rules of fractal symmetry hold, and if the human being is contained within the world, then an image of the whole human, which is part of that world, must have its own representation within every human being. This idea is represented symbolically in the following passage about the heart:

Lamed. Don't read LM"D but "Lev Meivin Da`at" – "the heart understands knowing", teaching that the heart weighs/shaqul equal to all the limbs of a person/Adam: For Adam has eyes, even so the heart has eyes; Adam has ears, even so the heart has ears, [... even so the heart has a mouth, speech, mourning, rest/comfort, crying out, walking, hearing, etc.]... and all the qualities... that belong to the limbs of adam, the heart has: [seeing, rejoicing, advising, healing, etc.][1016]

Nachman of Breslov drew on this image to build his Kabbalistic fable of the heart of the world (see p.294).

Leibniz uses the idea of fractal complexity (what he calls "monadology") to define the line between Nature and art – the difference between a living thing and a non-living human creation – in this way: "The machines of nature (namely, the living bodies) are... machines even in their smallest parts without any limit. Herein lies the difference between nature and art, that is, between divine and human art."[1017] Leibniz's definition of organic structure can be interpreted on many levels. Consider that every single cell of our bodies contains

---

[1015] ARNA ch.31, 91. Brackets reflect variants noted by Schechter. The passage may be read as a homiletical interpretation of the Biblical phrase, "YHVH Elohim formed the human, dirt from the ground" [Gn 2:7], especially in light of the preface: "R' Yosi Haglili says: All that the Holy One created in the earth He created in the human" (see p.244).

[1016] Midrash Otiyot d'Rabi Aqiva A, BM, vol.2, 376–7; cf. Aggadat `Olam Qatan, 57. The end of this section (377-8) lists twelve organs in the body, including the heart, that are either microcosms or symbolic of the microcosmic nature of the human body.

[1017] Monadology and Other Philosophical Essays, trans. Paul and Anne Martin Schrecker (Indianapolis IN: Bobbs-Merrill Company, 1965), 159. Leibniz's conceptualization of organic patterns is an important watershed in Western thought. He describes this more fully:

Thus every body of a living being is a sort of divine machine or natural automaton, which infinitely surpasses all artificial automata. For a machine made by human art is not a machine in all its parts. The cog on a brass wheel, for instance, has parts or fragments which for us are no longer artificial things.

Self-similarity, self-organizing systems, and the metaphor of the Sefirot 309

the full "instruction set" for human development and the maintenance of life, and Leibniz's words will become clear.

These frameworks can help us see multiple dimensions of sacredness and reach a greater depth of consciousness about our place in Creation. They can also be used to translate some of the basic ideas of complexity theory into terms that make sense within Judaism. Ideas about self-similarity and self-organizing systems are found throughout the Kabbalah. We have already seen how *qomah* can help relate the idea of wholeness to *tselem Elohim*. The pattern that emerges in a self-organizing system could be considered a *qomah*, at every level. Furthermore, the idea of *sheimot*, and the spelling out of God's name, as it were, on all levels within the structures of all organisms and ecosystems, teaches us about the fractal image of God, which is the divine pattern that in-forms (literally) the workings of every creature and system.

This idea of a self-organizing pattern is made more tangible when one thinks in terms of the structure of the Sefirot. The pattern of the Sefirot is understood to repeat itself within every existenz (every existent being from the perspective of its inner wholeness) and at every level of existence. The structures of the Sefirot are also repeated at many levels, for instance upper and lower, right and left, male and female, the model of the triadic scales or balances, all of which maintain their internal relationships and their relationships to each other, from the level of angels to that of rocks.

Especially in the notion of the *par'tsufim*, Lurianic Kabbalah suggests that at each level of dimensionality of the world there is a complete world system, which contains the structure of the whole within itself and sustains the whole that encompasses it. This pattern is a symbolic-religious correlate to physicist David Bohm's idea that there is an "implicate order" hidden behind the explicate order of the world.[1018]

The concept of fractal symmetry, often connected with holism or holographism (the idea that every part contains the whole), has been given spiritual or metaphysical meaning by many thinkers. For example, Ken Wilber writes,

Each and every holon in the Kosmos [sic] has equal Ground-value as a pure manifestation of Spirit or Emptiness. Further, as a part of *wholeness*, each holon possesses *intrinsic*

Leibniz speaks charmingly about ponds full of fishes where each fish is full of ponds of fishes, and, parallel to that, gardens full of fountains where each fountain is full of gardens full of fountains, when he tries to describe what we call fractal dimensionality. Leibniz's understanding is closely related to his conception of the infinitesimal, which was fundamental to his invention of calculus (see also n.903).

[1018] *Wholeness and the Implicate Order* (London: Routledge, 1980), chs.6–7. Bohm hypothesizes that the explicate or "unfolded" order of the world that can be defined in terms of equations, coordinates, particles, and so on, only describes what we can measure, whereas the implicate order is the whole that underlies what we can measure. It is intricately bound up with consciousness and characterized by holism. Bohm proposes this implicate order to explain entanglement, the "collapse" of the Schrödinger wave function, and other aspects of quantum theory.

value, depth value which is valuable precisely because it embraces aspects of the Kosmos as part of its own being (and the more aspects it embraces, then the greater its depth and the greater its intrinsic value, the greater its significance)... And finally, as a *part*, each holon possesses extrinsic or *instrumental value* because other holons... depend upon it in various ways for their own existence and survival.[1019]

This conception of wholeness within each being, and the potential for each being to embrace "greater aspects" of the whole, is resonant with the ideas discussed in this chapter. "Holographism" is one of the main hermeneutics of the Kabbalah and a primary tool used to extend the image of God beyond the human. Each spark contains the pattern of the Sefirot, and its *qomah* becomes more complete as it embraces more levels of Being. Every particle of Being contains the infinite within the finite.

For Kabbalah, there are sparks of the dimension of divinity in all things, whether appearing inanimate or alive, whether wholly of Nature or human-made. All things in this sense have some intrinsic value, but this value changes and increases through processes that deepen meaning and holiness. The concepts of complexity and fractals can help us distinguish this depth, in a way that would allow us to recognize divine sparks everywhere while understanding the greater dimensionality in what is alive, and what nurtures life, on the level of creatures, species, and ecosystems.

My purpose in drawing these connections is not to harmonize Judaism with science or to "update" the tradition, nor is it to claim that scientific ideas are foreshadowed by Jewish mysticism. Rather, by noticing correspondences between the patterns of science and the patterns of religion, we can build a religious language that is in conversation with science, and that can empower us to lift up what is truly wise, truly perceptive, truly understanding within science.[1020] Such language can also give us the power to resist what is destructive, exploitative, and ideological in science, what is called by some "scientism".

Lastly, these correspondences between science and Kabbalah create an image of what ritual and intention might mean. There are no hierarchies of scale in fractal theory, and from the perspective of complexity theory, there need not be any hierarchies of influence.[1021] Rather, a cause of the smallest scale and dimension may plausibly have an effect on the whole (the so-called "butterfly effect"). The Kabbalists believed that by attaching our minds and prayers to the self-organizing patterns of the Sefirot, we can bring blessing to the creatures, repair the sparks, and complete God's image in Creation. This idea may seem

---

[1019] *Sex, Ecology, Spirituality: The Spirit of Evolution* (Boston MA: Shambhala, 2000), 545–6, emphasis in original.

[1020] When the sacred guides our seeing, science readily becomes a way to open up to the world, rather than to control the world, just as understanding becomes an expression of humility, to "stand under" something, to listen and to wait faithfully upon it. This is the foundation of knowledge that comes from "the side of the Tree of Life", to use the Zoharic turn of phrase.

[1021] On this perspective as the correct view of all the sciences, see Mariam Thalos, *Without Hierarchy: The Scale Freedom of the Universe* (New York: Oxford University Press, 2013).

irrational, but the "butterfly effect" of human mind and intention upon the world, which can magnify or remediate our impact, enables us to postulate how ritual can be imbued with more than psychological or conventional meaning.

If indeed our minds and our bodies are fractal images of the universe, we have the potential to interact at a point of criticality and resonance with larger-scale patterns, and to change them. Indeed, one may say this potential was built into the Torah long before Kabbalah. The very fact that time is structured fractally in Judaism according to the seven "days" of Creation, from the weekly Sabbath to the seventh month of the High Holidays[1022] to the seventh or Sabbatical year to the seventh seventh of the Jubilee, means that human endeavor at every scale repeats and therefore sustains the pattern of Creation itself.[1023]

[1022] Tishrei, which begins with Rosh Hashanah, is actually the seventh month, starting from Nisan, "the beginning of months" (Ex 12:2). Of course, counting from Tishrei as we often do, Nisan, which includes Passover, is the seventh month.

[1023] On the idea that these practices structure time fractally, see Eisenberg, *The Ecology of Eden*, 101, 130. The Kabbalists extended this fractal pattern by depicting cosmic *Sh'mitot* of seven thousand years and more.

Intermediate conclusions
From Kabbalah to ecotheology

In Chapter 7 (in the section "First Conclusions"), I discussed how Kabbalists were able to find the image of God in any horizontal array of phenomena that represented the whole of Creation, and in any creature that represented Creation's vertical unification. We have also seen in the three preceeding chapters how the Kabbalists found the image of God in the entirety of Creation; how Gaia theory, by seeing the planet as an organic living whole, is congruent with Kabbalah and Maimonides; and how the Kabbalists and the Hasidic rebbes represented the potential for wholeness, and the potential for expressing God's image, through various constructs, such as *qomah sh'leymah*. In every dimension, Kabbalah emphasized holism.

Ecology, like Kabbalah, privileges holistic perspectives. Kabbalah looks at wholes within reality and sees the name of God, and it looks at parts that stand for the whole and sees the image of God. It sees the Sefirot at all levels of reality and all levels of meaning. Ecology looks at the phenomenon of Life and sees whole systems at many scales, expressed through the myriad relationships among creatures. Applying the principles of Kabbalah to constructive theology, we can train ourselves to see the image of God in all of these dimensions, in a species, in an ecosystem, in the water cycle, in the entirety of this planet, and so on.

As we have seen (p.55ff.), even in early midrashic literature, the human was imagined as the pivot of the world. In Kabbalah, our position as pivot means that we can strengthen the blessing that flows from upper realms to lower realms, and so strengthen the divine image in the world, or weaken that flow, and that image. As the continuation of the *Ra'ya Mehemna* passage (*Zohar* 3:123b) states, "all who wound His works wound His image. And the name YY (YHVH) does not rest on a wounded place..." The vision of human participation in blessing Creation is in some ways even stronger in *P'ri 'Ets Hadar* – as one might expect from the first Tu Bish'vat seder. Not only

Intermediate conclusions

can God's image in Creation be compromised by human action, but its full expression explicitly depends upon human consciousness.

At the same time, we heard from Shneur Zalman and Yaakov Lainer how the "lowest" levels of the *tachtonim*, the rocks and the soil, manifest the intense originary divinity of Creation, the *chesed* and *yir'ah*, the love and awe, that we can only limn in our most spiritual moments. One might say that our consciousness is an emergent property of the more recondite consciousness of the soil itself.

To think this way means to undo centuries of hierarchical thinking that has put human beings on a pedestal. But could expanding God's image to the more-than-human world (as Kabbalah hints at) and removing humanity from its pedestal have the unintended effect of trivializing human life? If we do so consciously, I think not. When we come to expand *tselem*'s reach, its original meaning is also intensified – in the language of the Talmud, *"ba' l'lameid v'nimtsa' limeid"*. Imagine, or remember, the awe you feel standing at the edge of the Grand Canyon, or descending into a forest, or witnessing an extraordinary storm or sunset. What would it be like to look at another person and feel that kind of awe? Imagine regarding a bus driver or a stranger who sits down beside you, or even an enemy, with those eyes. Imagine or remember what it is like to see a lover or a child with those eyes.

When we allow our innermost world to be penetrated by the World that is more-than-human, there is a mutual strengthening, as when mycelial hyphae interpenetrate the cells of a plant's roots, conveying nourishment to the plant and sucking nourishment from it. The more-than-human and the simply human can reflect and resound in each other's chambers, spiraling inward and upward, to the profoundest affirmation of Life. In Part III, I will explore some of the means through which we carry out this manifold expansion of God's image, including language, prayer, theology, and action, and look at where all this might lead us.

PART III

ECOTHEOLOGY

12

Nigun, shirah, the singing of Creation, and the problem of language

> These are the spheres in which the world of relation arises. The first: life with nature. Here the relation vibrates in the dark and remains below language. The creatures stir across from us, but they are unable to come to us, and the You we say to them sticks to the threshold of language.
>
> Martin Buber, *I and Thou*

> Said R' Chama bar Chanina: So difficult is the eloquence of lips, as weighty as the creation of the world and what fills it.
>
> *P'siqta Rabbati*[1024]

> Deep ecology involves learning a new language... to reanimate nature, we must have the courage to learn that new language.
>
> Christopher Manes, "Nature and Silence"[1025]

We are at the threshold of a new way of seeing the world. But in order to enter the land, to ground our lives in this new way of seeing, we must also find a new way of speaking **with** and **to** the world. We know language to be a vital component of our humanity, and one of the most powerful tools for transforming the world around us. From the earliest *midrashim* on, language was seen as an essential element of what makes us *b'tselem*. Buber also thought that language constituted a threshold separating us from an I–You relationship with the animals. This chapter will look at midrashic, Kabbalistic, and modern ideas about the presence of speech and conversation in the more-than-human

---

[1024] (Vienna: Yosef Kaiser, 1880), ch.33, 153a.
[1025] *Postmodern Environmental Ethics*, ed. Max Oelschlager (Albany NY: SUNY Press, 1995), 43–57; 51.

world, and use these ideas to further extend the meaning of *tselem*.[1026] How can they help us to construct an ecologically significant interpretation of God's image? If the image of God represents the potential to speak, as we saw in several teachings, in what ways is language limited to humanity, and in what ways may it be shared with other creatures? To answer these questions, I will engage more explicitly in doing theology than in preceding chapters.

The Torah itself, with its animistic view of the world, depicts non-human creatures talking (e.g., the snake in the garden and Bil`am's ass) and objects responding to speech (e.g., Miriam's well, which the Israelites sing to, and the rock that Moshe was commanded to speak to). The Psalms and many of the prophetic writings are full of trees, islands, seas, mountains, skies, earth that are singing, rejoicing, praising, and dancing. The Midrash and the *m'forshim* (commentators) on Genesis 2 understand the animals as receiving and responding to the names Adam gives them. Here again, language is conceived to be part of animals' lives, but not speech – the "speaking" of the animals is that they come when Adam calls them.

Ramban is sensitive to this point when he explains why the human could not find an `ezer k'negdo (Gn 2:20), a helper corresponding to himself:

[A]ny species that would call to him "*Ha'adam*" like his name, and say about him / *vayo'mer bo* that he (Adam) is a *nefesh chayah* like him (the animal)... he would be a help corresponding to him. [But Adam] called to all of them, and did not find for himself a helper that would call [back] to him.[1027]

Ramban poignantly describes Adam searching for an animal, a *nefesh chayah*, who would recognize him both as *ha'adam*, "human", and as a fellow animal. Adam's search resonates so deeply with the complex desire and feeling most people have toward animals.

[1026] Of course, according to Kabbalah, God places God's names and letters inside the creatures; this is a form of language. But this makes the other creatures not speakers but the spoken.

[1027] Ramban *ad* Gn 2:19 is responding to a difficulty in the verse, which, hyperliterally translated, reads: "and whatever would call to him the human an animal / *yiqra' lo ha'adam **nefesh chayah***, that [was] his name". In Hebrew, this should have been: "whatever the human would call *to* an animal / *l'nefesh chayah*". He begins his comment:

Maybe its explanation would be [found] in the matter of the helper, and the intent is to say that the *nefesh* of Adam is a *nefesh chayah*, like it said, "and the Adam became a *nefesh chayah*"... and [God] brought before him all of the species, and any species... (etc.).

There is a kind of contrapositive image of this interpretation in *TB Y'vamot* 63a, which states that the way Adam named the animals was that he "came upon them", that is, had sex with them (in rabbinic idiom, "coming" means penetration, not ejaculation). One interpretation of this I have heard (but have not been able to find a source for) is that in the act, whatever sound the animal made became its name. According to Ramban, Adam waited to be approached and none came to him; in the *Bavli*, he approached them all and none could fully meet him. In both cases, he dramatically discovers his loneliness. These interpretations could be woven into one story: Adam approached every animal intimately, but they could not name him, they could only name themselves.

The singing of Creation

If Adam wondered why the other animals did not try to name him, other passages in both Midrash and Kabbalah similarly wonder why the animals do not speak:

> [T]he Holy One has pity on the honor of the creatures/*b'riyot* (here meaning "people") and knows their needs. And He shut the mouth of the beast/*b'heimah*, for if she would speak, they could not make her serve or stand up to her /*bah*, for [there was] this silent one from the animals (the ass) and this wise one from the sages (Bil'am) – [and] when she spoke he could not stand up to her.[1028]

The implication of this midrashic passage is that animals really should speak, and that they have quite a bit to say. It is only because of God's concern for human honor that they are not given the chance to tell us what they think every single day. *Zohar Chadash* takes a less ironic tone in addressing the same question:

> R' Yosi said: What did Onkelos see, for it said "And the human became a *nefesh chayah*" and he translated, "a speaking spirit"? If there is a soul in the animals, why do animals not speak? R' Yitshak said: Because they were shaped from much thicker dirt/ *'afar* than the humans/ *b'ney nasha*, and they do not lift the head upright/*zaq'fin* or look up to the firmament as humans do. If they had been shaped from finer dirt, like humans, and they lifted their heads and looked up to the firmament, they would speak.[1029]

The reason why the other animals do not speak is because they cannot stand upright and so cannot behold the stars and the heavens! (See n.37.) More importantly, both passages see in all animals a potential for communicative speech – "if they lifted their head, they would speak" – a potential that can be read homiletically as a promise for a time to come, when we learn how to listen.

THE SINGING OF CREATION

What is more common, however, is the view that the animals, and all creatures, speak in some fashion. The Psalms abound with expressions of the heavens and earth (or "skies and land"), rivers, sea and land, trees and field, birds and beasts, singing out to God: "The heavens will rejoice and the earth sing out; the sea will roar out and all that fills him! The field will exult and that is in him; then all the trees of the forest will sing out!" [Ps 96:11–12], or "[T]he earth will

---

[1028] *BmR* 20:15.
[1029] *Midrash Hane'elam* 10d (WZ 727), riffing on Is 40:26 ("Lift up your eyes above and see. Come ask, Who created these?"). *Targum Onkelos* is discussed p.63. Further on, *Midrash Hane'elam* notes that *nefesh chayah* is created from the earth, meaning it is not divine. This passage resolves the "contradiction" in the Torah's labeling human and animal "*nefesh chayah*" by simply divorcing *nefesh chayah* from divine soul and *tselem*. See WZ 706ff., 720 (nn.174, 176), on what Tishby calls "this surprising differentiation between the intellectual soul and the speaking soul".

sing out, the many islands will rejoice!" [Ps 97:1].[1030] Many *aggadot* portray natural forces and beings speaking or singing, and Hillel was reported in a late aggadah to know not only the language of birds and animals, but also the language of mountains, trees, demons, and so on.[1031] *Pereq Shirah*, well known in Jewish environmental circles, places a verse of Psalms into the mouth of each species and force (including not only animals and trees but also clouds, thunder, islands, etc.).[1032] Several legends tell about the rivers and mountains talking (mostly arguing) with rabbis.[1033] In *Midrash Otiyot d'Rabi Aqiva A*, the very purpose of creation is song: "the world was only created for the sake of song and melody".[1034] But is this more than lovely lyricism?

While it would be hard to determine the Psalmist's intent, such verses were certainly understood in later texts to be making serious ontological claims. The prayer of *P'ri `Ets Hadar* gave full expression to this understanding when it imagined the trees exulting in response to the *tiqun* or repairing of the damage done to Creation by humans beings:

[M]ay all the sparks that were scattered by our hands, or by the hands of our ancestors, or by the sin of the first human against the fruit of the tree, return now to be included in the majestic might of the Tree of Life. "Then the trees of the forest will sing out" [Ps 96:12], and the tree of the field will raise a branch and make fruit, day by day.[1035]

The fruit that the tree creates is even part of its exultation. Here is an interpretation of the Psalmic image of exultant Nature that is both mystical and physical, and that is morally potent.

In a similar vein, Scholem detects an explicitly theological dimension in the aggadic tradition that the cows in 1Samuel sang a song as they pulled the Ark of the covenant from the territory of the Philistines back to the Israelites:

[1030] These images come from a culture embedded in a world seen as animate and ensouled; as I hope I have shown, taking these images to be merely poetic, rather than living statements about a living world, is historically inaccurate. Nevertheless, for *us* they tend to be more representative of poetry than theology.

[1031] *Masechet Sofrim* 16:9 (possibly composed in the Geonic period, but published with the *Bavli*). Similarly, late *midrashim* describe Shlomo speaking the languages of animals and demons – see p.325.

[1032] *Pereq Shirah* is found in many older prayerbooks. Everett Gendler takes it to be an expression of panpsychism, the idea that all things have a soul or awareness: "The song is consistent in ascribing sentience to the entirety of Creation" ("A Sentient Universe", 60). See also Natan Slifkin, *Nature's Song* (Jerusalem: Zoo Torah, 2009) and see herein, pp.162–3 and nn.497, 886, 1115 (end). Cf. Francis of Assisi, "Canticle of the Sun" For a scientific perspective on panpsychism, see Christof Koch, "Is Consciousness Universal?", *Scientific American Mind* 25:1 (Jan. 2014).

[1033] See TB *Chulin* 7a, quoted in n.1048. See also the story of Eliezer ben Dordya (TB `Avodah Zarah 17a), who, learning that his *t'shuvah* will never be accepted, asks the mountains and hills, heavens and earth, sun and moon, stars and constellations, to petition God that he be shown mercy. Each dyad responds, "Before we seek [mercy] for you, we need to seek for ourselves", since for each there is a prophecy that they will be destroyed. Finally, Eliezer expires in the throes of crying, and is accepted.

[1034] *BM*, vol.2, §*Alef*, 344. [1035] See Excursus 2.

R. Isaac Naptha, a Palestinian Amora of the middle of the third century, ascribed to the kine a song of a very different nature. In this song the kine are said to be addressing the Ark. And this is what they sing: "Rejoice Rejoice acacia [shrine]. Stretch forth in fullness of thy majesty..." This is an imitation of the setting in the Hekhaloth [*sic*] hymns. Just as the Holy Living Creatures (*chayot*), bearing the throne, sing hymns to the throne, so do these kine, bearing the Ark, sing hymns to the Ark.[1036]

As already discussed, the chariot or throne represents, among other things, the spectrum of the animal kingdom. According to Scholem, this very early tradition drew a connection between the heavenly *Chayot* (Animals) and earthly kine. Equally importantly for our discussion, the connection between heaven and earth is made through language, specifically song.

The following passage, from *Seder Rabbah d'B'rei'shit*, while in the realm of fable, delves more deeply into the question of language. Here, music, song, and praise are planted in every species of animal.

On the sixth [day] He created "animals/*b'heimot* in a thousand mountains / mountains of *Alef*" [Ps 50:10], and the rest of all the species of beast and seven [types of?] species of wild animal and creepers and crawlers as it is said, "The land will bring forth *nefesh chayah* by her species etc." [Gn 1:20], and at the end He created Adam to rule over all, and *hallel* and music He planted in their mouth, and song and praises in their throat... and for each and every one of them He commanded over its service/worship a prince/minister/*sar* at the head.[1037]

While up to here the animals are the ones who praise, in the next section a *sar* from every realm of being, who may be thought of as an angelic guardian, joins in celebration:

On the seventh [day] the Holy One sat on the throne of joy and made pass before Him the prince of water in great joy, the prince of rivers in great joy... the prince of mountains... of valleys... of wilderness... of the sun... of the moon... of [each constellation]... of plants... of *Gan`Eden*... of *Gehinom*... of trees... of crawlers... of fish... of grasshoppers... of birds... of angels... of each firmament... [of each type of celestial being]... and they were all of them standing in great joy in the wellspring of joy and rejoicing and dancing and singing and praising before Him... as it is said, "Majesty and splendor before Him, strength and delight and beauty in His holy place" (after Ps 96:6, 1Ch 16:27)—majesty and splendor corresponding to "[on the seventh

---

[1036] Scholem, *Jewish Gnosticism*, 25 (my parens.), analyzing a tradition found in TB `Avodah Zarah 24b, BR 54:4, Tanch Vayakhel 7, and *Seder Eliyahu Rabba'*, §11 (§12 in the edition Scholem used). Note that the cows sing a song exhorting the acacia trees (from which the ark is made) to themselves sing out: "*roni, roni hashitah!*" The image of the cows singing is derived from the phrase, "and the cows went straight /*vayisharnah*... going they went, and lowed / *hal'khu halokh v'ga`u*" [1Sa 6:12], where *vayisharnah* may also be read as "they sang".

[1037] BM, vol.1, §14, 26. Extant version reads, "On the sixth [day] He created deeps/*t'homot*", which Wertheimer corrects based on Ps 50:10.

day] He ceased /*shavat*", strength and beauty corresponding to "and He ensouled /*vay-inafash*" [Ex 31:17]. In that moment the Holy One brought the princess of Shabbat and sat her on the throne of glory.[1038]

The purpose of language is celebration, and the purpose of celebration is Shabbat, which is the completion of Creation.[1039] Language is both a response to the completion of Creation, and the final element that completes Creation.

The passage continues:

And He brought before her each and every prince of each and every firmament and of each and every abyss, and they were all of them dancing and rejoicing before her, and they said "Shabbat is YHVH's" [Lv 23:3], and the rest of the great princes said, "YHVH's is Shabbat". And even *Adam Harishon*, the Holy One brought him up to the heights of the heavens, the upper heavens, to celebrate and to rejoice in the joy of Shabbat.[1040]

If language corresponds to completion, wholeness, and joy, then *Adam Harishon* is the completion of language. Here the idea that Adam unites the upper and lower realms is given concrete expression in that only humankind represents itself in the heavenly court, whereas a ministering angel speaks on behalf of every other kind and species.[1041]

The following closely related section states:

The Holy One made a dedication for heavens and earth and all rejoiced in her and even *Adam Harishon* celebrated and rejoiced in the joy of Shabbat when [he] saw her praise... that all rejoiced in her and [that] she was the beginning and head of all joys.

[1038] §15, 26–7. Cf. *B'rei'shit Rabbati* (Jerusalem: Vegshel, 1984), 35 (see n.1043).

[1039] Enough cannot be said about the centrality of Shabbat to any Torah-based environmental ethics, and even more so the *Sh'mitah* and Jubilee years, the grand *Shabbatot* of every seventh year and fiftieth year, which delineate a radically eco-centric land ethic (see pp.11, 13, 152, 166–7, esp. nn.47, 549). Shabbat is not just an expression of the completion and wholeness of Creation in Genesis, a celebration of Creation, and, for us, an acknowledgment of gratitude to the Creator. It is also a rehearsal for living sustainably and justly in relation to the Earth and all her species. When one rests on Shabbat by refraining from all the categories of work defined by rabbinic tradition, one effectively relinquishes the power to manipulate the environment. Doing so, it is as if one draws closer to the more-than-human world, becoming in one sense more like the animals, who cannot create or exploit *techne* (arts and technology), while also becoming more like "our Creator", who rested on the first Shabbat. So one might say that as we grow in God's image we grow toward Creation.

[1040] *Seder Rabbah d'B'rei'shit*, §15, 27.

[1041] Several *midrashim* similarly frame the uniqueness of the people Israel: All other nations have an angel or "prince" who argues their case before God, or a constellation that determines their fate, whereas "there is no constellation/*mazal* for Israel", who stand directly before God (*TB Shabbat* 156a). This resonates with the dictum that every blade of grass has "a *mazal* that strikes it and says to it, 'Grow!'" (*BR* 10:6). Thus the nations are likened to the other species (i.e., part of the natural world), making Israel the essence of humanity. (Cf. *Zohar* 3:123b, n.747.) A related motif is that Israel's defender is the highest angel, Micha'el, who is also archangel over the whole Creation. One finds that ethno-archism and anthropo-archism are isomorphic in rabbinic tradition, and can be remedied through isomorphic shifts in meaning.

The singing of Creation

Right away they opened their mouths, and [Adam] said, "*Mizmor Shir* for the day of Shabbat" [Ps 92:1]... until Shabbat stood on her feet and fell on her face and said, "It is good to give thanks to YHVH..." [Ps 92:2], and all the orders of Creation[1042] replied, "... and to sing to Your high name".[1043]

Here, *Adam Harishon* initiates singing, rather than joining in as the celebration reaches its climax.[1044] Shabbat herself answers antiphonally, and "all the orders of Creation" sing, that is, the upper and lower creatures themselves, and *not* just their angelic representatives, form a single chorus. This passage telegraphs ideas seen in other contexts, that the role of the human is to unify creation, and to bring all the orders of Creation into prayer and song, that is, *into language*.

But in Kabbalah, one also finds the deeper perspective that all Creation, heavens and Earth and all creatures, are already born into song, born to sing:

> The Holy One created desiring songs with the creation of heavens and earth... [A]ll the world are desiring and rejoicing to beautify the One who formed them... and this is "In beginning /*B'Rei'ShiT* / בראשית"—look at the letters and see: Desiring Song / *ShiR Ta'eV* / שיר תאב.[1045]

Creation is woven out of the desire of song, out of en-chantment literally, and desiring songs are created at the beginning, *b'rei'shit*. All the creatures are created, as it were, to sing songs already created, waiting to be sung.[1046]

The speech of the waters and the trees

The following texts, about water and trees, further develop a midrashic picture of language in the more-than-human world. About the waters, we read,

> "[The rivers lift up their voice,] the rivers will lift up their waves /*dokhyam*" [Ps 93:3]...—R' Levi said: The waters whisper, these to these, and say, "Where will we go?" and they say "Seaward, seaward / *derekh yam, derekh yam*."[1047]

There are very many mythologically oriented descriptions of the anger, jealousy, or desire of the seas and waters in the Midrash, often describing how God

---

[1042] The phrase "*sidrey v'rei'shit*" or "orders of Creation" (lit. orders of 'In beginning') points toward the idea of a complex but coherent order, a sense of the "rightness of Nature", which is potentially sacred. See Kadushin, *The Rabbinic Mind*, 147–50, and discussion in n.936.

[1043] §16, 27. Wertheimer suggests amending to read, "Right away *he* (i.e., Adam) opened his mouth", following *B'rei'shit Rabbati*. *B'rei'shit Rabbati* also joins this section with §15.

[1044] What does it mean that "**even** *Adam Harishon* rejoiced"? One may read this, "most importantly, *Adam Harishon* rejoiced".

[1045] ZCh, *Midrash Hane`elam, B'rei'shit* 5d.

[1046] In a very real sense, song may be thought of as the information that encodes and is embedded in the structure of the universe.

[1047] *Midrash T'hilim* ad Ps 93:3, 415, n.29 (the standard published version) ‖ BR 5:3, YSh 2:848. Other suggestions for what the waters say include: "To that sea, to that sea / *l'hadeikh yama l'hadeikh yama*" (all); "[We] are broken, receive us; we are shattered, receive us / *Dukhim qablunu, m'dukhanim anu qablunu*" (BR; Jastrow translates the first part as "ye leaders, receive us", s.v. *dukh* III, 285. Cf. n.272).

has to rebuke, sunder, and restrain the waters in order for land to exist.[1048] However, this aggadah has an entirely different tone. The waters are in conversation with each other, not with human beings. The thoughts they have are utterly simple. The entire "mental being" of water (to use Walter Benjamin's phrase[1049]), is toward the other waters, and their entire intention is to join the sea, as though water were giving a poetic voice to the language of gravity and cohesion. Forces of Nature are imagined as languages, spoken through their effects on the creatures and elements.

We have already noted a few of the many passages in Psalms that ascribe speech to the trees. The idea that there is a "mental being" that belongs to the trees, parallel to that of the waters, can be found in the following midrashic passage:

"And every growth/*si'ach* of the field" [Gn 2:5]—All the trees as it were /*k'ilu* are conversing/*m'sichin*, these with these. All the trees as it were are conversing with the creatures / `*im hab'riyot*. All the trees were created to give pleasure to the creatures... All the conversations of the creatures are about nothing except the land... and all the prayers of the creatures are about nothing except the land... All the prayers of Israel are about nothing except the Temple/ *beyt hamiqdash*.[1050]

What does it mean that the trees speak? Even though the trees are "created to give pleasure", they are in "conversation" first with each other, and second with the other creatures (here probably meaning all creatures and not just humans). Thus, unlike the waters, the trees' being is also toward other creatures, toward humans and animals. This passage also tells us that all the creatures are conversing "about the land". According to another midrash, the trees of the garden lifted their voices after Adam ate the forbidden fruit, calling out "thief, thief".[1051]

Bracketing the idea of conversation in the first passage by using the phrase "as it were", the midrash indicates that it is not just personifying the trees

---

[1048] See p.86 and n.271. This motif also appears in specific stories, like the Red Sea's refusal to split (*ShmR* 21:6), or the Ginai River's refusal to part for R' Pinchas ben Yair (*TB Chulin* 7a). Pinchas, on his way to perform the mitsvah of freeing captives, encounters the Ginai, commanding it to split so he can cross. The river protests, "You are going to do the will of your Possessor /*qoneikh* and I am going to do the will of my Possessor. You – maybe you are going to do [God's will] and maybe you aren't (since Pinchas's success depends on others). I certainly am doing it"; that is, my mitsvah is more important than yours! Pinchas retorts, "If you don't split, I'll decree that water will not pass through you forever!" The river splits, under protest. This aggadah recognizes that when human needs prevail over the needs of other beings, this is determined by power, rather than by right or intrinsic moral value, even in the case of a righteous saint.

[1049] "On Language As Such and on the Language of Man", in *Reflections*, ed. Peter Demetz (New York: Schocken Books, 1978), 314–32. This essay delineates an idealized picture of Edenic language united with the essence of each thing, and hence shared by all, animate and inanimate.

[1050] *BR* 13:2; *YSh* 1:20. The Talmud also talks about "the conversation of date palms / *sichat d'kalim*" (*TB Bava Bat'ra* 134a, *Sukkah* 28a).

[1051] *BR* 19:8.

The singing of Creation 325

as one does in a children's tale, so that they can become characters in our stories. Rather, the passage expresses something substantive about how trees exist both for themselves and for other creatures. It recasts in midrashic terms the relationship between fruit-bearing and pollen/nectar-producing plants and the worlds of animals and insects. Angiosperms, the model trees of Kabbalah, did truly evolve in conversation with animal species, using animal and insect bodies to transport their fruit, seeds, and pollen in different directions and over longer distances than wind or water could carry them.[1052] Seen in the light of later developments in Kabbalah that ascribe God's image to fruit trees, this passage carries special weight for the question of how God's image might be present in non-human creatures. We have already seen that *P'ri `Ets Hadar* understood the very production of fruit by trees as a kind of exultation and prayer. Nachman certainly had a similar framework in mind when he instructed his followers to pray in the fields, as I will discuss further on (p.330ff.).

Understanding the speech of animals

It is almost universally assumed in folklore that the animals have their own languages. We have already discussed one midrash that ascribes the language of prayer and praise to the animals, who come to worship Adam and end up worshipping with him (p.65), and we have heard about the cows that sang to the ark of the covenant. Knowing the language of birds is a common theme in Jewish folklore.[1053] For our purposes, it is significant that some late *midrashim* interpret having dominion over the animals as having the ability to converse with them. Specifically, Shlomo's ability to understand the birds and animals is what enables his dominion over the world.[1054] If *r'diyah* or dominion means

---

[1052] See Michael Pollan, *The Botany of Desire* (New York: Random House, 2001) and Connie Barlow, *The Ghosts of Evolution* (New York: Basic Books, 2000). Pollan analyzes the hypothesis that some plant species have evolved or are evolving to use human agriculture as their means of propagation. Barlow explores the idea that many species of tree in the Americas evolved fruit suited to now-extinct megafauna. Both describe relationships between species as conversations.

[1053] Examples can be found in Howard Schwartz, *Elijah's Violin & Other Jewish Fairy Tales* (New York: Oxford University Press, 1994), 47, 59, 95, 156ff., 174, 203–5. The Talmud also speaks about understanding "the language of birds / *lishna d'tsiporey*" (TB Gitin 45a). Michael Swartz takes this and "the conversation of date palms" (n.1050) to be systems of divination, though in reference to *Gitin* he admits that "the Talmud ... presupposes that [the raven] knew what it was saying" ("Bubbling Blood and Rolling Bones", *Antike Mythen: Medien, Transformationen und Konstruktionen*, eds. Ueli Dill and Christine Walde (Berlin: de Gruyter, 2009), 445).

[1054] See *Targum Sheni* to Esther and YSh 2:182. Cf. *Shir Hashirim Rabbah* 1:9, as well as the Qur'an, *Surah* 27:16–26, though in those contexts Shlomo's ability is connected with wisdom rather than dominion. See Louis Ginzberg, *Legends of the Jews*, vol.6, trans. Henrietta Szold and Paul Radin (Philadelphia: JPS, 1956), 288–9, nn.34 and 38, who also cites texts that reject this claim, *viz.*: "'And He spoke concerning/with/ `al animals and birds' [1Kg 5:13]—And is it possible to talk with/ `al the animal and the bird? Rather [he explained the laws *about*

communicating with the animals, then it also entails a kind of parity between humanity and other animals, rather than hierarchy. Similarly, in Kabbalah, Noach was also said to understand "the whispering and chirping of every creature and their hints" (*Zohar Chadash* 22b), while Hasidic stories tell of the Baal Shem Tov's ability to do the same.[1055]

In Lurianic Kabbalah, this theme transcends folklore, at once becoming myth and metaphysics. Chayyim Vital, in *Sha`ar Ru'ach Haqodesh*, explains five ways one can learn Torah from "knowing bird songs / *tsif'tsufey `ofot*":

(1) [K]now that from the day the Torah was burned by the nations... her powers and secrets were passed into the hand of the shells/*q'lipot*, and therefore there is no creature in the world [without secrets of Torah]... for all of these [creatures] have princes placed over them, and those princes know the mysteries of the Torah and her secrets... [and] they insert into their mouths, through songs and sound/voice, deep secrets from the Torah... (2) Also know that whatever is decreed above, they (i.e., the heavenly hosts) announce the decree in all the worlds... [and] when the birds fly through the air, they cut through and split the air and divide it up by means of their flying and flapping, and then the announcing voice passes through there... (3) and [it can also be] the opposite, for the bird of the skies is the speaker/*ham'daber*, therefore it is said... "[the bird of the skies] will lead [with] the voice" [Ec 10:20], for his voice becomes mixed with the announcing voice... (4) And behold, sometimes the matter of the song of birds is another type, for there are human souls reincarnated in the these birds, or in any species of creature that they may be, and all is for the known reasons according to their punishment... and [they tell] of what they hear... from behind the veil/*pargod*... (5) Also there is sometimes another type, for a soul from some righteous person /*tsadiq* [may] come from the upper world and clothe herself in that form/*tsurah* and image/*dimyon* [of a bird], and he isn't an actual creature or bird, and he reveals and tells secrets of the Torah.[1056]

The beginning of this passage indicates that speech is present in animals only as a condition of exile. In the second and third explanations, the birds themselves are active agents, whether facilitating speech or actually speaking. Finally, Vital describes the incarnation of people into the forms of birds, whether as punishment or, in an almost illusionary sense, as a means that facilitates a divine visitation of the righteous.[1057] According to Vital's report, Luria experienced a kind of ecosystem of soul and speech that, for all its complication, courses in multiple directions and levels through the creatures.

animals and birds]" (*Tanch Chuqat* 6; *TanchB Chuqat* 15). *Tanchuma* may be specifically rejecting the Islamic story.
[1055] Dov Ber ben Shmuel of Linitz, *Shivchey Habesht* (Berlin: Ajanoth Verlag, 1922), 50–51.
[1056] *Sefer Sha`ar Ru'ach Haqodesh* (Jerusalem: Kitvey Rabeynu Ha'ar"i, 1963) *D'rush* 3, 22–3 (numbering my addition).
[1057] This book has not explored reincarnation. Many Kabbalistic and Hasidic systems of thought hold that human souls can be reborn in animals, plants, even objects. This trope, though significant for Jewish ecotheology (see p.142 and n.542), is beyond the scope of this work.

THE PHENOMENOLOGY OF SPEECH AND SONG

Exegetical texts about language such as these remain in the realm of poetry rather than theology. Delving further brings us to the realm of myth at the heart of the animate world of Midrash and Kabbalah. But can there be a theology that is more than poetry or myth, that coheres with "scientific reality"?

Buber's *I and Thou* and the more-than-human

Bridging the gap between myth and theology is no small challenge. Martin Buber, speaking about encountering the You in non-human creatures, wrestles with this exact problem:

> The question may be asked at this point whether we have any right to speak of a "reply" or "address" that comes from outside the sphere to which... we ascribe spontaneity and consciousness as if they were like a reply or address in the human world in which we live. Is what has here been said valid except as a "personalizing" metaphor? Are we not threatened by the dangers of a problematic "mysticism"?[1058]

Buber's attempts to answer these questions will guide the next part of this discussion.

Martin Buber's phenomenology of relationship is rooted in a very abstract idea of language, framed by the dichotomy between "the basic word I-It" and "the basic word I-You". These "basic words" have salience within the human interpersonal realm, where one can encounter another as an instrument to serve one's own ends (in which case our "I" is one pole of "I-It"), or as an end-in-itself (where our "I" is one pole of "I-You").

Obviously, the same dichotomies of I-You and I-It can be found in our encounters with the more-than-human world. However, for Buber, our encounters there cannot be divided by language in quite the same way. Buber explains:

> These are the spheres in which the world of relation arises. The first: life with nature. Here the relation vibrates in the dark and remains below language. The creatures stir across from us, but they are unable to come to us, and the You we say to them sticks to the threshold of language. The second: life with people. Here the relation is manifest and enters language. We can give and receive the You. The third: life with spiritual beings. Here the relation is wrapped in a cloud but reveals itself, it lacks but creates language. We hear no You and yet feel addressed; we answer – creating, thinking, acting: with our being we speak the basic word, unable to say You with our mouth. But how can we incorporate into the world of the basic word what lies outside language?[1059]

Beyond the threshold of language, there is Spirit, there is what calls us toward what we might define as the image of God. Yet Buber also suggests that we

---

[1058] *I and Thou*, trans. Walter Kaufman (New York: Charles Scribner's Sons, 1970), 177–8 (Afterword).
[1059] Ibid., 56–7, modified.

12 Nigun, shirah, *the singing of Creation, and the problem of language*

find God's presence in the mute encounters that "vibrate" below the language threshold. Though Buber divides the more-than-human realm into Nature and Spirit, separating both from the human realm, all three are united in "the eternal You": "In every sphere, through everything that becomes present to us, we gaze toward the train of the eternal You; in each we perceive a breath of it; in every You we address the eternal You, in every sphere according to its manner."[1060]

Notably, Buber does not employ the concept of *tselem* in *I and Thou*.[1061] For Buber, in every encounter, one is encountering "the eternal You", that is, not an image of God, but God in actuality.[1062] Nevertheless, one may consider the You one encounters in another individual to be a kind of image of the eternal You,[1063] and what Buber describes fits more than one aspect of God's image as it was defined in rabbinic literature. Roughly, it corresponds both to the divine image within oneself that becomes actualized in the presence of the You, and to the divine image in the Other that becomes manifest to one who recognizes the You within the Other. Elsewhere, Buber explains that in the more-than-human realm this presence is mediated not by speech but by its absence: "The demanding silence of the forms, the loving speech of human beings, the eloquent muteness of creatures – all of these are gateways into the presence of the word."[1064] This silence or muteness nonetheless brings us "into the presence of the word".

Buber struggled to define how this works with respect to Nature in an afterword to *I and Thou*:

[I]f we are to suppose that the beings and things in nature that we encounter as our You also grant us some sort of reciprocity, what is the character of this reciprocity, and what gives us the right to apply to it this basic concept?[1065]

[1060] Ibid., 57.
[1061] Where Buber does refer explicitly to *tselem* in other works, he seems to see it strictly in terms of *imitatio Dei*, of "man's having been made in the image of God, understood as deed, as becoming, as task" ("My Way Into Hasidism", *Hasidism and Modern Man* [New York: Horizon Books, 1958], 59).
[1062] Buber also does not use the term "God" in the first two parts of *I and Thou* (except in quotes, 101), but there is no doubt about what he means, even without his exploration of the concept of God in Part Three. Note that the phrase *der ewige Du*, "the eternal You", refracts the terms *der Ewige* (the Eternal) and *das ewige Wesen* (the eternal Being), which Mendelssohn used to translate YHVH in his Bible translation.
[1063] "Extended, the lines of relationship intersect in the eternal You. Every single you is a glimpse of that. Through every single You the basic word addresses the eternal You" (Buber, *I and Thou*, 123). This description is closer in analogy to a hologram than to any other kind of image.
[1064] Ibid., 150, my parens. Here the realm of Spirit is inhabited by "forms"; above, by "spiritual beings".
[1065] Ibid., 172. This afterword was written in response to critiques of his description of I-You in relation to a tree (57–8), where he concluded, "One should not try to dilute the meaning of the relation: relation is reciprocity."

The phenomenology of speech and song

He asserts here that the relationship with animals is one in which the You is latent, on "the threshold of mutuality".[1066] Buber then goes on to consider the more challenging question of other dimensions of Nature:

> It is altogether different with those realms of nature which lack the spontaneity that we share with animals. It is part of our concept of the plant that it cannot react to our actions upon it, that it cannot "reply." Yet this does not mean that we meet with no reciprocity at all in this sphere. We find here not the deed of posture of an individual being but a reciprocity of being itself – a reciprocity that has nothing except being. The living wholeness and unity of a tree that denies itself to the eye, no matter how keen, of anyone who merely investigates, while it is manifest to those who say You, is present when they are present: they grant the tree the opportunity to manifest it, and now the tree that has being manifests it.[1067]

For Buber, we can elevate this relationship to the level of reciprocity by our simple presence. Buber continues:

> Our habits of thought make it difficult for us to see that in such cases something is awakened by our attitude and flashes toward us from that which has being. What matters in this sphere is that we should do justice with an open mind to the actuality that opens up before us. This huge sphere that reaches from the stones to the stars I should like to designate as the pre-threshold, meaning the step that comes before the threshold.[1068]

Buber speaks of what "is awakened by our attitude and flashes toward us". He exhorts us to "do justice with an open mind" to this actuality. What does it mean to do justice in this context? Does it have a deontological component? How can we become sensitive to what is awakened? Again, Buber returns to the metaphor of the threshold.

In every one of Buber's examples, he singles out an individual, tree or animal, as the Other he relates to. His rhetoric also unites the upper and lower realms, "from the stones to the stars", under Nature, embracing as one the more-than-human world. Yet this whole is in its entirety the "pre-threshold". Buber has no language for relationships to greater wholes, to what is aggregate rather than individual. And Buber does not address the relationships we have with what is non-individual, with the entities that exist as shared spaces between life forms, such as atmosphere, land, oceans, which are the foundation of the

---

[1066] Ibid, 173. Buber explains:
> Instead of considering nature as a whole, as we usually do, we must consider its different realms separately. Man once "tamed" animals [...] Animals are not twofold, like man: the twofoldness of the basic words I-You and I-It is alien to them although they can both turn toward another being and contemplate objects. We may say that in them twofoldness is latent. In ... our You-saying to animals, we may call this sphere the threshold of mutuality.
(172–3)

[1067] Ibid., 173.
[1068] Ibid., 173–4. Note that in one place Buber speaks of "the threshold of language", and in the other, "the threshold of mutuality". These may or may not be the same.

community we call Life. Buber is lacking something we must create: a language that enables us to address as You those shared spaces, and to address Gaia itself.

Wherever we look – to planetary systems or to ecosystems of individuals, to ancient symbioses of mycelia and plants where fungal hyphae may penetrate root cell walls, to the microbiomes of individual animals, humans included, each carrying ten times as many bacterial cells as animal cells in symbiosis with us – there is more than meets the I of Buber's I-You. This too ecotheology must address: how do we speak to and with the invisible as well as the visible realms of the *tachtonim* – eubacteria and archaea, fungi and protists, as well as the four realms of life known to *Chazal*?[1069]

Prayer, melody, and the song of the grass

While Buber attempted to get at these questions from a phenomenological perspective, Nachman of Breslov took a more theological and midrashic approach to locating speech in the more-than-human realm. Nachman of Breslov claims that true speech, as exemplified by prayer, is actually a gathering up of the speech of the more-than-human world:

Know that when a person prays in a field, then all of the grasses/plants together come into the prayer, and they help him, and give him strength within his prayer. And this is what it means when prayer is called "conversation/*sichah*": it refers to "the growth of the field / *si'ach hasadeh*" [Gn 2:5], [meaning] that every shoot from the field gives strength and helps his prayer. And this is [what the verse means when it says,] "And Isaac went out to reflect in the field / *lasu'ach basadeh*" [Gn 24:63]: that his prayer (*sichah*) was made with the help and strength of the field (*si'ach*), that all the plants of the field gave strength and helped his prayer.[1070]

Prayer, which Hasidic thinkers often take to be the essence or purification of human language, is rooted in the earth itself, in the conversation of the plants. One could say that human beings are not the creators of language but tools of the creatures to fashion their language into prayer. We enter into *sichah*, conversation, which is also prayer, as Rebbe Nachman and the Midrash teach, and find that the creatures are already *m'sichin*, in conversation.

[1069] In all, that would make eight realms including the four traditional, all of which participate directly in the intelligence and wisdom of the natural world, or what Cordovero calls *chokhmat `elyon*. One might include viruses as a ninth realm. On an ecological scale, more weight should be given to the invisible realms. As Manes writes, "If fungus, one of the 'lowliest' of forms on a humanistic scale of values, were to go extinct tomorrow, the effect on the rest of the biosphere would be catastrophic... In contrast, if Homo sapiens disappeared, the event would go virtually unnoticied by the vast majority of Earth's life forms. As hominids, we dwell at the outermost fringes of important ecological processes".
("Nature and Silence", 51)

[1070] *LM* 2:11, 44.

The phenomenology of speech and song

Nachman calls the conversation of the grasses "song" in another teaching:

> Know that every shepherd has a unique melody/*nigun* according to the grasses and the place where he herds. For every animal/*b'heimah* has a grass unique to her that she needs to eat, and also a shepherd isn't always in one place, and according to the grasses and the place where he herds, so he has a *nigun*. For every grass there is a song/*shirah* which it speaks... and from the song of the grasses is made the *nigun* of the shepherd... And this is the dimension of "From the edge/wing/*kanaf* of the earth we heard songs/*z'mirot*" [Is 24:16]—[it means] that songs and *nigunim* come out from "the wing of the earth", for by means of the grasses growing in the land a *nigun* is made. And since the shepherd knows the *nigun*, by means of this he gives strength to the grasses... and there is pasture for the animals.[1071]

Nachman seems to describe a lived experience, even if it is propped up by scripture. The difference between *shirah* or song and *nigun* or melody is that a song has words but a *nigun* may not. There is a paradox in this teaching: humans extract music from the song of the grass, but not the "verbal" part, whatever that may be. Elsewhere, Nachman teaches that song and prayer, encumbered by words, cannot reach the highest levels, but that *nigun*, without words, can even cross the empty space that separates the universe from God, reaching all the way to *Eyn Sof*, to the infinite, primordial source.[1072] Together, these passages describe a kind of ecosystem of language and song in which the human being is one organ of a complex cycle that nurtures Life and divinity.

Understanding that we are in dialogue with the world around us – understanding this not just as metaphor but as phenomenology – opens new dimensions of experience. It is more than just psychological projection to say that the world has language. Rather, human language emerges from the rhythms and fluidity of a world that is constituted by relationship. In this sense, the challenge is not to learn to speak with the more-than-human world, but to realize that we are already speaking with it.[1073]

[1071] *LM* 2:63, 68–9. See also 2:11, which describes "the strength of the grasses", rather than their song, entering into one's prayer. Embedded in this teaching is the recognition that each ecosystem or place might make its own unique contribution to human prayer and melody, and so uniquely reveal divinity.

[1072] *LM* 1:64, Bo' El Paro`, 182–4. According to Nachman, through the process of *tsimtsum* or contraction, God creates an empty space that defines the universe. At the human level, *machloqet*, argument or debate between the sages, recreates this process. But a wordless *nigun* can actually reach a level that is beyond or prior to *tsimtsum*. In this light, *LM* 2:63 could be representing human participation in the song of the grasses as irenic and transcending the combativeness of intra-human language. Alternatively, Nachman may have meant that the language of the grasses only reaches to the height of the melody of human beings, or that only human beings can craft out of the grasses' song a melody that can cross the empty space. Also, whereas in *LM* 2:11 the conversation of the grasses gets raised further toward God by the conversation of human prayer, in *LM* 2:63 the human *nigun* gives strength back to the grasses.

[1073] See Abram, *The Spell of the Sensuous*, quoted n.102 and p.341.

13

Further theological reflections

CONTEMPORARY ECOTHEOLOGY

For people who are searching for the meaning of Nature within Jewish tradition, Kabbalah is a rich vein to draw on. Various authors have already written about the connections between Kabbalah and ecology or science (particularly cosmology).[1074] Much of this writing is homiletical; often the texts that serve as the ground for these connections are not quoted. For example, Waskow states:

> Luria saw the universe as itself an aspect of God – the enfolded *reshimu* [sic] or residue of the Divinity that was left-over in the void that emerged from the Infinite's *tzimtzum* [sic]... [T]he *tzimtzum* is the Infinite God's attempt to see Itself mirrored, reflected, through the unfolding God that emerges from the Divine *reshimu* – that is, through the finite universe that hazily reflects the Infinite... [T]he resulting aspect of God, God-embodied-in-the-universe, grows toward revealing Itself, toward becoming able to mirror the Infinite Beyond... For the universe to continue on this journey toward self-awareness, there needs to be a species capable of self-awareness... That is what it means to live in the Image of God – to reflect upon the Unity, and thus to mirror God's Own Self. Among the species on this planet, the human race so far bears this Image of God – the self-awareness of Unity – most fully. That does not mean other beings have no share in this Image, nor does it mean that the unfolding of the Image stops with us.[1075]

Luria was far closer to Gnosticism than he is depicted as being here (see p.277ff.), but Waskow's exposition can be supported by other sources in the Kabbalistic tradition. Though Waskow's theme, that the universe is on a

---

[1074] Such as Rav Kook, see the Introduction; on modern cosmology, see n.1013.
[1075] "The Emergence of Eco-Kabbalah" (Philadelphia: Shalom Center, 2001), www.the shalomcenter.org/node/170 (Aug. 2011).

journey toward self-awareness, is classically modernist-humanist and anthropocentric, the hubris of modernity is considerably softened.

Arthur Green also understands Kabbalah and science in terms of each other. His interpretation of DNA and evolution (see p.238) leads him to a contemporary "de-mythologized" reading of Kabbalah. For Green, even though "[t]he mythic universe of Kabbalah, for all its beauty, belongs to another age", "[the Kabbalist's] approach to spirituality can be appreciated more than ever today, not only for its beauty but for a certain dimly perceived accuracy as well."[1076] Green thus implies that science should be taken as Kabbalah's inner truth, its referent in the real world.[1077] Yet this also transfigures science: we must "embrace [the tale of evolution] and uncover its sacred dimensions".[1078]

To my mind, Waskow's and Green's interpretations suggest a fertile theological direction – not a way of interpreting the past or determining what is real, but a way of querying the future. However, merging scientific and theological images in this way suggests that the scientific frame of reference defines the best ("de-mythologized") interpretation of religious meaning. This can lead to a deracination of both science and Kabbalah, and it also risks a desacralization of Kabbalah.

Nevertheless, if one needs to be careful about collapsing science and Kabbalah into one, it seems to me that we must take that risk. Our cultural ideas about evolution and DNA already function on a mythic level, and can be manipulated for great harm. It is essential to ground our scientific knowledge in a context of humility and awe, to "uncover its sacred dimensions", so that the mythos underlying these ideas can be the source of a life-giving ethos and, in Kabbalistic terms, a force for *tiqun*, rectification.

The redemptive power that can come from connecting the sacred to science is diminished when one is reduced to the other; when we try to merge these dimensions, there is also a loss of the otherness of different texts and ideas.[1079] Moreover, if our approach is one of reconciling the "magisteria" of science and religion, to use Stephen Jay Gould's term, then it cannot help but be rooted in an idea of theological and scientific progress, which already assumes a role for humanity in Creation that we may need to question. At the same time, assuming with Gould that these magisteria are non-overlapping leaves so much potential for synergy on the table. Finally, in this happy embrace of science, there is also a loss of awareness that Nature may be tragic and unknowable. What

---

[1076] "A Kabbalah for the Environmental Age", *Tikkun* 14:5 (Sep./Oct. 1999): 33–40; 34.

[1077] As Green writes, "I understand the task of theologians to be one of *reframing*, accepting... the scientific consensus, but... guid[ing] us toward a more profound appreciation of that same reality" ("A Kabbalah", 19).

[1078] *Radical Judaism: Rethinking God and Tradition* (New Haven CT: Yale University Press, 2010), 16. The entire first chapter deals with evolution.

[1079] Aubrey Glazer critiques Green's *Radical Judaism* on these grounds, saying that "science [in Green's work] has unfortunately been 'aestheticized' rather than engaged in its own particularity" (*A New Physiognomy of Jewish Thinking: Critical Theory After Adorno as Applied to Jewish Thought* [New York: Bloomsbury Press, 2011], 115; see also 184, n.23).

is profoundly missing is the recognition that, in Walter Benjamin's words, "[N]ature is Messianic by reason of its eternal and total passing away".[1080]

My approach then differs from Green's and Waskow's. At the same time, our theologies have a lot more in common with each other than with ecotheologies that are simple statements of the new faith, like Brian Swimme's *The Hidden Heart of the Cosmos*.[1081] Swimme relies on an almost child-like belief in human progress, similar in many ways to Teilhard de Chardin's ideas about the "noosphere" and evolution, in order to tell what he calls "a new creation story". This story, about the universe achieving self-consciousness through unfolding evolution, culminates in us, the human species (with the next steps of consciousness perhaps leading into computers and beyond the solar system). Swimme treats scientific forms of knowing as theological facts that countermand traditional knowledge. Of course, it is possible to create a religious story out of the scientific imagination, just as it is possible with other types of imagination, but epistemologically, it seems to me to be a mistake to supplant religion with science. Religious or theological knowledge is not factual but hermeneutical, and an epistemology that tries to source such knowledge in what we think of as "facts" is rooted in a Western worldview that is inherently limiting.

There are solid Jewish sources, such as Rav Kook, that could be used to support de Chardin or Swimme's way of thinking, while perhaps improving upon it (see p.29ff.). The approach I have pursued, however, moves in the opposite direction, intimately working ways of being, perceiving, and thinking from the past into our own lives, and not simply rewriting, suspending, or annulling them. To achieve this, we must be changed by traditional ways of thinking.

TWO MORE THEOLOGICAL MAPS

In this book, I have explored the connection between God's presence and God's image, starting from the human as the central image of God, and then building up correspondences from there. If the image of God is somehow realized in those other creatures, it is because, in this anthropocentric paradigm, they become connected to our own divine image. We reflect or extend toward them

---

[1080] "Theological-Political Fragment" in Demetz, *Reflections*, 312–13.
[1081] (Maryknoll NY: Orbis Books, 1999); see also Thomas Berry and Brian Swimme, *The Universe Story: From the Primordial Flaring Forth to the Ecozoic Era – A Celebration of the Unfolding of the Cosmos* (San Francisco: Harper, 1994). My experience of Swimme's slideshow version of "The Universe Story", which I saw presented at the American Academy of Religion Conference in 1997, strongly informs these comments. I do think we need to tell a "universe story" that places our history within a sacred narrative of the history of Nature, but in a humbler key. "The Cosmic Walk", a ritual created by Sr. Miriam MacGillis of Genesis Farm, does exactly this. See a version of this ritual on neohasid.org (discussed n.1013), and other versions at www.threeeyesofuniverse.org/index.php?option=com_content&view=article&id=112&Itemid=214 (Mar. 2014).

Two more theological maps

the image in ourselves, from the image in ourselves, and they thereby participate in God's image.

This weak, or, one might say, enlightened anthropocentrism certainly provides a spiritual foundation for a holier and more whole relationship to the more-than-human world. It gives us a foundation for deeper ethical relationships between ourselves and the other creatures, one that recognizes that the Others are in some practical sense given into our hands. It leaves space for the idea that not only are they not ours to possess, but that even in the context of our dominion, we exist to serve them.

But can we go even further beyond our habits of thought? Are there other models of God's presence in Jewish tradition that are more egalitarian? Or, more to the point, models that are bio- or cosmo-centric, rather than anthropocentric? Here are two possibilities, also drawn from the language of Kabbalah.

All the world is fragrant with blessings

At the conclusion of *Idra Rabba*, one of the climaxes of the entire *Zohar*, the *chevraya*, the mystical fellowship of the *Zohar*, emerges from its seclusion into the world. Every place they look sends out fragrances/*reichin*. "The world is blessed because of us / `alma mitbareikh b'ginan*", exclaims R' Shimon bar Yochai when he smells the sweet smells.[1082] Like light, fragrance is also a symbol of blessing, but in the *Zohar* light is hierarchical and directional, whereas fragrances permeate all the worlds, "upper and lower". The sense of smell is egalitarian, and all the creatures benefit from it, just as all creatures benefit from the cosmic blessings engendered by the mystical practitioners of the *Zohar*.

When we generate blessing in the world, it can be more like light, meaning also enlightenment, which flows in a direction, and which we humans have (or

---

[1082] *Zohar* 3:144b. This statement, unique in the *Zohar*, was extraordinarily significant to later Kabbalists, as one can see in Cordovero, where it represents the essence of Kabbalah (p.37). However, the broader connection between fragrance (*reichin*) or giving forth sweet smell (*mitbasmin*) and blessing is repeated time and again in the *Zohar*. It often relates either to blessing reaching the lowest worlds (usually with reference to the smell of the Garden of Eden, etc.) or the lowest worlds becoming unified with the higher worlds (usually with reference to the smell of the sacrifices). Sweet smell (the root *BSM*) can indicate that blessing fills the earth ("the earth was repaired/arrayed and sweet smelling / *it'takanat ar`a' v'itbas'mat*", 1:31a), that all the worlds are unified ("the worlds will be sweet smelling and will all become one / *yitbas'mun almin viy'hon kola' chad*", 1:32b), and that the world is restored to wholeness (e.g., by the completion of the *mishkan*: "the world gave forth sweet smells and returned to its wholeness / *itbaseim alma' v'it'hadar b'ashl'muteyh*", 1:34a) – just to pick from the first few occurrences of *BSM*. This trope can also indicate the equalization of the worlds, e.g., when God dwells in the *mishkan*, upper and lower realms all become sweet smelling (3:4b), and it appears as an indicator of the arousal and intoxication of union in general.

believe we have) privileged access to. Or it can be more like fragrance, meaning also breath and immanence. Like the sense of smell, it is something that the other creatures may have more access to than we do.

When humans bring destruction, when we "scatter sparks and shatter vessels", we always find ways to make the world around us bear the brunt of our actions, deferring the consequences for ourselves as long as possible.[1083] Can we find ways to do this with blessing – that is, share abundant blessings first with the Others, and then let these blessings come round to us? Can we let them come round to us in good time, when they are ripe and full? This is a deeper way to construct our self-interest – not, protect the Others because you can use them and benefit from them, but, bless the Others and share in their blessing. This is being in God's image, at this time in human history.

A dwelling place below

A clear encapsulation of this goal can also be found in the idea that the purpose of human existence is to make a *dirah batachtonim*, "a dwelling place among the lower ones", for God. Within the homiletical framework I have developed, *dirah batachtonim* means causing God to dwell among the *tachtonim*, lower realms and creatures, by making God's image manifest in them.

This understanding may not be far from the earliest midrashic meaning of God dwelling "among the lower ones". *B'rei'shit Rabbah* states that "the root/essence of Shekhinah/God's presence was in the lower ones / `iqar sh'khinah batachtonim haytah*."[1084] This midrash goes on to teach that God's presence fled because of the sin of *Adam Harishon* – that is, if not for human corruption/consumption, the Shekhinah would have been fully manifest through the entirety of the lower realm.[1085]

Instead, it/She fled up to the next firmament, continuing to flee higher with each sinful generation, up through seven firmaments, until the generation of Avraham. Avraham "stood up and brought Her down" from the seventh firmament to the sixth, with each subsequent generation bringing Her down one more level.

The passage concludes with Moshe finally bringing the Shekhinah down "from above to below / *mil'ma`lah l'matah*". We have seen that the term

---

[1083] At least until such time as our actions overwhelm the resilience of a given ecosystem, so that it comes crashing down on us, as happened in pre-Biblical Mesopotamia.

[1084] BR 19:7 ‖ *Tanch Naso'* 12. The midrash does not specify the original locus of God's presence, though in *BR*, "lower ones" most often means all the earthly creatures. *PRK* 1:1, 1–2 does specify, however, explaining that the verse "I have come into My garden" [So 5:1] teaches us that the entire garden of Eden belonged to Shekhinah and was filled with Her presence.

[1085] The version of this midrash in *Midrash Alfa-Beitot* (BM vol.2, 426–7), underlines this point, describing how "all the *sidrey v'rei'shit*" (here meaning the earthly creatures), seeing Shekhinah flee upward, "wore mourning and wrapped [themselves] in anguish and groaning", while the heavens celebrated their boon. The parallel with Romans 8:20–24, esp. v.21, "For we know that the whole creation groans and suffers together" (netbible.org [Nov. 2014]), is striking.

"below/*l'matah*" is not necessarily synonymous with "among the lower ones /*batachtonim*" in *B'rei'shit Rabbah*. A possible implication of these terminologies here is that the Shekhinah was *not* fully restored by Moshe, and that another step remained to be bridged.[1086] Whether or not this was the intention behind the *B'rei'shit Rabbah* tradition, some Kabbalists did understand the passage this way. Here is Gikatilla's exegesis:

> Then Moshe our teacher came and all Israel with him and they made the Tabernacle/*mishkan* and its vessels. And they repaired the ruined channels, and they set in order the columns and prepared the pools, and they drew living water from the House of the drawing of the water. And they made the Shekhinah return to dwell /*l'shakhen* among the lower ones /*batachtonim*, in the tent, but **not on the ground / in the land** /*baqarqa*`, as in the beginning of the Creation. And this secret is, "Make me a sanctuary and I will dwell among/in them / *v'shakhanti b'tokham*" ... and for this [reason] it said, "and I will dwell in *them*" and it did not say, "and I will dwell below/ *l'matah*."[1087]

Though Gikatilla has actually reversed the valence of *batachtonim* and *l'matah* in his explanation, he interprets the phrase *batachtonim* as it is used within the midrash itself to mean that the original state of the Shekhinah was "in the land". For Gikatilla, the process of bringing the Shekhinah down became complete after the Temple was erected in Jerusalem and the Shekhinah had a fixed earthly home. In other words, Gikatilla saw the Temple as a sanctification of the earth itself.

Homiletically, we might respond to this by seeing ourselves bidden to follow the righteous and complete the process of "bringing the Shekhinah down", through concrete ecological action and spiritual insight.[1088]

The statement that the essence of the Shekhinah was to be found among the *tachtonim* was radical – as is made clear by the fact that later retellings of this midrash undermine this claim. *Sh'mot (Exodus) Rabbah* (approximately tenth century) even states, "the essence of the Shekhinah was *not* among the *tachtonim*".[1089] *Midrash Y'lamdeynu* resolved the ambiguity about the locus

---

[1086] Similarly, in *BmR* 12:6 R' Shimon bar Yochai states, "You find [that] from the beginning of the creation of the world the Shekhinah rested/*shartah* among the lower ones" – but this is preceded by a contrary teaching in the name of Rav, that from the time of creation until the *mishkan*, the Shekhinah had *never* rested among the *tachtonim* (cf. quote from *ShmR* further on). See also *Tanch P'qudey* 6 (|| *Naso'* 16), where Moshe completes the repatriation (rematriation?) of the Shekhinah upon completion of the *mishkan*. Thus, Moshe fulfills the promise that the upright "cause the Shekhinah to dwell in (on) the earth / *yashkinu hash'khinah ba'arets*" (cf. *BR* 19:7, n.1088). Parallel to Rav's position in *BmR*, R' Yosi in *TB Sukkah* 5a insists that the Shekhinah has never come closer than ten handbreadths to the earth ("*l'matah*"), even in the Temple. Heschel, following his method, understands the first view as Akivan and the second as Yishmaelian (*Heavenly Torah*, 365–7).

[1087] *Sha`arey Orah*, 16; *Gates of Light*, 24.

[1088] This interpretation is made more poignant by the ending of *BR* 19:7: "Said R' Yitshak: It's written, 'The righteous inherit the land/earth' [Ps 37:29] ... And what do the wicked do, float in the air?! Rather, the wicked do not cause the Shekhinah to dwell in the earth."

[1089] 13:2.

of the Shekhinah by claiming that human beings were meant to be the sole *dirah* for God – *because* they were meant to be rulers *batachtonim*.[1090] While Gikatilla bent this concept in the opposite direction, envisioning the Shekhinah becoming fully "grounded" in a redeemed physical world, often Kabbalah further narrowed God's *dirah* to Israel.[1091]

In some cases Hasidic interpretation personalized this concept: a person must prepare a dwelling place in their heart, so that they can become God's *dirah batachtonim*.[1092] Even within *Chasidut*, however, countertexts support a more eco- or biocentric interpretation. For example, Menachem Mendel Schneersohn (the Lubavitcher Rebbe, 1902–94, Russia, France, United States) taught:

Since the essence of [the *mitsvot*] is to make for [God], blessed be, a *dirah batachtonim*, it is necessary to fulfill them by means of Nature/*hateva`* really/*mamash*[1093] (i.e., physically), in order that the world's Nature itself / *teva` ha`olam `atsmo* be made into a dwelling place.[1094]

Understanding the physical world or Nature as an arena for transfiguration is characteristic of Hasidism. But Schneersohn takes this one step further when he equates the entirety of Nature with the *tachtonim*, making the whole world the divine *dirah*.

No strictly humanistic or anthropocentric interpretation adequately covers the concept of *dirah* described in these texts. According to some, the more-than-human world is or was already a dwelling place for the Shekhinah, already a

[1090] Explaining the same verse from scripture as *BR* 19:7, *Y'lamdeynu* teaches:

Said R' Ami: The Holy One desired that just as there is a dwelling place /*dirah* for Him in the upper ones above / *ba`elyonim l'ma`lah*, so there should be for Him below/*l'matah*, for so He says to *Adam Harishon*: "If you would merit, just as I am ruler in the `*elyonim* so I would make you ruler among the lower ones /*batachtonim*" ... [instead *Adam*] sinned. Immediately His Shekhinah fled.

(*BM*, vol.1, Midrash Ylam'deynu, B'rei'shit 9, 143; Tanch B'chukotai 3)

According to *Y'lamdeynu*, when Israel came, God returned to dwell **among them** – that is, not among the lower ones or humanity, but among Israel alone. See *Tanch Naso'* 16.

[1091] See *Zohar, Ra`ya Mehemna* 238b, *TZ* 22b, 69b–70a, 85a. In each case this is associated with keeping Shabbat.

[1092] The terminology is especially prominent in Chabad *Chasidut*. See, e.g., *Tanya*, ch.37, 178 (quoted p.263); ch.50, 266. We become in this schema the place within which God dwells in this world, and also that aspect of God that dwells here. In earlier Kabbalah, see *Yonat Eilem*, ch.9, 7b.

[1093] On the term *mamash* in Chabad and Schneersohn, see Elliot Wolfson, "Open Secret in the Rearview Mirror", *AJS Review* 35:2 (November 2011): 401–18, esp. 403–5.

[1094] *Liqutey Sichot*, vol.13 (Brooklyn NY: Kehot, 1998), 40. He also wrote that "the wholeness/completion/perfecting/*shleymut* of Nature [will be achieved when] it will be recognized openly that Nature is divinity" (*Torat Menachem: Sefer Ma'amarim M'luqatim*, vol.2 [Brooklyn NY: Otsar Hachasidim, 2002], 100) – not because Nature will take the place of God, but because it will be manifest that Nature is God's direct expression.

The image we make of God

home for the divine.[1095] Taken altogether, the various texts, whose foci range from the natural world to the earthly creatures to the human being to the service of the human heart, create a picture of levels within levels. Anthropocentrically, one could say that as the human heart becomes a *dirah batachtonim*, so too does the world surrounding us. But one could also say that we become able to perceive the indwelling of divinity that is already in the world when our hearts become dwelling places. Through this process, the divine image shines more and more through every level of the world in its fullness.

THE IMAGE WE MAKE OF GOD (MAP IS NOT TERRITORY)

If we become more alive to the world, and the world becomes, as it were, more alive to us, do we also become more alive to God? It would seem that we have taken several steps "away from" God, so to speak, into a sea of metaphor and metonym without solid ground. If what it means to be in God's image is that we see the image in all creatures, where and when do we encounter the horizon where our focus on the world reaches the limits of understanding, and turns back toward God as the goal of our contemplation? Or, are we necessarily moving toward a more "blurry" understanding of the divine, even as we engage in expanding the image of divinity? When we choose to opt out of theologically sponsored domination and ecological wasting of the planet, what God do we opt for?

According to Avraham Yehoshua Heschel of Apt, this is more of a psychological than a metaphysical question. He teaches that it is our hearts and our devotion that create an image of God:

"Know what is above (lit. 'above from') you / *mei`al mimekha*" (Mishnah Avot 2:1)—And what is above you? This is what Ezekiel says: "And upon the likeness/*d'mut* of the throne, [something] like the appearance /*k'mar'eh* of a human [sat] upon it from above" [1:26]. How can this be said with reference to God? For is it not written: "To whom will you liken me, that I should resemble him?" [Is 40:25.] But this [describes what happens] from our side (i.e., our perspective), through true service in the heart: for a likeness for our Creator, we make Him, as it were, "a human likeness / *d'mut adam*". By way of parable, if a person bestows kindness, he makes and prepares a right hand for the Holy One (*Tif'eret*) and his Shekhinah... and this is the secret that they hinted at [by the statement], "Know what is above [is] from you!" "What/*mah*" ($M + H = 45$) is the *gematria* of "human/*adam*" ($' + D + M$). So this means, "what is above the throne [comes] from you".[1096]

[1095] "Home" translates *oikos*, from which we get the word "ecology". In this light, one may interpret the term "ecotheology" quite literally, as the study of how one makes the world the home of divinity.

[1096] Quoted by Tsvi Hirsch of Zhidachov in `Ateret Tsvi (Lvov Ukraine [Galicia], 1871), 25a–b. Heschel of Apt is playing with the Besht's interpretation of *Avot* 2:1, which the Besht reads as "Know *that* what is above *comes* from you." This is one of the Besht's most radical

The Apter Rebbe cautions us that the image of God, whether in name, or form, or *tselem* or *d'mut*, is not a substantive category of being, independent of human devotion. "[T]hrough true service in the heart" we make "a likeness for our Creator" that is in our likeness, *d'mut Adam*. What likeness shall we fashion, in the twenty-first century? Will it be one in which God is a superhuman whose image feeds our egos and sustains our greed? Will it be one in which we find humility in relation to the other creatures, and show "God's mercy over all God's works", equally to all? And will it be one in which the divine and human likeness comes to include the likenesses of all creatures, as Kabbalah has taught? As Heschel of Apt's teaching suggests, this matter is one not only of overcoming our destructive anthropocentrism, but also of finally transcending that aspect of divine anthropomorphism that remains most entrenched in us, and with it, liberating ourselves to see more fully the divine.

apothegms; one good turn deserves another. For Buber's rendition of this teaching, see *Tales of the Hasidim: Later Masters*, 117–8; see also Arthur Green, *Radical Judaism*, 171, n.15.

Conclusions

A new ethos, a new ethics

> All who wound God's works wound God's image. And the name of YHVH does not rest on a wounded place.
>
> Zohar, Ra`ya Mehemna 3:123b

> Our bodies have formed themselves in delicate reciprocity with the manifold textures, sounds, and shapes of an animate earth – our eyes have evolved in subtle interaction with other eyes, as our ears are attuned by their very structure to the howling of wolves and the honking of geese. To shut ourselves off from these other voices, to continue by our lifestyle to condemn these other sensibilities to the oblivion of extinction, is to rob our own senses of their integrity, and to rob our minds of their coherence.
>
> David Abram, *The Spell of the Sensuous*, 22

I have explored many pathways in *Kabbalah and Ecology* for beholding and affirming the image of God in the other creatures and in the more-than-human world. This beholding is not merely a perceptive or receptive process but a creative and active one. As many of the Kabbalists saw, the universe in its diversity is the most significant and magnificent image of the divine that we have access to; the image of God in human beings is an echo of that greater image. Kabbalah developed this theme from *midrashim* that equate the human being with the world. But the Midrash itself was already rooted in an organic conception of the world, where humans were created in order to bring balance and make peace within the entire more-than-human Creation.

Tselem, according to the rabbis, was never limited to human beings, nor to souls or minds. Moreover, the cost of human sin, in Midrash and Kabbalah, was compared to the destruction of a whole world. The ultimate value was not human life but the world itself. If we equate the idea of God's image with imitating God, as later rabbinic and philosophical texts did, then we know what we must do. We can only fulfill the potential in us represented by God's image by acting and seeing with compassion, by honoring the intrinsic value of all lives and species, by beholding the image in each one and saying, this is good. *Tselem*, the image of God, is what we are and what we behold, when the lenses that focus our mind's eye are the lenses of awe and love.

Even if, like the medieval philosophers, we focus on how the mind images God, a mind that is torn from the world that feeds and embraces it, imagining its origins to be only human, a mind shaped by a world that is torn of its creaturely abundance, becomes a wounded place that cannot image God. Only a mind and spirit that cherish the fellowship of all other beings, that *behold* the world, exulting in the diverse bodies and lives and species of so many creatures in a world that was and will yet be very good, *tov m'od*, only such a mind and spirit can image God; only such a person can fully embody God. And a mind so embodied comes to recognize that it cannot be the sole or ultimate expression of God's image. Rather, as Kabbalah and Maimonides taught, the body of Creation in its entirety and its unity is the greatest possible image of God.

As these conclusions reframe tradition and scripture, they also reframe evolution, Gaia theory, and science in general. They lead us to the question, How can we increase God's presence, both as image and as living force, in and through our connection to all the creatures? The theological basis for this exists in Kabbalah, which mapped the image of God onto all levels of Creation and affirmed and recognized wholeness and self-similarity. In *Chasidut*, one also finds the belief that we redeem the sparks, and reveal the image of God in other creatures and things, through a right relationship with them. Though the texts most often apply this framework to how we use or consume other creatures, ecotheology can conduct us to the idea of restoring the *qomah* of another being, human or non-human, through our deep appreciation of its implicit divine nature.

This appreciation can also be understood as a way of speaking to and with the natural world. The challenge of redemption, so central to Judaism, may thus be interpreted as the challenge of finding the right language with which to speak with the more-than-human. Through dialogue, we may call forth in other creatures the "level" of God's image, which is itself a redemptive act.

This may seem like romanticism, more poetry than practice. However, when we search out new dimensions of our relationship with the more-than-human, realizing speech where we now perceive muteness, we may discover (or more deeply engage in) a kind of listening that is also scientifically and phenomenologically sound.[1097] This fulfills not just an ecological goal but also a deeply Jewish goal, emerging from the literal sense of *tiqun `olam*, cosmic repair – the goal of repairing not just the damaged human world but also the Earth itself.

Underlying all this is the Kabbalistic teaching that the purpose and promise of humanity is to bring blessing to all the orders of Creation and divinity.

[1097] Many scientists already experience this in varied forms, though the language I am using here may differ from what they would use.

Beyond stewardship (again)

When we actualize this promise, according to Kabbalah, we give substance to the divine intent that placed God's image in humanity. This fundamental purpose leads quite directly to lifting up the strands of Kabbalah that would inform – literally give form to – a renewed theology of Creation, engaged with the diversity of the world. Interweaving these strands, we find that *tselem*, which was rooted in our self-understanding as human beings, transcends humanity to embrace all other beings.

BEYOND STEWARDSHIP (AGAIN)

Uncovering this potential in *tselem* has been the intent behind the painstaking textual and theological work done here. I have reflected on the benefits of this kind of theology throughout the book. But there are also some losses and limitations. Most basically, the very act of extending the idea of God's image beyond the human realm is an act that extends human culture further into Nature. A possible consequence of this is that ecotheology may increase the degree to which we are trapped inside the circle of human culture. If we force all our experiences of Nature into such patterns of thought, we end up colonizing what is wild, imposing human patterns of thought on a world that is more-than-human in this sense as well. We may also risk losing (or fail to regain) the wildness within ourselves.[1098]

These spiritual stumbling blocks reinforce and are reinforced by the stewardship model, which quickly reduces caring for the Earth to a question of management and control. Such an approach is not likely to open us to "what flashes" beyond the threshold of human speech and symbol. While stewardship as a normative model may still be very useful for guiding our practical choices, theology has a different responsibility. Theology should help us find a way toward greater opening, beyond the confines of any tradition.[1099] As Buber suggested, what we need most is to be able to "step out of our habits of thought".[1100] Perhaps paradoxically, carefully rereading texts can be a

---

[1098] The way we most often come into contact with what is wild is through our sexuality. Modern society does a frighteningly thorough job of making sure that this wildness gets looped back into human culture, rather than leading us to feel our identity with the more-than-human. See Herbert Marcuse, *One Dimensional Man* (Boston MA: Beacon Press, 1964) on repressive desublimation. The opposite of this would be the more-than-human eroticism of the Song of Songs.

[1099] This is especially true on a pragmatic level, because, as humanity faces enormous ecological changes, we will need to draw on the wisdom of every culture and way of life in order to establish a sustainable society.

[1100] *I and Thou*, 177–8. Writing specifically about encounters with the more-than-human world, he says,

> [T]he I-You relationship, familiar to anyone with a candid heart and the courage to stake it, is not mystical. To understand it we must sometimes step out of our habits of thought, but not out of the norms that determine man's thoughts about what is actual... [W]hat acts on us may be understood as the action of what has being.

discipline that takes us beyond the tropes and figures we are habituated to, and helps us break those habits.

There is another advantage to doing this kind of theological work that I have only barely touched upon. If the Earth's climate has reached or does reach a tipping point – a point where the climate will be driven toward a new equilibrium that is both hotter and more chaotic, and that may cause massive extinctions (something no one can know for sure until after it is happening) – then we will need to face another level of spiritual crisis. This crisis will arise not only when we experience the very real tragedies of displaced humanity and impoverished communities. It will arise not only when we witness the suffering of species whose survival will be in jeopardy or who will not survive (this crisis is already facing all who are paying attention).[1101] It will also arise when we have to confront a world in which beauty has been driven from our presence, in which Spirit will seem to have abandoned us. In such a scenario, we will cross a different threshold, from a feeling of being embraced by Nature, which motivates so many of us who are striving to create a sustainable world, to an experience of Nature as fierce and fearsome, a literal equivalent of the Biblical curses for not letting the land rest: "And I will break the pride of your power, and I will set your heavens as iron, and your earth as brass" [Lv 26:19].[1102]

If this happens, humanity will also face the twin spiritual challenges of mourning for what has been lost and of sustaining compassion for each other and all Life. Anyone deeply engaged with environmental issues already has moments where they experience this. As Aldo Leopold wrote, "One of the penalties of an ecological education is that one lives alone in a world of wounds."[1103] In the face of such a wrathful image of God and Nature (*Elohim*), our theology may be what allows us to sustain our love for the more-than-human world and for one another. Under such circumstances – *rachmana*

[1101] The tipping point is not just a temperature measurement. It refers to the point at which positive feedback loops push us further and further away from the climate we now inhabit. For example, to mention what will be obvious to many readers: greater heat means drier forests means more wildfires means greater amounts of heat-trapping CO_2, meaning even greater heat. It is possible that the greenhouse gases we have already put into the atmosphere would drive such positive feedback and radically change our climate, even if we stopped using fossil fuels today. However, we should remember that a new climate does not mean the end of life or of "Gaia". Rather, it means the end of the climate system favorable to us.

[1102] This verse describes one consequence of not keeping the Sabbatical or *Sh'mitah* year. The parallel verse at Dt 28:23 is related to all the *mitsvot* generally. Broadly, one cannot help but hear something about contemporary climate change in these verses, and all the more so in Malachi 3:19: "for here, the day is coming, burning like an oven, and all the arrogant and all doing wickedness will be straw".

[1103] *Round River: From the Journals of Aldo Leopold*, ed. Luna Leopold (New York: Oxford University Press, 1993), 165. He continues: "Much of the damage inflicted on land is quite invisible to laymen. An ecologist must either harden his shell and make believe that the consequences of science are none of his business, or he must be the doctor who sees the marks of death in a community that believes itself well and does not want to be told otherwise."

lits'lan, may the merciful One save us from them – theological foundations like those explored here may be critical to sustaining our spirit.

If the worst outcomes do unfold, it will take great wisdom to remember and act on what Maimonides taught at the end of *The Guide*:

> [E]very benefit that comes from [God], may He be exalted, is called lovingkindness/ che͟sed... Hence this reality as a whole – I mean [the reality] that He, may He be exalted, has brought into being – is che͟sed. Thus it says: "The world is built up in lovingkindness" [Ps 89:3].[1104]

May we be so blessed to remember what we need to, to regret what we need to, to mourn what we need to, to celebrate what we need to, and to change what we need to, now, when the costs are still in the realm of what is livable, and when the ease of finding God's *che͟sed* in the life of this world is not as damaged as it may yet become.

Even if the Earth's climate does not take such a radical turn, we still have to confront the fact that we are living on a different planet than our ancestors, one in which it is we who decide about each species, about who will live and who will die.[1105] And so we are called to protect the lives of the species on Earth, even while we simultaneously are destroying those lives. In one sense this is an unavertable condition of Life. But now, as almost everyone realizes, people must intervene actively on behalf of many species, and not just refrain from destroying them, in order for those species to survive.[1106]

Whenever we have to manipulate the environment to save a species, we tend to think of the political or economic cost to ourselves. The following midrash, which I touched on in Chapter 5, is concerned with the loss to those creatures we help:

> "And again [Noach] sent forth the dove out of the ark... And the dove came in at evening, and here, an olive leaf torn off in her mouth" [Gn 8:11]. "An olive leaf torn off in her mouth"—From where did she bring it? R' Bibi said: The gates of *Gan Eden* were opened for her, and from there she brought it. Said R' Abahu: Had she brought it from *Gan Eden*, couldn't she bring something special, cinnamon or balsam? But she gave [Noach] a hint, and said to Noach: Better is bitterness from this and not sweetness from beneath your hand.[1107]

[1104] MN 3:53, 631.

[1105] See Bill McKibben, *Eaarth: Making a Life on a Tough New Planet* (New York: Henry Holt, 2010).

[1106] Eisenberg, *The Ecology of Eden*, 288–9.

[1107] BR 33:6. Another animal legend gives us a powerful image of what happens when we manipulate the natural world – even for holy ends. In *TB Gitin* 68b, Shlomo (King Solomon) devises to cut stone blocks for the Temple, which may not be touched by any metal implement, by using the *shamir* worm, which according to legend can cut through any stone. Ashm'da'i (Asmodeus), king of the demons, tells Shlomo how he can find the *shamir*: "It is not in my hands, it is in the hands of the Prince/Ruler of the Sea, who gives it only to the *tarn'gol bar* (lit. 'wild cock', usu. translated 'hoopoe'), whom he trusts because of his oath." At this point, the Talmud explains why the *shamir* is guarded by the hoopoe and how Shlomo steals it:

The dove rejects becoming dependent upon humankind in this story. Wildness is better than any captivity, even a captivity in which one is fed the sweetest of foods. Other stories depict the phoenix being blessed with immortality because it refuses food from human beings.[1108]

Though the gates of Eden are closed to humanity, they are open to the dove. Some *midrashim* also hold that the grapevine Noach planted was descended from the one in Eden. By planting the vine and sending out the dove, Noach tries to maintain his connection to the garden, even though he cannot go there. By connecting with and caring for other species, we may also gain a connection to that part of ourselves that still belongs to "the garden".[1109] However, the midrash also suggests that this connection is damaged and fragmentary as long as other creatures' lives and survival are up to us.

There is tension between "Adam the first", the human who controls and dominates, and "Adam the second", the human who nurtures and names, as Soloveitchik calls his pictures of humanity drawn from the first two chapters of Genesis. This midrash about Noach's dove clearly favors "Adam II", while still acknowledging the reality of "Adam I". Here I have attempted to chart a similar course, negating strong anthropocentrism while acknowledging the potential good that can flow from human power. A "weak" anthropocentrism rooted in tradition, which makes sense of the human role in Creation, may in fact

---

What does [the bird] do with it? He reaches mountains where nothing lives, and he puts it on the tooth (ridge) of the mountain and splits the mountain, and he brings seeds from trees and casts them there and (so) something lives, and this [*tarn'gol bar*] is what they translate (in Onkelos *ad* Lv 11:19) "mountain splitter" / *nagar tura* (for *dukhifat*, hoopoe). [So] they (Shlomo's servants) searched for a hoopoe's nest with young in it, and they covered over it with white (clear) glass. When the bird came he wanted to get through but could not find [a way]. He went to bring the *shamir* and set it on top [to split open the glass]. [The servant] shouted at him; he dropped [the *shamir*, and the servant] took it away. [The hoopoe] went and strangled himself because [he broke] his oath. (Cf. *Chulin* 63a, where the *dukhifat* brings the *shamir*, presumably willingly.)

Shlomo's holy task interferes with the hoopoe's, to deadly effect.
  Our tasks may all the more so interfere with the purpose and place of each species, each of which has its own symbiotic relationships with other species and with the Earth itself. Such relationships are represented in this aggadah as the fulfillment of a holy task. The *realia* behind the story is that the hoopoe makes its nest in rock crevices. See Jonathan Rosen, *The Life of the Skies: Birding at the End of Nature* (New York: Farrar, Straus and Giroux, 2008), 238–46, 250. Rosen also writes there about a Sufi parable, *The Conference of the Birds*, in which the hoopoe, representing a Sufi master, leads the other birds to spiritual awakening.

[1108] The phoenix or *chol* (based on Jb 29:18) gains the power of resurrection either because it declines to bother Noach for food in the ark (*TB Sanhedrin* 108b), or because it refuses to eat the fruit of the tree of knowing that Chava proffers (*BR* 19:5, see n.141). In both stories, the phoenix's power comes from choosing not to interact with humans. See also previous note on the hoopoe.

[1109] This garden, as Genesis portrays it, is much closer to what we might deem wilderness. See Eisenberg, *The Ecology of Eden*, 90–94.

be the most transformative theology.[1110] The idea of God's image suggests a model based neither on stewardship and control, nor on completely eschewing human power. Instead, our purpose is to bring blessing into the world through `avodah, service.

The image of God, in this sense, commands us to be aware and give attention. With awareness, we may come into a holy relationship with what lies before us. Without it, we may fail to connect with the divine image at all. In other words, the divine image is not inherent within the Other, nor within oneself, but rather comes into being through relationship with the Other. The *telos*, the goal, is a relationship that reflects the image of God, and the means for achieving this is relationship itself.

THE ORDERS OF CREATION

We established the premise that the entirety of Creation is a holy image of God, and each level of Being is also an image of God, associated with its own potential and its own quality of sentience and self-determination. From the perspective of Jewish tradition, the image of God implies moral responsibility, assigns intrinsic value, and demands respect. If every level of Being is or can become the image of God, or more broadly, if every aspect of Being can elicit a relationship that reflects the image of God, then what are the ethical, pragmatic, and halakhic responsiblities attendant upon that image? How do our responsibilities change from one level to the next, and how do they remain the same?

To take one example, if the image of God is found in the unification of the four "elements" (that is, fire, air, earth, and water),[1111] as the Shlah suggested, would this create a moral obligation not to separate the elements from each other? The simple answer is that one configuration of elements is not more in God's image than another, so there would be no responsibility to preserve them in a particular configuration. But that does not really scratch the surface of the question. For what the unification of the elements represents is the constant process of changing and recombining, or *t'murot*, that is the essence of Life. One might therefore say that we have a kind of obligation to the elements in themselves, to make sure that the processes of life are not disrupted by our actions, so that the unifications that come about through their combining and recombining can continue.

[1110] We cannot ignore the extraordinary difference between a traditional model of human power and dominion rooted in an organic view of Creation, which needs smaller corrections, and the model represented by Western industrialization that has reached its apogee in corporate capitalism.

[1111] If one were talking about the elements in the periodic table, one could also derive from this idea the obligation to not disperse elements that can harm life into the biosphere – not just from a human-centered perspective, but from the mystical perspective that the elements themselves have, as it were, a need to be used justly, to enhance life rather than destroy it.

A framework for this is suggested by a *Tiquney Zohar* passage already discussed (p.287), which states that when people "weaken their image above", they weaken the right side of Lovingkindness/*Chesed*, and it is "as if they were weakening the orders of Creation / *sidrey v'rei'shit*,[1112] and as if they diminished the likeness that is the [divine] stature above".[1113] *Chesed* is associated with the principle of Life itself, and Judgment/*Din* (*G'vurah*) with whatever undoes the capacity and potential for life.[1114] We need to ask ourselves what actions weaken *Chesed*, love and life, and what actions increase life, at every level of Creation.

We can apply this question, for example, to how we use water (itself a symbol for *Chesed*). One inference could be that we have an obligation not to remove water from the cycle of life. When we divert water to our uses, is that water being returned to the ecosystems to nurture life to at least the degree it would have without our intervention? This idea could have practical policy implications. For example, every well that gets hydrofracked permanently deletes millions of gallons of water from the biosphere.[1115] Certainly, that *is* a

---

[1112] See nn.936, 1042. [1113] *TZ* 70, 125b.

[1114] At issue is not whether death is good, but whether people act in a way that increases or strengthens death, so that death outstrips life. Such actions could be said to "weaken the orders of Creation", and the default should be to "forbid" them. Of course judgment in the Kabbalistic sense – that is, death, predation, competition, extinction – is also a necessary part of Nature, without which it would be impossible for life as we know it to exist and evolve. This is consistent with the midrashic teaching that the phrase "and here [Creation] is very good / *tov m'od*" [Gn 1:31] really means "and here, death is good / *tov mot* (*mavet*)" (*BR* 9:5; see also *BR* 9:10). *BR*'s perspective is quite opposite *ShmR* 30:3, which explains that the word *toldot* in Gn 2:4 is written out *malei'* – "fully", with two *Vav*'s (תולדות) – to show that "the Holy One created the world, and there was no angel of death" until Adam and Chavah sinned.

[1115] For every single wellhead, tens of millions of gallons of water mixed with chemicals and "proppants" are injected into the ground to "frack" or fracture rock formations and allow natural gas to be extracted. That water becomes poisoned with radioactive elements and hydrocarbons, and half or more of it remains permanently underground, never again to be part of life (Seidenberg, "Kabbalah and Fracking Don't Mix", www.huffingtonpost.com/rabbi-david-seidenberg/kabbalah-and-fracking-don_b_3642055.html [July 2013]). This concern applies to gas fracking and to shale oil extraction, and is completely independent of traditional environmental concerns, like whether gas fracking contaminates the aquifers and wells that supply people with water, or releases so much methane into the atmosphere (which is twenty times more powerful a greenhouse gas) that it cancels out natural gas's profile as a cleaner fuel. (See Jeff Tollefson, "Methane Leaks Erode Green Credentials of Natural Gas", *Nature* 493:7430 [Jan. 3, 2013]. Note that on top of this issue, the environmental problems with shale oil are far far worse. See David Bello, "How Much Will Tar Sands Oil Add to Global Warming?", www.scientificamerican.com/article/tar-sands-and-keystone-xl-pipeline-impact-on-global-warming/ [Jan. 23, 2013].) Just as fracking can be seen as a sin against the water, most people would see the Deepwater Horizon oil gusher at the bottom of the Gulf of Mexico – perhaps the worst environmental disaster in our lifetime so far – as a sin against the sea, and not just against the species it contains. Some theosophical mystics might go further in personifying the elements, and see an expression of panpsychism and "love" in the coming together of different elements, or even in the

kind of deprivation, not just for ourselves and the world, but for the "element" of water itself, contaminated and no longer available to sustain life. Even if the water that gets used up is non-potable, it is wrong from this perspective to remove water forever from the biosphere, unless the reason for doing so is to further life in some concrete, measurable, and permanent way.

We can also bring halakhah directly to bear on this question, in the form of the mitsvah of *kavod ladam*, "giving honor to the blood". According to Leviticus 17:13 (see discussion, n.476), one must bury the blood of a wild animal one has slaughtered. *Kavod ladam* means that one is also required to perform this mitsvah in a manner that shows honor – specifically, to effect burial with one's hand rather than one's foot.[1116] *Kavod ladam* implies a command to respect the processes and products of life. "Weakening the orders of Creation" is an effect of actions that violate *kavod ladam*, while properly respecting that which carries the *chiyut* or lifeforce is a halakhically mandated expression of bio- or ecocentrism.

In another example, we can apply these considerations to how we treat organic waste. When we compost, we honor the lifeforce in our food, enabling it to contribute again to life. If, as happens in our industrial society, we mix toxic chemicals (from batteries, cleaners, paint, etc.) into our landfills along with food scraps that could have decayed back into earth,[1117] then we are poisoning that which was created by Life, so that it cannot safely return to the soil as organic compounds to sustain future life. This would constitute "sinning" against our food. The problem in this light is not wasting food *per se*, but undoing the cycle that turns food back into life-giving earth. And this literally weakens the orders of Creation, just as it dishonors the blood – that is, the force of life – that courses through the elemental circuits of earth and water.

One might also wonder whether the concept of *sidrey v'rei'shit* should be applied to prohibit genetic modification of organisms. Certainly, the halakhic issue of *kilayim*, which prohibits both mixing agricultural species in a single plot of land and cross-breeding animal species, would suggest that there is an order of Creation that God cares for.[1118] But here I think the answer is more

---

attraction of protons and electrons (or protons and protons through the strong nuclear force, or all matter's attraction through gravity), so that they view substance itself as having a kind of moral (and erotic) orientation. On cosmic eroticism, see Leone Ebreo, *Dialoghi d'Amore*.

[1116] *TB Chulin* 87a, *Shabbat* 22a. Traditionally, this principle is applied to the honor due every mitsvah, but its source in the commandment of burying the blood speaks to the profound respect due to everything associated with life. Blood is repeatedly equated with and imagined as the element of life: "Only be strong against eating the blood, for the blood is the *nefesh* (life/soul) ... on the earth you will pour it out, like water ... in order that it will go well for you and for your children" [Dt 12:23–5]. See also Dt 12:16, 15:23.

[1117] Earth in this sense is not just the "element" earth, but the unification of water, fire (energy, light), earth (mineral), and air (oxygen, nitrogen, carbon dioxide) in both photosynthesis and decay – a full image of God.

[1118] The prohibitions on *kilayim* (Lv 19:19, Dt 22:9–11), according to Ellen Davis, should apply to genetic engineering (*Scripture*, 86–8). Indeed, these prohibitions have a universal dimension

complicated. We know that during the course of Earth's history, the orders of Life have changed many times over. If we take a long view of evolution, there is no essential "truth" to the array of species that define Life at this moment, even though they are the species with whom we create our home.

Moreover, though it will seem bizarre to environmentalists, creating GMOs (genetically modified organisms) in some abstract sense also adds to Life, and in fact genetic engineering may become a necessary if frightening tool for stewarding species so that they don't become extinct.[1119] Even if we were to take a more conservative view, and affirm sidrey v'rei'shit in some static sense to be sacred, this still would not mean that *all* genetic engineering should be prohibited. This is because one can (and should) distinguish between those GMOs that can both be completely isolated and be used to directly save life, such as bacteria modified so as to produce a certain drug in a laboratory reactor,[1120] and those GMOs whose goal is to merely (and questionably) "enhance" lives, like Bt corn.[1121] More broadly, the question of GMOs can be separated into two

---

in that they apply both in the land of Israel and outside the land (*Mishnah Qidushin* 1:9). However, in the eyes of Jewish law, because they are part of the holiness code, they apply only to Jews, which limits their moral impact.

[1119] Evan Eisenberg, in *The Ecology of Eden*, 321–5, forcefully argues that genetic engineering should be seen as being modeled on Nature to the same extent as any other human *techne*.

[1120] Genetic engineering is a much less complex matter, ethically and theologically, if we leave off modifying organisms that reproduce sexually (all plants, fungi, and animals), and instead modify bacteria. It is quite plausible on a practical level to isolate such strains in the lab, while it is impossible to do so with plants and animals that are used agriculturally. This corresponds in a concrete way to the distinction between the types of creatures enumerated in Genesis that reproduce sexually ("*mazri`a zera`* / seeding seed" [1:11] "*l'mineyhu*/ according to their kinds" [1:12,21,25]) – to which one might therefore apply the concept of sidrey v'rei'shit – and those that reproduce asexually through fissioning, which are therefore not *mazri`a zera `l'mineyhu*. Moreover, the fact that bacteria share genetic material through conjugation, a process completely separate from reproduction – even across species lines – means that the concept of species itself applies only approximately to bacteria. (The fact that bacteria can share genetic material across species may make other uses of genetic engineering more dangerous, however, including using GMO bacteria in the field.) This kind of literal/literary distinction based on Biblical phrases may seem odd if you are unfamiliar with *halakhah*, but it can be a powerful method for drawing fine ethical distinctions.

[1121] While the expression of Bt toxin in all the cells of such GMO crops could obviously have broad ecological effects on insects, and on the animals fed by these crops, not all genetic modification raises such red flags. In fact, the political and economic impact of GMOs, especially on subsistence farmers, may be more important in many cases than their ecological impact. Golden rice, which is engineered to contain beta-carotene and prevent malnutrition, is an interesting example, because its inventors insisted that the corporation controlling the patent allow "royalty-free local production by farmers who earn less than US $10,000 annually" and allow those farmers to save seed and replant it (www.goldenrice.org/Content3-Why/why3_FAQ.php [Mar. 2012]). The use of golden rice would still cut down on the varieties of rice being cultivated and the diversity of crops in general, and on the diversity of diet. See Davis, *Scripture*, 89. More importantly, the use of any GMOs opens the door for for-profit multinational companies to take control of food systems – something that is not likely be held in check under the rather loose morals of corporate capitalism and neoliberal "globalization".

The orders of Creation

levels: (1) What is the potential impact of any GMO on Life – that is, on other species and ecosystems? and (2) How does the impact of genetic engineering become exacerbated by (or exacerbate) human arrogance, which is a profound threat to all life? On both levels, the precautionary principle – the principle that one should not undertake actions that have the potential for great or widely spread harm, even if that potential is undefinable or uncertain – would apply. However, contemporary discussions in the Conservative and Orthodox movements about the halakhic status of genetic engineering hardly take into account any aspect of these questions.[1122]

We might contrast these higher or more abstract types of responsibilities with more specific obligations to not destroy individual animals or to protect members of a certain species. The image of God within (or in relation to) animals, which may include their varied capacities for compassion, mutual aid, and love, would imply multiple levels of responsibility, not simply because animals are more like us, but because these qualities themselves, which drive and subtend Life and evolution and holiness, image God and demand our respect. The fact that these same qualities play such a profound role in the lives of human beings, through our relationships with each other and with other species, is part of what makes each person a very significant expression of the image of God.

We started with a broad formulation of these issues: What is it that increases life, and what is it that decreases life – whether that be the life of each species we make use of and interact with, or the phenomenon of Life itself? That still looks like the right question. It is at the heart of the prayer in *P'ri `Ets Hadar*:

May the whole return now to his original strength . . . [a]nd may all the sparks that were scattered by our hands, or by the hands of our ancestors, or by the sin of the first human against the fruit of the tree, return now to be included in the majestic might of the Tree of Life.[1123]

In Kabbalistic terms, what we do that weakens the orders of Creation also weakens "our own image above", and it weakens divinity itself. These three strands – Life, humanity, and divinity – cannot be unraveled. In all three realms,

---

[1122] That is not surprising, given the overwhelmingly pro-science attitude taken by *halakhah*. Instead, these discussions have been limited to whether GMOs are *kosher*, that is, whether a cloven-footed ruminant, genetically modified with pig genes, is permissible for Jews to eat. But the relevant question is whether and when we should exercise the capacity, ability, or right to control Nature to this degree. Given the possible ecological (and spiritual) impact of these technologies, and the impossibility of knowing and limiting the consequences of GMOs released into the wild, where they can spread and displace non-GMOs or crossbreed with them, the precautionary principle would urge us not to take such risks. The reduction of this question to *kashrut* exemplifies how narrow and consumer-oriented the current halakhic discourse is on many issues. Of course, being pro-science is only problematic when it is misconstrued to mean that halakhah gives up the power to review and make moral judgments about the impact of science.

[1123] See Excursus 2.

we need to attend to what sparks we have scattered, wasted, or deleted from the Tree of Life that sustains all living things. How can we repair, reconnect, revive what has been scattered? How can we listen in a way that models God's *tsimtsum*, so that we may help create the womb space to gestate all Life and nurture the Tree of Life? Nurturing the Tree of Life – this is the theological equivalent of biocentrism. This challenge, so central to a Jewish theology of Nature, must become our practical and not just our theological concern.

INTO LIFE

Exploring one of Buber's metaphors, what threshold have we reached, or crossed, over the course of this work? In the journey toward a new theology, have we reached the threshold where we can imagine God's image in all Being and all beings? If so, crossing over this threshold would require us to bring our theology into lived experience and action. Developing and upholding new ethical and halakhic norms, redesigning our technology, embracing sustainability, and studying the more-than-human Earth so that we more deeply understand all that subtends Life – all these can assist in making this happen. But on the most direct level, we are called upon to open ourselves to simply encountering and listening to the creatures and orders of being that inter-penetrate our lives.

What does it mean, then, to try to hear "prayer" in the actions or lives of other creatures? How can we bear witness to the loss of freedom, of wildness, in those creatures that we must steward? How can we join our compassion with the humility that comes from knowing that it is the damage we have caused that forces us to take action? And how can we also learn to simply listen, celebrate, and mourn, as the processes of Nature, both of human-caused degeneration and world-generated *tiqun*, unfold on their own? Only when we can align ourselves in these ways can our theology really embrace the *tachtonim*, along with the `elyonim*, as sacred dimensions of God's image, as ends-in-themselves, in the more-than-human world.

Buber, in *I and Thou*, gives a second rendition of the three spheres of encounter.[1124] These spheres define the more-than-human world:

These are the spheres in which the world of relation is built. The first: life with nature, where the relation sticks to the threshold of language. The second, life with people, where it enters language. The third: life with spiritual beings, where it lacks but creates language.

In every sphere, in every relational act, through everything that becomes present to us, we gaze toward the train of the eternal You; in each we perceive a breath of it; in every You we address the eternal You, in every sphere according to its manner. All spheres are included in it, while it is included in none.

Through all of them shines the one presence. But we can take each out of the presence... even if we endow it with shining names: cosmos, eros, logos. For in truth there

---

[1124] *I and Thou*, 149–50; see also the final passage of Rosenzweig's *Star*.

Into life

is a cosmos for man only when the universe becomes a home for him with a holy hearth where he sacrifices; and there is eros for him only when beings become for him images of the eternal, and community with them becomes revelation; and there is logos for him only when he addresses the mystery of the world with service of the spirit.

The demanding silence of the forms, the loving speech of human beings, the eloquent muteness of creatures—all of these are gateways into the presence of the word. But when the perfect encounter is to occur, the gates are unified into one gate of actual life, and you no longer know through which one you have entered.

Unifying the gates – the gates of the senses, of learning, of culture, of wildness, of divinity and diversity, of creatureliness, of Other and friend, stranger and beloved, of death and life – this holds the promise of moving us beyond the threshold, into life.

EXCURSUS I

Nefesh and related terms

The primary meanings of *n'shamah* and *nefesh* in Torah can be understood by examining their relationship to *ru'ach*, meaning "spirit" and "wind". Let us assume for the sake of argument that the triad *ru'ach–nefesh–n'shamah* covers one and the same "semantic space" as the triad of spirit–wind–breath. How does this semantic space get divided differently in modern English and in Biblical Hebrew?

Starting from what is most similar, *n'shamah*, like "breath", denotes the respiration of a living, physical subject. From here the concepts diverge vastly. Breath is physical, while "spirit" denotes something metaphysical; breath is alive, while "wind" is not. One can visualize "breath" to be like a firmament, a flat plane, separating the metaphysical "spirit" above from the physical "wind" below. Thus a simple hierarchy is delineated: the metaphysical and animate spirit stands above the physical but still animate breath, which stands above the physical and inanimate wind. In this manner "spirit–wind–breath" defines its semantic space by dividing it into hierarchical levels, and it follows the history of conquest by reserving the Latin-derived word for the top of the hierarchy.

The fact that spirit and wind are unified in the single word *ru'ach* suggests a very different arrangement of semantic space. What spirit and wind share is that they both transcend physical bodies and are independent from any physical subject. Thus, *ru'ach* can be conceptualized as the external breath, the breath of Elohim, which both strikes the prophets and sways the tree branches. *Ru'ach*, which could be translated "spirit-wind", would mean any un- or disembodied invisible flow (which could therefore be attributed to God), including the wind. *N'shamah* as breath would contrast with *ru'ach*, not because one is physical and the other metaphysical, but rather because one exists in a body and one is disembodied.

We need to add a whole other dimension to our semantic space in order to make room for *nefesh*. One possible interpretation is that *nefesh* is the embodied breath, that is, the living animate subject, which is the body itself. Then *nefesh* would contrast both with *n'shamah*, the breath within the body, and *ru'ach*, the unembodied breath. This solution seems to neatly fit many many examples in Torah.

Using this understanding of *nefesh*, a coherent interpretation of Gn 2:7 is easily arrived at: Before God gave breath to the form of Adam, it was simply a *golem* of dirt, that is, not a body but a clod in the shape of a body. The union of the *golem* with breath is what creates the body itself, which is called "a living *nefesh*" (*nefesh chayah*). The breath of God, which was called *ru'ach*, becomes *n'shamah* when it enters the *golem*-body through its nostrils.

We can imagine a new map of the semantic space that makes sense of these interpretations. Similar to "breath", *nefesh* separates two realms, but it can be better visualized as a sphere than a plane, dividing internal from external, rather than metaphysical or higher from physical or lower. Its boundaries are the boundaries of the physical subject, consubstantial with the limits of the body. *Ru'ach* would be every aspect of spirit–wind–breath that is outside this subject, while *n'shamah* would be every aspect of spirit–wind–breath that comes into or comes from within the subject. Just as *nefesh* and *n'shamah* are not metaphysical, *ru'ach*/wind is also not metaphysical, even though, because it is not embodied, it bears an iconic relation to the God that is not bounded by a body. *Ru'ach* is the source or origin of every *n'shamah*, hence God is called "God of the spirits for all flesh / *Elohey haruchot l'khol basar*" [Nu 16:22, 27:16].

From this frame of reference, there is no difficulty understanding how *nefesh chayah* is applied both to the animals and to the first human (Gn 1:24, 2:7). Two other derived meanings are more difficult to explain, but still fit. One is *nefesh* as lifeforce or blood/*dam*: "for the *nefesh* of all flesh is his (its) blood / *ki nefesh kol basar damo hi*" [Lv 17:14]. Because blood is not breathed out but contained within the body, it is more like *nefesh* than *n'shamah*. Here, *nefesh* as *dam* means something like "soul" in the animistic sense, rather than in any philosophical or theological sense. (This is also the valence of sacrificial blood; see p.145.) *Basar* (flesh) may be regarded as the rough Biblical equivalent to *guf*. (See Robert Gundry, quoted in Stiegman, "Rabbinic Anthropology", 513.) *Nefesh* can also mean "affective state" (Gn 34:3, Ex 23:9, 2Kg 4:27), since this is a state of the *body*.

Four other uses of these terms appear more difficult. The first is that *ru'ach*, that is, the spirit of God, can be described as being "in" or "filling" someone, as in descriptions of Yosef, Betsalel, or Yehoshua (Gn 41:38; Ex 31:3, Nu 27:18). This makes sense because *ru'ach*, not being bounded by a body, can represent a continuous or prophetic connection with or communication from God, which reaches from outside a person to inside them (as opposed to *n'shamah*, which once it enters the body is in some senses separate from God). The second is that *n'shamah* is sometimes described as coming from within God (e.g., 2Sa 22:16; Ps: 18:16, though not in Torah) – this is associated with God's anger and seems to imply a specifically directed force. Third, there is one idiosyncratic use of *nefesh* in Torah, concerning Rachel's death: "when her *nefesh* [was] leaving / *b'tsei't nafshah*, for she died" [Gn 35:18]. Here *nefesh* seems to mean breath separate from (or at least separating from) the body, though more precisely it means "animating principle" (cf. Gn 1:30).

The last and most important is the use of *nefesh* to mean "human corpse". If *nefesh* is the animating principle in *basar*, why is a corpse not referred to as *basar*, but rather as *nefesh*, as in, "anyone impure/*tamei'* by (because of) a *nefesh* / *kol tamei' lanafesh*" [Nu 5:2] and "we are impure/*t'mei'im* by a human *nefesh*" [Nu 9:6–7]? The reason may be that the significance of a corpse is found in its wholeness as a once-living subject, whereas *basar* implies a way of seeing the body as matter that is divisible into parts. Since the Torah's Hebrew makes relatively few semantic distinctions between animate subject and inanimate object (see p.131). Here too, there is no sense in which a body ceases to be a *nefesh* when a person dies.

This picture fits almost all of the uses of *ru'ach*, *n'shamah*, and *nefesh* in Torah, though it fits some books of the Bible less well (e.g., Job). I share it here as a hypothesis worth testing, and as a model for reading Torah independently of our own modernist cultural lenses.

EXCURSUS 2

The prayer of *P'ri `Ets Hadar*

The *P'ri `Ets Hadar*, the first published Tu Bish'vat liturgy, includes a prayer unparalleled in Jewish history for its attunement to the more-than-human world. Here is an abridged translation (leaving out most of the references to angels and much of the conclusion) that includes all parts quoted in *Kabbalah and Ecology*.

Please, God, the One who makes /*ha`oseh*, and who forms /*hayotser*, and who creates /*haborei'*, and who emanates /*hama'atsil* the supernal worlds; And in their form (of the four worlds) and in their design You created their model on the earth below; You made all of them with wisdom, upper ones above and lower ones below, "to join [together] the tent to become one / *l'chaber et ha'ohel lih'yot echad*" [Ex 36:18].

And trees and grasses/plants / *ilanin ud'sha'im* You made bloom from the ground, with [the] stature and with [the] design/desire of what is above, to cause the children of Adam to know the wisdom and discernment that is in them, to reach what is hidden. And You appointed over them Your holy angels, to make them grow and bloom... And upon them You will drop the flow and strength of Your higher/upper vessels/*midotekha* (Sefirot): "And He made the harvest fruit" [Ps 107:37] and "the fruit tree making fruit by its kind" [Gn 1:11]; and "from the fruit of Your works the land is satisfied" [Ps 104:13], "to eat from her fruit and to satisfy from her goodness" (from the blessing after eating fruit); "to give life through them to the soul of all life / *l'hachayot bahem nefesh kol chai*" (from the blessing after all kinds of food), from the spiritual strength that is in them;... and from him/them Your fruit is found (after Ho 14:9), the reward of the fruit of the belly/womb, to cause life and to nourish the body: "and his fruit will be for eating and his leaves for healing" [Ez 47:12];

And this day [Tu Bish'vat] is the beginning of Your works [from now until Shavuot], to ripen her and to make her new: "a man will bring with his fruit" [So 8:11] "making fruit by their kinds" [Gn 1:12]; For thus will be filled the days of ripening for the supernal tree, "the Tree of Life in the midst of the garden" [Gn 3:3], and "he will make fruit above" [Is 37:31].

May the will [come] from before You, our God and God of our ancestors, that through the strength of the merit/*s'gulah* of eating the fruit which we will eat, and our blessing over them now, and our meditating in/over the secret of their roots above upon which they hang/depend, to cause the flow of desire and blessing and free gift to flow over them / *l'hashpi`a shefa` shel ratson b'rakhah un'davah*, to return again to make them grow and bloom from the beginning of the year until the end of the year, for good and for blessing, for good life and for peace.

And may You sustain the word which You promised us by the hands of Malachi Your seer: "and for you I will cast out the one who eats away, and the fruit of the earth will not be destroyed for you, and no vine in the field will be barren for you, said YHVH of hosts" [Ma 3:11].

"Look out from Your holy habitation / *m'on qodshekha*, from the heavens" [Dt 26:15] and bless for us this year for good and for blessing, "let them drink blessings forever, let them celebrate in joy Your presence" [Ps 21:7], "and [so] the earth/land will give her produce and the tree of the field his fruit" [Lv 26:4] – bring on them a blessing of goodness...

And may the might and majesty of the blessings for eating the fruits "become lights" [Gn 1:15] in the wellspring of blessings of the Righteous One, life of the worlds; "And may the [rain]bow appear" [Gn 9:14], joyful and beautified with his colors; And from there the flow of desire and mercy will flow over us, for pardon and forgiving our sins and errors. And may the Whole/*Hakol* return now to His/his first (original) strength / *v'yashuv `atah Hakol l'eitano harishon*, "and may His/his bow reside in strength / *vateishev b'eitan kashto*" [Gn 49:24], "for You are the one who will bless the Righteous One, YHVH, desire will crown him like a rampart" [Ps 5:13]. And may all the sparks that were scattered by our hands, or by the hands of our ancestors, or by the sin of the first human against the fruit of the tree, return now to be included in the majestic might of the Tree of Life...

"Then the trees of the forest will sing out" [Ps 96:12], and the tree of the field will raise a branch and make fruit, day by day; "And you will take from the first of all the fruits of the ground" [Dt 26:2] to bring the first-fruit offering "before the altar of YHVH" [Dt 26:4] with praise and thanks (after Ezr 3:11).

In *Chemdat Yamim* (Livorno, 1763; repr. Jerusalem: Makor, 1970), where *P'ri `Ets Hadar* was first published (see n.691), this prayer is found in vol.2, Shov'vim ch.3 on Tu Bish'vat, 109a–b. The prayer can be found in many Hebrew works on Tu Bish'vat. Published translations of the complete prayer can be found in Krassen, "*Peri Eitz Hadar*", 148–51 (www.opensiddur.org/tefillot/kavanot/pri-etz-hadar/, Nov. 2010) and Yitzhak Buxbaum, *A Person Is Like a Tree: A Sourcebook for Tu BeShvat* (Northvale NJ: Jason Aronson, 2000),146–8. Note that the first four descriptors of God correspond to the four worlds in Kabbalah (see the Appendix).

P'ri `Ets Hadar is introduced in Chapter 7, p.212ff. and discussed further on pp.220, 228–29 288, 351. Its potent interpretation of the Psalms' depiction of Nature exultant is discussed in Chapter 12, p.319ff. Many points in this prayer are significant for Jewish ecotheology. Poetically, it is unparalleled in its expression of the cosmic nature of blessing. A related point is the very direct

The prayer of P'ri 'Ets Hadar

connection made between human fertility and the fertility of trees and plants, where both are expressions of the fertility of the earth and hence manifestations of divine cosmic blessing. Note that "raising the sparks" happens not only through consumption, but also through "our meditating over the secret of their roots above" – see further discussion of this point on p.298. Also, the phrase "(may the sparks... return now) to be included / *l'hitkalel* in the majestic might of the Tree of Life" could with slight emendation be read as "to crown with majestic might the Tree of Life" or "to complete in majestic might the Tree of Life".

It is fair to imagine that the author intended to evoke these associations. Lastly, the words of this prayer could describe the evolutionary Tree of Life just as well as they describe the Kabbalistic Tree of Life. May the promise in these words be realized: that we learn how to truly sustain and support both Trees of Life, in all of their majestic might.

APPENDIX

THE SEFIROT, THE TREE OF LIFE, AND A BRIEF HISTORY OF KABBALAH

There are many resources online and in print that describe the structure of the Sefirot at an introductory level, and many excellent introductions to the study of Kabbalah. Here I will give just enough details to help orient anyone unfamiliar with Kabbalah to the historical figures and topics of discussion found in *Kabbalah and Ecology*.

The doctrine of the Sefirot distinguishes Kabbalah, starting with *Sefer Habahir* (twelfth century or earlier), from prior Jewish mysticism. The Sefirot are understood as qualities, powers, or vessels that structure how God unfolds Creation and interacts with the world. They represent a broad range of spiritual, emotional, and metaphysical concepts, arranged into a particular pattern that was standardized before the *Zohar* was written. Rather than being created by God as entities separate from God, these qualities and their pattern are emanated from God, are the image of God, and in some sense are God.

According to the standard depiction of the Tree of Life, there are ten Sefirot, arranged in seven levels and three columns (see figure). Within this pattern, right and left correspond to male and female, and move from love to judgment. Up and down also correspond to male and female, and move from transcendence to immanence, as well as from giving to receiving. The ten Sefirot by name, starting from the highest, are: *Keter* (Crown), *Chokhmah* (Wisdom), *Binah* (Understanding), *Chesed* (Love/Lovingkindness), *G'vurah* (Might or Power, also called *Din*, Judgment), *Tif'eret* (Beauty/Glory), *Netsach* (Eternity/Victory), *Hod* (Majesty), *Y'sod* (Foundation), and *Malkhut*/Shekhinah (Realm/Kingdom/Indwelling Presence). In the human body, the first nine correspond on the largest scale to the crown of the head, right brain/eye, and left brain/eye; right arm, left arm, and heart; right leg, left leg, and genitals (usually, but not always, the phallus). Lastly, Shekhinah may correspond to the Earth below, or to the Kabbalist's spouse, or to the divine Shekhinah that is understood to conjoin with the Kabbalist. Though all the Sefirot are mentioned in

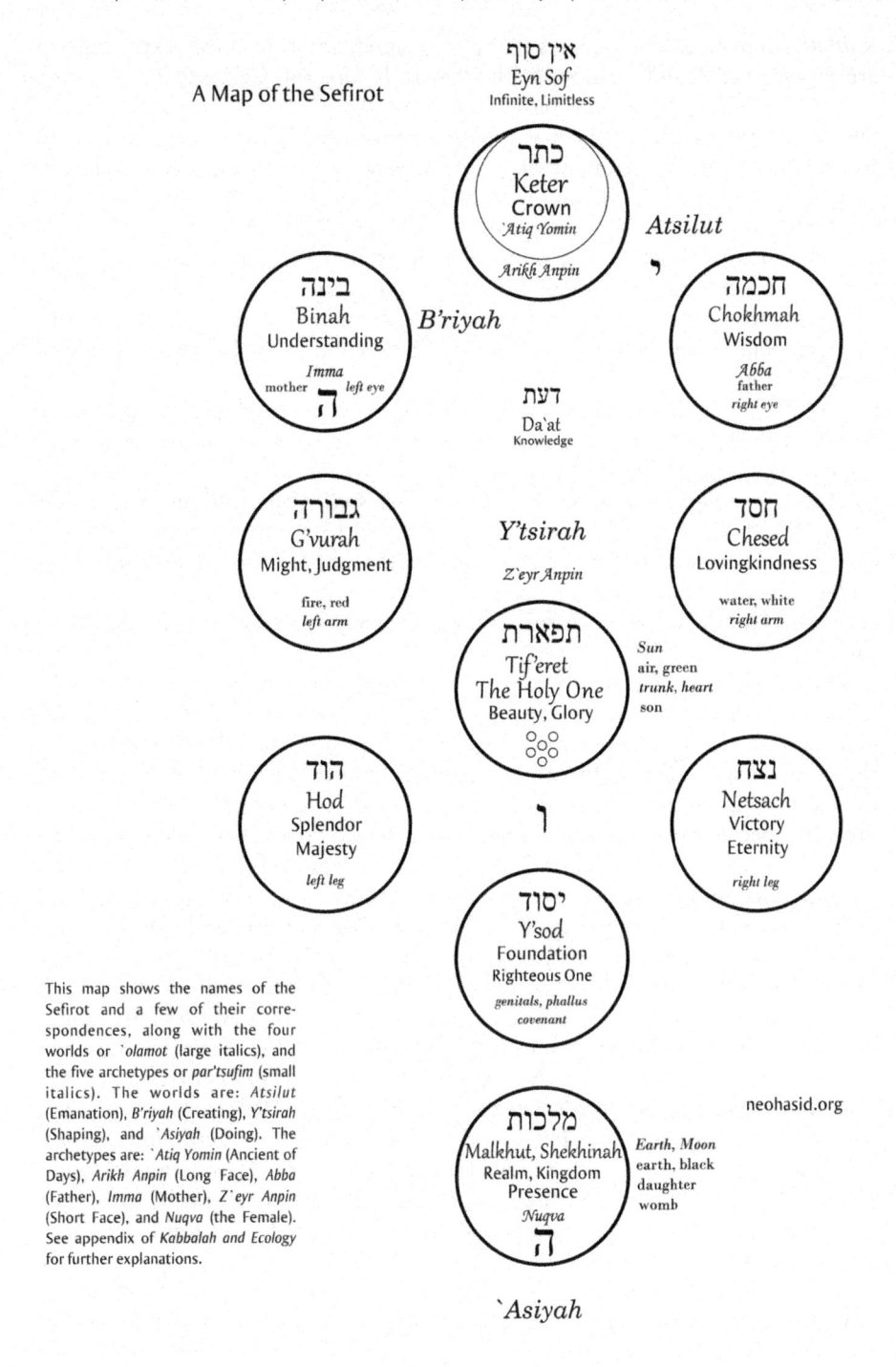

The Sefirot, the Tree of Life, and a brief history of Kabbalah

A Map of the Sefirot

אין סוף
Eyn Sof
Infinite, Limitless

כתר
Keter
Crown
`Atiq Yomin
Arikh Anpin

Atsilut

בינה
Binah
Understanding
Imma
mother — left eye
ה

B'riyah

חכמה
Chokhmah
Wisdom
Abba
father
right eye

דעת
Da`at
Knowledge

גבורה
G'vurah
Might, Judgment
fire, red
left arm

Y'tsirah
Z`eyr Anpin

חסד
Chesed
Lovingkindness
water, white
right arm

תפארת
Tif'eret
The Holy One
Beauty, Glory

Sun
air, green
trunk, heart
son

הוד
Hod
Splendor
Majesty
left leg

ו

נצח
Netsach
Victory
Eternity
right leg

יסוד
Y'sod
Foundation
Righteous One
genitals, phallus
covenant

neohasid.org

This map shows the names of the Sefirot and a few of their correspondences, along with the four worlds or `olamot (large italics), and the five archetypes or par'tsufim (small italics). The worlds are: *Atsilut* (Emanation), *B'riyah* (Creating), *Y'tsirah* (Shaping), and *`Asiyah* (Doing). The archetypes are: *`Atiq Yomin* (Ancient of Days), *Arikh Anpin* (Long Face), *Abba* (Father), *Imma* (Mother), *Z`eyr Anpin* (Short Face), and *Nuqva* (the Female). See appendix of *Kabbalah and Ecology* for further explanations.

מלכות
Malkhut, Shekhinah
Realm, Kingdom
Presence
Nuqva
ה

Earth, Moon
earth, black
daughter
womb

`Asiyah

Kabbalah and Ecology, the ones that play a significant role in the texts quoted are *Tif'eret* and *Malkhut*, along with *Che̱sed*, *Binah*, and *Chokhmah*.

In *Sefer Bahir*, where the basic outline of the Sefirot is first articulated, the main term used for Sefirot is *ma'amarot*. In the *Bahir* and in later Kabbalah, the Sefirot are thought of as the Cosmic Tree, which is understood to be a tree with roots in heaven that bears fruit on Earth. In addition to the Sefirot or Cosmic Tree, two other doctrines characterize the *Bahir* and all subsequent Kabbalah. The first is the belief that human beings can bring blessing into the world through ritual and right action, especially when they act with correct mystical intent (see §119, n.713). This doctrine is critical to the argument of *Kabbalah and Ecology*. The second is the belief in *gilgul* or reincarnation.

The *Zohar*, which emerged in Spain at the end of the thirteenth century, describes the Sefirot as being structured by threes in the form of triangles, so that they can be stable. The three triangles are *Keter–Chokhmah–Binah*, *Che̱sed–G'vurah–Tif'eret*, and *Netsach–Hod–Y'so̱d*, with *Malkhut* suspended below *Y'so̱d*. Each set of three is also compared to a balance scale, with its two pans suspended on either side of a central pillar. The Sefirot are also understood to have a fractal structure, where each Sefirah contains its own set of Sefirot. (Sarah Schneider describes this as the Sefirot being "interincluded in each other".)

Beyond all the Sefirot is *Eyn So̱f*, the infinite, limitless, beyond name and description. According to the myth of "the breaking of the Vessels" (*Sh'virat Hakeilim*), *Eyn So̱f* first emanated the Sefirot in a single chain, one below the other, or one within the other. Because of this, each one had to contain the entire force of creation by itself as it emerged. The first three Sefirot were protected because they were not separated in any way from their origin, but the next six shattered, landing upon and crushing the tenth Sefirah, *Malkhut*. This left *Malkhut* diminished, and receptive rather than active – two qualities that define what is female, according to Kabbalah, in the not-yet-redeemed world.

Cordovero (sixteenth century, Ts'fat, or Safed) emphasized a simpler picture of Kabbalah that divided the Sefirot into four worlds: the world of *Atsilut* or Emanation, the world of *B'riyah* or Creating, the world of *Y'tsirah* or Shaping, and the world of *`Asiyah* or Doing. These corresponded to the Sefirot and to the letters of the name YHVH in this manner: *Keter–Chokhmah* corresponds to *Atsilut* and *Yud* י; *Binah* to *B'riyah* and the first *Heh* ה; *Tif'eret*, along with the five Sefirot surrounding it (*Che̱sed* and *G'vurah* above, *Netsach*, *Hod*, *Y'so̱d* below), to *Y'tsirah* and *Vav* ו; and Shekhinah/*Malkhut* to *`Asiyah* and the final *Heh* ה. (Each world also comprises its own complete set of Sefirot.) Cordovero also emphasized the ethical lessons that could be learned from Kabbalah (see pp.163–5, 186–7, 189–90ff.).

In Lurianic Kabbalah, everything became much more complicated. Among other things, according to Yitshak (Isaac) Luria (also sixteenth century, Ts'fat), the shattered and crushed parts of the Sefirot resulting from *Sh'virat Hekeilim* were reconstructed into *par'tsufim*, persons or personalities: *Keter* became two – `*Atiq Yomin* (Ancient of Days, also called `*Atiqa Qadisha*, Holy Ancient One) and *Arikh Anpin* (Long Face); *Chokhmah* became *Abba* (Father); *Binah* became *Imma* (Mother); the six Sefirot centered on *Tif'eret* became *Z`eyr Anpin* (Short Face); and *Malkhut* became *Nuqva* (the Female). So while Cordovero merged the first two Sefirot into one, Luria divided the first Sefirah into two. (Other examples of how Luria magnified the complexity of Kabbalah can be found on pp.184–6, 196–7, 260–62 and n.942.) The shift from Cordovero to Luria is representative of a general trend in Kabbalah, which throughout its history oscillates between greater simplicity and (sometimes maddening) complexity.

The final stage of Kabbalah important for this book is *Chasidut* (Hasidism), emerging from the teachings of the Besht (Ba`al Shem Tov, eighteenth century, Ukraine). *Chasidut*, as a simplifying trend, focused on two dynamics: the quest to shift the energy of the cosmos from *G'vurah* to *Chesed*, that is, from judgment to love, and the quest to unify the Shekhinah/*Malkhut* with *Tif'eret*, that is, to unite cosmic male and female. As with each stage mentioned previously, in *Chasidut* there were swings between simplicity and complexity, with both Nachman of Breslov and Shneur Zalman of Liady (see n.760) swinging toward complexity (to wonderful effect as far as this book's purposes are concerned).

It may be helpful to the reader to place a few of the other authors and works cited in *Kabbalah and Ecology* in relation to the four junctures of Kabbalah just mentioned (the *Bahir*, *Zohar*, Cordovero/Luria, and the Besht). In earlier Jewish mysticism, before the *Bahir*, we have *Shi`ur Qomah* and *Sefer Y'tsirah* (as well as *Heykhalot* literature), which may go back as far as the early rabbinic period. (Traditionally, *Sefer Y'tsirah* is attributed to Avraham.) The "German Pietists" or *Chasidey Ashkenaz* (including Yehudah Hechasid and his disciple Elazar of Worms, twelfth to thirteenth century) received texts that may have been the sources of the *Bahir*, though they held a picture of mystical reality that differs somewhat from the *Bahir*. The *Bahir* was published by the mystics of Provence (who are not represented in *Kabbalah and Ecology*). When the *Bahir* came over the Pyrenees into Christian Spain, it catalyzed the development of Kabbalah there. The Spanish Kabbalists who received the *Bahir* up to the time around when the *Zohar* was published are quite important for this book, including Azriel of Gerona, Ramban (Nachmanides), Yosef Gikatilla, and most especially Yosef ben Shalom Ashkenazi.

Zoharic literature expanded beyond the *Zohar*, including *Zohar Chadash* and *Tiquney Hazohar*, which was written in the fourteenth century. The Kabbalists that lived after this period, but before Cordovero, only play a minor role in *Kabbalah and Ecology*. Luria, who arrived in Ts'fat (Safed) just months before Cordovero died, taught for less than three years there before his own passing. What we know of Luria comes mostly from his disciples, especially from Chayyim Vital, as well as figures like Azaryah deFano, who promulgated his Kabbalah in Italy.

Two other sources critically important for *Kabbalah and Ecology* appeared between this stage and the Besht: Yishayah Horowitz's *Sh'ney Luchot Hab'rit*, and *Chemdat Yamim*, which included *P'ri `Ets Hadar*. (*Tsadiq Y'sod `Olam* also appeared during this period.) Lastly, some of the Kabbalists who lived and wrote in the modern period, after the formation of Hasidism, pioneered the use of Kabbalah to reconcile science with Judaism, with Rav Kook following in their footsteps. These latter could also be considered "complexifiers", while the evolution of a liberal form of Kabbalah in Jewish Renewal can be seen again as part of a simplifying trend.

Here are a few suggestions for further introductory reading: Byron Sherwin, *Kabbalah: An Introduction to Jewish Mysticism* (Lanham MD: Rowman & Littlefield, 2006); Arthur Green, *A Guide to the Zohar* (Stanford CA: Stanford University Press, 2004); Tamar Frankiel, *Kabbalah: A Brief Introduction for Christians* (Woodstock VT: Jewish Lights, 2006); Perle Epstein, *Kabbalah: The Way of the Jewish Mystic* (Boston MA: Shambala, 2001); Daniel Matt, *The Essential Kabbalah* (New York: HarperCollins, 1996); and on the Internet, Jay Michaelson's website learnkabbalah.com, and neohasid.org.

Bibliography of primary Jewish sources

Classical rabbinic literature and pre-rabbinic literature

Adeni, David ben Amram. *Midrash Hagadol*. Jerusalem, 1975.
Avot d'Rabi Natan, ed. Salomon (Solomon) Schechter. Vienna, 1887. Reprint, Israel, n.d.
Batey Midrashot, ed. Shlomo Aharon Wertheimer, 2nd edn. Jerusalem: K'tav Yad v'Sefer, 1989.
Beyt Hamidrash, ed. Adolph Jellinek. Vienna: Bruder Winter, 1873.
B'rei'shit Rabbati, ed. Chanokh Albeck. Jerusalem: Vegshel, 1984.
Josephus, Flavius. *Antiquities of the Jews*, trans. William Whiston. www.earlyjewishwritings.com/text/josephus/ant3.html (Apr. 2010).
  The Wars of the Jews, trans. William Whiston. www.earlyjewishwritings.com/text/josephus/war5.html (Dec. 2011).
Midrash B'rei'shit Rabba' (*Bereschit Rabba*), 3 vols., eds. Julius Theodor and Chanokh Albeck. Berlin: Ts'vi Hirsch Itskovski, 1912.
Midrash Rabbah, including *B'rei'shit Rabbah*, *Sh'mot Rabbah*, *Vayiqra' Rabbah*, *B'midbar Rabbah*, *D'varim Rabbah*, *Kohelet Rabbah*, and *Shir Hashirim Rabbah*. Jerusalem: Avida` Da`at Umeyda`, 1994.
Midrash Tanchuma, ed. Solomon Buber. Vilna: Wittwe & Gebrüder Romm, 1885.
Midrash Tanchuma, ed. Chanokh Zundel. Reprint, Jerusalem: Levine Epstein, 1968.
Midrash Tanhuma, 2 vols, trans. John T. Townsend. Hoboken NJ: Ktav, 1989.
Midrash Tanhuma-Yelammedenu, trans. Samuel Berman. Hoboken NJ: Ktav, 1996.
Midrash T'hilim (*Tilim* or *Shocher Tov*), ed. Shlomo Buber. Vilna: Wittwe & Gebrüder Romm, 1891.
Miqra'ot G'dolot. Reprint, New York: Shulzinger Bros., n.d.
Mishnah. Jerusalem, 2002. www.mechon-mamre.org/b/h/ho.htm (Sep. 2011).
Mishnayoth, ed. Philip Blackman. New York: Judaica Press, 1963.
M'khilta d'Rabi Yishmael, ed. Chayyim Shaul Horowitz. Jerusalem: Bamberger and Wahrmann, 1960.

Philo of Alexandria. *On the Unchangeableness of God*, trans. C. D. Yonge. London: George Bell, 1890. www.earlyjewishwritings.com/text/philo/book10.html (Jan. 2012).
Pirkê De Rabbi Eliezer, trans. Gerald Friedlander. New York: Sepher-Hermon, 1965.
Pirqey Rabi Eli`ezer. Warsaw: Weissberg, 1874.
P'siqta d'Rav Kahana, ed. Mandelbaum. New York: Jewish Theological Seminary, 1962.
Sefer Y'tsirah. Reprint, Jerusalem: Monzon, 1961.
Shim`on of Frankfurt-am-Main. *Yalqut Shim`oni*. Jerusalem: Vegshel, n.d.
Sifrey d'Vey Rav (Sifrey `al Sefer B'midbar v'Sifrey Zuta), ed. Chayim Shaul Horowitz. Frankfurt-am-Main: J. Kauffman Verlag, n.d.
Sifra d'Vey Rav (Torat Kohanim), 2 vols. Jerusalem: Sifra, 1961.
Sifrey `al Sefer D'varim, ed. Louis Finkelstein. Berlin: Gesellschaft zur Föderung der Wissenschaft des Judentums, 1939. Reprint, New York: Jewish Theological Seminary, 1969.
Sifrey Lid'varim, ed. Zahava Gerlitz. Israel: Da`at, 2010. www.daat.ac.il/daat/vl/sifri-dvarim/sifri-dvarim01.pdf (Dec 2011).
Talmud Y'rushalmi. Krotoshin, 1866; Reprint, Jerusalem: Shilo, 1969.
Tana' d'Vey Eliyahu. Warsaw: Shmuel Shmelke Filitser, 1912.
Tanna Debe Eliyyahu, trans. William G. Braude and Israel J. Kapstein. Philadelphia: Jewish Publication Society, 1981.
Targum Onkelos. In *Miqra'ot G'dolot*.
Targum Pseudo-Yonatan. In *Miqra'ot G'dolot*.
Targum Y'rushalmi. In *Miqra'ot G'dolot*.

Medieval thought and Kabbalah

Ashkenazi, Yosef ben Shalom. *Peyrush L'parshat B'rei'shit*, ed. Moshe Hallamish. Jerusalem: Magnes Press, 1984.
Avraham ibn Ezra. *Longer and Shorter Peyrush*. In *Miqra'ot G'dolot*.
Azri'el ben Menachem of Gerona. *Peyrush Ha'agadot L'Rabi Azri'el*, ed. Isaiah Tishby. Jerusalem: M'qitsey Nirdamim, 1945.
Bahir, see Margaliot.
Bachya ibn Paquda (Pakuda). *Torat Chovot Hal'vavot* (Eng. title *Duties of the Heart*), trans. Moses Hyamson. Jerusalem: Feldheim, 1970.
Chavel, Chaim Dov (ed.). *Kitvey Ramban* (including *Igeret Haqodesh* and *Peyrush L'Shir Hashirim*). Jerusalem: Mossad Harav Kook, 1963.
Chemdat Yamim, 3 vols. (including *P'ri `Ets Hadar*). Livorno, 1763; Reprint, Jerusalem: Makor, 1970.
Cordovero, Moshe. *Or Ne`erav*. Jerusalem: Qol Y'hudah, 1965.
  The Palm Tree of Deborah, trans. Louis Jacobs. New York: Sepher-Hermon, 1974.
  Tomer D'vorah. Jerusalem: Or Yiqar, 1969.
  Shi`ur Qomah. Jerusalem: Dov Ze'ev ben Yosef, 1966.
David ben Yehudah Hechasid. *Mar'ot Hatsov'ot*, ed. Daniel C. Matt. Chico CA: Scholars Press, 1982.
deFano, Menachem Azaryah. *Yonat Eilem*. L'vov: n.p., 1858.
Donnolo, Shabtai. *Sefer Chakhmoni*. See *Sefer Y'tsirah*.

Bibliography

Duran, Shimon ben Tsemach. *Magen Avot*. Brooklyn NY: Light Publishing, 1946.
Elazar ben Yehudah of Worms. *Sefer Sodey Razaya*. Jerusalem: Makhon Sha`arey Ziv, 1985.
  Sodey Razaya Cheleq Bet: Sefer Hashem. Jerusalem: Makhon Sodey Razaya, 2004.
Ezra ben Solomon (Shlomo) of Gerona. *Commentary on the Song of Songs and Other Kabbalistic Writings*, ed. Seth Brody. Kalamazoo: Western Michigan University Medieval Institute Publications, 1999.
Gikatilla, Joseph (Yosef). *Gates of Light: Sha'are Orah*, trans. Avi Weinstein. New York: HarperCollins, 1994.
  Sha'arey Orah. Warsaw: Argelbrand, 1883.
Horowitz, Yishayah (Isaiah). *The Generations of Adam*, trans. Miles Krassen. New York: Paulist Press, 1996.
  Sh'ney Luchot Hab'rit. Reprint, Jerusalem: Book Export Enterprises, n.d.
Kimḥi, Joseph (Yosef Kimchi). *The Book of the Covenant*. Toronto: Pontifical Institute of Mediaeval Studies, 1972.
Loew, Yehudah. *G'vurot Hashem*. London: n.p., 1954.
  Derekh Chayyim. London: Honig and Sons, 1960.
Luria, Yitshak (attr). *Tsadiq Y'sod `Olam*, ed. Levi Yitshak Krakovsky. Jerusalem: Yeshivat Or Chozer, 1982.
Maimonides, Moses (Moshe ben Maimon). *The Guide for the Perplexed*, trans. Moses Friedlander. New York: Dover Books, 1980.
  The Guide for the Perplexed, trans. Shlomo Pines. Chicago: University of Chicago Press, 1963.
  Mishnah `Im Peyrush Harambam. Jerusalem: Mossad Harav Kook, 1963.
  Mishneh Torah. Jerusalem, n.d. www.mechon-mamre.org/i/o.htm (Sep. 2011).
  Moreh N'vukhim (Hebr.), trans. Yosef Kafich. Jerusalem: Mossad Harav Kook, 1977.
  Moreh N'vukhim (Hebr.), trans. Michael Schwartz. Jerusalem: Tel Aviv University Press, 2009. www.press.tau.ac.il/perplexed (Sep. 2014).
  Sefer Hamitsvot, trans. Yosef Kafich. Jerusalem: Mossad Harav Kook, 1957.
Matt, Daniel C. (ed.). *The Essential Kabbalah*. San Francisco: HarperCollins, 1996.
  (ed. and trans.). *Zohar: The Book of Enlightenment*. New York: Paulist Press, 1983.
Margaliot, Reuven (ed.). *Sefer Habahir and Tiquney Hazohar*. Jerusalem: Mossad Harav Kook, 1994.
  (ed.). *Sefer Hazohar*, 3 vols. Jerusalem: Mossad Harav Kook, 1984.
  (ed.). *Zohar Chadash and Sha`arey Zohar*. Jerusalem: Mossad Harav Kook, 1994.
Miqra'ot G'dolot. Reprint, New York: Shulzinger Bros., n.d.
Moshe ben Nachman (Ramban or Nachmanides). *Peyrush*. In *Miqra'ot G'dolot*.
Recanati, Menachem ben Binyamin. *Bi'ur `al Hatorah `al Derekh Ha'emet*. Venice: Marco Antonio Giustiniani (Justinian), 1545.
Saadyah Gaon (Saadyah ben Yosef). *Emunot v'Dei`ot*, trans. Yosef Kafich. Israel: Da`at, n.d. www.daat.ac.il/daat/mahshevt/kapah/4-2.htm (Sep. 2011).
Sforno, Ovadiah. *Peyrush*. In *Miqra'ot G'dolot*.
Shlomo Yits'chaqi (Rashi). *Peyrush*. In *Miqra'ot G'dolot*.
Shulchan `Arukh Shel Ha'ari, 2nd edn. Jerusalem: Makhon Chatam Sofer, 1987.
Vital, Chayyim. *`Ets Chayyim*. Reprint, Jerusalem: D'fus Levi, 1910.

Sefer Sha`ar Ru'ach Haqodesh (Sideret Kitvey Rabeynu Ha'ar"i Zatsa"l, vol.11), ed. Yehudah Ashlag. Jerusalem: Kitvey Rabeynu Ha'ar"i Zatsa"l, 1963.
Kabbalah of Creation: Isaac Luria's Earlier Mysticism (Sha`ar Hak'lalim), trans. Eliahu Klein. Northvale NJ: Jason Aronson, 2000.
Yehudah Hechasid. *Sefer Chasidim*, ed. Reuven Margaliot. Jerusalem: Mossad Harav Kook, 1992.
Zohar, see Margaliot.

Chasidut, early modern Jewish thought, and modern Kabbalah

Albaz, Rafa'el Moshe of Morocco. *Eden Miqedem*. Jerusalem: Makhon Yismach Lev Torat Moshe, 1996.
Baal Shem Tov, Yisrael. *Tsava'at Harivash* (Hebr.), ed. Jacob Immanuel Schochet. Brooklyn NY: Kehot Publication Society, 1998.
Tzava'at Harivash: The Testament of Rabbi Israel Baal Shem Tov, ed. and trans. Jacob Immanuel Schochet. Brooklyn NY: Kehot Publication Society, 1998.
Benamozegh, Elijah. *Israel and Humanity*, trans. Maxwell Luria. New York: Paulist Press, 1994.
Berlin, Naftali Tsvi Yehudah. *Ha`emeq Davar*. New York: Friedman, n.d.
Chayyim of Volozhin. *Nefesh Hachayyim*. Wickliffe OH: A. D. Goldberg, 1997.
Dov Ber ben Shmuel of Linitz. *Shivchey Habesht*, ed. S. A. Horodetsky. Berlin: Ajanoth Verlag, 1922.
Dov Ber of Mezritch. *Magid D'varav L'Ya`aqov*. New York: Otsar Hachasidim, 2003.
Eliyahu ben Shlomo of Vilna (the Vilna Gaon). *Aderet Eliyahu*. New York: Shulzinger Bros., 1950.
Siddur Hagr'a. Jerusalem: Yitshak Nachum Levi, 1926.
Feibush, Meshullam. *Yosher Divrey Emet*. Jerusalem: D'fus M'nachem Ra'ta, 5734 (1973).
Ginsburgh, Yitzchak. "*Mitsvat Kisui Hadam*", sec.8. www.malchuty.org/2009-06-16-14-01-37/821-2012-10-25-07-39-50.html (Nov. 2013).
Hakohen, Meir Simcha of Dvinsk. *Meshekh Chokhmah*. Riga: Menachem Mendel Dovber, 1927.
Heschel, Avraham Yehoshua of Apt. *Oheiv Yisrael*. Zhitomir: Nekhdei Harav Mislavita, 1863.
Hurwitz, Pinchas Eliyahu of Vilna. *Sefer Hab'rit Hashalem*. Jerusalem: Y'rid Has'farim, 1990.
Kook, Abraham Isaac (Avraham Yitshak). *Abraham Isaac Kook*, trans. Ben Zion Bokser. New York: Paulist Press, 1978.
Chazon Hatsim'chonut v'Hashalom, ed. David Cohen. Jerusalem: Nezer David, 1983.
The Essential Writings of Abraham Isaac Kook, trans. Ben Zion Bokser. Warwick NY: Amity, 1988.
Orot Hakodesh, 2 vols. Jerusalem: Ha'agudah L'hotsa'at Sifrey Hara'ya"h Kook, 1937.
A Vision of Vegetarianism and Peace, ed. David Cohen, trans. Jonathan Rubenstein. www.jewishveg.com/AVisionofVegetarianismandPeace.pdf (Sep. 2013).

Lainer, Yaakov ben Mordechai Yosef Me'izbitsa. *Beyt Ya`aqov `al Sefer Vayiqra'*, ed. Chanina Dovid Lainer. New York: Rabbi M. J. Lainer, 1991.
Nachman of Breslov. *Liqutey Moharan*. New York: R' Eli`ezer Shlomo Breslover, 1965.
The Thirteen Stories of Rebbe Nachman of Breslev, trans. Esther Koenig. Jerusalem: Hillel Press, 1978.
Sipurey Ma`asiyot Mishanim Qadmoniyot. Jerusalem: Mossad Harav Kook, 1971.
Noson (Natan) of Nemirov. *Liqutey T'filot*. Jerusalem: R' Yisra'el Dov Odesser, n.d.
Ricci, Immanuel Chai (Riqi). *Mishnat Chasidim*. Lemberg: M. F. Poremba, 1858.
Roth, Aharon (Arele). *Shulchan Hatahor*. Jerusalem, 1966.
Schneersohn, Menachem Mendel. *Likkutei Sichos (Liqutey Sichot)*. Brooklyn NY: Kehot, 1998.
Torat Menachem: Sefer Ma'amarim M'luqatim, vol.2. Brooklyn NY: Otsar Hachasidim, 2002.
*Sefer Ba`al Shem Tov (Ba`al Shem Tov `al Hatorah)*, ed. Shim`on Menachem Mendel. Reprint, Israel: Book Export Enterprises, n.d.
Shneur Zalman of Liady. *Likutei Amarim (Liqutey Amarim)* (also called *Tanya*), trans. Nissan Mindel et al. London: Otsar Hachasidim, 1972.
Liqutey Torah. Brooklyn NY: Kehot, 1973.
Torah Or. Brooklyn NY: Kehot, 1973.
Tcharek, Avraham ben Aharon Yosef. *Divrey Avraham*. Jerusalem, 1927.
Tsadok Hakohen. *Sefer Mach'shavot Charuts*. Pieterkov, Poland: Yachdut, 1911.
Tsarfati, Vidal. *Derekh Haqodesh*. Husiatyn, Ukraine: Dov'vey Sif'tey Y'sheinim, 1907.
Tsvi Hirsch of Zhidachov. *`Ateret Tsvi*. Lvov, Ukraine (Galicia), 1871.
Twersky, Dovid of Tolna. *Qohelet David*. Lublin, Poland, 1881.
Yaakov Yosef of Polnoye. *Ben Porat Yosef*. Pieterkov, Poland: Feivel Belchatovski, 1884.
K'tonet Pasim, ed. Gedaliah Nigal. Jerusalem: M'khon P'ri Ha'arets, 1985.
Zev Wolf of Zhitomir. *Or Hame'ir*, 4 vols. Warsaw: R' Me'ir Y'chi'el Halter, 1883.

Abbreviated titles

ARN *Avot d'Rabi Natan*
ARNA *Avot d'Rabi Natan* version A
ARNB *Avot d'Rabi Natan* version B
Ashkenazi *Peyrush L'parshat B'rei'shit*, Yosef ben Shalom Ashkenazi
BM *Batey Midrashot*
BmR *B'midbar Rabbah*
BR *B'rei'shit Rabbah*
ECh `*Ets Chayyim*, Chayyim Vital
LM *Liqutey Moharan*, Nachman of Breslov
MN *Moreh N'vukhim*, Maimonides
OHQ *Orot Haqodesh*, Avraham Yitshak Kook
PRE *Pirqey d'Rabi Eli`ezer*
PRK *P'siqta d'Rav Kahana*
SBST *Sefer Ba`al Shem Tov*
SCh *Sefer Chasidim*
ShLH *Sh'ney Luchot Hab'rit*
ShmR *Sh'mot Rabbah*
SifreyD *Sifrey D'varim*
Tanch *Tanchuma*
TanchB *Tanchuma Buber*
YSh *Yalqut Shim`oni*
TB *Talmud Bavli*
TY *Talmud Y'rushalmi*
TZ *Tiquney Zohar*
VR *Vayiqra' Rabbah*
ZCh *Zohar Chadash*

Modern titles:

Bernstein *Ecology and the Jewish Spirit*
BDB *A Hebrew and English Lexicon of the Old Testament*
Bokser (1978) *Abraham Isaac Kook*
Bokser (1988) *The Essential Writings of Abraham Isaac Kook*
EBR *Encyclopedia of the Bible and Its Reception*
EJ *Encyclopedia Judaica*
ERN *Encyclopedia of Religion and Nature*
OMG *On the Mystical Shape of the Godhead*, Gershom Scholem
MTJM *Major Trends in Jewish Mysticism*, Gershom Scholem
WZ *Wisdom of the Zohar*, Isaiah Tishby
Yaffe *Judaism and Environmental Ethics*

General index

(Note: In some cases references are grouped by literary/historical genre, into the categories of Torah and *Tanakh*, Midrash, medieval Philosophy, Kabbalah, Hasidism, and/or Contemporary thought. This is indicated by corresponding letters [T, M, P, K, H, C] preceding each such group of entries.)

Abba (Father, *par'tsuf*), see *Chokhmah*
Abraham (*Avraham Avinu*), 52, 87–8, 336
Abrahamic religions, 31–2, see also Christianity, Islam, Judaism, religion
anthropocentrism, God's image, and, 31
Abram, David, 2, 17, 34, 54, 96, 207, 231, 241
Abrams, Daniel, 188, 194
Abravanel, Don Yitshak (1437–1508), 148
Adam Ha'elyon (upper/supernal human), 183–5, 205, 206, 224–5, 251
Adam Harishon (the first human, Adam), 52–3, 57, 64, 99, 116–17, 118, 131, 158, 184, 210, 255, 296, 302, 304, see also *adamah*, *androginos*, Chavah, dominion, *du-par'tsufin*
  born circumcised, 87
  gigantic size and diminishment of, 89, 246–8, 283, 296
  language and, 65, 158, 322
  male and female, 79–80
  restoration of, 248–9, 297
  Shabbat and, 322–3
  sin of, 50, 184, 192, 243, 248, 283, 296, 320, 324, 336, 338, 351
  spirit of, 79, 137
Adam Qadmon (primordial/cosmogonic human), 189, 241–3, 248, 249–50,
255–9, 262, 264, 266–7, 277–8, 292, see also Adam Harishon, Or Chozer
Creation in God's image and, 215, 250–52
adamah (earth, ground, soil), 19, 44, 144, 197
  Adam and, 43, 64, 80, 81, 167, 197–8, 245, 272
  opposite *tselem*, 198
Adler, Rachel, 78
Aggadat 'Olam Qatan, 244, 308
agriculture, see also farming, *Sh'mitah*
  as sacrament, 167
  glyphosate (Roundup), 305
  GMOs and, 305, 350
  in ancient Israel, 10, 78
  in Palestine, 306
  laws of, see *kilayim*, *'orlah*, *migrash*, *Sh'mitah*, Jubilee
Akiva ben Yosef (c.40–c.135), 18, 39, 103–5
Alexandrian theology, 74, 133–6
  rejected by the rabbis, 134–5
androginos (androgyne), 79–80, 192, 195–6
angels, 188, 306, M: 47–8, 50–52, 55, 58–9, 61, 64–5, 68–9, 76–7, 79, 86, 89–90, 99, 101, 102, 136, 146, 155, 284, 321–2, P: 26, 27, 275, K: 146–7, 183, 296, 213, 223–7, 228, 230, 253, 285, 290–91, 306, 357, H: 292, see also chain of Being, *chayot*
Adam and, 31, 58, 64, 65, 79, 99, 248, 283

angels (cont.)
  angel of death, 27, 348
  animals and, 58–9, 65, 136, 146–7, 223
  archangels, 64, 115–16, 213, 221, 284, 322, see also Sama'el
  contrasted with heavens, 50–54
  created by people, 290–92, 306
  demons and, 59
  divine names in, 204–5
  humans in image of, 47–8, 54, 58–9, 60, 102, 176
  k'ruvim (cherubim on ark), 196
  stature of, 89–90, 283
  worship by, 31, 64–5, 248
animal rights, 5, 86, 143, 145, 155, 162
animal husbandry, 78
animals, T: 44, 98, 131, M: 83–5, 149–55, 157–9, 321, 325, 345–6, K: 146–7, 149, 153, 159–60, 164–5, 223–5, 228, 326, see also angels, birds, blood, Cordovero, Descartes, dominion, ethics, fish, insects, Isaac of Syria, Maimonides, n'shamah, Ramban, sacrifices, Sefer Chasidim, Tiquney Zohar, Torah, tsa`ar ba`aley chayyim, vision, Zoharic literature
  agency of, 85, 152–5
  as God's image, 122
  as subjects, 146
  Bil`am's ass, 153
  cognition in, 22
  compassion in, 22, 153–4, 351
  dog, 85, 91, 154–5
  dolphin, 77, 85, 116
  horse, 64, 91, 146, 226, 269
  justice in creation of, 286
  language in, 6, 22, 60–61, 153, 158, 159, 320, 326
  lion, 20, 100, 224, see also chayot
  "Love your fellow" applied to, 164–5
  naming of, 64, 318
  of the chariot (ox, lion, eagle), see also chayot
  other species, 56, 116, 154, 320
  ox, 64, 100, 227, see also chayot
  Pinchas ben Yair's donkey, 153
  prehistoric megafauna, 3, 4, 325
  primates, 49, 77, 88, 91, 116
  snake, 52, 56, 83–4, 86, 99, 158, 193, 318
  souls of, 74, 81, 103, 135, 139–42, 145
  vision compared to human, 77
  vivisection, 139
  whale/cetacean, 84–6

Yehudah Hanasi's calf, 146
animism, 131, 140, 145, 162, 235, 318, 355
anthropic principle, 267
anthropo-archism, 18, 26, 30, 32, 36, 56, 57, 61, 94–5, 112
  defined, 25–6
  ethno-archism and, 122, 322
anthropocentrism, 30–34, 99, 148, 188, see also anthropo-archism
  opposition to, see deep ecology, Maimonides, ethics
  transformation of, 25, 29–31, 35, 168, 253, 313
  "weak", 25, 57, 142, 346
anthropology, rabbinic (religious), 32, 46–103, 114–21, 127, 151–2, see also ethics, humanity, Kabbalah
anthropology, science of, 8, 87–8, 157, 192
Antiochean theology, 74, 133–5, 136, see also Irenaeus, the rabbis, Theodore of Mopsuestia
Aquinas, Thomas (1225–74), 16, 20, 27, 50, 161
Arikh Anpin (Long Face, par'tsuf), 362
Aristotle, 17, 67, 138, 271, 273
  animals in, 23, 50, 84–5
  human nature according to, 62–3
Artson, Bradley Shavit, 11, 15
Ashkenazi, Yosef ben Shalom (late thirteenth century), 5, 181, 194–6, 211, 215, 234, 238, 250–54, 255, 286, 301, 302, 363, see also index of rabbinic sources
  Creation as God's image, 181, 251–2
  idolatry, meaning of, 181, 238, 252
  Nature as Elohim, 275
  Zohar and, 181
`Asiyah (World of Action, Doing), 184, 257, 263, see also the four worlds
`Atiq Yomin and `Atiqa Qadisha (Ancient of Days, Holy Ancient One, par'tsuf), 362
Atsilut (World of Emanation), 184, 263, see also the four worlds
Augustine of Hippo (354–430), 140
Avot d'Rabi Natan, see index of rabbinic sources
  dating of, 46
awe, 2, 17, 37, 53, 72, 96, 117, 199, 210, 228, 235, 313, 333, 342

Baal Shem Tov, Yisrael (the Besht, 1698–1760), 206–7, 288–9, 292–4, 297–300, 339, 326, 363

General index

Bacon, Francis (1561–1626), 72, 94–5
Bachya ibn Paquda, *see* ibn Paquda
bacteria, 24, 214, 264, 330, 350
Bahir (Sefer Bahir), 176, 187, 219, 234, 360, 363, *see also index of rabbinic sources*
 blessing in, 37
 body in, 176, 187, 206
 Cosmic Tree, 209, 218
 Earth in, 209, 216, 237, 278
 Gnosticism, contrasted with, 278
 parable in, 209
bal tashchit (prohibition against wasting), 11–13, 162, 165
basar (flesh), 131, 144–5, 157, 184, 285, 355–6 *see also* blood
Bedouin, 12, 306
Belkin, Samuel, 112
Ben Azai, Shimon (second century), 103–5, 118, 162–3
Benjamin, Walter (1892–1940), 324, 334
Benstein, Jeremy, 11, 166, 270
Berlin, Naftali Tsvi Yehudah (the Netsiv, 1817–93), 254
Besht, *see* Baal Shem Tov
Bible (*Tanakh*), 2, 8, 9, 15, 33, 35, 44, 45, 52, 128, 167, 242, 319–20, 356, *see also* ecotheology, Torah, *and see index of scriptural verses*
Binah (Understanding, Sefirah), 147, 175, 178, 215, 234, 262, 288, 302, 360–62
 Imma, 180, 196, 362
 Leah, 289
biocentrism, 9–10, 15, 25, 38, 49, 119–20, 147, 270, 349, 352, *see also* theology of Nature
 ecocentrism and, 9
 limitations of, 15
biodiversity, *see* diversity
 origin of term, 17
biophilia, 17, 161, 171
birds, 4, 21, 77, 92–3, 94, T: 44, 97, M: 64, 99, 108, 150, 152, 154, 158, 160, 345–6, K: 100, 120, 146, 148, 153, 220–21, 326, *see also* animals, *shiluach haqein*
 eagle, 100, 223–6, 252, *see also chayot*
 hoopoe, 345–6
 moa, 3, 4
 Noach's dove, 150–51, 152, 345–6
 phoenix, 346
 raven, 152, 325
 speech of, 325–26
 ziz, 99

birth, 3, 77, 85, 116, 243, 276–7
blood, 137, 349
 Adam Harishon, 57
 circulation, in Kabbalah, 260
 honoring/burial of the blood of an animal, *see kavod ladam*
 menarche, 88, *see also nidah*
 nefesh (soul, life) as, 137–8, 140, 145, 147, 150, 355
 sacrificial, 82, 144–5
 tselem and, 102–3
body, 34, 343, M: 74, 76–82, P: 62, 67–8, K: 176–9, 182–3, 187–201, 250, *see also androginos*, blood, Creation:as one body, *du-par'tsufim*, *golem*, *guf*, *nefesh*, sex, soul:body and, *Taharah*, *tselem*
 as God's name, 188
 as microcosm, *see `olam qatan*
 female, *see* clitoris, female body, womb
 male, *see* circumcision, phallus
 parts of, in divine image, 187–8, 197–201
 sacrifices and, 144
 Torah as, 201
 upright stature, *see tselem*
Bohm, David, 309
Bookchin, Murray, 4, 113
breath, 17–18, 34, 44, 64
B'riyah (World of Creation, Creating), *see the four worlds*
Brown-Driver-Briggs Lexicon, 19, 106, 158
Bruegmann, Walter, 128
Buber, Martin (1878–1965), 113, 327–30
 debate with Scholem, *see* Scholem
 Hasidism and, 118, 299, 340
 imitatio Dei, 328
 I-You, 317, 327, 328
 Nature in, 327–9, 343, 352–3

Callicot, J. Baird, 33, 151–2
Calvin, John (1509–64), 96
Cambridge Declaration on Consciousness, 22
capital punishment, 114, 156
capitalism, 13, 33, 125, 347, 350
chain of Being, 25, 43, 54–9, 312
 angels and, 55, 58, 183, 309
chaos theory, 2–3, 6, 307
chariot, 182, 203, 205, 213, 221, 223, 226–7, 236, 254, 286, 321
Chasidey Ashkenaz (the German Pietists), 66, 191, *see also* Elazar of Worms, Yehudah Hechasid
 Bahir and, 363

Chasidut (Hasidism), 206, 227, 249, 260, 278, 282, 338, 363, see also Baal Shem Tov, Buber, Heschel of Apt, Lainer, Meshullam Feibush, Nachman of Breslov, Shneur Zalman, Schneersohn, Simchah Bunam, Tsadok Hakohen, Yaakov Yosef, Z'ev Wolf
   Breslover, 122
   Kabbalah in, 363
   Chabad (Lubavitch), 234, 256
Chavah (Eve), 80, 81, 84, 89, see also Eden
   Adam and, 90, 99, 100, 152, 158, 195, 196, 336, 348
   creation of, 80, 81
   forbidden fruit and, 50, 99
   Sama'el and, 52
   snake and, 84, 193
chayot, 121, 223–7, 236
   as God's image, 122
Chayyim of Volozhin (1749–1821), 168
Chazal, see the rabbis
Chaze, Micheline, 107
Chemdat Yamim, 212, 358
Cherry, Michael Shai, 25, 28
Chesed (Love, Sefirah), 175, 213, 222, 224, 234, 258, 261, 262, 264, 265, 285, 307, 348, 360–63
chesed (lovingkindness), 105, 258, 313, 345
chiyut (lifeforce), 233, 236, 239, 256, 259, 260, 275, 299, 349
Chokhmah (Wisdom, Sefirah), 175, 186, 215, 234, 261, 262, 360–62
   Abba, 180, 196, 362
chosenness, 121–2, see also Israel:the people, ethno-archism
   of humanity, 259
chotam (seal), 91, 104, 117, 181, 251, 302–3
Christianity, 9, 10, 14–15, 23, 31, 33, 38, 82, 100, 129, 140, 243–4, 274, see also ecotheology, feminism, *imitatio Dei*, *tselem*
   Anglican, see Fox, Habgood
   Catholic, 16, 134, 231, see also Aquinas, Augustine, Francis, Eckhardt
   early, 65, 101, 108, 132, see also Irenaeus, Justin Martyr
   God's image in, 44–5, 63, 101, 105, 108, 112, 186, 250
   kenosis, 231
   late ancient, 108, 133–6, see also Alexandrian theology, Antiochean theology, Augustine, Gregory of Nyssa, Isaac of Syria, Leo the Great, Theodore of Mopsuestia
   medieval, 231, 363, see also Aquinas, Eckhardt, Isaac the Syrian, Maximus the Confessor
   modern theology, 38, 45, 112, see also Callicott, Gregorios, Habgood, Linzey, McFague, Thielicke, Ware
   Orthodox, 56, 105, 164, 186, 250, see also Gregorios, Ware
   Protestant, 38, 111–12, see also Callicott, Calvin, Linzey, Luther, McFague, Thielicke
   scripture, 50, 108, 242, 336
circumcision
   anthropology of, 87–8, 192
   female body and, 89, 193
   tselem as, M: 87–9, K: 190–92,
climate change, 2–4, 6, 106
   as spiritual crisis, 344–5
clitoris, 80, 188
Cohen, Jeremy, 13, 33, 49–51, 55, 94, 136, 158
communism, 13, 125
compassion (*chemlah, chesed, rachamim*), 1, 105, 147, 154, 214, 342, 344, 351–2
   divine, 105, 149, 154, 189
   for all creatures, 164, 186, 298, 299
complexity (mathematics), 306–11
compost, 349 see also soil
constructive theology, 7, 19, 37, 49, 163, 171, 193, 194, 249, 264, 306, 342, see also methodology
Cordovero, Moshe (1522–70), 101, 149, 185, 215, 252–53, 262, 278, 301–2, 358, 362–3, see also index of rabbinic sources
   ethical standing of all creatures, 163–5
   human body in, 189–90
   on *imitatio Dei*, 186–7, 189–90
   purpose of Kabbalah, 37
Cosmic Walk, 306–7, 334
Creation (the Universe), 2, 5, 120, see also Earth, Nature, *sidrey v'rei'shit*
   as God's image, 175, 210–15, 223, 241, 250–55, 347
   as *mishkan* (sanctuary), 202–3, 213
   as one body, 203, 250, 271, 294, 297
   comprised in Adam, 250–55
   goodness of, 15–17, 254
   human participation in, 312–13
   telos of, 19, 25–7, 212

General index

unification of, 212–13, 226, 230–31, 238, 253
creation (of the universe), 175, 179–80, 194, 209, 211, 214, 217, 234–5, 242, 245, 256–9

Dan, Joseph, 178, 278
Davis, Ellen, 13, 19, 44, 127, 157, 167, 349–50
Dawkins, Richard, 24
death, 353, T: 356, M: 18, 50, 57, 58–9, 132, 137, 152, 156, 348, P: 141, 156, K: 92, 185, 147
environmental ethics and, 5, 344, 348
Declaration of Helsinki, 126
deep ecology, 14, 15, 167, 317
deFano (da Fano), Menachem Azaryah (1548–1620), 288, 363
derekh erets (proper behavior, "the way of the earth"), 161
Descartes, René (1596–1650), 62, 63, 72, 139
animals in, 6, 139
dirah batachtonim (dwelling place below/among the lower creatures), 263, 336–9
diversity, 3, 5, 6, 17–21, 28–9, 128, 239, 257, 350
aesthetics of, 305
of humanity, 21, 36, 117, 127, 225
of religions, 36
theology of, 17–21
within God, 34, 128
d'mut, 106–7, *see* tselem
contrasted with *tselem*, 179, 196, 197, 250
used independently of *tselem*, 48, 52, 59, 68–9, 74, 141, 206, 216, 222, 230, 284, 287, 339
Donnolo, Shabtai (913–82), 94, 100, 206, 269
domem (pl., *dom'mim*) (mineral, rock, stone), 131, 233, 235–7, 260, 262
domem-tsomei'ach-chai-m'daber (*DTsCh"M*; silent, growing, moving, speaking; i.e., mineral, vegetable, animal, human), 21, 149, 164, 186, 252, 253, 254, 263, 298
dominion, 49, 90, 95, 101, 156, 158–60, 325, *see also* Maimonides, *Zohar*
as taming, 86
as opposite of "terror and dread", 87
dualism, 132, 135, 207, M: 56, 246, K: 187, 207, 279, *see also* Gnosticism
du-par'tsufim (double-body/gender), 83, 246, M: 79–81, K: 192–7

Duran, Shimon ben Tsemach (1361–1444), 94, 249
d'yoqna, 44, 52, 159, 180, 182, 191, 194, 198–9, 205, 211, 224, 228, 250, 291, 301–3

Earth, 1–4, 6, 209, M: 137, 202–3, 243–5, 271–2, K: 215–17, 236–7, 266–7, 272–3, H: 257–9, *see also Bahir*, elements, Gaia, land, Nature, Zoharic literature
as co-creator with God, 93, 101, 167, 217, 258, 272–3
as a jewel, 236–37
carrying capacity, 3
fertility of, as echo of Eden, 258
heavens and, 121, 135, 180, 202–3, K: 37, 205, 210, 215, 216–17, 219–20, 221, 278
"saving" the, 5
usage of terms, "earth" vs. "Earth", 3
earth, element of (*'afar, adamah*), 197–8, 213, 255–7, 313, *see also* soil
Ebreo, Leone (Yhudah Leon Abravanel, c.1465–c.1523), 271, 349
Eckhart, Meister (c.1260–c.1328), 235
ecofeminism, 8–9, 14, 266
eco-kashrut, 10, 12
ecology, 23–4, 30, 40, 97, *see also* ecosystems, ecotheology, Nature, science
hermeneutics of, 24, 282, 312
ecosystems, 11, 163, 282, 305, 329–31
as microcosms, 282
as model of divine flux, 180, 326
ecotheology, 5, 25, 30–31, 35, 238, 273, 277, 297, 299, 331, 332–4, 339, 342–4, 352, *see also* ecology, Nature, Shekhinah, theology of Nature
Adam Qadmon and, 241, 256, 264
Creation spirituality, 31
Biblically-based, 43, 151–2, 346–7
Christian, 12, 26, 38, 134, 250, 274
contrasted with dualism, 278–9
Gaia and, 266–7, 271, 274–7
homiletics and, 49, 89
imitatio Dei and, 105
Jewish, 7–8, 12, 20, 27, 171, 282, 326, 330
contemporary, 7, 10, 34, 332–4
foundations for, 27, 30, 37–8, 54, 61, 68, 86, 334–5
justice in Nature, 286
Kabbalah and, 37–8, 274–9, 309–11, 342–3
Maimonides and, 27–9, 148, 270–71, 279, 342

ecotheology (*cont.*)
  mitsvot (commandments) and, 166
  Musar and, 7
  organicism and, 97
  pluralism and, 128
  raising the sparks, 299–300
  science and, 330
  Torah and, 43
Eden (*Gan Eden*), M: 50, 84, 119, 158, 243, 278, 321, 323, 348, K: 184, 278, 335, H: 259, *see also* Adam Harishon, Chavah
  Adam's cloak of skin, 158–9
  expulsion from, 91, 158
  fragrance of, 335
  gates of, 345–6
  human purpose in, 167
  language of, 324
  Noach's dove and, 150, 345
  origin of grapevine, 346
  redemption and, 300
  Sh'mitah as return to, 127
  trees of, 119
Eilberg-Schwartz, Howard, 8, 88
Eisenberg, Evan, 8, 19, 122, 150, 167, 267, 311, 345, 346, 350
Elazar of Worms (1176–1238), 100, 191, 224, 363, *see also Sodey Razaya in index of rabbinic sources*
elements, 256, 347, 348, *see also* greenhouse gases, stellar nucleosynthesis
  fire, air, water, earth (traditional/Aristotelian), 19, 115–16, 210, 213, 217, 222–4, 243, 253, 262, 272, 347, 349, *see also* earth, water:*tselem* in
  metals, 60, 94, 203, 344
  oxygen, 6, 18, 266, 349
Elior, Rachel, 256
Eliyahu ben Shlomo of Vilna, *see* Vilna Gaon
Elohim (God, attribute of judgment), interpretations of, 1, 103, 180, 181, 214, 215, 221, 286, *see also* Nature:Elohim as
embodiment, 135
  circumcision and, 88
  feminism and, 8
  of soul, 131, 137
  theurgy of dance, 21
endosymbiosis, 24
Enlightenment, 29, 111–12, 126
ethics, 15, 39–40, 166, 341–5 T: 126–7, 144–5, 162, 165, 322, M: 103–8, 146, 160–63, 287, P: 70–71, 147–8, K: 146, 149–50, 163–5, 189–90, C: 111–14, 147,

see also animals:as teachers, *imitatio Dei*, *halakhah*, humanity, justice, stewardship
human applied to animals, 146, 164–5
applied to all beings, 162–4, 168, 298, 309–10, 347–52
soul and, 129
evolution, 6, 17, 18, 88, 238–9, 325, 341, 350, *see also* Cosmic Walk, Dawkins, Gould, Kook, Maimonides, Margulis, neo-Darwinism, symbiosis, Creation:*telos* of, Tree of Life
  death and, 348
  image of God and, 239, 351
  in relation to Jewish thought, 25, 27–30, 238, 333, 342
  scientific interpretations of, 24, 28, 30, 334
extinction, 3–5, 28, 325, 330, 341, 344, 348, 350
  God's image and, 238–9
  Permian, 3
  sixth mass, anthropogenic, 4

farming, farms, 305, 350, *see also* agriculture, Israel:land of, *Keren Kayemet L'Yisra'el* programs, 11
female body, 80, 89, 193, 194, 262, 276, *see also androginos*, clitoris, *du-par'tsufin*, male and female, womb
  breasts, 194, 200
  divine image in, 188, 200, 276–7, 302
  vulva, 200
feminine images of God, 245, 276–7, *see also* female body, Goddess, Shekhinah
feminism, 8–9, 14, 266, *see also* embodiment
  Christian, 45, 78–9, 82, 274
  gender liberation and, 8, 78–9, 82–3
  Jewish, 8–9, 26, 78–9, 193, 194
fertility, 3, 44, 83, 85, 88, 357, 359, *see also* procreation
fish, 44, 83–4, 92, 93, 94, 158, *see also* animals:dolphin and whale
Fishbane, Michael, 21, 53, 294
Fleer, Gedaliah, 122
food, eating, 11–12, 157, 262–3, 349, *see also* Noach:permission to eat animals, vegetarianism
forests, 244, 297, 305–6, 319, 344
four worlds, the, 184, 215, 256, 357–8, 362, *see also* 'Asiyah, Atsilut
fracking, 348, 349
fractal symmetry, 230, 282, 306–11, 361
  defined, 307

General index

human, as fractal image of Creation, 267, 307–8
  in Kabbalah, 197, 211, 214, 221, 292, 307–9
  of time, 311
Francis of Assisi (1181/82–1226), 320
free will, 63, 69, 169, 284
fruit, T: 157, 274, 357–8, M: 12, 57–8, 99, 158, 162, 203, 217, 243, 284, 300, K: 221, 229, 298, 300, 320, 325, 351, 357–8, H: 258, *see* Adam Harishon:sin of, fertility, `orlah, tree of knowing, trees
Frymer-Kensky, Tikva, 8–9, 45, 78–9, 100, 107
fungi, 264, 313, 330, 350

Gaia, 266–7, 344, *see also* Adam Qadmon, Lovelock, Maimonides, Margulis
  science of, 24, 266–7
  Shekhinah and, 266, 274
Gamliel (V, fourth century, Palestine), 134–5
Gan Eden (Garden of Eden), *see* Eden
Gellman, Jerome, 299
gender, 32, 36, 80–83, 86, 190–97, *see also* androginos, circumcision, *du-par'tsufin*, feminism:gender liberation, heteronormativity, male and female, redemption:gender and, sex
  origin of, M: 80, K: 362
Gendler, Everett, 7, 14, 320
genetic engineering, 164, 305
  golden rice, 350
  halakhah and, 349–51
genetics, 6, 24, 237–8
Gikatilla, Yosef (1248–c.1310), 205, 219, 233, 237, 286, 337–8, 363
  justice in Nature, 286
gilgul, *see* reincarnation
Giller, Pinchas, 179, 187, 199, 250
GMOs, *see* genetic engineering
Gnosticism, 64, 123, 195, *see also* Zoharic literature
  Kabbalah and, 277–9, 332
God, *passim*, *see also* Elohim, *imitatio Dei*, Maimonides, Nature, *tselem*, world, YHVH
Goddess, goddesses, 8–9, 14, 27, 78–9, 267, 272, 274, *see also* neo-paganism, Shekhinah
golem, 164, 254, 355
  Adam as, 247, 251
  antithesis of *tselem*, 150, 304–6
  body as, 67, 254

Goodman, Len, 84, 119, 165
Goshen-Gottstein, Alon, 68, 74, 108, 132, 138, 170
Gould, Stephen Jay, 5, 24, 28, 333
grass, 220, 284, 288, 322, 330–31, 357
Green, Arthur, 7–8, 215, 217, 231, 238, 333–4, 340, 364
Greenberg, Irving (Yitz), 23, 110–14, 117, 127
  evolution of his thought, 113
  Holocaust in, 75
  human rights, humanism, and, 111, 121, 126
greenhouse gases, 3, 344, 348
Gregorios, Paulos Mar, 56
Gregory of Nyssa (fourth century), 56, 111
Grözinger, Karl, 66, 107
guf (body), 56, 130, 135, 184–5, 274, 355
G'vurah (Might, Judgment/*Din*, Sefirah), 86, 175, 213–14, 222, 224, 233, 234, 261, 264, 307, 348, 360–63

Habgood, John, 250
halakhah (Jewish law and jurisprudence), 47, 49, 103, 125, 156, 164, 166, 282, 350, *see also under particular laws* (*bal tashchit, kavod ladam, kilayim, kosher laws, migrash, `orlah, Shabbat, shechitah, Sh'mitah*)
Hamaqom (*Maqom*, "The Place", God), 88, 162, 166–8, 254
Hammer, Jill, 8, 10, 11
Hateva` (Nature), *see* Elohim, Nature
heavens, firmament, 60–61, 273, M: 48, 50–54, 55–6, 58, 59, 99, 101, 135, 169, 176, P: 26, 27, K: 183, 187, 206, 210, 215, 218, 319, H: 206, *see also* Earth, rain, spheres
  constellations and stars, 53–4, 57–8, 188, 206, 224–6, 228, 244, 300, 303, 320–21:
  science of, 59–60, 306–7
  gods/goddesses and, 78–9
  redemption and, 300
Hebrew thought and religion, 4, 8, 10, 78–9, 131, 144, 167, *see also* sacrifices, Shabbat, Sh'mitah, Torah:unitive vocabulary
Hegel, G. W. F. (1770–1831), 111–12
Hellenism, 79, 108, 116, 130, 132–6, 242, 246
Hellner-Eshed, Melila, 217
Heschel, Abraham Joshua (1907–92, Poland, United States), 7, 37, 76, 113, 116–17, 120, 337
  Nature in, 96

Heschel of Apt, Avraham Yehoshua
    (1748–1825), 297, 339–40
heteronormativity, 85, 195
Hfttermann, Aloys, 10, 147
hierarchy, 14, 25, 31–2, 52, 54, 86, 307, 310,
    326, 354, see also chain of Being
Hillel (first century BCE–c.10 CE), 136, 320
Hirsch, Shimshon Rafael (1808–88), 69
Hod (Majesty, Sefirah), 360–62
holiness, 105–6, 112, 144–5, 184, 218, 214,
    291, 297, 310, 350, 351
Holocaust, 26, 111, 124–5, 155
holographism, see fractal symmetry
homosexuality, see heteronormativity
Horowitz, Yishayah (Isaiah, the Shlah,
    1562–1630), 165, 198, 205, 214, 219,
    222–3, 224, 253, 255, 289–92, 306, 364
  Creation within Adam, 253
  origin of qomah sh'leymah, 290–92
  reincarnation in, 165, 291
human rights, see Greenberg, tselem:human
    rights
  tension with ecology, 112–13
humanism, see modernist humanism
humanity, 1, 5–7, 22, 23, 25, 32, see also
    anthropo-archism, anthropocentrism,
    anthropology, chain of Being, dominion,
    modernist humanism, `olam qatan,
    stewardship
  continuity with other animals, 22, 161, 223
  lifespan as a species, 5
  population, 3
  role and purpose, 17, 26–7, 34, 94–5, 249,
    312–13, 330–31, 332–3, 336–9, 342–3,
    346–7, 351–2
  sanctity of life, 32, 36, 119–20, 313, 351
Hurwitz, Pinchas (1765–1821), 29, 95–6
hydrofracking, see fracking

ibn Ezra, Avraham (1089–1164), 100, 269
ibn Paquda, Bachya (eleventh century), 7,
    18–19, 30, 91
Idel, Moshe, 170, 192–3, 194, 249, 252, 278,
    286–7
idolatry, 9–10, 13, 26, 231
  in Ashkenazi, 181, 238, 252
  modernist misinterpretation of, 9, 26
Igeret Haqodesh ("Ramban"), 215
Igeret Haqodesh (in Tanya), see Or Chozer,
    and see index of rabbinic sources
imitatio Dei, T: 105–6, M: 46, 97, 102,
    105–8, 149 P: 69–71 K: 149, 186–7,
    189–90, 195, 291, see also Buber

animals and, 152
ecology and, 109
in Christianity, 105, 108, 186
separate from tselem (imago Dei), 105–7
stewardship as, 149
tselem as, 105, 186–7, 189–90
Imma (Mother, par'tsuf), see Binah
indigenousness, 2, 4, 10, 131
infinite value, 110–12, 114, 120, 126–7
  in Christianity, 111
insects, 34, 77, 225, 305, 325, 350, see also
    shamir
intrinsic value, 5, 105, 112, 117, 145,
    155
Irenaeus (second century), 134
Isaac of Syria (d. c.700), 164, 186
Islam, 31, 63, 65, 88, 108, 325–6 see also
    Qur'an
Israel, Biblical, 13, 23, see also Hebrew
    thought, Israelites
Israel, land of, 10, 15, 19, 157, 166, 272, 274,
    305–6, 350, see also Sh'mitah,
    agriculture:laws, Keren Kayemet
    L'Yisra'el
  climate, 15
  ecology, 19
Israel, state of, 12, 124, 306, see also Bedouin,
    Keren Kayemet L'Yisra'el, promised land
Israel, the Jewish people, M: 52, 53, 88–9,
    106, 154, 238, 322, 324, K: 181, 191,
    199, 224, 260, 302, H: 21, 296
  ethno-archism, 21, 88, 100, 121–2, 191,
    228, 338
  holiness and, 105–7
Israelites, ancient, 23, 318, 320, 337, see also
    Hebrew thought

Jacob (Yaakov Avinu), 51, 87, 198, 215,
    289
Jastrow, Marcus (1829–1903), 50–51, 97,
    118, 283, 284, 323
Jewish continuity, 11
Jewish environmental movement, 10–13, 124,
    see also ecotheology:Jewish
JNF (Jewish National Fund), see Keren
    Kayemet L'Yisra'el
Jubilee, see Yovel
Judaism (contemporary), see also
    ecotheology:Jewish, feminism:Jewish,
    Jewish continuity, Jewish environmental
    movement
  Conservative, 82–3, 351, see also Heschel,
    Frymer-Kensky

General index

Orthodox, 23, 25, 26, 27, 111, 113, 128, 270, 351, *see also* Greenberg, Kook, Slifkin, Shneersohn, Soloveitchik
Reconstructionist, *see* Green
Reform, 2, 12, 132, *see also* Adler
Renewal, 11–12, 83, 188, 221, 364, *see also* Schachter-Shalomi, Waskow
justice, 13, 71, 95, 112–13, 126–7, 157, 166–7, 286, 329, *see also* social ecology, *tselem*:human rights
Justin Martyr (c.100–165), 101

Kabbalah, *see also* Adam Qadmon, fractal symmetry, male and female, *l'vush*, Maimonides, Nature, *nefesh*, *n'shamah*, *n'tsotsot*, Or Chozer, *par'tsuf*, science, Sefirot, *sh'virat hakeilim*, *qomah*, and *see index of rabbinic sources*
anthropology of, 66, 207, 250–55, 279–80, 307–11
consciousness and, 162, 312–15, 341–3
cosmic blessing in, 37–8, 175–7, 229, 310–11, 312, 335–6, 342–3, 358–9, 362
esotericism about *tselem*, 229
holism, 223, 231
hermeneutics of, 195, 205–6, 208–9, 226, 230
implications for civilization, 231–2, 312–15
limitations of, 122, 148, 240
nakedness and union, 191–2
philosophy, relation to, 169–70, 176–7, 182–3, 226, 254
reductionism in, 239–40
redemption and, 248–9, 262, 289, 295–7
Kadushin, Max (1895–1980), 48, 106
Kant, Immanuel (1724–1804), 62–3, 111–12
kashrut (kosher laws), 10, 12, 144, 145, 150, 349
kavod ladam (honoring/burial of the blood of an animal), 144–5, 146–7, 154, 349
Kepnes, Steven, 111, 114, 117, 119–20
Keren Kayemet L'Yisra'el (KKL), 12, 150, 305–6
Keter (Crown, Sefirah), 186, 189, 215, 234, 261, 262, 286, 360–62
kilayim (mixing species), 220, 349
Kimchi, Yosef (1105–70), 100
Kook, Avraham Yitshak (1865–1935), 25, 27, 29–30, 38–9, 113, 147–8, 150, 171, 332, 334, 364
kosher laws, *see kashrut*

Lainer, Yaaqov (1828–78), 227, 235–6, 239, 313
land, 2, 3, 19, 44, 51, 87, 93–4, 99, 101, 106, 121, 124, 125, 331, *see also* Earth, Gaia, indigenousness, Israel:land of, promised land, Leopold:land ethic, *Sh'mitah*, soil
as subject, 19, 126, 166–8, 272
precedence over people, 126–7, 272
language, speech, 39, 47, 140, 317, T: 63, 318, 319–20, M: 63–6, 73, 115–7, 158, 319–26, P: 62, 73, 138, 318, 320–23, K: 200, 210, 214, 231, 234–7, 254, 319, 323, 325–6, H: 293, 308, 330–31, C: 327–30, 343, 352–3, *see also* animals, Buber, Eden, trees, *nefesh chayah*
divine, 91, 115–6, 180, 214, 234–7, 254, 265
of/in all Creation, 298, 308, 318–31, 342, 352–3
of/in science, 237, 307, 310, 325
upright stature and, 47, 319
Leibniz, Gottfried Wilhelm (1646–1714), 72, 276, 308–9
Leo the Great (c.400–461), 108
Leone Ebreo, *see* Ebreo
Leopold, Aldo (1887–1948), 344
land ethic of, 152, 167, *see also Sh'mitah*
letters, 200, 204, 206, 234–5, 239–40
DNA and, 237
Creation as product of, 187, 235, 240
of God's name, *see* YHVH
Levinas, Emmanuel (1906–95), 155
Libanius (314–383), 134
lifeforce, *see* blood, *chiyut*
Linzey, Andrew, 26
liturgy, 19, 113, 242, *see also* prayer
borei' n'fashot, 242, 274, 357
Hoshana Rabbah (Sukkot), 284–5
Kaddish, 238
kedushah (*q'dushah*), 51–2
kiddush l'vanah, 23
morning blessings, 82–3, 164
Sh'ma`, 2, 127, 167
siddurim (prayerbooks), 2, 82–3, 188, 215, 230, 284–5, 320
Tu Bish'vat, *see P'ri `Ets Hadar*
wedding, 301
Lorberbaum, Yair, 47, 50, 81, 82, 103–4, 114, 132, 245
love, 1, 4, 19, 37–9, 88, 95, 103–5, 148, 157, 161, 165, 171, 199, 201, 313, 342, 344, 348, 351
Lovelock, James, 266–7

lulav (date palm branch), 287
Luria, Yitshak (Isaac) (1534–72), *see* Lurianic Kabbalah, Vital
  pseudepigraphic work attributed to, 289
Lurianic Kabbalah, 95, 138, 184–6, 191, 196–7, 200, 235, 257, 260–62, 278–9, 287–8, 309, 326, 362–3
  birthing imagery in, 276–7
Luther, Martin (1483–1546), 96
l'vush (clothing, illusion, materialization), 184, 210, 222–3, 235, 256, 258, 260, 296, 326

machloqet (debate) 52, 331
Magid, Shaul, 21, 185, 187, 191, 226, 295
Maharal (Yehudah Loew of Prague, 1525–1609), 33, 56–7, 69, 90–91, 100, 254
  Kabbalah and, 56
Maimonides (Moshe ben Maimun, Rambam, 1135–1204), 12, 15–16, 20, 23, 37, 68, 75, 92, 177, 243, 271, 275–6, *see also* diversity, *and see index of rabbinic sources*
  animals in, 23, 28, 67, 70–71, 140, 145, 148, 270
  anthropocentrism, opposition to, 15–16, 20, 21, 27, 28–9, 100, 148, 270
  apophatic theology and, 20, 67, 71–2, 269
  body in, 62, 67–8
  diversity in, 20, 28–9, 239
  dominion vs. *tselem*, 70–71, 92, 100, 160
  early work compared to *Guide*, 28, 177
  eternality of Creation, 28
  evolution and, 20, 21, 28–9, 239
  Gaia and, 27, 72, 251, 268–71
  goodness, 16
  of Creation, 15–16, 71–2, 171, 269
  humans as animals, 49, 70, 148
  imitatio Dei, 70–71
  intellect, 92–3, 269, 275–6
  tselem as, 62–3, 66–8, 70–71
  Kabbalah and, 24, 225–6, 266, 279, 312, 342
  knowing Creation, 20, 71–2, 171, 269
  knowing God, 71, 270, 275
  limitations of, 62, 68, 273
  Nature as *chesed* (lovingkindness), 71–2, 345
  Saadyah Gaon, opposition to, 26, 68
  Western science and, 29, 72, 270–71

male and female, 82–3, T: 78–9, M: 45, 48–50, 78–82, K: 193–7, 200, 202, 230, *see also androginos, du-par'tsufin*, gender, heteronormativity, sex, *tselem*
  redemption of/through the female, 289, 290, 295–7
male body, *see* circumcision, male and female, phallus
Malkhut (Realm, Sefirah), 175, 196, 213, 222, 230, 261, 262, 285, 289, 295, 302, 360–63, *see also* Shekhinah
  Daughter, 191
  matronita, 199
  Nuqva (par'tsuf), 196, 363
  Rachel, 287
Margulis, Lynn, 24, 29, 266–7
materialism, 22, 125, 131
Matt, Daniel, 29, 189, 195, 203, 211, 306
Maximus the Confessor, 56
McFague, Sallie, 38, 274
McLeod, Frederick, 56, 134–5, 210
medieval Jewish philosophy, *see* philosophy
Meir Simchah Hakohen of Dvinsk (1843–1926), 69
megafauna, *see* animals:prehistoric megafauna
menstruation, *see nidah*
mercy, 151, *see also* compassion
Meshullam Feibush of Zbarazh (d.1795), 259–60
Mesopotamia, 8, 10, 167, 336
methodology, 36, 52, 139, 194, 230, 282, 290, 295–6
metonymy, 205, 208–9, 214
Michaelson, Jay, 192, 195, 364
Midrash, 43–61, 63–6, 76–108, 131–42, 150–59, 202–3, 243–8, 283–4, 327, 336–8, 345–6, 348
  anthropology, 54–6, 109, 142, 169–72, 341–2
  contrasted with philosophy, 52–4, 73–5, 114–21, 124
  more-than-human in, 59–61, 150–51, 320–25, 345–6
  panpsychism in, 157, 162–3, 169–70, 320–25
Midrash Alfa-Beitot, 90, 336
Midrash Hagadol, 46, 56, 75, 162, 246
Midrash Otiyot d'Rabi Aqiva, 74, 141, 234, 248, 283, 308, 320
Midrash Y'lamdeynu, 46, 179–80, 337–8
migrash (communal urban farmland), 166
miqveh (ritual pool), 144, 178, 193, 287

General index

mishkan (sanctuary), 79, 145, 159, 191, 197, 216–17, 230, 245, 269, 335, 337
   Creation as, 203, 213
modernist humanism, xvi–xvii, 7, 15, 17, 34, 48, 53, 54, 94–6, 109, 110–14, 120, 121–6, 127–8, 170, 330, 338
   contrasted with rabbinic thought, 114, 117, 124–6, 169
   dependence on medieval philosophy, 34, 113, 129, 144–5, 147–8, 169–70
   defined, 112
   Holocaust and, 124–5
monotheism, 8–9, 30–32, 128, 148
Mopsik, Charles, 82
more-than-human world, 34, 54, 88, 111, 113, 121, 126, 232, *see also* Abram, biophilia, diversity
   defined, 2
   divinity and, 128, 207, 213, 322
   language in, 6, 22, 317–26, 328–31, 342, 352–3
Moshe ben Nachman, *see* Ramban
Moses (Moses, *Moshe Rabbenu*), 20, 23, 53, 71–2, 87, 186, 200, 303, 336–7
   striking the rock, 90, 162, 318
mourning, 106, 152, 344–5

Nachman of Breslov (1772–1810), 282, 294–5, 308, 363
   diversity in, 20–21
   song of the grass, 330–31
   tiqun `olam in, 118
Nachmanides, *see* Ramban
Narboni, Moshe (c.1300–62), 249, 254, 256
Nasr, Seyyed Hossein, 33
Nature, 17, 157, 226, T: 319–20, M: 5, 18–19, 160, 170, P: 15–16, 72–3, 275, 352, K: 217, 239–40, 275, H: 21, 206, 331, 338, C: 9–10, 95–6, 113, 324, 327–30, 352–3, *see also* Adam Qadmon, Creation, ecosystem, evolution, Gaia, Maimonides, more-than-human world, paganism:polemics against, panpsychism, Shekhinah, *sidrey v'rei'shit*, symbiosis, theology of Nature
   as *chesed* (lovingkindness), 258, 265, 345
   created for humanity, 6, 18–19, 25–6, 96, 148
   division from humanity/culture, 2, 7, 32, 33, 129, 150–51, 207
   Elohim as, 206, 214–15, 242, 254, 275, 344
   relation to God, 34, 149, 214

   fractal symmetry in, 267, 273, 308–10
   Hateva`, 206, 242, 275, 338
   philosophies of, 14
   right relation to, 30, 96, 152, 167, *see also Sh'mitah*
   seder `olam, 215, 255
   social construction of, 6
navel, 243, 245
nefesh (soul, body, person), T: 130–31, 140, 144–5, 147, 354–6, M: 133, 135–7, P: 67, 75, 103, 138, 141, 318, K: 131, 138–9, 184–5, 201, 221, 254, 319, H: 263, *see also* blood:*nefesh, nefesh chayah, n'shamah, ru'ach*, soul
   animal, 67, 140, 144
   body as, 130, 132, 355
   corpse as, 356
   life, 114, 125, 130
   "of all Life", 274
   person as, 102, 114, 131
nefesh chayah, T: 44, 321, 355, M: 131, 319, P: 67, 73, 318
   Adam as animal, 318
   from Shekhinah, 138–9, 221
   speech and, 63, 64, 319
neo-Darwinism, 24
neopaganism, 14, 267, 272, 274
Neoplatonism, 67, 214
Netsach (Eternity, Sefirah), 360–62
Neusner, Jacob, 51
Newton, Isaac (1643–1727), 72, 271
nidah (menstrual taboo, purification), 57, 193
Noach (Noah), 44, 88, 149–6, 218, 326
   as farmer, 87, 91, 99, 346
   Eden and, 346
   in the ark, 140, 149–51, 346
   loss of dominion, 158–9
   permission to eat animals, 98, 150, 158
   reproduction after the flood, 159
   stewardship and, 150–51, 161, 345–6
Novak, David, 117, 270–71
n'shamah, nishmat (soul, breath), T: 73, 130, 354–6, M: 50, 81, 132, 136–8, 247, 284, P: 74–5, K: 181, 182–5, 198–9, 205, 210, *see also nefesh*, soul, *tselem*, and *see* Gn 2:7, Pr 20:27 *in index of scriptural verses*
   animal, 74, 141
   B'rei'shit Rabbah and, 80, 136–7
   contrasted with *tselem*, 73–4, 136–8, 183–6
   liturgy, 285
n'tsotsot (sparks), 29, 111, 147, 152, 184, 296

nucleosynthesis, *see* stellar nucleosynthesis
Nuqva (Female, *par'tsuf*), *see* Malkhut

ocean, 6, 329, 348, M: 86, 93, 216, 221, 323
  acidification, 3
  climate change, impact on, 3, 6
  origin of life in, 18
`olam (world), 56, 242, 294–5
  hazeh (this world), 59, 136, 184, 227, 235, 242, 258, 266, 274, 278, 283, 338
  haba' (the coming world, world-to-come), 59, 136, 178, 242, 274, 287, 300
  `olamim (created worlds, worlds of divinity), 233, 242, 245, 273–4, 275
  `olam malei' (a full, complete world), 70, 114–16, 121, 123, 126–7, 245–6, 282
  `olam qatan (microcosm), 224, 230, 241–6, 250–51, 254, 269, 273, 282, 297, 308
Onkelos (c.35–120), 63, *see also* Targum Onkelos
Or Chozer (returning or reflected light), K: 260–62, H: 255–60, 262–5, *see also* Igeret Haqodesh 20 *in index of rabbinic sources*
`orlah (foreskin), 88, 191, 192
`orlah (sanctification of fruit tree), 88
organicism, 25, 56, 96–7, 126, 271, 274

paganism, 10, *see also* indigenousness, neopaganism
  polemics against, 8–10, 23–4, 26, 113, 122–3, 232, 272
panentheism, 168, 272, 276
panpsychism, 87, 153, 162–3, 284, 320, 348–9
  in Psalms, 318–20
par'tsuf, par'tsufim (Lurianic archetypes), 196, 208, 287, 288, 290, 295, 309, 363, *see also* Abba, Arikh Anpin, `Atiq Yomin, Imma, Nuqva, Z`eyr Anpin
par'tsuf (primordial face/s), *see* du-par'tsufin
Pereq Shirah, 155, 320
permaculture, 4, 13
Peyrush L'Shir Hashirim, 285–7, 288
phallus, 189, 192, 200, 229, 230, 362, *see also* circumcision, clitoris
Philo of Alexandria (c.20 BCE–40 CE), 67, 69, 87, 134, 136, 246, 247, 251
philosophy, *see also* Kabbalah, Renaissance
  ancient Greek, 242, *see also* Aristotle, Neoplatonism, Philo, Plato
  early modern, *see* Descartes, Hegel, Kant, Spinoza

  medieval Jewish, 26, 34, 55, 62, 67–8, 74–5, 100, 138–9, 144, 147–8, 169–70, 177, 189–90, 271, 342, *see also* Donnolo, Duran, ibn Ezra, ibn Paquda Maimonides, Narboni, Ramban, Saadyah Gaon
Pinchas ben Yair (second century), 153, 324
plants, 220, 228–9, 300, 357, *see also* kilayim, `orlah, domem-tsomei'ach
Plaskow, Judith, 8
Plato, 132–3, 212, 243, 268
pluralism 111, 127–8, *see also* diversity
Pollan, Michael, 325
Porton, Gary, 51, 79, 247
prayer, 65, 118, 188, 294, 296, 310, 313, *see also* liturgy, tsitsit
  more-than-human, 65, 323–5, 330–31, 352
P'ri `Ets Hadar, 203, 212–13, 220, 228–9, 284, 288, 298, 312–13, 320, 325, 351, 357–9, 364
procreation, 50, 81, 82
"promised land", 15, 272
Psalms, *see index of scriptural verses*
  Nature in, 318, 319–20, 358

Qayin and Hevel (Cain and Abel), 52, 114, 152, 154, 156, 158, 193
qomah (body, stature) 199, 254, 256, 281–310, M: 283–4, 300, K: 177–8, 188–9, 199, 254, 285–92, H: 254, 292–300
  self-similarity and, 282, 309–10
  sh'leymah, 201, 230, 282, 288–99, 312
  z'qufah (upright), 58, 89–90, 223–4, 283, *see also* tselem:upright stature
Qur'an, 31, 65, 152, 325

rabbis, the (*Chazal*, the sages of the classical rabbinic period) 13, 23–4, 47–9, 52, 54, 66, 74, 110, 125–6, 169–70, 284, 330, 341, *see also* animals:Pinchas ben Ya'ir's donkey and Yehudah Hanasi's calf, Akiva, Ben Azai, *halakhah*, Hillel, Midrash, Shimon bar Yochai, *and see index of rabbinic sources*
  animal souls and subjecthood in, 74, 140, 144, 284
  parallels with Antiochean theology, 134–6
rain, 15, 51, 87, 121, 125, 127, 203
rainbow, xii, 222, 230, 358
Ramban (Moshe ben Nachman, Nachmanides, 1194–c.1270, Spain), 16, 93, 216, 363

General index

animals in, 98, 103, 141, 145, 147–8, 150, 156, 318
dominion in, 93, 98
tselem in, 88, 93, 141
works attributed to, *see Igeret Haqodesh, Peyrush L'Shir Hashirim*
Rashi (Shlomo Yits'chaqi, eleventh century), 16, 46, 51, 63, 66, 78, 84, 85, 91, 99, 155, 156–7, 158, 183, 230, 272, 284, 303
"Rashi" on *B'rei'shit Rabbah*, 154, 158
Recanati, Menachem (1250–1310), 181, 196
red heifer (*parah adumah*), 144–5
redemption, 279, 290, 296–7, 300, 342, *see also* Kabbalah:redemption
gender and, 194, 290, 295–6
reincarnation, 142, 165, 176, 189, 291, 326, 360
religion, 7, 14, 17, 31–2, 34, 35, 124, *see also* Christianity, ecotheology, Islam, Judaism, theology of Nature
purpose of, 1–2, 4–5, 36, 343–4
science and, 2, 309–10, 333–4
Renaissance, 55–6, 63, 69, 243, 271
resurrection, 79, 121, 132, 135, 207
ritual 8, 88, 144–5, 177, 311, *see also* circumcision, liturgy, *nidah*, science
rocks, *see domem*, stones
Rosenzweig, Franz (1886–1929), 48, 113, 353
Roundup, *see* agriculture:glyphosate
r'shimu (tracing, impression), 149, 302
ru'ach (spirit, wind), 1, 63, 67, 285, T: 1, 130–31, 354–5, M: 81, 136–7, 284, P: 67, 93, K: 184, 201
as source of *tselem*, 93
of animal, 141
Ruether, Rosemary Radford, 78, 167
rulership, 84, 90, 91, 98–101, 107, 160, 286, 338, *see also* dominion

Saadyah Gaon (882–942), 26, 30, 68, 93–4, 98, 100, 113, 117, 158
Sabbatical year, *see Sh'mitah*
sacrifices, 78, 144–6, *see also* blood, red heifer, *taharah*
cheilev (sacred/visceral fat), 145
Sama'el (Satan), 52, 65, 290–91
Schachter-Shalomi, Zalman, 12, 32, 36, 95, 188, 221
Schechter, Solomon (1847–1915), 39, 105–6, 108, 116, 244
Schneersohn, Menachem Mendel (1902–94), 338

Schneider, Sarah, 194, 208, 295
Schochet, Immanuel, 260, 264, 299
Scholem, Gershom (1897–1982), 54, 142, 177, 183–4, 204, 249, 276–7, 278, 285, 291, 299, 302–3, 320–21
debate with Buber, 299
Schwartz, Eilon, 7–9, 13, 14, 26
science, 2, 6, 33, 72, 157, 271, *see also* Bacon, chaos theory, complexity, Descartes, DNA, ecology, Enlightenment, evolution, fractal symmetry, genetic engineering, Maimonides:Western science, Newton, religion, ritual
ecotheology and, 273
Kabbalah and, 29–30, 237, 307, 364
reductionism in, 22, 24–5, 72, 157
sea, *see* ocean
Seder Rabbah d'B'rei'shit, 86, 233, 321–3
Sefer Chasidim, *see also Chasidey Ashkenaz*, in index of rabbinic sources
animals in, 146–7
Sefer Y'tsirah (ancient text), 187, 190, 199, 206, 222, 234, 363, *see also* index of rabbinic sources
God's image and, 190
Sefirah, *s'firah* (sing.), *see* Sefirot (pl.)
Sefirot, 178–89, 191, 196, 360–64, *see also* Binah, body, Chesed, Chokhmah, G'vurah, Hod, Keter, Malkhut, Netsach, Tif'eret, tselem Elohim, Y'sod
defined, 175
fractals and, 309–11
extension of *tselem* via, 178–9, 201, 205, 212–14, 223, 229–30
holism of Creation and, 210–11, 223, 251–2, 312
map of, 361
names and correspondences, 360–63
seven lower, 187, 228, 285, 307
Seidenberg, David, 10, 12, 14, 34, 38, 68, 83, 113, 120, 127, 144, 145, 148, 157, 166, 193, 307, 348
self-similarity, *see* fractal symmetry
sex, sexuality, M: 80–82, 83–7, 89, 318, K: 178, 191–7, 200–1, 202, 289, *see also* body, *du-par'tsufin*, male and female, Shekhinah
connection to Nature through, 343
face-to-face, 82–4, 89, 200, 289, 295
kissing, as *tselem*, 200–1
other-than-human, 85–6

sex, sexuality (*cont.*)
  tselem and, 80–82, 84, 191–2, 194–6
  waters and, 86–7
Sforno, Ovadiah (1470–1550), 16, 47, 63–4, 68–70, 73, 103, 156, 159
Shabbat, 11, 13–14, 115, 127, 191, 278, 358
  celebration in Eden, 321–3
  meaning of, 115, 322
  pikuach nefesh (saving a life) and, 125–6
Shabtai Tsvi (1626–76), 278
shamir worm, 345–6
shechi̱tah (kosher slaughter), 12, 144, 146, 147, 150, 164–5, *see also* blood:burial of
Shekhinah (indwelling presence of God, divine feminine), M: 81–2, 83–4, 86, 89, 336–8, K: 178, 181, 186–8, 195, 211, 214, 221, 230, 260, 266, 283, 285, 302–3, 337, 339, *see also* Malkhut
  as chariot, 205, 286
  as Creator, 195
  building and redemption of, 295–6
  face of, 197–8
  feminism and, 38, 194, 290
  Nature as, 274
  qomah (stature/body) of, 178, 88, 199–200, 287, 289, 290, 295–7
  sex and, M: 83–4, K: 178, 195, 196
  soul as image of, 181
  union with, 186
Shem Tov ibn Shem Tov (c.1380–1441), 184, 245, 251
Shepard, Paul, 129, 143
shiluach haqein (or *haqan*, sending away the mother bird to take the eggs), 145, 147, 148
Shimon bar Yochai (midrash) (first century), 337
Shimon bar Yochai (*Zohar*), 37, 153, 182, 217, 290, 335
Shimshon Rafael Hirsch (1808–88), 69
Shi`ur Qomah (ancient text), 53, 178, 187, 190, 205, 249, 250, 254, 285, 363
Shlah, *see* Horowitz
Shlomo Hamelekh (King Solomon), 100, 159, 202, 320, 325, 345–6
Shlomo Yits'chaqi, *see* Rashi
Sh'ma`, *see* liturgy
Sh'mitah (Sabbatical year), 11, 12, 126–7, 152, 166–7, 272, 344, *see also* Leopold:land ethic
  consequences if not observed, 157

eco-centrism and, 322
permaculture and, 13
wild animals and, 76, 144
Shneur Zalman of Liady (1745–1813), 235, 236, 240, 264, 363
  "divine ecosystem" in, 262
  gardening and Eden, 259
  Or Chozer in, 255–9
Sh'ney Luchot Hab'rit, *see* Horowitz, *and see* index of rabbinic sources
Shoah, *see* Holocaust
sh'virat hakeilim (breaking of the Vessels), 184, 227, 277, 298, 306, 362
Sh'viti (mandala), 188
sidrey v'rei'shit (the orders of Creation), 5, 287, 323, 342, 347–52, *see also* Creation, Nature
  GMOs and, 349
  strengthening, 352
  weakening, 287, 312, 348–9, 350
Simchah Bunam of Przyscha (1765–1827), 118
sin, 99, 115, 147–8, 156, 185, 277, 291, 320, 351, *see also* Adam Harishon:sin of
sleep, 58, 64, 133, 136, 140
Slifkin, Natan, 25, 28, 147
Smith, Morton, 88–9, 108
social ecology, 14, 15, 113
soil, 19, 34, 151, 256–8, 264, 305, 313, 349, *see also* earth:element of
Sokol, Moshe, 27, 122, 123, 148
Soloveitchik, Joseph (1903–1993), 23, 111, 112, 122–4, 151, 346
  dominion vs. stewardship, 122
  moral standing of other creatures, 124
Song of Songs, eroticism of, 178, 343
soul, 129–42, T: 130–31, M: 73–4, 105, 132–9, P: 67, 103, 138, 73–5, 93, 104, 129, 138, 141, 169, 182, 266–70, K: 131, 138, 142, 181–6, *see also* animals, *nefesh*, *n'shamah*, reincarnation, *ru'ach*, *tselem*
  body and, 56, 93, 131–7
  B'rei'shit Rabbah on, 136–9
  in medieval philosophy, 138
sparks, *see* *n'tsotsot*
speech, *see* language
spheres and intellects, 58, 67, 72, 92–3, 94, 96, 266–7, 268–71, 275
  sublunar, 27, 67, 254, 273
Spinoza, Baruch (1632–77), 29, 139–40, 165, 274, 275, 276
stellar nucleosynthesis, 60, 271, 307
Stern, Josef, 268, 270

General index

Sternhartz, Noson (Natan) of Nemirov (1780–1844), 118
stewardship, 5, 83–4, 90, 107, 122, 149–50, 151, 161, 166, 347, 350
   citizenship vs., 151–2, 167
   critique of, 84, 150–51, 161, 345–6
Stiegman, Emero, 46–7, 89, 116, 117, 130–31, 160–61
stones, 53, 137, 163, 203, 216, 222, 233–4, 245, 329, 345, *see also domem*
Sukkot (fall harvest festival), 113, 284, 287
sustainability, 3, 4, 5, 10, 127, 322, 349, 352
Swimme, Brian, 334
symbiosis, 3, 24, 29, 267, 305, 330, 346

taharah and *tum'ah* (cultic purity and impurity), 77, 144–5, 193
Tanakh, *see* Bible
Tanchuma, *see also index of rabbinic sources*
   dating of, 46
   imitatio Dei in, 68
Targum Onkelos, 63, 180, 319, 346
targumim (Aramaic Bible translations), 44, 48, 59, 63, 90, 99, 180, 182, 325
   resistance to anthropomorphism, 48
tavnit (structure), 189, 251, 285, 301–2
t'cheilet (deep blue dye), *see tsitsit*
technology, 2, 94, 114, 322
telos, *see* Creation, evolution, *tselem*
Theodore of Mopsuestia (c.350–428), 134, 135, 210
theology of Nature, 11, 21, 38, 60–61, 166, 227, 238–40, 255, 264, 267, 276, 282, 297–300, 306–11, 313, 347–50, 351–2, *see also dirah batachtonim*, ecotheology, fractal symmetry, *sidrey v'rei'shit*
Thielicke, Helmut (1908–86), 112, 125
throne, 205, 321, 322
Tif'eret (Beauty, Sefirah), 56, 175, 178, 187, 196, 213, 214, 215, 222, 230, 234, 289, 302, 307, 360–63
   Holy One, 195, 295, 339
   Jacob, 289
   Son, 191
   Z'eyr Anpin (*par'tsuf*), 196, 288, 289, 295, 362
tiqun (*tikkun*) `olam (cosmic repair) 95, 118, 279, 297, 320, 342, 352
   humanistic, 95
Tiquney Zohar, 222, 230, 239, 250, 266, 363, *see also* Zoharic literature, *and see index of rabbinic sources*

animals in, 220–21, 224–6
body in, 188–9, 191–2
reincarnation and *tselem*, 291
Tirosh-Samuelson, Hava, 7, 9–10, 38, 92, 124, 194, 239, 240
Tishby, Isaiah, 48, 74, 138, 197, 319
to'ar (form), 54, 93, 210, 284–5, 303–4
toolmaking, 91–6
Torah, 8, 32, 44, 130–31, 151–2, *see also* Bible, Hebrew thought, *halakhah*, *nefesh*, *n'shamah*, *Sh'mitah*, *and see index of scriptural verses*
   animals in, 144–5, 147–8, 157
   animism in, 145, 162, 318
   scroll, as *tselem*, 202–4
   sustainability in, 1, 2, 127
   unitive vocabulary of, 130–31, 144, 354–6
Transition Town movement, 4
tree of knowing good and bad (tree of knowledge), 50, 90, 99, 192, 283, 346, *see also Adam Harishon*, Chavah
Tree of Life, 56, 175, 178–9, 181, 199–200, 218–19, 239, 310, 320, 351–2, 357, 359, 360–61
   evolutionary, 56, 239, 352
trees, 10, 229, 328, T: 12, 162, M: 154, 218, 284, K: 218–20, 288, 320, H: 21, 257, 296–7, *see also bal tashchit*, fruit, Keren Kayemet L'Yisra'el, `orlah, plants
   angiosperms, 325
   apple, 220, 300
   cedar, 144, 203, 218, 282
   date palm, 178, 188–9, 219, 283, 300, 319, 324, 325
   exulting, of fruit, 320
   fruit tree, "tree of the field", 12, 13, 88, 162, 165, 218–21, 284, 300, 306, 320, 325, 358
   olive, 150–51, 300, 345
   oren pine, 306
   speech of, 325
   willow, 220
Troster, Lawrence, 7, 50, 267
tsa`ar ba`aley chayyim (prohibition against animal suffering), 144, 146–8, 150
tsadiq (*tsaddik*, righteous person/creature), 20, 108, 153, 154, 218, 293, 326
Tsadiq (Sefirah), *see Y'sod*
Tsadiq Y'sod `Olam, 289–90, 292, 295, 364
Tsadok (Tsadoq) Hakohen of Lublin (1823–1900), 254

tselem Elohim (God's image, *imago Dei*),
  passim, T: 44–5, 97, *see also* body,
  circumcision, dominion, evolution,
  humanity:role and purpose, *imitatio Dei*,
  Maimonides:intellect, male and female,
  n'shamah, sex, stewardship, soul, *and see
  index of scriptural verses ad* Gn 1:26–7,
  5:1–3, 9:6–7
 Christianity and, 44–5, 105, 108
 Creation as, *see* Creation:as God's image
 compassion as, 164, 186, 189, 342
 esotericism and, 229–30, 287
 extension vs. unification, 210
 grace and, 105
 human rights and, 32, 76, 89, 111, 113, 126
 in the more-than-human, M: 52–4, 84–6,
  K: 203, 204–31, 250–55, 259, 264–5,
  272–3, 347
 physical/bodily interpretations, M: 74,
  76–91, 136, P: 69, 90–91, K: 176–8,
  187–201, 291–2
 ethical/behavioral interpretations, M: 97–9,
  102–9, P: 71, K: 149, 186–7, 189–90,
  195, 291
 intellect as, 69–73
 male and female as, 45, 78–83, 193–7
 n'shamah (soul) and, 73–5, 136–8
 participation in, of all beings, 5, 16, 157,
  214, 226, 233, 254, 267, 296, 330, 335
 relational vs. substantive content of, 45, 97,
  105, 340
 royal image/icon, 102, 108, 136, 183
 synonyms for, *see d'mut, d'yoqna, chotam,
  r'shimu, tavnit, to'ar, tsurah*
 upright stature, 47, 58, 89–91, 100, 178,
  189, 200, 224, 258, 285, 319
tsimtsum (divine contraction), 122, 256, 276,
  303, 331, 352
 defined, 296
tsitsit (prayer shawl fringes), 216, 230
tsorekh gavoha (divine need), 164, 177, 249
tsurah (form), 67, 70, 104, 189, 212, 301, 326
Tu Bish'vat, 11, 357, *see also* P'ri `Ets Hadar

Uffenheimer, Rivka Schatz, 261
unification, 217, 230, 335, *see also* Creation,
  tselem:extension
Upanishads, 246–7, 269

vegetarianism, 98, 124, 147–8, 150, 158
Vilna Gaon (Eliyahu ben Shlomo of Vilna,
  1720–97), 230, 252–3

vision
 animals, 48–9, 77
 human, 47, 76–8, 88
Visotzky, Burton, 107, 133, 135–6
Vital, Chayyim (1542–1620), 180, 185,
  196–7, 200, 237, 257, 260–62, 277, 287,
  288, 295, 326, 363

Ware, Kallistos, 250
Waskow, Arthur, 7–8, 11, 14, 17, 238, 240,
  332–4
water, waters, 1, 90, 93–4, 307, 312, 324,
  348–9, T: 162, M: 15, 51, 55, 85–7, 99,
  203, 321, 323–4, K: 86–7, 188, 209, 210,
  213, 216–17, 218, 221, 231, 272, 337,
  see also elements, *miqveh*, ocean
 male and female, upper and lower, 86–7
 mayin nuqvin, 258
 speech of, 323–4
Western civilization, 6–7, 17, 25, 32–3, 62–3,
  68, 72, 73, 131, 134, 144, 308, 334,
  347, *see also* capitalism, science,
  technology
White, Lynn Jr., 33, 95
Wilber, Ken, 249, 309–10
Wilson, E. O., 1, 4–5, 17, 29, 161, 171
Wissenschaft des Judentums, xix, 9, 28, 270
Wolfson, Elliot R., 38, 187, 192, 194, 195,
  212, 213, 230, 239, 295, 338
 feminism and, 194
womb, 141, 193, 277, 352, 357
world, 96, 180, 268, *see also* elements,
  more-than-human world, `olam,
  Creation, Nature
 as God's body, 276
 as God's child, 276–7
world-to-come, 276–7, *see* `olam haba'

yetser hara` (evil impulse/nature), 79, 108,
  291
Yehudah Hechasid (1150–1217), 92, 146–7,
  286, 363, *see also* Sefer Chasidim in index
  of rabbinic sources
 animals in, 146–7
Yehudah Loew of Prague, *see* Maharal
YHVH (God, God's name, attribute of mercy),
  180, 181, 214
 letters of, 179, 180, 188, 189, 197–200,
  204, 211, 215, 219–22, 224–5, 362
 name of, 199, 201, 205, 207, 214, 219,
  228
 substitutions for, 17

Yovel (Jubilee), 11, 13, 152, 166, 322
Yosef ben Shalom Ashkenazi, *see* Ashkenazi
Y'sod (Foundation, Sefirah), 178, 187, 229, 261, 285, 295, 360–63
   Tsadiq, 178, 189, 229
Y'tsirah (World of Formation, Shaping), *see the* four worlds
Y'tsirah (ancient text), *see Sefer Y'tsirah*

Zev Wolf of Zhitomir (the Or Hameir, d. 1800), 195–7
Z'eyr Anpin (Small Face, *par'tsuf*), *see Tif'eret*
Zohar, see also Zoharic literature, *and see* index of rabbinic sources
   dominion, 159–60, 228
   Idra Rabba, 186, 198, 335
   naming in, 237
   plants in, 219–20
   writing of, 160, 181
Zohar Chadash, *see also* Zoharic literature, and index of rabbinic sources
   cosmogony, 210, 217
   divine name, in the *tachtonim*, 211, 215
   philosophy and, 183
Zoharic literature, 57, 194, 206, 226, 363, *see also* Tiquney Zohar, Zohar, Zohar Chadash here and in index of rabbinic sources
   animals in, 224–6, 228, 319
   body in, 178, 187–9, 200, 250, 287
   colors, 222
   directions, 222
   Earth in, 138, 183, 217, 272–3, 277
   gnostic tendencies in, 183, 277–8, 279
   soul in, 138–9, 182–3, 217

Index of scriptural verses

(Note: pages where verses are cited without being quoted are given in italics.)

Genesis (Gn)
  1, 28, 122
  1:1, 55, 221, 272
  1:2, 137
  1:5, 55
  1:10, *101*
  1:11, 55, 258, 357
  1:11–12, *219*
  1:12, 258, 357
  1:14, 55
  1:15, 358
  1:16, *101*
  1:18, *101*
  1:20, 55, 93, 221, 321
  1:24, 131, 137, 355
  1:26, 48, 56, 68–70, 73, 75, 81, 93, 94, 97–100, 180, 191, 195–6, 252, 269, 273
  1:26–28, 44, 97
  1:27, 45, 48–50, 78–9, 192, 194–6
  1:27a, 91, 95, 108, 183, 303
  1:27b, 79, 81, 194, 195
  1:28, 49, 93, 97–8, 99
  1:29, 98, 141, 158
  1:30, *356*
  1:31, 17, 19, 72, 95, 171, 253–4, 269, 348
  2, 43, 122, *151*
  2:1, 121, 283, 286
  2:4, 120, 180, 278, 348
  2:5, 121, 324, 330
  2:6, 79, 200
  2:7, 44, 55, 56, 63, 73, 75, 93, 131, 137, 138, 182, 198, 205, 228, 308, 355
  2:7a, 43, 80, 81, 167, 272
  2:15, 167
  2:18, 64, 80, 115
  2:19, 93
  2:19–20, 64, 318
  2:21, 64, 79
  2:22, 79, 80, 81
  3, *151*
  3:1, 192
  3:3, 357
  3:5, 99
  3:8, 90, 248
  3:14, 84
  3:17, 84
  3:19, 91, 92
  3:22, 108
  4:4, *158*
  4:10, 137
  4:12, 193
  4:15, 156
  4:24, 284
  5:1, 70, 81, 103, 104, 120
  5:1–3, 44
  5:2, 80–81, 159, 194, 195
  5:3, 88
  6:6, 52
  7:22, 73
  8:1, 140, 153, 154
  8:8–11, *150*

Index of scriptural verses

Genesis (*cont.*)
8:11, 345
9:1–2, 150, 159
9:2, 100, 160, 228
9:4, *140*, *150*
9:5, 88, 103, 155, 157
9:6, 39, 44, 81, 82, 93, 97, 102, 103, 104, 110, 156
9:7, 44, 82, 103, 159
9:14, 358
17:1, 69, 88, 105
17:4, *185*
18:27, 118
24:63, 330
28:12, 198, 205, 228
34:3, 355
35:18, 356
41:38, 355
49:24, 358

Exodus (Ex)
1:7, 159
4:11, 66
10:5, 243
11:17, 154
12:2, 311
12:9, 298
12:19, *185*
15:2, 106
15:27, 188
17:6, 90
20:2, 102
20:12, 102
20:22, 163
22:30, 154
23:9, *355*
24:10, 216, 257
24:10–11, 44
25:17–21, *196*
26:6, 202
26:20, 79
26:24, 191
31:3, *355*
31:17, 322
32:12, *198*
33:19, 20, 71
36:13, 202
36:18, 212–13, *357*

Leviticus (Lv)
7:20–21, *185*
7:23–27, *145*
7:26–27, *145*

7:27, *185*
11:19, 346
14, *144*
17:10–12, *140*, *145*
17:13, *144*, 146–7, 349
17:14, 147, 355
19:2, 105, 106
19:18, 103, 164–5
19:19, 220, 349
19:23, *106*
19:23–25, 88
19:26, *145*
20:26, 105, 291
22:3, *185*
23:3, 322
25, *166*, 272
25:7, *127*, *144*
25:23, 10
25:34, *166*
26, *166*, 272
26:4, 300, 358
26:16, 157
26:19, 344
26:20, 157
26:22, 157
26:26, 157
26:29, 157
26:34, *127*, 166
26:38, 157
26:43, *127*, 166

Numbers (Nu)
5:2, 356
7:1, 202
9:6–7, 356
12:8, 44
13:20, 219
15:30, *185*
15:39, 216
16:20, 355
19, *144*
19:13, *185*
20:7–11, *162*
22:18, 66
22:28–30, *153*
23:5, 66
24:13, 66
27:16, 355
27:18, *355*

Deuteronomy (Dt)
4:24, 106
4:32, 247, 253

Deuteronomy (cont.)
4:35, 51
10:7, 224
11:10, 15
11:11, 15, 51
11:12, 15
11:13, 167
11:13–21, 2, 127
12:16, 145, 349
12:23–25, 140, 349
13:5, 105
14:1, 88
15:23, 349
20:19, 12, 162, 306
21:23, 103
22:6, 145
22:6–7, 147
22:9–11, 349
22:19, 200
25:4, 145
26:2, 358
26:4, 358
26:15, 358
28:23, 344
29:23, 198
30:19, 127
32:1, 59
33:26, 53

1 Samuel (1Sa)
16:7, 282
22:16, 321
28:20, 282

2 Samuel (2Sa)
22:16, 356

1 Kings (1Kg)
5:13, 325

2 Kings (2Kg)
4:27, 355

Isaiah (Is)
6:1, 205
6:3, 52, 65, 260, 283
34:4, 59
37:31, 357
40:26, 272, 319
44:13, 80
45:12, 57
45:8, 87
51:6, 59
66:8, 243

Jeremiah (Je)
14:21, 205
17:12, 205
17:13, 178, 193, 287
23:24, 256, 260

Ezekiel (Ez)
1, 205
1:5, 197
1:10, 100, 223, 224
1:12, 78
1:14, 221
1:26, 216
1:26–27, 44
1:28, 222
24:7–8, 137
31:3–8, 282
47:12, 357

Hoshea (Ho)
12:11, 197
14:9, 357

Jonah (Jo)
2:11, 84

Micah (Mi)
6:8, 105

Malachi (Ma)
3:11, 358
3:19, 344

Psalms (Ps)
5:3, 358
8:2, 208, 238
8:6, 183, 210
8:7, 210
8:10, 208
11:7, 149
16:8, 69
18:16, 356
19:6, 203
21:7, 358
25:10, 105
37:29, 337
39:1, 44
46:9, 237
49:21, 285

Index of scriptural verses

Psalms (cont.)
  50:10, 321
  78:20, 162
  82:6–7, 135
  84:11, 206
  89:3, 345
  92:1–2, 323
  92:13, 178, 189
  93:1, 65
  93:3, 323
  95, 91
  96:6, 321
  96:11, 252, 319
  96:12, 319, 320, 358
  97:1, 320
  102:26, 59
  103:1, 133
  104:13, 357
  104:24, 17, 65, 164, 203
  104:31, 284
  107:37, 357
  119:1, 91
  122:4, 224
  139:5, 79, 197, 247, 248
  139:16, 247
  139:5, 91
  144:4, 285
  145:9, 146, 149, 153

Proverbs (Pr)
  3:18, 199
  8:26, 243
  9:3, 100
  11:30, 140
  12:10, 140
  20:22, 290
  20:27, 74, 141
  21:23, 155
  29:7, 155

Job (Jb)
  16:8, 137
  26:11, 203
  29:18, 346
  38:4–7, 52

Song of Songs (So)
  3:9, 100, 202
  3:10, 100, 203
  3:11, 286
  4:5, 200
  5:1, 336
  5:10, 222
  5:11, 206
  5:14, 188
  5:15, 188
  7:8, 178, 283, 286, 287
  8:6, 302
  8:11, 357

Ruth (Ru)
  3:6–8, 289
  3:8, 295
  3:9, 289

Ecclesiastes (Ec)
  1:2, 228
  1:4, 119, 243
  3:11, 242
  3:14, 18
  3:21, 129, 137, 141
  5:8, 216
  7:13, 119
  7:14, 219
  7:29, 108
  10:20, 220, 326
  12:13, 117, 253, 263

Esther (Es)
  1:8, 164

Daniel (Da)
  7:9–10, 44
  12:7, 242, 275

1 Chronicles (1Ch)
  12:10, 130
  16:27, 321

Index of rabbinic sources

Tannaitic literature – see also Targum
Onkelos, targumim in general index

Mishnah
  Qidushin
    1:9, 350
  Sanhedrin
    4:5, 114, 117, 121, 137, 302
    6:5, 26
    6:6, 103
  Avot
    2:1, 339
    3:13, 39
    3:21, 305
    4:29, 284
    4:3, 163
    5:1, 114
    5:21, 91
  `Arakhin, 125

Tosefta
  Y'vamot 8:5, 82
  Sanhedrin
    8:4, 99, 100
    9:3, 164–5

Earlier midrashim – see also Midrash
Alfa-Beitot, Midrash Otiyot d'Rabi
Aqiva, Pereq Shirah, Seder Rabbah
d'B'rei'shit in general index

M'khilta d'Rabi Yishma'el
  Pischa 1, 79

Bachodesh
  8, 102
  11, 163
Kaspa 20, 154
Shirah 3, 106
Vayisa` 6, 90

Sifra (Torat Kohanim)
  Q'doshim
    1:1, 106
    4:12, 82, 103
  Sh'mini 5:7, 18

Sifrey D'varim
  37, 19
  203, 162
  306, 135
  355, 53

Sifrey B'midbar
  115, 205, 216

B'rei'shit (Genesis) Rabbah
  1:4, 205
  19:5, 346
  2:2, 51
  5:3, 323
  5:4, 86
  5:8, 101
  5:9, 99
  5:13, 87
  8:1, 79, 97, 99, 136, 137, 247, 248
  8:3–4, 101

Index of rabbinic sources

B'rei'shit (Genesis) Rabbah (cont.)
8:6, 99
8:7, 101
8:8, 51
8:9, 81, 84, 86
8:10, 64
8:11, 47–52, 54, 59, 61, 76–9, 86, 89, 136, 194
9:2, 242
9:3, 51
9:12, 253
10:6, 322
12:5, 57
12:6, 90, 248, 283–4
12:7, 60
12:8, 55, 73, 138
12:12, 51
13:2, 324
13:10, 51
13:13, 87
14:1, 57
14:3, 47, 136
14:7, 80
14:8, 247, 248
14:9, 136, 137, 138
14:10, 80, 136
15:1, 218
17:2, 80, 248
17:4, 64
17:8, 57
19:1, 84
19:4, 55, 99–100
19:5, 50
19:7, 336
19:8, 324
20:3, 83
20:5, 84
20:8, 50, 99
21:2, 80
21:3, 247
22:2, 81
22:9, 137
24:2, 247
24:7, 104
25:2, 99
27:4, 52
28:8, 52, 154
30:6, 140
30:7, 218
33:1, 125
33:3, 146, 149
33:6, 151
34:14, 82

38:6, 51
78:3, 51
79:8, 52

Vayiqra' (Leviticus) Rabbah
8:1, 79
9:9, 55, 138
14:1, 79, 99, 247
18:2, 247
24:8, 51
25:3, 106

Kohelet (Ecclesiastes) Rabbah
1:4, 119, 243
7:13, 119

Shir Hashirim (Song of Songs) Rabbah
1:9, 325
3:8:4, 203

Avot d'Rabi Natan A
ch.1, 91, 248
ch.2, 87
ch.31, 51, 114–15, 120, 244–5, 308
ch.37, 19, 47, 57–8, 89, 283
ch.43, 101, 272

Avot d'Rabi Natan B
ch.36, 115–16, 245
ch.43, 47, 58, 137, 245
ch.46, 107

Talmudic literature

Talmud Y'rushalmi
Dema'i 1:3, 153
Shabbat 2:4, 57
Nedarim 9:4, 103
Bava M'tsiy`a 2:2, 125
Horayot 3:7 (3:4), 134

Talmud Bavli
B'rakhot
6b, 117–18
61a, 79, 80
Shabbat
67b, 12
105b, 12
133b, 106
151b, 244
155b, 155
156a, 322

`Eruvin
  18a, 79, 80
  100b, 152
Pesachim 75a, 165
Yoma 54a, 196, 202
Sukkah 28a, 324
Ta`anit 7a, 121
Megillah 9a, 79
Mo`ed Qatan 15b, 182
Chagigah
  12a, 248
  16a, 59
Y'vamot
  62a, 260
  62b–63a, 81
  63a, 80
  63b, 82, 260
K'tubot 37b, 165
Sotah
  14a, 106
  17a, 216
  27b, 166
Qidushin 30b, 210
Bava Qama 91b, 12
Bava M'tsiy`a
  32b, 144, 150
  85a, 146
Bava Bat'ra
  16b, 193
  58a, 53, 91, 182
  99a, 196
  134a, 324
Sanhedrin
  38a, 99, 100, 248
  45a, 165
  52b, 165
  57b, 156
  59b, 88, 158
  108a, 57, 154
  108b, 151, 346
`Avodah Zarah
  5a, 260
  8a, 158
  27a, 89
M'nachot 43b, 216
Chulin
  7a, 324
  7a–b, 153
  89a, 216
  127a, 18
B'khorot
  8a, 83, 85
  8b, 84

Nidah
  13b, 260
  22b–23a, 49
  23a, 77
  31a, 81, 89, 171

Early Kabbalah – see also Shi`ur Qomah in general index

Sefer Y'tsirah
  1:3, 190, 199
  1:5, 199
  1:13, 222
  4:5–11, 187, 206
  4:12, 234
  5:2, 206
  6:2, 206

Geonic and earlier medieval midrashim – see also Midrash Y'lamdeynu in general index

P'siqta d'Rav Kahana
  1:1, 336
  1:2, 203, 216, 303
  4:4, 53
  12:1, 53

P'siqta Rabbati 153a, 317

Tanchuma
  B'rei'shit
    §7, 107–8
    §10, 152
    §11, 91
  B'shalach §22, 90
  Chuqat §6, 64, 326
  Emor §6, 125
  Ki Tisa' §27, 168
  Noach
    §2, 140
    §5–6, 149
    §7, 140
    §11, 87, 154
  P'qudey §3, 121, 202, 245
  Q'doshim §8, 106

Tanchuma Buber
  B'rei'shit §15, 56, 138
  Chuqat
    §12, 64
    §15, 326

Index of rabbinic sources

Noach
§2, 140
§4, 149, 155
§10, 140
§11, 154
§§17–18, 154

Pirqey d'Rabi Eli`ezer
ch.4, 205
ch.9, 93
ch.11, 65, 304
ch.12, 64, 167
ch.21, 52, 152
ch.29, 88
ch.34, 162

Midrash T'hilim (Psalms)
19:6, 53
42:6, 87
78:20, 162
93:3, 323

Later midrashim – see also Midrash Hagadol in general index

Sh'mot (Exodus) Rabbah
2:5, 303
5:9, 86
13:2, 337
21:6, 324
30:3, 348
30:13, 57
30:16, 48, 102
31:9, 154–5

B'midbar (Numbers) Rabbah
12:4, 100, 203, 216, 303
12:6, 337
12:8, 284
17:5, 216
20:15, 319

D'varim (Deuteronomy) Rabbah 7:7, 121

Yalqut Shim`oni
1:14, 78, 81
1:16, 87, 242
1:17, 88
1:19, 180
1:20, 324
1:23, 80
1:61, 156
1:80, 88
1:186, 243
1:187, 155
1:299, 102
1:764, 162
2:182, 325
2:287, 121
2:848, 86, 323

Parshanut (Torah commentaries) – see ibn Ezra, Rashi, Ramban, Sforno in general index

Medieval philosophy – see also Abravanel, Donnolo, Duran, ibn Ezra, ibn Paquda, Maharal, Narboni, Saadyah in general index

Maimonides
Peyrush Hamishnah
    Haqdamah, 27
Sefer Hamitsvot
    `Aseh 8, 70
Mishneh Torah
    Hilkhot M'lakhim 6:12–13, 12
    Y'sodey Torah
        4:14, 70
        4:14–15, 67
Moreh N'vukhim
    1:1, 67
    1:2, 70
    1:7, 70, 92, 160
    1:38, 72
    1:54, 20, 71–2, 171
    1:68, 92
    1:69, 275
    1:72, 92, 93, 268–70, 275, 276
    1:75, 23, 140
    2:6–7, 270
    2:30, 16
    2:40, 119
    3:1, 226
    3:8, 100
    3:12, 270
    3:13, 15–16, 27, 101, 160, 270
    3:17, 28
    3:25, 16, 20, 28, 239
    3:48, 148
    3:54, 71

Kabbalah – see also deFano, Gikatilla, Luria, Recanati, Peyrush L'Shir Hashirim, P'ri `Ets Hadar, Ramban, Recanati, Shem Tov ibn Shem Tov, Tsadiq Y'sod `Olam in general index

Sefer Bahir
  §3, 216
  §5, 209
  §6, 209
  §7, 216
  §22, 37, 209, 218
  §23-4, 278
  §24, 237
  §31, 278
  §81, 218
  §82, 176, 187, 218
  §95, 206, 218
  §95-6, 216
  §99, 218
  §106, 206
  §119, 37, 218
  §172, 187

Chasidey Ashkenaz
Sefer Chasidim
  §43, 115
  §44, 146
  §373, 147
  §530, 92
  §666, 158
  §§666-70, 146
Sodey Razaya
  Alef, 191
  Lamed, 100, 223
  Resh, 204
  Sefer Hashem 45, 66

Yosef ben Shalom Ashkenazi
Peyrush L'parshat B'rei'shit
  35b, 275
  36a, 194, 196
  37a, 251, 301
  38a, 254
  38b, 253
  41a, 251, 301, 302
  41b, 181, 238

Zoharic literature

Zohar
  1:13a, 211
  1:19a, 224
  1:29b, 87
  1:32b, 86
  1:34b, 222
  1:134b, 203, 250
  1:191a, 160
  1:201a, 291
  1:55b, 194
  2:5a, 216, 237
  2:15b-16a, 220
  2:64b, 233
  2:76a, 199
  2:162b, 202
  2:177a-b, 198
  3:19a, 86
  3:83a, 278
  3:118b, 224
  3:130b-134b, 198
  3:200b-202b, 153
  Ra`ya Mehemna
    3:123b, 182, 198-9, 205, 228, 312, 341
    3:252b, 287

Zohar Chadash
  12c, 86
  22b, 326
  31c, 188
  59a, 211
  Midrash Hane`elam
    5d, 323
    10d, 319
    16b, 217, 273
    16c, 183, 210, 277
  Sitrey Otiyot 2a, 211

Tiquney Zohar
  82b, 220-21
  83b, 180, 195
  84b, 190
  90b, 175, 182, 191
  91b, 209
  94b, 181
  99b, 192
  120a, 180
  120a-b, 210
  121a, 179, 181, 197, 224
  125a, 199, 222
  125b, 287, 348
  131a, 274
  132a, 291
  146a, 178, 188, 199-200, 287

Moshe Cordovero
Pardes Rimonim 89b, 91a, 262
Shi`ur Qomah shel Cordovero
  21, 131
  52, 149
Or Ne`erav, 26

Index of rabbinic sources

Tomer D'vorah
  ch.1, intro, 189
  ch.1, §13, 186
  ch.2, 164, 186
  ch.3, 37, 149, 164, 186
  ch.9, 186

Chayyim Vital
Sha`ar Ru'ach Haqodesh 22–3, 326
Sha`ar Hakavanot 106d–107a, 302
`Ets Chayyim
  Sha`ar Hak'lalim 1, 200
  Sha`ar Hak'lalim 2, 262
  3:2, 287
  6:5, 260–61
  6:6–7, 261
  7:1, 261
  22:1, 180
  26:1, 184
  26:3, 181, 196
  30:3, 288
  34:1, 287
  39:15, 261–2

Yishayah Horowitz
Sh'ney Luchot Hab'rit
  1:5b, 179
  1:6b, 188, 198, 219
  1:10b, 179, 205, 214, 222, 224
  1:14d, 193
  1:15a, 253
  1:15b, 198
  1:49a–b, 290
  1:52b, 291
  2:71b, 291
  3:82b, 165

Chasidut – see also Baal Shem Tov, Heschel of Apt, Meshullam Feibush, Lainer, Nachman of Breslov, Simchah Bunam, Tsadok Hakohen, Yaakov Yosef, Zev Wolf in general index

Sefer Ba`al Shem Tov
  1:100, 293
  1:132–3, 293
  1:163, 293
  1:166, 293
  1:267–8, 298
  1:43, 206
  1:76, 293

Shneur Zalman of Liady
Tanya
  ch.36, 263
  ch.37, 263
  ch.41, 265
  ch.49, 263
  ch.53, 264
Igeret Haqodesh
  ch.20, 255–59, 264–5
  ch.31, 260
Sha`ar Hayichud v'Ha'emunah, 234–5, 265

Nachman of Breslov
Liqutey Moharan
  1:5, 118
  1:10, 21
  1:17, 21
  1:64, 331
  1:169, 21
  1:178, 294
  1:277, 294
  2:11, 330–31
  2:63, 331

Other early modern thought – see Hurwitz, Maharal, Vilna Gaon in general index

Modern/contemporary thought –see Adler, Benamozegh, Berlin, Buber, Green, Greenberg, Heschel, Hirsch, Kook, Meir Simchah Hakohen, Plaskow, Kepnes, Rosenzweig, Soloveitchik, Waskow in general index